The Blue Guides

W9-ARG-128

BLUE GUIDE

ROME

Alta Macadam

A&C Black • London
WW Norton • New York

Eighth edition 2003

Published by A & C Black Publishers Limited
37 Soho Square, London W1D 3QZ
www.acblack.com

ISBN 0–7136–6276 X

Published in the United States of America by
WW Norton and Company, Inc
500 Fifth Avenue, New York, NY 10110

Published simultaneously in Canada by
Penguin Books Canada Limited
10 Alcorn Avenue, Toronto, Ontario M4V 3B2

ISBN 0–393–32473–7 USA

The author and the publishers have done their best to ensure the accuracy of all the information in *Blue Guide Rome*; however, they can accept no responsibility for any loss, injury or inconvenience sustained by any traveller as a result of information or advice contained in the guide.

Alta Macadam has been a writer of Blue Guides since 1970. She lives in Florence with her Italian family where she has been associated with the Bargello Museum, the Alinari photo archive, Harvard University at the Villa I Tatti, and New York University at Villa La Pietra. As author of the Blue Guides to Florence, Rome, Venice, Tuscany and Umbria she travels extensively in Italy every year to revise new editions of the books.

Timothy Potter (1945–2000), author of 'Ancient Rome: an introduction', was a renowned scholar of Roman archaeology. He was Keeper of the Romano-British department at the British Museum. He had a long and important connection with the British School at Rome, led numerous excavations in Italy, and made a fundamental study of the country in his *Roman Italy* (1987, 1992).

Cover pictures. Top: fragments of a colossal statue of Constantine the Great in the courtyard of Palazzo dei Conservatori on the Capitoline Hill, © Schuster, courtesy of Robert Harding Picture Library Ltd. Bottom: Roman Forum, detail of inscription, © Julia Davey, courtesy of the Hutchison Library.
Title page illustration: the Colosseum.

Printed in Great Britain by Butler & Tanner, Frome and London.

Contents

Practical information

Background information

The guide

Outer Rome

Days out of Rome

Maps and plans

Out of Rome

Historical maps

Introduction

Rome is one of the most celebrated cities of the world, and ever since her greatest days as the centre of the Roman Empire, and later as the home of the Roman Catholic Church, the city has had a role of the first importance in European history. The Eternal City was the *Caput Mundi* (Head of the World) in the Roman era, and from it law and the liberal arts and sciences radiated to the confines of its vast Empire, which covered the whole of the known western world. The ancient Roman city, with a population of over one million, was built over the famous seven hills on the left bank of the Tiber. The walls built to defend it by the Emperor Aurelian in the 3C AD still defined the urban limits of the city in the late 19C, and it was only in the 1940s that the population of the city began to reach (and supersede) that of ancient Rome.

The city today, the capital of Italy, preserves numerous magnificent Roman buildings side by side with palaces and churches from later centuries. Some of these are very well preserved—such as the Pantheon and Colosseum, together with commemorative columns and triumphal arches—while others are picturesque ruins in the very centre of the city. The Vatican, in part of the area of the city which from the 9C onwards became the stronghold of the popes, has, since 1929, been the smallest independent state in the world. Splendid basilicas and churches and beautiful palaces were built in Rome over the centuries by numerous popes, and the city has particularly fine Baroque churches, including masterpieces by Bernini and Borromini. Its delightful *piazze* are decorated with splendid fountains and Egyptian obelisks.

The large parks in the centre of Rome are a special feature of the city. Rome also has numerous fashionable shops, mostly in the elegant pedestrian streets which converge on Piazza di Spagna. The great museums in the city include superb collections of ancient Greek and Roman sculpture; the Vatican collections are famous for their Classical sculpture and their frescoes by Michelangelo and Raphael; and there are still some fine private patrician collections of paintings.

For centuries Rome has been visited by pilgrims and travellers, but now mass tourism threatens the enjoyment of the individual visitor to Rome (over three million people see the Sistine Chapel every year, with up to 20,000 in a single day). Traffic congestion has in part been solved since the 1970s by the closing of much of the historic centre to private cars, but there is still a lot to be done to cut down the volume of traffic in Rome, since the suburbs have become more congested than ever and air pollution has reached unacceptable levels. Pedestrians have to take extreme care when crossing roads because of the undisciplined and fast traffic.

For these reasons visitors are strongly advised not only to see the most famous sights of Rome, but also to spend as much time as possible exploring the quieter streets and piazze and the smaller museums and palaces: more than one hundred years ago Augustus Hare felt moved to give similar advice in his *Walks in Rome*: 'Many of those who are not mere passing visitors at Rome, will probably find that their chief pleasure lies not amid the well-known sights of the great basilicas and palaces, but in quiet walks through the silent lanes and amid the decaying buildings of [the] more distant hills.'

Since the last edition of *Blue Guide Rome* the splendid Musei Capitolini have been reopened on the Campidoglio, and many of the antique Roman statues cleaned. Another area of the museums will be made accessible when excavations are completed of the huge Temple of Jupiter. It is now possible to descend directly by the ancient road from the Campidoglio hill to the Roman Forum (and you no longer have to buy an entrance ticket). More areas of the Forum are now accessible and much of the restoration and excavation work there completed. There are plans to begin restoration of Santa Maria Antiqua, a church in the centre of the Forum with extremely important early wall-paintings, which has been closed for many decades.

A visit to the Colosseum is even more impressive since a platform has been built so that you can walk across the centre of the arena. It is now possible to climb the huge Monument to Vittorio Emanuele II in Piazza Venezia, from which there is a very fine view, and the Museo del Risorgimento has been reopened in the interior. The Etruscan Museum in Villa Giulia has been given a long-awaited face lift, and exhibitions are held in the adjoining Villa Poniatowsky. All the works in the Galleria Nazionale d'Arte Moderna have now been redisplayed following the original arrangement. The museum of the Accademia di San Luca has been reopened. Churches which have recently been restored include Santa Maria della Pace and Sant'Ignazio. Many more palace façades have been cleaned, including Palazzo Pamphilj in Piazza Navona, and even Palazzo Massimo on Corso Vittorio Emanuele II, for years blackened by the polluted air.

A bus has been provided from Piazza Venezia for visitors to the Via Appia Antica. The restoration and conservation of this wonderful old Roman road which leads directly out of the city into the Roman Campagna undoubtedly represents the most spectacular innovation in the city in the last few years, and a triumph for the conservationists who have battled for so long to preserve it. There is still much work to be done in the regional park here, but it is now possible to visit long stretches of the road, and part of the surrounding countryside (notably the Valle della Caffarella). There is a visitors' centre, where bicycles can also be hired. The Villa dei Quintili, owned by the State, has been restored and opened to the public, and there have been renovations to the Tomb of Cecilia Metella. A park traversed by a number of ancient Roman aqueducts is also now accessible.

How to use the Guide

The Guide is divided into 40 chapters: the first 34 describe **walks** within the historic centre of the city, almost all of which can be followed without the help of public transport. Chapters 35–38 cover outer Rome and the last two chapters its immediate environs, and for these details of public transport have been given.

Each important monument in the city is given a **map reference** in the text, relating to the 16-page atlas at the back of the book. Each page of the atlas is divided into numbered squares. The first figure in the reference denotes the page of the atlas, and the second denotes the square (e.g. **Map 1; 1**). References to ground plans are given in the text as a bracketed figure or letter.

The **opening times** of museums and monuments in force in 2002 are given in the text and in the list on pp 42–46. Telephone numbers have also been given, since opening times change frequently and it is always best to check them locally. Prices, which vary greatly (and can sometimes be high at private museums), are listed. The opening times of most churches have been given within the text.

The most important monuments in Rome have been highlighted in bold throughout the text, and **stars** are used to indicate works of art which are particularly beautiful or interesting. The highlights section on p 11 singles out the major monuments of each period which should not be missed.

All **churches** are taken as being orientated, with the entrance at the west end and the altar at the east end, the south aisle on the right and the north aisle on the left. Although many churches in Rome are not, in fact, orientated, this has seemed the simplest way of providing a standard description of church interiors, beginning at the entrance and following the right side up to the sanctuary and then returning down the left side to the entrance.

An exhaustive section at the beginning of the book lists all the practical information you are likely to need during a visit to Rome. A selection of **hotels** has been given on pp 26–31, listed according to location and category, which indicates the price range. They, too, are keyed to the atlas section (see above). The selection of **restaurants** on pp 35–40 is also listed according to price range and area: telephone numbers are supplied so that you can check opening times, and, if necessary, book a table.

Numerous popes, emperors and artists are referred to throughout the text: their dates can be found in the list of Roman emperors (p 68), the list of popes (p 476) and the index of artists (p 488). Architectural terms, Italian and Latin words and other specialised vocabulary are explained in the glossary on p 483.

Abbreviations and symbols used in the guide

APT	*Azienda di Promozione Turistica di Roma* (the Rome Tourist board)
ATAC	*Azienda Tramvie e Autobus del Comune di Roma* (the bus company which serves the city of Rome)
CIT	*Compagnia Italiano Turismo* (an Italian travel agency)
COTRAL	*Consorzio Trasporti Pubblici Lazio* (the bus company which serves Lazio)
ENIT	*Ente Nazionale Italiano per il Turismo* (Italian State Tourist Office)
FS	*Ferrovie dello Stato* (Italian State Railways)
fest.	*festa*, festival (i.e. holiday)
fl.	*floruit* (flourished); approximate period of an artist's career
€	Euro
☎	telephone
📠	fax
✉	web site/e-mail address

Highlights of Rome

Ancient Rome. The best place to start a visit to Rome is on the Capitoline Hill, the historic centre of the ancient city, with splendid views of the Forum and Palatine Hill and, in the other direction, of the modern city, with St Peter's on the skyline. In the piazza designed by Michelangelo are the Capitoline museums, with very fine collections of Roman sculpture.

The Forum and Palatine, with their remarkable ruined temples, palaces, triumphal arches and basilicas, evoke the spirit of the Roman Republic and Empire as nowhere else, and symbolise the grandeur of the ancient city. On the peaceful Palatine Hill the great monuments survive amid luxuriant vegetation. The Colosseum, a huge amphitheatre, is the most famous monument of ancient Rome. The Pantheon, with its extraordinary dome, is the best-preserved Roman building. The monumental Baths of Caracalla and the exquisitely carved Ara Pacis also represent some of the highest achievements of Roman architecture and sculpture (and are among the least visited, although the Ara Pacis is not at present open to the public). The commemorative columns of Trajan and Marcus Aurelius are still important features of the city, even though the very fine sculptured reliefs on them are difficult to appreciate with the naked eye. Beyond the impressive Circus of Maxentius and the Tomb of Cecilia Metella, the Via Appia still preserves its appearance as an important consular highway leading out of the city: it is best visited on Sundays when closed to traffic. The extensive ruins of Ostia Antica, west of Rome, are extremely interesting for their domestic and commercial architecture. Hadrian's Villa outside Tivoli is the most important Imperial villa in the Roman Empire.

Districts of Rome that are particularly attractive and typical of the city include Piazza di Spagna (and the neighbouring elegant streets of Via Condotti, Via Frattina, Via del Babuino, Via Margutta), Piazza Navona, the area around the Pantheon, Campo dei Fiori and its vicinity (including Piazza Farnese), and Trastevere (with Piazza di Santa Maria in Trastevere).

St Peter's and the Vatican Museums are of the highest interest. The huge 16C basilica of St Peter's, with its dome by Michelangelo and works by Bernini, is the most famous church in Christendom. The collections of the Vatican Museums cover all periods and are especially notable for their superb Greek and Roman sculpture, as well as for the Sistine Chapel frescoed by Michelangelo, and the Stanze frescoed by Raphael.

Churches. After St Peter's, the historic basilicas of Santa Maria Maggiore, San Giovanni in Laterano and San Paolo fuori le Mura are the most important churches in Rome, although the latter is a disappointing place to visit. Among smaller basilicas which have particularly attractive interiors are Santa Sabina and Santa Maria in Trastevere. Other churches which should not be missed include Santa Maria della Pace, Santa Maria del Popolo, San Giorgio in Velabro, Santo Stefano Rotondo, San Giovanni a Porta Latina, San Crisogono, San Lorenzo fuori le Mura and San Clemente.

Museums. Apart from the Vatican collections and the Capitoline museums, the most important museum of ancient Roman art is the Museo Nazionale Romano, now divided into four buildings: Palazzo Massimo alle Terme (sculpture, paintings, and mosaics), the Baths of Diocletian (epigraphs), Palazzo Altemps (sculpture collections) and the Crypta Balbi (excavations and medieval finds). Other museums of the highest interest include the Museo and Galleria

Borghese (for works by Bernini and Caravaggio), the Galleria Doria Pamphilj (a private Roman patrician collection), the Galleria Nazionale d'Arte Antica (13C–18C paintings) in Palazzo Barberini and Palazzo Corsini (Baroque paintings), the Museo Barracco (ancient sculpture, but closed in 2002), the Museo Nazionale Etrusco di Villa Giulia (Etruscan works), the Museo di Palazzo Venezia (decorative arts), Galleria Spada (17C and 18C works), and Castel Sant'Angelo. Specialised collections include a fine museum of musical instruments.

Rome has a wealth of beautiful **gardens and parks**. The largest parks include the extensive Villa Borghese and Pincio in the centre of the city, and the Villa Doria Pamphilj on the southern outskirts. The Farnese Gardens on the Palatine Hill are famous. The most important gardens attached to a villa which can be visited are those of the Villa Medici on the Pincio. For other gardens, see p 47.

The city is particularly famous for its **Baroque buildings**. Among Rome's Baroque churches are the Gesù, Sant'Andrea della Valle, Sant'Agnese in Agone and Sant'Ignazio. Bernini, the most important Baroque artist to work in Rome, designed the splendid piazza in front of St Peter's (as well as the baldacchino and tribune inside the church) and the church of Sant'Andrea al Quirinale. His sculptures can be seen in the churches of Santa Maria della Vittoria, Santa Bibiana and San Francesco a Ripa, as well as in the Museo Borghese. His delightful fountains include the Fontana del Tritone and Fontana dei Quattro Fiumi in Piazza Navona. Borromini was the architect of San Carlo alle Quattro Fontane, Sant'Agnese in Agone and the courtyard of the Palazzo della Sapienza (with the church of Sant'Ivo). Beautiful Renaissance palaces include Palazzo della Cancelleria, Palazzo Farnese and the Villa Farnesina.

There are many churches with lovely **mosaics** all over Rome: Santa Costanza and Santa Pudenziana (4C), Santa Maria Maggiore (5C and 13C), the baptistery of San Giovanni in Laterano (5C and 7C), San Marco, Santa Cecilia in Trastevere, Santa Prassede and Santa Maria in Domnica (9C), San Clemente, Santa Maria Nova and Santa Maria in Trastevere (12C).

Fountains are a special feature of the city as Rome has an abundant water supply. The most famous are the Fontana di Trevi and the Fontana dei Quattro Fiumi, in Piazza Navona, but there are numerous others in nearly every piazza. Outside Rome are the celebrated fountains of Villa d'Este in Tivoli. The River Tiber can best be seen from the picturesque little Isola Tiberina, or from Bernini's Ponte Sant'Angelo.

The **catacombs**, the underground cemeteries of the early Christians, are fascinating sights: the most important are those of San Callisto and San Sebastiano on the Via Appia; Santa Domitilla on Via delle Sette Chiese; Sant'Agnese on Via Nomentana; and Priscilla on the Via Salaria.

Artists who worked in Rome and are well represented here include Raphael, Michelangelo and Caravaggio. The remarkable frescoes in the Stanze in the Vatican are Raphael's masterpiece. Other works by him are found in the Vatican picture gallery and in Santa Maria del Popolo, Santa Maria della Pace and Sant'Agostino. Michelangelo designed the dome of St Peter's, Piazza del Campidoglio and part of Palazzo Farnese; there are sculptures by him in St Peter's (the *Pietà*), San Pietro in Vincoli (*Moses*) and Santa Maria sopra Minerva (*Christ Bearing the Cross*); and his greatest works are the beautiful frescoes in the Sistine Chapel. Caravaggio left works in San Luigi dei Francesi, Sant'Agostino and Santa Maria del Popolo, and there are paintings by him in the Pinacoteca Capitolina, Galleria Borghese, Palazzo Corsini, Palazzo Barberini and Galleria Doria Pamphilj.

PRACTICAL INFORMATION

Planning your trip

When to go

The climate of Rome is usually very pleasant except in the height of summer and periodically in the winter. The best months to visit the city are November or March: the most crowded periods, to be avoided if at all possible, are Easter, May and June, September, October and Christmas. July and August have become less crowded in the last few years, but the summer is usually uncomfortably hot.

Passports

Passports are necessary for all travellers from Britain and North America entering Italy. A lost or stolen passport can be replaced in a day or two with little trouble by the relevant embassy in Rome (see pp 56–57). You are obliged to carry some means of identification with you at all times. Visitors from Australia and New Zealand do not require visas, but those from South Africa do.

Italian tourist boards

The Italian State Tourist Office, ENIT (*Ente Nazionale Italiano per Il Turismo*) provides detailed information about Italy at 🖳 www.enit.it, or at the following addresses:

Australia   c/o Italian Chamber of Commerce and Industry, Level 26, 44 Market St, Sydney, NSW 2000, ☎ 0061 292 662 1666, 🖨 0061 292 625 745

Canada   1 Place Ville Marie, Suite 1914, Montreal, H3B 2C3, ☎ 001 514 886 7668, 🖨 001 514 392 1429, 🖂 initaly@ucab.net
175 Bloor Street East, Suite 907, South Tower M4W 3R8, Toronto (Ontario), ☎ 416 925 4882, 🖨 416 925 4799, 🖳 www.italiantourism.com

Netherlands   Stadhoudeskade 2, 1054 ES Amsterdam, ☎ 003 120 616 8244, 🖨 003 120 618 8515, 🖂 enitams@wirehub.nl

UK   1 Princes Street, WIR 8AY, ☎ 020 7408 1254 or 020 7355 1557; 🖨 020 7499 3567, 🖂 enitlond@globalnet.co.uk

USA   630 Fifth Avenue, Suite 1565, New York, NY 10111, ☎ 001 212 245 4822, 🖨 001 212 586 9249, 🖂 enitny@italian tourism.com
500 North Michigan Avenue, Suite 2240, Chicago I, IL 60611, ☎ 001 312 644 0996, 🖨 001 312 644 3019, 🖂 enitch@italiantourism.com
12400 Wilshire Boulevard, Suite 550, Los Angeles, CA 90025, ☎ 001 310 820 1898, 🖨 001 310 820 6357, 🖂 enitla@earth link.net

Web sites on Rome

www.romaturismo.com	Azienda di Promozione turistica di Roma
www.comune.roma.it	Municipality (Comune di Roma)
www.informaroma.it	Municipality (Comune di Roma)
www.romapreview.com	Municipality (Comune di Roma)
www.vatican.va	Vatican
www.capitolium.org	Excavations in the Imperial Fora
www.tour-web.com/accessibleitaly	For disabled travellers
www.romeguide.it	General website to Rome

Tour operators

Among the numerous tour operators which offer organised holidays to Rome from the UK are:

Magic of Italy, King's House, 12–42 Wood Street, Kingston-upon-Thames, Surrey KT1 1JF, ☎ 02700 270 500 for reservations, 0990 462 442 for brochures, ✉ www.magictravelgroup. co.uk

Citalia (CIT Holidays Ltd), Marco Polo House, 3–5 Lansdowne Road, Croydon, Surrey CR9 1LL, ☎ 020 8686 5533, ✉ www.citalia.co.uk

Travelscene, 11–15 St Ann's Road, Harrow Middlesex HA1 1LQ, ☎ 020 8863 2787, 🖷 020 8861 5083, ✉ www.travelscene.co.uk

Time Off, 1 Elmfield Park, Bromley, Kent BR1 1LU, ☎ 0870 584 6363, ✉ www.info@timeoff.co.uk

Prospect Music & Art Tours Ltd, 36 Manchester Street, London W1U 7LH, ☎ 020 7486 5704, 🖷 020 7486 5686, ✉ enquiries@prospecttours.com

Martin Randall Travel Ltd, 10 Barley Mow Passage, London W4 4PH, ☎ 020 8742 3355, 🖷 020 8742 7766, ✉ info@martinrandall.co.uk

Health and insurance

British citizens, as members of the EU, have the right to claim health care in Italy if they have the E111 form available from post offices. There are also a number of private holiday health insurance policies, certainly advisable for visitors from outside the EU. Keep the receipt (*ricevuta*) and medical report (*cartella clinica*) to present to your insurer if you have to make a claim.

Currency

On 1 January 2002 the Euro (€) replaced the Italian Lire as the official monetary unit. The fixed exchange rate for one Euro was Lire 1936.270, and the Lire was withdrawn from circulation at the end of February 2002. There are bank notes of 5, 10, 20, 50, 100, 200, and 500 Euro, and coins of 1, 2, 5, 10 and 50 Eurocents as well as 1 & 2 Euro.

Many banks in towns have cashpoints called *Bancomat* where you can withdraw money using your cashpoint card (check with your own bank about any charges associated with their use), and also automatic machines which change foreign bank notes. Travellers' cheques are the safest way of carrying money while travelling, and these can be changed at banks, larger hotesl and shops and foreign exhange bureaux in railway stations and airports. Most credit cards are now generally accepted in shops, hotels and restaurants, and at some petrol stations.

Planning an itinerary

Rome is best visited without a car, but you should choose a hotel in a central position (the best locations, and a selection of hotels are given on pp 26–31). Much of the city can then be explored on foot as described in the guide. Buses and trams are useful at times, as indicated in the text, but you should try to pick up a **bus map** on arrival as destination indicators at the bus stops are very unhelpful, and the bus routes in Rome often change. If you are travelling by car you will find it best to park on the outskirts (for long-term car parks, see p 23) and not use it while you are staying in Rome.

The tourist information offices (see p 19) supply a list of **opening times**, but these are always subject to change, and before making a special trip to a museum or monument it is wise to telephone first for confirmation of the opening hours.

The **Vatican**, which is at present one of the most crowded and uncomfortable places to visit, has very limited opening hours and is closed on odd days throughout the year (see p 365). If you have the energy, it is always a good idea to make a very early start in the mornings when you will find most of the **churches** open, since they almost all close at 12.00—except for the major basilicas including St Peter's—and many of them do not reopen until 16.00 or 17.00. Rome is busy with visitors at all times of the year, and tour groups can easily disturb the individual visitor's enjoyment of the city. There are many sites of great interest, and it is often much more rewarding to choose the lesser-known monuments, museums and churches to visit in peace, rather than attempt to visit the famous sites such as the Vatican.

If this is your first visit to Rome, it can be a good idea on your first day to see the city from one of the **electric mini-buses** (nos 116 and 117) which traverse the centre, or from bus no. 110 (see pp 20 and 22) which follows an itinerary which provides a tour of the main areas of the city.

The following is a suggestion for a very full (and tiring) **two-to-three-day itinerary**. One of the best places to start is at the Capitoline Hill, which has some very fine museums of ancient Roman sculpture and splendid views of the city and Roman Forum. From there you can descend directly into the Roman Forum and climb the Palatine Hill. Close by is the Colosseum. You can see Trajan's Column on the way back towards the Capitoline, and from Piazza Venezia take the Corso, turning off it to visit the Trevi fountain, the Spanish Steps and the elegant streets in this district, including Via Condotti. If you have time you can then visit the church of Santa Maria del Popolo at the end of the Corso in Piazza del Popolo.

The following day you could start with a visit to the Pantheon, Piazza Navona and, if time permits, the museum of ancient Roman sculptures in Palazzo Altemps, followed by the churches of San Luigi dei Francesi and Sant'Agostino to see works by Caravaggio. From Sant'Agostino you can walk north to visit the Ara Pacis (although this was closed in 2002). South of Piazza Navona you can see the exterior of Palazzo della Cancelleria, the market in Campo dei Fiori and the exterior of Palazzo Farnese close by. In the afternoon, you could visit the Museo Nazionale Romano famous for its ancient Roman works, displayed in Palazzo Massimo alle Terme and the Baths of Diocletian both very near Termini station. Close by are the basilica of Santa Maria Maggiore, and the church of

Santa Prassede with its lovely mosaics. On the Quirinal hill it is well worth visiting the Baroque churches of Sant'Andrea and San Carlo alle Quattro Fontane.

The last day could be devoted to St Peter's and the Vatican Museums. If, however, you are visiting Rome at a particularly crowded time, it may be best to limit your visit to the Vatican to Piazza San Pietro and the church of St Peter's only. If there is still time, a few hours could be spent on the quiet Aventine Hill and in the basilica of Santa Sabina.

Disabled travellers
Italy is at last catching up with the rest of Europe in the provision of facilities for the disabled. All new public buildings are now obliged by law to provide access and specially designed facilities for the disabled. In the annual list of hotels in Rome published by the *APT*, hotels which are able to provide hospitality for the disabled are indicated. Airports and railway stations in Italy provide assistance and certain trains are equipped to transport wheelchairs. The seats at the front of city buses are reserved for disabled passengers, as is *ATAC* bus no 590. There are free parking spaces for disabled drivers who display an official disc. In the list of current opening times of the museums and galleries in Rome available from the *APT*, those which are accessible to wheelchairs are indicated. The historic centre of Rome, however, remains a very difficult place to traverse in a wheelchair.

Travellers can contact *Co.In* (*Consorzio Cooperative Integrate*), ☎ 06 2326 7504, Mon–Fri 09.30–17.00, for a guide to Rome for the disabled in English. Other organisations in Italy with information on services for the disabled include: (in Rome) *ANTHAI* ☎ 06 6821 9168; (in Milan) *AIAS*, ☎ 02 5501 7564 and *RADAR*, ☎ 02 7250 3222. ✉ www.tour-web.com/accessibleitaly

Getting there

By air

Air services from the UK
Flights between London Heathrow and Gatwick and Rome Leonardo da Vinci/ Fiumicino are operated by:

Air France (via Paris)	☎ 0845 0845 111, ✉ www.airfrance.co.uk
Alitalia	☎ 0870 544 8259, ✉ www.alitalia.co.uk
British Airways	☎ 0990 444 000 (flight information), 0345 222 111 (reservations), ✉ www.britishairways.com
British Midland	☎ 0870 6070 555, ✉ www.flybmi.com
Go	☎ 0845 605 4321, ✉ www.easyjet.com
Lufthansa (via Frankfurt),	☎ 0345 737747, ✉ www.lufthansa.co.uk
Ryanair	☎ 0870 156 9569, ✉ www.ryanair.com

Air services from the US
Non-stop services from New York, Boston, Chicago and Los Angeles to Rome are operated by:

Alitalia	☎ 800 223 5730, ✉ www.alitaliausa.com

Flights from New York to Rome are also operated by:

Continental	☎ 800 525 0280,	✉ www.continental.com
Delta	☎ 800 241 4141,	✉ www.delta-air.com
TWA	☎ 800 221 2000,	✉ www. twa.com
United Airlines	☎ 800 538 2929,	✉ www.ual.com) operates

between Washington DC and Rome.

British Airways, *Air France* and *KLM* offer flights connecting through London, Paris, Amsterdam and Brussels which are often more economical than direct flights.

Arriving in Rome

Fiumicino airport (also called **Leonardo da Vinci**; ☎ 06 65951, ✉ www.adr. it), 26km south-west of Rome, is the airport for both international and domestic air services. Non stop trains run from Stazione Termini every half hour from about 07.00 to 21.15 (30mins) and metropolitana trains every 15mins from Stazione Roma Tiburtina via Ostiense and Trastevere from about 05.00 to 23.00 (41mins). There are also night bus services between Stazione Tiburtina and the airport. If you arrive late at night, however, it is usually best to take a taxi. Taxis cost standard meter charges plus an airport supplement, or a price by agreement in advance.

  Ciampino airport (☎ 06 794 941, ✉ www.adr.it), 13km south-east of Rome, is a subsidiary airport used mainly for domestic flights and international charter flights. It can be reached by underground Line A from Stazione Termini to Anagnina station, and from there by *COTRAL* airport bus from 06.00 to 22.00 (every 30mins), but this journey is not very convenient and most visitors prefer to take a taxi, for standard meter charges plus an airport supplement.

By rail

Rome can be reached via *Eurostar* train (from Waterloo, London, or Ashford, Kent, to the Gare du Nord, Paris where there is an overnight sleeper to Rome. For more information, contact *European Rail Travel*, ☎ 020 7387 0444, 📠 020 7387 0888, ✉ www.europeanrail.com

Websites

www.trenitalia.com   website of the Italian State Railways (FS)
www.freedomrail.co.uk
www.itwg.com/home.asp
www.railchoice.co.uk

Stations in Rome

Stazione Termini (Map 4; 6), Piazza dei Cinquecento, is the main station for all services of the State railways and for the underground railway (*la metropolitana*). It has left-luggage deposit facilities and a supermarket open 24hrs.

  Stazione Roma Tiburtina (beyond Map 5; 4), less central than Termini, is used by some trains which do not stop at the main station. It is well served by buses, and is on Line B of the underground, four stops from Termini. The stations of Ostiense and Trastevere are on the line to Fiumicino airport.

By coach

For details of coach services available from the UK to Rome, contact *Eurolines*, ☎ 020 7730 8235, ✉ www.gobycoach.com

Services operate from London's Victoria Coach Station on Mon, Wed, Fri and Sun (usually five days a week in summer) at 09.00 and arrive at Rome's Stazione Tiburtina, Piazzale Autolinee the next day at 18.00 (change bus in Milan).

By car

Rome is approached by a network of motorways, including the A1 from northern Italy. This joins the busy Rome ring-road (*Grande Raccordo Annulare*) at Settebagni, from which there are well-signposted exits to all districts of the city. For car parking, see below.

British drivers taking their own cars by any of the routes across France, Belgium, Luxembourg, Switzerland, Germany and Austria need the vehicle registration book, and a valid European Community pink version of the UK driving licence. The old style green licences, which were issued in the UK up to April 1991, are not valid for driving in Italy, neither are official translations of these licences which were previously issued by the *Italian State Tourist Office*. You can get the EC licence from the *DVLA*, ☎ 01792 772 134. Alternatively, you can get an International Driving Permit from the *AA*. You must also have insurance cover, and a nationality plate attached to the car. If you are not the owner of the vehicle, you must have the owner's permission for its use abroad.

A Swiss motorway pass needed for that country is obtainable from the *RAC*, *AA*, the *Swiss Tourist* office or at the Swiss border. The provisions of the respective highway codes in the countries of transit, though similar, have important variations, especially with regard to priority, speed limits, and pedestrian crossings. A Swiss motorway pass needed for that country is obtainable from the *RAC*, *AA* or at the Swiss border. Membership of the *AA* or *RAC* entitles you to many of the facilities of affiliated societies on the Continent.

AA   ☎ 01256 29123, 📧 www.theaa.com
RAC   ☎ 01345 333 1133 membership and insurance
          ☎ 01345 333 222 route information
          📧 www.rac.co.uk

Additional route information is available from 📧 www.autostop.it/

Motorways In Italy, motorways (*autostrade*) charge tolls according to the rating of the vehicle and the distance covered. There are service areas (open 24hrs) on all motorways. Most motorways have SOS points every 2km. Unlike in France, motorways are indicated by green signs and normal roads by blue signs. At the entrance to motorways, the two directions are indicated by the name of the most important (not the nearest) town, which can be momentarily confusing. The Autostrade del Sole (A1) which runs down the centre of Italy from Milan to Rome is narrower than some of the more recently built motorways and carries very heavy traffic, including numerous lorries, especially between Bologna and Florence. Driving on this road is easier on Sundays, when lorries are banned.

Dual carriageway Fast roads (*superstrade*) do not charge tolls. They do not usually have service stations, SOS points or emergency lanes. They are also usually indicated by green signs.

Petrol stations Stations are open 24hrs on motorways, on other roads 07.00–12.00 and 15.00–20.00 in summer, 07.30–12.30 and 14.30–19.00 in winter. There are now quite a number of self-service petrol stations open 24hrs and operated by bank notes or credit cards. Unleaded petrol (*senza piombo* or *ben-*

zina verde) is now available all over Italy. Petrol in Italy costs more than in Britain, and a lot more than in North America.

Rules of the road The Continental rule of the road is to drive on the right and overtake on the left. Italian law requires that you carry a valid driving licence when travelling. It is obligatory to keep a red triangle sign in the car in case of accident or breakdown. This serves as a warning to other traffic when placed in the road at a distance of 50m from the stationary car. Seatbelts are compulsory.

Driving in Italy is generally faster (and often more aggressive) than driving in Britain or North America. Road signs are now more or less standardised to the international codes, but certain habits differ radically. Unless otherwise indicated, cars entering a road from the right are given precedence, as they are at roundabouts. If a driver flashes his headlights, it means he is proceeding and not that he is giving you precedence. Italian drivers are very lax about changing lanes without much warning, and they tend to ignore pedestrian crossings. Beware of motorbikes, mopeds and Vespas, the drivers of which seem to consider that they always have the right of way.

Police The police (see p 55) sometimes set up road blocks to check cars and their drivers. It is important to stop at once if you are waved down by a policeman at the side of the road and you must immediately show your driving licence and the car documents.

Maps The *Italian Touring Club* publishes several sets of excellent maps: these are constantly updated and are indispensable to anyone travelling by car in Italy. They include the *Grande Carta Stradale d'Italia* on a scale of 1:200,000. This is divided into 15 sheets covering the regions of Italy. These are also published in a handier form as the *Atlante Stradale d'Italia*, an atlas in three volumes, with a comprehensive index: the volume entitled *Centro* covers Rome and Lazio. These maps can be purchased from Italian Touring Club offices and at many booksellers; in Britain they are available from *Stanfords*, 12–14 Long Acre, London WC2E 9LP, ☎ 020 7240 3611, ✉ www.stanfords.co.uk

 Local tourist offices

The official tourist agency for Rome is the *APT* (*Azienda di Promozione Turistica di Roma*), whose offices supply a list of hotels, a map (when available), a brief guide to the city and up-to-date opening times:
APT, 5 Via Parigi (**Map 4; 3**), ☎ 06 488 991, 🖨 06 481 9316, open Mon–Fri 08.15–19.00, Sat 08.15–13.45; closed Sun.
Tourist Information Service, ☎ 06 3600 4399
Stazione Termini, open daily 08.15–19.00
Fiumicino airport, open daily 08.15–19.00

There are also a number of **tourist information kiosks**, in the centre of the city, open daily 09.00–18.00: Via del Corso (Largo Goldoni), the Fori Imperiali, Castel Sant'Angelo, Piazza San Giovanni in Laterano, Trastevere (Piazza Sonnino), Via Marco Minghetti (Fontana di Trevi) and Via Nazionale (Palazzo delle Esposizioni), and Via dell'Olmata (Santa Maria Maggiore).

Getting around

By bus and tram

Rome is well served by a fairly efficient bus and tram service, since most of the centre of the city has been closed to private traffic. The service of orange **buses** is run by *ATAC* (*Azienda Tramvie e Autobus del Comune di Roma*). For information, freephone ☎ 800 431 784, ✉ www.atac.roma.it. Free maps of the principal routes (one for day-time services, and one for the night services) are usually available from the *ATAC* information kiosk on Piazza dei Cinquecento in front of Stazione Termini, open Mon–Sat 08.00–20.00.

Tickets are sold at tobacconists, bars and newspaper kiosks, as well as at *ATAC* booths and by automatic machines at many bus stops and metro stations. They are valid for 75mins on any number of lines and for one journey on the metro. They have to be stamped at automatic machines on board the vehicle. Those found travelling without a valid ticket are liable to a heavy fine.

It is usually well worthwhile purchasing a **one-day ticket**, a *BIG* (*biglietto giornaliero*) which expires at midnight of the day it was purchased. Available from the usual outlets, it must be stamped once on board. A seven-day ticket or *CIS* (*carta settimanale*) expires at midnight of the seventh day. Season tickets valid for one calendar month are also available.

As in other large cities, you should always beware of **pickpockets** on buses (take extra care on bus no. 64 from Stazione Termini to the Vatican). There are usually no bus or underground services in Rome on 1 May or on the afternoon of Christmas Day, and services are limited on other holidays. Night bus services operate from 00.10 to 05.30; the numbers on these routes are followed by 'N'.

The few **tramlines** which survive are charmingly old-fashioned and slow, but provide a very pleasant means of transport as they are almost always much less crowded than the buses and have more seats. A new line (with modern tramcars) to Trastevere from Largo Argentina has been introduced in the last few years.

Because of one-way streets, return journeys do not always follow the same route as the outward journey. A small selection of the 237 bus routes and six tram routes in the city is given below (some of them are described only in part).

Town buses

Two **blue electric mini-bus services** (nos 116 and 117) operate a circular route through some of the most beautiful districts of the centre of town on weekdays from 07.40–20.00:

116

Via Veneto	Piazza Farnese
Piazza Barberini	Via Monserrato
Via del Tritone	Viale Moretta
Piazza di Spagna	Piazza Farnese
Piazza San Silvestro	Campo dei Fiori
Piazza Ponte Umberto I	Corso Rinascimento
Corso Rinascimento	Piazza Rotonda
Campo dei Fiori	Piazza Colonna
	Via del Tritone

Piazza Barberini
Via Veneto
Villa Borghese (for the Galleria
  Borghese)
Via Veneto

117
Piazza San Giovanni in Laterano
Via Claudia
Piazza Colosseo
Via Serpenti
Via Milano
Largo del Tritone
Piazza di Spagna
Piazza del Popolo
Via del Corso
Piazza Venezia
Piazza Colosseo
Via Labicana
Piazza San Giovanni in Laterano

Orange bus routes (services from
05.30–24.00)
64
Stazione Termini
Piazza della Repubblica
Via Nazionale
Piazza Venezia
Largo Torre Argentina
Corso Vittorio Emanuele II
Largo Porta Cavalleggeri (for
  St Peter's and the Vatican)
Stazione di San Pietro

60 (express)
Piazza della Repubblica
Via Nazionale
Via IV Novembre
Piazza Venezia
Via dei Fori Imperiali
Piazza Colosseo
Via di San Gregorio
Piramide

85
Piazza San Silvestro
Piazza Venezia
Piazza Colosseo

Via Labicana
San Giovanni in Laterano

87
Piazza Cavour
Corso Rinascimento
Largo Torre Argentina
Piazza Venezia
Via dei Fori Imperiali
Piazza Colosseo
San Giovanni in Laterano

95
Piramide
Piazza Bocca della Verità
Via del Teatro di Marcello
Piazza Venezia
Via del Corso
Via del Tritone
Via Veneto
Villa Borghese

628
Largo Torre Argentina
Piazza Venezia
Via del Teatro di Marcello
Piazza Bocca della Verità
Terme di Caracalla

For buses to the Via Appia Antica, see
p 417.

Trams
3
Piramide
Viale Aventino
Piazza Colosseo
San Giovanni in Laterano
Santa Croce in Gerusalemme
Porta Maggiore
San Lorenzo fuori le Mura
Viale Regina Margherita
Viale delle Belle Arti
Piazza Thorvaldsen (for the
  Borghese Gardens, Galleria
  Nazionale d'Arte Moderna and
  Museo Etrusco di Villa Giulia)

8
Largo Torre Argentina
Via Arenula
Trastevere

19
Piazza del Risorgimento (near the Vatican)
Via Flaminia
Piazza Thorvaldsen (for the Borghese Gardens, Galleria Nazionale d'Arte Moderna, and Museo di Villa Giulia)

Night bus services
No. 116T is a blue electric mini-bus service for theatre-goers, which can be useful if you eat out at a restaurant in the town centre; it runs every day except Sun, 20.00–01.30)

116T
Via Veneto
Piazza Barberini
Via delle Quattro Fontane
Via Nazionale
Piazza di Spagna
Piazza San Silvestro
Corso Rinascimento
Campo dei Fiori
Piazza Farnese
Via Monserrato
Viale Moretta
Piazza Farnese
Campo dei Fiori
Corso Rinascimento
Piazza Rotonda
Piazza Colonna
Via del Tritone
Via Traforo
Via Nazionale

Piazza della Repubblica
Via XX Settembre
Via San Basilio
Via Veneto

60N
Piazza Venezia
Via del Corso
Via del Tritone
Piazza Barberini
Via Veneto
Via Nomentana
Corso Sempione

72N
Piazza Venezia
Largo Torre Argentina
Viale Trastevere

78N
Piazza Venezia
Via Nazionale
Stazione Termini

60N
Piazza Venezia
Via del Corso
Via del Tritone
Piazza Barberini
Via Nomentana
Corso Sempione

72N
Piazza Venezia
Largo Torre Argentina
Viale Trastevere

78N
Piazza Venezia
Via Nazionale
Stazione Termini

Sight-seeing tours of Rome
These are provided daily by bus no. 110, which departs from Piazza dei Cinquecento (**Map 4**; **3**) in front of Stazione Termini every half hour from 10.00–18.00. There are also night tours leaving at 20.00 (21.00 in summer). The circular route includes Piazza Barberini, Piazza del Popolo, San Pietro, Piazza Venezia and the Colosseum. The itinerary lasts 2hrs 30mins. There is no guide but a brochure is supplied. For bookings and information go to the *ATAC* information office beside Stazione Termini.

By underground railway

There are two lines in Rome's underground railway system (*metropolitana*), although if you want to visit the centre of the city, you are almost always better off taking a bus. The only really useful parts of the system if you are staying in the centre are from Stazione Termini to Piazza di Spagna, and from Stazione Termini to the Colosseum. The service begins at 05.30 and ends at 23.30; on Saturdays the last train is at 00.30.

Line A Opened in 1980 and extended in 2000 it runs from Battistini in the western suburbs to Via Ottaviano near the Vatican. From here it runs beneath the centre of Rome with stations at Piazzale Flaminio (Piazza del Popolo), Piazza di Spagna, Piazza Barberini, Piazza della Repubblica and Stazione Termini. It continues to San Giovanni in Laterano and traverses the southern suburbs of Rome along the Via Appia Nuova and Via Tuscolana to terminate beyond Cinecittà at Anagnina. It runs underground for the whole of its 14km length except for the bridge across the Tiber.

Line B The first part of Line B opened in 1952, runs south-west from Stazione Termini to Porta San Paolo, in Piazzale Ostiense, where it comes to the surface just beyond Ostiense station, running from there alongside the Rome Lido railway as far as Magliana, beyond the Basilica of San Paolo fuori le Mura. It then runs underground north-east to terminate at Tre Fontane (Laurentina) in EUR. In the 1990s it was extended north-east from Termini via Stazione Tiburtina through the suburbs of Rome as far as Rebibbia. The intermediate stops most useful to visitors serving the centre of Rome south of Termini station are Via Cavour, Colosseo, Circo Massimo, and Piramide (Porta San Paolo).

A service also runs from Porta San Paolo to Ostia Antica and Ostia Lido.

By coach

Coach services to the environs of Rome and Lazio start from and return to various underground railway stations. The blue coaches are run by **COTRAL** (*Azienda Consortile Trasporti Lazio*), which has an information office at 25 Via Portonaccio, ☎ 06 591 5551 or 06 57531 open Mon–Fri 07.45–16.40.

By car

You are strongly advised not to use a car in Rome: the city is invaded by some two million cars and there are often serious traffic jams. The inner area of the city (the *Centro Blu*) is closed to private cars without special permits Mon–Fri 06.30–18.00, Sat 14.00–18.00, and the use of many streets and lanes is restricted. Access is allowed for the disabled and visitors with a hotel reservation (some hotels have garages).

Parking

Parking is extremely difficult anywhere in the city. Some large car parks on the outskirts of the city are open 06.00–22.00 daily except festivals and charge a small daily tariff. These are mostly at underground stations and include Anagnina and Cinecittà on underground Line A, and Laurentina and EUR Maglaiana on underground Line B. There is a long-term car park, Verano, on Via Tiburtina which is open 07.00–19.00 and also charges by the day. There are very few large car parks in the centre of the city. The most central include Viale Giulio Cesare, near the Vatican; Viale del Muro Torto, under the Villa Borghese gardens; and Piazza dei Cinquecento, by Termini station. These have hourly tariffs. In many districts of the city—marked with a blue line on the kerb—you have to pay to park at the side of the road. You can pay the charge per hour either with coins or a card called *Roma per te* which you buy at newsstands or tobacconists. For information on car parking and car parks from *STA* (*Agenzia per la mobilità del Comune di Roma*) *Infososta*, ☎ 06 5711 8333.

Always lock your car when parked, and never leave anything of value inside it. It is forbidden to park in front of a gate or doorway marked with a blue-and-red *passo carrabile* sign. Once a week street-cleaning takes place at night, so cars have to be removed (or the owner may be fined and the vehicle towed away); ask locally for information. When driving in Rome, beware of motorcycles, mopeds and Vespas, the drivers of which seem always to assume the right of way.

Car hire

The principle car-hire firms have offices at Fiumicino airport and Stazione Termini Station as well as in the centre of Rome.
Avis, 25 Via della Giuliana, ☎ 06 3974 2361
Europcar, 7 Via Lombardia, ☎ 06 487 1274
Hertz, Via L. Vassallo 12, ☎ 06 438 6418
Maggiore, 8a Via Po, ☎ 06 854 8698

Motoring organisations

Italian Automobile Club (*ACI*), head office, 8 Via Marsala, ☎ 06 49981
Automobile Club of Rome, 261 Via Cristoforo Colombo, ☎ 06 514 971
For the *ACI* breakdown service, ☎ 116.

By bicycle and scooter

Bicycles can be hired at stands in Piazza del Popolo, Piazza San Silvestro, Piazza di Spagna and Piazza Augusto Imperatore on Via del Corso. Both bicycles and scooters can be hired from:
Scoot-a-long, 302 Via Cavour, ☎ 06 678 0206
Scooters for Rent, 84 Via della Purificazione, ☎ 06 488 5485
St Peter's Moto, 7 Via Fosse di Castello, ☎ 06 687 5714

By taxi

Taxis (white or yellow in colour) are provided with an identification name and number, the emblem of the municipality of Rome, and a meter; you should always make sure the latter is operational before hiring a taxi. The fare includes service, so tipping is not necessary. Licensed taxis are hired from ranks; there are no cruising taxis, and it is never advisable to accept rides from non-authorised taxis at the airports or train stations. There are additional charges for travel at night (22.00–07.00), on Sundays and for each piece of luggage.

To call a taxi, ☎ 06 3570; ☎ 06 4994; or ☎ 06 8822: you will be given the approximate arrival time and the number of the taxi.

Horse-drawn cabs are used exclusively by tourists, and you should agree the fare with the driver before starting the journey.

Where to stay

Information

Information about hotels and other accommodation in Rome can be obtained abroad from State tourist offices, *ENIT* (see above), and on arrival at the *APT* information offices at Stazione Termini, Fiumicino airport and 5 Via Parigi, or at the information kiosks in the city.

An annual, free publication by the *APT* of Rome, which is available from *APT* offices, lists all the hotels in Rome, with their charges.

Hotels

There are five official **categories** of hotels in Italy, from luxury five-star hotels to the most simple one-star establishments. These categories are bound to disappoint many travellers, however, for they are now based on the services offered (television in each room, private telephone and *'frigobar'*, for example), and often do not reflect quality. Three- and four-star hotels in Rome are not always on a par with hotels with the same designation in other large European cities.

It is essential to **book well in advance** for Easter and for September and October; you are usually asked to send a deposit or leave a credit card number to confirm the booking. You have the right to claim the deposit back if you cancel the booking at least 72 hours in advance. Accommodation booking services from the UK are offered by:

Hotel Connect, ☎ 020 8381 2233, 🖷 020 8381 1155, ✉ hotel.connect@ virgin.net

The Italian Connection, ☎ 020 7486 6890, 🖷 020 7486 6891, ✉ italian connection.london@btinternet.com, can arrange accommodation in hotels, pensions, and self-catering apartments

Once in Rome, *Hotel Reservation* provides a free booking service for about 500 hotels of all categories from a booth in front of platform 10 at Termini railway station and at Fiumicino airport, ☎ 06 699 1000; open daily 07.00–22.00.

Prices Every hotel has to declare its prices annually. Prices change according to the season, and can be considerably less in off-peak periods. In the foyer there should be a list of all the rooms in the hotel with their rates, and the total charge for a room should be displayed on the back of the room door. For tax purposes hotels are obliged by law to issue an official receipt (*ricevuta fiscale*) to customers; you should not leave the premises without this document.

In all hotels service charges are included in the rates, so tipping is not necessary. You should beware of **extra charges** added to the bill. Drinks from the *frigobar* in your room are extremely expensive, and it is always best to buy drinks yourself from a shop outside the hotel. Telephone calls are also more expensive if made from your room; there is usually a pay telephone in the lobby which is the most economical way of telephoning and is more convenient than using the public telephones in the streets (see below). You are usually also charged extra for garage parking.

You should be cautious about arranging to hire a car and guide with the hotel porter: everyone involved expects to take a large cut and a day in Rome spent in this way is bound to cost you a great deal and is hardly ever worthwhile.

Breakfast (*prima colazione*) can be disappointing and costly. By law it is an optional extra charge, although a lot of hotels try to include it in the price of the room. When booking, always specify if you want breakfast or not. If you are staying in a two- or three-star hotel, it is usually a good idea to go round the corner to the nearest *pasticceria* or bar for breakfast. In some of the more expensive hotels good buffet breakfasts are now provided, but even here the standard of the 'canteen' coffee can be poor: you can always ask for an espresso or cappuccino instead. A large supplement is usually charged for breakfast served in your room.

Rome has some 750 hotels and only a very small selection has been given below; omission does not necessarily imply any derogatory judgement. The hotels have been listed according to category and location. The most pleasant areas to stay in the city include the streets around Piazza di Spagna, the Pantheon and Campo dei Fiori. The numerous hotels near Termini Station and on Via Veneto are in much less attractive districts and further away from the main monuments. In the list below smaller hotels—many of which do not take groups—have usually been favoured, as have those in particularly pleasant positions. The map references refer to the street atlas section at the back of the book.

Prices per double room per night

☆☆☆☆☆   € 400–700
☆☆☆☆   € 200–300
☆☆☆   € 100–200
☆☆   € 50–100

Near Piazza di Spagna
☆☆☆☆☆

Hassler Villa Medici (**Map 3**; **3**), 6 Piazza Trinità dei Monti, 00187, ☎ 06 699 340, ▤ 06 678 9991, ✉ booking@hotelhassler.it. Famous old-established hotel at the top of the Spanish Steps. Stunning views from street-side rooms and the rooftop terrace/restaurant, and a well-earned reputation for luxury service. 85 rooms and five suites; no groups. Small summer garden. Garage and restaurant.
Plaza (**Map 3**; **5**), 126 Via del Corso, 00186, ☎ 06 6992 1111, ▤ 06 6994 1575, ✉ plaza@grandhotelplaza.com. Large, busy hotel, popular with businessmen and politicians which was until recently a four-star hotel. Rooms vary greatly in size and decor. Terrace and restaurant.
☆☆☆☆

De La Ville (**Map 3**; **3**), 69 Via Sistina, 00187, ☎ 06 67331, ▤ 06 678 4213, ✉ rome@interconti.com. One of the most luxurious hotels in the city. Many rooms with frescoes and stucco decoration. Splendid views from top-floor rooms. Garage and restaurant.
D'Inghilterra (**Map 3**; **5**), 14 Bocca di Leone, 00187, ☎ 06 699811, ▤ 06 6992 2243, ✉ reservation.hir@royaldemeure.com. One of the best-known old-established hotels, which retains its elegant atmosphere with rooms decorated with turn-of-the-century English furniture. In a quiet cul-de-sac surrounded by Rome's most fashionable shopping streets. The charming breakfast room in the basement is entirely frescoed with Roman garden scenes. Restaurant.
☆☆☆

City Nova (**Map 3**; **5**), 97 Via due Macelli, 00187, ☎ 06 679 7468, ▤ 06 679 7962. A solid, comfortable hotel on the street that runs between Piazza di Spagna and the Trevi fountain. Helpful and professional staff.

Gregoriana (**Map 3; 5**), 18 Via Gregoriana, 00187, ☎ 06 679 4269, 🖷 06 678 4258. A small, well-cared-for hotel on one of the quietest streets in the area. Three of the 16 rooms have balconies. There are no public rooms and breakfast is served only in your room. No groups. The staff could be more friendly.

Homs (**Map 3; 5**), 71 Via della Vite, 00187, ☎ 06 679 2976, 🖷 06 678 0482. A simple, family-run hotel in the heart of Rome's fashionable shopping area, with a beautiful terrace. Bathrooms and rooms are rather small.

Internazionale (**Map 3; 3**), 79 Via Sistina, 00187, ☎ 06 6994 1823, 🖷 06 678 4764, ✉ romint@flashnet.it. Housed in a 16C convent, this 42-room hotel retains a pleasantly old-fashioned atmosphere. All the rooms have wall-to-wall carpeting. The 11 rooms on the fourth floor have balconies, and several have jacuzzi tubs, a rarity in Rome. No groups.

Locarno (**Map 2; 4**), 22 Via della Penna, 00185, ☎ 06 361 0841, 🖷 06 321 5249, ✉ info@hotellocarno.com Located just off Piazza del Popolo, about 15mins' walk to Piazza di Spagna, the *Locarno* is a lovely hotel decorated in Art Deco style. An excellent place to stay. A pleasant roof bar and complimentary bicycles are available on loan.

Scalinata di Spagna (**Map 3; 3**), 17 Piazza Trinità dei Monti, 00187, ☎ 06 679 3006, 🖷 06 6994 0598, ✉ info@hotelscalinata.com. Some of the 16 rooms are a bit small, but this quiet, romantic hotel is right by the Spanish Steps, with a tiny roof garden. No groups. It has a very friendly atmosphere.

★★

Margutta (**Map 12; 4**), 34 Via Laurina, 00187, ☎ 06 322 3674, 🖷 06 320 0395. Lovely little hotel tucked away on a quiet street between Piazza di Spagna and Piazza del Popolo. The 21 double rooms are furnished with iron beds and dark wooden furniture.

Suisse (**Map 3; 5**), 56 Via Gregoriana, 00187, ☎ 06 678 3649, 🖷 06 678 1258. Spotless budget hotel in a prime location. Some of the 13 rooms have decorated ceilings and antique furniture.

Near the Pantheon, Piazza Navona and Campo de' Fiori

★★★★★

Grand Hotel de la Minerve (**Map 2; 8**), 69 Piazza della Minerva, 00186, ☎ 06 695 201, 🖷 06 679 4165, ✉ www.minervahotel.com. Right behind the Pantheon, a well-maintained 17C façade hides a dramatic, modern interior, designed by Paolo Portoghesi and full of marble and stained glass. The rooms are comfortable and quiet; many have views onto the narrow streets below. Beautiful roof garden. It has unfortunately lost all the atmosphere it had when, simply as the Hotel Minerva, it was throughout the 20C one of the best known moderately priced hotels in Rome.

★★★★

Sole al Pantheon (**Map 2; 8**), 63 Piazza della Rotonda, 00186, ☎ 06 678 0441, 🖷 06 6994 0689, ✉ hotsole@flashnet.it. Just steps away from the Pantheon (several of the 25 rooms have views), this hotel has been in business since the 15C. Rooms are cool and fresh, with whitewashed walls and terracotta decorations; jacuzzi tubs are a modern touch.

★★★

Del Senato (**Map 2; 8**), 73 Piazza della Rotonda, 00186, ☎ 06 678 4343, 🖷 06 6994 0297, ✉ info@albergodelsenato.it. An old-established hotel, much favoured by Italian politicians, it is usually very difficult to find a room here.

Many rooms look out onto the Pantheon, just a few steps from the hotel. The lower floors and entrance have been renovated tastefully; the upper floors remain a little dated.

Portoghesi (**Map 2**; **6**), 1 Via dei Portoghesi, 00186, ☎ 06 686 4231, ▤ 06 687 6976, ✉ info@hotelportoghesiroma.com. Unassuming hotel, well located on a quiet street between the Tiber and Piazza Navona. Lovely view from the terrace, where breakfast is served in summertime.

Santa Chiara (**Map 2**; **8**), 21 Via di Santa Chiara, 00186, ☎ 06 687 2979, ▤ 06 687 3144, ✉ info@albergosantachiara.com. An elegant, family-run hotel just behind the Pantheon. Well-appointed rooms have solid wood furniture and marble bathrooms. Many rooms have pleasant views, and a few have balconies.

Teatro di Pompeo (**Map 2**; **8**), 8 Largo del Pallaro, 00186, ☎ 06 6830 0170, ▤ 06 6880 5531, ✉ hotel.teatrodipompeo@tiscalinet.it. Located in a quiet small square between Campo de' Fiori and Corso Vittorio Emanuele, this tranquil hotel sits on the remains of a Roman theatre, whose original 55 BC circular structure is still visible in the breakfast room. All the 13 attractive rooms (only one single available) feature old wooden ceilings.

☆☆

Campo de' Fiori (**Map 2**; **8**), 6 Via del Biscione, 00186, ☎ 06 6880 6865, ▤ 06 687 6003, ✉ framar1@inwind.it A well-maintained, reasonably priced hotel just off the piazza of the same name. The 27 rooms are cosy (those on the first floor have the best decor), but only nine have full bathrooms. Views of the lovely square from the two common terraces.

Pomezia (**Map 6**; **6**), 12 Via dei Chiavari, 00186, ☎ & ▤ 06 686 1371, ✉ h.pomezia@libero.it. A very pleasant small hotel in a delightful position.

Sole (**Map 2**; **8**), 76 Via del Biscione, 00186, ☎ 06 6880 6873, ▤ 06 689 3787, ✉ info@solealbiscione.it. This medium-sized, cosy hotel is one of the best value in the area, although not all the rooms have bathrooms and there is no breakfast service. You can watch the sun set over the dome of the church of Sant'Andrea della Valle from the top terrace. There is also an enclosed garden. No credit cards.

On the Aventine Hill

☆☆☆

Domus Aventina (**Map 9**; **4**), 11b Via di Santa Prisca, 00153, ☎ 06 574 6135, ▤ 06 5730 0044, ✉ domus.aventina@italyhotel.com. Although housed in an ex-convent, the hotel is entirely modern and has no atmosphere. The 26 spacious rooms, some with balconies, face onto a courtyard and the wall of Santa Prisca. Reasonably priced.

Sant'Anselmo (**Map 9**; **3**), 2 Piazza Sant'Anselmo, 00153, ☎ 06 5743547, ▤ 06 578 3604, ✉ info@aventinohotels.com In the exceptionally quiet and peaceful residential district of the Aventine, this is a delightful hotel in a villa which was once a private residence. The 45 rooms are cheerfully decorated in Venetian style. Breakfast is served in the pretty garden. It is also an excellent place to stay if you have to come to Rome with a car as you can park on the road outside.

☆☆

Aventino (**Map 9**; **3**), 10 Via San Domenico, 00153, ☎ 06 5783214, ▤ 06 5441112, ✉ info@aventinohotels.com. Run by the *Sant'Anselmo* hotel, also in a lovely quiet position.

Via Veneto and the Parioli

☆☆☆☆☆

Ambasciatori Palace (**Map 7; 2**), 62 Via Veneto, 00187, ☎ 06 47493, 🖶 06 474 3601, ✉ ambasciatorirome@ambasciatoripalace.com. An elegant, old-style hotel, which until recently was a four-star hotel. Rich decor with plush carpets. Courteous and attentive staff.

Eden (**Map 7; 2**), 49 Via Ludovisi, 00187, ☎ 06 478 121, 🖶 06 482 1584, ✉ reservations@hotel-eden.it. The Eden is one of the finest hotels in Rome, very elegant with all the comforts and services of a luxury-class hotel. The roof restaurant, with adjoining piano bar, has a panoramic view of the city and is among the best in town. Gymnasium.

Excelsior (**Map 7; 2**), 125 Via Veneto, 00187, ☎ 06 47081, 🖶 06 482 6205, ✉ res070.excelsior.rome@westin.com. Opposite the American Embassy, this is one of Rome's most famous hotels. It continues to thrive although its reputation was made when the Via Veneto was the centre of fashionable Roman life in the 1960s. Owned by the Westin hotel group.

Lord Byron (**Map 12; 5**), 5 Via de Notaris, 00197, ☎ 06 322 0404, 🖶 06 322 0405, ✉ info@lordbyronhotel.com. This quiet, exclusive hotel with just 37 rooms in a converted mansion in the Parioli area, with views onto the Villa Borghese, seems far removed from the chaos of the centre of town. First-rate restaurant on the ground floor. Excellent, attentive service.

☆☆☆☆

La Residenza (**Map 3; 4**), 22 Via Emilia, 00187, ☎ 06 488 0789, 🖶 06 485 721, ✉ hotel.la.residenza@venere.it. A popular hotel which combines a central location with villa style decor and large, comfortable rooms. Good service.

Victoria (**Map 3; 4**), 41 Via Campania, 00187, ☎ 06 473 931, 🖶 06 487 1890, ✉ hotel.victoria@flashnet.it. Very close to the Via Veneto, this Swiss-run hotel offers excellent value: spacious, spotless rooms and friendly staff who attend to the smallest detail. Rooftop terrace with view onto the Villa Borghese across the street.

☆☆☆

Villa Borghese (**Map 3; 3, 4**), 31 Via Pinciana, 00198, ☎ 06 854 9648, 🖶 06 841 4100, ✉ hotel.villaborghese@tiscalinet.it. A pleasant hotel just off the park of Villa Borghese. Rooms are small but well cared-for. Breakfast is served on an ivy-covered patio.

Near the Vatican

☆☆☆☆

Atlante Star (**Map 1; 6**), 34 Via Vitelleschi, 00193, ☎ 06 687 3233, 🖶 06 687 2300, ✉ atlante.star@atlantehotels.com. The feature of this hotel is its glorious roof terrace on various levels with superb views, and the dome of St Peter's in the foreground. Efficient management, and friendly, helpful staff. Luxury-class restaurant on the roof.

Cicerone (**Map 2; 3**), 55/c Via Cicerone, 00193, ☎ 06 3576, 🖶 06 6880 1383, ✉ cicerone@travel.it. Reasonably priced, large modern hotel located near Castel Sant'Angelo in a side street off the busy Via Cola di Rienzo. The rooms are comfortable but without character. Covered parking in the basement.

Columbus (**Map 1; 6**), 33 Via della Conciliazione, 00193, ☎ 06 686 5435, 🖶 06 686 4874, ✉ hotelcolumbus@hotelcolumbus.net. Two minutes' walk from St Peter's. A pleasant hotel in an ex-convent with well-furnished rooms, and a terrace.

Farnese (**Map 2**; **3**), 30 Via Alessandro Farnese, 00192, ☎ 06 321 2553, 📠 06 321 5129, 🖥 www.travel.it/roma/hotelfarnese. A palazzo with comfortable rooms in the quiet, residential Prati district, not far from the shops on Via Cola di Rienzo and just across the river from the historic centre.

☆☆☆

Amalia (**Map 1**; **4**), 66 Via Germanico, 00192, ☎ 06 3972 3356, 📠 06 3972 3365, 🖥 hotelamalia@iol.it. Popular with Italians, this super-clean modern hotel is convenient for the Vatican and the Ottaviano metro stop. Friendly staff.

Sant'Anna (**Map 1**; **6**), 133–4 Borgo Pio, 00193, ☎ 06 6880 1602, 📠 06 6830 8717, 🖥 sant'anna@travel.it. In a delightful quiet pedestrian street, with local shops, very close to St Peter's, this has perhaps the most pleasant location of all the hotels in the otherwise rather unattractive district near the Vatican. A small hotel decorated in Art Deco style, the ample rooms on the top floor have small terraces. Parking.

Via Nazionale, Stazione Termini and Santa Maria Maggiore

☆☆☆☆☆

Le Grand Hotel ~ St Regis Grand (**Map 4**; **3**), 3 Via Vittorio Emanuele Orlando, 00185, ☎ 06 47091, 📠 06 474 7307, 🖥 www.stregis.com/grandrome. This old-fashioned, elegant hotel near Stazione Termini has long been one of the city's finest. Marble baths and Murano chandeliers recall a day when no expense was spared to decorate top-class hotels. Afternoon tea is still served in the richly decorated main salon. Owned by the Starwood hotel group.

☆☆☆☆

Massimo d'Azeglio (**Map 4**; **5**), 18 Via Cavour, 00184, ☎ 06 487 0270, 📠 06 482 7386, 🖥 dazeglio@bettojahotels.it. Serviceable hotel which has been in business since 1875; close to Stazione Termini, it has a decidedly dated feel. The 203 spacious rooms have solid furniture in the classic style. Attentive staff.

☆☆☆

Aberdeen (**Map 4**; **5**), 48 Via Firenze, 00184, ☎ 06 482 3920, 📠 06 482 1092, 🖥 hotel.aberdeen@travel.it. A hotel on two floors of a much larger building. Ample breakfast.

Impero (**Map 4**; **5**), 19 Via Viminale, 00184, ☎ 06 482 0066, 📠 06 483 762. Close to the Teatro dell'Opera, the Impero is a gracious hotel in a 19C building. Spacious common areas alternate with cosy living rooms. The doors are painted with scenes from ancient Rome, and the whole decor is done in Art Nouveau style.

Patria (**Map 4**; **3**), 36 Via Torino, 00184, ☎ 06 488 0756, 📠 06 481 4872, 🖥 infopatria@hotelpatria.it. Totally renovated in the last few years, with modern fixtures and double-glazed windows to keep out the noise of the traffic. 49 rooms on five floors, and a bar open 24hrs a day.

Villa delle Rose (**Map 4**; **4**), 5 Via Vicenza, 00185, ☎ 06 445 1788, 📠 06 445 1639, 🖥 villadellerose@flashnet.it. A quiet, friendly hotel housed in a villa with a garden near the station. The bar and lounge have original frescoes on the ceiling, in sharp contrast with the very simple decor of the 40 rooms, some of which are spacious enough to accommodate extra beds. One of the few hotels in Rome to have a non-smoking breakfast area.

Near the Colosseum and Forum

☆☆☆☆
Forum (**Map 7; 6**), 25 Via Tor dei Conti, 00184, ☎ 06 679 2446, 🖷 06 678 6479, 🖃 info@hotelforum.com. The Imperial Fora are just a few steps from the front door of the hotel, and many of the rooms and the rooftop terrace (with restaurant and bar service) offer some of the best views in the city onto the ruins of ancient Rome. The 76 rooms are comfortable but not particularly attractive, with slightly worn decor.

☆☆☆
Edera (**Map 10; 2**), 75 Via Poliziano, 00184, ☎ 06 7045 3888, 🖷 06 7045 3769, 🖃 leonardi@travel.it. Sober, medium-sized hotel with spacious double rooms and an inner garden. On a quiet street, two minutes' walk from the Colosseum.

☆☆
Casa Kolbe (**Map 9; 2**), 44 Via San Teodoro 00186, ☎ 06 679 8866, 🖷 06 6994 1550. Located on a tranquil street surprisingly out of the way even though it is at the foot of the Palatine Hill, and close to the Circus Maximus and Piazza Bocca della Verità, the *Kolbe* offers reasonably-priced double rooms, very sparsely furnished, but with bath. Small garden. No credit cards.

Bed and breakfast

This type of accommodation has recently been introduced into Italy and a separate list of authorised houses is published annually by the *APT*, with full details including prices (the name of the booklet is *Bed & Breakfast, Case per Ferie, Campeggi, Ostelli, etc.*).

Youth and students' hostels

The *Italian Youth Hostels Association*, *Associazione Italiana Alberghi per la Gioventù*, has its national headquarters at 44 Via Cavour, ☎ 06 487 1152, 🖷 06 4880492, 🖃 www.hostelbooking.com
Ostello del Foro Italico, 61 Viale delle Olimpiadi, ☎ 06 3236267, 🖷 06 3242613, 🖃 aig.sedenazionale@uni.net. This is the Rome youth hostel and regional headquarters of the association
Marello, 50 Via Urbana, ☎ 06 482 5361
YWCA, 4 Via Balbo, ☎ 06 488 0460, 🖷 06 4871028, a women's hostel
Protezione della Giovane, 158 Via Urbana; another women's hostel
  Religious organisations run some hostels for students and visitors (listed as *Case per ferie* in the *APT* booklet which includes Bed & Breakfast, etc), which are usually very reasonably priced.

Camping

Sites are listed in the annual APT booklet mentioned above, and full details of campsites in Italy are published annually by the *Touring Club Italiano* (*TCI*) in *Campeggi e Villaggi turistici in Italia*. The *Federazione Italiana del Campeggio* have an information office and booking service at 11 Via Vittorio Emanuele, Calenzano, 50041 Florence, ☎ 055 882 391, 🖷 055 882 5918. Rates charged must be displayed at the campsite office.
  Among the sites on the outskirts of Rome open all year are:
Roma Camping, 831 Via Aurelia, ☎ 06 662 3018, 🖷 06 664 18147,

guideuro@guideuro.it
Seven Hills, 1216 Via Cassia, ☎ 06 303 10826, 06 303 10039
Nomentano, 11 Via della Cesarina (corner of Via Nomentana), ☎ 06 414
69175, 06 336 13800
   In Lazio there are sites at Anzio, Nettuno, Bracciano and Subiaco.

Food and drink

Food in Rome, as in the rest of Italy, is generally extremely good, despite the fact that many Romans lament the disappearance in the last few decades of many typical Roman *trattorie* with their traditional food. There are still a great number of good restaurants although there tend to be fewer and fewer cheaper ones. Excellent pizzas are still made in numerous *pizzerie*. The least pretentious restaurant usually provides the best value.

   Most restaurants display a menu outside which gives you an idea of the prices; however, many simpler restaurants do not, and here, although the choice is usually limited, the standard of the cuisine is often very high. Some restaurants still have a cover charge (*coperto*) shown separately on the menu, which is added to the bill, although this practice has officially been discontinued. Prices include service, unless otherwise stated on the menu. Tipping is therefore not necessary, but a few Euro can be left on the table to convey appreciation. For tax purposes restaurants are now obliged by law to issue an official receipt to customers (*ricevuta fiscale*); you should not leave the premises without this document.

   Lunch is normally taken at about 13.00, while dinner is at 20.00 or 21.00. It is always acceptable to order a first course only, or to skip the first course and order only a main course.

The menu
Some of the best items of traditional Roman cuisine often served in Roman restaurants and trattorie are listed below.

First courses ~ *primi piatti*
Fresh **pasta** dishes, usually made on the premises, include:
fettuccine, ribbon noodles often served with a meat sauce or with porcini mushrooms
tonnarelli, fresh pasta in the form of spaghetti
bigoli, fresh pasta in the form of spaghetti
spaghetti alla carbonara, with a light sauce of salt pork, beaten egg, pecorino cheese and black pepper
penne all'arrabbiata, short pasta with a hot (piquant) tomato sauce
bucatini or *penne all'Amatriciana*, thick, hollow spaghetti or short pasta served in a light sauce of salt pork, tomatoes and pecorino cheese
pasta alla Checca, with diced mozzarella cheese, raw tomatoes and basil
pasta con broccoli, short pasta with broccoli, pine nuts and garlic
timballo, a rich pasta dish cooked in the oven, usually with peas and ham and a cheese sauce
   Another typical first course is *gnocchi alla Romana*, made from a dough of

semolina flour, eggs and milk, covered in cheese and baked. *Gnocchi di patate alla Romana* are potato dumplings served in a light meat and tomato sauce, and are traditionally made on Thursdays. *Agnolotti* are ravioli filled with meat.

A **soup** (*minestra*) often served in Rome is *stracciatella*, a meat broth with parmesan and a beaten egg. *Polenta*, made from yellow maize flour, is usually served with meat stews in a tomato sauce, or with grilled fish. A summer hors d'oeuvre (*antipasto*) is *fichi* or *melone* with *prosciutto*, figs or melon, with Parma ham.

Main courses ~ *secondi piatti*

The best known **meat** (*carne*) dish in Rome is *abbacchio arrosto* or *al forno*, roast suckling lamb

scottadito, grilled ribs or chops of suckling lamb

saltimbocca alla Romana, veal escalope with ham and sage

involtini, thin, rolled slices of meat in a sauce

stracotto, beef cooked in a tomato sauce, or in red wine

pollo or *coniglio alla cacciatora*, chicken or rabbit cooked in a tomato sauce, with herbs and onions

A number of traditional dishes using **offal** (*frattaglie*) are served in numerous restaurants in Rome:

coda alla vaccinara, oxtail in a celery and tomato sauce

pajata or *pagliata*, a dish made with the intestines of oxen and sheep (also often used as a sauce for pasta)

coratella d'abbacchio, a stew of young lamb's liver, heart, etc.

cervello, brains

rognoncini trifolati, sliced kidneys sautéed with parsley

animelle, sweetbreads

trippa, tripe

Fish ~ *pesce*

Fish is usually the most expensive item on the menu, but can be extremely good in restaurants specialising in it:

pesce arrosto or *pesce alla griglia*, roast or grilled fish: among the most succulent—and expensive—fish usually cooked in this way are *dentice* (dentex), *orata* (bream) and *triglie* (red mullet)

fritto di pesce or *fritto misto di mare*, various types of small fried fish, almost always including *calamari* (squid) and *seppie* (cuttlefish) is usually the most inexpensive fish dish on the menu

Seafood, often served cooked in white wine with garlic and parsley, includes:

cozze, mussels

vongole, clams

gamberi, prawns, usually grilled

anguilla (con piselli in umido), eel (stewed with peas)

filetti di baccalà fritti, fillets of salt cod fried in batter

zuppa di pesce, a rich fish stew made with a wide variety of fish

Vegetarian dishes ~ *platti vegetariani*

porcini, large wild mushrooms, an expensive delicacy served only in season, from October to December and around Easter. Best grilled, they are also often used as a sauce for pasta

pasta e fagioli or *pasta e ceci*, short pasta with white beans or with chick peas, are rich, warming dishes served in winter

scamorza al forno, cheese baked in the oven

melanzane alla parmigiana, aubergine cooked in the oven with a cheese and tomato sauce

Vegetables ~ *contorni*

Numerous delicious fresh vegetables are served in season:

carciofi, artichokes, an important part of Roman cuisine and cooked in a great variety of ways. They are always young and small and usually eaten whole. They may be *alla giudia* (deep fried) or *alla Romana* (stuffed with wild mint and garlic, and then stewed in olive oil and water)

zucchini, courgettes, sometimes served *ripieni* (stuffed) or fried

fritto di fiori di zucca, courgette flowers stuffed with mozzarella cheese and salted anchovies, dipped in batter and fried

insalata di puntarelle, a typical Roman salad made from the shredded stalks of locally grown chicory, with anchovy dressing

Particularly good cooked green vegetables found in Rome and Lazio include:

cicoria, chicory

broccoletti, broccoli

Cheeses ~ *formaggi*

Specialities include:

pecorino, a strong, hard cheese made from sheeps' milk

ricotta, the fresh by-product of *pecorino*, delicious on its own

mozzarella di bufala, made from buffalo's milk, which can also be *affumicata* (smoked)

Desserts ~ *dolce*

Italians usually prefer **fresh fruit** for dessert and in many simple restaurants and trattorie only fruit is served at the end of the meal. The fruit available varies according to what is in season:

fragole, strawberries are best served with fresh lemon juice or red wine rather than with cream. *Fragole di bosco* are tiny wild strawberries with a pungent flavour

cocomero or *anguria*, water melon, is particularly refreshing in summer

macedonia, fruit salad, is almost always made from fresh fruit in season

Sweets are considered the least important part of the meal, but may include the following:

crostata, tart, also usually made with fresh fruit

zuppa inglese, a rich trifle

tiramisù, a rich mixture of mascarpone cheese, egg, chocolate, biscuits and, sometimes, liqueur

gelato, ice cream, in restaurants is not always home-made

Wines ~ *vini*

Lazio used to be famous for its Vini dei Castelli, with their clear amber tint, but these wines have deteriorated drastically in quality and it is now very difficult to find a good bottled wine from this region. However, some restaurants still buy their wine in demijohns directly from vineyards in the Alban Hills and it is often a good idea to try this *vino della casa* before ordering a more expensive bottle. The house wine served in Rome is almost always white.

The few wines of Lazio still worth looking out for include the white from Capena, Colli Lanuvini and Monteliascone; the red **Cesanese** from Piglio, the strong red wine of Marino; and *L'Aleatico*, a red dessert wine from Gradoli near the Lago di Bolsena. It is no longer easy to find a good wine from Frascati or Velletri, but, as in other parts of Italy, the wine bottled by the local Cantina Sociale is usually of an acceptable standard. Good quality (but not cheap) bottled wines are available in most Roman restaurants: those from the Veneto, Puglia, Sardinia, Sicily and Tuscany are often the best.

Restaurants

In the simplest restaurants (*ristoranti, trattorie*) the food is usually as good, and considerably cheaper than in the more famous restaurants, though furnishings and surroundings can be a lot less comfortable.

The best guide to eating in Rome is *Roma del Gambero Rosso*, published annually by **Gambero Rosso Editore** (only in Italian).

A selection of a few restaurants—grouped according to location and divided into four categories according to price per person for dinner—is given below

€€€€	around € 100
€€€	around € 50–70
€€	around € 30–40
€	under € 30

Pantheon, Piazza Navona and Campo dei Fiori
€€€€

Camponeschi, 50 Piazza Farnese, ☎ 06 687 4927. Open evenings; closed Sunday. Carefully prepared dishes, mostly fish, are presented with elegance in this old Roman restaurant, although the real attraction here is the opportunity to dine outside on one of Rome's most charming piazze.

La Rosetta, 8 Via della Rosetta, ☎ 06 686 1002. Closed Sunday. A handsome restaurant a few steps from the Pantheon, La Rosetta is widely held to be top fish restaurant in Rome. Preparations are gracefully simple and accentuate rather than disguise the flavour of wonderfully fresh fish and seafood. Excellent list of wines and champagne.

Quinzi e Gabrieli, 5 Via delle Coppelle, ☎ 06 687 9389. Closed Sunday. Also considered one of the best places in Rome to eat fish, this is a fairly small restaurant so you should definitely book. Prices reflect the exceptional quality.

Toulà, 29b Via della Lupa, ☎ 06 687 3750. Closed Saturday and Monday lunchtime. Tastefully decorated with antiques and English prints, Toulà has an extensive menu which always includes several dishes from the Veneto region, where the Toulà group of restaurants originated. Excellent food and sure-handed service in a serene and classy atmosphere.

Papà Giovanni, 4/5 Via dei Sediari, ☎ 06 686 5308. Closed Sunday. One of the most original, and expensive, restaurants in Rome, famous for its fresh salads, truffles and Roman cuisine presented in the lightest possible manner. Intriguing wine list. One of the few restaurants in Rome with a non-smoking room.
€€€

Il Convivio, 44 Via dell'Orso, ☎ 06 686 9432. Closed Sunday and Monday lunchtime. A good, small restaurant with anything but anonymous food. Cooking that begins with traditional ingredients and ends up decidedly modern, with a *menù degustazione*—a many-course set menu—that changes weekly.

Vecchia Roma, 18 Piazza Campitelli, ☎ 06 686 4604. Closed Wednesday. Still worthy of the attention that has made it a favourite of locals and tourists for decades, the tables outside on Piazza Campitelli are among the most pleasant in town. The menu is varied and the service crisp.
€€

L'Eau Vive, 85 Via Monterone, ☎ 06 6880 1095. Closed Sunday. A long-established restaurant inside a 15C palace. The French nuns who run the restaurant for charity provide traditional French cuisine.

Al Pompiere, 38 Via Santa Maria dei Calderari, ☎ 06 686 8377. Closed Sunday. Only traditional Roman fare is served at this first-floor restaurant in the heart of the Jewish ghetto. *Potato gnocchi* (dumplings) on Thursdays, *pasta e ceci* (chickpea soup) and *baccalà* (salt cod) on Fridays, fried courgette flowers stuffed with anchovies, and *spaghetti cacio e pepe* (with pecorino cheese and plenty of freshly ground black pepper).

Il Bacaro, 27 Via degli Spagnoli, ☎ 06 686 4110. Closed Sunday. A tiny, bistro-like restaurant in the Piazza Navona neighbourhood with an ample choice of pasta dishes and imaginative second courses. Weather permitting, a couple of tables are set in the quiet alley outside.

La Carbonara, 3 Campo dei Fiori, ☎ 06 686 4783. Closed Tuesday. Pleasant dining out on Piazza Campo dei Fiori, and a menu with plenty of Roman and Italian standards to choose from.
€

Cul de Sac 1, 73 Piazza Pasquino, ☎ 06 6880 1094. Closed Monday lunchtime. The first wine bar in Rome. Long and narrow, warm and friendly, this place makes a pleasant change from pizza whenever an informal or frugal meal is required. Cheeses, cold meat, vegetable quiches, but also hearty lentil soup in wintertime. There are over 700 wine labels to choose from.

Anacleto Bleve, 9a/11 Via Santa Maria del Pianto, ☎ 06 686 5970. Open for lunch only; closed Sunday. In the heart of the Jewish ghetto, this old-style wine bar is perfect for a short rest. It offers a few hot dishes and a good selection of cheeses and cured pork meat from different Italian regions. The tables of the wine bar are surrounded by shelves of bottles of wine which you can buy to drink inside or take away.

La Tartaruga, 53 Via del Monte della Farina, ☎ 06 686 9473. Closed Monday. A friendly small restaurant and wine bar, with excellent food.

Piazza di Spagna
€€€–€€

Al Moro, 13 Vicolo delle Bollette, ☎ 06 678 3495. Closed Sunday. Situated near the Trevi fountain and very well known, Al Moro has the look of a restaurant but the feel of a trattoria. Service can be a little slow.

Dal Bolognese, 1/2 Piazza del Popolo, ☎ 06 361 1426. Closed Monday. One of the great dining spots in town, sited at the edge of Piazza del Popolo with a view up to the Pincio. As the name suggests, the cuisine is from Bologna, with excellent fresh pastas and a solid *bollito misto* (various types of meat stewed together, served with chutney or *salsa verde*, a sauce made with herbs).
€€

Porto di Ripetta, 250 Via di Ripetta, ☎ 06 361 2376. Closed Sunday. Close to Piazza del Popolo and popular with people who work in the area (there is a special business lunch menu). Chef Maria Romani provides innovative Italian cuisine based on traditional combinations. Excellent fish. Good wine list.

Al 34, 34 Via Mario de' Fiori, ☎ 06 679 5091. Closed Monday. Well-prepared Roman food at reasonable prices, which is rare in this part of town. A long-standing favourite with tourists.

Lounge del Roman Garden, 14 Via Bocca di Leone, ☎ 06 69981. Open every day. The small, elegant restaurant of the Hotel d'Inghilterra makes a great lunch-stop while shopping in the Piazza di Spagna area. Dinner is much more expensive.

Via Veneto and the Parioli
€€€€

Le Sans Souci, 20 Via Sicilia, ☎ 06 4201 4510. Open evenings only; closed Monday. This was the luxury restaurant of choice at the time of La Dolce Vita (late 1950s and '60s), and it is still doing well. The decor is an interesting combination of antique pieces and tacky details. Impeccable, elegant service. Very popular with American tourists and wealthy Romans in search of a very late meal.

La Terrazza dell'Hotel Eden, 49 Via Ludovisi, ☎ 06 478 121. Open every day. Having the best view in the city tends to distract attention from the food, but the modern interpretations of Italian classics are expertly prepared and beautifully presented.

Relais le Jardin, 5 Via G. de Notaris, ☎ 06 322 0404. Closed Sunday. The prestigious restaurant of the Hotel Byron. More suitable for dinner than lunch.

€€€–€€

Al Ceppo, 2 Via Panama, ☎ 06 841 9696. Closed Monday. A favourite with locals in the quiet Parioli quarter, Al Ceppo has been here for more than 30 years. The menu always features specialities from the Marche region, and the grilled meats are especially good.

Colline Emiliane, 22 Via degli Avignonesi, ☎ 06 481 7538. Closed Friday. This is a friendly, family-run trattoria located between Via Veneto and the Trevi fountain. It offers specialities from the Emilia region: an interesting selection of cured pork, home-made fettucine, pumpkin ravioli in wintertime, followed by a simple grilled beef fillet or *costoletta alla bolognese* (fried veal topped with ham and melted cheese) are always on the menu. Delicious home-made tarts for dessert.

Papà Baccus, 36 Via Toscana, ☎ 06 4274 2808. Closed Sunday. A fairly priced restaurant not far from Via Veneto, serving light Italian food. Good selection of appetizers and home-made pasta. Professional yet warm and friendly service. Very good desserts accompanied by a remarkable selection of wines by the glass. 'No smoking' room.

Monte Mario
€€€€

La Pergola, Hotel Cavalierei Hilton, 101 Via Cadlolo, ☎ 06 3509 2152. Open evenings only; closed Sunday and Monday. In the last few years this has become famous as perhaps the best restaurant in Rome (and among the top ten in the country). Unfortunately not in the historic centre, it has to be reached by car. The experts consider its very imaginative cuisine to be superlative. Impeccable service and elegant decor.

Trastevere
€€€€

Alberto Ciarla, 40 Piazza San Cosimato, ☎ 06 581 8668. Open evenings only;

closed Sunday. Mostly fish on this menu, which is always well prepared and beautifully presented in the elegant, candle-lit dining room. Several set menus as well as *à la carte* dishes, and a good selection of wines.
€€

Paris, 7a Piazza San Callisto, ☎ 06 581 5378. Closed Sunday evenings and Monday. A comfortable restaurant near Piazza Maria in Trastevere, *Paris* offers traditional Italian cooking with many good Roman dishes such as fried courgette flowers stuffed with mozzarella and anchovies and *zuppa di arzilla* (fish soup with broccoli). Excellent wine list.

Peccati di Gola, 7a Piazza dei Ponziani, ☎ 06 581 4529. Open evenings only; closed Monday. The slightly over-priced menu always features some specialities from Calabria, and pasta dishes are well made. Located on a pleasant, secluded little square (tables outside, of course) it is a particularly attractive option on a hot summer evening. One of the few restaurants in Rome that stays open throughout August.

Checco er Carettiere, 10 Via Benedetta, ☎ 06 581 7018. Closed Sunday evenings. An extremely popular and noisy restaurant, lined with photographs of past customers (the unknown as well as the famous). It offers traditional Roman dishes, such as *coda alla vaccinara* (oxtail stewed in a tomato and celery sauce), as well as lighter food, such as simple grilled fish. Home-made desserts.

Sora Lella, 16 Via di Ponte dei Quattro Capi, ☎ 06 686 1601. Closed Sunday. A small, neat, family-run trattoria located on the Tiberina island. Traditional Roman cooking, such as *amatriciana* (pasta in a tomato sauce with chunks of cured pork), *coda alla vaccinara* (see above); when in season, artichokes *alla romana* (stewed with mint) or *alla giudia* (deep-fried); home-made desserts.

Sabatini, 13 Piazza Santa Maria in Trastevere, ☎ 06 581 2026. Outside dining room on one of Rome's most animated piazze, opposite the wonderful church of Santa Maria in Trastevere. Customers come more for the view and atmosphere than the food.
€

Da Lucia, 2b Vicolo del Mattonato, ☎ 06 580 3601. Closed Monday. A basic, family-run trattoria in the heart of Trastevere, with tables outside on the narrow alleyway when the weather permits. Just a few dishes to choose from, but usually traditional Roman fare. No credit cards.

Testaccio
€€€

Checchino dal 1887, 30 Via di Monte Testaccio, ☎ 06 574 3816. Closed Sunday and Monday. Literally carved out of Monte Testaccio and run by the same family for over a hundred years, Checchino serves the most traditional Roman cuisine. Simple decor and one of the best wine lists in the city.
€€–€

Da Felice, 29 Via Mastro Giorgio, ☎ 06 574 6800. Closed Sunday. Owner Signor Felice does it all: he shops at the nearby Testaccio market, cooks excellent Roman dishes, sets the tables with strings of sausages as centrepieces, and looks customers in the eyes before allowing them to sit down and taste his daily efforts. No credit cards.

Vatican
€€

Girarrosto Toscano, 56 Via Germanico, ☎ 06 3972 5717. Closed Monday.

Typically Tuscan food from a great family restaurant not far from the Vatican museums; a welcome oasis in a neighbourhood of bad restaurants. Grilled meats, particularly the *bistecca alla fiorentina*, are wonderful. Outside dining.

Il Simposio, 16 Piazza Cavour, ☎ 06 321 1502. Closed Saturday lunchtime and Sunday. Close to Castel Sant'Angelo, this elegant wine bar has built its reputation on the sensational choice of first-quality cheeses (48 different kinds), smoked fish and cured meats. But for those who would rather have a full meal there is a real chef in the kitchen: soups, soufflés, duck breasts and beef, followed by very good desserts, are always on the menu. The wine shop in the basement deserves special attention.

Termini
€€–€

Trimani, 37b Via Cernaia, ☎ 06 446 9630. Closed Sunday. Located near Stazione Termini, Trimani is one of the oldest wine shops in town. The friendly wine bar round the corner was renovated in 1991 and has a decidedly modern feel. The wine list is great. The menu includes a few hot dishes, such as soups, quiches, grilled beef and seasonal vegetables, as well as a tempting selection of cheeses, smoked fish and cured pork. Friendly service and good air-conditioning.

Piramide
€€

La Sella del Diavolo, 102 Via Ostiense, ☎ 06 578 1260. Right beside the Centrale Montemartini, a splendid gallery with works from the Musei Capitolini (see p 410). Spacious rooms frequented by Italians who work nearby. Particularly good for fish and Sardinian specialities. Efficient, professional service.

Pizzerie

Most pizzerie are open only for dinner, usually from 20.00 to 00.30 or even as late as 02.00 in summertime. The Roman version of pizza is plate-sized, very thin, and usually baked for a scant minute in a very hot, wood-burning oven. Classic pizzas include the *margherita* (tomato sauce and mozzarella cheese) and the *napoletana* (tomato sauce, mozzarella cheese and anchovies), but all pizzerie seem to have their own combinations on offer. Without drinks, the cost of a pizza ranges from €13–15 depending on the toppings you choose. Italians typically wash down their pizza with beer or soft drinks, though most pizzerie also provide a small selection of inexpensive wines.

Other snacks available include *bruschette* (toasted bread drizzled with olive oil and served with various toppings), *crostini* (similar to *bruschette*, but done in the oven), and *filetti di baccalà fritti* (deep-fried salt-cod fillets).

Trastevere
Dar Poeta, 45 Vicolo del Bologna, ☎ 06 588 0516. Open evenings only. Credit cards accepted.
Acchiappafantasmi, 66 Via dei Cappellari, ☎ 06 687 3462. Open evenings only; closed Tuesday. No credit cards.
Panattoni, 53 Viale Trastevere, ☎ 06 580 0919. Open evenings only; closed Wednesday. No credit cards.

Esquiline
Alle Carrette, 14 Vicolo delle Carrette, ☎ 06 679 2770. Open evenings only.

Vatican

Il Bersagliere, 24 Via Candia, ☎ 06 3974 2253. Open evenings only; closed Monday.

L'Isola della Pizza, 47 Via degli Scipioni, ☎ 06 3973 3483. Open lunchtime and evenings; closed Wednesday. No credit cards.

Pantheon

Montecarlo, 12 Vicolo Savelli, ☎ 06 686 1877. Open lunchtime and evenings; closed Monday. No credit cards.

Piazza di Spagna

Leoncino, 28 Via del Leoncino, ☎ 06 687 6306. Open evenings and also for lunch during the week; closed Wednesday. No credit cards.

Parioli

Crilè, 44–46 Viale Maresciallo Pilsudski, ☎ 06 808 2690. Open evenings only; closed Sunday. One of the most popular places in Rome for the young and extremely crowded on Fridays and Saturdays.

Colosseum

Pizza Forum, 34–38 Via San Giovanni in Laterano, ☎ 06 700 2515. Open lunchtime and evenings. No credit cards.

Snacks ~ spuntini

For a slice of pizza and other good hot snacks go to a *rosticceria* or *tavola calda*; some of these have no seating and sell food to take away or eat on the spot. They often sell sliced *porchetta* (roast suckling pig) and other hot snacks including *supplì* (fried rice balls with mozzarella), *arancini* (fried rice balls with tomato), *calzoni* (a pizza 'roll' usually filled with ham and mozzarella) and *crocchette* (minced meat or potato croquettes).

There are a number of **self-service restaurants** in the centre of the city. These include:

Ciao/spizzico, 181 Via del Corso. Good for reasonably priced snacks, but the wine is not recommended.

Di fronte a..., 38 Via della Croce. Good salads and two or three hot dishes, and quality wine.

Il Delfino, 67 Corso Vittorio Emanuele, Largo Argentina.

Picnics

Excellent food for picnics can be bought at delicatessens (*pizzicherie*) and grocery shops (*alimentari*), and at bakeries (*fornai*). Sandwiches (*panini*) are made up on request, and bakeries usually sell delicious individual pizzas, rolls and cakes.

Some of the most pleasant spots in the city to have a picnic are found in its parks and gardens: for recommended sites, see p 47.

Cafés

Cafés (bars) are open all day. Most customers eat the excellent refreshments they serve standing up. You pay the cashier first, and show the receipt to the barman in order to get served. In almost all bars, if you sit at a table you are charged considerably more—at least double—and are given waiter service (you should not pay first).

Well-known cafés in the city, all of which have tables (some outside), include:
Caffè Greco, 86 Via Condotti. A famous café (see p 160).
Babington, Piazza di Spagna. English tearooms (see p 160).
Rosati, 4 Piazza del Popolo.
Tre Scalini, 31 Piazza Navona. Noted for its ices, including *tartufi* (truffles).
Giolitti, 40 Uffici dei Vicario. Also famous for its ice creams.
Camilloni a Sant'Eustachio, Piazza Sant'Eustachio.
Doney and **Caffè de Paris**, 90 and 145 Via Veneto.
Pascucci, Via di Torre Argentina. Justly famous for its fresh fruit milk-shakes.
La Casa del Caffè, Via degli Orfani, and **Il Caffè, Piazza Sant'Eustachio** (both near the Pantheon) serve particularly good coffee.
Bar della Rotonda, 68 Piazza della Rotonda. A pleasant, reasonably priced café in front of the Pantheon, with tables outside.
Vanni, in Via Frattina (corner of Via Belsiana). Good snacks and a yogurt bar.

Museums, galleries and monuments

Hours of admission to museums, collections and monuments in Rome are given in the text and in the table below. (This includes specialist museums, or those at present in restoration, and less important monuments not open regularly to the public.)

Opening times vary and often change without warning; those given below should therefore be accepted with reserve. An up-to-date list of opening times is always available at APT information offices and the information kiosks of the municipality, but even this can be inaccurate. To make certain the times are correct, it is worth telephoning first. The opening hours for Sundays given here usually apply also to holidays. All museums are usually closed on the main public holidays in Rome, Easter Sunday, 29 June and 15 August. They are sometimes open on holidays such as 1 January, 25 April, 1 May and Christmas Day (see below) but on others only in the morning (09.00–13.00). Monday remains the most usual closing day for the State museums and those owned by the municipality. The closing times given in the text indicate when the ticket office closes, which is usually 30–60 minutes before the actual closing time. Most opening times change between summer and winter. More and more museums are introducing longer opening hours: the major museums—except for the Vatican—are often open in summer after dark.

The **entrance charges** are also listed here and in the text (entrance is free if no price is given below). It has become much more expensive to visit museums in Italy in the last few years. British citizens under the age of 18 and over the age of 65 are entitled to free admission to State-owned museums and monuments, and all members of EU countries between the ages of 18 and 25 are entitled to a half-price ticket for all State-owned museums in Italy (you must show proof of nationality). The same terms apply in Rome to all the museums and monuments owned by the Municipality.

Students with ID (or ISIC) cards are given a discount at the **Vatican**.

An inclusive ticket, called the **Roma Archeologia Card**, valid for 7 days can be purchased which allows entrance to the main State-owned **archaeological sites and museums** in Rome. There is also a 7-day inclusive ticket for the four museums run by the Museo Nazionale Romano; for information ☎ 06 3996 7700. Up-to-date information on State museums is also available at 🖳 www. beniculturali.it. For information on the archaeological sites owned by the municipality, ☎ 06 6710 2070.

Lecture tours of museums and villas (sometimes otherwise closed to the public) are organised by various cultural associations: these are advertised in the local press. *La Settimana dei Musei Italiani* (**Museum Week**) has now become established as an annual event, usually held in March or April. Entrance to most museums is free during the week, and some have longer opening hours. Some private collections and monuments not generally accessible are normally opened at this time.

The office of the *Monumenti Antichi e Scavi Archeologici* of the Comune of Rome is at 29 Via Portico d'Ottavia.

Hours of admission, entrance charges and telephone numbers

The museums owned by the municipality (*Comune di Roma*) are marked (**C**). Sites of particular interest are marked with an asterisk.

Accademia di San Luca, ☎ 06 679 8850. Open 10.00–12.30, closed fest. See p 169.

Antiquarium Comunale del Celio (**C**), ☎ 06 700 1569. Closed for repairs. See p 304.

Antiquarium of the Forum, ☎ 06 699 0110. Officially open 09.00–2hr before sunset, but often closed. See p 108.

Antiquarium of the Palatine: *see* Palatine.

* **Ara Pacis** (**C**), ☎ 06 6880 6848. Closed for restoration. See p 152.

Auditorium of Maecenas (**C**), ☎ 06 487 3262. €2.58. Open 09.00–13.30; fest. 09.00–13.00; Apr–Sept also Tues, Thur and Sat 16.00–19.00, closed Mon. See p 277.

Aula Ottagonale: *see* Museo Nazionale Romano (Octagonal Hall).

* **Baths of Caracalla**, ☎ 06 575 8626. €5. Open 09.00–1hr before sunset, Mon 09.00–13.00. See p 311.

* **Baths of Diocletian** (Epigraph section of the Museo Nazionale Romano), ☎ 06 488 0530. €5. Open 09.00–19.00, closed Mon. See p 259.

Bioparco: *see* Zoo

Calcografia Nazionale. Open 09.00–13.00, closed Sun. See p 169.

Casa di Goethe: *see* Goethe Museum. See p 154.

Casa Museo di Giorgio de Chirico, ☎ 06 679 6546. €5. Open by previous appointment Tues–Sat and first Sun of month 10.00–13.00. See p 160.

Case Romane del Celio, ☎ 06 7045 4544. Open 10.00–13.00, 16.00–19.00, closed Tues and Wed. See p 305.

Casina delle Civette (Villa Torlonia; **C**), ☎ 06 4425 0072. €2.58. Open 09.00–17.00 or 19.00, closed Mon. See p 439.

Casino Pallavicini. Open first day of the month except Jan 10.00–12.00 and 15.00–17.00. See p 232.

* **Castel Sant'Angelo**, ☎ 06 681 9111. €5. Open 09.00–19.00, closed Mon. See p 336.

* **Catacombs**. €5. Normally open 08.30–12.00 and 14.30 or 15.00–dusk: **Priscilla**, ☎ 06 8620 6272. Closed Mon and in Jan. See p 443.

Sant'Agnese, ☎ 06 861 0840. Open Tues–Sat 9.00–12.00 and
16.00–18.00, closed Mon afternoon and fest. mornings. See p 441.
San Callisto, ☎ 06 5130 1580. Closed Wed and in Feb. See p 421.
Domitilla, ☎ 06 511 0342. Closed Tues and in Jan. See p 425.
San Sebastiano, ☎ 06 785 0350. Closed Sun and mid-Nov—mid-Dec. See
p 424.
The other catacombs may be visited by special permission only, see p 49)
* **Centrale Montemartini**, 106 Via Ostiense. Here some of the masterpieces
of Classical sculpture from the Palazzo dei Conservatori, Braccio Nuovo and
Museo Nuovo of the Musei Capitolini are displayed, ☎ 06 574 8030. €4.13
(or combined ticket with the Musei Capitolini). Open 09.30–19.00, closed Mon.
See p 410.
Circus of Maxentius (C), ☎ 06 780 1324. €2.58. Open Tues–Sun
09.00–17.00 or 19.00 in summer, closed Mon. See p 426.
Palazzo Massimo alle Terme: *see* Museo Nazionale Romano.
Collezione Ludovisi: *see* Palazzo Altemps.
* **Colosseum**, ☎ 06 700 5469. €8 (combined ticket with the
Palatine). Open 09.00 dusk. See p 123.
Crypta Balbi (Museo Nazionale Romano), ☎ 06 3996 7700. €4. Open
09.00–19.45, closed Mon. See p 200.
De Chirico's house: *see* Casa Museo di Giorgio de Chirico.
* **Domus Aurea**, ☎ 06 3996 7700. €5 (plus booking fee €1.50, booking
obligatory). Open 09.00–19.45, closed Tues. See p 278.
* **Forum** (Roman), ☎ 06 699 0110. Open 09.00–1hr before sunset. See p 91.
Forum of Trajan: *see* Markets of Trajan.
Gabinetto Comunale delle Stampe. Open by appointment. ☎ 06 6830
8393. See p 205.
Gabinetto Nazionale delle Stampe, ☎ 06 699 801. Open 09.00–13.00,
closed Mon, Sun. See p 225.
* **Galleria Barberini** (Galleria Nazionale d'Arte Antica), ☎ 06 482 4184. €5.
Open 09.00–19.00, closed Mon. See p 234.
* **Galleria Borghese** (Villa Borghese), ☎ 06 841 7645. €6.50 (plus booking
fee of €1.03). Booking obligatory, ☎ 06 328 101. Entrance every two hours
for limited numbers, 09.00–19.00, closed Mon. See p 239.
* **Galleria Colonna**, ☎ 06 678 4350. €7. Open Sat 09.00–13.00, closed in
Aug. See p 172.
Galleria Comunale d'Arte Moderna (Via Crispi; **C**), ☎ 06 474 2848.
€2.58. Open 09.00–18.30, fest. 09.00–13.30, closed Mon. See p 163.
Galleria Comunale d'Arte Moderna e Contemporanea (former Birreria
Peroni, 29 Via Cagliari; at present used only for exhibitions), ☎ 06 6710
7900. Open 09.00–19.00, summer 10.00–21.00, closed Mon. See p 442.
* **Galleria Corsini** (Galleria Nazionale d'Arte Antica), ☎ 06 6880 2323. €4.
Open 08.30–19.00, closed Mon. See p 222, 234.
* **Galleria Doria-Pamphilj**, ☎ 06 679 7323. €7.30 (reduction for students
and OAPs). Open 10.00 16.15, closed Thur. See p 143.
Galleria Nazionale d'Arte Antica: *see* Galleria Barberini and Galleria Corsini.
* **Galleria Nazionale d'Arte Moderna**, ☎ 06 322 981. €6.50. Open
08.30–19.30, closed Mon. See p 244.
Galleria Spada, ☎ 06 683 2409. €5. Open 08.30–19.00, closed Mon. See p 210.

Goethe Museum, ☎ 06 3265 0412. €3. Open 10.00–18.00, closed Tues. See p 154.

* **Hadrian's Villa** (Tivoli), ☎ 0774 530 203. €6.50. Open 09.00–dusk. See p 470.

Keats–Shelley Memorial House, ☎ 06 678 4235. €3. Open 09.00–13.00 and 15.00–18.00, Sat 11.00–14.00 and 15.00–18.00, closed Sun. See p 159.

Mamertine Prison, ☎ 06 679 2902. Open 09.00–12.00 or 12.30 and 14.00 or 14.30–17.00 or 18.30. See p 133.

* **Markets and Forum of Trajan** (**C**), ☎ 06 679 0048. €6.20. Open 09.00–1hr before sunset, closed Mon. See p 129, 131.

Mausoleum of Augustus (**C**). By appointment only, ☎ 06 6710 2070. See p 152.

Monument to Vittorio Emanuele II *see* Vittoriano.

* **Musei Capitolini** (**C**), ☎ 06 6710 2071 or 06 3996 7800. €6.20. Open 09.00–20.00, closed Mon. See p 78. See also Centrale Montemartini.

Museo dell'Alto Medioevo, ☎ 06 5422 8199. €2. Open 09.00–20.00, closed Mon. See p 435.

Museo dell'Arma del Genio, ☎ 06 372 5446. Open Tues, Thur and Sat 09.30–12.00. See p 344.

Museo di Arte Ebraica, ☎ 06 6840 0661. €5.16. Open 09.00–16.30, Fri 09.30–13.30, Sun 09.00–12.00, closed Saturday and fest. See p 328.

* **Museo Barracco** (**C**), ☎ 06 6880 6848. Closed for restoration. See p 205.

Museo Canonica (**C**), ☎ 06 884 2279. €2.58. Open 09.00–19.00, closed Mon. See p 243.

Museo della Casina delle Civette; *see* Casina delle Civette.

Museo Civico di Zoologia, ☎ 06 321 6586. €4.13. Open 09.00–17.00, closed Mon. See p 243.

Museo della Civiltà Romana (**C**), ☎ 06 592 6041. € 4.13. Open 09.00–18.45, Sun 09.00–13.30, closed Mon. See p 435.

Museo Hendrik Christian Andersen, ☎ 06 321 9089. €4. Open 09.00–18.30, closed Mon. See p 444.

Museo Mario Praz, ☎ 06 686 1089. €2. Open 09.00–13.00 and 14.30–18.30, closed Mon morning. See p 195.

Museo delle Mura (**C**), ☎ 06 7047 5284. €2.58. Open 09.00–19.00, fest. 09.00–17.30 winter, closed Mon. See p 315.

Museo Napoleonico (**C**), ☎ 06 6880 6286. €2.58. Open 09.00–19.00, Sun 09.00–13.30, closed Mon. See p 193.

Museo delle Navi Romane (Fiumicino), ☎ 06 652 9192. €2. Open Tues–Sun 09.00–13.30, Tues, Thur also 14.30–16.30, closed Mon. See p 461.

Museo Nazionale di Arte Orientale, ☎ 06 487 4415. €4. Open 08.30–14.00, Tues, Thur, & Sun 08.30–19.30, closed first and third Mon of the month. See p 277.

Museo Nazionale delle Arti e Tradizioni Popolari, ☎ 06 592 6148. €4. Open 09.00–20.00, closed Mon. See p 434.

Museo Nazionale di Castel Sant'Angelo: *see* Castel Sant'Angelo.

* **Museo Nazionale Etrusco di Villa Giulia**, ☎ 06 322 6571. €4. Open 08.30–19.00, closed Mon. See p 247.

Museo Nazionale del Palazzo di Venezia; *see* Museo del Palazzo di Venezia.

Museo Nazionale delle Paste Alimentari, ☎ 06 699 1119. €7.75. Open 09.30–17.30. See p 169.

Museo Nazionale Preistorico Etnografico Luigi Pigorini, ☎ 06 549 521. €4. Open 09.00–20.00. See p 434.

* **Museo Nazionale Romano** (combined ticket available):

   Palazzo Massimo alle Terme, ☎ 06 4890 3500. €6. Open 09.00–19.45, closed Mon. See p 253.

   Octagonal Hall of the Baths of Diocletian, ☎ 06 488 0530. Open 09.00–14.00, fest. 09.00–13.00, closed Mon. See p 264.

   See also Baths of Diocletian, Palazzo Altemps, and Crypta Balbi.

Museo Nazionale di Strumenti Musicali, ☎ 06 701 4796. €2. Open 08.30–19.30, closed Mon. See p 297.

Museo Nazionale di Villa Giulia: *see* Museo Nazionale Etrusco.

Museo Numismatico della Zecca, ☎ 06 4761 3317. Open 09.00–12.30, closed Mon & fest. See p 265.

Museo del Palatino: *see* Palatine.

* **Museo del Palazzo di Venezia**, ☎ 06 6999 4318. €4. Open 09.00 19.00; closed Mon. See p 139.

Museo del Risorgimento, ☎ 06 678 0664. Open 10.00–18.00, closed Mon. See p 138.

Museo di Roma (Palazzo Braschi), ☎ 06 8207 7304. €6.20. Open 09.00–18.00, closed Mon. See p 204.

Museo di Roma in Trastevere (C), ☎ 06 581 6563. €2.58. Open 10.00–20.00, closed Mon. See p 220.

Museo Storico Nazionale dell'Arte Sanitaria, ☎ 06 6835 2353. €3. Open Mon, Wed & Fri 10.00–12.00. See p 345.

Museo Storico delle Poste e Telecomunicazioni, ☎ 06 5422 1673. €0.52. Open 09.00–13.00, closed Sat & Sun. See p 436.

Museo Storico del Vaticano (Palazzo del Laterano), ☎ 06 6988 4947. €4. Open Sat and first Sun of the month, at 09.30, 11.00 and 12.15. See p 295.

Museo Teatrale del Burcardo, ☎ 06 681 9471. Open 09.00–13.30, closed Sat, Sun. See p 203.

Museo della Via Ostiense, ☎ 06 574 3193. Open 09.00–13.30, Tues, Thur also 14.30–16.30. See p 408.

Orto Botanico, ☎ 06 499 17107. €2.07. Open 09.30–17.30 or 18.30, closed Sun and Mon. See p 221.

* **Ostia Antica** (and Museo Archeologico Ostiense), ☎ 06 5635 8099. €4. Open 09.00–dusk, closed Mon. See p 447.

* **Palatine**, ☎ 06 699 0110. €8 (combined ticket with the Colosseum). Open 09.00–2hrs before sunset. See p 117.

* **Palazzo Altemps** (Museo Nazionale Romano), ☎ 06 683 3759. €5. Open 09.00–19.45, closed Mon. See p 188.

Palazzo Barberini: *see* Galleria Barberini.

Palazzo Madama (Italian Senate). Open first Sat of the month 10.00 18.00. See p 184.

Palazzo Massimo alle Terme; *see* Museo Nazionale Romano.

Palazzo di Montecitorio (Italian Parliament). Open first Sun of the month 10.00–17.30. See p 150.

Palazzo del Quirinale, ☎ 06 46991. Open Sun except in Aug 08.30–12.30

(gardens on 2 June). See p 230.

Palazzo Senatorio (Campidoglio, town hall), ☎ 06 6710 3018. Open Sun 09.00–15.30 (passport or identity card required); the tower can be climbed on the first Sun of the month. See p 88.

Palazzo Spada: *see* Galleria Spada.

Palazzo Venezia: *see* Museo del Palazzo di Venezia.

* **Pantheon**, ☎ 06 6830 0230. Open 08.30–19.30, Sun 09.00–18.00. See p 174.

Pinacoteca Capitolino: *see* Musei Capitolini.

Protestant Cemetery, ☎ 06 574 1900. Open 09.00–17.00 or 18.00, closed Mon. See p 408.

Priorato di Malta, ☎ 06 6758 1234. Church and gardens only open Sat at 10.00 and 11.00. See p 318.

Roman Forum: *see* Forum.

Teatro di Marcello (**C**). Closed for restoration. For information ☎ 06 6710 3819. See p 325.

Terme di Diocleziano: *see* Baths of Diocletian.

Theatre Museum: *see* Museo Teatrale del Burcardo.

Tomba di Cecilia Metella, ☎ 06 780 2465. €2. Open 09.00–1hr before sunset, closed Mon. See p 427.

Tomba dei Scipioni. Closed; for information ☎ 06 7047 5284.

University study collections (*see* p 302). Open by appointment, ☎ 06 5833 1022.

* **Vatican Museums**; see p 365.

* **Vatican City and gardens**; see p 404.

Villa Adriano (Tivoli): *see* Hadrian's Villa.

Villa d'Este (Tivoli), ☎ 0774 312 070. €6.50. Open 08.30–dusk. closed Mon. See p 464.

* **Villa Farnesina**, ☎ 06 683 8831. Open 09.00–13.00, closed Sun. See p 224.

Villa Giulia: *see* Museo Nazionale Etrusco di Villa Giulia.

Villa of Maxentius: *see* Circus of Maxentius.

Villa Medici (Accademia di Francia), ☎ 06 67611. Gardens only open Feb–May on Sat, Sun, guided tours at 10.30 and 11.30. See p 164.

Villa dei Quintili, ☎ 06 718 2273. €4. Open 09.00–15.30, summer 09.00–17.30, closed Mon. See p 429.

Villa Torlonia, ☎ 06 686 1044. Visits rarely granted and only by appointment. See p 442.

Vittoriano (Vittorio Emanuele II Monument), ☎ 06 699 1718. Open 10.00–16.00, summer 10.00–18.00, closed Mon. See p 230.

Zoo (Bioparco), ☎ 06 321 6586. €4.13. Open 09.00–17.00, closed Mon. See p 243.

Parks and gardens

Rome has many fine parks and gardens, most of which are well maintained. Among those described in the text are the **Villa Borghese**, the largest public park in the centre of the city (particularly attractive around the Giardino del Lago), with the adjoining **Pincio Gardens**. Another huge public park, south-west of the centre, is that of the **Villa Doria Pamphilj**. Parts of the Janiculum and Oppian Hills are occupied by parks. Smaller parks, beautifully kept, include the Villa Celimontana, the Parco Savello on the Aventine, the park by the Tomb of the Scipios between Via di Porta Latina and Via di Porta San Sebastiano, and the two parks off Via del Quirinale. The **Palatine Hill** is covered with luxuriant vegetation and fine trees, and here are the delightful Farnese Gardens laid out in the 16C and still beautifully maintained.

To the north of the centre are the large public parks of Villa Glori, with fine trees, and Villa Ada, which is partially open to the public. The park of **Villa Torlonia**, on the Via Nomentana, with Neo-classical buildings and the little Casina delle Civette, recently restored and opened to the public, is now better kept and the other garden buildings are being slowly restored. The gardens of the Villa Blanc, further out of Rome on the Via Nomentana, are still in an abandoned state. The Villa Sciarra, on the Janiculum, is open as a public park and has fine wistaria. The **Orto Botanico** is one of the most important botanical gardens in Italy. There is a rose and iris garden (May and June) in Via di Valle Murcia at the foot of the Aventine Hill above the Circus Maximus. The Spanish Steps are covered with a magnificent display of azaleas at the beginning of May. On the borders of the lake in EUR are a thousand Japanese cherry trees. A flower market is open on Tuesday mornings (10.00–13.00) in Via Trionfale.

A number of villas and palaces preserve their gardens, the most beautiful of which is that of the **Villa Medici** (for opening times, see above), which dates from the 16C. A formal 17C garden survives around the Casino del Bel Respiro (which can usually be visited only with special permission), in the Villa Doria Pamphilj public park. The charming little garden of the Priorato di Malta on the Aventine Hill is now open on Saturdays at 10.00 and 11.00. Other gardens which can normally be seen during the opening hours of their palaces include those of the Villa Farnesina in Trastevere, Palazzo Pallavicini Rospigliosi, Palazzo Colonna (although the garden can only be seen from the windows of the gallery), and the Villa Giulia. The formal garden behind the Palazzina Borghese in Villa Borghese has been restored. Tours can be taken of the rather disappointing Vatican Gardens. The beautiful gardens behind the Quirinal palace are only open on 2 June. It is difficult to get permission to see the hanging garden of the Villa Madama as it is used by the Italian Foreign Office. It is also extremely difficult to gain access to the park of the Villa Torlonia (formerly Albani)—not to be confused with that mentioned above—on the Via Salaria, with its umbrella pines, since it is privately owned by the Torlonia.

Some of the most pleasant spots in the city to have a **picnic** include: the Palatine Hill, the Parco degli Aranci on the Aventine, the Villa Borghese Gardens, the Pincio, the Belvedere di Monte Tarpeo on the Capitoline Hill, the Circus

Maximus, the park of the Villa Doria Pamphilj, the two public gardens off Via del Quirinale, the Parco Oppio (being replanted), the Villa Celimontana on the Celian Hill, Villa Torlonia on Via Nomentana, the Janiculum Hill, the Park of the Tomb of the Scipios (between Via di Porta Latina and Via di Porta San Sebastiano), and on the Via Appia (Valle della Caffarella or Parco degli Acquedotti).

 Churches and catacombs

Catholic basilicas and churches

The four great patriarchal basilicas are **San Giovanni in Laterano** (St John Lateran), the cathedral and mother church of the world, **San Pietro in Vaticano** (St Peter's), **San Paolo fuori le Mura** and **Santa Maria Maggiore**. These, with the three basilicas of San Lorenzo fuori le Mura, Santa Croce in Gerusalemme and San Sebastiano, comprise the Seven Churches of Rome. Among minor basilicas rank Sant'Agnese fuori le Mura, Santi Apostoli, Santa Cecilia, San Clemente and Santa Maria in Trastevere.

Some churches, including several of importance, are open only for a short time in the morning and evening (**opening times** have been given where possible in the text below, but might vary). St Peter's and the other three great basilicas are open all day 07.00–19.00, 07.00–18.00 winter. Other churches are closed 12.00–15.30, 16.00 or 17.00, but almost all of them open at 07.00.

Most churches now ask that sightseers do not visit the church during a service. **Dress**. If you are wearing shorts or have bare shoulders you can be stopped from entering some churches, including St Peter's. Closed chapels, crypts, etc., are sometimes unlocked on request by the sacristan. Many pictures and frescoes are difficult to see without **lights**, which often have to be operated with coins. When visiting churches it is always useful to carry a torch and a pair of binoculars. Churches in Rome are very often not orientated. In the text the terms north and south refer to the liturgical north (left) and south (right), taking the high altar as at the east end.

Roman Catholic services The ringing of the evening Ave Maria or Angelus bell at sunset is an important event in Rome, where it signifies the end of the day and the beginning of night. The hour varies according to the season. On Sunday and, in the principal churches, often on weekdays, Mass is celebrated until 13.00 and from 17.00 until 20.00. High Mass, with music, is celebrated in the basilicas on Sunday at 09.30 or 10.30 (the latter in St Peter's). The choir of St Peter's sings on Sunday at High Mass and at vespers at 17.00. The Sistine Chapel choir sings in St Peter's on 29 June and whenever the Pope celebrates Mass.

Roman Catholic **services in English** take place in San Silvestro in Capite, Piazza San Silvestro, ☎ 06 679 7775; San Clemente, 95 Via Labicana, ☎ 06 7045 1018; and Santa Susanna, 15 Via Venti Settembre, ☎ 06 488 2748; services in Irish are at St Patrick's, 31 Via Boncompagni, ☎ 06 488 4556; Sant'Isidoro; San Clemente; and Sant'Agata dei Goti. Confessions are heard in English in the four main basilicas and in the Gesù, Santa Maria sopra Minerva, Sant'Anselmo, Sant'Ignazio, and Santa Sabina.

Church festivals On saints' days Mass and vespers with music are celebrated in the churches dedicated to the saints concerned. The Octave of the Epiphany is held at Sant'Andrea della Valle. The Blessing of the Lambs takes place at Sant'Agnese fuori le Mura on 21 January around 10.30. On the evening of 6 January there is a procession with the Santo Bambino at Santa Maria in Aracoeli (the statue is a copy of the one stolen in 1994). The singing of the Te Deum annually on 31 December in the church of the Gesù is a magnificent traditional ceremony. In San Giovanni in Laterano a choral Mass is held on 24 June, in commemoration of the service held here on 24 June 1929 by Pius XI, and the Pope attends the Maundy Thursday celebrations in the basilica when he gives his benediction from the loggia on the façade. On 5 August the legend of the miraculous fall of snow is commemorated at Santa Maria Maggiore in a pontifical Mass in the Borghese Chapel. On Christmas morning in this basilica a procession is held in honour of the sacred relic of the Holy Crib. The church of Sant'Anselmo on the Aventine Hill is noted for its Gregorian chant at 09.30 on Sunday. Holy Week liturgy takes place on Wednesday, Thursday and Friday at St Peter's, San Giovanni in Laterano, Santa Croce and other churches.

For **papal audiences**, see p 347.

Non-Catholic churches and places of worship

American Episcopal	St Paul's Within the Walls, 58 Via Napoli, ☎ 06 488 3339
Anglican	All Saints, 153 Via del Babuino, ☎ 06 3600 1881
Baptist	35 Piazza San Lorenzo in Lucina, ☎ 06 687 6652
Jewish	Synagogue, Lungotevere dei Cenci, ☎ 06 684 0061
Methodist	Piazza Ponte Sant'Angelo, ☎ 06 686 8314
Muslim	Centro di Cultura Islamica, Via della Moschea (Parioli), ☎ 06 808 2167
Scottish Presbyterian	St Andrew's, 7 Via Venti Settembre, ☎ 06 482 7627

The catacombs

The catacombs are fascinating early Christian underground cemeteries that were established outside the walls of Rome, since burial within the walls was forbidden. (For a full description, see p 420.) The most famous catacombs—San Callisto and San Sebastiano on the Via Appia, and Domitilla on Via delle Sette Chiese—are all visited by **guided tours** in several languages and tend to be crowded with large groups, which can impair a visit if you are on your own. In some of them explanatory films are shown before the tour. Routes often vary and are shortened at the height of the tourist season. The two other catacombs open to the public—Sant'Agnese on Via Nomentana, and Priscilla on Via Salaria—of no less interest, are much more peaceful and rewarding places to visit since they are never crowded.

For information about catacombs not normally open to the public (which are mentioned in the main text), contact the *Pontificia Commissione di Archaeologia Sacra*, Via Napoleone III, 00185 Rome, ☎ 06 446 5610, 🖶 06 446 7625; ✉ pcomm.arch@arcsacra.va. Visits to the catacombs for research or study purposes can be arranged by written application—be sure to include requested dates and a contact number in Rome.

Warning. All the catacombs have some steep stairs and uneven narrow corridors, often poorly illuminated, making the visit not normally advisable if you have difficulty in walking.

Entertainment

Listings information

Concerts, theatre performances and exhibitions are advertised on wall posters throughout the city. Free up-to-date information in English is available from the *APT*, and in the excellent little leaflet called *L'Evento* published in Italian and English every two months by the municipality of Rome and available from their information kiosks or the *APT*. For up-to-date information: ☎ 06 36004399, ✉ www.romapreview.com or www.romaturismo.com

Un Ospite a Roma—a magazine in Italian and English with information on current events in the city—comes out once every fortnight and is given away free at hotels and information offices. There is also a monthly publication called *Romavision* (also in English) which provides much useful information. The most comprehensive source of information used by the Romans themselves is *Roma c'è*, which is published every Thursday. It can be bought at newsstands. The Italian listings are easily decipherable and there is a brief section in English at the back.

Opera takes place at the *Teatro Costanzi* (**Map 4**; **5**), Piazza Beniamino Gigli, off Via Nazionale (☎ 481601; open 09.00–13.00); ticket office open daily 09.00–20.00; closed Monday. ✉ www.opera.roma.it

Excellent **concerts** are held at the Accademia Nazionale di Santa Cecilia in their auditorium at 4 Via della Conciliazione; ☎ 06 6880 1044. The box office is open Thur–Tues 10.30–13.30 and 15.00–18.00; closed Wed. ✉ www.santa cecilia.it

Films in English are shown on Tuesdays (four progammes 15.30–22.30) at the *Cinema Augustus*, 203 Corso Vittorio Emanuele, ☎ 06 687 5455, and everyday (four programmes 16.20–23.20) at the *Cinema Pasquino*, 19 Vicolo del Piede, ☎ 06 580 3622.

Important **exhibitions** are held in Palazzo delle Esposizioni (Via Nazionale), the Scuderie Papali (on the Quirinal hill), and in the Vittoriano (Monument to Vittorio Emanuele II, Piazza Venezia).

Shops

The smartest shops are in Via Frattina and Via Condotti (the Bond Street of Rome), which lead out of Piazza di Spagna, in the area between the Corso, Piazza di Spagna and Piazza del Popolo. A good and less expensive shopping area is in the area of the Pantheon and Campo Marzio. Another important shopping street in the city (if in a less attractive area than the above) is Via Cola di Rienzo in the Prati district, between Piazza del Risorgimento and the Tiber.

Italy has notably few **department stores**: the best known in Rome (both open on Sunday) are *La Rinascente*, at Via del Corso and Piazza Fiume, and *Coin*, Piazza San Giovanni. There are branches of the chain department stores called *Oviesse* and *Upim* all over the city; these all have shoe repair departments, and also cut keys. The *Supermarket* at Termini station is open 24hrs a day.

English books are stocked at the following shops:

The Lion Bookshop, 33 Via dei Greci (just off Via del Corso), ☎ 06 3265 0437. Open 10.00–19.30; Mon 15.30–19.30. The shop also has a reading room and tea and coffee are available.

The Anglo-American Book Co., 102 Via delle Vite (near Piazza di Spagna), ☎ 06 679 5222. Open 09.00–13.00, 14.00–18.00; Sat 09.00–13.00; Closed Sun.

The Corner Bookshop, 48 Via del Moro, ☎ 06 583 6942. Closed Mon morning.

The Economy Book and Video Center, 136 Via Torino (near Via Nazionale), ☎ 06 474 6877. Closed Sun.

Feltrinelli International, 84 Via Vittorio Emanuele Orlando, ☎ 06 482 7878. Open daily 09.00–20.00. Claims to be the largest international bookshop in Italy.

Via del Babuino, Via dei Coronari, Via dei Banchi Vecchi and Via Margutta are known for their **antique shops**. Via del Governo Vecchio has numerous thrift shops selling second-hand clothes and 'junk'. For **markets** see below.

Telephones and postal services

There are numerous **public telephones** all over Rome in kiosks, and in some bars and restaurants, although many of these have been dismantled now that so many people use mobile phones. Most pay phones are operated by telephone cards which can be bought from tobacconists displaying a blue 'T' sign, bars, some newspaper stands and post offices, although a few old-style telephones still operate with coins. For international calls there are also now various prepaid telephone cards (available as above) which you do not insert in the public telephones, but they can be used from any telephone by dialling a toll free number.

Telephone numbers in Italy can have from seven to eleven numbers. All now require the area code, whether you are making a local call or a call from outside Rome.

Directory assistance (in Italian) is available by dialling 12. Most cities in the world can now be dialled direct from Rome. The telephone exchange at Termini station is open until midnight.

Rome area code	06
dialling UK from Italy	(00 44) + number
dialling US from Italy	(00 1) + number
dialling Rome from UK	(00 39) 06 + number
dialling Rome from US	(00 39) 06 + number

The **head post office** in Rome is in Piazza San Silvestro (**Map 3**; **5**), open every day 09.00–18.00. Branch post offices are open Mon–Fri 08.30–13.50, Sat 08.30–11.50, and on the last day of the month 08.30–12.00. For information about the Italian postal services, ☎ 160. Stamps are sold at tobacconists displaying a blue 'T' sign as well as post offices.

There is a **priority postal service** (for which special stamps must be purchased) for Italy and abroad, which promises delivery within three days. *CAlpost* is a guaranteed, but much more expensive, express postal service which gives you a receipt. Letters and postcards for outside Rome should always be posted into red boxes, or the blue boxes in the centre of town. The **Vatican postal service**—which has its own stamps which are not valid for the Italian State postal service—is usually thought to be more efficient: it costs the same and there are post offices in Piazza San Pietro and the Vatican Museums, as well as in Trastevere in the courtyard of Palazzo San Calisto, 16 Piazza San Calisto (blue letterboxes).

Visiting Rome with children

Children are much beloved by the Italians, who generally show great tolerance to even the naughtiest small visitor.

The **Roman remains** in the centre of the city cannot fail to fire the imagination of children of all ages: the Colosseum, Roman Forum and Palatine Hill provide an immediate picture of the splendour of the Empire. Begin at the Capitoline Hill with its views of the Forum and the Capitoline museums, which are particularly pleasant to visit. The Baths of Caracalla give a clear idea of the scale of ancient Rome. The Via Appia Antica (now part of a park) is a splendid place to spend a day with children (you can take the *Archeobus* from Piazza Venezia, or pick up a bicycle at the Visitors' Centre), and in particular the Valle della Caffarella, the Circus of Maxentius, the Tomb of Cecilia Metella, Villa dei Quintili, and the Parco degli Acquedotti. For children particularly interested in ancient Rome, the Museo della Civiltà Romana in EUR has a didactic chronological display (using casts) and a splendid scale model of the city in the 4C. You can walk along a stretch of the Aurelian Walls in the Museo delle Mura. At least one of the vast underground **catacombs** should be seen (preferably Sant'Agnese or Priscilla, as they are the least crowded); and the remarkable Roman remains of **Ostia Antica** and **Hadrian's Villa** at Tivoli are splendid places to spend a whole day with a picnic.

The **fountains** of Rome are particularly delightful. The element of surprise, and the noise, provided by the Trevi fountain are unforgettable. Children can discover how many different sculptural motifs were used in the decoration of fountains all over the city: boats in Piazza di Spagna and Piazza Santa Maria in Domnica; grotesque masks in Via Giulia and Piazza Pietro d'Illiria on the Aventine; tortoises in Piazza Mattei; bees in Piazza Barberini; and tritons in Piazza Barberini and Piazza Navona. Villa d'Este in the environs at Tivoli is famous for its fountains.

Piazza Navona and Piazza di Spagna (with the Spanish Steps) are perhaps the two most lively squares in the city, always fun to visit. The best place from which to see the **River Tiber** and some of its oldest bridges is the Isola Tiberina. A visit to the Galleria Doria Pamphilj gives a clear picture of how one of the great Roman patrician families lived, and the Keats-Shelley Memorial house, overlooking the Spanish Steps, preserves the atmosphere of a pensione in the last century.

Castel Sant'Angelo is one of the most exciting museums for children to visit: much of it is open for exploration—from the ramparts to the dungeons.

One of the most curious sights in the city is the **policeman** who, at certain times of the day, directs the traffic with great aplomb in Piazza Venezia at the head of the Corso. The exceptionally tall **President's guards** at the Palazzo del Quirinale can usually be seen outside the palace, and the **Swiss guards** with their splendid uniforms stand at the entrance to the Vatican beside St Peter's.

The **Aventine Hill** is a particularly peaceful place to visit, with several little gardens and a delightful view of the dome of St Peter's through the keyhole of the Priorato di Malta. The small Museo di Roma in Trastevere has charming life-size tableaux showing scenes of life in Rome in days gone by. A visit to the **Vatican** is exhausting for grown-ups and children alike, as it is almost always extremely overcrowded (never attempt to stay too long or see too much). The **dome of St Peter's** is well worth climbing.

There are a number of 'didactic' museums grouped near each other in **EUR**: an ethnographical museum related to Italy (Museo Nazionale di Arti e Tradizioni Popolari) and an ethnographical collection from the Americas, Africa and Oceania (Museo Etnografico Luigi Pigorini), as well as the Museo della Civiltà Romana mentioned above.

The Soprintendenza Archeologica di Roma has a didactic department with **special programmes** for the young and school children; for information, ☎ 06 39967700. There are also didactic departments at the Galleria Borghese and Castel Sant'Angelo. Postcards and interesting, colourful literature are now on sale in most museums.

The Biblioteca Centrale Ragazzi, 15 Via San Paola alla Regola, organises activities and games for children throughout the year, ☎ 06 686 5116. Both the Bioparco or zoo, ☎ 06 369 8211, and Museo Civico di Zoologia ☎ 06 321 6586, usually have interesting exhibitions about various aspects of wildlife.

Cinemas showing **films** for children include *Dei Piccoli*, 15 Viale della Pineta, ☎ 06 855 3485, and *Azzura Scipioni*, 82 Via degli Scipioni, ☎ 06 3973 7161. There are a number of puppet theatres, including *Teatro Mongiovino*, 15 Via Giovanni Genocchi, ☎ 06 513 9405, *Teatro Le Maschere*, 1 Via A. Saliceti, ☎ 06 5833 0817, and *Teatro Verde*, 10 Circonvallazione Gianicolense, ☎ 06 588 2034. Up-to-date information on activities for children are given in the free booklet *L'Evento* (p 50).

Among Rome's many splendid **parks**, the largest are the Villa Borghese, which also has a zoo, and the adjoining Pincio, where a band plays on Sunday morning in May and June. Open-air puppet shows are sometimes held in summer on the Janiculum Hill. The largest park of all is the Villa Doria Pamphilj. For all the other parks, see p 47. There is a pleasant little children's playground in the Villa Celimontana on the Celian Hill.

Breaks during a hard day's sightseeing should always be made at a *gelateria* which sells the best ice creams. Pizzas are generally excellent in Rome; for a selection of cafés and pizzerie, see pp 39–40. Children are welcomed in restaurants, where high chairs are provided and special food requirements catered for.

When choosing a means of public transport, try to take a **tram** (more interesting than a bus); no. 3 takes an unusual route near the Colosseum.

For annual festivals, see p 58.

Day excursions from Rome

Ostia Antica. Close to the sea due west of the city, Ostia Antica is one of the most important Roman sites, and can be reached easily by train in under an hour from the centre of Rome. (See p 447.)

Hadrian's villa at **Tivoli**. This is one of the most interesting Classical sites outside Rome and is the largest and richest known Imperial villa in the Roman Empire. (See p 470.)

Tivoli, on the hill above Hadrian's villa, is famous for the gardens of the Villa d'Este, decorated with spectacular fountains. (See p 464.)

Alban Hills. The Colli Albani are an isolated volcanic group rising from the Roman Campagna south of Rome, with foothills reaching to within 12km of the city. They enclose the two attractive crater lakes of Nemi and Albano, and 13 picturesque towns known as the **Castelli Romani** (Frascati, Monte Porzio Catone, Montecompatri, Rocca Priora, Colonna, Rocca di Papa, Grottaferrata, Marino, Castel Gandolfo, Albano Laziale, Ariccia, Genzano and Nemi), most of them founded by popes or patrician Roman families. Crossed by a confusing number of roads, the hills are now an elegant residential area with numerous villas amid chestnut woods. Many of the towns were damaged in the Second World War. They can be reached by train or bus from Rome (for information, ☎ *COTRAL* 06 57531).

Frascati, in a beautiful position on the northwest slopes of the Alban Hills, is perhaps the most elegant of the Castelli Romani, with fine villas and parks, the most famous of which is the Villa Aldobrandini, designed by Giacomo della Porta and built by Carlo Maderno in 1598–1603 for Cardinal Pietro Aldobrandini. Its superb garden can sometimes be visited. Outside Frascati are the ruins of *Tusculum*, an Etruscan site.

Grottaferrata has an important monastery of Basilian monks (Roman Catholics who celebrate according to the Byzantine Greek rite), with an interesting museum. The summer resort of **Rocca di Papa** is built up in picturesque terraces on the side of Monte Cavo, covered with chestnut woods. **Castel Gandolfo**, a lively little town built on the western lip of the Lake Albano crater, is famous as the summer residence of the pope, but the most important town near the lake is Albano.

Ariccia is in a charming position in wooded country, with numerous villas. Palazzo Chigi, with a lovely park, was restored by Bernini who also built a circular church close by in 1664.

The beautiful and unspoiled **Lago di Nemi** is surrounded by hills with woods of ilex and manna-ash, and no ugly buildings. The Temple of Diana Nemorensis in a grove on the north-east side of the lake became one of the most celebrated sanctuaries in central Italy, but only very scanty ruins survive. The attractive and quiet little resort of **Nemi** lies in a picturesque position above the lake. On the lakeside the Museo delle Navi Romane was built in 1936 to house two ancient ships constructed by Caligula (AD 37–41) to convey visitors across the lake for the festival of Diana. They were burnt in 1944 and little remains of them here. Genzano is built in terraces on the outer slope of the crater.

Additional information

Airline companies

Alitalia, 13 Via Bissolati, ☎ 06 65642. Fiumicino airport, ☎ 06 65631
British Airways, 54 Via Bissolati, ☎ 06 485 480. Fiumicino airport, ☎ 06 6501 1513
Canadian Airlines, 58 Via Veneziani, ☎ 06 655 7117. Fiumicino airport, ☎ 06 650 1462
Delta Airlines, 54 Via Bissolati, ☎ 800 864 114. Fiumicino airport, ☎ 06 6595 4095
KLM, ☎ 06 216 969. Fiumicino airport, ☎ 06 6501 1441
TWA, 59 Via Barberini, ☎ 06 47241. Fiumicino airport, ☎ 06 6595 4921

Banking services

Banks are usually open Mon–Fri 08.30 13.30, and for one hour in the afternoon, usually 14.30 or 15.00–15.30 or 16.00; closed Sat, Sun and holidays. A few banks are now open on Saturday mornings, including the **Banca di Roma** in Piazza di Spagna, and the **Banca Nazionale del Lavoro** at 266 Via del Corso. All banks close early (about 11.00) on days preceding national holidays.

The commission on cashing travellers' cheques can be quite high. Many banks now have automatic cash dispensers. Money can also be changed at exchange offices (*cambio*), travel agencies, some post offices, and main airports and railway stations. Some hotels, restaurants, and shops exchange money, but usually at a lower rate.

Crime and personal security

For all emergencies, dial 113 or 112.

As in large towns all over the world, **pickpocketing** is a widespread problem in Rome; it is always advisable not to carry valuables in handbags, and to be particularly careful on public transport (bus no. 64, which runs between Stazione Termini and the Vatican, has become notorious for pickpockets in recent years).

Cash, documents and valuables can be left in hotel safes. It is a good idea to make photocopies of all important documents in case of loss. Particular care should be taken when using a credit card to draw cash from an ATM.

There are three categories of **policemen** in Italy: *Vigili Urbani*, municipal police who wear blue uniforms in winter and white during the summer, and have hats similar to those of London policemen; *Carabinieri*, military police who wear black uniforms with a red stripe down the side of their trousers; and the *Polizia di Stato*, State police who wear dark-blue jackets and light-blue trousers. The central police station of the Polizia di Stato is at 15 Via San Vitale, ☎ 06 4686; foreigners' office, ☎ 06 4686 2102.

Municipal police ☎ 06 67691
Military police ☎ 112
Traffic police ☎ 55441
Railway police ☎ 06 481 9561

Crime should be reported at once, theft to either the *Polizia di Stato* or the *Carabinieri*. A detailed statement has to be given in order to get an official document confirming loss or damage (*denunzia di smarrimento*), which is essential for insurance claims. Interpreters are usually provided.

To report the loss or theft of a credit card, call:
Visa   ☎ 800 822056
Mastercard   ☎ 800 872 050
American Express   ☎ 06 7228 0371

If you are in difficulty, you can ask for help at your embassy in Rome (see below). They will replace lost or stolen passports, and will give advice in emergencies. For telephone numbers in case of other emergencies, see below.

Cultural organisations

British School at Rome, 61 Via Gramsci (Valle Giulia), ☎ 06 326 4939; see p 247.

American Academy in Rome, 5 Via Masina, ☎ 06 58461: organises lectures and exhibitions.

British Council, 20 Via delle Quattro Fontane, ☎ 06 478 141: with a library. It organises lectures, concerts and exhibitions.

French Academy, Villa Medici, 1 Viale Trinità dei Monti, ☎ 06 67611: see p 164.

Goethe Institut, 267 Via del Corso.

German Archaeological Institute, 79 Via Sardegna.

Istituto Nazionale di Archeologia e Storia dell'Arte, 3 Piazza Venezia; see p 141.

Accademia dei Lincei, 10 Via della Lungara; *see* p 224.

Società Italiana Dante Alighieri, 27 Piazza Firenze.

Società Geografica Italiana, Villa Celimontana, 12 Via della Navicella.

Accademia Nazionale di Santa Cecilia, 6 Via Vittoria.

Biblioteca Hertziana, 28 Via Gregoriana; an important art history library owned by the German government (closed for renovation).

Dress

It is forbidden to enter St Peter's and the Vatican museums wearing shorts, mini-skirts, or with bare shoulders. Some other churches can object to unsuitable dress also.

Electric current

The electricity supply is 220 watts. Visitors may need round, two-pin Continental plugs for any appliances.

Embassies

Australia   25/c Corso Trieste, ☎ 06 852 721. Open Mon–Thur 09.00–12.00 and 13.30–17.00; Fri 09.00–12.00

Canada   30 Via Zara, ☎ 06 4459 8421. Open Mon–Fri 08.30–12.30 and 13.30–16.00

Republic of Ireland	3 Piazza Campitelli, ☎ 06 697 9121. Open Mon–Fri 10.00–12.30 and 15.00–16.30
Netherlands	8 Via M. Mercati, ☎ 06 321 5827
New Zealand	28 Via Zara, ☎ 06 440 4035. Open Mon–Fri 08.30–12.45 and 13.45–17.00
South Africa	14 Via Tanaro, ☎ 06 852 541. Open Mon–Fri 08.30–12.00
United Kingdom	80/A Via Venti Settembre, ☎ 06 4890 3777. Open Mon–Fri 09.30–13.30
United States of America	121 Via Veneto, ☎ 06 46741. Open Mon–Fri 08.30–12.00

Emergency services

For all emergencies, ☎ 113: the switchboard will coordinate the help you need.

First aid services (*pronto soccorso*) are available at all hospitals, railway stations and airports. San Giovanni, in Piazza San Giovanni in Laterano, is the central hospital for road accidents and other emergencies: for first aid, ☎ 06 7705 5297. The American Hospital in Rome, 69 Via Emilio Longoni, ☎ 06 225 5290, is a private English-speaking hospital which accepts most American insurance plans. The International Medical Centre will refer callers to English-speaking doctors: ☎ 06 488 2371, nights and weekends ☎ 06 488 4051.

First-aid and ambulance service ☎ 118
Red Cross ambulance service ☎ 5510
Fire brigade ☎ 115
Road assistance ☎ 116

For all other emergencies, see under 'Crime' above.

Internet centres

Among numerous internet cafés in Rome are:
Internet Café, 12 Via dei Marruccini (near the University, **Map 5**; **5**). Open Mon–Fri 09.00–20.00, Sat, Sun 17.00–20.00
Bibli, 38 Via dei Fienaroli
Hackers, 16 Via Sebastiano Veniero

Markets

Open-air markets are open Mon–Sat 08.00–13.30. These include excellent **food** markets at Campo dei Fiori, Piazza Vittorio Emanuele II (with North African and Middle Eastern products), Via Andrea Doria and Testaccio. **New** and **second-hand clothes** are sold in Via Sannio (Porta San Giovanni), and **old prints** and **books** at the Mercato delle Stampe, Largo della Fontanella di Borghese. Porta Portese is a huge, chaotic **flea market** between Via Portuense and Viale Trastevere, open Sun 07.00–13.00.

Newspapers

The most widely read **Italian newspapers** in Rome are *La Repubblica*, *Corriere della Sera*, *Messaggero* (with a Tuesday supplement on events in the city, called *Metrò*) and *Il Tempo*.

Some important **foreign newspapers** arrive daily at many of the kiosks in the historic centre. The kiosk opposite Piazza Colonna (**Map 3**; **5**) is open 24hrs.

Wanted in Rome is a useful English magazine published every fortnight from 17 Via dei Delfini, and on sale at newsstands and the English bookshops (for which see above).

Nightlife

Up-to-date listings of discos and bars with live music open till late can be found in *Roma c'è*, a weekly magazine on sale at newsstands which provides detailed information about what's on in Rome. There are also listings in *Romavision*, published every month, and *L'Evento* published every two months.

Opening hours

Shops (for clothes and books, hairdressers, etc.) are generally open 09.00–13.00 and 16.00–19.30, including Saturdays, and for most of the year are closed on Monday mornings. Food shops are usually open 07.30 or 08.00–13.00 and 17.00–19.30 or 20.00, and for most of the year are closed on Thursday afternoons. From mid-June to mid-September all shops are closed instead on Saturday afternoons. Hardware shops are closed on Saturdays. In recent years, however, more and more shops have been staying open over the lunch hour, and some are now also open on Sundays.

Government offices usually work Mon–Sat 08.00–13.30 or 14.00.

For banking hours, museum and church opening times, see the relevant sections above.

Pensioners

There is free admission to all State-owned galleries and monuments for British citizens over the age of 65 (you should carry your passport for proof of age and nationality). There are no concessions for foreign pensioners on public transport.

Pharmacies

Pharmacies or chemists (*farmacie*) are identified by their street signs, which show a luminous green cross. They are usually open Mon–Sat 09.00–13.00 and 16.00–19.30 or 20.00. Some are open 24hrs a day, including the one outside Stazione Termini on Piazza dei Cinquecento. A few are open on Sundays and holidays, and at night: these are listed on the door of every chemist, and in the daily newspapers.

Photography

Rules about photography vary in musuems, so it is always best to ask first for permission (the use of a flash is often prohibited).

Public holidays and annual festivals

The main holidays in Rome, when offices and shops are closed, are as follows:

1 January (New Year's Day)	**1 November** (All Saints' Day)
25 April (Liberation Day)	**1 December** (Immaculate Conception)
Easter Monday	**25 December** (Christmas Day)
1 May (Labour Day)	**26 December** (St Stephen)
15 August (Assumption)	

In addition, the festival of the patron saints of Rome, Peter and Paul, is celebrated on 29 June as a local holiday in the city.

Museums are usually closed on 29 June, Easter Sunday and 15 August, and there is usually no public transport on 1 May and the afternoon of Christmas Day.

Annual festivals

5–6 January	Epiphany (Befana), celebrated at night in Piazza Navona
Shrove Tuesday	Carnival is celebrated in the streets and piazze
19 March	Festa di San Giuseppe, celebrated in the Trionfale district
21 April	Anniversary of the birth of Rome, celebrated on the Campidoglio
1 May	Open-air pop concert in Piazza San Giovanni in Lateran, celebrating Labour Day
23–24 June	Festa di San Giovanni, at night, near the Porta San Giovanni
First Sunday in June	Festa della Repubblica, a military parade in the Via dei Fori Imperiali
July	Festa di Noantri, celebrations in Trastevere for several weeks

Students and young visitors

EU members under 18 are allowed free entrance to state-owned museums, and EU students between the ages of 18 and 26 are entitled to half-price tickets for State-owned museums, and sometimes reductions for the young are available in other museums (including the Vatican). For youth hostels, see p 31.

Tipping

Most prices in hotels and restaurants include a service charge, and so tipping is far less widespread in Italy than in North America. Even taxi-drivers rarely expect more than one or two Euro added to the charge (which officially includes service). In restaurants prices are almost always inclusive of service, so always check whether or not the service charge has been added to the bill before leaving a tip (if in doubt, ask the waiter for explanation). In hotels, porters who show you to your room and help with your luggage, or find you a taxi, usually expect a tip of one or two Euros.

Toilets

There is a notable shortage of public toilets in Rome, as in the rest of Italy. All bars (cafés) should have toilets available to the public: generally speaking the grander the bar, the better the facilities. Nearly all museums now have toilets. There are also toilets (unlocked by coins) at the railway stations, and in Piazza di Spagna, Villa Borghese, the Colosseum, Piazza San Silvestro, Piazza Sonnino, Via Zanardelli and the Pincio.

Water

The water of Rome, brought to the city from springs many miles away by a series of aqueducts (see p 432), is particularly good. There are numerous public fountains known as *nasoni* ('hooked nose', from the shape of the tap) all over the city which provide a continuous flow of drinking water for everyone. The only water not drinkable is that labelled *non potabile*.

Ancient Rome: an introduction

by T.W. Potter

Few cities make quite so indelible an impression as Rome. Although in part brought about by the warm golden-brown hue of the soft volcanic *tufo* stone, and the cheerful, bustling, *vivante* atmosphere, it is above all the sense of history that is so pervasive. Every street brings a fresh and exciting vista, sometimes graced by a Classical building from the days of the Roman Empire, then an elegant Renaissance palazzo or a glorious church, next the imposing façade of a structure erected in the wake of Italy's reunification in 1870, when Rome once again became capital. History is writ large upon the streets and piazze of Rome, and it is impossible for the visitor, however casual, not to engage with it.

Our archaeological and historical appreciation of Rome's ancient and medieval landscape has in fact advanced enormously over the past decade or so. In response to enlightened proposals put forward by the Archaeological Superintendent for Rome, Professor Adriano La Regina, in March 1981, Parliament voted to release substantial funds for the investigation and, above all, conservation of the city's monuments. As inspection following an earth tremor in 1979 had showed, pollution from car emissions and central-heating fumes was having a devastating effect upon the marble and stone that face the monuments of the Eternal City. Visitors were to become all too familiar in the 1980s with the green gauze that draped many of Rome's most famous landmarks. But behind those screens were scholars and conservators, seizing the chance to study and preserve the past, in tandem with teams of archaeologists, Italian and foreign, who were opening new windows into earlier layers all over the city. Plans to close down and remove Mussolini's Via dei Fori Imperiali, which cuts across Rome's ancient centre, may not have come to pass, reflecting the modern dilemma between the conservation of the past and the needs of the present; but enormous strides have been made in our understanding of the evolution of one of the world's greatest cities.

Assimilating and interpreting all this new information has been one of the challenges of the 1990s. Coupled with it was the fresh scrutiny of documents and artefacts discovered by earlier generations of investigators, like the indefatigable Italian engineer and archaeologist Giacomo Boni ('excavation' in museum storerooms, as it has become known). This has shed much light on matters long considered settled. To know that the reliefs on Trajan's Column were almost certainly executed at the behest of his successor, Hadrian, is not a matter of dotting 'i's and crossing 't's, but a fundamental advance in knowledge. It shows how Hadrian, by honouring his adoptive father's military achievements, sought to render more secure his own precarious political position: for the Emperor Trajan, while bestowing upon Hadrian favours and high political office, had nevertheless not nominated him publicly as his successor. Countless rulers of Rome, whether consul, emperor, pope or president, have used architecture as symbolic statements of their power and prestige, a point that will not be lost upon those who gaze upon their monuments.

Rome's beginnings

Rome was to grow up at the one easy crossing-point along the lower reaches of the River Tiber. Excavations at nearby Sant'Omobono show evidence of settlement from as early as about 1500 BC. By the early first millennium BC, **villages of oval wooden houses** were emerging on the Palatine and Capitoline hills, both natural strongholds, the contours of whose once steep cliffs have been softened over the passage of time. There were also cemeteries on the spurs of the Quirinal, Viminal and Esquiline, which stretch like the fingers of a hand towards the Tiber, as well as on the low-lying ground beneath the Capitoline, where later the Roman Forum was to develop. The distinction between the settlements of the living and the burial grounds of the dead, maintained throughout the ancient history of the city for all but the greatest, was thus established at a very early date.

Traditionally, of course, Rome was founded by **Romulus and Remus**, perhaps in 753 BC (the ancients disagreed about the exact date). They are described as descendants of Aeneas who, as a fugitive from the Trojan Wars, settled at Lavinium, near the mouth of the Tiber; Roman historians thus provided their compatriots with a respectable ancestry, firmly locked into Greek mythology. It was one of the marvels of the early 1980s to see, emerging from the bottom of the great trench at the foot of the Palatine Hill, a high wall 1.4m in width, with a ditch in front. Datable to about 730–720 BC, on good archaeological evidence, it was rather convincingly proclaimed as the wall of Romulus, built to mark the pomerium, the sacred zone that surrounded the city. Archaeology and legend for once seem to cohere.

Six kings are supposed to have followed Romulus, and it is clear that some, including the last, Tarquinius Superbus, were **Etruscans** from the region to the north of Rome. To Servius Tullius (578–535 BC) is attributed the building of a great wall around the city (as yet unconfirmed by archaeology), and it was the Etruscans who drained the site of the Forum. The first paving stones were laid around 625 BC over a huge deposit of made-up ground (not a village, as was once supposed), and it rapidly developed into the religious, political and commercial centre of what was beginning to be a proper city-state. Nearby was the Regia, the sanctuary of the Rex Sacrorum, who was responsible for the official sacrifices of the State; it was constructed on the site of the Temple of Vesta, where the sacred flame of the community had been housed. Of the Agora in Athens, Sir Mortimer Wheeler could write that 'here, in a real sense, is the initial focus of the European mind'; of the Roman Forum in Rome we might observe that here lie the ground and monuments where the Romans inspired the creation of the first world state. It does require imagination to hear Caesar or Cicero speaking from the rostrum; but, by shutting out the noise of modern Rome, we know that it really did happen there.

The Romans establish control

But we are getting ahead of ourselves. It was therefore in the late 7C and 6C BC that Rome took on characteristics, such as public buildings, squares and fortifications, among others, that permit us to describe it as urbanised. To what extent

Etruscan rulers were ultimately responsible is a matter of scholarly contention; but there is no doubt that, while it was already a cosmopolitan place, the language and culture were predominantly Latin. Thus in 510 BC the Romans, themselves Latini, expelled their Etruscan tyrant, Tarquinius Superbus and, despite the famous—but perhaps apocryphal—siege of Lars Porsenna of Etruscan *Clusium* (modern Chiusi, in Tuscany), abolished the monarchy in 509 BC. In the **republic**, authority now became vested in the hands of two magistrates (later consuls), who were elected annually and chosen only from the aristocratic patrician class. As time went on, however, this exclusive concentration of power caused ever increasing resentment among the impoverished plebs. An intense class war ensued, which was to linger on for some 250 years. The Twelve Tables (451–450 BC) were an early attempt to introduce some legislative order, and were followed by a succession of new laws. Ultimately the sovereignty of the people was recognised, at least in theory; thus, while a patricio-plebeian élite effectively continued to hold the strings of power, via the magistrates and senate, democracy ostensibly prevailed. It was a typically Roman, pragmatic solution.

It was also during this period that, through wars and alliances, Rome gradually extended domination over Italy. By 275 BC control had been established all over the peninsula, leaving the way open for intervention overseas. Sicily (241 BC), Sardinia (238 BC), Spain (206 BC) and North Africa (146 BC) all were to become provinces, and during the 2C and 1C BC, large parts of the East Mediterranean also came under the Roman yoke. From being a parochial, somewhat rustic town in the 6C BC, Rome was now the wealthy mistress of a great **empire**.

The effect upon the city was to be profound. New **fortifications** had been built in the early 4C BC (still to be seen outside the Stazione Termini), following the sack of Rome in 390 BC by an army of Gauls. Enclosing about 400 hectares, they excluded the flattish ground of the Campus Martius, now Vecchia Roma in the bend of the Tiber, where the Roman youth received military training, and popular assemblies met. But the vast area within the walls is eloquent testimony to a fast-expanding population, as well as of a new sense of urban identity and purpose. Development was needed of the riverside dockyards and nearby cattle-market, the Forum Boarium, to feed the populace and promote commerce; and to Appius Claudius Caecus is due the credit for piping in water by building the city's first **aqueduct** in 312 BC. It must have seemed a miraculous achievement in a chaotic, crowded and, by Greek standards, still somewhat provincial Italo-Etruscan town.

It was contact through conquest, especially of the Greek world, that was to change this image. Huge profits were realised, not least through the sale of slaves, and Rome became an immediate beneficiary. Victorious generals were accorded triumphal processions into the city and, in return, often paid for the building of a temple, vowed in the midst of battle. This glorified both the city and their own names, and it was Greek deities that were frequently thus honoured. Likewise, Greek statues were brought back to grace the public places of the city, and paintings in the Greek style were commissioned to represent a military success. To the Roman, the Greek world, and its cities, appeared sophisticated and culturally illustrious. From the 2C BC in particular there was a conscious move to Hellenise the city of Rome, not least through literature, architecture and the arts. While moralist Romans like Cato (234–149 BC) denounced such developments, which seemed alien to the noble traditions of the strong farmer-soldier, most

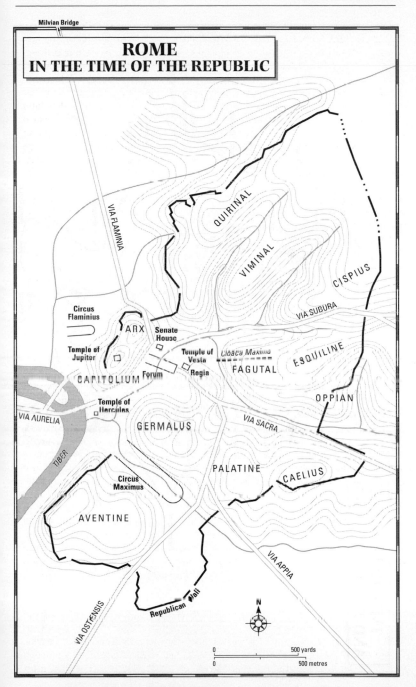

Milvian Bridge

ROME
IN THE TIME OF THE REPUBLIC

VIA FLAMINIA

QUIRINAL

VIMINAL

CISPIUS

VIA SUBURA

Circus
Flaminius

ARX

Senate
House

Temple of
Vesta

Cloaca Maxima

ESQUILINE

Temple of
Jupiter

CAPITOLIUM

Forum

Regia

FAGUTAL

OPPIAN

VIA AURELIA

Temple of
Hercules

GERMALUS

VIA SACRA

TIBER

Circus
Maximus

PALATINE

CAELIUS

AVENTINE

VIA APPIA

VIA OSTENSIS

Republican Wall

N

| 0 | 500 yards |
| 0 | 500 metres |

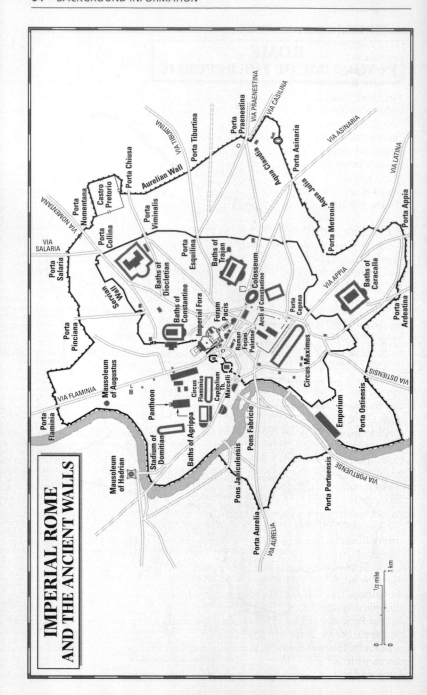

IMPERIAL ROME AND THE ANCIENT WALLS

accepted them with fervour. The elegant Graeco-Roman temples of Portunus (a god of commerce) and Hercules Victor, both built in the later 2C BC in the Forum Boarium, are still-standing reminders of this.

Rome's **population**, ultimately to reach a million or more in the 1C AD, was by now very substantial. The aristocracy lived in favoured areas like the Palatine, where their mansions were designed with atria; here their supporters (*clientes*) might be received. The plebeians inhabited squalid, multi-storey tenements, ever vulnerable to fire, and often cheek by jowl with great public monuments. Feeding and entertaining these poor classes became an important facet of public life. When the general Gaius Flaminius Nepos built a circus in the Campus Martius in 221 BC, he was to establish the area as a place of popular entertainment. Here Pompey provided the first stone theatre to be built in Rome, in 55 BC, and Caesar planned, and Augustus had constructed, the theatre of Marcellus, Augustus' nephew. Dedicated in 13 BC, it still remains a very imposing and impressive monument.

The building of Rome

The great generals of the 1C BC, particularly Sulla, Pompey and **Gaius Julius Caesar**, all sought to increase their prestige by embellishing Rome. Caesar's schemes were the most grandiose. Of lasting significance was his forum, near the old Roman Forum and by the Curia (which he rebuilt), where the senate met. His forum was dominated by a high temple of his divine ancestress Venus Genetrix, and the whole complex must have appeared a fitting symbol of the power and pre-eminence of the Julian family (see plan on p 130).

Caesar's murder in 44 BC brought his own high personal ambitions to an end; but his adoptive son and heir, Octavian, once he had seized the reins of power by defeating Antony and Cleopatra at Actium in 31 BC, was more than capable of resuscitating them. Bestowed with the title **Augustus** ('reverend') in 27 BC, he was to rule a largely peaceful empire for a further 41 years. Rome was particularly to benefit. His famous boast that he 'found a city made of brick and left it made of marble' was far from idle. The white marble quarries at Carrara, in north-western Italy, were greatly developed at this time, and huge quantities were shipped down to Rome. The building programme was on an enormous scale. Immediately initiated was the Forum of Augustus. It lay close to Caesar's forum, and was crowned (as it still is) by a temple of Mars Ultor, the Avenger of Caesar's murder. Filled with statues of Roman heroes, not least those of the Julian clan, it became the monumental focus of Augustan Rome, where proper respect was paid to the city's ancestors, and the great were received (see plan on p 130). Old buildings of historical and religious significance were restored, among them the House of Romulus, close to which, so as to emphasise his illustriousness, Augustus built his own residence; deliberately modest, it was the beginning of a process that was to transform the Palatine into an area of exclusive Imperial palaces.

Augustus was much aided by his devoted ally, the hugely wealthy Marcus Vipsanius Agrippa. Builder of Rome's first major public baths, two aqueducts, and the Pantheon (which still bears his name, although it is a Hadrianic reconstruction), he, like Augustus, was concerned to turn Rome into a well-run and elegant city that was a worthy capital of a great empire. The Ara Pacis (Altar of Peace), with its marvellous reliefs depicting legends concerning the foundation of Rome, and of Augustus and his family, symbolised the new stability. A food dole was provided for the needy, and Augustus' own mausoleum in the Campus Martius was a massive architectural statement of the legitimacy and authority of the empire's princeps, first citizen.

Many of the ancient standing buildings that one sees in Rome today are of course creations of the post-Augustan age. They are particularly characterised by the use of concrete faced with brick, an invention which seems to have taken place in Campania in the third century BC. It was, however, not until the days of Augustus' successor, Tiberius (AD 14–37), that the first large-scale building project using concrete was initiated in Rome: the construction of the Castra Praetoria, where the solders of the Praetorian Guard were housed. Set in the north-eastern part of the city, between the Via Nomentana and the Via Tiburtina, it was laid out like a legionary fortress. Troops had never before been based in Rome, for they potentially posed dangers for the unwary ruler. Indeed, when Claudius was proclaimed emperor in AD 41, it was the Praetorian Guard that did so.

Claudius, in AD 43 conqueror of Britain (an event which was commemorated with a triumphal arch), was to provide Rome with two new aqueducts to serve emerging residential areas on the Quirinal, Pincian and Aventine. He also built an all-weather harbour at **Ostia**, to facilitate importation of the vast supplies that the city needed: here was responsible civic management. Nero, by contrast, invested many of his energies into creating a vast palace and pleasure gardens, known as the **Domus Aurea** (Golden House), between the end of the Roman Forum and the Esquiline. The dark underground rooms that one can visit today hardly convey the once sumptuous splendour of this extraordinary place, which covered some 50 hectares; but it was architecturally a visionary, if megalomaniac, project. It was later blotted out by the **Colosseum** (dedicated in AD 80; it may have taken its name from a colossal statue of Nero set up nearby); the Baths of Titus (AD 79–81); and, in the early 2C, by the Baths of Trajan. The heart of the city was once more in the public domain.

Nero did rebuild many streets after the devastating fire of AD 64, including the Sacra Via which was provided with a great colonnade, like cities in the East. They were wider and straighter and, in combination with stringent new fire regulations, must have lent an altogether more organised impression to the city. The Flavian dynasty (AD 69–96), which under Vespasian seized power after a catastrophic civil war, were further to enhance that image. Thus Vespasian was to build a new forum, with as its centrepiece the Temple of Peace, echoing the message of Augustus's Altar of Peace. Although now largely buried, this once-elegant architectural creation lay not far from the huge Flavian Colosseum, an amphitheatre where 50,000 people might relish the lavish, if often gruesome, entertainments provided mainly from the emperor's pocket.

The last Flavian ruler, Domitian, also built facilities for entertainment; not least was a stadium for athletic competitions, the shape of which is now fossilised by the Piazza Navona. He also started to lay out a new forum, which was completed by his successor, Nerva. However, his most striking achievement was the construction of a vast palace on the Palatine, overlooking the Circus Maximus. Known as the Domus Augustana, it was to become the residence for rulers over the next 300 years, a symbolic reminder with its innovative architecture, and lavish decoration, of the achievements and power of the Flavian family.

But times were changing. When Trajan became emperor in AD 98, he was the first provincial to take the throne. A Spaniard by birth, he nevertheless left his stamp on Rome in a remarkable way. His enormous forum stretched north-east-wards from the Forum of Augustus, and included the Basilica Ulpia, 170m in length. His famous column, one of the mightiest monuments in Rome, stood just beyond the basilica, and was flanked by two libraries, one for Latin works, the other for Greek. Also still to be seen are his magnificent purpose-built market halls and shops, constructed beside his forum rather like a modern shopping centre; they underline how the fora had now become places of pomp and ceremony rather than humble commerce. Likewise, he attended to civic needs by building vast public baths over Nero's Golden House. As much, or more, places for social concourse as for cleanliness, they further enhanced Rome's image as a truly great city.

Trajan paid for these works largely with booty won in two wars from the Dacians, in the lower Danube region. But he by no means emptied the state coffers, and his successor Hadrian, also of Spanish origin, had plenty of funds to realise his own projects. Among them were the rebuilding of the **Pantheon**, justly described as one of the masterpieces of Roman architecture; and his mau-soleum, now **Castel Sant'Angelo**, which still dominates part of the skyline of Rome. But it was near Tivoli that he created his main residence, a huge villa whose buildings embodied the architectural ideals of the Greek and Eastern worlds that he so admired. Hadrian was above all a devoted philhellene, who ruled a united and largely harmonious empire. When Aelius Aristides delivered an encomium to Rome in AD 144, only six years after Hadrian's death, he could liken the empire to a single household, enjoying a perpetual holiday.

Yet the pre-eminence of the city of Rome was already beginning to wane. No more were there to be wars of conquest, bringing in fresh funds, and power was gradually slipping away to provinces like those of North Africa, which became ever more wealthy, especially through commerce. Septimius Severus, who ascended the throne in AD 193, was to be the first African emperor. His huge **triumphal arch**, dedicated in AD 203, is one of the more imposing monuments in the Roman Forum today (see plan on p 94), and he also built a great, three-tiered façade to a new wing of the imperial palace. Called the Septizodium, it held statues of seven planetary deities with, at the centre, the Sun, symbolically facing Africa; it was, alas, demolished in 1588.

It was Severus's son, Caracalla, who built the enormous **baths** that still bear his name; covering some 20 hectares, they remain one of the most impressive sights of ancient Rome. But with the demise of the last Severan, Alexander, in AD 235, much of the empire was to be plunged into nearly 50 years of anarchy, war-fare and chaos. It is to this period that the **Aurelian Wall** circuit belongs. Begun in the early 270s, it extends for 19km, and was so massively built that it remains as impressive today as in antiquity. Now Rome had become a stronghold in the new world of late antiquity and, when Diocletian restored order, the city lost its position as sole capital of the empire. Although he built his great baths (parts of which were converted into the church of Santa Maria degli Angeli by Michelangelo), he did not visit Rome until AD 303, and so disliked what he saw that he almost immediately departed. When Constantine founded his New Rome of Constantinople, modern Istanbul, dedicated in AD 330, a page of history was turned: after nearly a thousand years of pre-eminence Rome was no longer mis-tress of the world.

Constantine did of course endow Rome with many monuments, not least the **churches** of St Peter and St John Lateran, and his triumphal arch by the Colosseum; but we are here looking forward to the shaping of the medieval city, and away from its ancient past. Dark days were to lie ahead, especially in the 5C and 6C as the population dwindled away; but so too was a distinguished and brilliant future as, under Charlemagne and the popes, a renaissance gradually took place from the early 9C. Rome and the Romans have always shown a remarkable capacity for innovation, and survival, over an immense period of time. There is no other city with so sustained a record of achievements, surely a remarkable tribute to the founding fathers, and their innumerable distinguished successors.

Further reading

T. Ashby, *The aqueducts of ancient Rome* (Oxford 1935).

M.T. Boatwright, *Hadrian and the City of Rome* (Princeton 1987).

J. Carcopino, *Daily life in ancient Rome* (Harmondsworth, 1973 reprint).

A. Claridge, 'Hadrian's Column of Trajan', *Journal of Roman Archaeology*, vol. 6 (1993), pp 5–22.

F. Coarelli, *Il foro romano* (2 vols, Roma 1983, 1985).

M. Cristofani (ed.), *La grande Roma dei Tarquinii* (Rome 1990).

F. Lepper and S.S. Frere, *Trajan's Column* (Gloucester 1988).

R. Krautheimer, *Rome. Profile of a city 312–1308* (Princeton 1980).

R. Meiggs, *Roman Ostia* (2nd ed., Oxford 1973).

M. Pallottino, *The Etruscans* (London 1975).

T.W. Potter, *Roman Italy* (2nd ed., London 1992).

L. Richardson, Jnr., *A new topographic dictionary of ancient Rome* (Baltimore and London 1992).

J.E. Stambaugh, *The ancient Roman city* (Baltimore and London 1988).

M. Todd, *The walls of Rome* (London 1978).

J.B. Ward-Perkins, *Roman imperial architecture* (Harmondsworth 1981).

P. Zanker, *The power of images in the age of Augustus* (Ann Arbor 1988).

Roman Emperors

27 BC–AD 14	Augustus
14–37	Tiberius
37–41	Caligula
41–54	Claudius
54–68	Nero
68–69	Galba
69	Otho
69	Vitellius

Flavians

69–79	Vespasian
79–81	Titus
81–96	Domitian
96–98	Nerva
98–117	Trajan

Antonines

117–38	Hadrian
138–61	Antoninus Pius
161–80	Marcus Aurelius
161–69	Lucius Verus
180–92	Commodus
193	Pertinax
193	Didius Julianus

Severians

193–211	Septimius Severus
211–17	Caracalla
211–12	Geta
217–18	Macrinus
218–22	Elagabalus

222–35	Alexander Severus		306–07	Flavius Severus
235–38	Maximinus		306–12	Maxentius
238	Gordian I		308–14	Maximinus
	Gordian II		306–37	Constantine the Great
238	Pupienus		337–40	Constantine II
	Balbinus		337–50	Constans
238–44	Gordian III		337–61	Constantinus II
244–47	Philip I		350–53	Magnentius
247–49	Philip II		361–63	Julian
249–51	Decius		363–64	Jovian
251–53	Trebonianus Gallus		364–75	Valentinian I
253	Aemilian		364–78	Valens
253–60	Valerian		367–83	Gratian
260–68	Gallienus		375–92	Valentinian II
268–70	Claudius II		378–95	Theodosius I
270	Quintillus			
270–75	Aurelian		**Western Empire**	
275–76	Tacitus		395–423	Honorius
276	Florian		425–55	Valentinian III
276–82	Probus		455	Petronius Maximus
282–83	Carus		455–56	Avitus
282–85	Carinus		457–61	Majorian
283–84	Numerian		461–65	Libius Severus
285–305	Diocletian		467–72	Anthemius
286–305	Maximian		472	Olybrius
305–06	Constantius Chlorus		473	Glycerius
305–10	Galerius		474–75	Julius Nepos
308–24	Licinius		475–76	Romulus Augustulus

From the fall of the Roman Empire to the present

by Alta Macadam

The **Roman Church** was not recognised until the reign of the Emperor Constantine when, by his famous Edict of Milan in 313, Christians throughout the Empire were granted liberty of worship. A primitive shrine had been built between AD 160 and 180 over the tomb of St Peter, and the first basilica of St Peter was consecrated in November 326. Other early Christian places of worship were the churches of Santa Pudenziana, San Sebastiano, San Lorenzo fuori le Mura and Santi Giovanni e Paolo. To Constantine is attributed the foundation of San Giovanni in Laterano and its baptistery, St Peter's and Santa Croce in Gerusalemme. Public pagan worship was forbidden in the city in 346 and ten years later temples were closed. Christianity became the state religion under Theodosius (d. 395). The population of the city, in the 4C estimated at about 500,000, was gradually to diminish in succeeding centuries until the city began to expand again in the 11C.

Rome was sacked by the **Goths and Vandals** repeatedly during the 5C. In 476 Odoacar, king of the Goths, compelled Romulus Augustulus to abdicate and so effectively put an end to the Western Roman Empire.

Medieval Rome

The supremacy of the bishop of Rome was gradually recognised by a Christianised western world, and the 'Donation of Constantine' was used to prove that the **Papacy** had inherited territory from the Emperor: it was not until the 15C that this document was discovered to be a 5C forgery. The papacy of St Gregory the Great (590–604) marked the foundation of medieval Rome, although not much is known about the city in this period since little archaeological evidence has survived. Rome, the possession of which was disputed in the 6C by Goths and Byzantines, passed at the beginning of the 7C under the temporal protection of the popes, and from then, right up until the 19C, the history of the papacy became intricately connected with the history of Rome.

When Pope Stephen III was threatened by the Lombards, he appealed for help to Pepin, king of the Franks, who defeated them and granted the Pope a portion of Lombard territory (754). This marked the beginning of the temporal power of the popes over the States of the Church. On Christmas Day 800, Charlemagne, son of Pepin, was crowned by Leo III in St Peter's as Augustus and Emperor, and the Empire, known as the **Holy Roman Empire** from the 13C onwards, survived until the abdication of Francis II of Austria in 1806. The walls of the Leonine City, built to defend the Borgo and St Peter's, date from the 9C.

The strength of the papacy increased under Pope Nicholas I (858–67) but after his death the prestige of the popes declined and the German emperors took an active part in the papal elections thoughout the 10C and early 11C. Gregory VII (1073–85), with the help of some Roman noble families, reasserted papal authority, but was unable to prevent the Norman Robert Guiscard, who had conquered Sicily, from devastating the city in 1084. As in other large Italian towns during the 12C the **Commune of Rome** strengthened its administrative position, and in 1188 it received official papal recognition. During the splendid pontificate of Innocent III (d. 1216) Rome became the capital of the western Christian world, and the influence of the Empire in the Italian peninsula dwindled.

Boniface VIII proclaimed the **first jubilee** in 1300, which brought thousands of pilgrims to Rome from all over Europe, and provided a large income for the papal coffers. His bull *Unam Sanctam* asserted unequivocally the temporal power of the papacy. But in 1309 Pope Clement V removed the papacy from Rome to Avignon, where it remained under the protection of France for most of the 14C (the name 'Babylonian captivity' given to this period refers to the deportation of the Jews to Babylon by Nebuchadnezzar after which they were then allowed to return). Meanwhile Rome, and the surrounding countryside, was devasted by wars between rival Roman aristocratic families including the Colonna, Caetani and Orsini, and the Commune of Rome, in the absence of the pope, gained in strength. In 1347 Cola di Rienzo was made 'tribune' of the 'Holy Roman Republic', but he failed in his patriotic but utopian attempt to revive the ancient power and glory of the Imperial city and was killed on the Capitoline Hill in 1354. In 1378 Gregory XI was persuaded by St Catherine of Siena to return to Rome, and the Commune, while acknowledging the papal overlordship, at the same time attempted to retain its authority. Between 1378 and 1417, during the **Great Schism**, various popes fought over the chair of St Peter, while the city suffered both physically and socially and the population was reduced to some 20,000 inhabitants. The ruins of ancient Rome were used as pastureland, and plundered for use as building material or for lime.

The Renaissance period

Pope Martin V, a member of the important Roman Colonna family, began to restore the city in 1420, and the temporal power of the popes was gradually established in central Italy, where the Papal States now included Lazio, Umbria, the Marche and Romagna.

During the papacy of **Nicholas V** (1447–55) the supremacy of the pope over the Commune was finally recognised, and the city acknowledged its dependency on the papacy. Nicholas V not only carried out building work at St Peter's and the **Vatican**—where he established his residence—and strengthened the fortifications of Castel Sant'Angelo, but also restored the administrative offices of the Commune on the Capitoline Hill, and, under the guidance of Leon Battista Alberti, recognised the importance of preserving the buildings of ancient Rome. These, however, continued to be plundered for their stone and marble until the 16C.

Sixtus IV, a member of the Della Rovere family, was one of the richest patrons of his time. In 1471 he founded the oldest public art collection in the world when he donated to the city the sculptures which now form the nucleus of the Capitoline museums, and he considerably increased the holdings of the Vatican library and opened it to the public. He rebuilt the 'Sistine' Chapel (which is named after him) and constructed the Ponte Sisto across the Tiber. He also reorganised the streets of the city. The grandest of all the wealthy cardinals' residences erected at this time in the city was the splendid Renaissance Palazzo della Cancelleria, commissioned by Sixtus's nephew Cardinal Raffaello Riario. At the end of the century, Nero's Domus Aurea was discovered beneath the Baths of Trajan and the painted decoration on its walls had a great influence on Renaissance artists, many of whom imitated these 'grotesques'.

At the beginning of the 16C Cardinal Giuliano della Rovere was elected Pope **Julius II**: he spent untold riches on ambitious artistic projects designed to glorify the papacy as successor to the ancient Roman Empire. Rome became the centre of the High Renaissance while the three greatest artists of the age—**Bramante**, **Raphael** and **Michelangelo**—were at work here. Using Bramante as architect, Julius took the audacious decision to rebuild St Peter's, and he enlarged the Vatican palace on a magnificent scale. He commissioned the frescoes on the vault of the Sistine Chapel from Michelangelo, and the frescoes in the 'Stanze' in the Vatican from Raphael. He planned the long and straight Via Giulia and Via della Lungara on either side of the Tiber. The Medici Pope Leo X appointed Raphael as commissioner responsible for the preservation of the ancient buildings of Rome.

After Clement VII took sides with Francis I of France against the Emperor Charles V, German mercenary troops captured Rome in the devastating **Sack of Rome** in 1527, when great damage was wrought to the city. It lost its prestige as a centre of humanism, and its population fell to around 30,000 inhabitants. This humiliation for Clement VII (who had to take refuge in Castel Sant'Angelo) as well as the attacks on the papacy by Martin Luther—who had visited Rome in 1511—preluded the period of the Counter-Reformation. The Farnese Pope Paul III introduced the idea of Rome as the 'Holy City', and many fine buildings were erected, including the splendid Palazzo Farnese, perhaps the most dignified and impressive palace in Rome. The very heart of the ancient city, Piazza del Campidoglio, was redesigned in 1538 by Michelangelo, and the ancient Roman statue of Marcus Aurelius was set up here. Paul III approved the founding of the Order of the Jesuits in 1540, and later in the century the great Jesuit church of the Gesù was built.

Pope **Sixtus V** did more than any of his predecessors to improve and adorn the city in celebration of the Catholic Church. With the help of Domenico Fontana, he built new long and straight streets (including the Strada Felice, part of which is now called Via Sistina, over 3km long, which ran up and down four hills of the city) and set up obelisks to close the vistas at the end of them or as focal points in piazze. He also completed the dome of St Peter's, and enlarged the Vatican and Lateran palaces. He brought the water of the Acqua Felice by aqueduct from the Alban Hills into the centre of Rome. The district of the Borgo between the Vatican and Castel Sant'Angelo, which had been the stronghold of the papacy since 850, was formally incorporated into the city of Rome in 1586. By now the population of the city was around 100,000 and Rome became the most cosmopolitan city of its time.

Baroque Rome
Paul V (1605–21) completed St Peter's (consecrated by Urban VIII in 1626), and reactivated an aqueduct from Lake Bracciano, built by Trajan, which ends on the Janiculum Hill. The Acqua Paola still supplies water to the Vatican and its fountains. It is to the 17C popes Urban VIII, Innocent X and Alexander VII that Rome owes its Baroque aspect of today. Urban VIII (1623–44) was the patron of **Bernini**, one of whose most remarkable works was the colonnade in Piazza San Pietro. He also designed numerous delightful fountains in the city, the most elaborate of which is in Piazza Navona. **Borromini**, the other great architect of this time, built the courtyard of Palazzo della Sapienza, San Carlo alle Quattro Fontane, the church and dome of Sant'Ivo, Sant'Agnese in Agone, and the Oratorio dei Filippini.

The flamboyant staircase beneath Trinità dei Monti, known as the **Spanish Steps**, dates from the 18C, as does the **Fontana di Trevi**. This was the century of the Grand Tour when numerous rich young men from Britain came to Rome on a leisurely visit to complete their education, admire Rome's Classical remains, and, where possible, acquire some antiquities. The city came to be regarded as a centre of European culture at this time, although its population was little over 150,000. In February 1798, the **French** entered Rome and proclaimed a republic: Pius VI was taken as a prisoner to France where he died in 1799. In 1809 Napoleon annexed the States of the Church, already diminished, to the French Empire: in 1810 the French Senate proclaimed Rome to be the second capital; and in 1811 Napoleon conferred the title of King of Rome on his newborn son. On the fall of Napoleon in 1815, Pius VII returned to Rome, to which were also restored almost all the works of art that had been removed by the Emperor.

The Risorgimento
The city took an active part in the agitated period of the Risorgimento, the political renaissance of Italy, and shared with the rest of Europe the revolutionary ideas of liberty and independence. A republic was proclaimed by an elected assembly in Rome under the guidance of Giuseppe Mazzini and the pope fled to Gaeta. When the French sent an army in support of the pope in 1849, the defence of the city was entrusted to the able hands of **Giuseppe Garibaldi**, who made a heroic stand against the foreigners on the Janiculum Hill. The inhabitants of Trastevere were particularly enthusiastic supporters of Mazzini and Garibaldi. In the first half of the 19C important restoration work was carrried out on the Colosseum and Pantheon.

In 1867 Garibaldi made another attempt to rouse the Romans against the papal government with the help of the Cairoli brothers, who were killed in the same year. In 1870 the French garrison, who had occupied Castel Sant'Angelo since 1849, withdrew from the city, and a month later the Italian army, under Raffaello Cadorna, entered Rome through a breach in the walls beside the **Porta Pia**. This brought an end to the papal rule of the city, although an agreement was made on the same day with the papacy that the Leonine City was excluded from the jurisdiction of the Italian troops. Rome, still contained within the Aurelian Walls, was proclaimed the capital of united Italy in 1871.

At the end of the 19C the ugly Via Nazionale, Via Cavour and Corso Vittorio Emanuele II were all built, and the embankments constructed along the Tiber. An obtrusive monument to the first king of Italy, Vittorio Emanuele II, was set up in the centre of the city in 1885–1911, and after the First World War became also the burial place of Italy's Unknown Soldier. By 1911 the population of the city was around 500,000 inhabitants.

The twentieth century

After the First World War the movement known as Fascismo, the creation of **Benito Mussolini**, rapidly developed. He organised the 'March on Rome' on 28 October 1922, after which the king, Vittorio Emanuele III, invited Mussolini to form a government. In 1929 the Lateran Treaty (the 'Concordat') was signed, by which the Vatican City became an independent sovereign state. The Classical Roman period was glorified by Mussolini who attempted to imitate it through his building activities and his ambition to create a new foreign 'Empire'. Numerous disastrous interventions of 'urban planning' were perpetrated in the 1930s; the Capitoline Hill was flanked by two broad thoroughfares—Via dei Fori Imperiali and Via del Teatro di Marcello—both opened in 1933. Beyond the Tiber, the old medieval district of the Borgo was transformed by the building of Via della Conciliazione (1937), which also altered irrevocably the dramatic effect of Bernini's piazza in front of St Peter's. The district of EUR and the Foro Italico are typical of the grandiose conception of Fascist Rome.

Italy entered the **Second World War** on the German side on 10 June 1940; the Fascist regime was finally overthrown in 1943 and Mussolini was killed by partisans in 1945. In 1944, 335 civilians were shot by Nazi troops at the Fosse Ardeatine near the Via Appia, as a reprisal for the killing of 32 German soldiers in Rome by members of the Italian Resistance movement. After the landings at Anzio and Nettuno in 1944, the American 5th Army entered the capital. In 1946 Vittorio Emanuele III abdicated, and less than a month later a general election, with a referendum on the form of government, was held. The referendum approved the establishment of a **republic**, with an elected president. In 1947 the Constituent Assembly passed the new republican constitution.

In the 1950s the population of Rome grew from 1.6 million to 2.1 million inhabitants, and by 1981 was around 3 million. The metropolitan area of the city expanded enormously (when it was mistakenly predicted that by the year 2000 the population would be in the region of 5 million), and is now about ten times greater than it was in the 1950s. However, in recent years the population has decreased to around 2,600,000, and most of the residents live in the sprawling suburbs which have spread into the Roman Campagna in an uncontrolled way. The historic centre suffers from depopulation (it is estimated that only some

150,000 residents now live here), and many of the buildings are used as offices. However in the last few years immigrants from Europe, Asia, America and Africa have come to live in the city.

In 1978 Aldo Moro, President of the Christian Democrat Party, the largest political party in Italy at that time, was kidnapped and assassinated and his body abandoned in a street in the centre of the city. In the same year John Paul II was elected, the first non-Italian pope since 1522, and the only Polish pope in the Church's history. In 1993 the mayor of Rome was for the first time elected directly by the inhabitants of the city.

Since the 1980s interesting **excavations** have been carried out in the Roman Forum on the Palatine Hill, and in the Imperial Fora, and important **restoration projects** have been completed on numerous monuments and works of art, including Trajan's Column, the Arch of Constantine, the Domus Aurea (reopened to visitors in 1999 after fifteen years closure), the equestrian statue of Marcus Aurelius, the frescoes by Michelangelo in the Sistine chapel, and the frescoes by Raphael in the Stanze in the Vatican. In the 1990s many church and palace façades and fountains, blackened by the polluted air, were carefully cleaned. During Holy Year in 2000 24 million pilgrims and tourists visited the city. In the same year an urban plan for the city was approved by the town council, the first in 38 years.

The circulation of traffic in the city still has to be resolved, and there are long-term plans to increase transport by train (both underground and light railway), which is still only a tenth of that provided in Paris, Berlin, and London.

In 2002 the long-awaited regional park of the Via Appia Antica was at last a reality and represents one of the most significant achievements of conservationists in recent years.

Further reading

M. Andrieux, *Daily life in papal Rome in the 18th century* (London 1968).

B. Boucher, *Italian Baroque sculpture* (London 1998).

E. Bowen, *A time in Rome* (London 1960).

Lord Byron, *Selected poems* (London 1996).

B. Cellini, *Autobiography* (London 1964).

E. Clark, *Rome and a villa* (London 1953).

P. Ginsborg, *A history of contemporary Italy: society and politics 1948–1988* (London 1990).

J.W. Goethe, *Italian Journey* (London 1962).

A. Hare, *Walks in Rome* (London 1883).

H. Hibbard, *Bernini* (London 1965).

C. Hibbert, *Rome. The biography of a city* (London 1987).

J.N.D. Kelly, *Oxford Dictionary of Popes* (London 1986).

R. Krautheimer, *Rome. Profile of a city 312–1308* (Princeton 1980).

E. Male, *The early churches of Rome* (London 1960).

H.V. Morton, *A traveller in Rome* (London 1959).

H.V. Morton, *The fountains of Rome* (London 1966).

P. Partner, *Renaissance Rome 1500–59. Portrait of a society* (California 1980).

G.M. Trevelyan, *Garibaldi's defence of the Roman Republic, 1848–49* (London 1988).

B. Wall, *A city and a world* (London 1962).

R. Wittkower, *Art and architecture in Italy 1600–1750* (revised, in 3 volumes, London 1999).

THE GUIDE

1 • The Capitoline Hill

The Capitoline Hill (Map 7; 5, 7; and see p 76), in Italian, Campidoglio, is the best place to start a visit to Rome. It was of the first importance in the early history of Rome, and today it provides good views of the city and of the Roman Forum. The splendid Roman bronze equestrian monument to Marcus Aurelius, already famous in the Middle Ages, was provided with a fitting setting in the piazza on the summit of the hill by Michelangelo, who also designed the palaces here. These contain the town hall of Rome and the Capitoline museums, with the city's superb collections of ancient sculpture. Also on the hill is the important church of Santa Maria in Aracoeli, of ancient foundation, which has a beautiful interior. There are delightful peaceful gardens off the quiet street which encircles the summit of the hill.

History of the Capitoline Hill

The Capitoline Hill was the political and religious centre of ancient Rome, and is the most important, even if the smallest, of the Seven Hills of Rome. Already inhabited in the Bronze Age, since the end of the 11C it has been the seat of the civic government of the city.

On its southern summit (the Capitolium) stood the **Temple of Jupiter Optimus Maximus Capitolinus**, remains of which still exist. This was the most venerated temple in Rome, since 'the best and greatest of all Jupiters' was regarded as the city's special protector. The northern summit of the hill—altered at the end of the 19C by the construction of the monument of Vittorio Emanuele II—was occupied by the Arx, or citadel of Rome. During a siege by the Gauls in 390 BC the Capitolium was saved from a night attack by the honking of the sacred geese of Juno that were kept here, which alerted the Romans to the danger. In 343 BC a temple was erected to Juno Moneta; the name came to be connected with the mint later established here. In the Middle Ages the church of Aracoeli on this summit was the meeting place of the Roman Council.

Formerly the hill was accessible only from the Roman Forum but since the 16C the main buildings have been made to face the north, in conformity with the direction of the modern development of the city. There are three approaches to the hill from Piazza d'Aracoeli (**Map 7; 5**). On the left a long flight of steps mounts to the church of Santa Maria in Aracoeli, and on the right, Via delle Tre Pile (a road opened for carriages in 1873) winds up past a fragment of Archaic tufa wall. In the middle the stepped ramp known as the **Cordonata**, designed by Michelangelo and modified c 1578 by Giacomo della Porta, provides the easiest way up the hill. At its foot are two Egyptian lions in black granite veined with red, dating from the Ptolemaic period (3C BC), that were formerly in the Temple of Isis which once stood near the Pantheon. The water they now blow from their

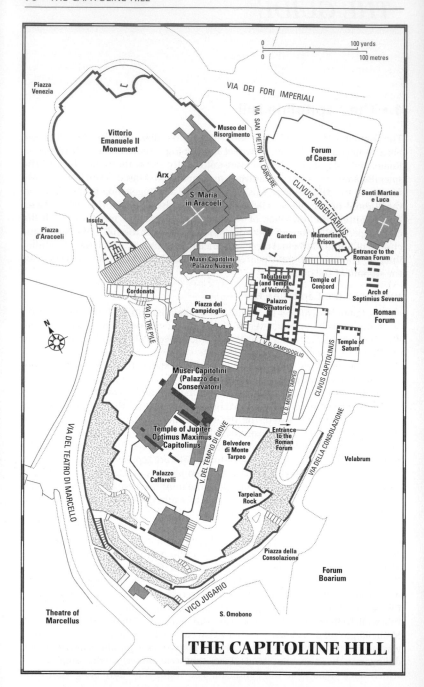

THE CAPITOLINE HILL

mouths (except in winter) comes from the Acqua Felice, an aqueduct which was constructed to provide water for the hill in the late 16C (see p 433). In the garden on the left, where there is a group of fine trees and another flight of steps, shaded by a pergola, a 19C statue of Cola di Rienzo marks the spot where he was killed in 1354. He had been appointed 'tribune' of a 'Holy Roman Republic' in 1347 and addressed the assembly in the church of Santa Maria in Aracoeli, but his ambition to recreate a glorious period of republican rule modelled on ancient Rome was very short-lived.

At the top of the ramp is **Piazza del Campidoglio**, beautifully designed by Michelangelo in 1538, just after he had been made a citizen of Rome, to add grandeur to the historical centre of the city (it was completed to his design in the 17C). It is surrounded on three sides by stately palaces and a balustrade defines its open end. The attractive pavement with an oval star design gave prominence to the famous gilded bronze statue of Marcus Aurelius, which has been displayed under cover since its restoration (see below); it was replaced here by a disappointing copy in 1997. Michelangelo provided its small and elegant base.

On the **balustrade** are a miscellany of statues. The colossal sculptures of the twin heroes Castor and Pollux with their horses, known as the Dioscuri, are much-restored late Roman works that were found in the 16C in the Ghetto (where a temple to them once stood). Beside them are two Roman sculptures modelled on the enemy arms and armour which used to be displayed as trophies in processions held in honour of victorious generals after battle. They have been known for centuries as the *Trophies of Marius*, since it was traditionally thought that they depicted the war booty of General Marius after his victory over Germanic tribes in 101 BC, but in fact they date from the time of Domitian (late 1C AD). The statues of the Emperor Constantine and his son Constantine II come from the Baths of Constantine, and the two milestones are the first and seventh of the Via Appia.

At the back of the piazza is Palazzo Senatorio; on the left is Palazzo Nuovo; facing it on the right is Palazzo dei Conservatori. The latter has a very unusual design with Ionic columns supporting a flat open loggia below, and handsome windows with coupled columns on the *piano nobile*, below a prominent entablature with a balcony. The two storeys are united by columns which rise from the ground as far as the entablature, the earliest example of the giant order being used in secular architecture. The Palazzo Nuovo opposite, also designed by Michelangelo, was not built until the mid-17C.

Piazza del Campidoglio

The Capitoline Museums

The collections housed in **Palazzo Nuovo** and **Palazzo dei Conservatori** (with the adjoining Palazzi Clementino and Caffarelli), are grouped under the comprehensive title of the **Musei Capitolini**, famous for their magnificent Roman sculptures. Founded in 1471, they constitute the oldest public collection in the world.

Opening times

09.00–20.00, closed Mon. ☎ 06 3996 7800, ✉ www.capitolium.org. The ticket includes entrance to all the sculpture galleries in both the Palazzo Nuovo and Palazzo dei Conservatori, as well as the Tabularium and the Pinacoteca.

There is a **café** (not cheap) on the delightful roof terrace of Palazzo Clementino, with splendid views.

Note An important collection of Classical sculptures, part of the Musei Capitolini and formerly exhibited here, is now permanently displayed at the **Centrale Montemartini**, described on p 410, and should on no account be missed (Combined ticket.).

History of the museums

In 1471 Sixtus IV made over to the people of Rome a valuable group of bronzes (including the famous *Spinario* and the She-wolf of Rome, see below), which were deposited in Palazzo dei Conservatori. This nucleus was later enriched with finds made in Rome and by various acquisitions, notably the collection of Cardinal Alessandro Albani. A second museum was opened in 1876, and in 1925 the Museo Mussolini (also known as the Museo Nuovo) was opened on the ground floor of Palazzo Caffarelli adjoining Palazzo dei Conservatori (given a new wing, the Braccio Nuovo in 1950–52). The superb contents of these two museums, closed to the public in 1984, are now permanently displayed at the Centrale Montemartini, see p 410. The Pinacoteca Capitolina was founded in the mid 18C with the Pio and Sacchetti collections, formed respectively by Prince Gilberto Pio of Savoy and Cardinal Sacchetti. In the 19C it lost some of its treasures to the Vatican picture gallery and to the Accademia di San Luca. It was later enriched by the Cini bequest, which included some interesting 14C–15C paintings from the Sterbini collection, as well as ceramics.

The museums were restored and many of the Classical statues cleaned in 2001 when the tunnel which connects the two buildings beneath the piazza was reopened so that remarkable remains of the Tabularium beneath Palazzo Senatorio can now again be visited (and from which there are superb views over the Roman Forum). Since excavations during restoration work brought to light more of the Temple of Jupiter Capitolinus (see below) and Bronze Age sepulchres, part of Palazzo Caffarelli is still closed to the public. When it reopens these excavations will be visible, and a new Pavilion, designed by Carlo Aymonino, will probably display the original equestrian statue of Marcus Aurelius, and other large sculptures at present kept in the Sala degli Orazi e Curiazi. The top floor is used for important exhibitions. The Medagliere, with a very important collection of coins and medals is soon to be opened in Palazzo Clementino, which is also used for small exhibitions.

Palazzo Nuovo

Palazzo Nuovo, on the left side of the piazza, built in the reign of Innocent X

(1644–55), contains an extremely interesting collection of ancient sculpture begun by Clement XII and added to by later popes. It was opened to the public in 1734 during Clement's pontificate.

Large Roman sculptures, including (on the right) Hadrian in a toga which also covers his head, as Pontifex Maximus (or high priest), and (on the left) Faustina, wife of Antoninus Pius represented as the goddess Ceres (beneath is a bas-relief of a sow feeding her young) are displayed in the **atrium** on the ground floor. Beyond, facing each other, are two statues of women after Greek originals, with portrait heads of the 2C–3C AD. Looking onto the courtyard is a colossal statue of Minerva, from a 5C original.

In the **courtyard** is the colossal statue of a river-god (probably 2C AD), which in 1596 was moved by Giacomo della Porta from the foot of the Capitoline Hill, where it had lain since the days of the Empire and incorporated in the fountain here. Known as *Marforio*, its name is thought to be derived from *Martis forum*, since the statue was once in the Forum of Augustus dedicated to Mars. This was one of Rome's 'talking' statues, used for the display of satirical comments and epigrams. Marforio 'conversed' with another statue called *Madama Lucrezia*, still at the bottom of the hill (see pp 141 and 198). In the side niches are two figures of Pan (telamones), from the Theatre of Pompey. Unhappily displayed here (awaiting a definitive arrangement in a new covered courtyard in Palazzo dei Conservatori, see above) is the **equestrian statue of *Marcus Aurelius**, formerly in the centre of Piazza del Campidoglio. Since its restoration in 1981–90, when the gilding was returned to its surface, it has been decided to protect it under cover. This magnificent colossal gilded bronze is a masterpiece of Roman sculpture. It is now thought to date from the latter part of the Emperor's reign (AD 161–80), or possibly from the year of his death; it is the only Roman equestrian statue of this period to survive. This popular statue appears time and again in

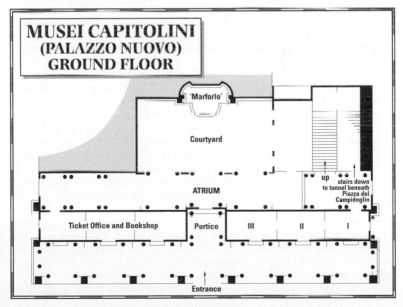

medieval representations of the city, and it is first documented in the 10C when it was believed to represent the Christian emperor Constantine the Great. It is thought to have stood on the Lateran Hill as early as 782 and was certainly there by the 10C, and it was greatly admired, together with other classical bronzes, throughout the Middle Ages. In his description of Rome entitled *Meraviglie di Roma* at the end of the 12C or beginning of the 13C, a visitor, thought to have been an Englishman known as Maestro Gregorio, dedicates much space to this statue (his work is known from one manuscript transcription dating from the late 13C which is preserved in St Catherine's College in Cambridge, England). The statue was moved from the Lateran to the Capitoline Hill by order of Paul III in 1538. In 1873 Henry James commented, 'I doubt if any statue of King or captain in the public places of the world has more to commend it to the general heart.'

At the foot of the stairs is a colossal statue of Mars, dating from the Domitian period. On the right are three small rooms. **Room I** displays portraits of Roman citizens, and a funerary relief of three men, probably from the same family. On the walls are fragments of calendars from the Palatine and Ostia, including a finely preserved Order of Precedence of the citizens of Ostia (from the time of the emperor Pertinax). In **room II** there is a cippus of a master-mason called Titus Statilius Aper, with his tools. In **room III** there is a colossal double *sarcophagus, a splendid work of the 2C AD, with portraits of the deceased and reliefs representing the story of Achilles.

Stairs lead down to the tunnel which runs under the Piazza to Palazzo dei Conservatori, and also gives access to the Tabularium (described on p 87).

Roman classical sculpture

As early as the 3C BC the Romans showed an interest in Greek art, and ancient sculpture was brought to the city as war booty from Sicily and Greece. When the supply of bronze originals by famous Greek sculptors diminished, the idea arose of copying Classical masterpieces in marble, which was imported from Greece until Julius Caesar opened the Luni marble quarries near Carrara. Most of the copyists were Greek slaves or freedmen, and very few are known by name or easy to distinguish as individual artists. Since the Roman copies are usually of extremely high quality, it is often very difficult to tell the difference between them and the Greek originals themselves. The Romans were also particularly skilled in reusing old statues for new dedications, and repairing or restoring Greek works.

In Greek art the entire human figure was portrayed, but the Romans invented the portrait bust, numerous examples of which are exhibited in the Capitoline museums, many of them masterpieces. They document various changes over the centuries, for instance, different fashions in hair-style: Hadrian was the first emperor who chose to be portrayed with a beard, and every emperor who succeeded him was shown in the same manner.

The **Galleria** on the **first floor** retains its old-fashioned arrangement of statues, busts, and inscriptions. The decorative vase (krater) of the 1C AD, rests on a very fine well-head from Hadrian's Villa, with archaistic decoration representing the procession of the 12 gods (Dii Consentes). The colossal statue of *Hercules* was restored and altered to show him slaying the Hydra by Alessandro Algardi (it was probably orginally intended to represent Hercules capturing the hind). Cupid

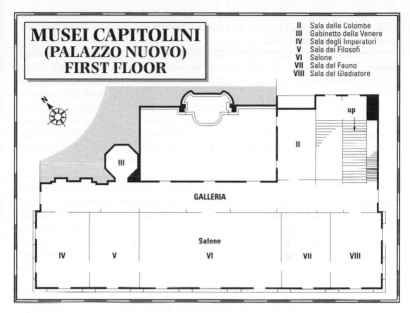

MUSEI CAPITOLINI (PALAZZO NUOVO) FIRST FLOOR

II Sala delle Colombe
III Gabinetto della Venere
IV Sala degli Imperatori
V Sala dei Filosofi
VI Salone
VII Sala del Fauno
VIII Sala del Gladiatore

GALLERIA

Salone

as an archer is a good copy of a celebrated work by Lysippos. The torso of the *Discobolos* of Myron, was badly restored in the late 17C as a fighting gladiator. Outside room II is a statue of *Leda with the Swan*, a replica of the work attributed to Timotheos (4C BC).

Room II, the Sala delle Colombe, is named after the exquisite small *mosaic of four doves at a fountain, found in Hadrian's villa at Tivoli, after a work by Sosias of Pergamon. The other mosaic here depicts two theatrical masks. In show cases below the windows are inscriptions, including the Tabula Iliaca, a plaque with small reliefs representing the Trojan cycle, by Theodorus (1C AD). In the centre of the room is a charming little statue of a young girl protecting a dove, a Roman copy of a Greek work of the 2C BC, wrongly restored with a snake.

Outside the door, in the Galleria, is a seated statue of a drunken old woman, perhaps after Myron the Younger, a Pergamene sculptor of the end of the 3C BC. Near the door into Room VI, displayed opposite each other, are two colossal heads of female divinities, the one of Aphrodite, perhaps an original of the Hellenistic period.

Off the far end of the Galleria is the **Gabinetto della Venere (III)** which displays the celebrated *Capitoline Venus*, found in the 17C in a house near San Vitale and purchased by Benedict XIV in 1752. A superbly modelled statue of Parian marble, it is a Roman replica of a Hellenistic original, thought to be derived from the Cnidian Aphrodite of Praxiteles. For centuries it has been one of the most famous statues in the city. It is thought to be the statue admired by Maestro Gregorio (see above) in the late 12C or early 13C: in his *Meraviglie di Roma* he describes how he went back to see her no fewer than three times during his stay in the city, thoroughly seduced by her modesty. In 1835 a much later visitor to Rome, the French painter Ingres, complained that he was not admitted to see the statue since the prudish pope had locked her away because of her nudity; he tells us that Gregory XVI had also attached 'enormous vine leaves' to numerous other sculptures.

At the end of the corridor, on the left, is the entrance to the **Sala degli Imperatori (IV)** with very fine Roman Imperial busts, interesting as portraits and also in some cases because of the precious materials used. They are arranged chronologically, starting on the top shelf in the far corner by the door into Room V. Here two portraits of *Augustus* (one showing him wearing a wreath of myrtle) flank a portrait of his wife Livia. In the next corner is a portrait of *Agrippina Maggiore*, and, displayed on a pedestal, *Marcus Aurelius as a boy*. Also on this wall, displayed on a pedestal is a *woman of the late Flavian period, with a splendid head-dress. On the opposite wall is the bearded *Marcus Aurelius* (top shelf, third from the right), and on the shelf below *Trajan Decio*, distinguished by his worried expression. In the centre is a beautiful seated figure of *Helena*, mother of Constantine, inspired by the Aphrodite of Pheidias.

In the **Sala dei Filosofi (V)** is another splendid display of Roman busts, this time of philosophers and poets, some identified as Socrates, Sophocles, the blind Homer, and Euripides. On the lower shelf in the corner opposite the windows is a very fine bust of Cicero. The double portrait portrays *Epicuros and Metrodorus*.

The **Salone (VI)** is the largest room in this museum and has a splendid display of Roman statuary. In dark marble in the centre are the *Infant Hercules*, a colossal ugly figure in green basalt, of the late Imperial epoch, on a base decorated with scenes from the myth of Zeus. The *Young* or *Laughing Centaur* and *Old* or *Weeping Centaur* are two remarkable works from Hadrian's Villa, signed by his contemporaries Aristeas and Papias of Aphrodisias in Caria. Around the walls are statues of *Apollo*, one an Archaic statue, a copy of the so-called *Omphalos Apollo* in Athens; an *Old woman in terror*, a striking example of the Hellenistic period; a *Huntsman* (with a dead hare), with the head of the period of Gallienus on a body of the late Archaic type; and a *Wounded Amazon* signed by the copyist Sosicles (from a 5C original).

The **Sala del Fauno (VII)** is named after the statue of the laughing *Silenus*, in red marble, of the Imperial period derived from a Hellenistic bronze, displayed in the centre of the room. Also here is the **Lex Regia** of Vespasian, inscribed on a bronze plaque, the historic decree conferring sovereign power on the emperor; the text was used by Cola di Rienzo to demonstrate the greatness and the rights of the citizens of Rome. Claiming that Boniface VIII had hidden it away beneath an altar, Rienzo had it installed inside San Giovanni in Laterano for all to see. The two statues of young boys show one with a goose (copy of a bronze by Boethos of Chalcedon, 2C BC), and one with a mask (a Hellenistic work).

In the centre of the **Sala del Gladiatore (VIII)** is the *Dying Gaul*, an exquisitely modelled figure of a Celtic warrior who lies mortally wounded on the ground. It was discovered in 1622 in the Gardens of Sallust near the Villa Ludovisi and is a copy from the Roman period of one of the bronze statues dedicated at Pergamon by Attalos I in commemoration of his victories over the Gauls (239 BC). The statue was formerly called the Dying Gladiator, 'butcher'd to make a Roman holiday', in Byron's phrase. It was beautifully restored in 1986 when the position of the right arm, altered in a 17C restoration, was rectified. Also displayed in this room: *Satyr Resting*, a good replica of an original by Praxiteles, found in Hadrian's Villa near Tivoli. This is the Marble Faun of

Nathaniel Hawthorne's novel (there are other replicas are in the Vatican). The group of *Eros and Psyche* is a Hellenistic work, and the statue of a Greek Cynic Philosopher is thought to date from the 2C BC (probably a copy in marble of a bronze original). The *Amazon* is a Roman work after an original attributed to Pheidias (wrongly restored), and the statue of *Hermes* or *Antinouos*, once owned by Cardinal Albani, is a Hadrianic version of a 4C original.

Palazzo dei Conservatori

The Palazzo dei Conservatori, on the right side of Piazza del Campidoglio, was rebuilt by Nicholas V about 1450 and remodelled after 1564 by Giacomo della Porta and Guidetto Guidetti from a design by Michelangelo. It contains the Appartamento dei Conservatori on the first floor, and the Pinacoteca on the second floor. Considerable remains of the 6C BC Temple of Jupiter Capitolinus are incorporated into the building, and more of the temple is at present being excavated, and will one day be visible to the public.

In the **courtyard** of the ground floor are fragments of a colossal statue of *Constantine the Great* (c 12m high), including the head, hand and foot, which were brought from the Basilica of Constantine in 1486. The body of the statue was made in wood. Near the head is an inscription from the time of Boniface VIII (1294–1303). Opposite are bases and transennae with sculptured representations of provinces and nations subject to Rome, which once decorated the Temple of Hadrian in Piazza di Pietra (see p 149). Above is an inscription from the arch erected in AD 51 on Via Lata to celebrate the conquest of Britain by Claudius. Beneath the portico is a seated statue of *Roma* from the time of Trajan or Hadrian, and two colossal statues in grey marble of *Barbarians*, all three acquired by Clement XI in 1720.

Stairs lead up to the **first floor**, past four reliefs from triumphal arches, three of them celebrating Marcus Aurelius and his military victories and triumph in 176—including a scene of the Emperor sacrificing before the Temple of Jupiter Capitolinus—and one from an arch in Via di Pietra.

On the stair landing of the first floor is a relief of *Hadrian* from the demolished Arco di Portogallo, and a statue of *Charles of Anjou*, by Arnolfo di Cambio or his workshop, made for Santa Maria in Aracoeli c 1270.

The **Appartamento dei Conservatori**, the rooms where the governing magistrates of the city carried out their administrative duties, were decorated from the 16C onwards with scenes of Roman history. The **Sala degli Orazi e Curiazi (I)** has frescoes by the Cavaliere d'Arpino, representing episodes from the reigns of the early kings. The marble statue of *Urban VIII* is a studio work begun by Gian Lorenzo Bernini; and the bronze statue of *Innocent X* is by Alessandro Algardi. It was in this room in 1957 that the Treaty of Rome, the foundation of the European Economic Community, now the European Union, was signed by Italy, Belgium, France, West Germany, Luxembourg and Holland. Some important bronzes, destined to be exhibited in a new pavilion in Palazzo Caffarelli, are temporarily exhibited here. The colossal statue of *Hercules* in gilded bronze was found in the time of Sixtus IV during the demolition of the Ara Maxima, near the Forum Boarium. It is a Roman work derived from a Greek bronze. The colossal bronze *Head of Constantine* has recently been restored (the hand and globe probably came from the same statue).

Room II (Sala dei Capitani) has frescoes (1594) from Roman history by

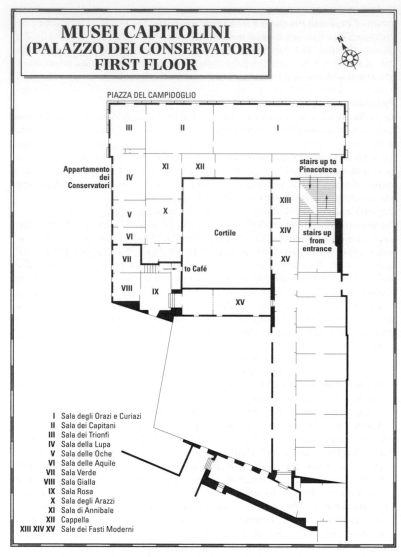

**MUSEI CAPITOLINI
(PALAZZO DEI CONSERVATORI)
FIRST FLOOR**

PIAZZA DEL CAMPIDOGLIO

III   II   I

Appartamento dei Conservatori

IV   XI   XII

stairs up to Pinacoteca

V   X   XIII

VI   Cortile   XIV   stairs up from entrance

VII   XV

to Café

VIII   IX   XV

I Sala degli Orazi e Curiazi
II Sala dei Capitani
III Sala dei Trionfi
IV Sala della Lupa
V Sala delle Oche
VI Sala delle Aquile
VII Sala Verde
VIII Sala Gialla
IX Sala Rosa
X Sala degli Arazzi
XI Sala di Annibale
XII Cappella
XIII XIV XV Sale dei Fasti Moderni

Tommaso Laureti, and handsome 17C doors. On the entrance wall are statues of *Gianfrancesco Aldobrandini* and *Tommaso Rospigliosi* by Ercole Ferrata. In the far corner are memorials to Virginio Cesarini (with his portrait attributed to Gian Lorenzo Bernini or Duquesnoy) and Carlo Barberini, with a Roman statue restored by Alessandro Algardi (and a portrait head by Bernini).

Room III (Sala dei Trionfi). Frieze by pupils of Daniele da Volterra representing the *Triumph of Emilius Paulus over Perseus of Macedon*, and a fine wood ceiling, all dating from 1569. The two paintings of the *Deposition* and

St Francesca Romana were commissioned for this room in 1614 from Paolo Piazza. The *Battle between Alexander the Great and Darius* is by Pietro da Cortona. The most famous of the bronzes presented to the Conservatori by Sixtus IV are exhibited here. In the middle is the celebrated *Spinario*, a sculpture of a boy plucking a thorn from his foot, formerly known as the *Fedele Capitolino*, because it was thought to be the portrait of Marcius, a Roman messenger who would not delay his mission though tortured by a thorn. It is a delicate Hellenistic composition in the eclectic style of the 1C BC. Also here is a bronze head, known as *Junius Brutus*, of Etruscan or Italic workmanship of the 3C BC, and a statue of *Camillus*, or an acolyte, dating from the 1C AD. There is also a fine sarcophagus of the 3C AD.

Room IV (Sala della Lupa). The fine wood ceiling dates from 1865. Here are displayed fragments of the *Fasti Consulares et Triumphales*, from the inner walls of the Arch of Augustus in the Forum, in a frame designed by Michelangelo. These are records of Roman magistrates and of triumphs of the great captains of Rome in the period of 13 BC–AD 12. Here since at least the 16C has been displayed the famous *She-wolf of Rome* thought to be an Etruscan bronze of the late 6C or early 5C BC, probably belonging to the school of Vulca, an Etruscan sculptor of Veio. It originally stood on the Capitoline Hill and may be the figure that was struck by lightning in 65 BC, when the hind feet are said to have been damaged. It was taken to the Lateran Palace some time in the Middle Ages. The figures of the twins Romulus and Remus were added by Antonio del Pollaiolo c 1509.

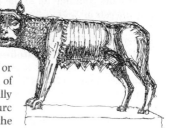

The She-wolf of Rome, in the Sala dei Conservatori

Room V (Sala delle Oche). This is an interesting example of a 17C apartment: it contains a figure of Isis and antique bronzes of two geese, or more probably ducks; a bronze bust of *Michelangelo*; and a marble head of *Medusa* by Bernini.

Room VI (Sala delle Aquile) displays two Roman eagles on cipollino columns and Roman sculpture including *Diana of Ephesus*. Beyond the **Sala Verde (VII)** with busts of Roman emperors, including one of Hadrian in rare Egyptian alabaster, is the **Sala Gialla (VIII)** with a table top in the centre (resting on a capital), with reliefs of the life of Achilles, incorporated in a Cosmatesque design. In the display cases are examples of rare antique marbles. The **Sala Rosa (IX)** has, in the centre, a group of two girls playing, a Hellenistic work. Plaques on the walls commemorate Michelangelo, Bernini, and Titian.

It is now necessary to return to the Sala Verde from which there is access to the **café** in Palazzo Clementino, worth visiting for the view from the delightful terrace. From right to left can be seen the Monument of Vittorio Emanuele II, the squat dome of the Gesù, the Pantheon (with Monte Mario in the distance behind), the spiral tower of Sant'Ivo, then the four domes of Sant'Andrea della Valle, St Peter's, San Carlo ai Catinari, and Santa Maria in Campitelli. Further round is the hill of the Gianicolo, and, nearby, the Synagogue in front of which is the Theatre of Marcellus.

Also from the Sala Verde and the Sala delle Oche there is access (right) to the **Sala degli Arazzi (X)** decorated with tapestries made in Rome showing the goddess Roma, and the Birth of Romulus and Remus (from the painting by Rubens in the Pinacoteca Capitolina). The frescoes and wood ceiling date from 1544. The very well preserved bust of *Commodus as Hercules* is flanked by two fragments of statues of tritons. The **Sala di Annibale (XI)** has early 16C frescoes and the oldest ceiling in the palace (1519). A beautiful bronze krater with an inscription, the gift of King Mithridates to a gymnastic association, part of the booty from a Mithridatic war, found at Anzio, is exhibited here. Off this room is the **Cappella (XII),** decorated with frescoes and stuccoes in 1578. On the left wall is a lovely 15C *Madonna and Child with angels*, attributed to Andrea d'Assisi (l'Ingegno).

From the Sala di Annibale we return through rooms II and I to reach the stairs. The three small rooms known as the **Sale dei Fasti Moderni (XIII–XV),** which contain lists of the chief magistrates of Rome since 1640, are closed for restoration.

The stairs continue up to the **second floor**. On the landing is a relief of the *Apotheosis of Sabina*, from the Arco di Portogallo (see p 151), and two splendid marble intarsia panels of a bull attacked by a tigress from the basilica of Junius Bassus on the Esquiline (4C AD).

The **Pinacoteca Capitolina** is a gallery of paintings founded in 1749 by Benedict XIV, with the help of his Secretary of State Cardinal Silvio Valenti Gonzaga, a famous collector. It is particularly important for its 16C–18C Italian and foreign works, and its most precious possessions are two paintings by Caravaggio.

Room I. *Death and Assumption of the Virgin* by Cola dell'Amatrice; *Presentation in the Temple* by Francesco Francia and Bartolomeo Passerotti; and *Trinità* by Niccolò di Pietro Gerini. **Room II.** Paintings by Scarsellino, Garofalo (including an *Annunciation*), Domenico Panetti, Dosso Dossi and Lodovico Mazzolino. There is also a *Portrait of a girl* by a 16C painter from Ferrara.

Room III. *Strength, Temperance*, and *Rape of Europa* by Paolo Veronese; *Portrait of a Lady as St Margaret* by Girolamo Savoldo; *Woman Taken in Adultery* by Palma Vecchio; *Baptism of Christ*, an early work by Titian; *Man with a Crossbow* by Lorenzo Lotto; *Scourging of Christ, Crown of Thorns, Baptism of Christ*, and *St Mary Magdalene* all by Domenico Tintoretto.

Room IV. Works by Giovanni Francesco Romanelli and Pier Francesco Mola.

We now return to room II, on the right of which is **room V** which has Emilian paintings, including *Diana* by Cavalier d'Arpino. **Room VI** has works by the Bolognese school, including Annibale, Agostino and Ludovico Carracci, (the *Head of a boy* is a very fine early work by Ludovico) and Guido Reni (*St Sebastian, Cleopatra*, and *Anima Beata*).

The large **room VII** is named after the huge canvas of *St Petronilla* by Guercino which was formerly in St Peter's, and four more works by the same artist are displayed here. The painting of the *Gipsy Fortune-teller* is one of the most delightful of Caravaggio's works. It is displayed beside his *St John the Baptist* (there is a replica of this painting in the Galleria Doria Pamphilj). The painting of *Romulus and Remus Fed by the She-wolf* by Peter Paul Rubens was finished by pupils. There are also paintings by Domenichino and Francesco Albani in this room. On the other side of room IV is **room VIII**, another large room named after Pietro da Cortona, here represented by a number of fine works (including the *Rape of the Sabines*).

The last room, the **Galleria Cini (IX)**, contains part of the bequest of Count Giuseppe Cini (1881), including a fine collection of bronzes and *ceramics from various sources, and excellent Saxon porcelain, clocks and tobacco boxes. On the walls are Flemish tapestries made in the middle of the 17C. The paintings here include portraits of the engravers Pieter de Jode, father and son, and of the painters Luke and Cornelius de Wael by Anthony Van Dyck, and a self-portrait by Federico Zuccari. The very fine *Portrait of a Man* is attributed by some scholars, as a self portrait, to Velasquez, and by others to the 17C Roman school. A small 15C portrait of a man by Marescalco is displayed beside the *Portrait of a Young Man* by Giovanni Bellini (c 1500). At the end of the gallery is a portrait of **Cardinal Silvio Valenti Gonzaga** (see above), by Pierre Subleyras.

Upper floor rooms in the adjoining Palazzo Clementino are to be reopened to display the **Medagliere**, a rich collection of Roman, medieval and modern coins and medals.

Other parts of Palazzo Caffarelli, adjoining Palazzo dei Conservatori, where excavations of the basement of the huge **Temple of Jupiter Capitolinus** are in progress, are also to be opened to the public (see p 75). This was the temple where the investiture of consuls took place, and where the triumphant procession awarded to victorious generals terminated. According to tradition, it was founded by Tarquinius Priscus, completed by Tarquinius Superbus, and dedicated in 509 BC. It is the largest temple known of this period. It was destroyed by fire in 83 BC during the civil wars, rebuilt by Sulla, destroyed again in AD 69, rebuilt by Vespasian and again by Domitian, and was still standing in the 6C. Remains of the temple are incorporated in Palazzo Caffarelli and part of it can be seen from Via del Tempio di Giove (see p 90).

Stairs lead down from both Palazzo dei Conservatori and Palazzo Nuovo to a **tunnel beneath the Piazza**, built in 1938. This was arranged in 1952 with a display of epigraphs, which are to be returned here, and there are remains of a Roman wall. From here there is access to the **Tabularium** and **Temple of Veiovis**, both beneath Palazzo Senatorio (see below). At the top of the stairs, on the right, can be seen considerable remains of the Temple of Veiovis, erected first in 196 BC and then rebuilt after a fire in the 1C BC. The pronaos is orientated towards the west, and the podium and cella are well preserved. Also here is the colossal marble statue of Veiovis (1C AD, after a 5C BC type) found in the cella in 1939. The external wall of the Tabularium may be seen on two sides of the temple: only a small gap was left between it and the Temple. In the corridor beyond are two large fragments of the friezes from the temples of Concord, and of Vespasian, the remains of which are below in the Roman Forum (see p 95). From the arcaded gallery of the Tabularium there is a splendid view of the Roman Forum.

The Tabularium was the depository of the Roman state archives, and its great blocks of porous tufa built into the unhewn rock dominate the view of the hill from the Roman Forum. On two storeys, with a rectangular plan and a central court, it was erected in 78 BC by Lutatius Catulus: an inscription stone of this date has survived. Part of the building was used from the Middle Ages onwards as a prison. A staircase (no admission) of the Republican period led steeply down to the Forum. It was blocked at the bottom by a tufa wall (still in place) when the Temple of Vespasian was built.

Palazzo Senatorio

Palazzo Senatorio, the central palace in Piazza del Campidoglio, is the official seat of the Mayor of Rome. An 11C fortress was built by the Corsi on the remains of the ancient Tabularium (see above), and the Senate was probably installed here c 1150. The medieval castle with four towers was renewed in the 13C and redesigned by Michelangelo in the 16C. The present **façade**, by Giacomo della Porta and Girolamo Rainaldi (1592), is a modification of Michelangelo's design. In front of the **double staircase** with converging flights, Michelangelo placed two colossal Roman statues of reclining river-gods representing the Nile and Tiber, formerly in Constantine's baths on the Quirinal Hill. The figure of the Nile to the left, in grey marble, is particularly successful and well-proportioned. The figure to the right used to represent the River Tigris but was given the attributes of the Tiber in the 16C; the she-wolf has been very damaged. In 1589, when the Acqua Felice aqueduct reached the hill, the two Greek marble fountain basins were added and a colossal statue of Jove in the central niche was replaced by the small seated figure of Minerva, a Roman work in porphyry from Cori in Lazio, which was transformed into the goddess Roma.

The palace is crowned by a **bell-tower** (1582) with a clock, another statue of Minerva and a gilded cross; two bells (1803–04) replace the famous Patarina, which was installed in 1200 to summon the people to *Parlamento*. The tower can be climbed on the first Sunday of the month.

The first-floor **interior** (open Sun 09.00–15.30; document required) is in fact of very little interest. At the top of the steps is the Council Chamber which preserves, above the mayor's dais, a colossal marble statue of *Julius Caesar*—the only statue of him which survives—dating from the period of Trajan. The Room of the Flag contains a fragment of the 14C flag of St George, from the church of San Giorgio in Velabro.

From Piazza del Campidoglio the short Via del Campidoglio skirts the right side of Palazzo Senatorio and runs downhill to a terrace with an excellent view of the Roman Forum backed by the Colosseum. From Via di Monte Tarpeo here there is an entrance to the Forum (described on p 93). On the left side of Palazzo Senatorio is Via San Pietro in Carcere, which has another splendid view of the Forum, and another entrance to the Forum.

Santa Maria in Aracoeli

Santa Maria in Aracoeli, an austere, brick-built church dating from before the 7C, when it was already considered ancient, stands on the highest point of the Capitoline Hill. Open daily 07.00–17.30 or 18.00. A flight of steps leads up behind Palazzo Nuovo to the inconspicuous south side door of the church; its main west door is approached by the long, tiring flight of steps which rise from the foot of the hill to the left of the Cordonata.

History of Santa Maria in Aracoeli

The church occupies the site of the Arx, or Roman citadel, and stands on the spot where, according to medieval tradition, the Tiburtine Sibyl foretold to Augustus the imminent coming of Christ in the words '*Ecce ara primogeniti Dei*': hence the name Aracoeli (Altar of Heaven). In the 10C the church belonged to the Benedictines; in 1250 Innocent IV handed it over to the

Franciscans, who rebuilt it in the Romanesque style. 'It was here, as Gibbon himself tells us, that on the 15th of October, 1764, as he sat musing amidst the ruins of the Capitol, while the bare-footed friars were singing vespers, the idea of writing the "Decline and Fall" of the city first started to his mind.' (Augustus Hare)

The **façade**, never completed, overlooks a very steep flight of 124 steps from Piazza d'Aracoeli, built in 1348 as a thank-offering for deliverance from a plague. There is a good view from the top. In the tympanum of the south door is a mosaic of the *Madonna and two angels* by the school of Pietro Cavallini.

Although freely restored the **interior**, hung with chandeliers, has retained its grandeur and severity. It contains a large number of very fine tombs. The ceiling of the **nave**, with naval emblems and much gold ornamentation, dates from 1575 and commemorates the naval victory over the Turks at Lepanto in 1571; Marcantonio Colonna celebrated his triumph in the church. The 22 antique columns in the nave, of varying sizes and styles, were taken from pagan buildings; the third on the left bears the inscription *a cubiculo Augustorum*, which seems to suggest it belonged to a Roman public building, and the fourth on the left has a 15C Sienese fresco of the *Madonna and Child*. Many tombs are set in the Cosmatesque pavement.

On the **west wall** is the *tomb, with a reclining effigy, of Cardinal d'Albret by Andrea Bregno (1465). Beside it, set into the wall, is the very worn *pavement tomb of the archdeacon Giovanni Crivelli signed by Donatello (1432). The tomb of the astronomer Lodovico Grato Margani (1531) by the school of Andrea Sansovino, bears a figure of Christ by Sansovino himself.

In the **south aisle**, the first chapel (Bufalini) has frescoes from the *Life of St Bernardino*, considered among the finest works of Bernardino Pinturicchio (c 1486; restored by Vincenzo Camuccini, and again recently restored). Between the second and third chapels there is a colossal statue of *Gregory XIII* by Pier Paolo Olivieri. In the fifth chapel are 16C paintings by Girolamo Muziano; the sixth chapel is a pretty 17C work designed by Giovanni Battista Contini. By the south door are the monument of *Pietro da Vicenza* by Andrea Sansovino (left) and the tomb of Cecchino Bracci (d 1545) by Pietro Urbano after a design by Michelangelo (right). The last chapel on this side, dedicated to San Pasquale Baylon, is being restored. Extremely important early frescoes have been discovered here attributed to Pietro Cavallini.

In the **crossing**, on the pilasters facing the high altar, are two *ambones by Lorenzo and Giacomo di Cosma (c 1200). In the **south transept**, the Capella Savelli (or Cappella di San Francesco di Assisi) contains two fine *tombs: on the left is that of Luca Savelli attributed to Arnolfo di Cambio, with a 3C Roman sarcophagus beneath, and on the right, the 14C tomb of Vana Aldobrandeschi, wife of Luca, with an effigy of her son Pope Honorius IV. The Cappella di Santa Rosa, seen through the Cappella del Santissimo Sacramento, to the right, has a fine mosaic of the *Madonna Enthroned between St John the Baptist and St Francis* (13C).

Over the high altar in the **choir** is a small *Madonna*, known as the *Madonna d'Aracoeli*, usually attributed to a 10C master. From 1512 to 1565 Raphael's *Madonna of Foligno* (now in the Vatican picture gallery) hung here; it was commissioned by Sigismondo Conti, whose tomb is in the pavement near the stalls on the south side. In the apse, on the left, is the fine monument of *Giovanni Battista Savelli* by the school of Andrea Bregno (1498).

In the centre of the **north transept** is the little Temple of St Helena, or Santa Cappella, a 17C shrine (reconstructed in the 19C) with eight columns. Beneath it are remains of an altar (12C or 13C) showing the apparition of the Virgin to Augustus. At the end of the transept is the beautiful Cosmati *tomb of Cardinal Matteo di Acquasparta (d. 1302), mentioned by Dante in *La Divina Commedia* (*Paradiso*, xii, 124), with a fresco by Cavallini. To the right is the entrance to the Cappella del Santissimo Bambino, which contained a figure of the Infant Christ reputed to have been carved from the wood of an olive tree in the Garden of Gethsemane and an object of immense veneration (see below). This was stolen in 1994, and has been replaced by a copy.

In the **north aisle**, the fifth chapel (being restored) contains a painting of *St Paul* by Muziano, and to the left the fine tomb of Filippo Della Valle by Michele Marini or the school of Andrea Riccio (1494). The third chapel has a fresco of *St Anthony* by Benozzo Gozzoli and to the right the Renaissance tomb of Antonio Albertoni (1509). Between the third and second chapels stands a statue of *Paul III*. During the Christmas festival, in the second chapel, the Cappella del Presepio, the copy of the Infant Christ figure from the Cappella del Santissimo Bambino is exhibited, and children recite little poems and speeches in front of its crib.

The rest of the Capitoline Hill can be seen by taking Via di Monte Tarpeo and then **Via del Tempio di Giove** back uphill from the terrace beside Palazzo Senatorio, or by the staircase which ascends from Piazza del Campidoglio to a portico named after the architect Vignola, the arches of which have been closed in with glass.

At the top of Via del Tempio di Giove, enclosed by a modern wall and very much below the level of the road, are the remains of the eastern angle of the façade of the Temple of Jupiter Optimus Maximus Capitolinus (see p 87).

From the peaceful gardens on the terrace known as the **Belvedere di Monte Tarpeo**, there is another extensive view of Rome to the south and south-east, taking in the Forum, the Palatine, the Baths of Caracalla, the Aventine and the Tiber. The precipice below is thought to be the notorious Tarpeian Rock of ancient Rome, from which condemned criminals were flung to their death, although some scholars suggest this was on the north side of the hill. The delightful quiet road continues past a little 19C temple to the edge of the hill (where steps lead down to Via di Teatro di Marcello), and then turns right under an arch to skirt the side of the hill above gardens and paths which descend to its foot.

From in front of the 16C Palazzo Caffarelli, another splendid panorama of Rome, this time towards St Peter's, can be seen. Here is an entrance to the café in the Musei Capitolini, and to the museum offices.

From the right side of Palazzo Senatorio Via del Campidoglio descends towards the Forum, and Via di Monte Tarpeo leads up right to the steps which descend to **an entrance to the Roman Forum**, approached by the Clivus Capitolinus (described below, in Chapter 2).

2 • The Roman Forum

The Roman Forum (Map 7; 8; see also plans on pp 94–104) is one of the most evocative places in Rome. Its ruins stand in the centre of the modern city as a romantic testament to her past greatness. The Roman Forum was the heart of ancient Rome, and here is reflected almost every event of importance in Rome's development, from the time of the kings through the Republican and Imperial eras to the Middle Ages. Many buildings survive from these times, some with their columns or huge vaults still standing, others only identified by their foundations. The huge paving stones of Rome's most important ancient road, the Sacra Via, remain visible here and pass the well-preserved triumphal arches dedicated to Titus and Septimius Severus.

The Forum is open to the public free of charge so it can become rather crowded.

Opening times

09.00–dusk. ☎ 06 699 0110. Free entrance (you need an admission ticket for the Palatine, described in Walk 3). There are now **five entrances** to the Forum: from the Capitoline Hill (Via di Monte Tarpeo), from Via San Pietro in Carcere beside the Mamertine prison, from Via dei Fori Imperiali, from Piazzale del Colosseo, and from Via San Teodoro. The description below begins at the entrance on Via di Monte Tarpeo from the Capitoline Hill along the Clivus Capitolinus since this was the ancient road which connected the hill with the Forum.

You need at least half a day for a complete visit. In summer the Forum is occasionally floodlit and tours are available; for information call the number above.

The best comprehensive **view** of the Forum is from the Capitoline Hill: from the Tabularium (which is now included in the visit to the Capitoline Museums, see p 87), or from Via San Pietro in Carcere or Via di Monte Tarpeo. The view from the Palatine is, at present, restricted as the edge of the hill is fenced off.

There are very few helpful **signs** in the Forum, and only some of the buildings are discreetly labelled with marble plaques. This makes the ruins all the more romantic to visit, but means that their history and original appearance can only be fully appreciated by studying the plans and description provided below. The Forum runs west-north-west and east-south-east, following the direction of the Capitoline end of the Sacra Via and that of the Nova Via. For simplicity's sake, in the following description it is taken as running west and east, the left side, as you look towards the Colosseum, being north and the right side south. The **plans** on pp 94 and 104 have been given this orientation. The following description takes into account the fact that most of the monuments are now surrounded by low fences and in some cases cannot be seen in their entirety from one side.

Although there are no refreshments available in the Forum or Palatine, there are a number of pleasant drinking fountains.

History of the Roman Forum

The site of the Forum was originally a marshy valley lying between the Capitoline and Palatine Hills. It was bounded on the north and east by the foothills of the Quirinal and Esquiline and by the low ridge of the Velia, which connected the Palatine with the Esquiline. In the Iron Age it was used as a necropolis. During the period of the last of the six kings of Rome—traditionally considered to have succeeded Romulus—the area was first paved as a market-place (*forum*) c 625 BC. The Etruscan king Servius Tullius (578–535 BC) made the area habitable by canalising its stagnant waters into a huge drain called the Cloaca Maxima. The first monuments of the Forum also date from the period of the kings: they include the Lapis Niger, the Vulcanal, the Temple of Janus, the Regia, the Temple of Vesta and the Curia.

The original Forum was a rectangle bounded on the west by the Lapis Niger and the Rostra, on the east by a line through the site of the Temple of Julius Caesar, and on the north and south by two rows of shops (*tabernae*) approximately on the line of the Basilica Emilia to the north and the Basilica Julia to the south. This area measured approximately 115m by 57m. Adjacent to it, on the north-west, was a second rectangle including the Comitium, or Comitia Curiata, reserved for political assemblies, the Curia, or senate house, and the Rostra, or orators' tribune. Beyond these limits, to the east, were the Regia, seat of the Pontifex Maximus (head of a college of priests who presided over the public State cult), the Temple of Vesta and the House of the Vestals.

In this direction ran the Sacra Via. Other streets were the Argiletum to the north; the Vicus Jugarius and the Vicus Tuscus leading to the Velabrum (see p 321); the Clivus Argentarius, which ran between the Capitol and the Quirinal to the Via Flaminia and the Campus Martius; and the Nova Via, to the south, which ran along the side of the Palatine Hill.

The Forum was therefore divided into three distinct areas: the Comitium, or political centre; the religious centre of the Regia; and the commercial centre of the Forum proper. The area of the Forum gradually lost its character as market-place and became a centre of civic importance and the scene of public functions and ceremonies. The greengrocers and other shopkeepers were moved to the Velabrum and replaced by money-changers (*argentarii*).

In the 2C BC a new type of building, the basilica, was introduced. This large covered space was used for judicial hearings and public meetings when these could not be held outside. The new construction involved the demolition of private houses behind the *tabernae*. The first basilica was the Basilica Porcia, built by the censor Cato in 185 BC and destroyed in 52 BC. Others were the Basilica Emilia (179 BC) and the Basilica Sempronia (170 BC), later replaced by the Basilica Julia. The last to be built was the Basilica of Constantine (4C AD).

After Julius Caesar's assassination his body was cremated in the Forum. Caesar had begun the enlargement of the Forum which Sulla had planned some years before, and which was completed by Augustus. Between 44 and 27 BC the Basilica Julia, the Curia and the Rostra were completed, the Temple of Saturn and the Regia restored, the Temple of Julius Caesar dedicated and the Arch of Augustus erected. In his biography of the Roman emperors *De vita Caesarum*, published around 121 AD, Suetonius states that Augustus found the city brick and left it marble: he also made the forum a fitting centre of the expanding Empire.

Nevertheless, the area of the Forum soon became inadequate for the growing population and succeeding emperors were obliged to build their own Fora (see Walk 5). Important work was carried out between the Forum and the Palatine by Hadrian in 125–130, and a fire in the old Forum in the 3C caused much damage, which was repaired by Diocletian. In the following centuries the area reflected the general decline of the city, and the temples and sanctuaries were neglected under Christian rule and robbed of most of their treasures. The few that remained were finally despoiled in the barbarian invasions and the abandoned buildings were further damaged by earthquakes.

Medieval Roman barons, such as the Frangipani family, used the tallest of the ruined buildings as foundations for their fortress-towers, and a few churches were constructed, but most of the Forum was used as a cattle-pasture, and so became known as the Campo Vaccino. Its monuments were used as quarries and its precious marbles were burned in limekilns. In the Renaissance the Forum provided inspiration to numerous artists. Many buildings erected from the 15C to 18C took their plans from monuments here, and often parts of the Roman edifices were reused in these buildings. It is extraordinary to think that even in Augustus Hare's time (1883) the 'meek-faced oxen of the Campagna' were still to be found among the ruins.

At the end of the 18C systematic excavations of the site began, and continued with little interruption through the 19C, especially after 1870. The distinguished archaeologist Giacomo Boni conducted the excavations from 1898 to 1925, and found archaic monuments of great interest; his work was continued by Alfonso Bartoli. Since 1980 excavations have been carried out (some still in progress) at the west end of the Forum at the foot of the Capitoline Hill, in the area of Santa Maria Antiqua and the Temple of Castor, behind the Basilica Emilia and the Curia, and on the northern slopes of the Palatine, between the Sacra Via and the House of the Vestals.

The western section of the Forum

From Piazza del Campidoglio (see p 88), Via del Campidoglio descends towards the Forum, and Via di Monte Tarpeo leads up right to the steps which descend to an entrance to the Forum. By the elimination here in 1980–2000 of a road, the Via del Foro Romano, the Forum was reconnected with the Capitol via the ancient road, known as the **Clivus Capitolinus**, which was uncovered beneath the modern road. Built in the 2C BC, it preserves many of its huge old paving stones. It was the western continuation of the Sacra Via in the Forum (see p 99), and the only way up to the Capitol in ancient times. It was used for triumphal and other processions to the Temple of Jupiter Capitolinus (see p 87) at the top of the hill.

On the descent to the Forum we first pass on the left the **Portico of the Dei Consentes** (12 Gods) which preserves 12 white columns forming an angle; the seven original columns are in marble, the restorations in limestone. Rebuilt on the pattern of a Flavian structure in AD 367 by the prefect Vettius Praetextatus

The Roman Forum from the Capitoline hill

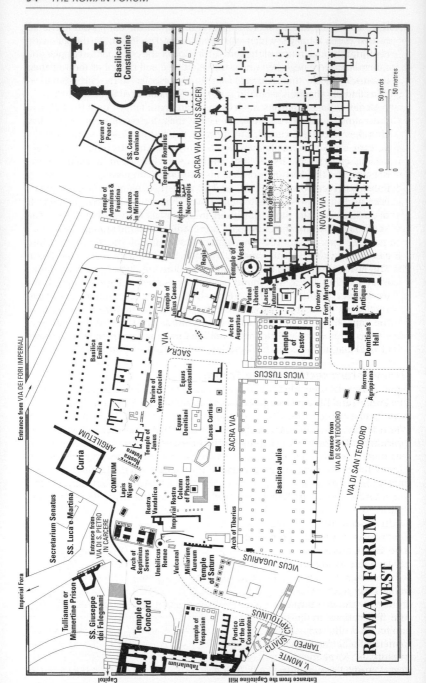

ROMAN FORUM
WEST

(known for his opposition to Christianity), this was the last pagan religious monument in the Forum. It was decorated with statues of 12 Roman deities—probably Jupiter, Juno, Neptune, Minerva, Mars, Venus, Apollo, Diana, Vulcan, Vesta, Mercury and Ceres—to whom the monument was dedicated. The portico was reconstructed in 1858 and was restored in 2000. Beyond, on the side of the Capitol Hill the mighty wall of the Tabularium (described on p 87) with Palazzo Senatorio towering above can be seen.

On the right is an area of new excavations, where a deposit of ex-votos from the Archaic period, probably connected with an ancient cult of Saturn, has been found, and an interesting 12C district of the city has been revealed. Beyond rise the eight columns, nearly 11m high, of the **Temple of Saturn**, one of the most ancient sanctuaries in the Forum, which may have been inaugurated in 498 BC in honour of the mythical god-king of Italy, whose reign was the fabled Golden Age. The temple was rebuilt, after several previous reconstructions, by Lucius Munatius Plancus in the year of his consulship, 42 BC. It was again restored after fires in 283 and c 400 AD. The high podium and eight columns of the pronaos with part of the entablature, all dating from the time of Plancus, survive. Six columns in grey granite are in front; the other two, in red granite, are at the sides. The Ionic capitals were added in the 5C restoration. The temple was the State treasury, where gold and silver ingots and coined metal were kept. The treasury itself (*aerarium*) was a room east of the narrow stairway of the temple: the holes for the lock can still be seen. The 'Saturnalia', a day of festivities when temporary freedom was given to slaves and presents were exchanged, was celebrated here every year on 17 December: it later came to be associated with New Year's Day and Christmas.

On the other side of the Clivus Capitolinus are three high columns, all that remains of the hexastyle pronaos of the sumptuous and elegant **Temple of Vespasian** erected in honour of that emperor at the foot of the Tabularium staircase by his sons Titus and Domitian after his death in AD 79. The front part of the basement has recently been excavated.

Next to it is the site of the **Temple of Concord**. This was a reconstruction by Tiberius (7 BC–AD 10) of a sanctuary which traditionally was thought to have been built in 366 BC by Camillus, a famous military leader and politician in early Roman history, to commemorate the concordat between the patricians and the plebeians. Instead it is probable that the temple was built for the first time in 218 BC. It was then rebuilt in 121 BC with the consent of the consul Lucius Opimius after the murder of the plebeian Gracchus. It became a museum and gallery of paintings and sculptures by famous Greek artists. Only the pavement remains *in situ*; part of the frieze is in the Tabularium.

On the level of the Forum a path continues left passing a semicircular wall or hemicyclium, formed by alterations during the building of the Arch of Septimius Severus. Behind it, now mostly a mound of rubble and brick arches, are the ruins of the **Imperial Rostra**, or orators' tribune, brought from its original site in front of the Curia during Caesar's restoration. It is 3m high, 24m long and 12m deep. The original structure, of very early date, was decorated with *rostra*, the iron prows of the ships captured at the battle of Antium (modern Anzio) in 338 BC, when Rome finally subjected the Volsci, who had formerly controlled the territory in southern Lazio, to their rule. On the platform rose columns surmounted by commemorative statues, and its parapet was probably decorated with the sculptured *Plutei* of Trajan (see p 97). At the north end was the **Rostra Vandalica**, an extension of the 5C AD; the modern name is taken from an inscription commemorating a naval victory over the Vandals in 470.

In front of the semicircular wall, close to the triumphal arch, is a cylindrical construction, the **Umbilicus Urbis** (?2C BC) supposed to mark the centre (the *umbilicus* or navel) of the city. Next to it is a quadrangular area protected by a roof, thought to be an **Altar of Saturn**, dating from before the 6C BC. Two trees grew here in Republican times, a lotus and a cypress, said to be older than the city itself. Opposite the other end of the wall is the site of the Miliarium Aureum (golden milestone), a bronze-covered column set up by Augustus as the symbolic starting-point of all the roads of the Empire, with the distance from Rome to the chief cities engraved in gold letters on its base.

Arch of Septimius Severus

We can now walk through the triple Arch of Septimius Severus, nearly 21m high and over 23m wide, entirely faced with marble, erected in AD 203 in honour of the tenth anniversary of that emperor's accession, and dedicated by the senate and the people to Severus and his sons Caracalla and Geta in memory of their military victories, notably in Parthia, now Iran. It was restored in 1988–2000. The name of Severus's elder son, Geta, who was murdered by Caracalla in 212, was replaced by an inscription in praise of Caracalla and his father, but the holes made for the original letters are still visible. On the well-proportioned arch the four large reliefs depict scenes from the two Parthian campaigns: in the small friezes are symbolic Oriental figures paying homage to Rome, and at the bases of the columns are captive barbarians. A small interior staircase (no admission) leads up to the four chambers of the attic.

Near the arch is another entrance to the Forum from Via San Pietro in Carcere. Just beyond the arch on the left is a conspicuous marble base of an equestrian statue with a dedicatory inscription celebrating the victory of Arcadius and Honorius over the Goths in 403. On the right is a large marble **column base**, with reliefs showing a procession of senators and scenes of sacrifice (it was provided with a modern brick plinth at the end of the 20C). This is the only one left of five original bases which bore columns set up here by the Emperor Diocletian. As the inscription *Caesarum Decennalia Feliciter* records, they celebrated the felicitous tenth anniversary in AD 303 of the rule of a tetrarchy instituted by Diocletian, which made provision for four co-emperors.

Curia Senatus

On the left is the most impressive and conspicuous building in the entire Forum, the **Curia Senatus** or Curia Julia, the senate house. Replacing the original Curia Hostilia said to have been built by Tullus Hostilius, traditionally held to be the third king of Rome (673–642 BC), it was begun by Sulla in 80 BC and rebuilt after a fire by Julius Caesar in 44 BC. Fifteen years after Caesar's death it was completed by Augustus, who dedicated a statue of Victory in the interior. The present building dates from the time of Domitian and was restored by Diocletian after a fire in 283. In 630 it was converted into the church of Sant'Adriano. In 1935–39 Alfonso Bartoli restored to it the form it had under Diocletian.

The lower part of the brick façade was originally covered with marble and the upper courses with stucco. It was preceded by a portico. The existing doors are copies of the originals, removed by Alexander VII to San Giovanni in Laterano. A simple pediment with travertine corbels crowns the building.

The remarkable interior, 27m long, 18m wide and 21m high, has a beautiful green-and-maroon *pavement in opus sectile, which has been preserved since it was beneath the floor of the church. The three broad marble-faced steps on the two long sides provided seats for some 300 senators. At the end, by the president's tribune, is a brick base which may have supported the golden statue of Victory presented by Augustus. The side walls with niches were partly faced with marble. The porphyry statue of Hadrian or Trajan dating from the 1C–2C AD was found in excavations at the end of the 20C behind the building.

Also exhibited here are the *Plutei of Trajan, or Anaglypha Trajani, two finely sculptured balustrades or parapets, found in the Forum in 1872 between the Comitium and the Column of Phocas. Both their date and original location are uncertain. On the outer faces (visible from the doorway) are scenes showing emperors carrying out public duties: the first (on the left) appears to represent an emperor burning the registers of outstanding death duties, an event which took place in 118, during Hadrian's reign; in the second (on the right) an emperor standing on a Rostra with a statue of Trajan is receiving the thanks of a mother for the founding of an orphanage. The architectural backgrounds systematically depict the buildings on the west, south and east sides of the Forum (from the right of the first panel to the left of the second): the Temple of Vespasian, an arch without decoration, the Temple of Saturn, the Vicus Jugarius, and the arcades of the Basilica Julia (continued on the second panel), followed by an interval which may represent the Vicus Tuscus, then the Temple of Castor and Rostra or the Temple of Julius Caesar on which the emperor is standing and, at the end, his attendants mounting the ramp of the Rostra through the Arch of Augustus. On both sides the statue of Marsyas is depicted beside the sacred fig tree (see below). On the inner faces (not visible from the doorway) are depicted the animals used as offerings during public sacrifices (suovetaurilia), a boar, a ram and a bull.

In recent excavations behind the Curia, remains of the Augustan building have come to light. Two doors at the rear end opened into a columned portico of the Forum of Caesar (see p 133), providing an entrance from the old Republican Forum to the new Imperial one. Connected to the Curia was the **Secretarium Senatus** used by a tribunal set up in the late Empire to judge senators.

In front of the Curia building was the area of the **Comitium**, the place where the Comitia Curiata, representing the 30 districts or curiae into which the city was politically divided, met to record their votes. The earliest political activity of the Republic took place here and this was the original site of the Imperial Rostra (see above). During the Empire the Comitium was restricted to the space between the Curia and the Lapis Niger; under the Republic the area was much more extensive.

A pavement in black marble, protected by upright marble slabs and a modern iron fence, which mark the site of the Lapis Niger and the oldest relics of the Forum can be seen here. The **Lapis Niger** (Black Stone) was a pavement of black marble laid to indicate a sacred spot. This was traditionally taken to be the site of the tomb of Romulus, or of Faustulus, the shepherd who found the infant Romulus and Remus, or of Hostus Hostilius, father of the third king of Rome, but is now identified as the ancient sanctuary of Vulcan, known as the **Vulcanal**. The pavement and the monuments below it were discovered in 1899. Below ground level (reached by a flight of iron steps, but kept closed) are a truncated column, possibly the base for a statue, an altar and a square stele with inscriptions on all four sides. These provide the most ancient example of the Latin language (probably mid 6C BC) and seem to refer to a *lex sacra* (holy law) warning against profaning a holy place. In the space between the pavement and the monuments, bronze and terracotta statuettes and fragments of 6C vases were found (now exhibited in the Terme di Diocleziano, see p 261), mixed with profuse ashes indicating a great sacrifice.

Excavations to the east of the Lapis Niger have revealed some remains of the Republican Rostra, dating partly from 338 BC, and partly (the curved front and steps) from the period of Sulla, who became dictator in 81 BC.

In front of a small group of trees can be seen the paved **Argiletum**, once one of the Forum's busiest streets, which leads north between the Curia building and the west end of the Basilica Emilia. It originally continued north to the district of the Subura through the Forum of Nerva (see p 134). The area to the north is still being excavated: the **Macellum**, a market building paved in peperino and surrounded by columns, built in the late 3C or early 2C BC, has recently been unearthed.

The open space to the south was the original **Forum**. As the meeting-place of the whole population, and a market-place, the Forum was kept free of obstructions in Republican days. Here all important ceremonies and public meetings took place. Orators spoke from the Rostra, where magistrates' edicts, legal decisions and official communications were published. The Forum was where all the main religious festivals were held, where political offenders were executed, and where the funerals of important people took place. During the Empire the Forum lost its original character, and new buildings encroached on the area. It remained merely an official centre, and was to a great extent replaced by the new Imperial Fora (see Walk 5).The few columns and monuments which survive in the area of the Forum are best seen from the other side, so are described below.

A path of dirt and ancient paving stones continues east between the area of the Forum on the right and a row of shops, the **Tabernae Novae** on the left, still well-preserved. These used to stand under a two-storeyed portico of the **Basilica Emilia**, which was restored during the late Empire, and the scant remains of which lie to the north (see the plan on p 94). The basilica was built by the censors Marcus Aemilius Lepidus and Marcus Fulvius Nobilior in 179 BC, restored by members of the Aemilia gens—including another Marcus Aemilius Lepidus—in 78 BC and rebuilt in the time of Julius Caesar. It was again rebuilt in AD 22 after a fire and nearly destroyed by another fire during Alaric's sack of Rome in 410.

Much of this ancient building was demolished during the Renaissance in order to reuse its marble. It comprised a vast rectangular hall 70m by 29m, divided by columns into a central nave and aisles, single on the south side and double on the north. It was paved in coloured marble slabs.

Only some broken marble columns and part of its marble paving are left, but enough to show its original plan. At the end nearest the Curia (not at present accessible) are some mottled columns, and the covered remains of its fine pavement, in coloured marble, in which are embedded some coins that fused with the bronze roof-decorations during the fire of 410 AD. At the opposite end, visible from the path which leads up to the gate on the Via dei Fori Imperiali, casts of fragments of a frieze of the Republican era have been assembled below the terrace.

Our path in front of the Tabernae Nuove passes the presumed site of the **Shrine of Janus**, the bronze doors of which were closed only in peace-time, which is said to have occurred only three times in the history of Rome. Just beyond the foundations of the circular **Shrine of Venus Cloacina**, which stood on the point where the Cloaca Maxima entered the Forum, can be seen. This great drain, installed by the Etruscans, crossed the Forum from north to south on its way to the Tiber (see p 321). At the far end three granite columns which date from the time of the late Empire, have been set up in front of the shops, and a large dedication inscription from the Senate in 2 BC to Lucius Ceasar, son of Augustus, which probably once decorated a triumphal arch.

The Temple of Julius Caesar

The path now bends right in front of all that remains (protected by a roof) of the Temple of Julius Caesar, the site of which marks the eastern limit of the original Forum. The body of Julius Caesar was brought to the Forum after his assassination on the Ides of March in 44 BC, and it was probably here that his body was cremated and his will read by Mark Antony. The temple was dedicated by Augustus in 29 BC in honour of *Divus Julius* (the 'Divine' Julius Caesar). Tiberius gave a funeral oration here over Augustus's own body before it was buried in his mausoleum in AD 14.

The temple (probably Corinthian prostyle hexastyle) was preceded by a terrace which was an extension of the podium. This was called the **Rostra ad Divi Julii**, from the prows of the Egyptian ships of Antony and Cleopatra, captured by Augustus at Actium in 31 BC, with which it was decorated. Only the central block of the podium and the round altar (under cover) survive, probably marking the spot where Caesar was cremated. Here you can often find fresh floral tributes to this the most famous of all the great Romans. Fragments, thought to belong to the frieze, are in the Antiquarium of the Forum. Remains of foundations on the north and south sides of the temple are thought to be those of the arcaded **Porticus Julia**, which surrounded the temple on three sides.

We now follow the path which returns towards the Capitol hill passing between the area of the original Forum on our right and the Basilica Julia on our left. The path follows the **Sacra Via**, the oldest street in Rome, and a continuation of the Clivus Capitolinus, which traverses the length of the Forum. It was lined with important sanctuaries. Its oldest section is that between the Temple of Castor and the Velia. The winding road now visible, at a lower level than the later monuments on either side, dates from the late Republican era; the later Imperial road took a slightly different course between the Forum and the Arch of Titus. At the eastern end, the Republican road left the Forum to the south of the Velia. In late Imperial times it was continued by another road beyond the Arch of Titus to the Arch of Constantine, near the Colosseum.

It was along the Sacra Via that a victorious general awarded a triumph passed in procession to the Capitol to offer sacrifice in the Temple of Jupiter. He rode in a chariot drawn by four horses, preceded by his captives and spoils of war, and followed by his soldiers. In the Sacra Via, by the south-east corner of the Basilica Emilia, is a dedicatory inscription to Lucius Caesar, grandson and adopted son of Augustus, set up in 2 BC; there was probably an arch here dedicated to him and his brother Gaius.

Basilica Julia

On the left is the huge platform, raised above a stepped basement, of the Basilica Julia, which occupies the area between the Vicus Jugarius and Vicus Tuscus (see below). All that remains of this large building are the steps and some column bases.

History of the Basilica Julia

The basilica, built on the site of the Basilica Sempronia (170 BC) named after its builder, the censor Tiberius Sempronius Gracchus, was begun by Julius Caesar in 54 BC and finished by Augustus. After a fire, it had to be reconstructed and rededicated by Augustus in AD 12. It was again damaged by fire in AD 283 and reconstructed by Diocletian in 305. It was damaged yet again in the sack of Rome by the Visigoths and their king Alaric in 410 and was restored for the last time by the prefect of the city, Gabinius Vettius Probianus six years later.

The Basilica Julia was the meeting-place of the four tribunals of the Centumviri, a special court of justice which dealt with civil cases. In the Middle Ages the church of Santa Maria in Cannapara was built on its west side. The surviving remains mostly date from 305; the brick piers of the central hall are 19C reconstructions.

The basilica was even larger than the Basilica Emilia, measuring 101m by 49m. It had a central hall 82m long and 18m wide, bordered all round by a double row of columns which formed aisles. On the long side, facing south, was a colonnade of arches and piers with engaged columns; this contained a row of shops. Graffiti on the marble steps show that the Romans used to while away their time here playing 'board' games.

On the other side of the Sacra Via, opposite the Basilica Julia, is a row of **seven brick bases** dating from the 4C. These used to bear columns with statues of illustrious citizens; two of these have been re-erected. They mark the southern limit of the original Forum which was first paved in the Etruscan period. In one of the pavement slabs is incised the name of Lucius Naevius Surdinus, *praetor peregrinus* in the time of Augustus, who possibly had his tribunal here. This legal dignitary had to deal with cases involving *peregrini*, that is, individuals who were not Roman citizens.

In the middle on the right can be seen the covered, paved area of the **Lacus Curtius** (Lake of Curtius), with the substructure of the parapet of a well, surrounded by a 12-sided structure of peperino blocks. The lake must have been a relic of the marsh drained by the Cloaca Maxima. According to one tradition, in 362 BC a great chasm opened here, which the soothsayers said could be closed only by throwing into it Rome's greatest treasure. A young Roman called Marcus Curtius, announcing that Rome possessed no greater treasure than a brave citizen, rode his horse into the abyss, which promptly closed. A bas relief of a horse and rider was found here: a cast is shown *in situ*. Livy suggests the name comes from the consul Curtius who fenced off this area in 445 after it had been struck by lightning.

Nearby, surrounded by iron railings and below ground-level, are three travertine blocks formerly taken to be the base of an equestrian statue of Domitian (AD 91) but now considered by some scholars to be the base of the equestrian statue of Constantine or *Equus Constantini*, probably dedicated in AD 334 (Domitian's statue is now thought to have been in the centre of the Forum). To the west rises the **Column of Phocas**, not only a conspicuous feature of the Forum but the last of its monuments. The fluted Corinthian column, probably taken from some building of the best Imperial era, is 13.5m high. It stands on a high base, formerly faced with marble and surrounded by steps. A long inscription states that it was crowned with a statue which was placed on its summit in 608 by Smaragdus, exarch of Italy, in honour of the centurion Phocas who had seized the throne of Byzantium; its erection may have been a mark of gratitude for the usurper Phocas's gift of the Pantheon to Boniface IV.

Close to the column is a small, square, unpaved space, which may be where a statue of Marsyas once stood next to the sacred fig tree, the olive and the vine (all replanted here in 1956) mentioned by Pliny the Elder.

The path ends at the south-western corner of the original Forum, where the **Vicus Jugarius** runs south to the Velabrum between the Basilica Julia on the left and the Temple of Saturn on the right. Near the Temple of Saturn stood the **Arch of Tiberius**, erected in AD 16 in honour of the Emperor and of his nephew Germanicus after a victory over German tribes. Its foundations can be seen below ground level. Behind the temple, excavations are in progress in an area formerly covered by houses; it is possible another temple may be found beneath the medieval constructions.

We now return to the east end of the Basilica Julia, where the ancient Vicus Tuscus lead south past the three tall columns with their entablature which survive of the **Temple of Castor**, or Temple of the Dioscuri (also known as the *Castores*).

History of the Temple of Castor

It was almost certainly built in 484 BC by the dictator and general Aulus Postumius in honour of the twin heroes Castor and Pollux, revered in Greece as sons of Zeus and brothers of Helen, whose miraculous appearance at the battle of Lake Regillus (496 BC) resulted in victory for the Romans over the Tarquins and their Latin allies. Roman knights regarded the Dioscuri as their patrons; every year, on 15 July, they staged an impressive parade in front of the temple. This temple, which had three cellae and a deep pronaos, built on a high podium, was restored after 200 BC. It was reconstructed by the consul Metellus Dalmaticus in 117 BC, when a tribune for orators was installed, and according to Cicero it was also used by money-changers. This temple was destroyed by fire in 14 or 9 BC, and the present building was inaugurated by Tiberius during the reign of Augustus (AD 6).

Peripteral in plan, and approximately 26m by c 40m in area, the temple had eight Corinthian columns at either end and eleven at the sides. The wide pronaos, excavated in 1982–85, was approached by a flight of steps. The three remaining columns, which are 12.5m high and have a beautifully proportioned entablature, date from the time of Tiberius. Fragments of statues of the Dioscuri found here are now in the Antiquarium: the twins are usually depicted as giants with white horses. (Other statues of them in Rome survive on the balustrade of the Capitoline Hill and at the foot of the obelisk on the Quirinal Hill.) Excavations and restoration work were carried out on the Temple in 1983–87.

In front of the east end of the Basilica Julia can be seen another entrance to the Cloaca Maxima (see above). Beyond there is a splendid view of **Domitian's Hall**, a large rectangular brick building, 21m by 28m, originally vaulted. With an entrance on the Vicus Tuscus, it was intended as a monumental entrance to Domitian's palace on the Palatine (see p 113). The hall was never completed and was transformed into a warehouse. Excavations here in 1983–87 clarified that this was the site of a large atrium built by Caligula in front of the Temple of Castor which also provided an extension to the Imperial palace on the Palatine. Traces were found of the 26.5m by 22.3m perimeter wall, built of blocks of travertine. On a lower level were Republican buildings facing the Vicus Tuscus, demolished to make way for Caligula's atrium.

Also on the Vicus Tuscus is a vast brick building known as the **Horrea Agrippiana**. This was a grain warehouse built around three courtyards, each provided with three storeys of rooms, built by Agrippa. The church of San Teodoro (entered from outside the Forum enclosure, see p 323) stands in the second courtyard. Near here is another entrance to the Forum from Via di San Teodoro.

The remains to the east of the Temple of Castor and Domitian's hall (the Lacus Juturnae and Santa Maria Antiqua) are not at present open. From the path can be seen (in the distance) an apsidal building of the late Empire, converted into the **Oratory of the Forty Martyrs** (no admission) and preserving remains of 8C–9C frescoes. The 40 martyrs were Christian soldiers frozen to death in an icy pool at Sebaste, in Armenia in AD 303. The building closes the west end of the Nova Via (see p 112).

To the south of the oratory are the considerable remains of the church of **Santa Maria Antiqua**, the oldest and most important Christian building in the Forum. This has been closed for many years but is to be restored and reopened. The 7C–8C wall-paintings inside are of the first importance in the history of early Christian art. Excavations were carried out here in 1983–87.

To the north of the oratory is a little restored shrine with two small columns, preceded by a well and an altar, belonging to the **Lacus Juturnae** (Pool of Juturna), closely connected to the story of the Dioscuri: a legend related how they were seen watering their horses here immediately after their appearance at the battle of Lake Regillus (see above). Juturna, the nymph of healing waters, was venerated in connection with the springs here. The fountain has a square basin of opus reticulatum lined with marble; a statue probably stood on the rectangular base in the centre. On the parapet is a small marble altar (a copy; the original is in the Antiquarium), with reliefs of the Dioscuri and their sister Helen on two of its sides, and of their parents Jupiter and Leda on the other two. In the 4C the Lacus Juturnae was the seat of the city's water administration. In the late Empire a series of rooms was built here presumably for the accommodation of invalids who came to take the waters. These rooms contain fragments of statues of gods and other sculptures. To the south is the shrine itself, an aedicule, restored in 1953–55, with the front built into the brick walls and two columns. In front is a marble well-head, with a dedicatory inscription to Juturna by the magistrate Marius Barbatius Pollio, and a marble altar with a relief of Juturna and her brother Turnus.

The eastern section of the Forum

The Vicus Tuscus returns north between the Basilica Julia and the Temple of Castor, and then east, past the bases of the Arch of Augustus, to reach the religious centre of the Forum. Here are the Temple of Vesta, the House of the Vestals and the Regia.

The few flat stones to the south of the Temple of Julius Caesar are the foundations of the **Arch of Augustus**, which had a central arch flanked by lower and narrower side passages surmounted by pediments. After excavations here at the end of the 20C, this is thought to date from 20 BC, after the standards captured by the Parthians had been returned. The consular and triumphal registers known as the *Fasti Capitolini* (see p 85), which date from this period, may have belonged to the arch. Another, single, triumphal arch was erected in another part of the Forum by Augustus in 30 BC to commemorate the victory over Antony and Cleopatra at Actium two years earlier. Next to the south pier foundation of the arch is a rectangular monument in the shape of a well-head, which is a remnant of the *Puteal Libonis*, a monument which stood beside the tribunal of the *praetor urbanus*, who dealt with cases involving Roman citizens.

Temple of Vesta

Of the Temple of Vesta, a number of columns on high bases supporting a fragment of entablature, as well as part of the curving cella wall, survive (they have been reconstructed).

History of the Temple of Vesta

The temple was a circular edifice of 20 Corinthian columns, its design recalling the form of the huts used by the Latin people, traces of which have been found on the Palatine and elsewhere in Rome. The first temple on this site was possibly made, like these, of straw and wood. The temple was burned down several times, notably during Nero's fire of AD 64 and in 191. It was rebuilt as often, the last time by Septimius Severus and his wife Julia Domna. It was closed by Theodosius and was in ruins by the 8C. The circular basement surmounted by tufa blocks and a few architectural fragments survived up until 1930, when it was partially reconstructed by Alfonso Bartoli.

Here the Vestals guarded the sacred fire and Vesta, goddess of the hearth, protected it. In the interior was an *adytum*, or secret place, containing the *Palladium*, a statue of Pallas Athena supposedly taken from Troy by Aeneas. No one was allowed inside the adytum except the Vestals and the *pontifex maximus*, and its contents were never shown. The *Palladium* was an object of the highest veneration, as the safety of the city depended on its preservation. When the Emperor Elagabalus tried to steal it, the Vestals are supposed to have substituted another statue, keeping the cult statue of Vesta in a small shrine near the entrance to the House of the Vestals.

Immediately east of the Temple of Vesta are the considerable remains of the **House of the Vestals** (not at present accessible) where a charming rose garden is planted in its ruined courtyard. The house seems too large for just six Vestals, and part of it may have been reserved for the *pontifex maximus*, whose official seat during the Republican era was in the Regia (see below). It dates from Republican times, but was rebuilt after the fire of Nero in AD 64, and was last restored by Septimius Severus.

The house has a spacious courtyard, 61m long and 20m wide, in the middle of which are three ponds irregularly spaced and unequal in size. The central pond was once partly covered by an octagonal structure of unknown purpose. The

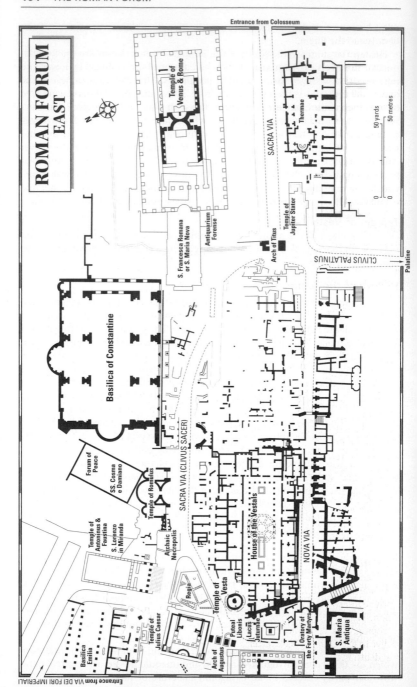

ROMAN FORUM EAST

Entrance from Colosseum

Temple of Venus & Rome

SACRA VIA

Thermae

S. Francesca Romana or S. Maria Nova

Antiquarium Forense

Temple of Jupiter Stator

Arch of Titus

50 yards

50 metres

CLIVUS PALATINUS

Palatine

Basilica of Constantine

SACRA VIA (CLIVUS SACER)

Forum of Peace

SS. Cosma e Damiano

Temple of Romulus

Temple of Antoninus & Faustina

S. Lorenzo in Miranda

Archaic Necropolis

House of the Vestals

NOVA VIA

Temple of Vesta

Regia

Puteal Libonis

Lacus Juturnae

Oratory of the Forty Martyrs

S. Maria Antiqua

Temple of Julius Caesar

Arch of Augustus

Basilica Emilia

statue-bases and statues of Vestals date from the 3C AD onwards; from one of them (near the entrance) the name of the Vestal has been removed, possibly because she became a Christian.

A two-storey portico surrounded the courtyard. In the middle of the short east side is a large hall paved with coloured marbles and flanked on either side by three small rooms, thought to be the sacristy of the priestesses. Behind this hall, towards the Palatine, are an open courtyard with a fountain, and other rooms. Along the south side, which abuts on the Nova Via, is another series of rooms opening out of a corridor. In the first of these are the remains of a mill; the second was probably a bakery. On this side staircases lead to the upper floor and to the Nova Via. Near the last staircase is a small shrine. In the middle of the west side is a large room, perhaps the dining-room, leading to the kitchen and other rooms. The north side of the building is less well preserved; stairways on the second floor show that it had more than two storeys.

The **Nova Via** (described on p 112) runs parallel with the Sacra Via along the southern slope of the Palatine Hill: it is not accessible here as excavations are in progress. It provided a means of communication with the buildings on the Palatine. The visible remains of this road probably date from the Flavian period, but recent excavations at the point where it crosses the Clivus Palatinus have revealed paving which seems to date from the Republican era.

The Vestal Virgins

The task of the Vestals, the virgin priestesses of Vesta, was to keep the fire that symbolised the perpetuity of the State constantly alight: its extinction was the most fearful of all prodigies, as it implied the end of Rome. The origin of the cult is supposed to go back to Numa Pompilius, second king of Rome, or even to Aeneas, who brought the eternal fire of Vesta from Troy, together with the images of the *penates* (household gods).

There were six Vestals who were chosen by the king, and later, during the Republic and Empire, by the *pontifex maximus*, a post held by the emperor himself. Girls between six and ten years of age from patrician families could be candidates. After her election a Vestal lived in the House of the Vestals for 30 years; ten learning her duties, ten performing them and ten teaching novices. During this period she was bound by the vow of chastity. At the end of the 30 years she was free to return to the world and even to marry. The senior Vestal was called *vestalis maxima* or *virgo maxima*. If a Vestal let the sacred fire go out, she was whipped by the *pontifex maximus*, who then had to rekindle the fire by the friction of two pieces of wood from a *felix arbor* (propitious tree).

The Vestals' other duties included making offerings to Vesta, sprinkling her shrine daily with water from the Egerian fountain, assisting at the consecration of temples and other public ceremonies, and guarding the *Palladium* (see above). Maintained at the public expense, they had many privileges, such as an exalted order of precedence and the right of intercession. Wills—including the emperor's—and treaties were entrusted to their keeping. If a Vestal broke her vow of chastity, however, she was immured alive in the Campus Sceleratus (see p 303) and the man was publicly flogged to death in the Forum.

Between the Temple of Vesta and the huge Temple of Antoninus and Faustina (see below) was the site of the **Regia**, identified only by very scanty remains. It was traditionally supposed to be the palace of Numa Pompilius, the second king of Rome, and the official headquarters of the *pontifex maximus* (see above). Primitive huts, similar to those on the Palatine (see p 121) were found here, and the earliest permanent construction excavated dates from the 7C BC. The edifice, rebuilt by the consul Domitius Calvinus after a fire in 36 BC, retains its 6C form. The elegance of its architecture can be seen from the few scattered fragments here. Other parts of the building date from a reconstruction of the time of Septimius Severus.

The Regia may have been the depository of State archives and of the *Annales Maximi*, written by the *pontifex maximus*. It also included the Sacrarium of Mars, with the *ancilia* (sacred shields), and the chapel of Ops, goddess of plenty. At the south-east corner of the Regia were discovered the foundations of a triumphal arch, erected in 121 BC by the censor and military commander Quintus Fabius Maximus Allobrogicus to span the Sacra Via.

To the north of the Regia rises the huge **Temple of Antoninus and Faustina**, complete with its pronaos of ten huge columns above a flight of steps, one of the best-preserved temples in the Forum. In AD 141 the Senate dedicated it to the memory of the Empress Faustina and, after his death in 161, also to Antoninus Pius, and it was a famous temple of Imperial Rome. A reconstructed flight of steps leads up to the pronaos, which has monolithic Corinthian columns (17m high) in cipollino, six in front and two on either side. The architrave and frieze of vases and candelabra between griffins, and the side walls of the cella, of peperino blocks originally faced with marble, also survive. Sculptures, including a female torso, have been placed in the pronaos.

The temple was converted into the church of **San Lorenzo in Miranda** (no admission) before the 12C, and given a Baroque façade in 1602. The dedication of the church to St Lawrence may commemorate the trial of the saint which is thought to have taken place in this temple before his martyrdom in 258. Famous as one of the earliest Christian martyrs, Lawrence is frequently portrayed in Christian art being burned alive on a gridiron. His death seems to have signalled an important moment in Rome for the advance of Christianity and decline of pagan worship.

The Sacra Via continues east past an **Archaic necropolis**, discovered in 1902. This was the cemetery of the ancient inhabitants of the Esquiline or of the original settlement on the Palatine, and dates back to the Early Iron Age, before the date of the traditional foundation of Rome. Tombs were found for both cremations and burials. Cremated ashes were discovered in urns surrounded by tomb furniture, in small circular pits. The burials here were either in tufa sarcophagi, hollowed-out tree trunks or trenches lined with tufa slabs. The finds are kept in the Forum Antiquarium.

From here the Sacra Via begins to ascend the Velia to the Arch of Titus. The Velia was a low ridge which connected the Palatine Hill with the Esquiline and was levelled by Mussolini (see p 128). On either side of the road are the ruins of private houses and shops, some under cover, including one dating from the Republican era.

On the left is the so-called **Temple of Romulus** (the interior can be seen from the church of Santi Cosma e Damiano, see p 135), a well-preserved 4C building with a curving pronaos in which two porphyry columns supporting an architrave taken from some other building flank the doorway, which still preserves its splendid original bronze doors, a remarkable survival from ancient Rome. This was formerly thought to have been a temple dedicated to Romulus, son of Maxentius who died in AD 309, but it has recently been suggested that it may instead have been the audience hall of the city prefect, or it could be identified with a Temple of Jupiter. It is a circular building built of brick and covered by a cupola flanked by two rectangular rooms with apses, each originally preceded by two cipollino columns (only those on the right survive). Behind there is a rectangular hall, probably the library of the Forum of Peace built by Vespasian in AD 70 (see p 134), where the city plans and public property registers may have been kept. It was converted in the 6C into the church of Santi Cosma e Damiano (see p 135), the temple serving as a vestibule. The *Forma Urbis*, a famous Roman plan of the ancient city, fragments of which survive in the Antiquarium Comunale (see p 304), used to decorate the far wall of the hall towards the modern Via dei Fori Imperiali.

Basilica of Constantine

We pass a medieval portico lining the road and take the old shady path on the left, with lovely paving stones, to visit the three huge barrel-vaulted niches of the Basilica of Constantine, or Basilica of Maxentius, also called the Basilica Nova, which dominates the Forum. The arches—20.5m wide, 17.5m deep and 24.5m high—are one of the largest and most impressive examples of Roman architecture to have survived anywhere. The skill and audacity of their design inspired many Renaissance builders, and it is said that Michelangelo studied them closely when he was planning the dome of St Peter's. They formed the north aisle of the basilica which was begun by Maxentius (AD 306–10) and completed by Constantine, who considerably modified the original plan.

History of the Basilica of Constantine

This huge building was a rectangle 100m long and 65m wide, divided into a nave and two aisles by massive piers supported by buttresses. As first planned, it had a single apse, on the west side. Against the central piers were eight Corinthian columns 14.5m high; the only survivor was moved by Paul V to Piazza Santa Maria Maggiore. The original entrance was from a side road on the east; on the south side Constantine added a portico with four porphyry columns (which partly survive), which opened onto the Sacra Via. It was used as the seat of prefects of the city, and, in the 4C AD, of the *Secretarium Senatus*, the tribunal which heard cases against senators, formerly connected to the Curia (see above). In the middle of the north wall Constantine built a second apse, which was shut off from the rest of the building by a colonnaded balustrade; here the tribunal probably held its sittings.

The interior walls, decorated with niches, were faced with marble below and with stucco above. The arches of the groin-vaulted nave, whose huge blocks have fallen to the ground, were 35m high and had a radius of nearly 20m. Parts of a spiral staircase leading to the roof can also be seen on the ground, having collapsed in an earthquake. A tunnel was built under the north-west corner of the basilica for a thoroughfare which had been blocked by its construction. The entrance to the tunnel, walled up since 1566, can still be seen. In 1487 a colossal statue of Constantine was found in the west apse, fragments of which are now in the court-yard of the Palazzo dei Conservatori (see p 83). The bronze plaques from the roof were removed in 626 by Pope Honorius I for the old basilica of St Peter's.

On the opposite side of the Sacra Via are scattered ruins, among which there are remains of a large portico, the vestibule to the Domus Aurea of Nero (see p 278). Domitian reused the portico when he built the **Horrea Piperataria**, a bazaar for oriental goods, pepper and spices, to the north of the Sacra Via. Later, the area to the south also became commercialised. Domitian's building was finally destroyed in 284. A small circular base with a relief of a Maenad and an inscription record-ing its restoration by Antoninus Pius (originals in the Antiquarium), close to the Sacra Via, may be the remains of a Sanctuary of Bacchus.

On the ascent to the Arch of Titus is the church of Santa Francesca Romana, or Santa Maria Nova (entered from Via dei Fori Imperiali and described on p 136). The former convent of this church is now the seat of the Forum and Palatine excavation offices and contains the **Antiquarium of the Forum** or Antiquarium Forense; admission see p 42. Most of it has been closed for a number of years; there are long-term plans to rearrange it but meanwhile it is kept in a neglected state. In the first room are a model and finds from the Archaic necropolis near the Temple of Antoninus and Faustina. Rooms II and III contain objects found near the House of the Vestals: yields from wells, Italo-geometric and Etrusco-Campanian vases, votive objects, glassware and lamps. Room IV (beyond Room II) looks into the impressive cella of the Temple of Venus and Roma (see p 127), which cannot otherwise be seen. Here are displayed objects from the area of the Lapis Niger, Comitium, Cloaca Maxima, Regia and Basilica Emilia.

The rest of the collection, not at present on view, includes a large capital from the Temple of Concord; a marble basin reconstructed from original fragments found near the Lacus Juturnae, and sculptures from the fountain, among them a headless statue of Apollo from a Greek original of the 5C BC; fragments of the frieze of the Basilica Emilia, and part of its architectural decoration; and part of

The Arch of Titus in the Roman Forum

a *fresco from Santa Maria Antiqua.

Dominating the summit of the Sacra Via is the well-preserved **Arch of Titus**, presumably erected by Domitian just after the death of Titus in AD 81 in honour of the victories of Titus and Vespasian in the Judaean War, which ended with the sack of Jerusalem in AD 70. In the Middle Ages the Frangipani family incorporated the arch into one of their castles, but the encroaching buildings were partly removed by Sixtus IV (1471–84) and finally demolished in 1821. The arch was dismantled and then restored by Giuseppe Valadier, who used travertine instead of marble to repair the damaged parts so that they are easily distinguishable.

The beautiful, perfectly proportioned

single archway with Composite columns is covered with Pentelic marble. The two splendid reliefs inside the arch are very worn. One of them shows the goddess Roma guiding the Imperial quadriga with Titus and the winged figure of Victory; and the other shows a triumphal procession bringing the war booty from Jerusalem, which includes the altar of Solomon's temple decorated with trumpets, and the seven-branched golden candlestick (or Menoràh), the symbol of Judaism. In the centre of the panelled vault is the Apotheosis of Titus, showing the deified Emperor mounted on an eagle. On the exterior frieze is another procession in which the symbolic figure of the vanquished Jordan is carried on a stretcher.

A large area on the northern slopes of the Palatine between the Nova Via and the Sacra Via, from west of the Arch of Titus as far as the House of the Vestals, has been excavated since 1985 beneath the visible remains of *horrea*, large ware houses on several floors. The building nearest the House of the Vestals probably dates in its present form from the time of Hadrian. The larger building to the east may be the **Horreum Vespasiani**, a market which fronted the Horrea Piperataria (see above), destroyed when the Basilica of Constantine was built. A row of shops against the Palatine Hill is prominent: almost in the centre can be seen a well-preserved vaulted edifice, beside which steps led up to the Nova Via and the upper floors.

The most important result so far of the excavations in this area has been the discovery of **Archaic walls** on three levels: the oldest traces date from 730–675 BC, when Romulus is supposed to have founded Rome; above these was a wall in red tufa defended by a ditch (675–600 BC). The latest wall may have been part of the boundary defences of the first city—which was roughly rectangular in shape and hence known as Roma Quadrata—dating from the time of Servius Tullius (530–520 BC). It was constructed with large blocks of red tufa. Subsequent levels have shown interesting remains of at least four Archaic houses and at least four Republican houses, one of which, facing the Clivus Palatinus, may eventually be opened to the public (see p 112). Evidence was also discovered here of the destruction of numerous buildings by Nero for his huge Domus Aurea which invaded the centre of the Roman city, extending from the Oppian and Celian Hills across the Velia to the Palatine (see p 278). The *horrea* were part of a general plan of the Flavians to reinstall public edifices in this area after the death of Nero.

The Forum can be left by the gate beyond the Arch of Titus. The path descends along an extension of the Sacra Via, with the high platform of the Temple of Venus and Roma (described on p 127) on the left, to the Colosseum. Otherwise the Palatine (see Walk 3) is reached directly from the Arch of Titus by the Clivus Palatinus, where there is a ticket booth.

3 • The Palatine Hill

The Palatine Hill (Map 7; 8; and see plan on pp 114–115), to the south of and above the Roman Forum, is a beautiful park containing impressive ancient ruins. It was here that the primitive city was founded, and splendid Imperial palaces were later built over its slopes, so that the word Palatine came to be synonymous with the palace of the emperor (and hence 'palace'). The gardens are spectacular and beautifully kept, with a profusion of wild flowers and fine trees, and are inhabited by many birds (and cats). Wonderful views of Rome can be seen from the edge of the hill. The Palatine is usually less crowded than the Forum and is one of the most romantic and charming spots in the centre of the city, remarkably isolated from the traffic-ridden streets at the foot of the hill.

The Palatine Museum provides a fascinating history of the hill. Houses with important Roman wall-paintings can be visited by appointment.

Opening times

09.00–2hrs before sunset. ☎ 06 699 0110 (the ticket includes admission to the Palatine Museum and the Colosseum). For the *Archaeological Card*, see p 41. The **entrances** to the Palatine are in the Roman Forum near the Arch of Titus, and on Via San Gregorio (see plan on pp 114–115).

Of the **areas normally kept locked**, the Aula Isiaca and Loggia Stati Mattei are opened on request at the Palatine

Museum. The House of Augustus, the House of the Griffins and the House of Marcus Aemilius Scaurus can only be seen by previous appointment, ☎ 06 3996 7700. There are excellent tours of these sites on certain days throughout the year: see their programme. The House of Livia has been closed for a number of years for restoration. Several of the more interesting sites are apt to be fenced off, because of fresh excavations or damage of some kind.

History and topography of the Palatine Hill

The topography of the Palatine is intricate, one level after another of multi-storey buildings having been erected on and through the previous levels. It now has the appearance of a four-sided plateau, rising to a height of 40m above the Roman Forum and 51m above sea-level. It is about 1750m in circumference.

In ancient times the central summit was called the Palatium. It sloped down towards the Forum Boarium (cattle-market) and the Tiber, with a declivity called the Germalus, now occupied by the Farnese Gardens, on the west and north looking towards the Capitoline. The Velia, a second, lower summit, was connected with the Esquiline by a saddle through the Roman Forum. The intervening hollows have since been filled in by successive constructions in the Imperial era.

Recent research suggests the hill was inhabited sporadically by the Late Bronze Age (13C–12C BC), and traces of occupation going back to the 9C BC have been discovered during excavations. The earliest Paleolithic material has been found since 1989 in the area of the Temple of Victory (near the Temple of Cybele) and at the northern foot of the hill.

According to legend the hill was settled from Greece. Sixty years before the Trojan War (traditional date 1184 BC), Evander, son of Hermes and an Arcadian nymph, led a colony from Pallantion in Arcadia, and built a town at the foot of the Palatine Hill near the Tiber, naming it after his native village. Aeneas, who escaped from burning Troy after the Trojan War sailed to Italy, and according to Virgil was welcomed here by Evander.

Some Classical authors give another explanation of the name Palatium, that it is derived from Pales, the goddess of flocks and shepherds, whose festival was celebrated on 21 April, the day on which the city of Rome is supposed to have been founded in 754 or 753 BC by Romulus and Remus.

The twins were traditionally thought to have been found by the shepherd Faustulus on the hill, and the cave where they were nursed by the she-wolf was located at its foot. When they grew up and decided to found a new city, they contested its site, Remus advocating the Aventine and Romulus the Palatine. It was decided that the first to see a flight of birds as an omen would be given the choice, and when twelve vultures flew over the Palatine Romulus was given the honour of naming the city, killing his brother and becoming the first king of Rome.

Some time after its foundation on the hill, the city was surrounded by a strong wall forming an approximate rectangle, hence the name Roma Quadrata. Three gates were provided in the walls: the Porta Mugonia on the north-east and the Porta Romanula on the north-west (neither of these has been yet identified by the archaeologists), and the Scalae Caci at the south-west corner overlooking the valley of the Circus Maximus. Excavations begun in 1985 on the lower northern slopes of the hill would appear to have identified a stretch of this wall, as well as traces of even earlier fortifications and four huts dating from the 9C–8C BC (see p 109).

The northern slopes of the Palatine, in the area nearest to the Forum, were for centuries considered one of the most prestigious residential districts. During the Republic many prominent citizens lived here, including the great orator and writer Cicero, the statesman and philosopher Quintus Lutatius Catulus, the orators Crassus and Hortensius, the demagogue Publius Clodius and the triumvir Antony. Remains of some of these residences have recently been unearthed. Augustus, who was born on the Palatine, acquired the house of Hortensius and enlarged it. His new buildings included the renowned Temple of Apollo, with Greek and Latin libraries attached. Part of his palace has also been excavated. The example of Augustus was followed by later emperors, whose residences became more and more magnificent, and the Palatine tended to become an imperial reserve.

Recent excavations have revealed that the first palace on the Germalus summit, still called the Domus Tiberiana, was in fact part of Nero's huge Domus Aurea (see p 278), which he built after his Domus Transitoria burned down in 64 AD. This was reconstructed by Domitian. Hadrian added buildings towards the Nova Via and on the north-west side of the hill, but preferred to live on his estate near Tivoli.

The whole of the Palatium was reserved for the constructions of the Palace of the Flavian emperors (now called the Palace of Domitian), which comprised the official palace, the emperor's residence and the stadium. To provide a water supply, Domitian extended the Acqua Claudia from the Celian Hill to the Palatine. Septimius Severus increased the area of the hill to the south by means of a series of arcades. Other remarkable edifices were the emperor's box overlooking the Circus Maximus and the monumental Septizodium. Elagabalus built a new temple in the Adonaea, in which he placed the most venerated treasures of Rome.

Odoacer, first king of Italy after the extinction in 476 of the Western Empire, lived on the Palatine; so for a time did Theodoric, king of the Ostrogoths, who ruled Italy from 493 to 526. The hill later became a residence of the representatives of the Eastern Empire. From time to time it was favoured by the popes, and some Christian churches were built here. In the 12C there was an important Greek monastery on the hill.

In the course of time, after a period of devastation, the Frangipani and other noble families erected their castles over the ruins. In the 16C most of the Germalus was laid out as a villa for the Farnese.

Systematic excavations were begun about 1724 by Francesco Bianchini, shortly after Duke Francis I of Bourbon Parma had inherited the Farnese Gardens. Little more was done in a scientific fashion until 1860; in that year the gardens were bought by Napoleon III, who entrusted the direction of the excavations to Pietro Rosa. He continued his work after 1870 when the Palatine was acquired by the Italian Government.

In 1907 the Germalus was explored, and later Giacomo Boni worked on the buildings below the Domus Flavia of the Palace of Domitian. Between the two world wars Alfonso Bartoli carried out research under the Domus Augustana of the same palace and elsewhere and brought to light much information about the earliest inhabitants. In the 1960s important work was done in the House of Augustus and the adjacent Temple of Apollo was identified. Excavations have been in progress since 1985 on the lower northern slopes of the hill, beneath the Domus Tiberiana, on the south-west corner of the hill in the area of the Temple of Cybele, and near the Vigna Barberini. For a description of recent excavations on the northern slopes, see p 109.

The usual approach to the hill is by the Clivus Palatinus which leaves the Forum near the Arch of Titus (see Walk 2) and ascends past the **Nova Via** on the right, which can be followed for part of its length. This ancient road runs parallel with the Sacra Via in the Roman Forum, along the southern slopes of the Palatine. It provided a means of communication between the Forum and the buildings on the Palatine. The visible remains probably date from the Flavian period, but at this point, where it crosses the Clivus Palatinus, recent excavations have revealed paving which seems to date from the Republican era. There are considerable ruins of shops and buildings which faced on to the road. Its western end is fenced off during restoration work.

A Republican house, close to the Nova Via and facing the Clivus Palatinus, was excavated in 1985. With some 50 bedrooms it is thought that it may have been the servants' quarters attached to the **House of Marcus Aemilius Scaurus**. He was a *quaestor* (official) under Pompey, whose former wife he married, and may have built this *domus* (house) in 58 BC before he fell into disgrace and was exiled in 52 BC. His residence is mentioned frequently by Roman writers as being the most splendid on the hill in the Republican era. The house has been restored but can only be visited by previous appointment (see above).

On the other side of the Clivus Palatinus, and outside the enclosure, is the Via di San Bonaventura which leads up to the north-eastern summit of the Palatine (described on p 122).

The Farnese Gardens, Domus Tiberiana and western Palatine

Beyond the ticket booth, on the right, paths and steps lead up to the **Farnese Gardens**, or Orti Farnesiani, laid out by Vignola in the middle of the 16C for Cardinal Alessandro Farnese, grandson of Paul III. They extended from the level of the Forum, then much higher, to the slopes of the Germalus; the various terraced levels were united by flights of steps. Vignola's work was completed by Girolamo Rainaldi at the beginning of the 17C. The modern stairs lead up to the first terrace (the former approach, by a monumental ramp from the Nova Via, has been fenced off) with a nymphaeum. Above another terrace with a fountain stand the twin pavilions of the aviary, on the highest level of the gardens, over-looking the Forum. The pleasure-gardens instituted by Alessandro Farnese—modelled on the Classical *viridarium* of ancient Roman villas and replanted here by the archaeologist Giacomo Boni—are still very beautiful. Boni's tomb stands beneath a palm tree in the part overlooking the Roman Forum. Delightful paths continue through the gardens to the western limit of the hill. There is a partial view of the Forum from here (although access to the edge of the hill has been fenced off for many years).

The gardens cover the site of the so-called **Domus Tiberiana**, very little of which is visible here, although its substructures are clearly seen from the Forum. Recent excavations have revealed that the first palace on this site, which was for-merly occupied by Republican houses, was part of Nero's Domus Aurea. This was reconstructed by Domitian (who seems to have called it the Domus Tiberiana), and extended by Hadrian to the north-west towards the ancient road known as the Clivus Victoriae. A cryptoporticus, a vaulted passage with entrances on Via di San Teodoro (no admission), dates from the period of Nero. Under Domitian a ramp on four levels was constructed to connect the Domus Tiberiana with the Forum.

Paths lead south through the gardens, past an ancient palm tree beneath which is a box-hedge maze reproducing that in the peristyle of Domitian's Palace. From the southwest corner of the hill there is a good view of Rome including the dome of St Peter's, but since restoration work and excavations are in progress there is at present no access from here (by a modern flight of steps) to the Temple of Cybele and the hut village on the lower southern slopes of the hill nor to the House of Augustus and so-called House of Livia (all described on pp 120–122). There is an oval fishpond in the south-east corner of the gardens where a modern flight of steps leads onto a small bridge above another cryptoporticus 130m long, built by Nero (no admission). The vault is decorated for part of its length with fine stuc-coes, now replaced by casts. It receives light and air from windows set high on the east side, and is one of the most interesting features of the palace, since it is rela-tively well preserved. A later branch corridor connected it to the Palace of Domitian, covering the huge raised open area beyond.

The Palace of Domitian

The ruins of the vast Palace of Domitian occupy nearly the whole of the summit of the Palatium hill, roughly in the centre of which is a former convent building which houses the Palatine Museum. Also in this area is part of a 17C loggia. Dotted here and there are some fine pine trees. There is a good view of the trees of the Farnese Gardens, looking towards the Forum.

The Palace of Domitian which covered the Palatium summit and the former depression between it and the Germalus, was a vast collection of buildings, bril-liantly planned for Domitian in 81–96 AD by the architect Rabirius, who levelled the central part of the hill to fill up the depression on the west. In the process he demolished or buried numerous earlier constructions, from private houses to Imperial palaces; some of these have been revealed by excavations.

The original entrance was to the north, towards the Forum, by a monumental staircase of three flights. Recent excavations have confirmed that the palace extended as far as the area of the Vigna Barberini (now outside the Palatine enclo-sure, see below), and another entrance hall was begun by Domitian in AD 80 on

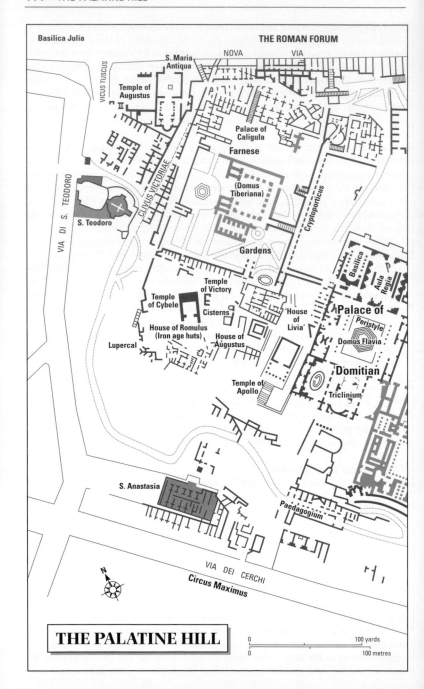

Basilica Julia

THE ROMAN FORUM

NOVA VIA

VICUS TUSCUS

S. Maria Antiqua

Temple of Augustus

Palace of Caligula

Farnese

CLIVUS VICTORIAE

VIA DI S. TEODORO

(Domus Tiberiana)

Crypoporticus

S. Teodoro

Gardens

Basilica

Aula Regia

Temple of Victory

Temple of Cybele

Cisterns

House of Romulus (Iron age huts)

House of Augustus

Lupercal

'House of Livia'

Palace of

Peristyle

Domus Flavia

Domitian

Temple of Apollo

Triclinium

S. Anastasia

Paedagogium

VIA DEI CERCHI

Circus Maximus

N

THE PALATINE HILL

0 ___ 100 yards
0 ___ 100 metres

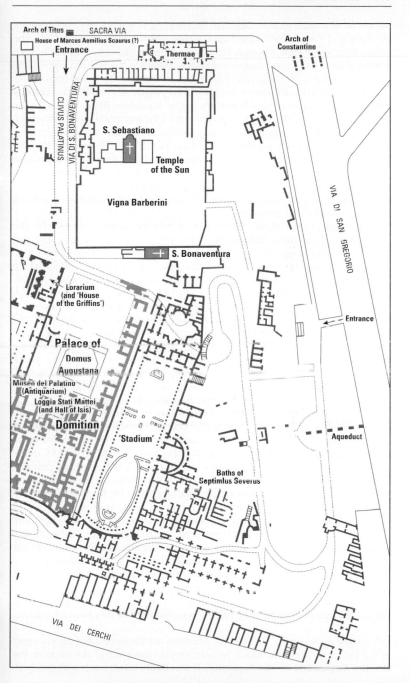

the site of an atrium built by Caligula. This was excavated in 1983–87 between the Temple of Castor and Santa Maria Antiqua in the Forum (see p 102). The palace covered the earlier Domus Transitoria built by Nero in AD 54 but burned down ten years later, some remains of which survive at the western corner, and the House of the Griffins and Aula Isiaca both dating from the Republican era.

In the south-western area was the official palace, also called the **Domus Flavia**, the splendour of which was praised by numerous Roman poets. In the centre of this palace is the spacious peristyle with an *impluvium* (pool) in the middle in the form of an octagonal maze surrounding a fountain. A box-hedge reproduction of this maze is in the Farnese Gardens (see above). The peristyle was surrounded by a portico and because of Domitian's constant dread of assassination he is supposed to have had the walls covered with slabs of Cappadocian marble, the mirror-like surface of which enabled him to see anyone approaching. On the west side is a series of small rooms with apses, statue-bases and baths; on the east side are traces of three more rooms.

To the north of the peristyle are three large halls facing north (fenced off). The central hall is the so-called **Aula Regia**, or throne room, originally decorated with 16 columns of pavonazzetto and 12 black basalt statues: two of the statues were found in 1724 and are now in Parma. In the apse was the imperial throne where the emperor sat when he presided over meetings of his council and received foreign ambassadors. To the east is the so-called **Lararium** (under cover), in fact thought to be another room used for public ceremonies, or a guardroom protecting the main entrance to the palace. Beneath this is the earlier House of the Griffins (described below; admission only by previous appointment). To the west is the **Basilica Jovis**, divided by two rows of columns of giallo antico; it has an apse at the further end, closed by a marble screen. This may have been used as an auditorium, for political and administrative meetings. A flight of steps (no admission) connects the basilica to the cryptoporticus in the Farnese Gardens. A portico of cipollino columns, also on the north, may have served as a loggia.

To the south of the peristyle is the **Triclinium**, or banqueting-hall. It has an apse reached by a high step; in this was placed the table where the emperor dined. The hall was paved with coloured marbles, which are well preserved in the apse. Leading out of the hall on either side was a court with an oval fountain. Around the fountain on the west side, which is also well preserved, is a magnificent pavement in opus sectile belonging to the earlier Domus Transitoria of Nero. The conspicuous pavilion here, with a double loggia looking north-west and decorations attributed to the Zuccari, was constructed by the Farnese in the 16C as part of their gardens. A staircase (no admission) leads down from the Triclinium to a court beneath it with a partly restored nymphaeum, decorated with rare marbles, which was also part of Nero's palace; the exquisite frescoes from the vault have been detached and are now exhibited in the Palatine Museum.

Behind the Triclinium is a row of partly restored columns belonging to the Flavian palace. Further south are two rooms with apses, once thought to be Domitian's reconstruction of the Greek and Latin libraries of the Temple of Apollo, but now considered to be reception rooms used by Augustus for legates.

Behind and to the east of the Palatine Museum are the remains of another part of the Palace of Domitian which was the private residence of the emperor, the **Domus Augustana** or 'the Augustus'. It was built on two levels with two peristyles, one on the upper level and one much lower. On the upper level, only the bases of the columns of the open peristyle, in front and to the east of the Palatine Museum building, and various small rooms survive. A path leads to the south-west edge of the hill between the Museum and the Triclinium from where there is a splendid view of another court (closed to the public), some ten metres below ground-level, in the middle of which is a large basin with a quadrangular shrine. Numerous living-rooms and fountain courts can be seen here. A doorway in the bottom wall leads to the exedra of the palace overlooking the Circus Maximus; this was originally decorated with a colonnade.

The Museo Palatino

The Palatine Museum, formerly called the Palatine Antiquarium (same opening times as the Palatine Hill, see above), houses material from excavations on the Palatine. The collection was founded in the mid-19C by Pietro Rosa. It was moved to its present building, a former convent, in 1868, and in the 1930s was under the direction of Alfonso Bartoli. It was reopened in 1997 and the collection is beautifully displayed and well-labelled, and includes material from the most recent excavations of the earliest settlements on the hill, as well as Roman wall-decorations and frescoes, stucco, marble intarsia and sculptures, all of them found in buildings on the hill.

On the **ground floor** are finds dating from the earliest prehistoric hut-villages up to the Republican era. The 1C AD masonry which can be seen beneath the floor in some of the rooms was part of the Palace of Domitian, which formerly covered this part of the hill. **Room I** has fragments of Paleolithic finds made since 1989 in the area near the Temple of Victory and at the foot of the hill by the Forum. **Room II** has models of huts and finds from the huts on the Germalus (see above). There are also finds dating from 900–830 BC from a cremation grave found in 1954 under the House of Livia, including an urn with a lid in the form of the circular roof of a hut. **Rooms III** and **IV** display cooking ware and domes-tic utensils (9C–late 7C BC) from recent excavations on the northern slopes of the Palatine, where more huts have been found (9C–8C BC), and terracottas including exquisite heads of Zeus and Apollo (3C BC) from excavations near the Temple of Victory. The altar dedicated to an unknown god was found in the south-west corner of the hill, towards the Velabrum.

Finds from the period of the Emperors are on the **upper floors**. **Room V** dis-plays material from the Augustan period (29 BC–14 AD) from the House of Augustus and Temple of Apollo, excavated in the 1960s, including beautiful painted terracotta *panels (38–28 BC) with reliefs of paired figures. Also here are three black marble herms, excavated in 1869 near the site of the Temple of Apollo, and now identified as part of the series of 50 Danaids which decorated its portico, and two fragments from a colossal statue of Apollo, which some schol-ars think might be the famous Greek original by Skopas (360 BC) which is known to have been set up in this temple. There is also a fragment of a statue of Pallas Athene, which may be another Greek original (6C BC). The fragments of wall-paintings (1C BC) include Apollo with his Lyre. **Room VI** contains beautiful mar-ble intarsia pavements and *frescoes of Homeric subjects all from Nero's Domus Transitoria, found beneath the Triclinium of the Palace of Domitian (54 AD).

Room VII displays finds dating from the 1C–2C AD, including marble intarsia panels which were once wall-decorations, two busts of Nero, a beautiful head of

Agrippina, daughter of Marcus Aurelius (mid-1C AD), carved fragments in giallo antico marble, and two heads of Vestals from a Hadrianic relief.

Room VIII covers the period from the Antonine emperors up to the 4C AD, with portraits and reliefs. Also here is a caricature of the Crucifixion, a graffiti found in the Paedagogium in 1855: it shows a young man standing before a cross on which hangs a figure with the head of an ass, and bears a blasphemous inscription in Greek stating 'Alexamenos worships his god.'

Room IX, in the **gallery**, displays a fragment of a female statue, which probably served as an acroteria, a Greek original (on a pedestal in the middle of the room by the entrance to room VIII) and a fine collection of Roman statues, all of them copies of Greek originals, including the graceful statuette of a *Satyr* turning round to look at his tail, after a Hellenistic bronze. The headless seated statue of *Cybele* from her temple is also displayed here.

The Loggia Mattei, Hall of Isis and House of the Griffins

Close to the museum building is the **Loggia Stati Mattei** (for admission, ask at the museum), a winter loggia formerly part of the Villa Mattei, built in 1520 with a vault decorated with grotesques on a white background by the circle of Peruzzi. The tondi with the Signs of the Zodiac were detached in 1846 and ended up in the Metropolitan Museum of Art in New York: the museum has recently generously returned them here. The frescoes from the walls found their way to St Petersburg at the same time and are still in the Hermitage.

The loggia now overlooks a room which contains murals detached from the **Hall of Isis** (*Aula Isiaca*) beneath the Basilica Jovis of the Palace of Domitian. This was a large rectangular hall with an apse at one end, erected in the Republican era and modified probably under Caligula, and dedicated to the cult of Isis. The murals were painted just before the edict of 21 BC banning the worship of Isis, were discovered in 1724, and were the subject of further investigation in 1912. The fantastic architectural paintings, which have panels with scenes of the cult of Isis and especially interesting designs on the ceiling, were detached in 1966. When they were in much better condition in the 18C they were copied by Gaetano Piccini and Francesco Bartoli: Bartoli's watercolours are preserved in the Topham Collection at Eton College in England.

Beneath the Lararium (see above) is the **House of the Griffins** or *Casa dei Griffi* (for admission ask at the Palatine Museum, but normally shown only by appointment). Named after the two griffins in stucco which decorate a lunette in one of the rooms, this is the oldest Republican building preserved on the Palatine (2C or 1C BC). Its wall-paintings, like those in the House of Livia, are in the second Pompeian style, with red, purple and yellow dominating. The house is on two levels, the decorations being on the lower level. Of the several rooms reached by a steep staircase, the large hall is the best preserved. In the centre of a mosaic floor there is an opus sectile pavement. The mural paintings simulate three planes of different depth, while the columns imitate various marbles. Round the top of the room runs a cornice and the ceiling is stuccoed.

The stadium and eastern edge of the hill

The eastern part of the Palace of Domitian, well below ground-level, is the so-called **stadium**, which most scholars now believe was a garden used occasionally as a hippodrome. There is a splendid view of it from above, although there is no admission to the ground-level. It is an enclosure 160m long, with a series of rooms at the north end and a curved wall at the south. The interior had a two-storeyed portico with engaged columns covering a wide ambulatory or cloister. The arena has a semicircular construction at either end, presumably once supporting a *meta* (turning-post). In the centre are two rows of piers of a late Empire portico. Towards the south are the remains of an oval enclosure of the early Middle Ages which blocked the curved end. Columns of granite and cipollino, Tuscan, Corinthian and Composite capitals, and fragments of a marble altar with figures of divinities now lie on the ground. In the middle of the east wall is a wide exedra shaped like an apse, of two storeys, and approached from the outside by a curved corridor. This structure is traditionally identified as an imperial box, used by the emperor when he commanded the races and athletic contests here.

East of the stadium was the so-called **Domus Severiana**, which was built over a foundation formed by enlarging the southern corner of the hill by means of enormous substructures that extended almost as far as the Circus Maximus. The scant remains include part of the **Baths of Septimius Severus**. To the north (near the exit onto Via di San Gregorio) is the aqueduct built by Domitian to provide water for his palace; it was an extension of the Acqua Claudia which ran from the Celian Hill to the Palatine. The aqueduct was restored by Septimius Severus.

To the south is the site of the imperial box built by Septimius Severus, from which he could watch the contests in the Circus Maximus. In the south-eastern corner of the Palatine is the site of the **Septizodium** (or Septizonium), also built by Septimius Severus in AD 203, an ornate building set up to impress visitors to Rome arriving by the Via Appia. Renaissance drawings show that it had three floors, each decorated with columns. The ornamental façade, some 90m long, was divided vertically into seven zones, the number corresponding either to that of the known planets or to the days of the week. In 1241 Matteo Orsini imprisoned the cardinals here and forced them to elect Pope Celestine IV; the new pope and three of the cardinals died as a result of the conditions. In 1588–89 Sixtus VI ordered Domenico Fontana to demolish the Septizodium and the columns and blocks of marble and travertine were reused in various buildings in the city.

The buildings on the southern edge of the hill can only be seen from a distance, from Via dei Cerchi or the Circus Maximus. They include the Severian arches, the south end of the stadium, the exedra of the Domus Augustana and, halfway down the hill, the **Paedagogium** (1C or 2C AD) supposed to have been a training-school for the court pages. Other inaccessible rooms on the edge of the hill above Via dei Cerchi include the so-called **Schola of the Praecones**. These buildings erected by Septimius Severus represent the last important monuments to be built on the Palatine.

If the southwestern part of the hill is closed, with its very important monuments, including the Temple of Cybele, the House of Augustus and the so called House of Livia, all described below, the Palatine can be left from here either by descending the hillside to the east of the Palace of Domitian and the stadium to the exit on Via di San Gregorio (through a portal built by Vignola for the Farnese Gardens, and later moved here) or by returning north across Domitian's Palace and descending the Clivus Palatinus to the exit at the Arch of Titus in the Forum.

The Temple of Cybele and the hut village

Steps (at present closed) lead down from the gardens of the Domus Tiberiana (see p 113) past a series of rooms with brick vaults which were built by the Antonines in the 2C AD for the accommodation of the Praetorian Guard, who protected the emperor and his family; graffiti in them indicate their occupation by soldiers.

The ruins of the **Temple of Cybele** or *Magna Mater* on a mound covered by a thicket of dark ilex trees can be seen from here. Cybele, the Magna Mater, mother of the gods, was the great Asiatic goddess of fertility and was worshipped in the town of Pessinus in Phrygia (Asia Minor). She, and her young lover Attis, were served by eunuch priests, and the festival of Cybele and Attis was celebrated annually (22–24 March) with primitive orgies. During a critical period of the second Punic War, an oracle had foretold that the battle could only be won if the Romans obtained from Phrygia the black stone which was the attribute of the goddess Cybele. Once in possession of this sacred cult image the Romans were in fact victorious, and the temple was built in 204 BC and consecrated in 191 BC. Burned down in 111 BC, it was rebuilt by Quintus Caecilius Metellus (consul in 109), and restored again after another fire in the reign of Augustus (AD 3).

The temple, raised on a high podium, had six Corinthian columns in antis, as can be seen on a Roman relief now on the garden façade of the Villa Medici (see p 166). Excavations have clarified the various dates of the building. The podium and the walls of the cella date from after the fire of 111 BC. At this time a large platform for athletic games and theatrical performances in honour of the goddess was built in front of the temple, beneath which was a district with an underground road, shops and baths. Pavements and external architectural decorations survive from the Augustan period. The statue of *Cybele* and fragments of a marble lion found here are now exhibited in the Palatine Museum.

Just to the east of the temple, on lower ground and under cover, are the remains of the **Temple of Victory**, one of the earliest temples so far found on the hill, built in 294 BC by the consul Lucius Postumius Megellus, after a Roman victory over Italic tribes. Precious finds made in this area since 1989 are now exhibited in the Palatine Museum. Between the two temples is the base of a much smaller temple, recently identified as the **Temple of Victory Virgo** dedicated by Marcus Porcius Cato in 193 BC. Cato was well known for his wise politics while serving as censor, and is also famous for his writings.

A short way further east and under cover are two **cisterns** dating from the 6C BC, one of which is particularly well preserved. It is circular in form, with a bee-hive vault of blocks laid in gradually diminishing courses; the top was closed with a single slab. The construction recalls Mycenaean tholos tombs.

The area at the south-western edge of the hill is the most ancient part of the Palatine, and excavations have been in progress here since 1978. Some of the ruins are protected by roofs, and the area is fenced off. Here are traces of a wall of tufa and the site of the **Scalae Caci**, one of the three gates of Roma Quadrata (see above). The gate is named after Cacus, a giant monster who according to legend had his den in the Forum Boarium at the foot of the hill and terrified the populace by his pillaging. It was only when he dared to steal the cattle which had belonged to the monster Geryon, and which Hercules had obtained as one of his Twelve Labours, that he was finally put to death by the Greek hero.

Excavations in 1907–49 revealed the traces of a hut-village of the Early Iron Age (9C BC). Numerous holes and channels in the tufa indicate the plan of three huts (now protected by iron roofs). Poles supporting the hut roofs were placed in the holes; the channels carried away rain-water from the roofs.

It is known that the **Lupercal** was also in this part of the hill, although traces of it have not yet been found. This was the cave sanctuary of the she-wolf connected with the legend of Romulus and Remus and sacred to Rome. There was an altar here which was surrounded by a grove sacred to the god Lupercus. Here the annual festival of the Lupercalia was held on 15 February, when the priests of the god, the *luperci*, dressed in goatskins, processed around the hill whipping whomever they met. (It was believed that the castigation of women encouraged fertility.) The Latin *Februarius* means purification and expiation. A hut at the top of the Scalae Caci near the Temple of Mater Matuta is known as the **House of Romulus**: it was restored periodically and up until the 4C AD was mentioned as being the hut that belonged to the shepherd Faustulus who found the legendary twins and brought them up.

The House of Augustus and the House of Livia

The part of the hill further east has also been fenced off while excavations of the **House of Augustus**, begun in 1961, have been in progress. It is significant that the Emperor chose this corner of the hill for his residence, close to the traditional site where Romulus and Remus were found. From Augustus's time the hill became the official residence of the emperors. It can only be visited by previous appointment, see p 110.

Augustus, who had been born in his father's house on the other side of the Palatine Hill, acquired the orator Hortensius's house in 23 BC, and incorporated it into his new palace after 36 BC. The house was reconstructed by the emperor (at public expense) after a fire in 3 AD. Some rooms of the palace have been found with wall-paintings of the highest interest, dating from 25 BC–AD 25, remarkable for their vivid colour (mostly red, yellow, and black), intricate designs and refined figure studies. Considerable fragments of the stuccoed vaults and pavements of marble inlay have also survived. In the west wing of the house, thought to be the private quarters of the Emperor, are two small adjacent rooms (seen behind glass), one with architectural and theatrical motifs including masques, and the other with a charming frieze of pine-cones. A series of larger rooms were probably used for public ceremonies and included two libraries and a little nymphaeum decorated with shells. Here are more very fine wall-paintings, stucco vaults and marble intarsia floors; a (modern) flight of stairs leads up to the exquisite little *studiolo*, beautifully restored, which has the most refined decoration so far found in the house.

After a building of the late Republican era was found beneath them, the ruins to the south-east of the House of Augustus were identified as the famous **Temple of Apollo** vowed by Augustus in 36 BC and dedicated eight years later, after the Battle of Actium in which he defeated Antony. A corridor which is thought to have connected the temple to the House of Augustus has been excavated here, and more wall-paintings have been discovered near the temple podium. Fragments of a colossal statue of *Apollo*, now in the Palatine Museum, were found near the site. All that survives of the temple itself is its basement, 44m by

24m, reached on the south side by a long flight of steps (no admission; the existing flight is a modern reproduction).

The Temple of Apollo was surrounded by the Portico of the Danaids, on which were statues (or herms) of the 50 daughters of Danaus: three herms, found in 1869, have recently been identified with these, and are exhibited in the Palatine Museum, along with some magnificent painted terracotta panels also found here. Nearby were the renowned Greek and Latin libraries, rebuilt by Domitian.

To the north of the House of Augustus a conspicuous modern flat-roofed building protects the so-called **House of Livia** (closed many years ago for restoration), famous for its wall-paintings. When it was discovered by Pietro Rosa in 1869, it was identified as the house of the wife of Augustus from some lead pipes bearing the inscription *Iulia Augusta*. It is now considered to be part of the House of Augustus itself. The masonry dates from the 1C BC; the mural paintings are Augustan.

An original staircase descends into the rectangular courtyard, in which there are two pillar bases and architectural paintings. The most important rooms open onto it. In front are the three rooms thought to belong to the *tablinum*, or reception suite; on the right is a room which was probably the *triclinium*, or dining-room.

The decorations of the *tablinum* are in the second Pompeian style (1C BC), which imitates in painting the marble of Greek and Roman domestic architecture, and introduces figures. They have been detached but are exhibited *in situ*. The paintings in the central room are the best-preserved, especially that on the right wall. It has panels separated by columns of fantastic design in a free interpretation of the Corinthian style. In the central panel Hermes is seen coming to the rescue of Io, the lover of Zeus, who is guarded by Argus of the hundred eyes; in the left panel is a street scene; the right panel is lost. In the intercolumniations are small panels with scenes of mysterious rites. The central painting on the rear wall of this room, now almost obliterated, shows Polyphemus pursuing Galatea into the sea; on the left wall, which lost its paintings in ancient times, are exhibited the lead pipes which gave the house its name.

The room on the left has some very ruined architectural decorations with panels of griffins and other fantastic creatures. The room on the right is also architectural in its decorative scheme. The delicate yellow frieze depicts small landscapes and genre scenes. Below is the representation of a Corinthian portico; between the columns are rich festoons of fruit and foliage. In the *triclinium* the decorations are also mainly architectural. On the wall opposite the entrance is a portico with an exedra; in front is a trophy with spoils of the chase, and below is a pond with ducks. Above are branches of trees.

The Vigna Barberini

Near the Arch of Titus in the Roman Forum (but not included in the Forum or Palatine enclosures), Via di San Bonaventura ascends to the north-eastern summit of the Palatine. Here, approached by a 17C portal in the wall of the Vigna Barberini, the former Barberini vineyard, is the small medieval church of **San Sebastiano al Palatino**, with interesting murals (c 970) in the apse. Excavations (1985–99) in the churchyard have unearthed the probable site of the **Adonaea**, or gardens of Adonis, where the god was worshipped. Later, Elagabalus built a **Temple of the Sun** in the centre of the gardens. Here he placed numerous treasures from the most ancient cults of the city, including the sacred stone from the Temple of Cybele, and what he took to be the *Palladium* (see p 103). The district acquired the name *Palladii* or *in Pallara* in the Middle Ages, and this was given also to the church of San Sebastiano. Excavations here have revealed a semicircular exedra which has the same dimensions as the south exedra of the Domus Augustana overlooking the Circus Maximus, and is therefore probably part of the same palace. The last section of Via di San Bonaventura, which ends at the church, is flanked by 18C terracotta Stations of the Cross.

4 • The Valley of the Colosseum

The famous Colosseum is probably the most visited monument in Rome. Although in the centre of the city on Piazzale del Colosseo (partly closed to traffic), which lies in a valley between the Velia on the west, the Esquiline on the north and the Celio to the south, it is now in a rather unattractive setting in part dating from the 1930s, beside a station of the *Metropolitana* and near busy roads. The piazza is usually crowded with tour groups and souvenir stalls.

Nevertheless, the interior of the Colosseum still retains an extraordinary atmosphere. In addition, Hadrian's Temple of Venus and Roma, the largest temple in Rome, and the well-preserved Arch of Constantine, are close by. Excavations are in progress on the south side of the Colosseum, but there are plans to rebury the basement of the huge circular fountain known as the Meta Sudans, unearthed during earlier excavations.

The Colosseum

The Colosseum (Map 10; 1) is the most famous monument of ancient Rome, although to this day it is still one of the least-studied works of the Roman period. It is the largest amphitheatre ever built by the Romans, and its design was copied in similar buildings all over the Empire. Despite being pillaged for centuries for its stone, the huge building preserves its remarkable grandeur and the north-east side appears almost undamaged.

The Colosseum has been an emblem of Rome's eternity for centuries. The historian and scholar known as the Venerable Bede (c 673–735) quotes a prophecy made by Anglo-Saxon pilgrims: 'While the Colisaeus stands, Rome shall stand, when the Colisaeus falls, Rome shall fall; when Rome falls, the world shall fall.' Although the name presumably referred to Nero's colossal statue, which used to stand beside the amphitheatre, it soon became the popular name applied to the building itself. Its original name, Flavian Amphitheatre, commemorated the family name of Vespasian, who began the building, and of his son Titus, who completed it.

Opening times

Daily 09.00 dusk. ☎ 06 700 4261 or 06 700 5469 (ticket includes entrance to the Palatine on the same day, see p 110; but if you visit the Colosseum after 13.30, then the ticket allows admission to the Palatine the following day). For information on the Archaeological card', see p 41. The **entrance** is at present in the middle of the south side, but may be moved to the north side. The first storey is open to the public (reached by various flights of stairs, or by the lift on the northeast side), but the highest storeys, which provide by far the best view of the building, have been closed to the public for many years.

History of the Colosseum

The amphitheatre, begun by Vespasian in AD 70 on the site of the lake in the gardens of Nero's Domus Aurea (see p 278), was completed by Titus ten years later. The expense of the monument was in part covered by the sale of war booty. The inaugural festival lasted 100 days, during which many gladiators and 5000 wild beasts were killed.

The gladiatorial combats and wild animal hunts (*venationes*) which took place in the Colosseum throughout the Imperial period were very popular forms of entertainment with the Romans, and grand ceremonies and processions preceded them. Gladiators, who were mostly prisoners of war, slaves, or condemned convicts, fought man to man in single combat, and it was only when one was killed that the other was declared winner. They carried different types of arms, and usually wore helmets. The spectacles with wild animals included crocodiles, lions, elephants and tigers shipped to Rome for the purpose. The arena was also sometimes flooded for mock sea-battles (*naumachiae*). Gladiatorial combats were suppressed in the 5C and fights with wild beasts in 523.

The amphitheatre was restored after a fire in 217 under Alexander Severus and in 248 the thousandth anniversary of the foundation of Rome was celebrated here. The damage from an earthquake in 443 was probably repaired by Theodosius II and Valentinian III. The building was again shaken by earthquakes in 1231 and 1349. It was converted into a castle by the Roman aristocratic families of the Frangipani and the Annibaldi.

In 1312 the Colosseum was presented to the senate and people of Rome by the Emperor Henry VII. By the 15C it had become a recognised quarry for building material. Its travertine was used during the construction of Palazzo di Venezia and Palazzo della Cancelleria. Other parts of the building were reused in St Peter's and Palazzo Barberini. In 1749, however, Benedict XIV dedicated the Colosseum to the Passion of Jesus and pronounced it sanctified by the blood of martyrs, although there is no historical basis for the tradition that Christians were killed in the arena. Pius VII, Leo XII, Gregory XVI and Pius IX carried out restorations, erecting buttresses and other supports. In 1893–96 it was freed from obstructive buildings by Guido Baccelli, and the structures beneath the arena were revealed. Further clearances were carried out after the construction in 1933 of Via dei Fori Imperiali. The Colosseum is again undergoing a long process of restoration and study expected to take many years, based on a detailed elevation, the first ever made of the whole building.

The Colosseum was particularly admired by 19C travellers to Rome because of its romantic ruined state. Lord Byron dedicates many stanzas of *Childe Harold's Pilgrimage* (Canto iv, 1818) to this 'vast and wondrous monument' ... 'a ruin—yet what ruin!' Dickens in 1846 declared: 'It is the most impressive, the most stately, the most solemn, grand, majestic, mournful sight, conceivable. Never, in its bloodiest prime, can the sight of the gigantic Coliseum, full and running over with the lustiest life, have moved one heart, as it must move all who look upon it now, a ruin. God be thanked: a ruin!' Augustus Hare was disgusted by the 'tidying up' of the Colosseum in

1882 and the eradication of its 'marvellous flora' (in fact, the monument used to be covered with an extraordinary variety of plants and flowers, some of them unknown elsewhere in Rome). Since the time of Paul VI the Pope has visited the Colosseum on Good Friday to re-enact the Passion of Christ Carrying the Cross (the Via Crucis) which is televised throughout the world.

The **exterior** is roughly 189m long, 156m wide and 48–50m high (the total circumfence measuring 545m). It is built of travertine outside and of brick-faced concrete and tufa in the interior. The travertine blocks were originally held together with iron clamps; these were torn out in the Middle Ages and their sockets are conspicuous. The mighty exterior wall, which supports the complicated interior, has four storeys. The lower three have rows of arches decorated with **engaged columns** of the three orders superimposed: Tuscan Doric on the lowest storey, Ionic on the middle and Corinthian on the top. The fourth storey, dating from the restoration of Alexander Severus, has no arches but is articulated by slender Corinthian pilasters. The projecting **corbels** supported 240 wooden poles which, when inserted through the holes in the cornice, protruded above the top of the building to support an awning which gave protection to the audience (see below). Statues originally occupied the arches of the second and third storeys.

All 80 arches on the ground floor were numbered and served as **entrance arches**. The numbered arches led to the concentric vaulted corridors giving access to the staircases. Each spectator entered the arch which corresponded to the number of his ticket, ascended the appropriate staircase and found his seat in the cavea by means of one of numerous passages. In addition there were four main entrances at the ends of the diameters of the ellipse, situated north-east, south-east, south-west and north-west. That on the north-east (between arches XXXVIII and XXXIX), which was without a cornice and was wider than the others, opened into a hall decorated with stuccoes: it was reserved for the emperor.

Though more than two-thirds of the original masonry has been removed, the magnificence of the **interior** of the amphitheatre, which could probably hold more than 50,000 spectators, can still be appreciated. The spectacular view is less effective than it might be because most of the wooden floor which formerly covered the underground passages beneath the arena is now missing, leaving them conspicuous. However, since 2000 a small part of the floor has been reconstructed, and there is now a walkway across the middle of the arena. Modern staircases lead up to the first storey (or there is a lift).

The **arena** measures 83m by 48m. Its name comes from the sand (*arena*) which covered the floor in order to prevent combatants from slipping and to absorb the blood. The substructures which can now be seen beneath the arena were used for the arrangement of the spectacles: they provided space for the complicated mechanism by which scenery and other apparatus was hoisted into the arena; cages for animals; and access passages.

The arena was surrounded by a wall c 5m high that protected the spectators from the animals. At the top of this wall was the **podium**, a broad parapeted terrace on which was set the emperor's couch, or *pulvinar*. The rest of the terrace was reserved for senators, pontiffs, Vestals, and foreign ambassadors.

Above the podium was the vast **cavea**, with seats (now missing) for all the other spectators. It was divided into three tiers (*moeniana*). The lowest tier was reserved for knights (*equites*), the middle one for Roman citizens (*plebieans*), and the top one, constructed in wood, for the populace, including women and slaves. The tiers were separated by landings (*proecinctiones*) reached by several staircases. Each tier was intersected at intervals by passages left between the seats, 160 in all. The section between two passages was called a *cuneus* (wedge, from its shape). Above the topmost tier was a colonnade, and at the very top was the narrow platform for the men who were responsible for the awning (*velarium*) that kept off the sun; it was attached to poles on the exterior.

The **cross** replaces an earlier one which was set up to commemorate the martyrs who were supposed to have died in the Colosseum. The chapel of **Santa Maria della Pietà** opens for services at 14.00 on Saturdays and 10.00 on Sundays. A model of the Colosseum and a few architectural fragments can be seen (behind glass) in a hall on the first storey.

Outside the southern end of the Colosseum excavations are in progress, which have revealed an entrance constructed by Commodus.

Between the Colosseum and the Temple of Venus and Rome, and marked by a raised lawn planted with ilexes, is the huge brick base (7m square) of the **Colossus of Nero**, the remains of which were demolished in 1936. This gilt-bronze statue of Nero as god of the Sun, by the Greek sculptor Zenodorus, is thought to have been nearly 35m high and the largest bronze statue ever made (it had a concrete core); it was even larger than its model, the Colossus of Rhodes. The statue was provided with a new base and moved here from the vestibule of the Domus Aurea by Hadrian when he built the Temple of Venus and Rome. Twenty-four elephants were needed to shift the statue.

Nearby a little garden has been planted with three cypresses. On the other side of a square lawn is an area of recent excavations surrounded by a fence and planted with olive trees, although there are plans to cover part of this area again. The visible ruins belong to the vestibule of the Domus Aurea. Beneath these were found extremely interesting remains of a temple and a Roman road. A circular fence surrounds the base of the **Meta Sudans**, the remains of which were demolished in 1936 by order of Mussolini, and re-excavated since 1982. This marble-faced fountain, probably around 17m high, was erected by Domitian and marked the boundary of four regions of the Augustan city (II, III, IV and X). It was restored by Constantine, and received its name from its resemblance to the conical turning-post for chariot races in circuses (*meta*), and from the fact that it 'sweated' water through numerous small orifices. It was surrounded by a circular fountain basin, and its shape is known from its representation on some ancient Roman coins. In 2002 another circular structure made from red tufa, about 3metres in diametre was found here and dated to the time of Augustus.

The triple **Arch of Constantine** (**Map 10; 1**) was erected in AD 315 by the senate and people of Rome in honour of Constantine's victory over a rival emperor, the 'tyrant' Maxentius, at the Milvian Bridge just outside Rome in 312. A triumphal arch of excellent proportions, it was decorated with fine sculptures and reliefs reused from older Roman monuments. Because of this it is often taken as an example of the decline of the arts in the late Imperial period.

The splendid large *****reliefs** on the inside of the central archway and the two above on the sides of the arch come from the frieze of a monument commemorating Trajan's victories over the Dacians and are probably by the sculptor who carved Trajan's Column. The eight large *medallions on the two façades, with finely carved hunting scenes and pastoral sacrifices, belonged to an unknown monument erected by Hadrian. The eight high-reliefs set into the attic were taken (like the three in Palazzo dei Conservatori, see p 83) from a monument to Marcus Aurelius, and represent a sacrifice, orations to the army and to the people, and a triumphal entry into Rome. The small bas-reliefs of the frieze, and the victories and captives at the base of the columns, are the only sculptural decorations carved at the time of Constantine.

The summit of the Velia has been transformed into a terrace with gardens (145m by 100m), the area of which virtually coincides with that of the enormous **Temple of Venus and Roma** (Map 10; 1), the largest temple ever built in Rome. It is being restored, and may one day be opened to the public. Probably designed by Hadrian himself, it stood on the site of the vestibule of the Domus Aurea, where Nero had placed a colossal bronze statue of himself as the Sun. The statue had therefore to be moved (see above). The temple was built in honour of Venus, the mother of Aeneas and the ancestor of the gens Julia, and of Roma Aeterna, whose cult appears to have been localised on the Velia. Begun around 125, and dedicated in 135, it dominated this end of the Roman Forum. Its Classical proportions show the strong influence Greek architecture had on the emperor. Damaged by fire in 283, it was restored by Maxentius in 307. It is said to have been the last pagan temple which remained in use in Rome, as it was not closed until 391 by Theodosius. It remained virtually entire until 625, when Honorius I stole the bronze tiles off its roof for the old basilica of St Peter's.

To counteract the unevenness of the ground, it was necessary to build a high platform; this was of rubble, with slabs of peperino and marble-faced travertine. The temple was dipteral, with ten granite Corinthian columns at the front and back and 20 on each of the sides. It had two cellae placed back to back; that facing the Forum was the shrine of Roma Aeterna and the other that of Venus. The visible remains date from the time of Maxentius. The two cellae (the apses and diamond-shaped coffers were added by Maxentius) are still standing. That facing the Roman Forum has been partly restored, and is visible from a room of the Antiquarium in the Forum (see p 108). The brick walls were formerly faced with marble and provided with niches framed with small porphyry columns. The apse contains the base of the statue of the goddess. The floor is of coloured marbles. The temple was surrounded by a colonnaded courtyard, with propylae on the north and south sides; in 1935 some of the columns and column fragments on the south were re-erected, and can be seen from the extension of the Via Sacra which leads up from the Colosseum towards the Arch of Titus in the Forum (see p 108).

The Domus Aurea, on the Oppian Hill a few steps from the north side of the Colosseum, is described in Walk 22.

5 • The Imperial Fora

The Imperial Fora were laid out by Julius Caesar, and then by the emperors Augustus, Vespasian, Nerva and Trajan, as extensions to the Roman Forum, and occupy the huge area between it and the lower slopes of the Quirinal and Viminal. They were uncovered only in 1933 when Mussolini constructed the wide Via dell'Impero, now Via dei Fori Imperiali (Map 7; 6, 8) between Piazza Venezia and the Colosseum.

There are long-term plans to eliminate the Via dei Fori Imperiali and open the whole area as an archaeological park: debate continues between archaeologists, urban planners and public administrators as to what should be done about the traffic along the road. Meanwhile, part of the area is still in the process of being re-excavated. The most impressive monument visible at present is the beautifully restored Trajan's Column. The Markets of Trajan are also particularly well preserved.

Opening times

At present only the Markets and Forum of Trajan are open (Tues–Sun 09.00–1hr before sunset). It is likely that parts of the other fora, which are all visible from the outside, will also soon be opened to the public. Since 1994, Via dei Fori Imperiali has become a pedestrian precinct on Sundays. In summer the fora are often floodlit at night. ✉ www.capitolium.org

History of the Imperial Fora

With the population of the city ever increasing, by the end of the Republican era the Roman Forum had become too small for its purpose. It was congested with buildings and overcrowded by citizens and by visitors from abroad. The purpose of any new forum was to be the same as that of the Roman Forum, namely to serve, with its basilicas, temples and porticoes, as a judicial, religious and commercial centre. The only direction in which expansion was possible was to the north, even though numerous buildings had to be demolished here.

The first step was taken by Julius Caesar, who built his Forum during the decade before his death in 44 BC. In it he placed the Temple of Venus Genetrix in commemoration of the victory at Pharsalus in Thessaly (48 BC) when, despite his smaller army, Caesar was victorious over Pompey. Caesar's example was followed by his successors, most of whom erected temples in memory of some outstanding event in Roman history for which they took the credit. The Forum of Augustus, with the Temple of Mars Ultor, commemorated the battle of Philippi (42 BC); the Temple of Peace was erected by Vespasian with the spoils of the campaign in Judaea (AD 70); and the Forum of Trajan, completed by Hadrian, had a temple to the deified Trajan in honour of his conquest of Dacia (AD 106). The Forum of Nerva had a Temple of Minerva. All the fora were connected and the whole area was arranged in conformity with a definite plan.

During the Middle Ages and the Renaissance the fora were pillaged for building material and robbed of their marbles and bronzes, and the area was later built over. Until the 20C only parts of the Fora of Trajan and Augustus and the so-called 'Colonnacce' were visible; the clearance of the area was begun in 1924 to make way for Via dei Fori Imperiali. During the construction of this thoroughfare, built to add dignity to Fascist military parades, numerous 16C buildings were demolished, the Velia Hill levelled, and the Imperial Fora hastily and inconclusively excavated, leaving only about one-fifth of them visible.

In 1980 projects were first mooted to eliminate the stretch of road between Piazza Venezia and Via Cavour, and systematic **new excavations** of the fora at a considerably lower level was begun in 1985. The new excavations have revealed important information about how the Forum of Augustus was linked to that of Trajan, and the form of the portico which lined the southern end of the Forum of Trajan (fragments of huge columns of giallo antico and a statue of a Dacian in Luni marble have been found here). Considerable new areas of the Fora of Caesar and Nerva have been revealed, including stretches of original pavement in grey granite, Republican houses, the Temple of Peace built by Vespasian and part of the Cloaca Maxima (see p 321). Important traces of the medieval city have also been found.

At the west end of Via dei Fori Imperiali, opposite the corner of the Vittorio Emanuele II monument, two domed churches of similar design flank Trajan's Column. The first, **Santa Maria di Loreto**, by Antonio da Sangallo the Younger, with a lantern by Giacomo del Duca (1582), is a fine 16C building. It is usually open in the afternoon. It contains an altarpiece attributed to Marco Palmezzano, and a statue of St Susanna by François Duquesnoy (1630). The second church, dedicated to the **Nome di Maria** is by Antonio Dérizet (1738).

Trajan's Column, and the Forum and Markets of Trajan

In front of the churches there is a good view of the **Forum of Trajan**, built between 107 and 113 and the last and most splendid of the Imperial Fora. It was designed by the architect Apollodorus of Damascus to celebrate the military victories of Trajan, in a site excavated in the saddle between the Capitol and Quirinal hills. The forum itself is in the form of a rectangle 118m by 89m, with a portico and exedra on each of the long sides. In the centre was a colossal equestrian statue of Trajan, the base of which in travertine was found during excavations in 1999. At the west end, occupying the whole of its width, was the Basilica Ulpia. Adjoining on the west were the Greek and Latin libraries with Trajan's Column between them, and, still further west, beneath the area of the two churches, the Temple of Trajan. The entrance was from the east, adjoining the Forum of Augustus, through a monumental arch. To the north of the forum and virtually adjoining it is the semicircle of the Markets of Trajan. In the opinion of ancient writers these constructions made up a monumental group unequalled in the world, although scholars are now uncertain about their exact design. Important excavations are being carried out in the eastern and southern parts of the forum, formerly covered by roads and public gardens.

Trajan's Column, still almost intact, and carefully restored in 1980–88, is generally considered to be the masterpiece of Roman sculptural art. It was dedicated to Trajan by Hadrian in memory of his conquest of the Dacians, the inhabitants of what is now Romania. Around the column shaft winds a spiral frieze 200m long and between 0.89m and 1.25m high, with some 2500 figures in relief illustrating in detail the various phases of Trajan's remarkable military achievements in the Dacian campaigns (101–102 and 105–106). The carving was carried out in less than four years by an unknown Roman master and his workshop. It is known that the column could originally be seen from buildings which surrounded it on various levels in the Forum of Trajan: from ground-level it is now more difficult to appreciate the beautiful details of the carving with the naked eye. Casts of each panel (made before restoration) are kept in the Museo della Civiltà Romana.

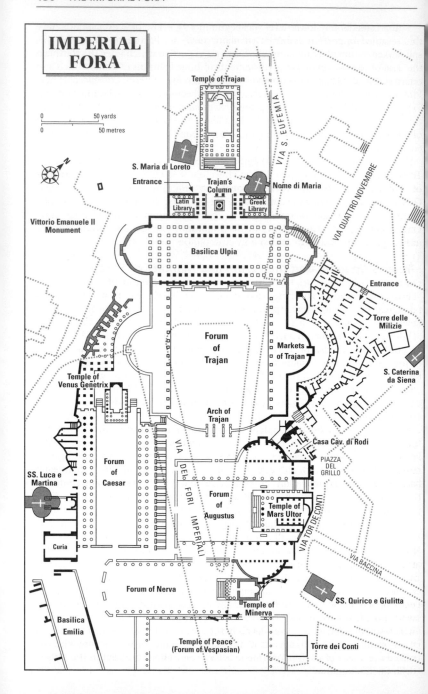

IMPERIAL FORA

| 0 | | 50 yards |
| 0 | | 50 metres |

N

VIA S. EUFEMIA

VIA QUATTRO NOVEMBRE

Temple of Trajan

S. Maria di Loreto

Entrance

Trajan's Column

Nome di Maria

Latin Library

Greek Library

Vittorio Emanuele II Monument

Basilica Ulpia

Entrance

Torre delle Milizie

S. Caterina da Siena

Forum of Trajan

Markets of Trajan

Temple of Venus Genetrix

Arch of Trajan

Casa Cav. di Rodi

PIAZZA DEL GRILLO

SS. Luca e Martina

Forum of Caesar

VIA DEI FORI IMPERIALI

Forum of Augustus

Temple of Mars Ultor

VIA TOR DE' CONTI

VIA BACCINA

Curia

Forum of Nerva

Temple of Minerva

SS. Quirico e Giulitta

Basilica Emilia

Temple of Peace (Forum of Vespasian)

Torre dei Conti

The column is 100 Roman feet (29.7m) high, or, with the statue of St Peter that surmounts it, 39.8m high. It is constructed of a series of marble drums. A spiral stair of 185 steps (no admission) carved in the marble ascends to the top of the Doric capital on which the statue of Trajan—replaced by St Peter in 1588—once stood. The ashes of the Emperor, who died in Cilicia in 117, and of his wife Plotina, were enclosed in a golden urn and placed in a vault below the column. Trajan was the first and probably the only emperor to be buried in the centre of the city. An inscription at the base has been interpreted as indicating that the top of the column reached to the original ground-level, thus giving an idea of the colossal excavations necessary for the construction of the forum.

Although there is an entrance by the column and Markets of Trajan, this is at present closed. But from here there is a good view of the **Forum of Trajan**. On the right of the column is the Latin Library and on the left the Greek Library, both rectangular, with wall-niches surmounted by marble cornices to hold the manuscripts. Behind the column is a fragment of a colossal granite column with its marble Corinthian capital, one of the largest ever found in Rome, virtually all that remains of the huge **Temple of Trajan** erected after Trajan's death by Hadrian. Dedicated to the deified Emperor and his wife Plotina c 118, the temple stood between Trajan's Column and the Via Lata (now the Corso). This magnificent temple probably had columns over 14.5m high.

Behind the column are the extensive remains of the **Basilica Ulpia** (Trajan's family name was Ulpius), dedicated to the administration of justice, and the largest in Rome. Though not as spacious as the Basilica of Constantine (see p 107), at 120m, not counting the apses at either end, it was longer; its width was 60m. It was divided by rows of columns into a nave and four aisles. The front of the basilica, towards the interior of the forum, had three doors; at the back, towards Trajan's Column, there were two doors. Part of the pavement in coloured marbles has survived, as has a fragment of the entablature, with reliefs depicting scenes of sacrifice and candelabra. The roof, covered with bronze tiles, may have been some 50m high.

On each short side was an extensive apse or portico; the north portico was found under Palazzo Roccagiovine beside Via Magnanapoli. It conforms to the semicircular shape of the markets. In the Middle Ages the portico was stripped of its precious marbles: all that survives are the remains of three steps of giallo antico, a column base, traces of the polychrome marble pavement and a column of the apse. Behind the portico part of the wall of the enclosure is visible. The site of the south portico is under Via dei Fori Imperiali, where excavations are in progress.

To visit the **Markets of Trajan** (for admission times, see above) at present you have to go up the stepped Via Magnanapoli to the entrance in Via Quattro Novembre. The buildings are at present rather ill-kept, and the sculptures and architectural fragments once displayed in the rooms have been removed. The markets were built before the forum, at the beginning of the 2C AD, and consisted of 150 individual shops used for general trading. The entrance is through a **rectangular hall** of two storeys, with six shops on each floor; on the upper storey is a large covered hall which may have served as a bazaar. Steps emerge on an ancient paved road, the **Via Biberatica**, which passed in front of the markets but is now blocked by Via Quattro Novembre. Beyond is the large semicircle of three superimposed rows of shops with arcaded fronts, built on the slopes of the Quirinal. The semicircle ends on either side in a well-preserved apsidal hall (only one of which can be visited). The portico of the fourth shop on the left of the bottom row has been reconstructed. The apsidal buildings on the second floor are particularly well preserved.

The passageway which leads from the markets into the area of the Forum of Trajan itself and the site of the monumental entrance arch which connected it to the Forum of Augustus is at present closed.

The **Torre delle Milizie** (no admission) behind the markets is a massive brick-built tower, a conspicuous feature in the skyline of Rome, and one of the most important civic medieval buildings to have survived in the city. It is thought to have been rebuilt in the 13C by the Caetani. In 1312 the Emperor Henry VII stayed here. The tower, which acquired its lean after an earthquake in 1348, later belonged to the Conti family, and was restored and isolated from the convent of St Catherine by Antonio Muñoz in 1914. It originally had three storeys: two of these survive.

Forum of Augustus

Adjoining the Forum of Trajan is the Forum of Augustus, built to commemorate the victory of Philippi (42 BC). It was dedicated to Mars Ultor (the 'Avenger'; at the battle Caesar's assassins, Cassino and Brutus, were defeated). Closed since 1984, there are long-term plans to reopen access to it from the Markets of Trajan. At present it can be seen from the railings along Via dei Fori Imperiali, which covers half its area.

This forum is dominated by the octastyle **Temple of Mars Ultor**, dedicated in 2 BC, which has columns on three sides. It had a large pronaos and an apsidal cella. It became one of the most honoured temples throughout the Empire, and as a centre of solemn ceremonies and the Imperial sanctuary, it became a museum of art and miscellaneous relics; among these were the sword of Julius Caesar and the Roman standards surrendered by the Parthians in 20 BC. Three columns at the end of the right flank are still standing. Of the eight Corinthian columns in front, four (the two middle and the two end ones) have been partly reconstructed from antique fragments. A broad flight of steps ascends to the capacious pronaos. In the cella, where the effect of undue width is lessened by a colonnade on either side, are the stepped bases of the statues of Mars, Venus and perhaps Divus Julius. Behind is the curve of the large apse. A stairway on the left descends to an underground chamber once thought to be the temple treasury. The huge wall behind was built to isolate the forum from the Subura district.

On either side of the temple, marble steps lead up to the site of twin **basilicas** which were almost completely destroyed during the Renaissance for their marble; each had a great apse, which Augustus decorated with statues of Roman heroes from Aeneas onwards (some of the niches can still be seen). On the ground between the surviving columns of the temple and the right-hand basilica are architectural fragments of great interest. Behind these is the Arch of Pantanus, formerly an entrance to the forum. The left-hand basilica had an extension at the north end known as the Hall of the Colossus, a square room which held a colossal statue of Augustus or of Mars, the base of which remains. Two ancient columns have been re-erected at the entrance.

Behind the Forum of Augustus, in Piazza del Grillo, is the **Casa dei Cavalieri di Rodi**, ancient seat of the Roman priorate of the Order of the Knights of St John of Jerusalem (see p 318). The house was built over a Roman edifice at the end of the 12C, and restored in 1467–70 by Cardinal Marco Balbo, nephew of Paul II. It has a well-preserved colonnaded atrium dating from the time of Augustus; the roof is a Renaissance addition. It is now used as a chapel by the Knights of St John. Open for services, Sun 10.30.

At the top of a flight of restored Roman stairs is a fine **Renaissance hall** (not at present open to the public as it is being restored, for information, ☎ 06 6710 2634), off which are several contemporary rooms; one of these, the Sala del Balconcino, contains part of the attic storey of the portico of the Forum of Augustus, with caryatids. Stairs lead up to a loggia with restored frescoes and fine views over the Fora.

Forum of Caesar

At the other side of Via dei Fori Imperiali, near the Vittorio Emanuele II monument, the steep Via di San Pietro in Carcere—open only to cars with special permits—diverges right to climb above the Mamertine Prison (see below) to the Capitoline. Here, well beneath the level of the road, can be seen the remains of part of the Forum of Caesar, where important excavations are in progress: some of the original grey granite paving has been exposed, and also medieval houses. This was the first of the Imperial fora, said by Dio Cassius to have been more beautiful than the Roman Forum. Recent excavations behind the Curia building in the Roman Forum (see Walk 2) have shown that Caesar created an entrance to his forum from the Curia. The focal point of the new forum was the **Temple of Venus Genetrix** (from whom Julius Caesar claimed descent), which was the most important building erected in the city by him. The high base remains, and although it has lost its marble facing, three of its Corinthian columns have been re-erected. In the temple, dedicated in 46 BC, two years after the battle of Pharsalus, were exhibited a statue of the goddess by Arcesilaus, a statue of Julius Caesar, a gilded bronze statue of Cleopatra and two pictures of Ajax and of Medea by Timomachus of Byzantium (1C BC). In front of the temple stood an equestrian statue of Caesar. Trajan rebuilt the temple and forum and added the **Basilica Argentaria**, or exchange building, and five large shops over which was an extensive, heated public lavatory (*forica*), remains of which survive.

From Via di San Pietro in Carcere a well-preserved stretch of the **Clivus Argentarium**, the Roman road which ran between the Capitoline and the Quirinal hills, is open to pedestrians. Lined with the remains of shops and a nymphaeum dating from the time of Trajan, it descends to the little church of **San Giuseppe dei Falegnami** (often closed). This was built in 1598, perhaps by Giovanni Battista Montano, above the **Carcere Mamertino** or the **Mamertine Prison** (open daily 09.00–12.00, 14.00–17.00; summer 09.00–12.30, 14.30–18.30). Known as the Tullianum, this is thought originally to have been a cistern, like those at Tusculum and other Etruscan cities. On the lower level can be seen the form of a round building that may have had a tholos, which could date it as early as the 6C BC. A spring still exists in the floor. In Roman times the building was used as a dungeon for criminals and captives awaiting execution. According to Christian tradition, St Peter and St Paul were also imprisoned here, and in the Middle Ages the building was consecrated as San Pietro in Carcere.

Opposite is the handsome church of **Santi Luca e Martina** (Map 7; 6; often closed), probably founded in the 7C by Honorius I. It was rebuilt in 1640 by Pietro da Cortona, and is considered one of his masterpieces. The façade, built of travertine, and the dome are particularly fine. The two storeys, the upper dedicated to St Luke and the lower to St Martina, have an original and complex design. The church of St Luke has a centralised Greek-cross plan. It contains a marble statue of St Martina, martyred under Alexander Severus in 228, by Niccolò Menghini (1635). The lower church of Santa Martina is reached by a staircase to the left of the high altar. Here there is a tabernacle by Pietro da Cortona, and the side chapel, with a pretty scallop motif, has a fine terracotta group of three saints by Alessandro Algardi. In the corridor is the tomb of Pietro da Cortona, and in the vestibule, statuettes by Cosimo Fancelli and a bas-relief of the *Deposition* by Alessandro Algardi.

Beside the church is an entrance to the Roman Forum (see Walk 2), and steps lead up to the Capitoline Hill (described in Walk 1). From the terrace there is a good view of the Arch of Septimius Severus and the other monuments at the west end of the Roman Forum. Excavations of the Forum of Caesar are in progress behind the church of Santi Luca e Martino.

Forum of Nerva

Behind the Curia building in the Roman Forum a terrace provides a fine view of the new excavations of the south-western part of the Forum of Nerva. It was, in effect, a development of the Argiletum, the street that led from the Roman Forum to the Subura district (see p 274). Begun by Domitian and completed in AD 97, it was also called the **Forum Transitorium** because it led into Vespasian's Temple of Peace. From the terrace can be seen the large marble slabs which provided the paving of the forum and part of the Cloaca Maxima drain. The excavations carried out in 1991–97 revealed excellent evidence of the various uses of this land over the centuries: both remnants of the Forum of Nerva and medieval houses were found. A sewage conduit laid in the Renaissance was also discovered, and this has been restored and now serves to connect the new excavations with those done in the 1930s on the other side of Via dei Fori Imperiali. There are plans to open this area to the public.

Since 1988 more excavations have been in progress nearby, beneath the gardens in Via dei Fori Imperiali, and traces of Republican houses destroyed in the fire of AD 64 have been found here, as well as medieval and 16C buildings.

Another part of the Forum of Nerva can be seen on the other side of Via dei Fori Imperiali, adjoining the Forum of Augustus. This includes the massive basement of the **Temple of Minerva**, which rose in the centre of the forum and was still standing at the beginning of the 17C, when it was pulled down by Paul V to provide marble for the Fontana Paolina on the Janiculum. Beside the railing on Via dei Fori Imperiali are two enormous Corinthian columns, the so-called **Colonnacce**. In the attic between the columns is a high-relief of Minerva, after an original of the school of Skopas. In the rich frieze of the entablature Minerva (Athena) is seen teaching the arts of sewing and weaving and punishing Arachne, the Lydian girl who excelled at weaving and dared to challenge the goddess. In front of the Colonnacce is a section of the Argiletum.

Forum of Peace and Santi Cosma e Damiano

To the east of the Forum of Nerva extended the Temple of Peace, also called the Forum of Peace or **Forum of Vespasian**, built with the spoils of the Jewish War by Vespasian and inaugurated in AD 75 to commemorate peace at the end of the civil wars which followed the death of Nero. Excavations on the north side of Via dei Fori Imperiali revealed and identified a shrine under the Torre dei Conti, some prone columns and remains of a pavement in opus sectile. South of Via dei Fori Imperiali a large hall was converted in the 6C into the church of Santi Cosma e Damiano. New excavations are in progress here beside an entrance to the Roman Forum.

A stairway on the left of one of the entrances to the Roman Forum leads to the church of San Lorenzo in Miranda, which encloses the Temple of Antoninus and Faustina in the Roman Forum (see p 106).

Further on, towards the Colosseum, is the church of **Santi Cosma e Damiano** (Map 7; 8), dedicated to two brothers from Cilicia who were miraculous healers. The church occupies a large rectangular hall, probably a library, of the Forum of Vespasian, which St Felix IV adapted in 527, adding mosaics to the apse. It was rebuilt in 1632, when the pavement was added to make it a two-storeyed building. The church is reached through the early-17C cloisters of the adjoining convent, decorated with a fountain and palms and contemporary frescoes by Francesco Allegrini.

The church is celebrated for its 6C **'mosaics**, copied in several Roman churches, especially in the 9C; there are lights in each chapel. On the triumphal arch is the *Lamb Enthroned*, surrounded by seven candlesticks, four angels and the symbols of the Evangelists. In the apse are *St Cosmas* and *St Damian, being presented to Christ at His Second Coming by St Peter and St Paul; St Theodore* (on the right); and *St Felix IV*, presenting a model of the church (on the left, restored). There are also mosaics of palms and the phoenix, symbol of the Resurrection. Below is the Lamb on a mount from which four rivers symbolising the Gospels flow; 12 other lambs represent the Apostles, with Bethlehem and Jerusalem on either side.

The **ceiling** of 1632 has a fresco by Marco Montagna who also painted frescoes in the nave. The Baroque high altar by Domenico Castelli (1637) is adorned with a 13C *Madonna and Child*.

At the west end a huge window was installed in 2000 to provide a view of a remarkably well preserved circular Roman temple, the so called Temple of Romulus in the Roman Forum (see p 106) which served as a vestibule to the church up until the end of the 19C. The original bronze doors can be seen.

In the first chapel in the right aisle is a striking fresco of *Christ Crowned on the Cross*, derived from the Volto Santo in Lucca. It dates perhaps from the 13C, but more probably from a repainting in the 17C by an unknown Lucchese artist. In the vault are frescoes by Giovanni Battista Speranza. In the second chapel are paintings of 1644 by Giovanni Baglione. The third chapel has an altarpiece of *St Anthony of Padua* by Giovanni Spadarino, and frescoes by Francesco Allegrini, who also painted the frescoes in the first and second chapels in the left aisle. In a domed Roman vestibule off the cloister is part of an 18C Neapolitan **presepio** or crib (closed in August). The models and figures in wood, terracotta and porcelain are of exceptionally fine workmanship.

Via dei Fori Imperiali now leaves the area of the Imperial Fora and passes on the right the colossal ruins of the Basilica of Constantine, which can be visited from the Roman Forum (described on p 107). The four interesting **relief maps** on a modern brick wall facing the street were set up here in 1932. They show the extent of Roman power at four stages in history: in the 8C BC; in 146 BC, after the

Punic Wars; in AD 14, after the death of Augustus; and in the time of Trajan, AD 98–117.

Santa Maria Nova

Adjoining the Basilica of Constantine, and reached by a flight of steps from Via dei Fori Imperiali, or by a short road from Piazzale del Colosseo, is the church of **Santa Maria Nova** or Santa Francesca Romana (**Map 7; 8**). Open 09.30–12.30 and 15.30–19.00; 15.00–17.00 in winter. It stands on the summit of the Velia and encroaches on the Temple of Venus and Roma (see p 127); a fine stretch of ancient Roman road is conspicuous on the approach to the west door. The church incorporates an Oratory of St Peter and St Paul built by Paul I (757–67) in the west portico of the Temple of Venus and Roma. In 847, after grave structural damage to the church of Santa Maria Antiqua in the Roman Forum, that church was abandoned and the diaconate was transferred to the oratory, which became Santa Maria Nova. The church was enlarged and the apse mosaic and campanile added before it was consecrated anew in 1161. The façade, designed by Carlo Lombardi, was added during his reconstruction in 1615.

St Francesca Romana (1384–1440)—Francesca Buzzi, wife of Lorenzo Ponziani—founded the Congregation of Oblates here in 1421, and joined it herself after her husband's death in 1436. Canonised in 1608, she is the patron saint of motorists, and on her festival (9 March) the street between the church and the Colosseum is congested with cars lining up for a blessing. The painter Gentile da Fabriano was buried in the church in 1428. The former conventual buildings now contain the excavation offices and Antiquarium of the Roman Forum.

There is a restored Cosmatesque pavement in the raised east end. In the vestibule of the side entrance (right) are the **tombs** of Cardinal Marino Bulcani (d. 1394) and of Antonio da Rio (or Rido), castellan of Castel Sant'Angelo (c 1450). In the south transept are the tomb of Gregory XI by Pietro Paolo Olivieri, set up in 1585 by the Roman people in honour of the pope who had restored the seat of the papacy to Rome from Avignon in 1377. Let into the south wall behind grilles are two flagstones from the Sacra Via which are supposed to show the imprint of the knees of St Peter, made as the saint knelt to pray for the punishment of Simon Magus, who was demonstrating his wizardry by flying. The legendary site of Simon's consequent fall is in the neighbourhood. From here stairs lead down to the crypt with the body of St Francesca Romana, and a bas-relief of her with an angel (17C). The confessio, an early work by Bernini, has a marble group of the same subject by Giosuè Meli (1866).

In the apse are **mosaics of the Madonna and Saints* (probably completed in 1161), and on either side, statues of angels of the school of Bernini. Above the altar is a 12C *Madonna and Child*, detached in 1950 from another painting found beneath it. The earlier painting, a colossal **Virgin and Child*, which may have come from Santa Maria Antiqua, is now kept in the sacristy. Probably dating from the end of the 6C, it is one of the most ancient

Santa Maria Nova

Christian paintings in existence. Also in the sacristy, on the left wall, are paintings of **Paul III** and **Cardinal Reginald Pole** attributed to Perino del Vaga; fragments of medieval frescoes; and a **Miracle of St Benedict** by Pierre Subleyras. On the entrance wall are Madonnas by Girolamo da Cremona and Sinibaldo Ibi of Perugia (1545).

The Colosseum and Temple of Venus and Roma are described in Walk 4.

6 • Around Piazza Venezia

Piazza Venezia is usually considered the centre of Rome. It is dominated by the colossal and rather ugly monument of Vittorio Emanuele II, one of the tallest buildings in Rome: the exterior terraces from which there are good views, are now open to the public. Palazzo di Venezia, a Renaissance palace built for a Venetian cardinal, which gave its name to the piazza, houses a museum of paintings, sculptures and decorative arts, and is also used for important exhibitions. The basilica of San Marco has a remarkable early mosaic in its apse.

Piazza Venezia (Map 7; 5), a huge and busy square, is the focus of the main traffic arteries of the city. It was transformed at the end of the 19C when parts of the Renaissance city were demolished and the Capitoline Hill itself encroached upon to make way for the huge Vittorio Emanuele II monument, an unforgivable intrusion into the centre of the city. At the busiest times of the day a policeman still regulates the traffic at the head of Via del Corso, which runs straight from the north side of the piazza for nearly 2km to Piazza del Popolo (see Walk 7).

Monument to Vittorio Emanuele II

The overwhelming Monument to Vittorio Emanuele II, also called the **Vittoriano** (Map 7; 5) was inaugurated in 1911 to symbolise the achievement of Italian unity, and the exterior terraces were reopened to the public in 2000 (10.00–16.00 or 18.00, closed Mon). Some 80m high, the building changed irrevocably the aspect of the city, throwing out of scale the Capitoline Hill itself, and causing indiscriminate demolition in the area. Familiarly known as 'the wedding cake' or 'Mussolini's typewriter', it can only be described as a colossal monstrosity. It was begun in 1885 by Giuseppe Sacconi, winner of an international competition in which there were 98 entries. He used an incongruous dazzling white botticino marble from Brescia to further alienate the monument from its surroundings. However, now that both the exterior and interior are open to the public it has become more acceptable, and it provides very fine views of the city. The entrance to the terraces is through the gate at the front of the building, but the entrance to the interior, with the Museo del Risorgimento and exhibition halls, is on the left side, reached from Via di San Pietro in Carcere.

The individual sculptures, described below, are interesting examples of official Academic Italian art of the period. At the sides of the monument are fountains representing the Tyrrhenian Sea, by Pietro Canonica, and the Adriatic, as well as the remains of the tomb of Gaius Publicius Bibulus, dating from the early 1C BC. At the foot of the wide flight of steps are two colossal groups in bronze, **Action**, by Francesco Jerace on the right, and **Thought** by Giulio Monteverde on the left. Midway are two winged lions and at the top sculptured bases for flagstaffs with bronze Victories. The four sculptural groups on the extreme left and right represent *Law* by Ettore Ximenes, *Sacrifice*, by Leonardo Bistolfi, *Concord* by Ludovico Poliaghi and *Strength* by Augusto Rivalta. The grave of Italy's **Unknown Soldier** (*il Milite Ignoto*) from the First World War, is perpetually guarded by two sentinels (each one is on guard for one hour). Above is the Altare della Patria by Angelo Zanelli, with a figure of Rome enshrined in the pedestal and friezes on either side: the *Triumph of Patriotism* on the right and the *Triumph of Labour* on the left. Steps to the right and left continue up flanking the equestrian statue of *Vittorio Emanuele II*, in gilt bronze 12 metres high, by Enrico Chiaradia (completed by Emilio Gallori). Around the base are figures by Eugenio Maccagnani representing historic towns of Italy; from the centre to the left; Turin, Florence, Naples, Amalfi, Pisa, Ravenna, Bologna, Milan, Genoa, Ferrara, Urbino, Mantua, Palermo, and Venice, and on the pedestal are military emblems. The two *quadrigae* crowning the monument are by Paolo Bartolini (representing *Liberty*, on the right) and Carlo Fontana (representing *Unity* on the left). Decorating the portico are a frieze with eagles and a cornice with lions' heads and sixteen colossal statues symbolising the Italian provinces.

From the portico at the top there are very fine **views**. Beyond the huge equestrian monument the Corso can be seen leading straight to Piazza del Popolo. Near at hand rises the huge Palazzo Venezia, and in the distance Monte Mario is prominent on the skyline, with its television masts. To the left can be seen the huge dome of the Pantheon and large church of the Gesù with its squat dome. Further left is St Peter's on the skyline and the high dome of Sant'Andrea della Valle. To the right of the Corso can be seen in the distance the light-coloured Villa Medici (the French Academy) with its two towers in pine trees, the façade of the church of Trinità dei Monti, and further round, the tall upper part of the façade of the Quirinal palace is very conspicuous, from which three flags are flown when the President is in residence. Near at hand are the two small domed churches and column of Trajan beside the Forum of Trajan.

From the left corner of the building there is a view in the other direction of the Roman Forum backed by the Palatine, and the Colosseum, with the top of the façade (crowned with statues) of San Giovanni in Laterano in the distance. Nearer can be seen the Fori Imperiali and the medieval brick Torre delle Milizie behind the Markets of Trajan and Via Nazionale running straight to Piazza della Repubblica and the huge church of Santa Maria degli Angeli. From the right corner of the building there is a close view of the exterior of the church of the Aracoeli and part of the hill of the Campidoglio.

The building houses the **Museo del Risorgimento** (open 10.00–18.00; closed Mon), which is entered around the corner to the left, in Via di San Pietro in Carcere. The museum was founded in 1906 but not opened until the 1970s. It was reopened in 2000 and is very well arranged (with explanations also in English) to illustrate the history of Italy's struggle for independence, as well as the First World War. Stairs, hung with prints, lead up past a small theatre where fascinating early films (*Film Luce*) of the First World War are shown. Up more stairs is a grand rectangular room with mementoes of Giuseppe Garibaldi, Mazzini, and Cavour. In the long curving corridor, with busts of war heroes, are various well labelled sections on moments of historic significance in Italian history from 1848 onwards. The second rectangular room at the other end of the corridor is devoted to the First World War. Exhibitions are often held in other parts of the building.

Dwarfed by the monument, and to the right of it, is the Capitoline Hill (see Walk 1). This is separated from **Piazza d'Aracoeli**—where there is a fountain of 1589 designed by Jacopo della Porta—by the wide, modern, traffic-ridden Via del Teatro di Marcello, one of the most difficult roads in the city to cross on foot, which runs south to the Tiber past the foot of the hill. Beside the monument here are the ruins, discovered in 1927, of a **Roman insula** (tenement house) built in the 2C AD and over four storeys high. This is particularly interesting as one of the few remains found in Rome itself of a service building with shops on the ground floor and simple living-quarters above.

Across Piazza Venezia is the battlemented **Palazzo di Venezia** (Map 7; 5), the first great Renaissance palace in Rome. Giuliano da Maiano, Bernardo Rossellino and Leon Battista Alberti have all been suggested as its architect, but it has recently been attributed to Francesco del Borgo. The palace was begun in 1455, enlarged in 1464 and finally finished in the 16C. It was built, partly of stone from the Colosseum, for the Venetian Cardinal Pietro Barbo, afterwards Paul II (1464–71), the first of the great High Renaissance popes. Barbo is said to have built the palace in order to view the horse races in the Corso. He used it as a papal residence and rebuilt the church of San Marco here, providing it with a loggia for papal benedictions. The palace was often occupied as such even after it had been given by Pius IV (1559–65) to the Venetian Republic for its embassy. Charles VIII of France stayed here after entering Rome with 20,000 soldiers in 1494. From the Treaty of Campoformio in 1797 until 1915 it was the seat of the Austrian ambassador to the Vatican. In 1917 Italy resumed possession and the palace was restored. During the Fascist regime it was occupied by Mussolini, who had his office in the Sala del Mappamondo. Some of his most famous speeches were made from the balcony overlooking Piazza Venezia.

The door on Piazza Venezia is finely carved and attributed to Giuliano da Maiano. The picturesque **inner court** (reached from 49 Piazza di San Marco), with its tall palm trees, has a large, unfinished 15C loggia on two sides, of beautiful proportions. In the centre is a fountain by Carlo Monaldi (1730). Special permission is needed to visit the courtyard and garden; apply in advance to the Direttrice del Museo di Palazzo di Venezia, 49 Piazza San Marco, Rome 00100. ☎ 06 679 8865, 📠06 6999 4221.

Adjoining the palace and facing the Via and Piazza di San Marco, to the south and east, is the **Palazzetto di Venezia** (c 1467). This was originally in Piazza Venezia, but was moved to its present position in 1911 because it obstructed the view of the Vittorio Emanuele II monument.

Museo del Palazzo di Venezia

The Museo del Palazzo di Venezia is the city's museum of decorative arts. It occupies several of the papal apartments in Palazzo Venezia and many rooms in the Palazzetto di Venezia. Its collections include Romanesque and 14C ivories, majolica, church silver and terracottas, and it also has paintings, wood sculptures and bronzes.

Opening times

09.00–19.00; closed Mon. ☎ 06 6999 4318. The items, displayed in modern showcases designed by Franco Minissi, are of very high quality but the museum has a neglected feel. Some of the 30 rooms are often closed, and not all of the collection is on display: rooms 27–30 are closed for restoration for an indefinite period. The rooms are unnumbered but the works are all labelled, although the display is subject to change. The State rooms are open only for exhibitions. The **entrance** is in Via del Plebiscito (ticket office on the first floor).

A monumental staircase by Luigi Marangoni (1930) leads up to the **first floor**. To the left is the **Appartamento Cibo**, the apartments of the Cardinals of San Marco, with some good ceilings and colourful floors, where the paintings (including the Sterbini collection) are arranged by Italian regional schools.

Room 1. Works of the Veneto school, including an exquisite early 14C *diptych by an artist named from it, the Maestro del Dittico Sterbini. Also here are a fresco fragment with a female head by Pisanello; a triptych attributed to Jacopo da Montagnana; *Christ and the Woman Taken in Adultery* by Nicolò dei Barbari; a double portrait attributed to Giorgione, and *St Michael Archangel*, and *Rape of Europa* by Girolamo da Santacroce.

Room 2. Works by artists from Emilia Romagna: Cristoforo da Bologna (*Madonna of Humility*); Bernardino Zaganelli (*Christ Carrying the Cross*); and Lelio Orsi (*Deposition*).

Room 3 (left). Works from Lazio, Umbria and the Marche. These include a painted Crucifix and a fragment of the *Head of the Redeemer*, both by the 13C Roman school; one half of a diptych which served as a reliquary, by the Master of Beata Chiara di Montefalco; works by Giovanni Antonio da Pesaro; and a very worn painted Crucifix by the Maestro Espressionista di Santa Chiara.

Room 4 (with a ceiling with signs of the zodiac) has paintings of the Tuscan school. *Madonna and Child with Saints* by Nanni di Jacopo; two works by the Maestro del 1419; the Marriage of St Catherine by the Maestro dell'Incoronazione di Christ Church (14C); and a fragment of a prophet by Gherardo Starnina. More works by the Tuscan school are displayed in **room 5**: fresco fragment of the *Head of the Redeemer* by Benozzo Gozzoli; *Martyrdom of St Catherine of Alexandria* by Bicci di Lorenzo; and *Visitation of St Bernard* by Bachiacca.

Room 6. 17C–18C canvases by Donato Creti (*Dance of Nymphs*); Giuseppe Maria Crespi (*Finding of Moses*); Guercino (*St Peter*); and Giulio Carpioni. In the niche is a terracotta bust of *Innocent X* by Alessandro Algardi.

Room 7, the Salone Altoviti, has *grotteschi* on the ceiling attributed to Giorgio Vasari. Here are displayed church silver, a Byzantine ivory casket, a rock crystal cross (10C–11C), and a reliquary by Jacopo Tondi. Charming portraits in pastels dating from the 17C to 19C are exhibited in **room 8**.

The long corridor (**11**) which connects these apartments to the Palazzetto di Venezia has a splendid view of the delightful courtyard, with palms and a fountain. Here is displayed a representative collection of Italian ceramics with examples from all the main workshops—Faenza, Urbino, Montelupo, Deruta, Pesaro, Casteldurante, etc. The second half of the corridor displays porcelain, including Meissen, Sèvres and Staffordshire.

The first rooms (**12–13**) of the Palazzetto contain some furniture, including 15C *cassoni* (dower chests), and 18C Neapolitan wax figurines. **Room 14** has a 15C marble bust of the Venetian *Cardinal Pietro Barbo* (afterwards Paul II) who built Palazzo di Venezia, and **room 15** displays 19C church silver.

In **room 16** begins the splendid display of small *bronzes, continued in **room 17**. Here are works by Il Riccio, Nicolò Roccatagliata, Girolamo Campagna, Giovanni Francesco Susini, Pietro Tacca, Pietro Bracci, Il Moderno, Tiziano Aspetti, Giambologna, François Duquesnoy, Alessandro Algardi, Antonio Susini, Gian Lorenzo Bernini and Alessandro Vittoria.

Room 18 has sculptures by Baccio da Montelupo (*Head of the Redeemer*) and Francesco Segala, and two reliefs of the *Miracle of St Mark* by Jacopo Sansovino (models for the bronze reliefs in the chancel of the basilica of San Marco in Venice). Beyond room 19, **room 20** displays small terracottas, some by Baccio Bandinelli. **Room 21** displays numerous busts, statuettes, and terracotta *bozzetti* by Bernini (models for an angel on Ponte Sant'Angelo and for details of his Roman fountains) and Algardi (bust of *Giacinta Sanvitali Conti* and *St Agnes Appearing to St Constance*). **Rooms 22–24** have 17C 18C models including works by Rusconi and Pierre Le Gross. **Room 26** displays a bust of *Benedict XIII* by Pietro Bracci (1724), and models for the Trevi fountain by him and Filippo della Valle. From the little **room 25**, with a pretty barrel vault, is the entrance to the **study collections and deposits**. The Enrichetta Wurts collection of silver, presented to Mussolini in 1930 which consists mostly of German, English and American ware dating from the 17C to the late 19C, and ivories, oriental porcelain and ceramics are kept here.

Numerous other works not at present on display include: architectural fragments dating from the early 8C–end of 9C; a marble transenna with donors attributed to Giovanni di Stefano (fl. 1366–91); a seated statue of a pope, sometimes identified as Nicholas IV or as Boniface VIII, a Roman work of the late 13C; the *Madonna of Acuto*, an early 13C wood polychrome seated statue, the earliest known work of its kind; a *Head of a Woman* by Nicola Pisano; and fine wooden statues, including two of the *Magi* dating from the 14C, from the Marche. Also a 10C ivory triptych of the *Deësis and Saints*; a 13C relief of an angel in gilded bronze and cloisonné enamel; 13C *Byzantine crosses; a *relief of the *Crucifixion*; *Christ Pantocrator*, an unusual Byzantine work in metal and enamel (13C); and a gilded bronze incised *lunette from the Santuario della Mentorella near Palestrina, thought to be an early 13C German work, possibly the back of an episcopal seat. There is also a collection of 12C–13C seals. Other paintings include a *Portrait of a Young Man* by Giovanni Bellini; and a *Child with a Puppy* by Cornelius Johnson. There is also an important collection of arms and armour, some left to the city by the Odescalchi in 1976, and 15C–17C German, Flemish and Italian tapestries.

The palace is also the seat of the **Istituto Nazionale di Archeologia e Storia dell'Arte** (entered at 49 Piazza San Marco), founded in 1922. The institute's library, the most important of its kind in Italy, with about 350,000 volumes, was partially reopened here in 1993, but is in urgent need of new premises; part of it has been moved to the Collegio Romano (see below).

At the corner of Piazza San Marco is a colossal mutilated bust of Isis, known as **Madama Lucrezia**. It has been here since the 15C and was once one of Rome's 'talking' statues: she carried on witty 'conversations' with Marforio on the Capitoline Hill (see pp 79 and 198). In the garden in front is a fountain (1927) with a pine-cone, the emblem of this district, the Rione della Pigna.

Also in Piazza San Marco is the basilica of **San Marco** (Map 7; 5), which forms part of Palazzo di Venezia. Open 07.30–12.30, 16.00–19.00; closed Thur afternoon and Tuesday morning. It was founded in 336 by St Mark the Pope, restored in 833, rebuilt in the 15C by Paul II, and again restored in the 17C and in 1744. The campanile is Romanesque, and the façade an elegant Renaissance work with a portico and a loggia built by Paul II for the papal benediction ceremony when he moved into Palazzo di Venezia. Under the portico are sculptural fragments and inscriptions, and the beautiful central door incorporates a relief of *St Mark Enthroned* attributed to Isaia da Pisa (1464).

Steps lead down to the fine **interior**, which retains its ancient basilican form with a raised sanctuary. There is a good Renaissance ceiling and remains of a Cosmatesque pavement at the east end. The bright columns of Sicilian jasper and the stucco reliefs in the nave (between 17C frescoes) date from the Baroque restoration in the 18C. The well-head dates from the 9C–10C.

On the **south side**, the first altarpiece is a *Resurrection* by Palma Giovane; in the third chapel is the *Adoration of the Magi* by Carlo Maratta. Beyond a niche with a monument to *Cardinal Vidman* (d. 1660) by Cosimo Fancelli, the fourth chapel contains 17C works by Bernardino Gagliardi. By the steps up to the presbytery is the funerary monument of *Leonardo Pesaro* by Antonio Canova. The chapel to the right of the high altar, by Pietro da Cortona, contains a painting of *St Mark the Pope* by Melozzo da Forlì and frescoes by Borgognone. In the **apse**, where there is a coin-operated light, is a mosaic (c 829–30) representing *Christ with Saints and Gregory IV*, offering a model of the church. Beneath are the *Lamb of God*, with 12 sheep representing the Apostles, and, on the arch, *Christ between St Peter and St Paul*.

The niches on the **north side** contain notable Baroque monuments, and here the fourth chapel has works by Francesco Mola and Borgognone. The second chapel was decorated by Emidio Sintes (1764). Remains of the earlier churches have been found beneath the pavement.

7 • The Corso and Piazza del Popolo

The Corso, an incredibly long and straight road with grand palaces, Baroque churches, elegant shops and a busy atmosphere is one of the streets which best characterises the city. From Piazza Venezia it runs past the Italian prime minister's official residence, in a square decorated with the splendidly carved Column of Marcus Aurelius, and, just beyond, the Italian parliament. About half-way along delightful pedestrian streets open on the right with vistas of the Spanish Steps; many fashionable shops are concentrated in the area between the Corso, Piazza di Spagna and Piazza del Popolo. Off the other side is the Ara Pacis, one of the masterpieces of Roman sculptural art. At its far end, the Corso passes the house where Goethe lived on his visits to Rome in the 18C and ends in the spacious Piazza del Popolo, with its Egyptian obelisk and fountains. The church of Santa Maria del Popolo here has important works by Caravaggio, Raphael and Pinturicchio. The most interesting palace in the Corso is at the other end, close to Piazza Venezia: this, the Doria Pamphilj family residence, has a magnificent patrician collection of paintings.

Via del Corso (Map 7: **5**, **3**, **1**), now called simply *Il Corso*, has been one of the most important thoroughfares in the city since Roman times. It is fairly narrow but remains one of the busiest streets in Rome; the pavements are hardly wide enough to accommodate the almost incessant stream of pedestrians in either direction during working hours and at weekends.

History of the Corso

The Corso represents the urban section of the Via Flaminia (221 BC), the main road to northern Italy. In Latin it was called the Via Lata (broad way) because of its width, exceptional in ancient Rome. Many palaces were built along the street from the 16C to the 18C, and the straightness of its line between Piazza Venezia and Piazza Colonna was perfected by Alexander VII, when he demolished two Roman triumphal arches that formerly spanned it.

Its present name is derived from the riderless horse races inaugurated here by Paul II in 1466, which became a celebrated event (*corso* means race). The Corso has since given its name to the principal street in numerous other Italian cities.

The carnival celebrations in the street from the 17C onwards became famous spectacles; John Evelyn, Goethe, Dickens and Henry James have left vivid descriptions of the festivities. James found it all a bit too much, and complained about the 'sport' of the masqueraders packed into the balconies lining the street, 'solemnly [shovelling] lime and flour out of bushel-baskets and down on the heads of the people in the street ... The scene was striking, in a word; but somehow not as I had dreamed of its being. I stood regardful, I suppose, but with a peculiarly tempting blankness of visage, for in a moment I received half a bushel of flour on my too-philosophic head.' Dickens, on the other hand, entered into the spirit, declaring 'anything so gay, so bright, and lively as the whole scene there, it would be difficult to imagine.'

Looking north up the Corso from Piazza Venezia, on the left corner is Palazzo d'Aste Rinuccini Bonaparte by Giovanni Antonio dei Rossi (17C), where Letizia Ramolino, mother of Napoleon I, died in 1836. On the right, beyond Vicolo del Piombo, are Palazzo Salviati, by Carlo Rainaldi (1662), and Palazzo Odescalchi, dating from the 17C–18C, but with a façade (1887–88) in the Florentine 15C style.

Palazzo Doria Pamphilj

On the opposite side of the Corso is the huge Palazzo Doria Pamphilj (**Map 7: 5**), which dates from 1435 but has suffered many vicissitudes. It has been the residence of this important Roman noble family since the 17C. The façade towards the Corso, by Gabriele Valvassori (1731–34), is perhaps the finest and most balanced Rococo work in Rome. The south façade is by Paolo Ameli (1743); that on the north in Piazza del Collegio Romano is by Antonio del Grande (1659–63), with two very fine wings.

The Palazzo contains the **Galleria Doria Pamphilj**, the most important of the Roman patrician art collections to have survived in the city. The period rooms, richly decorated in white, red and gold, and beautifully maintained, provide a sumptuous setting for the fine paintings.

Opening times

Fri–Wed 10.00–16.15; closed Thur. ☎ 06 679 7323. The private apartments have been closed indefinitely. The works are not labelled but are numbered as in the text below. An audio-guide is lent to visitors. The **entrance** is at no. 2 Piazza del Collegio Romano, reached off the Corso by Via Lata beyond the church of Santa Maria in Via Lata (described below).

History of the Doria-Pamphilj collection

The collection was initiated in 1651 by the Pamphilj Pope Innocent X, who decreed that the pictures and furnishings in Palazzo Pamphilj in Piazza Navona should be inherited by his nephew Camillo, son of the Pope's acquisitive sister-in-law Olimpia Maidalchini. Important additions were made to these works of art when Camillo married Olimpia Aldobrandini, widow of Paolo Borghese, and in 1760 with the Doria family bequests. The Doria family still live here, and the collection has been protected by the State since 1816.

The period rooms were restored in 1996, nine more rooms were opened for the first time, and the collection was rehung as it had been arranged after 1760 by the Doria prince Andrea IV, with the Flemish and Italian works side by side.

The grand staircase leads up to the first floor. The first series of rooms forms part of the **Appartamento di Rappresentanza**. The walls of the Sala del Poussin are covered with 17C landscapes by Gaspard Dughet, brother-in-law of Nicolas Poussin (see below), and often known as 'Il Poussin'. The **Sala del Trono** (right) displays more landscapes, this time in tempera, most of them by Crescenzio Onofri, pupil of Dughet. In the **Sala Azzurra** (right) are 19C family portraits. The **Sala dei Velluti**, which retains its late 18C red velvet wall-hangings, contains paintings by Giuliano Bugiardini, and *busts of *Innocent* X and *Benedetto Pamphilj* by Alessandro Algardi. The Rococo **Saletta Verde** (right), decorated in an elegant 18C Venetian style, has Venetian scenes, including a view of *Piazza Venezia* by Josef Heintz the Younger.

The **Sala da Ballo**, together with the adjacent smaller ballroom, was decorated at the end of the 19C with silk hangings. The smaller room has an 18C ceiling fresco of *Venus and Aeneas* by Antonio Nessi, and a Gobelins tapestry woven for Louis XIV from a 16C Flemish design, representing the month of May. The large family **Cappella** or chapel was designed by Carlo Fontana (1691) but altered in the 18C–19C. The altar of rare marbles dates from the 17C and the ivory crucifix is by Ercole Ferrata. In the **Saletta Gialla** (right), the 12 tapestries of the *Signs of the Zodiac* by Claude Audran were executed in the Gobelins workshops by order of Louis XV. The **Saletta Rossa** has a 17C Gobelins tapestry, four allegorical paintings of the *Elements* by Jan Brueghel the Elder, and a portrait of *James Stuart, the Old Pretender* by Alexis Simon Belle. In the **Stanza di ingresso alla Galleria** are works derived from David Teniers the Younger, and two paintings of the *Holy Family* by followers of Andrea del Sarto (**g12.**) and Fra' Paolino (**g11.**).

The **Galleria**, with the most important paintings, is arranged around four sides of a courtyard, redesigned by Gabriele Valvassori in 1731–34. The arrangement now follows that of the late 18C. **First gallery**. Left wall: (**i1.**) Annibale Carracci, *Mary Magdalene*; (**i3.**) Garofalo, *Madonna in Glory*; (**i4.**) Claude

Lorrain, *Landscape with Dancing Figures*; (i5.) Annibale Carracci, *Flight into Egypt*; (i10.) Lodovico Cigoli, *Christ in the House of the Pharisee*; (i15.) Paris Bordone, *Venus, Mars and Cupid*; (i17.) Claude, *Meeting with Diana*; (i19.) Annibale Carracci (attrib.), *St Jerome*; (i21.) Claude Lorrain, *Mercury Stealing the Oxen of Apollo*; (i22.) Garofalo, *Holy Family*; (i28.) Guercino, *Herminia and Tancred*; (i30.) Carlo Saraceni, *St Roch and the Angel*. Window wall: (i47.) Quinten Massys, *Userers*; (i63.) Jan van Scorel, *Portrait of Agatha van Schoonven*; (i64.) Domenico Beccafumi, *St Jerome*.

The **second gallery**, the delightful **Galleria degli Specchi**, was created in the 18C by Gabriele Valvassori; the vault is decorated by Aureliano Milani. In the **Cabinet** is the *Portrait of Innocent X* commissioned by the Pope in 1650 from Velázquez—the gem of the collection. Also displayed here is a sculpted bust of *Innocent X* by Bernini. In the gallery are displayed Roman statues and two paintings: a portrait of *Joan of Aragon, princess Colonna* (after Raphael), and the *Crossing of the Red Sea* painted on stone by Antonio Tempesta.

At the end of the Galleria degli Specchi is a series of four rooms overlooking the Corso with prettily decorated ceilings. Works grouped according to period (but in reverse chronological order) are exhibited here. The **Saletta del Settecento** displays Italian views by Hendrick Frans van Lint, Jan Frans van Bloemand, and Gaspar van Wittel. The **Saletta del Seicento** contains two masterpieces by Caravaggio, (M5.) *Rest on the Flight into Egypt* and (M6.) *Penitent Magdalene*. The *San Sebastian* (M8.) is by Ludovico Carracci. The **Saletta del Cinquecento** displays a *double portrait* (N1.) by Raphael; a *Portrait of a Young Man* (N2.) by Tintoretto; *Salome with the Head of St John the Baptist* (N4.) by Titian; and the *Return of the Prodigal Son* (N5.), by Jacopo and Francesco Bassano. The **Saletta del Quattrocento** contains 15C works: Lodovico Mazzolino, (0/1.) *Pietà*, (0/5.) *Massacre of the Innocents* and *Rest on the Flight into Egypt*; (0/2.) Antoniazzo Romano, *Madonna and Child*; (0/3.) Garofalo, *Holy Family*; (0/4.) Gian Battista Benvenuti Ortolano, *Nativity and Saints*; (0/9.–0/11.) works by Bernardino Parentino; (0/12.) Hans Memling, *Deposition*; (0/13.) Massys, *The Hypocrites*, and works by Giovanni di Paolo. At the end is a little cabinet with three busts, portraits of Filippo Andrea Doria V, his wife Mary Talbot, and her sister.

Third gallery. Left wall: (q2.) Correggio, *Triumph of Virtue*, an unfinished sketch for the painting now in the Louvre; (q3.) Claude Lorrain, *Rest on the Flight into Egypt*; (q10.) Lorenzo Lotto, *St Jerome*; (q13.) Guercino, *Return of the Prodigal Son*; (q19.) Guido Reni, *Madonna in Adoration of the Child*; (q21.) Pieter Bruegel the Elder, *Battle in the Port of Naples*; (q23.) Guercino, *St John the Baptist in the Desert*; (q25.) Garofalo, *Marriage of St Catherine of Alexandria*; (q31.) Alessandro Allori, *Calvary*; (q32.) Marcello Venusti, *Crucifixion*; Sassoferrato, (q34.) Holy Family, (q39.) *Madonna in Prayer*. Window wall: (q46.) Giovanni Bellini and his *bottega*, *Madonna and Child with St John the Baptist*; (q49.) Paul Brill, *Landscape with a Hunting Scene*; (q53.) Garofalo, *Holy Family with Saints*; (q56.) Leandro Bassano, *Sacrifice of Noah*; (q57.) Guercino, *St John the Evangelist*; (q58.) Brill, *Landscape with a Hunting Scene*; (q59.) Jacopo Bassano, *Adam and Eve in Earthly Paradise*, (q61.) Boccaccio Boccaccino, *Holy Conversation*; (q65.) and (q67.) Jan Frans van Bloemen, *Landscapes*; (q66.) Federico Barocci, *Study of a Head*.

Fourth gallery. (I) Algardi, bust of *Olimpia Aldobrandini Pamphilj*; (s43.) Jan Brueghel the Elder, *Madonna and Child with Animals*. Left wall: (s60.) Jan

Brueghel the Elder, *Landscape*; (**s57**.) Caravaggio, *Young St John the Baptist*, a replica of the painting in the Pinacoteca Capitolina; (**s71**.) Parmigianino, *Madonna and Child*; (**s80**.) Mazzolino, *Christ in the Temple*; (**s83**.) Jan Brueghel the Elder, *Earthly Paradise*; (**s84**.) David Ryckaert III, *Rural Feast*.

The charming little **Saletta degli Specchi** was decorated by Stefano Pozzi in the early 18C, and contains the following paintings by Jan Brueghel the Elder; (**s90**.) *Creation of Man*; (**s92**.) *Temptations of St Anthony*; (**s94**.) *Vision of St John on Patmos*; (**s.95**.) *Allegory of Fire*; (**s96**.) *Allegory of Water*; (**s111**.) *Allegory of Air*; (**s112**.) *Allegory of Earth*. Also in this room are (**s4**.) Domenichino, *Landscape* and, on the window wall: (**s13**.) Guercino, *St Joseph*; (**s14**.) Marco Basaiti, *St Sebastian*; (**s16**.) Titian, fragment of an *Angel*; (**s21**.) Marcello Venusti, *Christ in the Garden*; (**s22**.) Ludovico Carracci, *Madonna and Child with Saints*; (**s31**.) Nicolò Rondinelli, *Madonna and Child*.

Steps lead down from the fourth gallery into the **Salone Aldobrandini** which displays antique sculptures—not yet fully catalogued—including three large sarcophagi, busts and statues: in the centre stand a young *Bacchus* in red basalt and a *Centaur* in red and black marble. Four Brussels tapestries illustrating the Battle of Lepanto have been removed, but on the far wall are marble reliefs by François Duquesnoy.

In the **Private Apartments** (at present closed) red dominates the decorations. The **Winter Garden** or conservatory is decorated with antique busts, a 16C Brussels tapestry and an 18C sedan chair. The **Fumoir** or smoking-room was created by Mary Talbot, wife of Filippo Andrea Doria V, in the 19C: her portrait hangs here. In the adjoining room is a large polyptych of the *Madonna and Child with Saints and Angels*, of the early 15C Tuscan school, attributed to the Maestro di Borgo alla Collina, and *St Bernardine* by Sano di Pietro. The 16C Brussels tapestry depicts the month of February. In the **Room of Andrea Doria**, with a 16C ceiling, a glass case contains some of Filippo Andrea Doria's possessions, and there are two more Brussels tapestries with scenes of Lepanto. The portrait of *Christopher Columbus* is by Mabuse (Jan Gossaert).

The **Small Dining-Room** contains a bust of *Princess Emily Doria* by Pietro Canonica, a collection of Trapani corals, ambers and ivories, and a 19C frieze showing the fiefs of the Doria-Pamphilj family. The **Green Salon** contains a *Madonna* by Domenico Beccafumi; a *Deposition* by Memling; a large mid-15C Tournai tapestry with the medieval legend of Alexander the Great; a bronze bust of *Innocent X* by Algardi; and a *Portrait of a Man* by Lorenzo Lotto. In the centre is a rare 18C cradle in carved and gilded wood. In the recess to the left is a beautiful *Annunciation* by Filippo Lippi.

On the north side of Piazza del Collegio Romano (**Map 7**; **5**) is the **Collegio Romano**, a large building erected in 1585 by order of Gregory XIII for the Jesuits. The architect was probably the Jesuit Giuseppe Valeriani. It is now partly used by the Cultural Ministry. The founder of the Jesuit College was St Francis Borgia, duke of Gandia, third in succession after Ignatius Loyola as General of the Jesuits. The college was extremely important during the Counter Reformation when the Catholic Church placed renewed emphasis on learning. Its pupils included eight popes: Urban VIII, Innocent X, Clement IX, Clement X, Innocent XII, Clement XI, Innocent XIII and Clement XII. The Jesuit library founded here formed the nucleus of the Biblioteca Nazionale Centrale Vittorio

Emanuele, which was moved to new premises near the Castro Pretorio in 1975. The Salone della Crociera, with its original bookcases, has been used to house part of the library of the Istituto Nazionale di Archeologia e Storia dell'Arte in Palazzo di Venezia (see p 141).

On the south side of the piazza is the former church of **Santa Marta** by Carlo Fontana, with a good doorway. It has been restored as an exhibition centre, and is closed when not in use. Inside is a pretty vault decoration designed by Baciccia, with paintings by him and Paolo Albertoni. Just beyond, on the left of Via del Piè di Marmo, in Via di Santo Stefano del Cacco, is a colossal marble foot, perhaps from an ancient Roman statue of Isis.

Back on the Corso, next to Palazzo Doria, rises **Santa Maria in Via Lata** (Map 7; 5), a small church of ancient foundation, rebuilt in the 15C. Open daily 17.00–19.00. The graceful façade and vestibule are by Pietro da Cortona (1660). In the pretty little **interior**, at the end of the left aisle, is the tomb (1776) of the poet Antonio Tebaldeo (1463–1537), tutor of Isabella d'Este, secretary of Lucrezia Borgia, courtier of Leo X and friend of Raphael, who painted his portrait in the Vatican, a copy of which is placed here. The church also contains tombs of the families of Joseph and Lucien Bonaparte. The high altar and apse, decorated with coloured marbles, were once attributed as an early work of Bernini, but they are now thought to be by Santi Ghetti.

The **lower level** (closed for restoration) has remains of a large Roman building, some 250m long, which probably served as a warehouse, was converted in the 5C into a Christian chapel and welfare centre, and was rebuilt and enlarged as a church in the 7C and 11C. The interesting 7C–9C murals discovered here are now exhibited in the Crypta Balbi (see p 201). A tradition that St Paul was guarded on this spot during his second visit to Rome led to excavations as early as the 17C, when a high-relief by Cosimo Fancelli was put in place.

Here the Corso was spanned by the **Arcus Novus**, erected by Diocletian in 303–304, and demolished in 1491 when the church was rebuilt.

In the Corso, beyond Via Lata, a bank now occupies Palazzo Simonetti (no. 307), once the property of the Boncompagni-Ludovisi and for years the residence of Cardinal de Bernis, ambassador of Louis XV at the papal court. Low down on the corner of the palace, in Via Lata, is the **Fontanella del Facchino**, with the figure of a sturdy porter holding a barrel; water issues from the bung-hole. Water-sellers are supposed to have resold Tiber or Trevi water from their barrels. Il Facchino was one of Rome's 'talking' statues (see p 198); with his flat beret, he was once thought to be a caricature portrait of Martin Luther, but the figure more probably represents Abbondio Rizio, a heavy drinker. In 1751, Vanvitelli attributed the sculpture to Michelangelo.

Opposite Palazzo Simonetti is **San Marcello** (Map 7; 3), a very old church, rebuilt on a design by Jacopo Sansovino after a fire in 1519, with a façade by Carlo Fontana (1683). Open daily 07.00–12.00 and 16.00–19.00.

The **interior** was frescoed in the 17C by Giovanni Battista Ricci da Novara, including the *Crucifixion* on the west wall, the scenes of the *Passion* between the windows, and the apse. On the west wall is the tomb of Cardinal Giovanni Michiel (d. 1503) and his nephew Bishop Antonio Orso (d. 1511), by Jacopo Sansovino. On the **south side**, in the third chapel, is a 15C fresco of the *Madonna and Child* in a marble frame, and, on the altar wall, frescoes by

Francesco Salviati. On the ceiling of the fourth chapel are frescoes of the *Creation of Eve*, *St Mark* and *St John the Evangelist* begun by Perino del Vaga and completed after the *Sack of Rome* by Daniele da Volterra and Pellegrino Tibaldi. Beneath the altar, which has a fine 14C Crucifix, is an interesting Roman cippus. The fifth chapel has paintings by Aureliano Milani (c 1725). The fourth chapel on the **north side** has frescoes by Taddeo Zuccari and on the right wall busts of three members of the Frangipani family by Algardi. Excavations of the medieval church may one day be opened to the public.

Via del Caravita diverges to the left to the delightful Rococo **Piazza di Sant'Ignazio**, a theatrical masterpiece by Filippo Raguzzini (1728). The buildings (recently cleaned) have curving façades which fit into a careful decorative scheme in relation to the streets between them. The central building is now used by the Cultural Ministry and the special *carabinieri* police force in charge of safeguarding Italy's cultural heritage.

The Jesuit church of **Sant'Ignazio** (**Map 7; 3**) rivals the Gesù in magnificence. Open daily 07.30–12.30 and 16.00–19.15. It was begun in 1626 by Cardinal Ludovico Ludovisi as the church of the Collegio Romano (see above), to celebrate the canonisation of St Ignatius Loyola by the cardinal's uncle Gregory XV. The design by Carlo Maderno and others was carried out by Orazio Grassi, a Jesuit mathematician from the college, who is also responsible for the fine façade.

The spacious aisled **interior** is sumptuously decorated. In the vaulting of the nave and apse are remarkable paintings representing the missionary activity of the Jesuits and the **Triumph of St Ignatius*, the masterpiece of Andrea Pozzo. The amazing trompe l'oeil perspective projects the walls of the church beyond their architectural limits, and Pozzo even provided a cupola, never built because of lack of funds, in a canvas 17m in diameter. The vaulting and 'dome' are best seen from a small yellow disc set in the pavement about the middle of the nave. On the west wall are two allegorical figures by Alessandro Algardi. The second chapel on the south side, lavishly decorated with rare marbles, has an altarpiece of the *Death of St Joseph* by Francesco Trevisani.

In the ornate **transept chapels**, also designed by Andrea Pozzo, with marble Solomonic columns, are large marble high-reliefs: on the south side, the *Glory of St Louis Gonzaga* by Pierre Le Gros, with a lapis lazuli urn containing the remains of the saint, and two figures of angels, 18C works by Bernardo Ludovisi; on the north side, the *Annunciation* by Filippo della Valle, and another lapis lazuli urn with the relics of St John Berchmans (d. 1621), and two 18C angels by Pietro Bracci. In the chapel to the right of the high altar is the elaborate funerary monument to Gregory XV and his nephew Cardinal Ludovisi, the founders of the church, by Le Gros. From the sacristy there is a lift (access by request) to a chapel frescoed by Borgognone.

On the right side of the Corso is Palazzo Sciarra-Colonna (no. 239), built in the late 16C by Flaminio Ponzio, under which part of the Acqua Vergine was found in 1887. Opposite is a bank building by Antonio Cipolla (1874). Here, on the ground floor, the ambitiously named and much publicised Museo del Corso is in fact an exhibition space in modernised rooms, with a collection of paintings (of relative interest) acquired by the bank. Open daily 11.00–20.00. The street here was once spanned by an arch of the Acqua Vergine, transformed by Claudius into a triumphal arch after his conquest of Britain in 51–52 AD. Via delle Muratte leads off to the right to the Fontana di Trevi (see p 167).

In Piazza di Pietra, a few metres to the left of the Corso, reached by Via di Pietra, are the splendid remains of the huge **Temple of Hadrian**, built by Antoninus Pius in 145 and dedicated to his father. Now incorporated in the façade of the chamber of commerce building, the high wall of the cella survives, along with the peristyle of the right side with 11 disengaged fluted *Corinthian columns (15m high). The houses in front follow the line of the portico which used to surround the temple.

Piazza Colonna

Via Bergamaschi leads north from Piazza di Pietra to Piazza Colonna (**Map 7: 3**) on the Corso, which for centuries was the centre of the city. On the north side rises the great flank of **Palazzo Chigi**, the official residence of the prime minister. Begun in the 16C by Matteo di Castello (and also possibly Giacomo della Porta and Carlo Maderno), it was finished in the 17C by Felice della Greca. The famous Chigi Library, founded by Alexander VII, was presented by the State to the Vatican in 1923. The main façade of the palace faces the Corso and Largo Chigi, from which the busy Via del Tritone leads towards Piazza Barberini. Although the public is not allowed access, the interesting 17C courtyard can sometimes be glimpsed through the entrance.

In the centre of the piazza, beside a graceful **fountain** with a particularly attractive veined pink-and-grey marble basin designed by Giacomo della Porta (the dolphins are a 19C addition by Achille Stocchi), rises the monument from which the piazza derives its name, the majestic **Column of Marcus Aurelius**, or Colonna Antonina. It is made entirely of Italian marble from Luni, and is formed of 27 blocks. The ancient level of the ground was nearly 4m lower than at present. The shaft measures 100 Roman feet (29.6m), and the total height of the column, including the base and the statue, is nearly 42m. In the interior (no admission) are 203 steps lit by 56 tiny windows.

History of the Column of Marcus Aurelius

The column was erected between AD 180 and 196 in honour of Marcus Aurelius's victories over the Germans (169–73) and Sarmatians (174–76), and dedicated to him and his wife, Faustina. The philosopher-emperor Marcus Aurelius led his troops in all these important battles, which delayed the barbaric invasions of Italy for several centuries.

The column was inspired by Trajan's Column (see p 129), but instead of being the focal point of a forum, it was in the centre of an important group of monuments of the Antonine period. The ancient base was decorated with Victories, festoons and reliefs. The summit was originally crowned with figures of Marcus Aurelius and Faustina, but in 1589 Domenico Fontana replaced the imperial statues with one of St Paul.

Around the shaft a bas-relief ascends in a spiral of 20 turns, interrupted half-way by a Victory; the lower part of the relief commemorates the war against the Germanic tribes, the upper that against the Samaritans. On the third spiral (east side) the Roman soldiers are represented as being saved by a rainstorm, which in the 4C was regarded as a miracle brought about by the prayers of the Christians in their ranks. Casts of the reliefs are kept in the Museo della Civiltà Romana (see Walk 37), but these are not at present on view.

On the west side of the piazza is the façade of **Palazzo Wedekind** (1838), incorporating on the ground floor a handsome portico with 12 Ionic marble columns, brought from a Roman building at Veio. The little church on the south side is San Bartolomeo dei Bergamaschi (1561). The east side of the piazza across the Corso is closed by the huge Galleria Colonna (1914), a covered shopping arcade in the form of a Y. This is at present closed and the shops and cafés not accessible. At the beginning of Via del Tritone is **Santa Maria in Via**, rebuilt in 1594, with a good Baroque front, completed in 1670.

Adjoining Piazza Colonna to the west is Piazza di Montecitorio with the old façade of **Palazzo di Montecitorio** (**Map 7**; **3**), which, since 1871, has been the seat of the *Camera dei Deputati* (Italian Chamber of Deputies). This, together with the *Senato della Repubblica* (see p 185), represents the parliament of Italy: both houses have identical legislative duties and exercise political control over the government of the country. The 630 deputies, who have to be at least 25 years old, are elected every five years by Italians over the age of 18. The two houses sit together to elect the president of the Republic.

The original palace was begun for the Ludovisi family in 1650 by Bernini, who was responsible for the general plan of the building and for the idea of enhancing the effect of the façade by giving it a convex, slightly polygonal form. The north façade of the palazzo is in Piazza del Parlamento. In 1918 it was enlarged and given its new façade, with an art nouveau red-brick front, by Ernesto Basile; the principal entrance is now on this side. In the interior (open to the public on the first Sunday of the month, 10.00–17.30) the chamber, also of this period, is panelled in oak and brightly illuminated from above by a row of windows in the cornice, below which is an encaustic frieze by Aristide Sartorio, begun in 1908, representing the development of Italian civilisation. The fine bas-relief in bronze in honour of the House of Savoy is by Davide Calandra.

The **obelisk** (22m high) in the centre of the piazza was originally erected at Heliopolis by Psammetichus II (c 590 BC). It was brought to Rome by Augustus to celebrate his victory over Cleopatra, and set up in the Campus Martius, where it served as the gnomon of an immense sundial. In 1748 it was discovered underground in the Largo dell'Impresa (an open space north of the Palazzo di Montecitorio) and in 1792 it was erected on its present site.

In the Corso, beyond Largo Chigi, stand Palazzo Marignoli (1889), on the right, and on the left, Palazzo Verospi, where a plaque records Shelley's residence here in 1819. Via delle Convertite leads off right to **Piazza San Silvestro**, not an attractive piazza, but the site of the central post office and an important bus terminus.

The church of **San Silvestro in Capite** (**Map 7**; **3**) was originally erected here by Pope Stephen III (752–57) on the site of a Roman building, possibly Aurelian's Temple of the Sun. It was bestowed on the English Roman Catholics by Leo XIII in 1890, and is now administered by the Irish order of the Pallottini. Open daily 07.00–12.30; fest. 09.00–12.30 and 15.30–19.30; services also in English. The name of the church refers to the relic of the head of St John the Baptist which is preserved in a side chapel. The 12C–13C campanile is surmounted by a 12C bronze cock. The interior contains interesting 17C works, including the organ. The nave vault was painted by Giacinto Brandi. In the second south chapel is an altarpiece of *St Francis* by Orazio Gentileschi. The cupola was painted by Pomarancio. The north transept and third north chapel have works by Lodovico Gimignani, and the first north chapel has a *Crucifixion* by Trevisani.

Further along the Corso, now less busy, and beyond Piazza del Parlamento is Palazzo Fiano, on the left, which was built over the remains of the Ara Pacis (see below). This was also the site of the Roman Arco di Portogallo, demolished in 1662 by order of Alexander VII. Opposite is the pretty Via Frattina, the first of several long straight pedestrian streets which open off this side of the Corso and end in Piazza di Spagna (see Walk 8).

A small square opens out just beyond the Palazzo Fiano. On the left is **San Lorenzo in Lucina** (**Map 7; 3**), a church probably dating from the time of Sixtus III (432–40) or even earlier, rebuilt in the 12C, and again in 1650. Of the 12C church there remain the restored campanile, which has several rows of small loggie with colonnettes, the portico with six Ionic columns, and the doorway. In the first chapel on the south side a reliquary contains part of a gridiron on which St Lawrence was supposed to have been martyred. In the second chapel on the left pillar is the tomb of Nicolas Poussin (1594–1665) by François Lemoyne, erected by Chateaubriand in 1830. The fourth chapel, designed by Bernini for Innocent X's doctor Gabriele Fonseca, is decorated with pretty stuccoes and has a fine portrait bust (left of the altar) by Bernini. The *Crucifixion* on the high altar is by Guido Reni. On the north side, the decorative fifth chapel was designed by Simon Vouet and contains two good paintings of *St Francis* by him, on the left and right walls. In the second chapel the altarpiece is by Carlo Saraceni. Pompilia, in Browning's *The Ring and the Book*, was married in this church. Excavations have revealed interesting remains of the early Christian basilica (2C 3C) above Roman edifices, including a private house and a market building of brick-faced concrete, thought to date from the time of Hadrian. These are usually open at 16.30 on the last Saturday of the month.

Beyond, at no. 418A on the left, is **Palazzo Ruspoli**, designed by Bartolomeo Ammannati, with a great marble staircase by Martino Longhi the Younger and frescoes by Jacopo Zucchi. Since 1990 it has been the seat of the Fondazione Roberto Memmo which holds exhibitions here. At Largo Carlo Goldoni three streets converge on the Corso: Via Condotti, with its fine shops, leading past the church of the **Santissima Trinità dei Spagnoli**, with an 18C elliptical interior (open daily 07.00–12.00 and 16.30–19.30; closed July, Aug), to Piazza di Spagna; Via Fontanella di Borghese, ending in Piazza Borghese (see below); and Via Tomacelli, which runs to Ponte Cavour, an important bridge over the Tiber leading to the Prati district.

Further on, where the street widens, stands **Santi Ambrogio e Carlo al Corso** (**Map 7; 1**), built in 1612 by Onorio Longhi and completed by his son Martino. Open daily 09.30–12.00 and 17.00–19.00; 08.00–12.00 and 16.00–19.00 in winter. The fine cupola is by Pietro da Cortona and the heavily restored façade by Giovanni Battista Menicucci and Fra Mario da Canepina (1690). The poorly lit altarpiece of the *Madonna Presenting San Carlo to Christ* is one of Carlo Maratta's best works, and on an altar behind it is a rich urn containing the heart of St Charles Borromeo. In the neighbouring **Oratory of Sant'Ambrogio**, at no. 437 to the left of the church (ring for the porter), on the site of the old church built by the Lombards in 1513 on a piece of land granted them by Sixtus IV, is a marble group of the *Deposition* by Tommaso della Porta (1618).

Mausoleum of Augustus and Ara Pacis

Behind the apse of San Carlo is the ugly Piazza Augusto Imperatore (**Map 7; 1**), now used by tourist buses. It was laid out by the Fascist regime in 1936–38 around the **Mausoleum of Augustus**, or *Tumulus Caesarum*. Open by appointment, ☎ 06 6710 3819 or 06 6710 2070.

History of the Mausoleum of Augustus

This was the tomb of Augustus and of the principal members of his family, the gens Julia-Claudia, and was one of the most sacred monuments of ancient Rome. The last Roman emperor to be buried here was Nerva in AD 98. It dominated the north end of the Campus Martius and used to be surrounded in Roman days by a huge public park. Erected in 28 BC, it is a circular structure 87m in diameter (330 Roman feet), the largest mausoleum known. The smaller cylinder above was originally surmounted by a tumulus of earth some 45m high, planted with cypresses and probably crowned with a bronze statue of the emperor.

In the Middle Ages the tomb became a fortress of the rich Roman Colonna family. Later it was pillaged to provide travertine for other buildings, and a wooden amphitheatre was built on top of it, where Goethe watched animal-baiting in 1787. In the 19C a theatre was constructed here which was used as a concert hall from 1908 to 1936. When these structures were demolished and excavations began it was left open to the sky.

Nowadays the mausoleum is rather neglected and the interior less interesting than it might be. The circular base, which incorporated a series of large niches, was built of opus reticulatum and was once faced with travertine. On either side of the entrance were two obelisks—one of which is now in Piazza del Quirinale, and the other in Piazza dell'Esquilino—and pilasters on which was inscribed in bronze lettering the official will of Augustus, a copy of which was found at Ankara in Turkey (it is reproduced on the outside wall of the pavilion protecting the Ara Pacis; see below). A corridor leads to the centre of the building where the opus reticulatum walls can be seen, with numerous abandoned marble architectural fragments which used to decorate the upper part of the mausoleum, and finely carved fragments of inscriptions. The sepulchral cella in the centre had three niches, two of which can still be seen: that on the left preserves the inscription to Augustus's sister Octavia and his beloved nephew Marcellus, who was the first to be interred here in 23 BC; the other niches contained the cinerary urns of Augustus himself and of his wife Livia and his nephews Gaius and Lucius Caesar. The central pillar also survives.

To the west of the mausoleum, between Via di Ripetta and the Tiber, work has been in progress since 2000 to provide a new museum building (designed by Richard Meier) for the monumental altar called the **Ara Pacis**, reconstructed in 1937–38 from scattered remains and from reproductions of other, dispersed fragments. The carved decoration is a splendid example of Roman sculpture, influenced by Classical Greek and Hellenistic art, which characterises the supreme achievement of Augustan art. It is not expected to be reopened until at least 2004; for information, ☎ 06 6880 6848.

History of the Ara Pacis

The Ara Pacis Augustae was consecrated in the Campus Martius on 4 July 13 BC, and dedicated four years later, after the victorious return of Augustus from Spain and Gaul, in celebration of the peace that he had established within the Empire. This much is known from the document (*Res gestae Divi Augusti*) which the emperor had engraved on bronze tablets in Rome a year before his death at the age of 76 in AD 14 (a copy of which is displayed here).

In 1568, during excavations for the foundations of Palazzo Fiano on the Corso, nine blocks belonging to the frieze of the altar were found and bought by Cardinal Ricci da Montepulciano for the Grand Duke of Tuscany. To facilitate transport, each block was sawn into three pieces. These went to the Uffizi Gallery in Florence. The cardinal overlooked two other blocks unearthed at the same time. One of these eventually passed to the Louvre in Paris; the other to the Vatican Museum.

Three hundred years later, during a reconstruction of Palazzo Fiano in 1859, other parts of the altar were found, and these were acquired in 1898 by the Italian Government for the Museo Nazionale Romano. In 1903 and 1937 excavations brought to light the basement of the altar and further fragments. The pieces from the Museo Nazionale Romano and the Uffizi were recovered; those in the Louvre, the Vatican and the Villa Medici were copied, and the altar was reconstructed, as far as possible, in its original form. It is not in its original position, however; this was further south, close to the Via Lata, between the present Piazza del Parlamento and Piazza di San Lorenzo in Lucina. A pavilion, with glass walls, was built here in 1938 to protect the altar, but this was demolished in 2000.

The monument, built throughout of Luni marble, has a simple **base** with two horizontal bands. On the base is an almost square-walled enclosure, with two open and two closed sides. The **external decoration** of the enclosure is in two zones divided by a horizontal Greek key-pattern border. The lower zone is covered with an intricate and beautiful composition of acanthus leaves on which are swans with outstretched wings. In the upper zone is a frieze of reliefs with a decorated cornice above it. Between the jambs of the main or north entrance (approached by a flight of steps) are scenes illustrating the origins of Rome. The left panel, which is almost entirely lost, represented the Lupercalia; the right panel shows **Aeneas Sacrificing the White Sow*. The panels of the south entrance depict **Tellus the Earth Goddess*, possibly an allegory of Peace, on the left, and much-damaged Rome on the right. The side panels illustrate the ceremony that took place during the consecration of the altar itself: the procession includes Augustus, members of his family including women and children, state officials and priests.

The **interior** of the enclosure is also in two zones; because sacrifices took place here, the lower part has no decoration other than simple fluting. The upper zone, however, is decorated with beautifully carved bucrania. The altar is an exact reconstruction of all recovered fragments. Approached by a flight of steps, it has a back and two side walls; a further flight of narrow steps leads up past the walls to the altar proper. The cornice and the anta of the left side wall are the best-preserved; the reliefs indicate the *Suovetaurilia*, or sacrifice of a pig, a sheep and an ox. Little else of the decoration survives.

To the south, on Via di Ripetta, in a district once inhabited by the Serbs (Schiavoni) who came here as refugees after the battle of Kossovo on 15 June 1389, are two churches, **San Girolamo degli Schiavoni**, rebuilt in 1587, and **San Rocco**, with a Neo-classical façade by Giuseppe Valadier (1834) and an early altarpiece by Baciccia in the sacristy.

Further south, Via Borghese diverges left from Via di Ripetta—the name of which is a reminder of the vicinity of the old river bank and port—to **Palazzo Borghese** (Map 7; 1), called from its shape the 'harpsichord of Rome'. It was begun perhaps by Vignola (c 1560) and completed by Flaminio Ponzio, who designed the beautiful terrace on the Tiber front. The palace was acquired by Cardinal Camillo Borghese, who became Pope Paul V in 1605, and was renowned for its splendour. For nearly two centuries it contained the paintings from the Galleria Borghese; they were restored to their former residence in 1891. It is now the seat of the Circolo della Caccia, an exclusive club for men, founded in 1869 (open only to members). The pretty courtyard has long lines of twin columns in two storeys, and colossal statues representing *Ceres* and the empresses *Sabina* and *Julia*; a garden beyond contains fountains and Roman sculpture.

In Via Vittoria, across the Corso, is the **Accademia Musicale di Santa Cecilia**, a renowned musical academy. Further north the Corso passes on the left the church of **San Giacomo in Augusta**, so called from its proximity to the Mausoleum, with a façade by Maderno; it is known also as San Giacomo degli Incurabili from the adjoining hospital. Opposite is the small church of **Gesù e Maria** with a façade by Girolamo Rainaldi, who was also responsible for the interior decoration completed c 1675.

At no. 18 is the **Casa di Goethe** (Map 2; 4), a museum dedicated to the poet, who lodged on the upper floor of this house with his friend the painter Johann Hienrich Tischbein during his trip to Italy in 1786–88. Open 10.00–18.00; closed Tues. ☎ 06 3265 0412.

Although the house was altered in 1833 some of the rooms are probably those in which Goethe lived. The **museum** has material relating to the poet's travels in Italy and copies of some of his drawings, and numerous delightful informal sketches by Tischbein of Goethe made while he was staying with him here. It has a copy (1996) of the artist's most famous work, his portrait of Goethe as a traveller in the Roman Campagna, which was also painted here (the original is now in Frankfurt). Also on display are two paintings by Jakob Philipp Hackert, Goethe's friend, whom he met in 1787 and who accompanied him on some of his travels and taught him to draw (Goethe later wrote a biography of Hackert). The copy of the colossal head of Juno, three times natural size, in the Ludovisi collection recalls the cast Goethe had made of this work, which he particularly admired (he called it his 'first love in Rome'). Winckelmann had attributed it to a Greek master, but in fact it is now recognised as a Roman work and a portrait of Antonia, mother of the Emperor Claudius, and the original is displayed in Palazzo Altemps (see p 192). The last room is a reconstruction of Goethe's study in Weimar where he had a house from 1775 until his death. The apartment overlooks a charming little courtyard planted with banana trees and

Goethe In Rome

The poet Johann Wolfgang Goethe (1749–1832) stayed in Rome from October 1786 to February 1787, and again from June 1787 to April 1788, where he spent his time sight-seeing and writing. His *Italian Journey* (various editions of which are preserved in the museum), published later, in 1828, is one of the most important descriptions of Italy of its time.

When Goethe came to Italy he was already a famous literary figure in Germany—although the first part of his *Faust*, his most famous work, was not published until 1808—and a leading politician in Weimar. He was one of the last and most serious 'Grand Tourists': besides his attraction to Italy because of its Classical past, he was also a keen naturalist. In his *Italian Journey* he describes his journey down through Italy from the Lago di Garda, where he saw olive trees for the first time, and his visits to the botanical gardens of Padua and the Giusti garden in Verona. He admired the works of Palladio in Vicenza, and was particularly impressed in Assisi by the Temple of Minerva, the first complete Classical monument he had ever seen.

Goethe's circle of friends in Rome included Angelica Kauffmann (1741–1807), the most famous woman painter in Europe in her time, whose portrait of Goethe is now in Weimar, and Johann Winckelmann (whom Angelica also painted), the founding father of Classical archaeology who made some fundamental studies of ancient Roman sculpture. Goethe left a drawing showing his grave at the Protestant Cemetery (see p 409), but in fact his only son August was buried there when he predeceased him, aged 42, while staying in Rome in 1830.

palms. Exhibitions are held here and there is also a **library** specialising in the works of Goethe, open to students.

Piazza del Popolo

Piazza del Popolo (**Map 2; 2**), at the end of the Corso, provides a scenic entrance to the city from Via Flaminia and the north. The piazza was created by Latino Giovenale Manetti in 1538 for Paul III in strict relationship to the three long straight roads which here penetrate the city as a trident. The two twin-domed churches were added in the 17C. The piazza was given its present symmetry by Valadier after the return of Pius VII from France in 1814. It was here that most visitors to Rome used to enter the city, and numerous famous 19C travellers recorded their first arrival in Rome through the Porta del Popolo.

Between four fountains with lions by Valadier (1823) after a 16C design by Domenico Fontana rises an **obelisk** (24m), the hieroglyphs on which celebrate the glories of the pharaohs

Santa Maria dei Miracoli and Santa Maria in Montesanto, Piazza del Popolo

Rameses II and Merenptah (13C–12C BC); Augustus brought it from Heliopolis, after the conquest of Egypt, and it was dedicated to the Sun in the Circus Maximus. Domenico Fontana moved it here in 1589, as part of the urban plan of Sixtus V.

The three streets which converge on the piazza from the south are Via di Ripetta on the left, the Corso in the middle, and Via del Babuino from Piazza di Spagna (see Walk 8) on the right. The ends of the streets are separated by a pair of decorative Baroque churches (not always open), **Santa Maria dei Miracoli** to the left or west, and **Santa Maria in Montesanto** to the right or east; the façades were modified by Bernini and Carlo Fontana (1671–78), after Carlo Rainaldi. In the centre of each hemicycle is a fountain with marble groups, on the left, *Neptune with Two Tritons*, on the right, *Rome between the Tiber and the Anio*, both by Giovanni Ceccarini (1824), and at the ends are more Neo-classical statues of the *Four Seasons*. A winding road designed by Valadier, Viale Gabriele d'Annunzio, descends from the Pincio Hill past the abundant monumental fountain or *mostra* at the termination of the Acqua Vergine Nuova. From here there is a good view of the piazza, in which there is the well-known fashionable café, *Rosati*.

Santa Maria del Popolo

Across the piazza, to the right of the gate, rises the flank of Santa Maria del Popolo (**Map 2**; **2**). The early Renaissance façade is attributed to Andrea Bregno. Open daily 07.00–12.00 and 16.00–19.00; fest. 08.00–13.30 and 16.30–19.00. The church stands on the site of a chapel erected by Paschal II in 1099 over the tombs of the Domitia family. Because Nero was buried there it was believed to be the haunt of demons. The Pope solemnly cut down a walnut tree that was supposed to shelter them in the form of black crows. The church, dedicated to the Virgin, was built at the expense of the city (the *popolo Romano*), hence its name. It was rebuilt in 1227 and again under Sixtus IV (1472–77).

The interior was renovated by Bernini and has many important works of art. There are lights in some chapels and in the apse. In the **south aisle** the first chapel (Della Rovere) has *frescoes by Pinturicchio (1485–89); over the altar, the *Adoration of the Child*; in the lunettes (very worn and restored), scenes from the *Life of St Jerome*; on the right, the tomb of Cardinal de Castro (1506), perhaps by Antonio da Sangallo the Younger; on the left, the tomb of Cardinals Cristoforo and Domenico della Rovere (1477) by Mino da Fiesole and Andrea Bregno. The well-designed second chapel (Cybo) has architecture by Carlo Fontana; its marbles are especially rich and varied. The huge altarpiece of the *Assumption and Four Doctors of the Church* is by Maratta; at the sides are the tombs of the Cybo family, and of Bishop Girolamo Foscari (d. 1463).

The third chapel, with a worn majolica pavement, has beautiful and recently restored frescoes by the school of Pinturicchio (1504–07). To the right is the tomb of Giovanni della Rovere (1483) by the school of Andrea Bregno. In the fourth chapel (Costa) the altarpiece (1489) is also by the school of Andrea Bregno. On the right, is the tomb of Marcantonio Albertoni (1485); on the left, the tomb of the founder, Cardinal Giorgio Costa (1508). In the lunettes are frescoes by the school of Pinturicchio (1489). The bronze *effigy of Cardinal Pietro Foscari, formerly attributed to Vecchietta, is now thought to be by Giovanni di Stefano (c 1485).

In the **south transept**, the altarpiece of the *Visitation* by Giovan Maria Morandi is in a frame supported by two angels by Ercole Ferrata and Arrigo

Giardè. On the right is the tomb of Cardinal Lodovico Podocataro of Cyprus (1508). In the dome over the crossing are frescoes by Raffaele Vanni. A corridor, passing an altar from the studio of Andrea Bregno, leads to the sacristy (opened on request) which contains a *tabernacle by Bregno, with a painted *Madonna* of the early Sienese school, and the monuments of Bishop Rocca (d. 1482) and Archbishop Ortega Gomiel of Burgos (d. 1514).

The **triumphal arch** is decorated with fine 17C gilded stuccoed reliefs, and over the high altar is the venerated *Madonna del Popolo*, a 14C painting. The apse of the church behind the altar, with a shell design, is one of Bramante's earliest works in Rome, commissioned by Julius II (there is a light on the left). Here are the two splendid *tombs of Cardinal Girolamo Basso della Rovere (1507) and Cardinal Ascanio Sforza (1505), signed by Andrea Sansovino. The *frescoes high up in the vault—illustrating the *Coronation of the Virgin*, *Evangelists*, *Sibyls*, and *Four Fathers of the Church*—are by Pinturicchio (1508–09). The stained glass, commissioned by Julius II, is by Guillaume de Marcillat.

In the **north transept**, the first chapel to the left of the choir, with a pretty vault, has two dramatic paintings by Caravaggio, the *Crucifixion of St Peter* (right wall) and *Conversion of St Paul* (left wall). These famous masterpieces were executed in 1600–01. The altarpiece of the *Assumption of the Virgin* is by Annibale Carracci, who also designed the frescoes in the barrel-vault above, with attractive stuccoes. In the second chapel to the left of the choir, with another pretty vault, is a marble statue of *St Catherine of Alexandria* by Giulio Mazzoni and two paintings of the *Annunciation* by Giacomo Triga (early 18C). The altarpiece of the *Holy Family* in the north transept, by Bernardino Mei, is in another frame supported by two angels, by Antonio Raggi and Giovanni Antonio Mari, on the left wall is the tomb of Cardinal Bernardo Lonati (late 15C).

In the **north aisle**, the fourth chapel has a 14C wood crucifix, and frescoes by Pieter van Lint. The third chapel has fine monuments to the Mellini family. The earliest ones are low down on the right wall: to the right of the altar is the exquisite small tomb of Cardinal Pietro Mellini (1483). To the left of the altar is a bust of *Urbano Mellini* by Algardi. The *tomb of Giovanni Garzia Mellini on the left wall, with a half-figure of the cardinal, is also by Algardi. The second chapel is the well-lit, octagonal *Chigi Chapel**, founded by the great banker Agostino Chigi (1465–1520). It was designed as a fusion of architecture, sculpture and painting by Raphael (1513–16). Work on the chapel was interrupted in 1520 with the deaths of both Agostino and Raphael, and it was only completed after 1652 for Cardinal Fabio Chigi (Alexander VII) by Bernini. Raphael prepared the cartoons for the *mosaics in the dome, executed by the Venetian artist Luigi de Pace in 1516. These represent *God the Father as Creator of the Firmament*, surrounded by symbols of the seven known planets, each of which is guided by an angel, as in Dante's conception. The frescoes depicting the *Creation* and the *Fall*, between the windows, and the medallions of the *Seasons*, are by Salviati (1552–54). The altarpiece of the *Nativity of the Virgin* is by Sebastiano del Piombo (1530–34); the bronze bas-relief in front, depicting *Christ and the Woman of Samaria*, by Lorenzetto, was intended for the base of the pyramidal tomb of Agostino, but was moved here by Bernini. By the altar are statues of the prophets *Jonah* (left), designed by Raphael and executed by Lorenzetto, and *Habakkuk* (right) by Bernini; by the entrance are the prophets *Daniel*, with the lion, by Bernini and *Elijah*, by Lorenzetto. The remarkable pyramidal form of the tombs of Agostino

Chigi and of his brother Sigismondo (d. 1526), executed by Lorenzetto, were dictated by Raphael's architectural scheme and derived from ancient Roman models. They were altered by Bernini. The unfinished burial crypt below the chapel, with another pyramid, would in Raphael's original design have been visible and illuminated from the chapel above. The lunettes above the tombs were painted by Raffaele Vanni in 1653. The marble intarsia figure of *Death*, with the Chigi stemma, in the centre of the pavement was added by Bernini.

On the left of the chapel is a colourful funerary monument, erected in 1771 in memory of Princess Odescalchi. In the **baptistery** are two ciboria by Andrea Bregno, and the tombs of Cardinals Francesco Castiglione (1568) to the right and Antonio Pallavicini (1507). The former Augustinian convent adjoining the church was the residence in Rome of Martin Luther during his mission as a priest here in 1511. It was only nine years later that Leo X issued a bull against his writings which Luther burnt publicly in the square of Wittenberg: his subsequent excommunication marked the beginning of the German Reformation.

At the back of the church, near the steps from the Pincio, the Sala del Bramante is used for exhibitions.

Beside the church stands the monumental and historic **Porta del Popolo** (Map 2; 2), which occupies almost the same site as the ancient Porta Flaminia. The outer face is by Nanni di Baccio Bigio (1561), who followed a design by Michelangelo. Two colossal statues of *St Peter* and *St Paul* in the niches, late works by Francesco Mochi, were removed in 1979. The two side arches were opened in 1879. Outside the gate, in the busy Piazzale Flaminio, is an entrance to the huge park of the Villa Borghese (see Walk 17).

Queen Christina of Sweden

Queen Christina of Sweden (1626–89) was the daughter of the Protestant King Gustavus Adolpus, whom she succeeded in 1632. A clever and beautiful woman, she abdicated in 1654, and converted to Roman Catholicism. In 1655 she made a triumphant entry into Rome through Porta del Popolo, on horseback and dressed as an Amazon: the inner face of the gate was redesigned in her honour by Gian Lorenzo Bernini, who was her great admirer and close friend. In the 1660s she took up permanent residence in the city, under the aegis of the pope, and received the leading artists and writers of Rome in Palazzo Riario alla Lungara. She was an important intellectual figure in the city, and founded an academy in 1680 for literary and political discussions (see p 330). She died in Palazzo Corsini, is buried in the grottoes of St Peter's, and left her library to the Vatican.

---

8 • Piazza di Spagna and the Pincio

Piazza di Spagna was for centuries the focus of the artistic and literary life of the city. Foreign travellers usually chose their lodgings in the pensioni and hotels in its vicinity, and here the English colony congregated. John Evelyn, on his first visit to Rome in 1644, stayed near the piazza, Keats died in a house on the square and the British Consul formerly had his office here. The Brownings' Roman residence was nearby (at the corner of Via Bocca di Leone and Vicolo del Lupo). To this day a delightful English 'tea-room' is still open in the square, and the English church is in the neighbouring Via del Babuino.

Today the piazza is the place which perhaps best characterises the opulent air of Rome, since it is in the pedestrian streets which lead from it down to the Corso—Via Condotti, Via Frattina and Via Borgognone—that the most elegant shops are to be found, and some of the grandest old-established Roman hotels are nearby. The famous Spanish Steps provide a theatrical background to the piazza, always busy with tourists and Romans. In addition to Keats' house, the elegant apartment of the painter Giorgio de Chirico almost next door can also be visited. Both give a remarkable insight into Roman residences of their day. Close to the top of the Spanish Steps is the Villa Medici which retains its splendid 16C garden (limited access, see below), the most important one to have survived in the middle of Rome. The public gardens of the Pincio, a famous promenade in the 19C, still offer splendid views of Rome but have lost some of their atmosphere.

Piazza di Spagna

In the centre of the long and irregular Piazza di Spagna (**Map 3**; **3**) is the **Fontana della Barcaccia**, a delightful fountain, once thought to be the masterpiece of Pietro Bernini, but now usually considered to be the work of his famous son Gian Lorenzo. The design of a leaking boat is well adapted to the low water-pressure of the fountain. The theatrical **Scalinata della Trinità dei Monti** or **Spanish Steps** were built in 1723–26 by Francesco de Sanctis to connect the piazza with the church of the Trinità dei Monti and the Pincio, and are a masterpiece of 18C town planning. The monumental flight of 137 steps, which rises between picturesque houses, some with garden terraces, has always been a well-loved haunt of Romans and foreigners. The steps are covered with tubs of magnificent azaleas at the beginning of May.

In an elegant pink 18C house marked with a plaque, on the right as you look up the steps, is the apartment with a little vine-covered terrace where the poet John Keats spent the last three months of his life. It is now the **Keats-Shelley Memorial House** and retains the atmosphere of that time. Open Mon–Fri 09.00–13.00 and 15.00–18.00; Sat 11.00–14.00 and 15.00–18.00; closed Sun. ☎ 06 678 4235. The entrance is at no. 26 in the piazza; the museum is on the second floor. The house was a small *pensione* in 1820, when Keats booked rooms for himself and his friend Joseph Severn, having been advised by his doctor to spend the winter in Rome. Keats led what he himself described as a 'posthumous life' here until his death from tuberculosis on 23 February 1821, aged 25. He was buried in the Protestant Cemetery (see p 109). Severn came back to Rome as British Consul 1860–72, and when he died in 1879 at the age of 85 he chose to be buried next to Keats.

The house was purchased in 1906 by

The Spanish Steps

the Keats-Shelley Memorial Association and first opened to the public in 1909 as a delightful little museum and library dedicated to the English writers Keats, Percy Bysshe Shelley, Lord Byron and Leigh Hunt, all of whom spent much time in Italy.

The library contains over 9000 volumes and numerous autograph letters and manuscripts. Material relating to Shelley and Byron, including a painting of *Shelley at the Baths of Caracalla* by Severn, is displayed in the Salone. The kitchen was in the small room opening onto a terrace on the Spanish Steps, and Severn's room now contains mementoes of Severn, Leigh Hunt, Samuel Taylor Coleridge and William Wordsworth. Here is displayed a reliquary of Pius V which was later used as a locket for the hair of John Milton and Elizabeth Barrett Browning and was owned by Leigh Hunt (see Keats' poem *Lines on Seeing a Lock of Milton's Hair*). The death mask of Keats, and a sketch by Severn of the poet on his deathbed, are preserved in the little room where he died. The Landmark Trust in the UK has the use of the apartment above the museum, and it is available for short rents; for information, ☎ (44) 01628 825 925.

The house opposite across the Spanish Steps, which retains its fine deep russet colour, was built by De Sanctis to form a pair with Keats's house. Here, *Babington's English Tea Rooms*, a charming old-fashioned café (which also serves lunch), survive. Open daily 09.00–20.30. You pay extra for your memorable surroundings.

At no. 31 Piazza di Spagna, a few doors along from the Keats museum, is the **Casa Museo di Giorgio de Chirico**, opened to the public in 1998. The apartment on the fifth floor was the home and studio of Giorgio de Chirico (1888–1978), one of the most important European painters of the early 20C, famous as the inventor of the Metaphysical style of painting before the First World War. Visits (maximum of 15 people) by previous appointment Tues–Sat 10.00–13.00. ☎ and 🖷 06 679 6546.

De Chirico lived here from 1947 until his death and is buried in the church of San Francesco a Ripa (see p 228). His Polish wife Isabella Far, who died in 1990, established a foundation dedicated to the artist in 1986. The house gives a fascinating glimpse of a delightful Roman residence, as well as providing a very clear idea of the artistic achievements of De Chirico, since the 50 works here were chosen and hung by the painter himself, and his home and studio remain as they were furnished at his death. Most of the works date from the 1960s and 1970s: his earliest period is less well documented. The house has three floors, with the bedrooms and studio—containing objects and terracotta models as he left them—on the upper floor with a terrace above. On the main floor the living-room has some important self-portraits dating from the 1940s (and one painted in 1959), as well as portraits of his wife. The dining-room has numerous lovely still-lifes, and the last room has some Metaphysical works, including copies made by the artist of his earliest paintings.

In the fashionable **Via Condotti** (**Map 3; 5**), named after the conduits of the Acqua Vergine, is the renowned *Caffè Greco*, founded in 1760 and a national monument since 1953. It retains its delightful interior, with numerous little sitting-rooms with small round marble tables. It is decorated with personal mementoes and self-portraits of some of its most famous patrons who included Goethe (see p 155), Nikolai Gogol, Hector Berlioz, Stendhal, Hippolyte Taine, Charles Baudelaire, Bertel Thorvaldsen and Richard Wagner. The 17C palace at no. 68 is the headquarters of the Sovereign Military Order of Malta, or the order of the Knights of St John of Jerusalem, which is accorded extraterritorial rights by the Italian State (see p 318).

North of Piazza di Spagna: Via del Babuino

The piazza is particularly attractive at its northern end, where there is a row of 18C houses and four tall palm trees, and a flower stall. **Via del Babuino** (Map 3; 3), opened in 1525, connects Piazza di Spagna with Piazza del Popolo and is famous for its antique shops. The street takes its name from one of Rome's 'talking' statues (see p 198) known as **Babuino**, from the word for baboon, signifying 'dolt' or 'fool'. This is in fact a very worn Roman statue of a reclining Silenus, which was used to decorate a fountain set up here after 1571 by the local residents by order of Pius V, in return for the Pope's concession of water from the newly restored Acqua Vergine for the numerous gardens and orchards that used to exist in this district at the foot of the Pincio. It was one of the first fountains in the city erected by private citizens for the use of the public. It was recomposed in the street in 1957 above a small antique marble fountain basin next to a florist's stand; on the wall behind (which was once an artist's studio) it is still the custom to write up slogans against the present rulers of Rome and Italy.

The church of **Sant'Atanasio dei Greci** was designed by Giacomo della Porta. On the right, near Vicolo Alibert, was the studio in which the Danish sculptor Thorvaldsen succeeded his English colleague John Flaxman as occupant. The neo-Gothic Anglican church of **All Saints** (Map 3; 3) was built in 1882 by G.E. Street.

Parallel to Via del Babuino (on the right) is the 16C **Via Margutta**, the residence of Dutch and Flemish painters in the 17C. Here, at no. 53, Sir Thomas Lawrence founded the British Academy of Arts in 1821. It is still a street of artists with art galleries and studios with interesting courtyards and gardens towards the Pincio, and in spring and autumn a street fair is held where paintings are for sale.

South of Piazza di Spagna

The southern end of Piazza di Spagna runs into Piazza Mignanelli, where the **Column of the Immaculate Conception** (1857) commemorates the establishment by Pius IX in 1854 of the dogma of the Immaculate Conception of the Virgin Mary. Here is Palazzo di Spagna, the residence since 1622 of the Spanish ambassador to the Vatican, which gave the main piazza its name. It is a good building with a fine courtyard by Antonio del Grande (1647).

Between Via Due Macelli and Via di Propaganda running off the southern end of the piazza is the Collegio di Propaganda Fide, with a façade by Francesco Borromini on Via di Propaganda (1622). The detailed friezes are particularly fine. The college, which has the privilege of extraterritoriality, was founded for the training of missionaries (including young foreigners) by Urban VIII as an annexe to the Congregazione di Propaganda Fide established by Gregory XV in 1622.

Beyond, in Via Capo le Case, is the church of **Sant'Andrea delle Fratte** (Map

3; 5), which belonged to the Scots before the Reformation. The composer Alessandro Scarlatti was married here in 1678. The unfinished tower and refined, fantastical campanile, both by Borromini, were designed to make their greatest impression when seen from Via Capo le Case.

In the second chapel on the right is the tomb of Judith Falconnet (1856), with a recumbent figure by the American artist Harriet Hosmer. To the left of the side door is the epitaph of Angelica Kauffmann (1741–1807). The Swiss painter came to live in Rome in 1781 and soon became the centre of the foreign artistic community in the city, where she was greatly admired by Goethe. She was extremely wealthy and one of the most successful Neo-classical painters of her time, well-known for her portraits. Earlier in her career she had lived in London where she had been a founding member of the Royal Academy and a close friend of Sir Joshua Reynolds. Works by her can still be seen in Rome at the Accademia di San Luca and the Galleria Nazionale in Palazzo Barberini.

Rubens and Poussin in Rome

The famous Flemish painter **Peter Paul Rubens** (1577–1640) spent his last two years in Italy (1606–08) in a house on Via del Babuino. The eight years Rubens stayed in Italy were essential to his formation as an artist—indeed, he usually signed his works in Italian (PietroPaolo)—and were to have a lasting influence over the development of his very successful career. He collected antiquities, read widely in the classics, and even wrote a book on the customs of the ancient Romans. While in Rome he met Adam Elsheimer, who taught him etching, and bought Caravaggio's *Death of the Virgin*, and his style on his return to Antwerp on the death of his mother was indebted to both Caravaggio and the Carracci. The only paintings by him still in a church in Rome are the three commissioned from him in 1608 for the Chiesa Nuova (see p 207). The first version of the altarpiece was not a success because it caught the light, and was replaced by another painted on slate: Rubens took the rejected painting back to Antwerp and placed it on his mother's grave. Other works by him in Rome are in the Galleria Borghese, Pinacoteca Capitolina, Palazzo Corsini, Galleria Pallavicini, Galleria dell'Accademia di San Luca, and the Pinacoteca Vaticana.

The painter **Nicolas Poussin** (1594–1665), who was to have such a fundamental influence on French painting, first came to Rome in 1624, taking lodgings in Via del Babuino two years later. At first he worked in the studios of Domenichino, but by 1628 had been commissioned to produce an altarpiece for St Peter's (see p 355). After a brief visit to France in 1640 he returned to Rome in 1642 and remained there the rest of his life. He worked mainly in the city under the patronage of Cardinal Maffeo Barberini (later Urban VIII) and his secretary, Cassiano dal Pozzo, who became his closest friend. From Rome Poussin absorbed the influence of antique cameos, of Titian and Raphael, and the Roman Campagna. He became famous for his Classical landscapes and historical paintings based on ancient mythology. Poussin married his landlord's daughter, Anne Marie Dughet, sister of Gaspard Dughet, who became a well-known landscape painter (known as 'Il Poussin'). Poussin died in Rome and is buried in the church of San Lorenzo in Lucina (see p 151).

The cupola and apse were decorated in the 17C by Pasquale Marini, and the three huge paintings depicting the *Crucifixion, Death* and *Burial of St Andrew* are by Giovanni Battista Lenardi, Lazzaro Baldi and Francesco Trevisani. By the high altar are two beautiful *Angels* by Bernini, sculpted for Ponte Sant'Angelo but replaced on the bridge by copies. The **cloister** has a pretty little garden with cypresses and orange trees.

South of the church, in Via del Nazareno, can be seen remains of the **Acqua Vergine** aqueduct. For admission, ☎ 06 6710 3819.

Via Capo le Case ascends to Via Francesco Crispi where, in the former Carmelite convent of San Giuseppe, the **Galleria Comunale d'Arte Moderna** (Map 3; 5) is temporarily arranged in seven rooms. Open 09.00–18.30; fest. 09.00–13.30; closed Mon. ☎ 06 474 2848.

Although the paintings are interesting as representative of some of the best 20C Italian artists, the arrangement is poor and the rooms are shabby. The sculpture on the **ground floor** includes a work by Giacomo Manzù. On the **first floor**, room 1 exhibits paintings by Nino Costa, Ercole Rosa and Aristide Sartorio; sculptures by Ettore Ximenes and Vincenzo Gemito; and two busts by Rodin. Room 2 has some landscapes by Sartorio. Room 3 displays Giacomo Balla's *portrait of Ernesto Nathan* (1910) and *Il Dubbio* (1907–08) and a bronze, *Conca dei Bufali*, by Duilio Cambellotti. On the **second floor**, room 4 has works by Armando Spadini and Primo Conti. On the **third floor**, room 5 has paintings by Francesco Trombadori, Felice Casorati, Ferruccio Ferrazzi, Virgilio Guidi, Emanuele Cavalli, Mario Mafai, Scipione, Mario Sironi, Carlo Carrà, Filippo De Pisis, Antonio Donghi and Felice Carena. Room 6 has more works by Cavalli, and paintings by Alberto Savinio, etchings by Giorgio Morandi, and a mosaic by Gino Severini.

Via Crispi and Via Due Macelli meet at the busy Via del Tritone, across which Via del Traforo leads to the Traforo Umberto I (**Map 3**; 5), a road tunnel under the Quirinal Gardens, 347m long, built in 1902–05. The area to the south of Via del Tritone, with the Fontana di Trevi, is described on p 169.

Piazza della Trinità dei Monti

On the terrace at the top of the Spanish Steps is Piazza della Trinità dei Monti with its church. From the balustrade there is a fine view of Rome with the dome of St Peter's in the distance, beyond the dome of Santi Ambrogio e Carlo al Corso, and to the left the top of the Column of Marcus Aurelius. On the near right can be seen the Villa Medici (described below). The **obelisk** here, probably brought to Rome in the 2C or 3C AD, when the hieroglyphs were copied from those on the obelisk in Piazza del Popolo, formerly stood in the Gardens of Sallust (see p 265). It was set up here in 1788 by Pius VI.

The church of the **Trinità dei Monti** (Map 3; 3), attached to the French Convent of the Minims, was begun in 1493 by Louis XII. It was restored at the expense of Louis XVIII after damage caused by Napoleon's occupation in 1816. Usually open daily 10.00–13.00 and 16.00–18.30; when closed, ring at the door of the small side staircase on the left.

The unusual 16C façade has a **double staircase** by Domenico Fontana. The interior is divided by a grille into two parts, only one of which may ordinarily be visited. The first chapel on the **south side** has an altarpiece and frescoes by

Giovanni Battista Naldini. The third chapel is decorated to a plan by Daniele da Volterra (executed by his pupils) and contains an **Assumption* by him that includes a portrait of Michelangelo (the last figure on the right). The painting has a remarkable design but is in very poor condition. In the second chapel on the north side is a **Descent from the Cross* by the same painter, possibly executed from a design by his master: it is an especially fine work although very damaged, since it was transferred to canvas in 1811.

The other part of the church contains **frescoes by Perino del Vaga, Giulio Romano and others, in finely decorated chapels. In the **north transept** the fourth chapel on the left has the *Assumption* and *Death of the Virgin* by Taddeo Zuccari, finished by his brother Federico. The vault is painted by Perino del Vaga. Excavations by the French Academy beneath the convent have revealed traces of a Roman building which seems to have had a terrace on the hillside similar in form to the Spanish Steps (see below).

From the piazza there is a good view of the long and straight **Via Sistina** (**Map 3**; **3, 5**), which descends to Piazza Barberini (see Walk 16) and then ascends the Quirinal Hill as Via delle Quattro Fontane. This handsome thoroughfare was laid out by Sixtus V as the Strada Felice, which ran for some 3km via Santa Maria Maggiore all the way to Santa Croce in Gerusalemme. Most of the illustrious visitors to Rome between the days of Napoleon and 1870 seem to have lodged in this street. Gogol (1809–52) lived at no. 126; no. 48 housed in succession Giovanni Battista Piranesi (1720–78), Thorvaldsen and the architect and archaeologist Luigi Canina (1795–1856). At the top end the street still has some old-established luxury hotels and elegant shops.

In the triangle formed between Via Sistina and Via Gregoriana is the charming and bizarre **Palazzo Zuccari**, built by the artist Federico Zuccari as his residence and studio. Sir Joshua Reynolds lived here in 1752–53 and the German archae-ologist Winckelmann in 1755–68. In 1900 it was bought by Enrichetta Hertz, who left her library, with the palace, to the German government. The **Biblioteca Hertziana** is now one of the most famous art history libraries in the country (closed for several years for restoration). The entrance on Via Gregoriana has an amusing portal and two windows in the form of gaping monsters.

Villa Medici
In the other direction, Viale della Trinità dei Monti leads along the edge of the hill to the Villa Medici (**Map 3**; **3**), the seat of the French Academy since 1803. It is still one of the most important cultural institutes in Europe, and the most beautiful villa to have preserved its garden in the centre of Rome. The garden front, which can only be seen on a guided tour, is particularly handsome and interesting for its Classical sculptures. Its two towers make it one of the most conspicuous buildings on the skyline of Rome, almost always visible from a distance.

Opening times
Guided tours of the gardens Feb–May on Sat, Sun at 10.30 and 11.30. These times are subject to change: to check, ☎ 06 67611. The villa is only open for exhibitions, but these are normally of the highest interest.

History of the Villa Medici

The villa built by Nanni di Baccio Bigio and Annibale Lippi for Cardinal Ricci da Montepulciano in 1564–74 was bought in 1576 by Cardinal Ferdinando dei Medici, who succeeded his brother Francesco I as Grand-Duke of Tuscany in 1587. He enlarged it with the help of Bartolomeo Ammannati and the villa became known as one of the grandest residences in the city. Cardinal Ferdinando's famous collection of ancient Roman sculpture was kept here: he had the garden façade decorated with Classical sculpture and the garden itself decorated with ancient busts and statues. In 1775 the masterpieces of the collection (including the so-called *Medici Venus*, the *Wrestlers* and the *Niobe* group) were transferred to the Uffizi gallery in Florence, while the less important pieces were used to decorate the Boboli gardens in the same city. Apart from the colossal statue of the *Dea Roma* still in the garden, the only piece which has remained in Rome is a head of *Meleager*, which might even be an original by Skopas (it is now in a private room of the villa). The apartment of Ferdinando was decorated by Jacopo Zucchi. Cardinal Alessandro dei Medici, who became Pope Leo XI in 1605, also lived in the palace. In the 17C Velázquez was a tenant, and Galileo was confined here by the Inquisition in 1630–33.

In 1801 the villa was bought by Napoleon and the French Academy, founded in 1666 by Louis XIV, was transferred here. Students at the École des Beaux-Arts in Paris, who are aged between 20 and 35 and who win the Prix de Rome for painting, sculpture, architecture, engraving or music (or, since 1968, for cinema, history of art, restoration, photography or stage design), are sent to study here for periods of between six months and two years at the expense of the French government. Well-known French artists and musicians who stayed here as scholars (known as *pensionnaires*) included Berlioz, Claude Debussy and Ingres. Women were admitted for the first time in the early 20C. The famous painter known as Balthus was director here 1961–77. Of Polish origin, his real name was Baltazar Klossowski de Rola and he was born in Paris in 1908, and died in 2001. He was responsible for a number of important restoration projects, the decoration of many of the rooms and the exhibition gallery on the ground floor.

The villa is famous for its beautiful 16C **garden**, with long vistas through hedged walks of laurel and box and numerous ilex trees. The tall umbrella pines were planted in the 18C. The custom of decorating gardens with sculpture originated in Hellenistic times and numerous gardens in ancient Rome were famous for their sculptures. The grand Renaissance villas continued this tradition. The busts and statues once here have now all been replaced by copies except for the colossal Roman statue of the **Dea Roma**, which was given by Pope Gregory XIII to Ferdinando dei Medici. The group of *Niobe and her Children* on the lawn nearby are copies of the originals found in a vineyard near the Lateran in 1583 and formerly kept in the garden but transferred to the Uffizi in Florence in the 18C. The little **garden pavilion** on the Aurelian Walls, used as a retreat by Ferdinando dei Medici (but now disturbed by the busy road below), is also shown to visitors: its charming painted decoration by Jacopo Zucchi (1576–77), with a pergola inhabited by numerous birds, was discovered in 1985. In the vestibule are grotesques and three interesting painted views of the villa, showing it in

1564 as it was when first built for Cardinal Ricci da Montepulciano; the modifications, including the garden, made by Ferdinando dei Medici in 1574; and the original layout of the garden in three distinct parts, the labyrinth with hedges, the formal garden in front of the villa, and the ilex *bosco* beyond.

The splendid **garden façade** of the villa overlooking the formal garden—recently restored to its ivory colour—was decorated by Ferdinando dei Medici with numerous ancient Roman statues, medallions, columns, garlands and bas-reliefs from sarcophagi, including four delicately carved panels dating from AD 43. Some of the reliefs are thought to have come from a Roman altar similar to the Ara Pacis (see p 152). In front of the loggia was placed Giambologna's famous bronze statue of *Mercury*, commissioned for this site and now replaced by a copy; the original is in the Bargello museum in Florence. The obelisk in the formal garden in front (recently replanted) was made in 1961 by Balthus. Excavations of a Roman house, from which mosaic pavements have been found, as well as edifices dating from the 5C AD are being carried out here as part of a major research programme funded for the period between 1981 and 2006. The Roman statues of Dacian prisoners are copies of the originals taken to Florence in 1788, and now in the Boboli gardens. Above a beautiful terrace—the library wing of the villa—is the well-preserved ilex *bosco* (not usually shown on the tour of the garden) in which steps lead up to a belvedere from which there are splendid views over the tops of the trees. In the garden beyond are the residences of the students of the Academy.

In a group of ilexes across the road in front of Villa Medici is a charming **fountain**, with an ancient Roman red granite vase, which was designed in 1589 by Annibale Lippi. The lovely view—with the fountain in the foreground in a bower of trees and the rooftops of Rome beyond stretching as far as the dome of St Peter's—is familiar from many paintings, including one by Camille Corot dated 1828, although it is now impaired by a scraggy line of ugly fir trees which have grown up in a garden just below. The cannon ball is said to have been shot from Castel Sant'Angelo by Queen Christina of Sweden, when late for an appointment with the painter Charles Errard who was staying at the French Academy.

The gently sloping Viale della Trinità dei Monti ends at a monument by Ercole Rosa (1883) to the brothers Enrico and Giovanni Cairoli, who, as supporters of Garibaldi, died in 1867. From this point Viale d'Annunzio descends to Piazza del Popolo while Viale Mickiewicz ascends to the Pincio.

The Pincio

The Pincio (**Map 3**; **1**) was laid out as a Romantic park by Giuseppe Valadier in 1809–14 on the Pincian Hill (46m). Adjoining the Villa Borghese, it forms the largest public garden in the centre of Rome and it is especially crowded on holidays. The *view from the terrace of the Piazzale Napoleone is dominated by the dome of St Peter's.

History of the Pincio

The Pincian Hill was known as the *Collis Hortulorum* of ancient Rome because it used to be covered with the monumental gardens of the Roman aristocracy and emperors. In the 4C it was owned by the Pinci family, from whom the name of the hill is derived. Excavations have found traces of 1C walls here.

The Pincio was the most fashionable Roman *passeggiata* in the 19C, when the aristocracy and foreign visitors came here in their carriages to hear the band play and admire the sunset. Nathaniel Hawthorne was one of many foreign visitors who observed the crowded scene: 'Here, in the sunny afternoon roll and rumble all kinds of carriages, from the cardinal's old fashioned and gorgeous purple carriage to the gay barouche of modern date.' Joseph Severn described his walks here with Keats in 1820–21 while they were staying above the Spanish Steps, during which they frequently met Pauline Borghese, Napoleon's sister.

On a terrace is the ***Casina Valadier*** (1813–17), now an open-air café, though often closed. Among the habitués of its most sumptuous period as a fashionable restaurant were Richard Strauss, Benito Mussolini, King Farouk, Mahatma Gandhi and Chiang Kai-shek. The view from its terrace is even better than that from Piazzale Napoleone. Nearby can be seen the monumental entrance to the garden of Villa Medici with the colossal Roman statue of ***Dea Roma***.

The park is intersected by broad avenues passing between magnificent trees, many of them remarkable specimens of their kind. One of these avenues, Viale dell'Obelisco, runs east to join Viale delle Magnolie in the park of the Villa Borghese (see Walk 17). The **obelisk** which gives the avenue its name was placed here in 1822: it was found in the 16C outside the Porta Maggiore, where it may have decorated the Circus Varianus. The hieroglyphs suggest that it was originally erected by Hadrian on the tomb of his lover Antinous, who drowned in the Nile in 130. It may have been transported from Egypt by Elagabalus in the 3C. Throughout the park are busts of celebrated Italians from the days of ancient Rome to the present time. Of the fountains, the most notable are the Water Clock, in Viale dell'Orologio, and the Fountain of Moses.

The Pincio is bounded on the north and east by massive walls, part of which is the **Muro Torto**, or *Murus Ruptus*, the only stretch of the Aurelian Wall that was not fortified by Belisarius against the Goths: he was prevented from doing so by the Romans who told him it would be defended by St Peter. The wall has for centuries seemed on the point of collapsing. Viale del Muro Torto, at the foot of the Pincio, is a busy road running outside the wall from Piazzale Flaminio to Porta Pinciana.

9 • The Fontana di Trevi district

The Trevi fountain is the most famous of all the fountains of Rome, and its most magnificent. In a tiny piazza closed to traffic it is also one of the most accessible fountains in the city. This chapter also describes two interesting but little-visited picture galleries, that of the Accademia di San Luca and the Galleria Colonna (open only on Saturdays). The church of Santi Apostoli has a Baroque interior and interesting papal tombs.

Fontana di Trevi

The huge Fontana di Trevi (**Map 3; 5**) is one of the most famous sights of Rome, and one of the city's most exuberant and successful 18C monuments. The abundant water, which forms an essential part of the design, fills the little piazza with its sound.

History of the Fontana di Trevi

The name Trevi may come from *tre vie*, referring to the three roads which converged here. Its waters are those of the Acqua Vergine Antica aqueduct, almost entirely underground, which Agrippa brought to Rome from a spring some 20km east of the city to supply his public baths near the Pantheon in 19 BC. It remained in use throughout the Middle Ages, was restored by Pius V in 1570, and still feeds the fountains of Piazza di Spagna, Piazza Navona and Piazza Farnese.

The original 15C fountain was a simple and beautiful basin by Leon Battista Alberti; it was restored by Urban VIII, who is said to have obtained the necessary funds from a tax on wine. Many famous architects, including Bernini, Ferdinando Fuga and Gaspare Vanvitelli presented projects for a new fountain. In 1732 Clement XII held a competition and the little-known Roman architect and poet Nicola Salvi was given the commission. His theatrical design incorporated, as a background, the entire Neo-classical façade of Palazzo Poli, which had been completed in 1730.

The fountain was completed in 1762, after Salvi's death, by others including Pietro Bracci, who carved the tritons. It was restored for the first time in 1989–91.

The palace façade has niches containing the figures of **Neptune** flanked by statues symbolising **Health** and **Abundance**; on the enormous artificial rock built out of tufo two giant tritons, one blowing a conch, conduct the winged chariot of Neptune pulled by horses which appear to gallop through the water. The bas-reliefs above represent the legendary virgin from which the aqueduct took its name, pointing out the spring to the Roman soldiers, and Agrippa approving the plans for the aqueduct. The four statues above these represent the **Seasons** with their gifts. At the summit are the arms of the Corsini family, with two allegorical figures.

There is still a rooted tradition—which seems to have grown up only at the end of the 19C—that if you throw a coin into the fountain before your departure

from the city it will bring good luck and ensure your return. The coins are collected every Monday morning when the fountain's pump mechanism has to be turned off for cleaning by the city's waterworks department. The Euros go into the municipality's coffers, while the foreign coins are donated to the Italian Red Cross. The last scene of the American film *Three Coins in the Fountain* (1954) was filmed here, and the Trevi fountain has been a feature of numerous Italian films, including Federico Fellini's *La Dolce Vita* (1959), which has a famous scene in which Anita Ekberg takes a dip in its waters.

The Fontana di Trevi

Opposite the fountain is the church of **Santi Vincenzo ed Anastasio**, rebuilt in 1630, with a Baroque façade by Martino Longhi the Younger. In the crypt of this church, the parish church of the neighbouring pontifical palace of the Quirinal, are preserved the hearts and lungs of almost all the popes from Sixtus V (d. 1590) to Leo XIII (d. 1903).

Via del Lavatore diverges right to Vicolo di Scanderbeg which leads to Piazza Scanderbeg, where the **Museo Nazionale delle Paste Alimentari**, despite its name, is a private museum that illustrates the history of pasta. Open daily 09.30–17.30. ☎ 06 699 1119.

Via della Stamperia runs north to the right of the Fontana di Trevi past the garden of the Accademia di San Luca (see below), opposite the **Calcografia Nazionale** or Calcografia di Roma, the most important collection of copper-plate engravings in the world. Open Mon–Sat 09.00–13.00; closed Sun. The collection was formed in 1738 by Clement XII and moved in 1837 to its present site; the building is by Luigi Valadier. It contains almost all the engravings of Giovanni Battista Piranesi (1432 plates) and examples of the work of Marcantonio Raimondi, Rossini, Bartolommeo Pinelli and many others among a total of more than 19,600 plates. Exhibitions are often held; any items not on display can be seen on request, and copies purchased. The institute also owns Palazzo Poli next door.

Galleria dell'Accademia di San Luca

The street opens out into Piazza dell'Accademia di San Luca. Here is **Palazzo Carpegna** (Map 3; 5), seat of the Accademia di San Luca, founded in 1577 by the painter Girolamo Muziano of Brescia, which incorporated the 15C Università dei Pittori (Painters' University) whose members used to meet in the little church of San Luca. Muziano's successor, Federico Zuccari, gave the academy its first statutes, and it soon became famous for its teaching and for its prize competitions.

The eclectic **Galleria dell'Accademia di San Luca** (open Mon Sat 10.00–12.30. ☎ 06 679 8850) contains gifts and bequests from its members, together with donations from other sources. It is arranged on the third floor, reached by a delightful spiral ramp (once used by horse-drawn carriages), lined with busts of former Academicians. In the **first room** are recently restored works including a portrait (of Ippolito Rimanaldo) attributed to Titian; *Mary Magdalene* by Anton Raphael Mengs, and works by Pier Francesco Mola, Sassoferrato, and Bronzino. In **room II** are works awaiting restoration, or of doubtful attribution. **Room III** displays a *Madonna and Child with Angels* by Anthony van Dyck, a plaster sculpture of the *Three Graces* by Bertel Thorvaldsen, and genre scenes by Michel Sweerts. In **room IV** is a *putto*, a fragment of a fresco by Raphael (1512), an imaginary view by Canaletto, *Judith and Holofernes* by Giovan Battista Piazzetta, and works by Sebastiano Conca and Carlo Maratti. **Room V** displays 18C terracotta reliefs including two by Innocenzo Spinazzi and Richard Westmacott. The largest work, trapezoidal in shape, is by Alessandro Algardi. In the **gallery** are a small selection of the Academy's large collection of portraits, with two notable self-portraits by Federico Zuccari, and Elisabeth Vigée le Brun. Here also is a bust of *Piranesi* by Joseph Nollekens.

A painting of *St Luke Painting the Virgin*, begun by Raphael and finished by assistants is kept in the Aula Magna, and on the stairs are works by Thorvaldsen, Francesco Hayez and Aristide Sartorio (Monte Circeo).

Via della Stamperia ends at the busy Via del Tritone: the area on the other side of this street is described, together with Piazza di Spagna, in Walk 8.

From the piazza in front of the Trevi fountain, Via San Vincenzo leads south, crossing Via dell'Umiltà, which leads right to the Corso, and Via della Dataria, which leads left up to the Quirinal Hill. Via dei Lucchesi continues south into Piazza della Pilotta, with the large Università Gregoriana Pontificia (1930). In Via della Pilotta is the entrance to Palazzo Colonna (see below). Via del Vaccaro leads right into the long, thin Piazza dei Santi Apostoli (**Map 3; 7**) beside the little Baroque Palazzo Balestra (formerly Muti), once owned by the Stuarts of Scotland and England.

The Jacobites in Rome

The exiled house of Stuart was descended from James I of England (and VI of Scotland), whose grandson James II was forced to abdicate from the English throne in 1688 because of his Roman Catholic sympathies. Members of this royal line and their supporters became known as Jacobites. James II's son, James Stuart, nicknamed the 'Old Pretender' (1688–1766), first lived in France and then came to Rome where Clement XI presented him with Palazzo Balestra on the occasion of his marriage in 1719 to Clementina Sobieska. Although his wife died in 1735 he continued to live here until his own death, when he was given a grand funeral in St Peter's with no fewer than 22 cardinals present. A portrait of him survives in the Galleria Doria Pamphilj on the Corso (see p 144).

His son, Charles Edward (the Young Pretender or Bonnie Prince Charlie), who was born in Palazzo Balestra in 1720, led the last Jacobite rebellion in Scotland in 1745–46 which ended in his decisive defeat at Culloden, after which he was forced to escape to France and then return to Rome. Here he married Louise de Stolberg and they moved to Florence, where the Prince led a dissolute, drunken life and his wife escaped to a convent with the help of Count Vittorio Alfieri, the Italian poet. Years later, when Alfieri was giving a private performance of one of his plays in the Spanish embassy in Piazza di Spagna, he met Louise again and they lived together for the rest of their lives. Charles died in Palazzo Balestra in 1788.

The Young Pretender's younger brother was Henry, Duke of York (also born in Palazzo Balestra, in 1725), who was made a cardinal, and as 'Henry IX' was the last of the Stuarts. Known as Cardinal York he was given the bishopric of Frascati, just outside Rome in the Alban Hills, where he died in 1807. When the Young Pretender died, his brother saw that his body was buried in the Duomo of Frascati (where his cenotaph remains) before it was moved to the Vatican Grottoes. The Cardinal built a convent on Monte Cavo near Frascati, and restored a chapel in Santa Maria in Trastevere. The three last Stuarts are commemorated in St Peter's with a monument by Antonio Canova (see p 359), paid for in part by King George IV.

On the western side of the piazza is Palazzo Odescalchi, which extends to the Corso; the façade on the piazza is by Bernini, with additions by Niccolò Salvi and Luigi Vanvitelli (1750). The east side of the piazza is occupied by the huge building of Palazzo Colonna (**Map 3; 7**), which incorporates the church of Santi Apostoli.

Santi Apostoli

The church of Santi Apostoli was built by Pelagius I, c 560, to commemorate the defeat and expulsion of the Goths by the Byzantine viceroy Narses, and dedicated to the Apostles James and Philip. It was restored and enlarged in the 15C and 16C and almost completely rebuilt by Carlo and Francesco Fontana in 1702–14. Open daily 07.00–12.00 and 16.00–19.00.

The unusual **façade**, which has the appearance of a palace rather than a church, consists of a stately Renaissance double loggia of nine arches. This is attributed to Baccio Pontelli, and was built at the cost of Cardinal della Rovere, afterwards Pope Julius II. The upper storey was filled in with Baroque windows c 1665 by Carlo Rainaldi, who also added the balustrade with statues of the Apostles. Behind this and above it the Neo-classical façade of the church added by Valadier in 1827 can be seen. In the **portico** (closed by an iron grille), on the left, is the tomb of the engraver Giovanni Volpato, by Antonio Canova (1807). On the right are a *bas-relief found in Trajan's Forum dating from the 2C AD, representing an eagle holding an oak-wreath in its talons; and a lion, signed by Pietro Vassalletto. Two 12C red marble lions flank the entrance portal.

The Baroque **interior** is on a vast scale, with a nave 18m broad. The effect of immensity is enhanced by the manner in which the lines of the vaulting continue those of the massive pillars, and the lines of the apse those of the nave. From the end near the entrance the surprising effect of relief attained by Giovanni Odazzi in his contorted group of *Fallen Angels*, on the vault above the high altar, can be seen. On the ceiling are the *Triumph of the Order of St Francis* by Baciccia and the *Evangelists* by Luigi Fontana.

In the **south aisle**, the first chapel contains a beautiful late-15C *Madonna and Child* by Antoniazzo Romano donated to the church by Cardinal Bessarion (see below). Against the second pillar is a monument to Clementina Sobieska, wife of James Stuart, the Old Pretender, by Filippo della Valle. The chapel at the end of the aisle has eight columns from the 6C church. In the sanctuary the high altar-piece, supposed to be the largest in Rome, of the *Martyrdom of St Philip and St James*, is by Domenico Muratori. On the right are the tombs of Count Giraud de Caprières (1505) and Cardinal Raffaele Riario, perhaps to a design of Michelangelo; on the left is the beautiful monument of Cardinal Pietro Riario, by the school of Andrea Bregno, with a *Madonna* by Mino da Fiesole. Fragments of the exquisite frescoes by Melozzo da Forlì which formerly covered the 15C apse are preserved in the Quirinal and in the Vatican picture gallery.

Steps in front of the sanctuary lead down to the **confessio**. The relics of the Apostles Philip and James are preserved here, and, in the chapel to the left, the beautiful *tomb of Raffaele della Rovere (d. 1477), brother of Sixtus IV and father of Julius II, by Andrea Bregno. The other chapels were charmingly decorated in 1876–77 in the style of the catacombs, and foundations of the earlier church can be seen here.

At the east end of the **north aisle**, around the door into the sacristy, is the first important work in Rome by Canova, the *mausoleum of Clement XIV, a master-piece of Neo-classical art (1783–87). On the second pillar is an epitaph of 1682 dedicated to Cardinal Bessarion (1389–1472), the illustrious Greek scholar, with a 16C portrait of him: his remains were translated here in 1957. In the second chapel is an altarpiece of *St Joseph of Copertino* (the 'flying monk'), by Giuseppe Cades (1777), between two columns of verde antico that are the largest known.

The two Renaissance **cloisters** (entered at no. 51) contain a bas-relief of the *Nativity* by the school of Arnolfo di Cambio; an early Christian sarcophagus; and, in the second cloister, a memorial to Michelangelo, whose body was temporarily placed here in 1564 before his burial in Santa Croce in Florence. Also here is a double inscription in Latin and Greek which was dictated by Cardinal Bessarion for his own tomb.

Galleria Colonna

The Galleria Colonna is one of the most important of the patrician collections in Rome. The very fine collection of paintings is arranged in magnificent Baroque galleries, sumptuously decorated with frescoes, mirrors and antique sculpture, and is beautifully maintained.

Four arches spanning Via della Pilotta connect Palazzo Colonna with the Villa Colonna (no admission), which has a beautiful garden with tall cypresses, part of which can be seen from the Galleria Colonna. In the garden are the remains of the huge Temple of Serapis, built in the time of Caracalla.

Opening times

Sat 09.00–13.00; closed Aug. ☎ 06 678 4350. The Apartment of the Principessa Isabelle can be seen by previous appointment, 🖷 06 6794 638.

The **entrance** is at 17 Via della Pilotta. The paintings, most of them not labelled, are all numbered, and a hand-list in numerical order is given to visitors.

History of the Palazzo and Galleria Colonna

Palazzo Colonna was built by Oddone Colonna, later Martin V, who lived here as pope from 1424 until his death in 1431. It was rebuilt in 1730, and here, on 4 June 1802, after the cession of Piedmont to France, Carlo Emanuele IV of Savoy, King of Sardinia, became a Jesuit and abdicated in favour of his brother Vittorio Emanuele I.

The Galleria Colonna was begun in 1654 by Cardinal Girolamo I Colonna, who employed the architect Antonio del Grande, but it was not completed until nearly 50 years later. On Del Grande's death in 1671, Girolamo Fontana took over direction. In 1703 the gallery was opened by Filippo II Colonna.

From the entrance, stairs mount to the **vestibule**, in which is displayed on an easel a painting (142.) of *St Julian*, attributed to Perino del Vaga.

From the **Hall of the Colonna Bellica**, named after a 16C column of rosso antico surmounted by a statue of *Pallas Athena*, there is a view of the splendid main hall. The ceiling frescoes of the *Reception into Heaven of Marcantonio II Colonna* are by Giuseppe Chiari. On the right of the door, (139.) *Madonna and Child, with St Peter and Donor* by Palma Vecchio; opposite, on the window wall, (25.) *Holy Family, with St Jerome and St Lucy* by Bonifacio Veronese. Between the windows: (32.) *Venus with Cupid and a Satyr* by Bronzino; opposite, (117.) *Venus and Cupid* by Michele di Ridolfo del Ghirlandaio; above, also between the windows and by Ghirlandaio, (116.) *Night* and, opposite, (115.) *Dawn*; below, (189.) *Narcissus* by Jacopo Tintoretto. On the right and left of the steps, (106.) portrait of *Cardinal Pompeo Colonna* attributed to Lorenzo Lotto, and (147.) portrait of *Pius V* by Scipione Pulzone.

On the steps leading down to the Great Hall is preserved a cannon ball which fell here on 24 June 1849, during the siege of Rome. The **Great Hall** is superbly decorated with mirrors, chandeliers, antique sculpture (fine bas-reliefs and sarcophagi fragments are set into the walls beneath the windows, and into statue pedestals), as well as paintings. The ceiling paintings, by Giovanni Coli and Filippo Gherardi, depict incidents in the *Life of Marcantonio II Colonna*, who commanded the papal contingent at Lepanto (1571); the central panel illustrates the battle. On the walls are four Venetian mirrors with flower paintings by Mario de' Fiori and Giovanni Stanchi, and putti painted by Carlo Maratta.

The paintings include, at the beginning of the left wall, (162.) *St John the Baptist* by Salvator Rosa, once thought to be a self-portrait; above the first mirror on the left wall (46.) *St Irene Taking the Arrows from St Sebastian* by Giovanni Domenico Cerrini; and, on the opposite wall, (165.) an equestrian *portrait of Carlo Colonna, Duke of Marsi*, a copy of a work by Rubens (formerly attributed to Van Dyck).

The **Room of the Desks**, or Room of the Landscapes, derives its name from two valuable *desks displayed here. The first, in ebony, has 28 ivory bas-reliefs by Francis and Dominic Steinhard after drawings by Carlo Fontana; the central relief is a copy of Michelangelo's *Last Judgement*, the other 27 are copies of works by Raphael. The second desk, in sandalwood, is adorned with lapis lazuli, amethysts and other semi-precious stones; in front are 12 small amethyst columns and at the top gilt-bronze statuettes representing the *Muses* and *Apollo* seated under a laurel tree. The ceiling frescoes, by Sebastiano Ricci, are of the battle of Lepanto. In this room is a fine series of *landscapes by Gaspard Dughet (54–65), distinguished by their pale colours, on the two walls on either side of the columns and on the right wall. There is a further series by J.F. van Bloemen, with figures probably by Placido Costanzi (21–24), on the left and end walls. Other landscapes here include works (49, 50.) by Borgognone, and (113.) a *View of the Campo and Scuola di San Rocco* in Venice by the circle of Michele Marieschi (formerly attributed to Canaletto). The sculpture includes a copy in bronze of the *Farnese Bull*, by Susini.

From the **Room of the Apotheosis of Martin V** there is a view of the attractive courtyard planted with palms and bay trees. This room takes its name from the subject of the central ceiling painting by Benedetto Luti; the other ceiling panels show *Fame Crowning Victory* by Pietro Bianchi, and *Time Discovering Truth* by Pompeo Batoni. Between the windows are two portraits (187, 188) by Domenico Tintoretto. On the next wall: (190.) *Onofrio Panvinio, the Augustinian* by Jacopo Tintoretto, (formerly attributed to Titian) and (170.) *Portrait of a Man* by Francesco Salviati. On the wall opposite the windows: (83.) *Guardian Angel* by Guercino; (43.) *Peasant Eating Beans* by Annibale Carracci (also attributed to Bartolomeo Passarotti); and (169.) *Raising of Lazarus*, a small painting by Francesco Salviati. On the last wall: (197.) *Man in Venetian Costume* by Paolo Veronese.

The **Throne Room** is reserved, as in other princely houses, for the pope; the chair is turned to the wall so that no one else can sit in it. The three Colonna portraits are (144.) *Martin V, Oddone Colonna*, a copy from a work by Pisanello, (149.) *Marcantonio II Colonna* by Scipione Pulzone, and (150.) *Felice Colonna Orsini*, thought to be a copy of a work by Pulzone. The nautical chart was presented by the Roman people to Marcantonio II and the parchment diploma given him by the Roman senate after the battle of Lepanto.

In the **Room of Maria Mancini**, or Room of the Primitives. On the window wall, (**143**.) *Resurrection of Christ*, with members of the Colonna family, by Pietro da Cortona. On the next wall, (**198**.) **Madonna Enthroned* by Bartolomeo Vivarini. Opposite the windows: (**107**.) **Madonna and Child with St Elisabeth and the Young St John*, a small work by Bernardino Luini; (**35**.) **Madonna* by Giuliano Bugiardini; (**154**.) **Young Man in Profile*, traditionally identified as Guidobaldo della Rovere, Duke of Urbino, attributed to Rocco Zoppo; (**179**.) **Madonna and Child Enthroned with Angels* by Stefano da Zevio; (**166**.) *Reconciliation of Esau and Jacob*, a copy from Rubens; and (**90**.) *Holy Family with St Francis* by Innocenzo da Imola.

The **Appartamento della Principessa Isabelle** (for admission, see above) consists of eleven sumptuously decorated and furnished rooms on the ground floor of Palazzo Colonna, named after Isabelle Sursock, wife of Marcantonio Colonna, who restored the apartment in the early 20C. It contains paintings by Gaspar van Wittel, the Dutch painter known as Vanvitelli, who carried out 107 works, including numerous views of Rome, for the Colonna between 1681 and 1732. In the **Sala Rosa** are small paintings by Jan Brueghel the Elder dating from the 1590s, and a self-portrait by Sofonisba Anguissola. The vault of the **Sala della Fontana** is painted by Pinturicchio (c 1485–92). The red granite crocodile dates from the 3C AD, and the superb painting of *Two Saints with Abbot Niccolò Roverella* (part of a polyptych) is by Cosmè Tura. The **Sala del Tempesta** is named after the artist who painted the seascapes on the walls in the 17C. The adjoining room was decorated by Gaspard Dughet with delightful landscapes. The **Dining-room**, formerly used as a library, has a vault decorated in the late 16C by a group of artists including Pomarancio, Giovanni Baglione, Jacopo Zucchi and Ferraù Fenzoni. The **Sala del Mascherone** has a Roman pavement (4C AD) and various ancient marble fragments.

10 • The Pantheon and Santa Maria sopra Minerva

The small area covered in this chapter surrounds the Pantheon, the best preserved monument of ancient Rome, and one of the most beautiful buildings in the city. Beside it is the church of Santa Maria sopra Minerva, interesting for its frescoes and sculptures.

In **Piazza della Rotonda** in front of the Pantheon is a fountain (1575), on a model of Giacomo della Porta, surmounted by an obelisk of Rameses the Great, formerly belonging to the Isaeum (see below) and erected here in 1711.

The Pantheon

The Pantheon (**Map 7; 3**) survives virtually intact as the most magnificent symbol of the Roman Empire. Dedicated to all the gods (Pan-theon), it was conceived as a secular Imperial monument as much as a shrine. In 609 it was converted into a church, the first temple in Rome to be Christianised. Open Mon–Sat 08.30–19.30; Sun 09.00–18.00. ☎ 06 6830 0230.

History of the Pantheon

The original temple, apparently of travertine, was built during the third consulate of Agrippa (27 BC) to commemorate the victory over Antony and Cleopatra at Actium. This building was damaged by fire in AD 80, restored by Domitian, and struck by lightning and destroyed by another fire in 110.

It has been conclusively proved by examination of the brick stamps that the existing temple, including the pronaos, is not that of Agrippa, but a new one of brick, built and probably also designed by Hadrian on a larger scale and on different lines. This second building, begun in AD 118 or 119 and finished between AD 125 and 128, received and retained the name of Pantheon. Hadrian characteristically set up the dedicatory inscription on the pediment of the pronaos—M. AGRIPPA, L.F. COS. TERTIUM FECIT ('Marcus Agrippa, son of Lucius, consul for the third time, had [this building] made')—in honour of its original builder.

The Pantheon was restored by Septimius Severus and Caracalla. Closed and abandoned under the first Christian emperors and pillaged by the Goths, it was given to Boniface IV by the Byzantine emperor Phocas, whose column is in the Roman Forum (see p 101). Boniface consecrated it as a Christian church in 609. It was dedicated to Santa Maria ad Martyres—there was a legend that some 28 wagonloads of martyrs' bones had been transferred here from the catacombs. On a 12-day visit to Rome in 667, Constans II, emperor of Byzantium, robbed the temple of what the Goths had left, and in particular stripped off the gilded roof-tiles, which were probably of bronze. Benedict II restored it (684), Gregory III roofed it with lead (735); and Anastasius IV built a palace beside it (1153).

When the popes took up residence in Avignon the Pantheon served as a fortress in the struggles between the rival Roman aristocratic families of Colonna and Orsini. In 1435 Eugenius IV isolated the building, and from then on it was the object of such veneration that a Roman senator on taking office swore to preserve 'Maria Rotonda' intact for the pontiff, together with the relics and sacred treasures of the city.

The monument was greatly admired during the Renaissance; Pius IV repaired the bronze door, and had it practically recast (1563). The Barberini pope Urban VIII, however, employed Bernini to add two clumsy turrets in front, which became popularly known as the 'ass-ears of Bernini'. Urban also melted down the bronze ceiling of the portico to make the baldacchino at St Peter's and 80 cannon for Castel Sant'Angelo, an act of vandalism that prompted the 'talking' statue Pasquino's stinging gibe, '*Quod non fecerunt barbari fecerunt Barberini*' ('What the barbarians did not do, the Barberini did').

Alexander VII had the portico restored by Giuseppe Paglia (1662), and the level of the piazza lowered to provide a better view of the façade; Clement IX surrounded the portico with an iron railing (1668); Benedict XIV employed Paolo Posi (1747) to restore the interior and the atrium. The first two kings and the first queen of Italy are buried here. The incongruous turrets added by Bernini were removed in 1883.

A pedimented pronaos precedes a gigantic domed rotunda, with a rectangular feature as wide as the pronaos and as high as the cylindrical wall inserted between the two. This combination of a pronaos and rotunda gives the building a special place in the history of architecture. Originally the pronaos was raised by several steps and preceded by a large rectangular paved forecourt much larger than the present piazza, although the huge dome was only ever visible from the interior.

The **portico** is nearly 34m wide and 15.5m deep, and has 16 monolithic Corinthian columns of red or grey granite, without flutings, each 12.5m high and 4.5m in circumference. The superb capitals and the bases are of white marble. The three columns on the east side are replacements, one by Urban VIII (1625), the others by Alexander VII (1655–67); the arms of these popes may be seen in the decoration of the capitals. Eight of the columns stand in front, and the others are disposed in four rows, so as to form three aisles, the central one leading to the bronze door, which dates from the time of Pius IV, and the others to the two great niches which may formerly have contained colossal statues of Augustus and Agrippa.

The visual impact of the domed **interior** is unforgettable. The use of light from the opening in the roof displays the genius of the architect. The great **dome** has five rows of coffers diminishing in size towards the circular opening in the centre, which measures almost 9m across. The intricate design of the coffers is mainly responsible for the effect of space and light. They were probably ornamented with gilded bronze rosettes. The height and diameter of the interior are the same—43.3m. The diameter of the dome, the largest masonry vault ever built, exceeds by more than one metre that of the dome of St Peter's. Its span, which contains no brick arches or vaults, begins at the level of the highest cornice seen on the outside of the building, rather than, as it appears in the interior, at the top of the attic stage.

The **cylindrical wall** is 6m thick. It contains seven great niches, or recesses; except for the central apse, each is preceded by two Corinthian columns of giallo antico and flanked by pilasters. The apse instead has two free-standing columns. Between the recesses, which originally contained statues, are eight shrines (*aediculae*), those flanking the apse and entrance with triangular pediments, and the others with segmented pediments. These are supported by two Corinthian columns in giallo antico, porphyry or granite. Above the recesses is the entablature with a beautiful cornice, and still higher is an attic, unfortunately restored in 1747, making this stage more pronounced than was intended. Part of the original decoration can be seen over the recess to the right of the apse: between the rectangular openings (fitted with grilles) were shallow pilasters of reddish marble alternating with three marble panels. More than half of the original coloured marble sheets on the walls are still in place. The floor, though restored, retains its original design.

On the **right side**, in the first chapel is the *Annunciation*, a fresco attributed to Melozzo da Forlì or Antoniazzo Romano, and two 17C marble angels. In the aedicule there is a 14C fresco of the *Coronation of the Virgin*. The second chapel houses the tomb of Vittorio Emanuele II, first king of Italy (d. 9 January 1878), designed by

The Pantheon

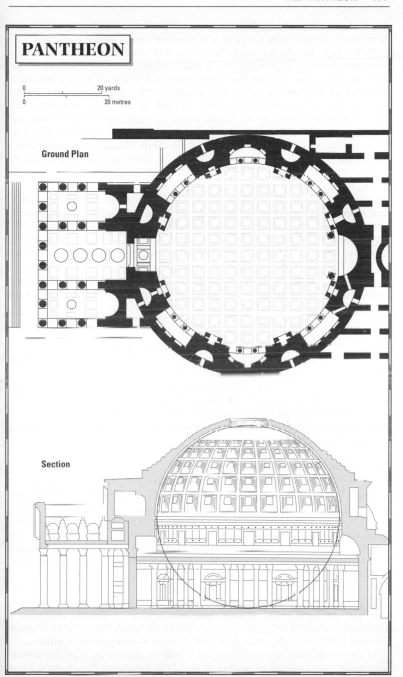

PANTHEON

0 ————————— 20 yards
0 ————————— 20 metres

Ground Plan

Section

Manfredo Manfredi. The third chapel has a 15C *Madonna and Saints*. In the main apse, above the high altar, is a 7C icon of the *Virgin and Child*.

On the **left side**, in the third chapel, is a 16C crucifix and, on the right, a monument by Bertel Thorvaldsen to Cardinal Consalvi (d. 1824), secretary of Pius VII, who represented the Holy See at the Congress of Vienna. The third aedicule is the **tomb of Raphael**, inscribed with a Latin distich (couplet) by Pietro Bembo, translated by Alexander Pope in his '*Epitaph on Sir Godfrey Kneller*' (the portrait-painter): 'Living, great Nature feared he might outvie Her works, and dying, fears herself may die.' On the altar is the statue of the *Madonna del Sasso*, by Lorenzetto, probably with the help of Raffaello da Montelupo, from Raphael's original design. The bronze bust is by Giuseppe de Fabris. A fresh red rose usually honours the tomb. Below the empty niche on the right is the short epitaph of Maria Bibbiena, niece of Cardinal Dovizi da Bibbiena, who was to have married Raphael but predeceased him. Among other artists buried in the Pantheon are Giovanni da Udine, Perino del Vaga, Taddeo Zuccari, Annibale Carracci and Baldassare Peruzzi.

In the second chapel is the tomb of Umberto I (assassinated at Monza on 29 July 1900), designed by Giuseppe Sacconi. Below Umberto's tomb is that of Margherita di Savoia, first queen of Italy (d. 5 January 1926).

In Via della Palombella, attached to the back of the Pantheon, can be seen remains of another Roman structure, which was named the **Basilica of Neptune** when it was unearthed in 1938, and attributed to Agrippa. It has similarities to the pronaos of the Pantheon and is now known to date from Hadrian's time, but its purpose is unclear.

Piazza Minerva, where excavations are in progress, contains a bizarre but delightful work by Bernini (1667), a marble elephant supporting a small **obelisk** which belonged to the Isaeum Campense, or Temple of Isis, that formerly stood nearby. Other relics from the temple are in the Capitoline museums, Piazza dei Cinquecento and the Egyptian Museum in the Vatican. The hieroglyphic inscription on the obelisk relates to Apries, the last of the independent pharaohs of Egypt (the Hophrah of the Bible), who was the ally of Zedekiah, king of Judah, against Nebuchadnezzar (6C BC).

Santa Maria sopra Minerva

Santa Maria sopra Minerva (**Map 7; 3, 5**) stands on the site of a small oratory probably built here before AD 800 on the ruins of a Temple of Minerva. It was rebuilt in 1280 by the Dominicans who modelled it on their church of Santa Maria Novella in Florence (according to Vasari it was by the same architects, Fra Sisto and Ristoro). It was altered and over-restored in the Gothic style in 1848–55. On the right side of the simple **façade** (1453) small marble plaques register the heights reached by floods on the Tiber before it was canalised. Open daily 07.00–19.00.

In the **interior** (with coin-operated lights in some chapels) the vault, rose-windows and excessively colourful decorations date from the 19C restoration. On the right of the central door is the tomb of Nerone Diotisalvi, a Florentine exile (d. 1482), and, on the right of the south door, that of Virginia Pucci Ridolfi (1567), the latter with a fine bust by an unknown Florentine.

In the **south aisle**, the baptistery has a *Noli me tangere* by Marcello Venusti and the bust of *Ladislao di Aquino* (d. 1621) by Francesco Mochi. By the first chapel, with an altarpiece by Baciccio, is the tomb of the archivist Castalio, with a fine portrait. The second chapel was decorated by Lazzaro Baldi in the late 17C. The third chapel has vault frescoes by Girolamo Muziano. The fourth chapel was designed by Carlo Maderno. The altarpiece of the *Annunciation* is by Antoniazzo Romano (1500): the painting shows Cardinal Juan de Torquemada (uncle of Tomás de Torquemada, the inquisitor) presenting three poor girls to the Virgin, and commemorates the Confraternity of the Annunziata, founded in 1460 to provide dowries for penniless girls. On the left is the tomb of Urban VII by Ambrogio Buonvicino.

The fifth chapel has a frescoed ceiling by Cherubino Alberti and an altarpiece of the *Institution of the Eucharist* by Federico Barocci. At the sides are the tombs of the parents of Clement VIII, by Giacomo della Porta, and in a niche to the left a statue of *Clement*. The statue of *St Sebastian* in a niche on the right wall is probably by Nicolas Cordier. In the sixth chapel, on the right, is the tomb of Bishop Juan Diaz de Coca (1477) by Andrea Bregno, and his workshop, with a fresco by the school of Melozzo da Forlì; on the left is the tomb of Benedetto Sopranzi, Bishop of Nicosia (d. 1495), by the school of Bregno.

In the **south transept**, the first chapel contains a wooden crucifix (early 15C). The **Cappella Carafa** is preceded by a fine marble arch attributed to Giuliano da Maiano, with a beautiful balustrade. It contains celebrated *frescoes by Filippino Lippi (1489). On the right wall, below, is *St Thomas Confounding the Heretics*, the central figures being Arius and Sabellius: the two youths in the right-hand group are probably portraits of the future Medici popes, Leo X and Clement VII, both buried in this church. In the lunette above is *St Thomas Aquinas in Prayer*, and in the vault, the *Sibyls*. On the altar wall is the *Assumption*, with a splendid group of angels, and an altarpiece of the *Annunciation*, with St Thomas Aquinas presenting Cardinal Olivieri Carafa to the Virgin, also by Filippino. On the left wall is the monument of Paul IV (d. 1559) by Giacomo and Tommaso Cassignola, from a design by Pirro Ligorio.

To the left of this chapel is the *tomb of Guillaume Durand (d. 1296), bishop of Mende, by Giovanni di Cosma, with a beautiful 13C mosaic of the *Madonna and Child*. The third chapel has Carlo Maratta's *Madonna and Saints*. The fourth chapel has a frescoed ceiling by Marcello Venusti and, on the right, the tomb of Cardinal Capranica (1458).

In the **choir**, at the foot of the steps on the left, is *Christ Bearing the Cross* by Michelangelo (1514–21), commissioned at a cost of 200 ducats by Metello Vari and Pietro Castellani. The bronze drapery is a later addition. Under the 19C high altar lies the body of St Catherine of Siena (see below). In the apse are the tombs of the Medici popes Leo X (left) and Clement VII, designed by Antonio Sangallo the Younger, with statues by Raffaello da Montelupo and Nanni di Baccio Bigio respectively. In the pavement is the slab-tomb of Cardinal Pietro Bembo (1547), secretary to Pope Leo X from 1512 to 1520, and friend of Michelangelo, Raphael and Ariosto.

To the left of the choir in the **north transept**, in a passageway which serves as an exit, are several large monuments, including those of Cardinal Michele Bonelli (Alexandrinus) by Giacomo della Porta, and of Cardinal Domenico Pimentel designed by Bernini. Here is the pavement **tomb of Fra Angelico**, attributed to Isaia da Pisa. The painter died in the convent here in 1455, and the charming epitaph was composed by Pope Nicholas V whose chapel in the Vatican the friar had frescoed. In the second chapel to the left of the choir is a 15C altar-piece (a processional standard painted in tempera on silk) of the *Madonna and Child* attributed to Benozzo Gozzoli. The tomb of Giovanni Arberini (d. c 1470) is by a Tuscan sculptor (Agostino di Duccio?), who incorporated a splendid *bas-relief of *Hercules and the Lion*, probably a Roman copy of an original Greek work of the 5C BC. To the left is the entrance to the 17C **sacristy**, behind which is the room (opened on request) in which St Catherine of Siena died in 1380; it was brought here from Via di Santa Chiara by Cardinal Barberini. The poorly preserved frescoes are by Antoniazzo Romano and his school (1482). At the end of this transept is the Cappella di San Domenico, containing the monument of Benedict XIII (d. 1730), with sculptures by Pietro Bracci. At the corner of the nave and transept is the charming small tomb of Andrea Bregno (1421–1506). On the second nave pillar is the tomb of Maria Raggi, a colourful early work by Bernini.

Between the fourth and third chapels of the **north aisle** is the tomb of Giovanni Vigevano (d. 1630), with a bust by Bernini (c 1617). The third chapel has a tiny altarpiece of the *Redeemer*, attributed to Perugino or Pinturicchio; on the right, a statue of *St Sebastian*, attributed to Michele Marini; on the left, *St John the Baptist*, by Ambrogio Buonvicino; and against the side-walls, the tombs of Benedetto and Agostino Maffei, attributed to Luigi Capponi (15C). In the second chapel (being restored) the tomb of Gregorio Naro, showing the cardinal kneeling at a prie-dieu, has recently been attributed to Bernini. In the first chapel is a bust of *Girolamo Bottigella*, perhaps by Jacopo Sansovino. Near the door is the tomb of Francesco Tornabuoni (1480) by Mino da Fiesole, and above is that of Cardinal Tebaldi (1466) by Bregno and Giovanni Dalmata.

The **monastery** was once the headquarters of the Dominicans, and was the scene of Galileo's trial in 1633. In the **cloister** (sometimes shown on request) are two funerary monuments attributed to Andrea Bregno, and the Sala dei Papi with a colossal statue of the *Madonna and Child*, an unfinished work attributed to Bernini.

The Dominicans were left a library by Cardinal Girolamo Casanate which they opened in the convent in 1701. The **Biblioteca Casanatense** specialises in theological texts and works on the history of Rome and has some 350,000 volumes. It is now entered at 52 Via Sant' Ignazio.

From Piazza Minerva, the narrow Via dei Cestari—where a number of shops sell liturgical articles—runs south towards the busy Corso Vittorio Emanuele. On the right, in Via dell'Arco della Ciambella, part of the circular wall of the central hall of the **Baths of Agrippa** is charmingly incorporated into the street architecture. These were the first public baths in the city, begun by Agrippa in 29 BC, and restored by Hadrian. The brick-faced concrete dates from the 3C. Agrippa, who was born around 64 BC, was a very close friend of Augustus. He supported the emperor by financing numerous ambitious building projects in Rome including the Pantheon, the Baths of Agrippa, three aqueducts and hundreds of fountains. He married Augustus's only child Julia and was considered his obvious successor, but he and his two children all predeceased Augustus.

Opposite, Via della Pigna leads past the 16C Palazzo Maffei Marescotti to a little piazza in front of the Baroque church of **San Giovanni della Pigna** (usually closed), which has interesting tomb slabs inside the entrance wall. At no. 6,

Mussolini met Cardinal Gasparri in 1923 to initiate discussions on the Concordat (see p 404). In Via del Gesù there is a beautiful Renaissance doorway at no. 85, and at no. 62 a curious fountain in the form of a water-clock, which is no longer functioning. The street ends beside Palazzo Altieri (1650–60) which has interesting courtyards, on the traffic-ridden Piazza del Gesù (see p 199).

North of the Pantheon

From behind the Pantheon, Via della Palombella leads to Piazza Sant'Eustachio, from where there is a good view of the spire of Sant'Ivo (see p 185), and a charming palace with fine windows, a pretty cornice and remains of its painted façade. No. 83 is a house built by Giulio Romano for the Maccarani family. The church of **Sant'Eustachio**, of ancient foundation, preserves its campanile of 1196. The pretty **interior** was designed by Antonio Canevari after 1724. The two large 18C altarpieces in the transepts are by Giacomo Zoboli.

In Via del Pantheon, no. 63 on the right is a hotel where the poet Ariosto stayed in 1513 (marked by a plaque). The street leads from Piazza della Rotonda to the church of **Santa Maria Maddalena** (Map 7; 3) with a Rococo façade by Giuseppe Sardi (1735). Open daily 07.30–11.45 and 17.00–19.45; fest. 09.00–11.00.

The pretty **interior** (1695–99), on an original plan, was designed by Giovanni Antonio de'Rossi and Giulio Carlo Quadrio. The statues of *Virtues* in the nave are attributed to Paolo Morelli, except for the first and third on the left which are by Carlo Monaldi, and by Giuseppe Raffaelli. The vault was frescoed by Michelangelo Cerruti (1732) and the cupola by Stefano Parrocel (1739). The confessionals are by Giuseppe Palma (1762).

On the **south side**, the second chapel has a 16C painting of the *Madonna and Child* and the third chapel an elaborate marble altar with a vault fresco by Sebastiano Conca. By the side door is a fine wooden statue of *Mary Magdalene* (15C). Over the high altar is *Mary Magdalene in Prayer* by Michele Rocca and, above, a fresco by Aureliano Milani. On the **north side**, the third chapel contains *St Nicholas of Bari* by Baciccio and the second chapel *St Lawrence Giustiniani in Adoration of the Child* by Luca Giordano (1704). The elaborate cantoria and organ date from the early 18C. The sacristy, entered from the left aisle, is a charming room which preserves intact its decoration and furnishings from 1741.

Via delle Colonnelle (passing the right side of the church which dates from the late 17C) leads to Piazza Capranica, which is dominated by Palazzo Capranica, built by Cardinal Domenico Capranica (c 1450) and partly Gothic and partly Renaissance in style. The tower has a delightful loggia.

Via della Maddalena continues north past Via delle Coppelle, where no. 35 is Palazzo Baldassini, a smaller version of Palazzo Farnese by Antonio Sangallo the Younger (1514–23), with a handsome courtyard and loggia. Garibaldi lived here in 1875. Via della Maddalena ends at the church of **Santa Maria in Campo Marzio** (Map 7; 3). The church, of ancient foundation, was rebuilt in 1685 by Giovanni Antonio de' Rossi on a Greek cross plan, and has a good portico and court. Over the high altar is a *Madonna*, part of a triptych probably of the 12C–13C. Since 1920 the church has belonged to the Roman Catholic Patriarchate of Antioch of the Syrians (services on fest.).

11 • Piazza Navona and its district

This chapter covers one of the loveliest parts of the city, centering on the delightful Piazza Navona, one of the places which best illustrates the spirit of Rome: the entirely successful adaptation of a Classical building (in this case a Roman circus) to the urban structure of succeeding centuries; the triumph of Bernini's Baroque style with his splendid fountain of the Four Rivers, which also provides a setting for an Egyptian obelisk brought to the city by a Roman emperor; and the relaxed festive atmosphere typical of the Romans, who come here to enjoy the scene.

The superb Baroque architectural style of Francesco Borromini can be seen both in the façade of Sant'Agnese in Agone in the piazza, and in the courtyard of the Sapienza and church of Sant'Ivo nearby. The two churches of San Luigi dei Francesi and Sant'Agostino contain very fine paintings by Caravaggio, while frescoes by Raphael are preserved in Santa Maria della Pace (which also has a delightful façade by Pietro da Cortona) and Sant'Agostino. The Renaissance roads Via dei Coronari and Via del Governo Vecchio are well worth exploring. To add to the interest of this district, Palazzo Altemps is now part of the Museo Nazionale Romano and here, beautifully displayed, the Ludovisi collection is of particular interest in showing how numerous antique Roman statues have been restored or integrated over the centuries. Nearby are two small museums; one vividly illustrates the Napoleonic period in Italy, and the other the personal taste of the art historian Mario Praz, who died here in 1982.

Piazza Navona

Piazza Navona (**Map 6; 4**) occupies the site of the Stadium of Domitian. It is the most animated square in Rome, beloved of the Romans as well as visitors, and the cafés and restaurants have tables outside throughout most of the year.

History of Piazza Navona

Its form, preserving the dimensions of a Roman circus building which could probably hold some 30,000 spectators, represents a remarkable survival within the modern city. The name is derived from the athletic games, the *Agoni Capitolini*, held here after the stadium was inaugurated in AD 86. In the Middle Ages the piazza was called the Campus Agonis; hence agone, *n'agona* and *navona*. Historic festivals, jousts and open-air sports took place here, and it was also used as a market-place from 1477 until 1869. From the 17C to the late 19C the piazza was flooded every weekend in August for the entertainment of the Romans; the nobles enjoyed the spectacle from their carriages. Nowadays, during the Christmas festival statuettes for the Christmas crib are sold here, and the fair and toy-market of the Befana (Epiphany) is held.

Three splendid fountains decorate the piazza. The **Fontana del Moro** at the south end was designed by Giacomo della Porta in 1576, with sculptures by Taddeo Landini, Simone Moschino, Silla Longhi and Egidio della Riviera. In 1874 these were replaced by copies made by Luigi Amici, and in 1909 the originals were moved to the Giardino del Lago in Villa Borghese (see p 243). The fountain was altered by Bernini in 1653 when he designed the central figure, known as *Il Moro* (the Moor), executed by Antonio Mari.

The central **Fontana dei Quattro Fiumi** (Fountain of the Four Rivers) is one of Bernini's most famous works. Four colossal allegorical figures are seated on a triangular base of travertine rock. They represent the four most famous rivers of the time—the *Danube*, *Ganges*, *Nile* and *Rio della Plata*—symbolising the four continents Europe, Asia, Africa and America, and were carved by Bernini's assistants, Antonio Raggi, Giacomo Antonio Fancelli, Claude Poussin and Francesco Baratta. A horse and a lion with long flowing tails inhabit the caves in the hollow rock below, seen from both front and back, and near a scaly sea monster with a snout there is a sea serpent in the water. The rock is overgrown with various carved plants and a palm tree.

The fountain was designed as a support for the tall **obelisk**, which was cut in Egypt and had been brought to Rome by order of Domitian. The Emperor had Roman stonemasons carve the hieroglyphics, which refer to Domitian as 'eternal pharaoh' and Vespasian and Titus as gods. It then lay for centuries in five pieces in the Circus of Maxentius on the Via Appia, before the Pamphilj pope, Innocent X, decided to move it here. It is crowned with the dove, the emblem of the Pamphilj family, who also had their palace in the square (see below). The popular story told to illustrate the rivalry between Bernini and Borromini—that the Nile is holding up an arm to block out the sight of Sant'Agnese—is apocryphal, since the fountain was finished in 1651 before Borromini started work on the church.

The fountain at the north end of the square, representing Neptune struggling with a marine monster or giant octopus, Nereids and sea-horses, is by Antonio della Bitta and Gregorio Zappala (1878).

On the west side of the piazza is **Sant'Agnese in Agone** (**Map 6, 4**), an ancient church built on the ruins of the stadium which Christian tradition marks as the spot where St Agnes was exposed (see p 440). It was reconstructed by Girolamo and Carlo Rainaldi in 1652. The splendid concave façade, which adds emphasis to the dome, was begun by Borromini (1653–57). The lantern of the dome is by Carlo Rainaldi, and the twin bell-towers are by Giovanni Baratta and Antonio del Grande. Only the lower part of the façade has been restored.

The small Baroque **interior** (often closed) has an intricate Greek-cross plan in which a remarkable effect of spaciousness is provided by the cupola. The fresco on the dome is by Ciro Ferri and Sebastiano Corbellini; the pendentives are by Baciccia. Above the seven altars 17C bas-reliefs or statues (including an antique statue of *St Sebastian* altered by Paolo Campi) take the place of paintings. The high altar-piece is a *Holy Family* by Domenico Guidi. Above the entrance is the monument of Innocent X, who is buried here, by Giovanni Battista Maini. Beneath the church the **Oratory of St Agnes**, built before 800, survives, although poorly restored, in a vault of the Stadium of Domitian. It contains badly damaged 13C frescoes and the last work of Alessandro Algardi, a bas-relief of the *Miracle of St Agnes*.

Next to the church is the splendid façade of **Palazzo Pamphilj**, sometimes called Palazzo Doria, which was started

Piazza Navona

by Girolamo Rainaldi and completed by Borromini for Innocent X in the mid-17C. It is now the Brazilian Embassy. The very pale blue colour of the façade has been rediscovered in its recent restoration. The interior is of the greatest interest for its architecture and painted decorations (for permission to visit, write to Piazza Navona 14, Rome 00100; ☎ 06 686 7858). It includes the Sala Palestrina, a magnificent example of Borromini's secular architecture, using the minimum of surface decoration, decorated with busts by Algardi. It has had an interesting history as a music room, since the first performance of the Concerti Grossi of Corelli took place here in the 17C. The long gallery, also designed by Borromini, has a splendid fresco of the *Story of Aeneas* by Pietro da Cortona, who also frescoed the ceiling of the charming papal bedroom. The State rooms overlooking Piazza Navona were decorated between 1634 and 1671. The palace was later occupied by the sister-in-law of Pope Innocent X, the notorious Olimpia Maidalchini.

On the opposite side of the piazza is the church of the **Madonna del Sacro Cuore**, formerly San Giacomo degli Spagnoli, which was rebuilt in 1450 and restored in 1879. On the south side the choir-gallery is almost certainly by Pietro Torrigiani; the chapel off the north side is by Antonio da Sangallo the Younger.

Bernini and the decoration of Rome

Gian Lorenzo Bernini (1598–1680), one of the most famous Italian architects and sculptors of all time, was born in Naples but came to Rome as a boy and remained here almost all his life, except for a short stay in France in 1665 at the invitation of Louis XIV. He began work with his father Pietro, who was an able sculptor, but Gian Lorenzo was considered an *enfant prodige*: in 1617 the Borghese pope Paul V ordered him to carve his bust, and the Pope's nephew, Cardinal Scipione Borghese, commissioned Bernini's first important sculptures, which are still in the Galleria Borghese. He was at once recognised as the greatest artist working in Rome.

Subsequently the Barberini pope Urban VIII became his most important patron as well as a close friend, and called on Bernini to work on St Peter's. Many artists came to Rome to benefit from his guidance and his workshop was busy carrying out the numerous commissions he received as the most celebrated sculptor and architect in Europe. After the death of Urban VIII, however, Bernini fell out of favour, and when Urban's successor Innocent X had the idea of decorating Piazza Navona with a fountain to incorporate a restored Egyptian obelisk, he deliberately excluded Bernini from the list of leading sculptors of the day whom he asked for designs. Bernini decided to produce a model anyway, and a nephew of the pope managed to show it to Innocent, who was unable to resist giving Bernini the commission in 1648.

Bernini also carried out a great deal of work for the Chigi pope Alexander VII, including Piazza San Pietro, a wing of the Quirinal palace, the church of Sant'Andrea and the Chigi chapel in Santa Maria del Popolo, as well as more work in St Peter's and the Vatican. Today his remarkable buildings, fountains, sculptures and funerary monuments can be seen all over the city.

East of Piazza Navona

The modern Corso del Rinascimento runs parallel to the piazza to the east. Here is the main Baroque façade of the huge **Palazzo Madama** (**Map 6: 4**). Open to the public on the first Saturday of the month, 10.00–18.00. Originally this was a house belonging to the powerful Roman Crescenzi family, and it passed to the Medici in the 16C as part of the dowry of Alfonsina Orsini. In the 17C the building was enlarged and decorated by Lodovico Cardi and Paolo Marucelli, who are responsible for the interesting façade. It owes its name to the residence here of 'Madama' Margaret of Parma, illegitimate daughter of Charles V, who married first Alessandro de' Medici and afterwards Ottavio Farnese, and was Regent of the Netherlands from 1559 to 1567. Benedict XIV bought the palace in 1740, and it became successively the residence of the Governor of Rome and the seat of the Ministry of Finance (1852–70). The right wing was added in 1931.

The palace has been the seat of the **Senato della Repubblica** (Italian Senate) since 1871. This, together with the Camera dei Deputati in Montecitorio (see p 150) represents the parliament of Italy. The 315 senators, who must be over the age of 40, are elected every five years by Italians over the age of 25. In addition, the president of the Republic is allowed to nominate five life senators, who are citizens who have excelled in social, scientific, artistic or literary fields. Former Italian presidents also become life senators at the end of their term of office.

Via degli Staderari, which separates the senate building from Palazzo della Sapienza, has a tiny wall-fountain carved in 1927 to mark the *rione* or district of Sant'Eustachio, and a splendid, huge antique basin which was set up here as a **fountain** in 1987 by the Senate to commemorate the fortieth anniversary of the Italian Constitution, and is the most recent fountain to be inaugurated in central Rome.

Palazzo della Sapienza (Map 6; 6) has a fine Renaissance façade, also on Corso del Rinascimento, by Giacomo della Porta. Until 1935 it was the seat of the University of Rome, founded by Boniface VIII in 1303, and the university is still known as La Sapienza after it. It now houses the Archivio di Stato, and exhibitions are held in a library designed by Borromini. The beautiful **court**, which can always be seen from the open doorway, also designed by Borromini, has porticoes on three sides, and the church of **Sant'Ivo** is at the far end. Begun for the Barberini pope, Urban VIII, both the courtyard and the church incorporate his device (the bee) into their design, as well as Alexander VII's Chigi device of mounds. The dome is crowned by an ingenious spiral tower that has been copied many times, especially in German architecture. The church (open on Sun 09.00–12.00) is a masterpiece of Baroque architecture, with a remarkable light interior.

On the other side of Palazzo Madama, Via del Salvatore leads to the church of **San Luigi dei Francesi** (Map 6; 4), the French national church (1518–89). The **façade**, attributed to Giacomo della Porta, has two superimposed orders of equal height. Open daily 07.30–12.30 and 15.30–19.00; closed Thur afternoon.

The **interior** was heavily encrusted with marble and decorated with white and gilded stucco on a design by Antonio Dérizet (1756–64). Against the first pillar in the south aisle is the monument to the French who fell in the siege of Rome in 1849. The second

The tower of Sant'Ivo

chapel has *frescoes (damaged by restoration) by Domenichino—to the right, *St Cecilia Distributing Garments to the Poor* and *St Cecilia and her Betrothed Crowned by Angels*; to the left, *St Cecilia Refusing to Sacrifice to Idols*, and her *Martyrdom*; on the ceiling, *St Cecilia in Paradise*. The altarpiece is a copy by Guido Reni of Raphael's *St Cecilia* at Bologna. In the fourth chapel the altarpiece is the *Oath of Clovis* by Jacopino del Conte; to the right, the *Army of Clovis* is by Pellegrino Tibaldi; the *Baptism of Clovis*, to the left, by Girolamo Sermoneta.

The high altarpiece is an *Assumption of the Virgin* by Francesco Bassano. In the north aisle the fifth chapel contains three famous and very well preserved *paintings of scenes from the *Life of St Matthew* by Caravaggio (1597–1603), commissioned for this chapel by Cardinal Matthieu Cointrel's heirs. On the left is the *Calling of St Matthew*; on the right, *St Matthew's Martyrdom*; and the altarpiece is *St Matthew and the Angel*. They can only be seen by a coin-operated light. On the first pillar is a monument to Claude Lorrain (1600–82) by François Lemoyne.

Nearly opposite the church is the orange **Palazzo Giustiniani**, designed by Girolamo Fontana; the main doorway is by Borromini. The palace was built in 1590 by Vincenzo Giustiniani, Caravaggio's patron, and he kept his important collection of antique sculpture here (dispersed in the early 19C).

Sant'Agostino
From here, Via della Scrofa continues north to Piazza Sant'Agostino (on the left), in front of the church of Sant'Agostino (**Map 6**; **4**), which was built for Cardinal d'Estouteville by Giacomo da Pietrasanta (1479–83). The severely plain façade is one of the earliest of the Renaissance. The church is dedicated to St Augustine, author of the *Confessions*, whose mother, St Monica, is buried here. Open daily 07.45–12.00 and 16.30–19.30.

The **interior**, renovated by Luigi Vanvitelli (1750), contains good frescoes on the vault and **nave** by Pietro Gagliardi (1855), including five prophets on the nave pilasters which accompany the *Prophet Isaiah* frescoed on the third pillar on the north side by Raphael. This was commissioned by the Humanist scholar Giovanni Goritz in 1512 for his funerary monument, and shows how much the painter was influenced by Michelangelo's frescoes in the Sistine Chapel. It was restored by Daniele da Volterra. Beneath it is a *Madonna and Child with St Anne*, sculpted from a single block of marble by Andrea Sansovino.

At the **west end** is the so-called *Madonna del Parto* by Jacopo Sansovino (1521), a greatly venerated statue and the object of innumerable votive offerings. The two angels holding stoups at the west end are by Antonio Raggi.

In the **south aisle**, the first chapel contains paintings by Marcello Venusti; and the second chapel, the *Madonna della Rosa*, a copy by Avanzino Nucci of the original painting by Raphael, which was stolen from Loreto and subsequently disappeared. The third chapel has an altarpiece by Giacinto Brandi, and two paintings by Pietro Locatelli. In the fourth chapel, *Christ Giving the Keys to St Peter* was sculpted by Giovanni Battista Cotignola. The fifth chapel has a 16C crucifix.

In the **south transept** is the Chapel of Sant'Agostino, with an altarpiece by Guercino and side panels by his school; 18C stuccoes; and the Baroque tomb of Cardinal Renato Imperiali by Paolo Posi. On the high altar (1628), below two angels designed by Bernini, is a Byzantine *Madonna* brought from Constantinople. In the chapel to the left of the choir is the tomb of St Monica by

Caravaggio

Michelangelo Merisi da Caravaggio (1571–1610) was always known simply as Caravaggio, since it was thought he had been born in the town of the same name near Bergamo in Lombardy, although he may in fact have been born in Milan. He was the most important painter in Italy in the 17C and made Rome the most influential centre of art in the country during his lifetime. He also had a profound influence on a large school of painters who came to be known as the *Caravaggeschi*. His works are characterised by a striking use of light and shadow, and for their dramatic realism. He produced superb still-lifes and genre scenes, and (mostly after 1601) numerous paintings of religious subjects.

Caravaggio came to Rome around 1592, and his first public commission was for the Cointrels' chapel in San Luigi dei Francesi. These paintings are considered by many scholars to be his masterpiece. At the same time (1599–1602) he was working on two paintings of *St Peter* and *St Paul* for Tiberio Cerasi for another chapel in Santa Maria del Popolo, and shortly afterwards (1604) received a commission to paint the Madonna di Loreto for an altar in Sant'Agostino, very close to San Luigi dei Francesci. Other masterpieces by him in Rome are now preserved in the Galleria Doria Pamphilj, the Pinacoteca Capitolina, the Galleria Corsini and the Galleria Borghese. Apart from his numerous Italian followers, the influence of his style of painting can be seen in other great painters such as Velázquez and Rembrandt.

Caravaggio had a violent temperament and, after a quarrel, he murdered a certain Ranuccio Tomassoni in 1606. He was condemned to death and forced to flee Rome. He went in disguise to Naples before setting sail for Malta, where he was caught and imprisoned for a time. He escaped to Sicily in 1608. He still managed to paint, however, and several of his masterpieces of this period are preserved on both islands. He died, not yet 40 years old, in mysterious circumstances, possibly of a fever, on the beach near Porto Ercole on his way back to Rome.

He was a famous painter in his lifetime and one of his patrons was the wealthy banker Vincenzo Giustiniani, who lived in the palace opposite San Luigi dei Francesci and who owned no fewer than 13 of his works, including the first version of *St Matthew and the Angel* painted for the Cointrel chapel which was rejected (Giustiniani's painting was taken subsequently to Berlin where it was destroyed in the Second World War). Caravaggio's works were largely ignored by 18C and early 19C travellers, but he was 'rediscovered' in the 1950s, after an exhibition in Milan and the publication of numerous studies of his paintings.

Isaia da Pisa, and vault frescoes attributed to Giovanni Battista Ricci. The next little chapel—seen through a gate—was decorated by Giovanni Lanfranco (1616–19). The chapel in the north transept has a marble group on the altar finished by Ercole Ferrata.

The fifth chapel in the **north aisle** has an altarpiece by Giacinto Brandi; the fourth chapel, a *St Apollonia* by Girolamo Muziano; the third chapel, an altarpiece by Sebastiano Conca; and the second chapel, designed by Bernini, a crucifix by Ventura Salimbeni. In the first chapel is the *Madonna di Loreto*, or *Madonna* *dei Pellegrini*, commissioned for this altar by Ermete Cavalletti from Caravaggio (there is a light on the right). This is one of the most beautiful paintings by Caravaggio in the city: the graceful figure of the Madonna appears at the door of her house to show the blessing Child to two kneeling peasants who have come here on a pilgrimage. According to legend, in 1294 the Santa Casa or House of the Virgin was miraculously transported by angels from Nazareth to near Rijeka, in Croatia, and from there across the Adriatic to a laurel wood in the Marche. This place became known as Loreto and is still one of the great pilgrimage shrines in the Catholic world. As in many of Caravaggio's works, the iconography is extremely unusual; in most other paintings of this subject the house itself is shown being transported through the sky. Caravaggio's detractors were very critical of the peasant's dirty feet when the painting was first exhibited on this altar.

In the little vestibule at the north door are *Four Doctors* by Isaia da Pisa, statues belonging to the tomb of St Monica, and a crucifix by Luigi Capponi (15C).

Via dei Pianellari skirts the left side of Sant'Agostino as far as Via dei Portoghesi. Here are a delightful 15C doorway and tower and, behind a pretty balustrade, the ornate façade of the 17C church of **Sant'Antonio dei Portoghesi** (usually closed). The good Baroque interior has a painting of the *Madonna and Saints* by Antoniazzo Romano over the first altar on the left.

Palazzo Altemps

Near Sant'Agostino, in a small piazza beyond the north side of Piazza Navona, is the entrance to Palazzo Altemps (**Map 6; 4**), which houses the Ludovisi collection of ancient Roman sculptures from the **Museo Nazionale Romano** (see p 253). The remains of Cardinal Altemps' collection, part of the Mattei collection, and the pieces of Egyptian sculpture which belong to the Museo Nazionale Romano are also displayed here. The arrangement of the works has, as far as possible, attempted to illustrate 17C antiquarian taste. There are plans to exhibit other former private collections in the building. Open 09.00–19.45; closed Mon. ☎ 06 683 3759.

The collection is beautifully displayed and very well labelled, with excellent diagrams (also in English) in each room showing where the antique statues have been restored.

History of Palazzo Altemps and the Ludovisi collection

The palace was begun before 1477 by Girolamo Riario. Building was continued by Cardinal Francesco Soderini of Volterra (1511–23) and completed after 1568 by Cardinal Marco Sittico Altemps and his descendents, for whom Martino Longhi the Elder worked. Longhi was responsible for the charming belvedere in the form of a turret, an innovative architectural feature and later much copied. The palace was carefully restored after its acquisition by the State in 1982.

Here in the 16C Cardinal Altemps started collecting antique sculptures and so it is fitting that the palace now houses the private Roman collections of Classical sculpture later bought by the State, notably the Ludovisi collection. The 16 statues that survive from Altemps' collection (all the rest have been dispersed, and some of the finest are now in the Vatican, British Museum and Louvre) are preserved here.

The Ludovisi collection was begun in 1621 by Cardinal Ludovico Ludovisi, nephew of Pope Gregory XV, to decorate his villa and garden near Porta Pinciana (see p 237). He acquired part of the Altemps collection, and other pieces from the Cesi and Mattei families. The collection was further enriched by finds from excavations, some of which were carried out in his own garden. He employed Bernini and Algardi to restore and integrate the statues. The first pieces were dispersed in 1665 but the collection and villa (which became the property of Gregorio Boncompagni) became famous as a place to visit among travellers to Rome. A fashion grew up for copying the statues and making casts of them: Goethe was able to obtain a cast of the colossal head of Juno when he visited the city (see p 192). His friend Johann Winckelmann, the distinguished German scholar who was considered the greatest expert on Classical works in Rome during the 18C, made a detailed study of the statues, and the collection continued to grow in the 19C. In 1883, however, the Villa Ludovisi and its garden were destroyed for building land. In 1901 the State managed to buy the last 104 pieces of the collection, which include some very fine Greek and Roman pieces, although in most cases the provenance is unknown. The collection is particularly interesting as a reflection of 17C taste for the antique, and shows the skill with which so many of the pieces were restored at that time.

Alessandro Algardi

Alessandro Algardi (1598–1654) was one of the four most important sculptors active in Rome in the early 17C (along with Bernini, Francesco Mochi and François Duquesnoy). He was called to Rome in 1625 by the Bolognese Cardinal Ludovico Ludovisi and spent the next six years restoring his collection of antique sculpture. Many of these statues can be seen in Palazzo Altemps, as well as the *Dadoforo* (see below), which was created by Algardi from an antique Greek marble torso.

Although Pope Urban VIII favoured Bernini as a sculptor, Algardi designed the tomb of Leo XI in St Peter's and that of Giovanni Garzia Millini in the church of Santa Maria del Popolo, and executed the statues of **St Philip Neri** in the sacristy of Santa Maria in Vallicella and of **Innocent X** in Palazzo dei Conservatori on the Campidoglio. After 1646 he carried out the high-relief of the **Meeting of Pope Leo the Great with Attila in St Peter's**, and designed the Casino del Bel Respiro in Villa Pamphilj, his most important architectural work, for which he also executed the very fine stuccoes. Another work by him—a black marble putto personifying sleep—can be seen in the Galleria Borghese.

The handsome **courtyard** was begun by Antonio da Sangallo the Elder (1513–17), continued by Baldassare Peruzzi and completed by Martino Longhi at the end of the century. Some statues which were part of the original Altemps collection, and some very damaged statues which formed part of the Mattei collection, removed from the Villa Celimontana in 1996, are displayed here.

In the **atrium** (**3**) on the ground floor, a statue of *Antoninus Pius*, which was in the Mausoleum of Augustus in the 16C and was restored in 1621, begins the exhibition of pieces from the Ludovisi collection. In **room 4** is a high-relief of *Zeus* (2C AD) and a head of *Pluto*. **Room 5** has portrait busts, many of them

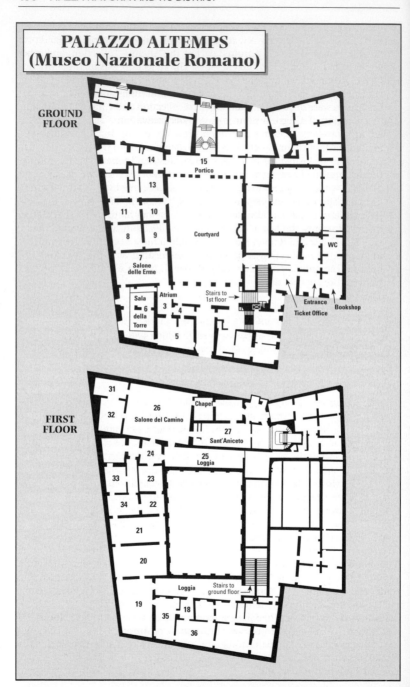

PALAZZO ALTEMPS
(Museo Nazionale Romano)

GROUND FLOOR

14
15
Portico

13

11 10

8 9 Courtyard

7
Salone delle Erme

WC

Sala 6 della Torre | Atrium 3 4

Stairs to 1st floor

5

Entrance
Ticket Office

Bookshop

FIRST FLOOR

31

32 | 26 Salone del Camino | Chapel

27 Sant'Aniceto

24

25 Loggia

33 23

34 22

21

20

19 | Loggia | Stairs to ground floor

35 18

36

restored. The colossal bronze head of *Marcus Aurelius* is one of the most famous pieces of the Ludovisi collection: the porphyry bust dates from the 4C BC, but the bronze cloak and other additions were made in the 17C. The other works are later: a bust made in the 17C has been added to a head of *Giulia* (90 AD); the portrait of *Julius Caesar* dates from the 16C, and that of *Antinous* is even later. Beneath the floor of the **Sala della Torre** (**6**), part of a medieval tower on the site of the palace can be seen. There is a case of exquisite fragments of Roman wall-paintings on a red ground found during the excavations (2C AD), and a case of 16C–17C ceramics also found here.

The **Salone delle Erme** (**7**) exhibits six herms dating from the 2C BC. In the centre are an antique vase and Roman fountain basin in rare Egyptian marble. Also here are two seated statues of *Apollo with his Lyre*. **Room 8** (once the entrance to the palace) displays three sculptures, only the central one of which is a Roman original. **Room 9** (on the right) contains a Roman statue of *Athena*, with the head, hands, feet and serpent's head all by Algardi. **Room 10** displays a copy of a renowned statue of *Athena* made by Phidias for the Parthenon in Athens. This is one of the very few copies of this famous work to have survived: it was made by an Athenian sculptor called Antiochos (the arms date from the 17C). **Room 11** displays a fine sarcophagus with Dionysiac scenes including a charming procession of elephants (190–220 AD). It is very ruined as it was formerly used as a fountain. Also here are two graceful small statues of the seated *Muses* (2C and 1C AD); the heads, although ancient, do not belong. Beyond a closed room is **room 13**, with a colossal torso from the Altemps collection, probably representing Polyphemus or Atlas. In **room 14** is a colossal group with Dionysius, a Satyr and a Panther. This was found on the Quirinal Hill during the late 16C. The *Satyr* and *Torso of Dionysius* are mostly original Roman works. In the portico (**15**) is a *Dacian Prisoner* in giallo antico: the black marble face and hands are later restorations.

From the other side of the courtyard stairs lead up to the **first floor**. In the loggia are important reliefs from the del Drago and Brancaccio collections. They were known and studied as early as the 15C, and were published by Winkelmann, but were only aquired by the Italian State in 1964. The sarcophagus with Mars and Venus dates from 160–180 AD. The relief from the end of a sarcophagus (of uncertain significance), with two female figures, one washing the feet of the other, who is covering her face, was made in the same century. It was well known in the Renaissance (drawings of it by Andrea Mantegna and Raphael survive), and the round hole was made when it was adapted for use as a fountain. The relief illustrating a funerary banquet (which includes the horse which belonged to the dead man) dates from the 4C BC. Another relief shows divinities and *Zeus Enthroned*, derived from a work by Phidias, but with additions of later date. The relief with the *Dioscuri* (Castor and Pollux) and their sister Helena is a Greek work (5C–4C BC) found in 1885 on the Esquiline Hill. The small room on the left (**18**) contains a kneeling statue of *Venus* made in the Hadrianic era, but derived from a 4C BC work.

Some frescoed rooms of the palace can be entered from the loggia. **Room 19** has remains of painted perspectives on the walls dating from the 16C. Here the bust of a *Satyr* in grey bigio marble, thought to have been restored by Bernini, is displayed on top of a funerary urn and altar dating from the 1C AD. The beautiful figure of *Hermes*, dating from the late 1C or early 2C AD, was carefully restored by Algardi, who probably had his workshop restore the statue of *Asclepios* (late 2C AD) in 1627.

Room 20 has a delightful 15C fresco attributed to the circle of Melozzo da Forlì, showing a tapestry covered with wild flowers, behind a sideboard on which are displayed plates, ewers and candlesticks which were wedding presents given to Girolamo Riario and Caterina Sforza when they were married in 1477. Three important statue groups are displayed here. A Roman statue of a seated male, formerly thought to represent Ares, the Greek war-god, is now displayed beside a female statue (2C BC) which has recently been identified as Thetis, the mother of Achilles. Scholars now believe this was the statuary group representing *Achilles with his mother, Thetis* which was described by Pliny as adorning the Temple of Neptune in the Campus Martius. The statue of Achilles was found in the early 17C and restored by Bernini. The standing group of *Orestes and Electra* is signed by the Greek artist Menelaos, pupil of Stephanos. Pliny mentions Stephanos as being the assistant of Pasiteles (early 1C AD). Winkelmann was the first to identify the figures as Orestes with his sister Electra at the tomb of their father Agamemnon. The head of the statue of the *Seated Warrior* (2C AD) is not original, although it, too, is an antique work.

Room 21 has a painted frieze by Pasquale Cati (1591). Here is exhibited the famous Ludovisi Throne, found at the end of the 19C in the Villa Ludovisi. It is thought to have been intended for the statue of a divinity, and is usually considered to be a Greek original of the 5C BC. The back and sides are adorned with reliefs. The central subject is apparently the birth of Aphrodite, who rises from the sea supported by two figures representing the Seasons. On the right side is the figure of a young woman sitting clothed on a folded cushion; she is taking grains from a box and burning them in a brazier. On the left side is a naked flute girl, also sitting on a folded cushion, playing a double pipe. On either side are displayed two colossal heads, one of them, the Juno Ludovisi, three times natural size. Winkelmann supposed this to be a Greek work and it was greatly admired by Goethe on his visit to Rome; he had a cast made of it which is now in the Casa di Goethe (see p 154). Its subject has now been identified as Antonia, mother of the Emperor Claudius, who deified her as Augusta after her death. The other colossal head of an acrolith is a Greek original of 480–470 BC, which may have been taken from Erice in Sicily after the Roman conquest there in 241 BC.

Room 22 has another 16C frescoed frieze, attributed to Antonio Viviani, and two more colossal heads: that of *Heracles* is much restored, but that of *Hera* (late 2C BC or early 1C BC) is a beautiful work. The sarcophagus fragment shows the *Myth of Phaedra and Hippolytus* (3C AD). **Room 23** has another frieze by Francesco Allegrini to a design by Antonio Tempesta. The striking red marble relief of the mask of *Dionysius*, which dates from the time of Hadrian, was used as a wall fountain, hence the two round holes. The two colossal busts and sarcophagus fragment with the *Judgement of Paris* also date from the same period. In **room 24**, with more pretty frescoes dating from 1590, a beautiful marble circular base is displayed with delicate reliefs of winged dancers dating from the Augustan period. The loggia (**25**) has charming frescoed decoration dating from 1595 with a pergola and numerous putti with garlands, and an elaborate fountain. Twelve busts, nine of them of emperors, are displayed here. The **Salone del Camino** (**26**) has a fireplace by Martino Longhi the Elder. The fine sculpture here includes a high relief with a head of *Mars* (2C AD; the bust was added in the 16C), and a splendid huge sarcophagus showing a battle between Romans and Barbarians, in excellent condition. It was found in 1621 near the Porta Tiburtina and dates from the 3C AD. The fragment of a female head, that of the dead Amazon Erinnyes, dates from the 2C AD. The dramatic figure of the nude *Galatian Committing Suicide* is a Roman copy of the time of Julius Caesar (46–44 BC) of an original Greek bronze. It formed part of the same group as the famous *Dying Gaul*, now in the Musei Capitolini (Palazzo Nuovo; see p 82). The church of Sant'Aniceto (**27**) was frescoed by Pomarancio and Ottavio Leoni (1604–17). **Room 31**, beyond a chapel (**30**), displays two very fine sarcophagi with battle scenes in high and low relief (170–180 AD). Also here is a statue of a seated *Man in a Toga*, signed in Greek (1C BC); although the head is ancient it is not the original. The two reliefs date from the 2C AD. In **room 32**, the sculptural group of a *Satyr and Nymph* is a Roman copy of a Greek original (the head of the satyr, added in the 17C, is attributed to Bernini). The other group of *Pan and Daphne* dates from the 1C AD. Also here are statues of two Muses, *Urania* and *Calliope*. The *Dadoforo* or Torch-bearer was created by Algardi from an original antique torso.

It is now necessary to return to room 22, from which a door leads into **rooms 34** and **33**. Here are displayed a *Child with a Goose* from the Hadrianic period; *Venus at her Bath* dating from the 1C BC (the head and arms restored); and a carved twisted column (2C AD). The entrance to **room 35** is from room 19: here are two statues of *Bacchus*: the one with a panther was made up from antique pieces in the 17C, and the other dates entirely from the 17C and was made as a fake Classical work. The satyr dates from the 2C AD but the arms are modern. **Room 36** exhibits a splendid bull (the god Apis) in serpentine porphyry, an Egyptian work (2C BC) brought to Rome during the Empire and discovered in 1886 on the Esquiline Hill. The remaining rooms (**37** to **48**) are still closed: they will display the rest of the Egyptian collection of the Museo Nazionale Romano. The Teatro Goldoni, which preserves its 17C decoration, will also be opened. It is one of the oldest private theatres in Rome, rebuilt in 1575, restored in 1890, and used as one of the first cinemas in the city in 1905.

Palazzo Primoli

The busy Via Giuseppe Zanardelli leads north from Piazza Navona to Ponte Umberto I on the Tiber. Here is **Palazzo Primoli** which houses the Museo Napoleonico and Museo Mario Praz. On the ground floor is the **Museo Napoleonico** (Map 6; 4), created and presented to the city of Rome in 1927 by Count Giuseppe Primoli (1851–1927), a descendent of Napoleon I who frequented the court of Napoleon III. This interesting collection illustrates the various periods of Napoleonic rule in Italy, but is particularly important as a record of the prolonged stays in Italy of Napoleon's numerous brothers and sisters and their descendents, and it documents the history of the Roman branch of the Bonaparte family. Open Mon–Sat 09.00–19.00; Sun 09.00–13.30. ☎ 06 6880 6286.

Although Napoleon Bonaparte never came to Rome himself (a trip was planned in 1812 but never took place), he led some brilliant military campaigns in northern Italy, and in 1798 the French entered the city and remained here for a year. Rome was again occupied in 1808–09.

The 16C palace was acquired by the Primoli family in 1820–28, and reconstructed in 1901 by Raffaello Ojetti, who added the monumental entrace on Via Zanardelli and a new façade overlooking the Tiber. The interior arrangement has been left more or less as it was in Giuseppe Primoli's time (the majolica floors were made in Naples in the early 19C).

Room 1 illustrates the Empire of Napoleon I (1804–14) with official portraits (c 1810) of him and his family, including an equestrian portrait of the Emperor, and of his sister Elisa Baciocchi and her daughter in the Boboli Gardens by François Gérard. The marble bust of *Napoleon* is by Houdon and that of *Elisa* by Lorenzo Bartolini. The portrait of Napoleon's mother, *Letitia*, is by Robert Lefèvre; the court robe also belonged to her. After the fall of Napoleon she came to live in Rome and remained here until her death in 1836. Also displayed here are numerous small wax portraits (some of them by Giovanni Antonio Santarelli) and several snuff boxes used by Napoleon. **Room 2** contains portraits of Napoleon's brothers, including Luis and his son by Jean-Baptiste Wicar, and his brother Lucien (see room 10) by François Xavier Fabre (1808).

Room 3 is dedicated to the Second Empire (1852–70). The official portraits of the Emperor Napoleon III and his Empress Eugénie are by Franz Xavier Winterhalter. A number of prints illustrate historic occasions at this time. **Room 4** records Napoleon I's son who was born in 1811 from his second marriage to Marie Luise of Austria and baptised as King of Rome. He had to leave Paris in 1815 and died aged 21. **Room 5** illustrates the Jacobin Republic of Rome, which was set up in 1798 and lasted a year. At this time the Pope, Pius VI, was forced to leave the city for France and 100 works of art and 100 codexes were seized from the Vatican and taken to France.

Room 6 is dedicated to Napoleon I's sister Pauline Bonaparte who lived in Rome from 1816 to 1825. As widow of General Leclerc she married the Roman prince Camillo Borghese in 1803. The bust of her exhibited here, by Antonio Canova, dates from 1805–07 and is contemporary with his famous portrait of her as *Venus Victrix*, now in the Galleria Borghese. **Room 7**. The French Kingdom of Naples was established in 1806 when Napoleon's brother Joseph took the throne. The portrait of him and his wife is by Jean-Baptsite Wicar. When Joseph became King of Spain in 1808 his sister Caroline and her husband Gioacchino Murat succeeded him to the throne.

Room 8 has material which illustrates the myth of Napoleon I, with caricatures and satirical drawings. **Room 9** preserves its neo-Gothic decoration dating from 1830–40, the period when Joseph's daughters Zenaide (grandmother of the founder of the Museum) and Charlotte were living in Rome and Florence. The portrait of the sisters by Jacques-Louis David dates from 1821, and there are also watercolours by Charlotte herself, and a portrait by her of her grandmother, Letitia.

Room 10 is dedicated to Lucien Bonaparte (1775–1840), a cultivated man and a convinced republican who disapproved of his famous brother. It was through him that the Primoli and Roman branch of the Bonaparte family are descended. He took up residence in Rome in 1804, and after he moved in 1808 to the castle of Canino near Viterbo became known as the Prince of Canino. He was an accomplished archaeologist, and carried out excavations at Veio. The last rooms document the lives of his descendents (he had 13 children), including Charles (1803–57), also a Republican who took part in the defence of Rome against the French army in 1849 but had to flee to Paris where he remained until his death. He had married Zenaide, daughter of Joseph, Napoleon's eldest brother and one of their children Charlotte Bonaparte (1832–1901) married Count Pietro Primoli. Their son, Giuseppe was founder of this museum.

The second and third floors of Palazzo Primoli are entered from Via Zanardelli. On the second floor is the **Fondazione Primoli**, with an important library, and on the top floor (there is a lift) is the **Museo Mario Praz** (Map 6; 4), the residence of the art historian and man of letters from 1969 until his death in 1982. Open daily on the hour 09.00–13.00 and on the half hour 14.30–18.30; closed Mon morning. ☎ 06 686 1089. A maximum of ten visitors are accompanied and lent a handsheet (in Italian only). The tour lasts about 30–40mins. There are no labels.

Although he was a Shakespeare scholar and wrote books on Charles Lamb and Lord Byron, Praz is perhaps best remembered for his *History of Interior Decoration* (1945). The apartment is filled with his remarkable collection of decorative arts, paintings, sculpture, drawings, miniatures, fans, wax portraits, porcelain and furniture, particularly representative of the Neo-classical period (late 18C and early 19C), which up until his time had been out of vogue and largely ignored by scholars. The house and its contents as Praz left them were bought by the State in 1986.

The nine rooms here, crowded with possessions and rather gloomy in atmosphere, give a clear idea of his taste. Praz formed his collection while living in the more spacious Palazzo Ricci on Via Giulia, described in his autobiographical book *La Casa della Vita* (published in 1958; translated into English as *The House of Life* in 1964). The works of art include a marble statue of *Cupid* attributed to Adamo Tadolini, a portrait of *Foscolo* by Fabre, and early 19C watercolours of period interiors. His daughter Lucia's room (he married a Scottish wife, Vivyan) has Biedermeier furniture.

Nearby, on the corner of Via di Monte Brianzo, is a medieval building (altered c 1460) which was the **Osteria dell' Orso**. It first became a hotel in the 16C and Rabelais, Montaigne and Goethe were among its later patrons.

Returning to the northern end of Piazza Navona, the remains of the north curve of the stadium, with the entrance gate, can be seen beneath modern buildings in **Piazza di Tor Sanguigna**. The not particularly interesting ruins can be seen only by appointment (☎ 06 6710 3819). From this piazza, **Via dei Coronari** (Map 6; 4), a beautiful Renaissance street on the line of the Roman Via Recta, runs due west. It is now famous for its antique shops, and is well worth exploring. At the beginning, there are interesting streets parallel to the north: Via della Maschera d'Oro with Palazzo Sacripante Ruiz, a fine building attributed to Bartolomeo Ammannati; and the medieval Vicolo dei Tre Archi. Via dei Coronari runs through the Piazzetta di San Simeone with Palazzo Lancellotti, begun by Francesco da Volterra and finished by Carlo Maderno.

Further on is a piazza in front of **San Salvatore in Lauro**, a church with a Palladian interior by Mascherino (1594). To the left of the church, at no. 15, is the entrance to the fine Renaissance cloister (in poor repair). A small courtyard beyond has two Renaissance portals. The refectory contains the *tomb of Eugenius IV (d. 1447) by Isaia da Pisa, one of the earliest sepulchral monuments to exhibit the characteristic forms of the Renaissance. The street continues past nos 122–23, on the left, the so-called House of Raphael and ends in Piazza dei Coronari, off which Via di Panico leads left into Via di Monte Giordano. Here the 18C Palazzo Taverna, formerly Gabrielli, has a beautiful fountain by Antonio Casoni (1618) in the court. The palace stands on **Monte Giordano**, a small, apparently artificial hill that was already inhabited in the 12C. It takes its name from Giordano Orsini (13C) whose legendary fortress stood here. Dante mentions the 'Monte' (*Inferno*, xxviii, 12) in his description of the pilgrims crossing the Ponte Sant'Angelo on the occasion of the jubilee of 1300. The Orsini continued to own the castle until 1688, and the buildings, here still crowded together, betray their medieval origins.

West of Piazza Navona

Off the western side of Piazza Navona, in the street of the same name, is the German church of **Santa Maria dell'Anima** (**Map 6**; **4**), rebuilt in 1500–23. The façade may have been designed by Giuliano da Sangallo. Above the door is a cast of the *Virgin* attributed to Andrea Sansovino, a copy of a highly venerated *Madonna between Two Souls in Purgatory*, which was formerly in the church and was the origin of its name. The original is kept in the sacristy. The entrance is through a pretty little courtyard behind the church at 20 Vicolo della Pace. Open daily 08.00–19.00; fest. 08.30–12.30 and 15.00–19.00.

The **interior** has an unusual plan, derived from late Gothic German churches. The paintings in the vault and on the walls are by Ludovico Seitz (1875–82), who also designed the window over the central door.

On the **south side**, the first chapel has a painting of *San Benno* by Carlo Saraceni; the second chapel, a *Holy Family*, by Giacinto Gimignani, and two funerary monuments by Ercole Ferrata; the third chapel a Crucifix by Giovanni Battista Montano, and 16C frescoes by Girolamo Siciolante da Sermoneta; and the fourth chapel a *Pietà*, by Lorenzetto and Nanni di Baccio Bigio, in imitation of Michelangelo.

In the **sanctuary**, over the high altar, is a *Holy Family with Saints* by Giulio Romano. On the right is the magnificent **tomb of Hadrian VI** (d. 1523), born in Utrecht and the last non-Italian pope until the present Pope John Paul II. He was a learned professor who, after his unexpected election, tried to reform the Church in answer to Luther's criticisms. He lacked support in his short papacy of under two years and could do little to resolve the problems of the Church: the inscription on his tomb reads 'How important, even for the best of men, are the times in which he finds himself.' The tomb, which was designed by Baldassare Peruzzi, has sculptures by Michelangelo Senese and Niccolò Tribolo. On the left is the tomb of Karl Friedrich of Clèves (d. 1575), by Gilles de Rivière and Nicolas d'Arras; a bas-relief from this tomb is in the corridor leading to the sacristy.

On the **north side**, the fourth chapel contains a *Descent from the Cross* and frescoes by Francesco Salviati; the third chapel, a *Life of St Barbara*, and frescoes by Michiel Coxie; and the first chapel a *Martyrdom of St Lambert*, by Carlo Saraceni.

Santa Maria della Pace

In the peaceful little piazza here, in a delightful part of the city, is the beautiful church of Santa Maria della Pace (**Map 6**; **4**). The church was rebuilt by Sixtus IV (1480–84) to celebrate victory over the Turks. There was also a popular legend that a miraculous image of the Virgin in the portico of the old church bled on being struck by a stone. The architect is believed to have been Baccio Pontelli. The church was partly rebuilt in 1611 and again later in the century by Alexander VII, under whose auspices the façade and beautiful semicircular porch with Tuscan columns were erected by Pietro da Cortona; his design for the delightful little piazza and the surrounding area was never completed.

The **cloisters**, commissioned in 1504 by Cardinal Oliviero Carafa, are among Donato Bramante's finest works in Rome. They have two rows of arcades one above the other—columns of the upper row rise from the centres of the arches in the lower row. The tomb of Bishop Bocciaccio (1497) on the right is by the school of Luigi Capponi.

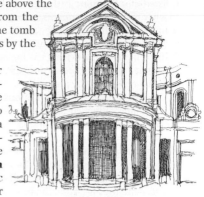

The **interior** (services are no longer held here and it is usually opened by a cus- todian Tues–Fri 10.00–13.00 only; the entrance is sometimes beyond the arch to the left of the façade, at 5 Via Arco della Pace). It consists of a domed octagon pre- ceded by a simple rectangular nave. Above the arch of the first chapel on the **south side** are frescoes of *Sibyls* by Raphael (c 1514), painted for Agostino Chigi, founder of the chapel. They are covered for restora-

Santa Maria della Pace

tion in 2002. They represent (beginning on the left) the Cumaean, Persian, Phrygian and Tiburtine Sibyls, to whom the future is being revealed by angels; their varying shades of awe and wonder are beautifully conveyed in look and gesture. The paintings were restored in 1816 by Palmaroli. Above them are four *Prophets*, by Raphael's pupil Timoteo Viti: on the right, Daniel and David, on the left, Jonah and Hosea. On the altar, is a fine bronze of the *Deposition* by Cosimo Fancelli. The second chapel (Cesi) was designed by Antonio da Sangallo the Younger, and has remarkable marble deco- ration by Simone Mosca (1540–42). The ruined frescoes in the window lunette are by Rosso Fiorentino. The Cesi tombs and sculptures are by Vincenzo de Rossi.

In the niche in the first chapel on the **north side** is a fresco of the *Virgin, St Bridget and St Catherine*, with the donor Ferdinando Ponzetti, by Baldassare Peruzzi, who also painted the small frescoes of Old Testament subjects on the vaulting of the niche. At the sides of the chapel are the little *tombs* of the Ponzetti family (1505 and 1509), with delicately carved decoration and four busts. The second chapel has a much-darkened altarpiece of the *Madonna and Saints* by Marcello Venusti, perhaps from a design by Michelangelo.

In the **octagon**, above the high altar by Carlo Maderno, is the highly venerated 15C image of the *Madonna della Pace*. The beautiful marble tabernacle in the Chapel of the Crucifix (left) is attributed to Pasquale da Caravaggio. On the octagon, to the right of the high altar, is Baldassare Peruzzi's *Presentation in the Temple*.

Via Santa Maria dell'Anima leads south to Piazza Pasquino. Here is a statue which has been known as *Pasquino* since it was placed here in 1501. Apparently named after a tailor who lived in the vicinity, it is a fragment of a marble group thought to represent Menelaus with the body of Patroclus, a copy of a Hellenistic work of the Pergamene school which may once have decorated the Stadium of Domitian (see above). Gian Lorenzo Bernini admired it as the finest Classical work he had seen. It is the most famous of Rome's 'talking' statues, and labels ridiculing contemporary Italian politicians are still often attached to it.

Rome's 'talking' statues

The tailor Pasquino is thought to have originated the custom of attaching witty or caustic comments on topical subjects to the pedestal of this statue, and this method of public satire came to be known by the term *pasquinade*. This effective (and anonymous) way of getting at the rulers of the city, and in particular of criticising the papacy, was much in vogue in the 17C before the days of the free press. Many printing houses and bookshops were opened in the vicinity of the piazza.

Pasquino was the most famous of the 'talking' statues in the city, but labels were attached to various other statues so that they could carry on witty 'conversations'. *Madama Lucrezia*, a colossal antique bust now in Piazza San Marco, conversed with the colossal statue of a river god called *Marforio* which is now in the courtyard of Palazzo Nuovo on the Capitoline Hill. Other statues with this characteristic included *Abbot Luigi*, a statue of a Roman in a toga, which is still outside the church of Sant'Andrea della Valle, and the *Facchino*, the bust of a 16C water-vendor in Via Lata, just off the Corso. The only other 'talking' statue to have survived as such is *Babuino*, a very damaged Roman statue of a reclining Silenus, in Via del Babuino: on the wall behind the fountain here it is still the custom to write up political slogans against the present rulers of Rome and Italy. Stendhal noted on his visit to Rome in 1816: 'What the people of Rome desire above all else is a chance to show their strong contempt for the powers that control their destiny, and to laugh at their expense: hence the dialogues between "Pasquino" and "Marforio".'

From Piazza Pasquino the narrow **Via del Governo Vecchio**, an ancient papal thoroughfare with many traces of the early Renaissance, leads west. At no. 39 on the right is Palazzo Nardini or Palazzo del Governo Vecchio, built in 1473 by Cardinal Stefano Nardini, made Governor of Rome by Paul II. It has a splendid Renaissance portal. Opposite is the remarkable Palazzo Turci (1500), once attributed to Bramante.

The area to the south of Piazza Navona on Corso Vittorio Emanuele II is described in Walk 12.

12 • Along Corso Vittorio Emanuele II

Although the monuments described in this chapter are all in busy and unattractive positions, most of them on the Corso Vittorio Emanuele II (Map 7; 5, and 6; 6, 3), which was laid out in 1876 and is now one of the main traffic arteries of Rome running from Piazza Venezia to the Tiber, the three churches of the Gesù, Sant'Andrea della Valle and the Chiesa Nuova are particularly worth a visit. They were all built in the 16C for the most important new religious orders founded in the Counter Reformation, and it is interesting to compare their sumptuous decorations, funded by wealthy clerics. The charming little Museo Barracco has an exquisite, little-visited collection of ancient Egyptian, Greek and Roman sculpture, although it is at present closed for restoration, and the Museo di Roma, dedicated to the history of the city, was reopened in 2002 after a long period of closure. The museum (part of the Museo Nazionale Romano) known as the Crypta Balbi was opened in 2000, dedicated principally to medieval Rome.

The Gesù

The Gesù (**Map 7; 5**), or the church of the Santissimo Nome di Gesù, is the principal Jesuit church in Rome and the prototype of the sumptuous style to which the order has given its name. Both the façade by Giacomo della Porta and the interior by Vignola were important to the subsequent development of the design of Baroque churches in Rome. It was built between 1568 and 1575 at the expense of Alessandro Farnese. The cupola planned by Vignola was completed by della Porta. Open 06.00–12.30, 16.00–19.15.

The heavily decorated **interior** has a longitudinal plan, with an aisleless nave and lateral chapels. On the **vault** is a *fresco of the *Triumph of the Name of Jesus*, a remarkably original work with marvellous effects of foreshortening by Baciccia. The frescoes of the cupola and the tribune are by the same artist. He also designed the stucco decoration, executed by Ecole Antonio Raggi and Leonardo Retti. The marble decoration of the nave dates from 1858–61.

The first chapel on the **south side** has an altarpiece and frescoes by Agostino Ciampelli. In the third chapel, the altarpiece, vault and walls were all painted by Federico Zuccari; the lunettes and pendentives are by Ventura Salimbeni. The four marble festoons incorporated in the decoration are supposed to have come from the Baths of Titus. The elegant **sacristy** is by Girolamo Rainaldi.

In the **south transept**, the altarpiece is from a sketch by Pietro da Cortona with the *Death of St Francis Xavier* by Carlo Maratta. The high altar and presbytery were redesigned in 1840 by Antonio Sarti. Over the high altar, sumptuously decorated with coloured marbles, is the *Circumcision* by Alessandro Capalti (1842). On the left, a bust of *Cardinal Roberto Bellarmine* by Bernini was placed in a Neo-classical setting after the tomb was destroyed during the rebuilding in the 19C. The two pretty little circular domed chapels on either side of the main apse were decorated by Giuseppe Valeriani (1584–88).

In the **north transept** (being restored) is one of the most elaborate Baroque altars in Rome. The *altar-tomb of St Ignatius is by the Jesuit lay brother Andrea del Pozzo with the help of many assistants (1695–1700) and is resplendent with marble and gilded bronze; the columns are encrusted with lapis lazuli and their bronze decorations are by Andrea Bertoni. The statue of *St Ignatius* is a stucco copy by Adamo Tadolini of the original in silver and gilded copper by Pierre Legros, which was melted down by order of Pius VI in 1798. Above is a group of the *Trinity* by Retti with a terrestrial globe covered with lapis lazuli. In front of the altar is a magnificent balustrade, and at the sides are marble groups: *Religion Triumphing over Heresy* by Pierre Legros the Younger (right), and *Barbarians Adoring the Faith* by Jean Baptiste Théodon (left).

On the **north side**, the third chapel has

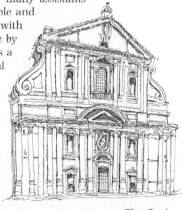

The Gesù

an altarpiece of the *Holy Trinity* by Francesco Bassano, and a *Baptism of Christ* by Salimbeni on the right wall. The second chapel has vault frescoes by Pomarancio, 17C paintings by Giovanni Francesco Romanelli, and interesting sculptures. The first chapel also has a vault frescoed by Pomarancio and two paintings by Francesco Mola. The singing of a Te Deum in this church annually on 31 December is a magnificent traditional ceremony.

To the right of the Gesù's façade, at no. 45 Piazza del Gesù, is the entrance to the rooms where St Ignatius lived from 1544 to his death in 1556. They contain mementoes, paintings and documents. Open Mon–Sat 16.00–18.00; fest. 10.00–12.00. An adjoining corridor was decorated by Andrea Pozzo c 1680.

Via d'Aracoeli leads from Piazza del Gesù towards the Capitoline Hill: off it, to the right, is Via delle Botteghe Oscure, which until 2000 housed the headquarters of the former Italian Communist Party (*Partito Comunista Italiana*), renamed the *Partito Democratico della Sinistra* after the fall of the Berlin Wall in 1989. Nearby are the remains of a **temple** (seen from the railings), probably a Temple of Nymphs, dating from the 1C BC, found in 1938.

Crypta Balbi

At no. 31, in Palazzo Paganica is the so-called Crypta Balbi, a museum of medieval Rome, on a site where systematic excavations were begun in 1983 by the Italian State to study the various levels of development in the urban history of Rome above a Roman theatre built by a certain Balbus, and a cryptoporticus (known as the Crypta Balbi). Apart from the scant Roman remains on this site, the finds from later buildings including a church and monastery, are particularly interesting as illustrations of the early medieval period in Rome, about which relatively little is known since excavations in other parts of the city have tended in the past to concentrate on unearthing Roman remains, destroying the later levels of occupation above them. The museum is part of the Museo Nazionale Romano, and the medieval exhibits, beautifully displayed, include finds made here, as well as from other collections in Rome.

Opening times

09.00–19.45; closed Mon. ☎ 06 3996 7700. When you buy the ticket you are told when you can visit the excavations (see below) below ground level, but these are, at present, the least interesting part of the museum.

The exhibits on the **ground floor** illustrate the archaeology and history of this urban site in the centre of Rome, from Roman times to the present day. Two delicately carved Roman altars found during excavations here are displayed near the ticket office. **Room 1** illustrates the ancient history of the area of the Campus Martius, or Plain of Mars. At first it included the whole area between the Capitoline Hill, the Tiber, and the Quirinal and Pincian hills, but came to refer more precisely to the low-lying ground enclosed in the Tiber bend. It was said originally to have been the property of the Tarquins, and to have become public land after the expulsion of the kings. The area at first had a predominantly military nature: it took its name from the sacred area devoted to Mars, the god of war, to whom an ancient altar here was dedicated. After the 2C BC many temples and edifices for public entertainments were built, and on other parts of the land military exercises and athletic competitions were held. Since the low-lying area to the north was subject to flooding from the Tiber, Hadrian raised the ground level and made numerous other improvements. The southern part of the Campus Martius was the Prata Flaminia, with the Circus of Flaminius. The area was not included in the walls of Rome until Aurelian built his famous wall round the city (AD 272–79).

Room 2 illustrates the building of the small Theatre of Balbus inaugurated in 13 BC, adjoined to the west (behind the stage) by a cryptoporticus known as the Crypta Balbi, remains of which have been uncovered here (in the courtyard the excavations and a pilaster from the portico can be seen). This theatre was the smallest of the three theatres which were built at this time in Rome (the other two were the Theatre of Marcellus and the Theatre of Pompey).

The large room to the left of the corridor is divided into sections, illustrating the history of the site of the theatre and cryptoporticus from Roman times through the medieval period and up to the present day. **Section 3** describes the buildings after their reconstruction by Domitian following a fire in 80 AD. Here is exhibited a fragment, showing this area, of the Forma Urbis, a marble 'map' of ancient Rome in AD 193–211 found in the Forum of Peace in 1562, and one of the most important documents for our knowledge of the topography of the Roman city. **Sections 4** and **5** have finds from the medieval monastery of San Lorenzo and the church of Santa Maria on the site, including fragments of 9C plutei and 13C frescoes. In **section 6** is a case full of ceramics from dwellings dating from the 11C–18C. **Section 7** has documents relating to the conservatory of Santa Caterina built on this site in 1549 by Nanni di Baccio Bigio to house the daughters of Roman prostitutes, and maiolica used in the institute found during excavations. The last **section 8** gives the history of the site in the 19C, the widening of Via delle Botteghe Oscure in 1935, and the archaeological investigation of the entire area from 1983 to the present day, a remarkable project intent on revealing all periods of the history of this urban area.

Rooms 9–11, to the right of the corridor display architectural fragments found on the site including a very fine huge Corinthian capital, probably once part of the theatre, and a model of the site. In the last room can be seen part of the wall of the Roman cryptoporticus.

The sections on the **second floor**, mostly in a large hall with a fine wood roof, illustrate the history of Rome in the Middle Ages (from the 5C to the 10C).

Room 1, in two sections, displays household objects, including cutlery and kitchen utensils from various sites in the city, including 4C–6C jewellery, some 6C ceramics found recently in the House of the Vestals in the Roman Forum, oil lamps, glass, and coins. In the second section are finds from sporadic tombs in the city from 5C–8C. **Room 2** is devoted to the Byzantine period, with 7C lead seals found on this site, ceramics, tools, jewellery, and lamps. In **room 3** are displayed interesting 7C–9C frescoes detached from a building below the church of Santa Maria in Via Lata (see p 147) on the Corso. In **room 4** are exhibits related to Papal Rome from the 8C onwards. These include pilgrims' phials (made out of lead, terracotta or glass), commemorative inscriptions, and 8C and 9C architectural fragments from Roman churches. The last part of the hall is devoted to the economic life of the city in the Middle Ages, with coins, and a rare (reconstructed) bishop's throne dating from the 9C, decorated in incised bone, found on this site. On the platform above (**5**) are medieval finds from the area of the Fori Imperiali and Roman Forum which prove these areas were still densely inhabited in medieval times.

The (rather uninteresting) Roman remains below ground level are shown by a custodian. Excavations continue on this site, and so far the exedra in the centre of the Balbi cryptoporticus, and a Mithreum have been identified.

In Via Caetani a plaque and bas-relief mark the place where the body of the Italian Prime Minister Aldo Moro was abandoned by his murderers in 1978.

Around Largo Argentina

Via delle Botteghe Oscure ends at Largo Argentina (**Map 7**; **5**), a traffic-ridden square with numerous buses and the tram terminus from Trastevere, and an impressive group of four Republican temples, known as the **Area Sacra di Largo Argentina**. The site was demolished in 1926–29 for a new building which, after the temples had been discovered and excavated, was never built. The ruins can be seen clearly from the railings outside. Since 1994 the large cat colony here has been looked after by a voluntary association which has its headquarters in an underground shelter beside the temples and welcomes visitors. About 450 cats are abandoned every year in Rome and many of them find refuge here. ☎ 06 687 2133; ✉ www.romancats.com.

All the temples face a courtyard to the east paved with travertine. It is not yet known with certainty to whom they were dedicated, so they are usually identified by letters. **Temple A** is peripteral and hexastyle; most of the tufa columns and stylobate are preserved. In the Middle Ages the church of St Nicholas was built over it; the apses of the church (otherwise demolished) may still be seen. **Temple B**, the most recent temple, is circular; six columns survive, as well as the original flight of steps and the altar. A podium behind this temple, near Via di Torre Argentina, almost certainly belongs to the Curia Pompei where Julius Caesar was murdered. **Temple C**, oldest of the four, was built at a lower level; it dates from the end of the 4C or the beginning of the 3C BC. In the Imperial era the cella was rebuilt and the columns and podium covered with stucco. The altar, with an inscription relating to c 180 BC, was discovered in 1935; even this was a replacement of an older altar. **Temple D**, in travertine, is the largest; it has not been completely excavated as part of it is under Via Florida, to the south. During the excavations the medieval Torre del Papito here was restored and isolated.

Just off the north side of the square, at the beginning of Via dei Cestari, is the church of the **Santissime Stimmate**, rebuilt at the beginning of the 18C by Giovanni Battista Contini. It contains paintings by Francesco Trevisani, including the high altarpiece of *St Francis Receiving the Stigmata* (1714).

On the west side of Largo Argentina is the **Teatro Argentina** dating from 1730, the most important theatre in Rome during the 18C. The façade is by Pietro Holl (1826). In 1816 the first performance of Rossini's *Barber of Seville* was given here, and in 1851 that of Verdi's *Rigoletto*. The theatre is now noted for drama productions—the Teatro di Roma is the resident company. It has a small museum usually open 10.00–13.30; closed Mon, but best to telephone first: ☎ 06 6840 0061.

On the right of the theatre, Via del Sudario leads out of the square past the handsome south façade of Palazzo Caffarelli Vidoni, attributed to Lorenzo Lotti (c 1515). Opposite is the little **Chiesa del Sudario** (1604) which was the court church of the House of Savoy from 1871 to 1946. The façade is by Carlo Rainaldi, and inside (closed) are late 19C works by Cesare Maccari.

Beyond is the delightful **Palazzetto del Burcardo** (Map 6; 6), built in 1503 for Bishop Hans Burckardt or Burckhardt, who was born in Strasbourg. When he came to live in Rome in 1479, he wrote a remarkable account of the papal court under Innocent VIII and Alexander VI. He called the house the Torre Argentina from the Latin name for Strasbourg (*Argentoratum*), which in turn became the name of the piazza. The back doors of the Teatro Argentina (see above) open on to the courtyard. It houses the *Italian Authors and Publishers Society*, and a library of some 40,000 volumes, the earliest of which date from the 16C, including nearly all the editions of Carlo Goldoni's works, as well as a photographic archive. On the ground floor there is an interesting little theatrical museum which contains statuettes of characters from the *commedia dell'arte*, puppets, costumes, autograph texts, prints, drawings, paintings, and costumes. Open Mon–Fri 09.00–13.30. ☎ 06 681 9471.

Sant'Andrea della Valle

Via del Sudario ends in the little Piazza Vidoni, where a Roman statue called *Abate Luigi*, one of Rome's 'talking' statues (see p 198), has been placed against the side wall of the church of **Sant'Andrea della Valle** (Map 6; 6), which faces Corso Vittorio Emanuele II. Open 07.30–12.00 and 16.30–19.30. The church was begun in 1591 financed by Cardinal Alfonso Gesualdo, for the religous Order of the Theatines, which had been founded in 1524 by Giampietro Carafa (afterwards Paul IV). Architects involved included Giacomo della Porta and Pier Paolo Olivieri. It was continued by Carlo Maderno, who crowned it with a fine dome, the highest in Rome after that of St Peter's. The façade was added in the following century (1665) by Carlo Rainaldi

The aisleless **interior** has a high barrel vault and spacious apse. Inspired by the Gesù it gives the impression of a sumptuous reception hall rather than a house of prayer. On the **south side**, the first chapel, by Carlo Fontana, has green marble columns and fine 17C sculptures by Ercole Antonio Raggi. The design of the second, the Strozzi chapel, shows the influence of Michelangelo and contains reproductions in bronze of his *Pietà* and of his statues of *Leah* and *Rachel* from the projected tomb of Julius II. The third chapel has a Neo-classical monument attributed to Giuseppe de Fabris and Rinaldo Rinaldi. At the east end of the nave, high up, are similar monuments of two popes of the Piccolomini family: on the right, Pius III (d. 1503) attributed to Francesco Ferrucci and his son Sebastiano; on the left Pius II (d. 1464) attributed to Paolo Taccone and a follower of Andrea Bregno

In the **dome**, high up above the crossing, is the *Glory of Paradise* by Lanfranco; and in the pendentives, the *Evangelists* by Domenichino (1623). Domenichino also designed the splendid presbytery and painted the *Six Virtues* and the scenes from the *Life of St Andrew* in the vault of the apse; the gigantic frescoes on the wall below are by Mattia Preti. The **sacristy** has 17C decorations. In the little chapel on the right of the presbytery is a 17C crucifix, and in the north transept is an altar by Cesare Bazzani (1912) in the Baroque style.

On the **north side**, the third chapel has an altarpiece of *St Sebastian* by Giovanni de'Vecchi, and the second chapel an altarpiece by Francesco Manno (early 19C). The first chapel, frescoed by Passignano, has four good late 16C–early 17C sculptures: on the left, *Mary Magdalene* by Cristoforo Stati, and *St John the Baptist* by Pietro Bernini; and on the right, *St John the Evangelist* by Ambrogio Bonvicino and *Santa Marta* by Francesco Mochi.

Opposite the church façade, at the beginning of Corso del Rinascimento, is a fountain (covered for restoration) by Carlo Maderno decorated with an eagle and a dragon. Corso Vittorio Emanuele II continues past **Palazzo Massimo alle Colonne**, skilfully set in a narrow, irregular site, by Baldassare Peruzzi (1532–36). The convex façade, being restored, follows the line of the cavea of the Odeon of Domitian which stood here. The beautiful portico is decorated with stuccoes. The palace has two courtyards: one a charming Renaissance work with a frescoed loggia and a Baroque fountain, and the second (in very poor repair) with 17C decorations. The interior is being slowly restored, and a fresco has been uncovered which may be the work of Giulio Romano. In Piazza dei Massimi, behind the palace (reached from Corso Rinascimento) is the **Palazzetto Massimi**, called the Palazzo Istoriato because it has remains of a painted façade by the school of Daniele da Volterra (1523). Here Pannartz and Sweynheim transferred their press from Subiaco in 1467 and issued the first books printed in Rome. The marble cipollino column set up in the piazza belonged to the Odeon of Domitian.

The Corso Vittorio Emanuele II widens at a little piazza in front of the church of **San Pantaleo** dating from 1216 (open only early in the morning). It was rebuilt in 1681 by Antonio de Rossi and preserves its 17C interior with a vault fresco by Filippo Gherardi. The façade was added by Giuseppe Valadier in 1806.

Museo di Roma

The huge **Palazzo Braschi** built after 1792 by Cosimo Morelli houses the Museo di Roma (**Map 6;6**), founded in 1930 to illustrate the history and life of Rome from the Middle Ages to the present day. It was closed for restoration in 1988 and finally partially reopened in 2002 (open 09.00–18.00, closed Mon). Most of the exhibits relate to the 17C–19C.

At the foot of the staircase is a colossal sculptural group of the *Baptism of Christ* by Francesco Mochi. The magnificent **staircase** (1791–1804), by Cosimo Morelli, incorporates 18 antique columns of red granite. The ancient Roman statues decorating the staircase are the only works from the huge Braschi collection to have survived. The fine neo-Classical stuccoes are by Luigi Acquisti (perhaps on a design by Valadier).

First floor. **Rooms 1** and **2** are devoted to Pius VI who commissioned Palazzo Braschi and died in exile in 1799. Here are three huge paintings by Gavin Hamilton illustrating the story of Helen and Paris from Villa Borghese, and a portrait of the Pope by Giovanni Domenico Porta. In the oval **room 3** are busts of popes and cardinals including works by Filippo Della Valle, and Francesco Duquesnoy. **Room 4** contains 17C portraits and scenes of tournaments in Rome. The 17C and 18C portraits of cardinals in **room 5** include two by Baciccio and Carlo Moratti. **Room 6** illustrates the history of the magistrates who presided over the Roman Senate, including some 19C ceremonial robes. The 17C–19C prints in **room 7** include works by Giovanni Paolo Pannini. Beyond **room 8**, with 18C views of celebrations in Piazza del Popolo, there are more 18C and 19C paintings of Rome by Ippolito Caffi and Gaspar van Wittel in **room 9**. From the window in **room 10** there is a splendid view over Piazza Navona. Here are exhibited busts by Christopher Hewitson (1776), a painting of the Vitali family by Antonio Canova and portraits by Stefano Tofanelli. Thre is also a painted self–portrait by Canova (c 1799) and a plaster model by him for a colossal self-portrait bust in marble he made for his tomb (1811–12). The portrait of *John*

Staples (1773) is by Pompeo Girolamo Batoni. **Room 11** contains 19C portraits by Francesco Podesti and Guglielmo de Sanctis. In **room 12** is a very fine ceiling fresco of the fable of Psyche by Cigoli (1610–13) detached from Palazzo Borghese on the Quirinal Hill, and some costumes dating from 1760–80.

Second floor. Here are displayed remnants of collections once owned by the great patrician families of Rome. **Room 1** contains 17C cabinets with a series of miniature scenes of Rome, and paintings of processions in the city. In **room 2** is a 17C cabinet which once contained the Barberini collection of medals. The busts of the Barberini in **room 3** include one of Carlo Barberini by Francesco Mochi. **Rooms 4–7** are dedicated to the Rospigliosi family, and include a model of their chapel in the church of San Francesco a Ripa, portraits of their horses, and paintings of their residences. **Room 6** was decorated in the mid 19C with a chinoiserie vault. The costumes exhibited here date from 1770–90. In **room 8** are two mirrors and four divans all dating from around 1840 which once decorated the Torlonia residence in Piazza Venezia (demolished in 1902). The series of large drawings are by Francesco Podesti. In **room 9** are 12 tempera lunettes executed for the Torlonia by Filippo Bigioli in 1839 and plaster models by Pietro Tenerani of monuments to the Torlonia. **Room 10** contains a lovely alcove designed by Giovanni Battista Caretti and painted by Filippo Bigioli, also once in Palazzo Torlonia. **Room 11** is devoted to the Giustiniani Bandini and Brancaccio families, including the bust of a girl attributed to Bertel Thorvaldsen, reliefs by Pietro Tenerani, and portraits by Francesco Gai (1879). The last **room 12** has 19C costumes, and a fine collection of 19C photos.

There are long-term plans to open more rooms to exhibit the rest of the collection.

The **Gabinetto Comunale delle Stampe e archivio fotografico** is housed in the same building. Admission only by appointment, ☎ 06 6830 8393.

Museo Barracco

Opposite Palazzo Braschi is the elegant little Renaissance palace sometimes called the **Piccola Farnesina** (Map 6; 6). Since 1948 the palace has contained the Museo Barracco, a museum of ancient sculpture, at present closed for restoration (due to reopen in 2004; for information, ☎ 06 6880 6848). The collection, not large but choice, was formed by Senator Giovanni Barracco (1829–1914) and presented by him to the city of Rome in 1902.

History of the Piccola Farnesina

It was built in 1523 to the order of the French prelate Thomas Le Roy; the architect was almost certainly Antonio da Sangallo the Younger. Le Roy, the son of a French peasant, held important posts at the pontifical court and played a significant part in the concordat of 1516 between Leo X and Francis I of France. For his services he was ennobled and permitted to augment his coat of arms with the lilies of France. This heraldic privilege is recorded in the architectural details of the palace: the three floors are divided horizontally by projecting bands displaying the Le Roy ermines and the Farnese lilies, which were substituted for the lilies of France and gave the palace the name by which it is best known. It has no connection with the Villa Farnesina in Trastevere. The palace is also called the Farnesina ai Baullari and Palazzo Le Roy or Regis.

The Piccola Farnesina was built to face Vicolo dell'Aquila, to the south. The construction of the Corso Vittorio Emanuele II left exposed the north side of the palace, which backed on houses that had to be pulled down to make room for the new street. A fine new façade on the Corso was therefore built in 1898–1901; the architect was Enrico Guj, who also modified the side of the palace facing Piazza dei Baullari and added the steps and balustrade. At this time a Roman building of the late Imperial period (with 4C frescoes) was discovered beneath the foundations, which can be visited when the museum reopens.

Only some of the most important pieces in the collection are mentioned below. There is a very fine collection of **Egyptian sculpture** from the beginning of the 3rd millennium to the end of the Roman era, including a head of *Rameses II*, as a young man, with a blue chaplet (1299–1233 BC), the head of a *Priest Wearing a Diadem*, once thought to be a portrait of Julius Caesar (an interesting example from Roman Egypt), and a *Sphinx of Queen Hatshepsut*, with the seal of Thutmosis III (1504–1450 BC), as well as bas reliefs, statuettes, canopic vases, amulets, seals and scarabs. Among the **Greek originals of the 5C** BC is a fragment of an Attic sepulchral stele with a horseman; an Archaic head of a youth; a head of Athena (perhaps from southern Italy); a head of an *Athlete*; a head of *Marsyas*, replica of the head of the famous statue by Myron; and a head of *Apollo*, after an original by Pheidias, possibly the bronze statue seen by Pausanias near the Parthenon (Athens, before 450 BC). There are also good copies of works by Polykleitos: a statuette of *Hercules*, and the upper part of a statue of an *Amazon*, after the original in the Temple of Diana at Ephesus, and part of a leg of this statue. A replica of the *Westmacott Athlete* in the British Museum, is also derived from an original by Polykleitos, possibly a portrait of Kyniskos, victor at Mantinea.

There are also early works from the Cyclades and Mycenae. The ceramics include two amphorae of the 5C BC, one attributed to the Berlin Painter, and works from Magna Graecia. Among the 4C Attic works are a *votive relief to Apollo, and the head of *Apollo Kitharoidos*, the best existing replica of the statue by Praxiteles.

Hellenistic sculptures include *Bitch Licking her Wounds*, perhaps a replica of the masterpiece by Lysippos, formerly in the Temple of Jupiter on the Capitoline, and portrait heads.

There are **Sumerian and Assyrian works** in bronze, terracotta and alabaster, and fine Assyrian reliefs; as well as works dating from the 6C–5C BC from Cyprus; and Etruscan finds from Chianciano and Chiusi, and a Phoenician work found in Sardinia (an alabaster lion mask). Roman works include a statuette of *Neptune of the 1C BC (from a 4C Greek original) and the head of a *Roman Boy*, perhaps Nero. There are also sepulchral reliefs from Palmyra (3C AD).

The **medieval** exhibits include two charming marble reliefs from the Duomo of Sorrento (10C–11C); and a fragment of a mosaic from old St Peter's with the representation of the Ecclesia Romana.

Chiesa Nuova

The huge Renaissance Palazzo della Cancelleria on the Corso Vittorio Emanuele II is described in Walk 13. The Corso continues past the 16C Palazzo Sora, at no. 217 on the right, to a piazza with a charming fountain in the shape of a soup tureen in front of the Chiesa Nuova or Santa Maria in Vallicella (**Map 6; 4**).

History of the Chiesa Nuova

The church was built under the inspiration of St Philip Neri, born in Florence in 1515, who came to Rome c 1530 and founded an 'oratorio' here (see below). He was an outstanding figure of the Counter Reformation and in recognition of his Oratorian order, in 1575 Gregory XIII gave him Santa Maria in Vallicella, which he proceeded to rebuild with the patronage of Cardinal Pier Donato Cesi and his brother Angelo. Among the architects were Matteo Bartolini da Città di Castello and Martino Longhi the Elder (1575–1605), but the façade is by Fausto Rughesi.

The vault, apse and dome in the **interior** were decorated by Pietro da Cortona (1664) and the whole church is brilliantly gilded. In the sanctuary are three *paintings by Rubens, commissioned by the Oratorians before he left Rome in 1608 (see p 162). Resplendent with colour they represent the **Madonna and Angels** (over the high altar), **Saints Domitilla, Nereus and Achilleus** (to the right); and **Saints Gregory, Maurus and Papianus** (to the left). They are the only paintings by Rubens still in a church in the city.

On the right of the apse, under the fine 18C cantoria, is the Cappella Spada, designed by Carlo Rainaldi, with an altarpiece of the **Madonna between St Charles and St Ignatius** by Carlo Maratta. St Philip Neri is buried beneath the altar of the sumptuous Cappella di San Filippo (1600–04) on the left of the apse; his portrait in mosaic is copied from a painting by Reni. In the north transept is the *Presentation of the Virgin in the Temple* by Federico Barocci. In the fine 17C sacristy, with a fresco by Pietro da Cortona, is a statue of *St Philip Neri and an Angel*, by Alessandro Algardi. From here there is access to another chapel and the rooms of St Philip Neri with works by Guercino, Pietro da Cortona, Reni and Garofalo, and mementoes of the saint.

In the neighbouring **Oratorio dei Filippini**, rebuilt largely by Francesco Borromini (1637–52), St Philip instituted the musical gatherings which became known as oratorios, and have given their name to a form of musical composition. The façade, between that of a church and a palace, has a remarkably subtle design. The delightful clock-tower can be seen from Via dei Banchi Nuovi, on the right. The extensive convent buildings, also by Borromini, are now occupied by the Vallicelliana Library, specialising in books on the history of Rome, the Municipal Archives and various learned societies.

The Corso Vittorio Emanuele II continues past a little piazza on the left with Palazzo Sforza Cesarini, with a 15C courtyard, to end at Ponte Vittorio Emanuele II over the Tiber. The interesting area to the west and south of Corso Vittorio Emanuele II is described in Walk 13.

13 • Campo dei Fiori, Piazza Farnese and Via Giulia

Campo dei Fiori is one of the most attractive old squares in Rome with a characteristic busy food market. The two most important Renaissance palaces in Rome, with splendid courtyards—Palazzo della Cancelleria and Palazzo Farnese, in an elegant little piazza—are close by. Both were built by wealthy cardinals, but both are normally inaccessible to the public. Palazzo Spada, dating from the following century and with beautiful exterior stucco decorations, is open regularly. It contains an important gallery of 17C and 18C paintings and a trompe l'oeil perspective by Francesco Borromini in the garden. Via Giulia, laid out in the early 16C, is one of the most beautiful streets in the city. This area also includes numerous churches of interest, including San Giovanni Battista dei Fiorentini, San Carlo ai Catinari, Sant'Eligio degli Orefici (designed by Raphael) and Santa Maria di Monserrato.

Palazzo della Cancelleria

Roughly half-way along Corso Vittorio Emanuele II (see Walk 12) is Piazza della Cancelleria, along one whole side of which is the graceful façade of Palazzo della Cancelleria (**Map 6**; **6**), a masterpiece of the Renaissance. It was built for Cardinal Raffaello Riario by an unknown architect, probably in 1486, with a double order of pilasters. Showing Florentine influence, it is thought that Donato Bramante may have helped at a late stage, possibly designing the beautiful courtyard; it is also probable that Andrea Bregno was involved in the building. The magnificent **courtyard**, always visible from the main doorway, has double loggie with antique columns. The palace is now the seat of the three Tribunals of the Vatican, including the Sacra Rota, and of the Pontificia Accademia Romana di Archeologia.

Incorporated into the palace is the basilica of **San Lorenzo in Damaso**, which is entered by a doorway at the right end of the main façade. The ancient basilica founded by Pope St Damasus I in the 4C, was one of the most important and largest early Christian churches in Rome. Remains of this building dating from the 4C and 5C as well as a cemetery in use from the 8C to the 15C were discovered beneath the courtyard of the palace in 1988–91. It was finally demolished in the 15C when the present church—built on part of the site and contemporary with the palace—had been completed. It was entirely restored in 1868–82, and again in the 20C after a fire. It has a double atrium, and over the fine doorway in the right aisle is a detached lunette fresco of *Angel Musicians* by Cavaliere d'Arpino, which was formerly in the nave. The adjoining chapel has a 14C crucifix in wood. In the main apse, the *Coronation of the Virgin with Saints* by Federico Zuccari was commissioned by Cardinal Alessandro Farnese in 1568.

In the chapel at the end of the left aisle is a 12C icon of the Virgin brought here from Santa Maria di Grottapinto in 1465. On the aisle wall here is the tomb of Cardinal Ludovico Trevisan, called Mezzarota Scarampi (1505).

Campo dei Fiori and Palazzo Farnese

At the southern end of Piazza della Cancelleria, beyond the interesting old Via del Pellegrino which skirts the side of the palace, with shops set into the façade on street level, opens **Campo dei Fiori** (Map 6; 6). Once a meadow, it became one of the most important piazze in Rome in the 15C. Executions were occasionally carried out here: in the centre, the fine monument to *Giordano Bruno*, by Ettore Ferrari (1889), stands on the spot where Bruno was burned alive as a

Campo dei Fiori

heretic by the Inquisition in 1600. Campo dei Fiori has been a market-place since 1869, and it still has attractive old stalls where some of the merchandise is sold in lovely old baskets, under canvas shades. The fountain in the form of a soup-tureen, in pink porphyry and granite, was installed here in 1898. Campo dei Fiori is the centre of a distinctive district of the city, with numerous artisans' workshops. The beautiful old Via dei Cappellari, which leads out of the north-west side of the piazza, and the parallel Via del Pellegrino are worth exploring.

The huge 15C **Palazzo Pio** (Righetti), at the east end of the piazza, was built over the ruins of Pompey's Theatre (see below), which was surmounted, on the highest part of the cavea, by a Temple of Venus. The late 16C façade of the palace by Camillo Arcucci faces Piazza del Biscione, where at no. 89 there is a small house with a painted façade. The impressive remains of the theatre can be seen on request at the restaurant in the piazza. From here a frescoed archway leads into a dark passageway by the old (deconsecrated) chapel of **Santa Maria di Grottapinta** to Via di Grotta Pinta. If this is closed it is necessary to reach Via di Grotta Pinta by way of Via del Biscione (where the *Albergo Sole* is thought to be the oldest hotel in the city), Piazza del Paradiso and Via dei Chiavari, from where there is a good view of the dome of Sant'Andrea della Valle. The semicircular Via di Grotta Pinta follows the line of the auditorium of the **Theatre of Pompey** (55 BC), Rome's first stone-built theatre; to the east of it formerly stood the great rectangular Porticus of Pompey, off which opened the Curia (the remains of which have been identified in Largo Argentina; see p 202), where Julius Caesar was murdered on 15 March 44 BC at the foot of a statue of Pompey, perhaps the one now in Palazzo Spada. The modern Teatro dei Satiri is here.

Via dei Baullari connects Campo dei Fiori with **Piazza Farnese**, created by the Farnese in front of their splendid palace. Here are two huge baths of Egyptian granite, brought from the Baths of Caracalla in the 16C and used by the Farnese as a type of 'royal box' for the spectacles which were held in the square. They were adapted as fountains (using the Farnese lilies) in 1626.

Palazzo Farnese (Map 6; 6), the most magnificent Renaissance palace in Rome, is now the French Embassy; it was first used as such in 1635.

History of Palazzo Farnese

The palace was designed by Antonio da Sangallo the Younger for Cardinal Alessandro Farnese, afterwards Paul III (the pope who excommunicated King Henry VIII of England in 1538.) Sangallo designed the vestibule, with a beautiful colonnade and stuccoed ceiling, and the first two storeys of the courtyard. He also began the piazza façade and the two sides, and after his death in 1546 Michelangelo finished the upper storeys and added the superb entablature. Work on the back of the palace was continued by Vignola and Giacomo della Porta.

In the 18C the palace became the property of the Bourbons of Naples, who transferred the magnificent Farnese collection of antique sculpture (which included the *Farnese Bull* found in the Baths of Caracalla in 1545) to that city. On his visit to Rome in 1787 Goethe records this loss for the city of Rome, lamenting: 'If they could detach the Gallery with the Carracci from Palazzo Farnese and transport it, they would.'

In the **interior** (not at present open to the public) the huge Salon d'Hercule is named after the gigantic statue of the *Farnese Hercules*, which was also taken by the Bourbons to Naples. It has a fine wooden ceiling by Sangallo, and two statues representing *Piety* and *Abundance* by Guglielmo della Porta.

The Galleria has a magnificent *frescoed ceiling of mythological subjects which is the masterpiece of Annibale Carracci (1597–1603). The ingenious treatment of the angles, and the impressive overall scheme centring on the *Triumph of Bacchus*, demonstrate the great imagination of the artist. This work had a profound influence on later Baroque ceiling decorations. Carracci was assisted by his brother Agostino, and—in the frescoes above the doors and niches—by Domenichino.

Palazzo Spada

Vicolo de'Venti leads out of the piazza to Piazza Capodiferro, with the huge Palazzo Spada (**Map 6; 6**), built for Cardinal Girolomo Capodiferro in 1544, probably by Giulio Mazzoni. The palace was acquired in the 17C by Cardinal Bernardino Spada and is now owned by the State. It has been the seat of the Council of State (or Supreme Court) since 1889. The courtyard and façade are by Giulio Mazzoni or Girolamo da Carpi and are outstanding examples of stucco decoration.

Borromini restored the palace for his friend Cardinal Spada, and designed a painted niche with a statue on a wall in Piazza Capodiferro to close the view from the garden entrance on Via Giulia. The design of the niche has been found beneath the intonaco, and reconstructed here above an ancient sarcophagus which serves as a fountain in the piazza.

The entrance is reached through a door in the side street, and a spiral staircase from a corridor at the back of the palace leads up to the **Galleria Spada** a collection of paintings formed by Cardinal Spada and augmented by successive generations of his family. Arranged in four rooms which preserve their 17C decoration and furnishings, the important collection of 17C and 18C paintings (and 2C and 3C Roman sculpture) is a fascinating example of a 17C Roman patrician family's private collection, which survives almost intact. It was acquired by the State in 1926.

Opening times

Gallery open 08.30–19.00; closed Mon.
☎ 06 683 2409, ✉ www.galleria
borghese.it. The State Rooms on the first
floor (used by the Italian government)
are only open by appointment;

☎ 06 682 7568.
The works are numbered to
correspond with the handlists
available in each room.

Room I. The two portraits of *Cardinal Bernardino Spada* are by Guido Reni (**32**) and Guercino (**35**); *St Jerome* (**29**) is also by Reni. **Room II**. (**56**) *Visitation*, by Andrea del Sarto; (**77**) *Portrait of a Young Man* by Jan van Scorel; (**60**) *Musician*, an unfinished work by the school of Titian. The portrait of *Pope Paul III* is a copy of a work by Titian. Also here are works by Sigismondo Foschi, Lavinia Fontana, Marco Palmezzano and Hans Durer (**78**. *Young Man*). On the wall opposite the window are fragments of a larger painted frieze by Perino del Vaga, designs for tapestries originally intended for the wall below Michelangelo's *Last Judgment* in the Sistine Chapel.

Room III contains a *sketch for the vaulting of the Gesù by Baciccia (**133**) and a *Portrait of a Cardinal* by the school of Rubens (120). Also works by Niccolò dell'Abate, Ciro Ferri, Pietro Testa, Antonio Carracci, Francesco Trevisani, Guercino (132. *Death of Dido*), Francesco Furini, J.F. Voet, Nicolò Tornioli, P. Snayers and Jan Breughel the Elder. Among the Roman sculpture are a *Seated Philosopher*, a bust of a woman of the 2C AD, and two Roman statuettes of boys, one dressed in the lion-skin of Hercules, and another in the philosopher's pallium.

Room IV displays a number of works by Michelangelo Cerquozzi, including (161) *Masaniello's Revolt in Naples*. Also here are works by Orazio Gentileschi and his daughter Artemisia, and Mattia Preti. The Roman bust of a boy dates from the Julio-Claudian period.

On request to the custodian in the gallery you can see Borromini's ingenious trompe l'oeil perspective in the garden, planted with orange trees. This little garden building makes use of the waste space between the Spada garden and the adjoining Palazzo Massari. The dimension of the tunnel is perspectively multiplied more than four times through the use of light and spacing of the columns.

Of the **State Rooms** on the first floor (for admission, see above), the General Council Chamber has magnificent trompe l'oeil frescoes by the 17C Bolognese artists Agostino Mitelli and Michelangelo Colonna, with birds and figures peering into the room from around columns and window ledges. The colossal statue of *Pompey* is traditionally thought to be the one at the foot of which Caesar was murdered. The Corridor of Stuccoes is a delightful work by Giulio Mazzoni (1559), complemented by his ornamentation of the façade of the court seen through the windows. The Meridiana is a corridor decorated by Giovanni Battista Ruggeri, mapping the time at various places in the world. The eight very fine Hellenistic reliefs (2C AD) here of mythological subjects are in a particularly good state of preservation.

Via Capo di Ferro continues to another small piazza in front of the church of **Santissima Trinità dei Pellegrini** by Paolo Maggi (1603–16). Open only for services on Sunday. The façade was added in 1723 by Francesco de Sanctis. The interior contains 17C works by Guido Reni (*The Trinity*), Borgognone and Cavaliere d'Arpino. In the neighbouring hospice (1625), the poet Goffredo Mameli, author of the national hymn which bears his name, died at the age of 22 from wounds received fighting for the Roman Republic in 1849.

Via dell'Arco del Monte di Pietà skirts the flank of the **Monte di Pietà** (now a bank), which has a long history as a pawnshop. The façade, in Piazza del Monte di Pietà, by Ottaviano Nonni (Il Mascherino) was enlarged by Carlo Maderno, with a clock and small marble bell-tower attributed to Borromini. A fine domed chapel (admission on request) by Carlo Maderno (1641; restored 1725) contains high reliefs by Domenico Guidi, Pierre Legros and Jean-Baptiste Théodon.

Several streets continue to the animated Via de' Giubbonari, a busy local shopping street closed to cars, which connects Campo dei Fiori with Via Arenula. It leads right to the domed church of **San Carlo ai Catinari** (Map 6; 6), built by Rosato Rosati (1612–20) for the Barnabites and many times restored. It takes its name from the basin-makers (*catini*) who used to work in the area. The façade was erected in 1636 by Giovanni Battista Soria. Open daily 07.30–12.00 and 16.30–19.00.

The spacious interior is interesting for its 17C works. On the **south side**, the first chapel, decorated in 1698–1702 by Simone Costanzi, has an altarpiece of the *Annunciation* by Giovanni Lanfranco, and the second chapel a *Martyrdom of St Biagio* by Giacinto Brandi. Between the second and third chapels is the Hamerani monument, with exquisite Classical carved decoration by Luca Carimini (1830–90). The third chapel, the Cappella di Santa Cecilia, beautifully lit from its little oval dome, was designed by Antonio Gherardi. In the sanctuary, the high altarpiece, illustrating *St Charles Carrying the Sacred Nail to the Plague-stricken*, is a good late work by Pietro da Cortona. The apse bears a fresco of *St Charles Received in Heaven* by Giovanni Lanfranco. In the pendentives of the dome over the crossing are the *Cardinal Virtues* by Domenichino.

The **sacristy** contains a little bronze crucifix attributed to Alessandro Algardi, and the *Mocking of Christ* by Cavaliere d'Arpino; in an adjoining room (shown by the sacristan) is a tondo of *St Charles in Prayer*, a fresco detached from the façade, attributed to Guido Reni, and another painting of *St Charles* by Andrea Commodi.

On the **north side**, the third chapel, decorated in the 17C, has frescoed lunettes attributed to Giacinto Gimignani. The altarpiece in the second chapel, of the *Death of St Anne*, is by Andrea Sacchi.

Opposite the church is Palazzo Santacroce, by Carlo Maderno (1602).

It is now necessary to return to the church of Santissimo Trinità dei Pellegrini (see above). From here Via San Paolo alla Regola leads past the church of San Paolo alla Regola to the Case di San Paolo, a group of over-restored 13C houses now used as offices. Other medieval buildings were demolished to make way for the huge Ministry of Justice built here in 1920 by Pio Piacentini. To the left is the ancient church of **Santa Maria in Monticelli** (closed indefinitely), with a 12C campanile, radically restored in 1860. In the apse is a mosaic head of *Christ*, and fragments of mosaic decoration dating from the 12C. In the second chapel to the right is a detached fresco of the *Flagellation* by Antonio Carracci; opposite is a 14C wooden crucifix.

From the church of Santissima Trinità dei Pellegrini, Via dei Pettinari leads to the Tiber, here crossed by Ponte Sisto (pedestrians only; see p 221). The little church of **San Salvatore in Onda** (usually closed) was built at the end of the 11C but transformed in the 17C. The interesting crypt was built over a Roman building of the 2C AD.

Via Giulia

The long and straight Via Giulia (**Map 6**; 3, 5, 6), which runs parallel to the Tiber for over one kilometre, begins in Piazza Pallotti at the foot of Ponte Sisto. It was laid out by Julius II (1503–13) and was for a long time the most beautiful of the 16C streets of the city. It has a number of fine palaces with lovely courtyards.

A short way along, a picturesque **arch** hung with creeper spans the road. This was the only arch of a viaduct planned, but never realised, by Michelangelo to connect the Palazzo Farnese with the Villa Farnesina by a bridge across the Tiber. Here, the lovely garden of Palazzo Farnese (see above) with magnolias, orange trees, cypresses and pines can be seen through a gate, as can the palace's rear façade, adapted from Michelangelo's designs by Giacomo della Porta.

Via dei Farnese, where there is a charming small palace at no. 83, skirts the right flank of Palazzo Farnese as far as Piazza Farnese (described above). The fountain in the pretty wall niche on the left, the **Mascherone**, was erected by the Farnese; both the colossal mask of a girl with long hair and the porphyry basin are Roman, although the figure's mouth was enlarged when it was adapted as a fountain. The church opposite the end of Via del Farnese, **Santa Maria dell'Orazione e Morte** was rebuilt in 1733–37 by Ferdinando Fuga. Open Sun and fest. at 18.00.

Palazzo Falconieri, enlarged by Borromini, is distinguished by the giant falcons' heads, the emblem of the Odescalchi family, at either end of its façade. It has been the seat of the Hungarian Academy since 1928. Several rooms inside have fine ceilings decorated in stucco by Borromini. Cardinal Fesch, Napoleon I's uncle, lived here in the early 19C and amassed a splendid collection of paintings which was, however, dispersed after his death.

A narrow road leads right to Piazza Santa Caterina della Rota where there are no fewer than three churches. **Santa Caterina della Rota** (usually closed) has a fine ceiling from a demolished church and 18C works. Just off the square, on Via di Monserrato, is the exterior in Romanesque style, including an elaborate portal by Luigi Poletti.

On Via di Monserrato is the church of **St Thomas of Canterbury** (Map 6; 6), attached to the Venerabile Collegio Inglese (entrance at no. 45). The ground on which they stand has been the property of English Catholics since 1362, when a hospice for pilgrims was built here. Thomas Cromwell came here in 1514. The college was founded in 1579 by the Jesuits, with funding from Gregory XIII, as a seminary for the training of priests as missionaries to England. The record of visitors shows the names of Thomas Hobbes (1635), William Harvey (1636), John Milton (1638), John Evelyn (1644) and Cardinal Manning (late 19C).

The church was rebuilt to a design by Virginio Vespignani in 1866–88, a free adaptation of a Romanesque basilica, with elaborate gilded decorations. The frescoes of English martyrs in the matroneum are based on an earlier cycle, lost when the old church was destroyed, which were painted by Niccolò Circignani and included scenes of the death of Edward Campion in 1581. The beautiful *tomb effigy of Cardinal Christopher Bainbridge, Bishop of York (d. 1514), borne on two Romanesque lions, is attributed to Nicola Marini. The monument to Thomas Dereham (d. 1739) was designed by Ferdinando Fuga, with sculptures by Filippo della Valle. The high altarpiece is by Durante Alberti. In the college, of which Cardinal Howard and Cardinal Wiseman were both rectors, are portraits of English cardinals.

Also in the piazza is the church of **San Girolamo della Carità**, rebuilt in the 17C by Domenico Castelli, with a façade by Carlo Rainaldi. If closed, ring at 63 Via San Girolamo. The funeral chapel of the Spada (first on the right), formerly attributed to Borromini, is now thought to be the work of Cosimo Fanzago. To the left of the high altar is a decorative chapel (1710) dedicated to St Philip Neri, by Filippo Juvarra; there is a light to the left.

Further along Via Giulia is the church of **Santa Caterina da Siena** (open only on fest. at 10.30), rebuilt by Paolo Posi in 1766. It stands opposite **Palazzo Varese** by Carlo Maderno (c. 1617). A street on the left leads to **Sant'Eligio degli Orefici** (Map 6; 6). Open Mon, Tues, Thur, Fri 10.00–12.00; closed Wed. Ring for the *custode* at 9 Via di Sant'Eligio. In 1509 the confraternity of Roman goldsmiths was given permission to erect a church dedicated to their patron saint, St Eligio, by Julius II. Raphael was commissioned by them in 1514 to design this beautiful small church, surmounted by a cupola and Greek-cross in plan, and clearly influenced by Bramante. After Raphael's death Baldassare Peruzzi finished the building, including the cupola. The façade, following Raphael's designs, was rebuilt by Flaminio Ponzio after it collapsed in 1601.

The **interior** is particularly interesting for its architecture, but it also contains some 17C frescoes and a few goldsmiths' tombs.

From the Lungotevere, the road which follows the Tiber embankment, there is a fine view of the Gianicolo, the dome of St Peter's and the Villa Farnesina. Via della Barchetta, on the other side of Via Giulia, leads to Via di Monserrato, on the right of which stands the church of **Santa Maria di Monserrato** (Map 6; 6), the Spanish national church. Open only on Sun; for admission apply at 151 Via Giulia.

It was begun by Antonio da Sangallo the Younger (1518) but altered later, with a façade by Francesco da Volterra. In the **interior**, the first south chapel contains an altarpiece of *St Diego*, by Annibale Carracci, and the 19C tombs of the two Borgia popes, Calixtus III (d. 1458) and Alexander VI (d. 1503), and of King Alfonso XIII (d. 1941). In the third north chapel is a statue of *St James* by Jacopo Sansovino, and two fine wall-tombs attributed to Andrea Bregno. The first north chapel contains a group of the *Madonna and Child with St Anne* by Tommaso Boscoli (1544), and a ciborium (behind wooden doors) attributed to Luigi Capponi. In the court, reached through the sacristy at the end of the nave on the right (or at 151 Via Giulia), are several fine tombs, notably that of Cardinal Giovanni de Mella attributed to Bregno. In a room off the courtyard is the monument to Pedro de Foix Montoya; this incorporates a remarkable portrait bust, an early work (c 1621) by Bernini.

Via Giulia continues past the church of the **Spirito Santo dei Napoletani** on the left, begun by Il Mascherino in 1619, restored by Carlo Fontana, and again in the 19C, when the façade was built by Antonio Cipolla. It contains paintings by Pietro Gagliardi and a *Martyrdom of St Januarius* (San Gennaro) by Luca Giordano. The street opposite leads to the 16C Palazzo Ricci with a painted façade by Polidoro da Caravaggio, heavily restored and now badly faded. Via Giulia next traverses an area demolished before 1940 for a new road, never built; the 18C façade by Filippo Raguzzini of San Filippo Neri survives here.

Opposite the church of Santa Lucia del Gonfalone on Via dei Banchi Vecchi is Vicolo Cellini, named after the famous sculptor Benvenuto Cellini who had his workshop in the area.

The **Carceri Nuove** on Via Giulia, built in 1655 by Antonio del Grande, were long considered a model prison. The **Museo Criminologico** is arranged in an adjacent prison building designed in 1827 by Giuseppe Valadier. The entrance is at 29 Via del Gonfalone. Open 09.00–13.00; Tues & Thur also 14.30–18.30; closed Mon and fest. ☎ 06 6830 0234. It illustrates the history of criminology.

The 16C **Oratorio di Santa Lucia del Gonfalone** has a façade by Domenico Castelli. The entrance is on Vicolo della Scimmia. Concerts are given here by the Coro Polifonico Romano. The interior has a fine pavement, and a carved and gilded ceiling by Ambrogio Bonazzini. It is particularly interesting for its frescoes of the *Passion of Christ* by painters of the late 16C Tuscan-Emilian school, including Jacopo Bertoia, Raffaellino da Reggio, Federico Zuccari (*Flagellation*), Livio Agresti, Cesare Nebbia and Marco Pino.

On Via del Gonfalone and beyond the church of **Santa Maria del Suffragio** by Carlo Rainaldi, several large, rough blocks of masonry protruding into the street are all that remains of a great court of justice designed for Julius II by Bramante but never finished. Here is yet another church, the small San Biagio della Pagnotta. At no. 66 rises Palazzo Sacchetti by Antonio Sangallo the Younger (1543).

At the end of Via Giulia is **San Giovanni Battista dei Fiorentini** (Map 6; 3), the church of the Florentines. Open daily 07.00–11.00 and 17.00–19.30. Leo X ordered a competition for its erection. Raphael and Peruzzi were among the contestants, but Jacopo Sansovino was successful and began the work. It was continued by Antonio da Sangallo the Younger and completed by Giacomo della Porta; Carlo Maderno added the transept and cupola. The façade is by Alessandro Galilei (1734).

In the south aisle, above the door into the sacristy, is a 16C Tuscan statuette of *St John the Baptist*. On either side of the arch here is a portrait bust; that on the left by Pietro Bernini (1614), and that on the right by his son Gian Lorenzo (1622). The third chapel contains a *St Jerome* by Santi di Tito; on the right wall another by Lodovico Cigoli; and on the left wall, the *Construction of the Church* by Passignano. In the south transept is a picture of *St Cosmas and St Damian at the Stake*, by Salvator Rosa. The first chapel in the north aisle has an altarpiece by Giovanni Battista Vanni; the fourth chapel has putti on the wall-tombs of the Bacelli, carved by François Duquesnoy. Behind the high altar is a crypt sepulchre of the Falconieri family, a fine late work by Borromini.

14 • Trastevere

Trastevere (Map 8; 2 and 9; 1), the area 'across the Tiber' (*trans Tiberim*) on its right bank, is enclosed between the Gianicolo and the Vatican. Since the Middle Ages it has been essentially the popular district of Rome, and its inhabitants seem to retain the characteristics of the ancient Romans, who are said to have been proud and independent. This area of the city has been distinguished by its numerous artisans' houses and workshops since Roman times. It is a fashionable place to live, and has a cosmopolitan atmosphere, with numerous popular *trattorie*.

The most important church in Trastevere, and one of the oldest in Rome, is Santa Maria in Trastevere, in a piazza in the heart of the district; it has very important 12C mosaics and numerous precious works of art. The little-visited church of San Crisogono, with a fine pavement and the fascinating remains of a very early Christian church beneath it, is also well worth visiting. Nearer the Tiber is the Renaissance Villa Farnesina, with beautiful early 16C frescoes by Raphael and his school, and Palazzo Corsini which houses the 17C and 18C paintings of the Galleria Nazionale d'Arte Antica. Its gardens are now occupied by beautifully kept botanical gardens, open regularly. In the eastern part of Trastevere is the important church of Santa Cecilia in Trastevere (with limited opening hours), in the convent of which there is a remarkable medieval fresco of the *Last Judgement* by Pietro Cavallini. The church of San Francesco a Ripa has a fine late work by Bernini.

History of Trastevere

This was the 'Etruscan side' of the river, and only after the destruction of Veio by Rome in 396 BC did it come under Roman rule. In earliest Republican days, this bank of the Tiber was occupied by Lars Porsenna in his attempt to replace the Tarquins on the Roman throne. On the higher ground at the foot of the Janiculum Hill, and along the waterfront, suburban villas were built by the aristocracy. The magnificent wall-paintings from a villa dating from the Augustan age—excavated at the end of the 19C next to the Villa Farnesina and then destroyed—are preserved in the Museo Nazionale Romano at Palazzo Massimo. Under the Empire the district became densely populated by artisans and dock-workers. It was probably not entirely enclosed by walls before the time of Aurelian (270–275). Trastevere was home to a great number of Jews, who are recorded here as early as the 2C BC, before they were confined to the Ghetto on the other side of the river. It was the stronghold of independence during the Risorgimento; here Mazzini found support for his Republic of 1849, and here in 1867 Giuditta Tavani Arquati, with her family, made an attempt to incite the city on Garibaldi's behalf. In July, the lively festival of Noantri ('We others') takes place here.

Ponte Garibaldi (Map 8; 2), a modern bridge with small obelisks, leads across the Tiber to the busy Piazza Gioacchino Belli, named after the Roman poet (1791–1863) who wrote popular verses and satirical sonnets in the Roman dialect. The delightful monument here, which shows him in a frock coat and top hat, is by Michele Tripisciano (1913). The wide and busy Viale Trastevere leads from here for nearly 2km through an uninteresting part of the city, as far as the Stazione Trastevere. A smart new tram line (no. 8) with frequent services now connects Viale Trastevere with Largo Argentina across the Tiber. On either side of the viale for the first few hundred metres is the beautiful old district of Trastevere described below.

In Piazza Belli is the over-restored 13C **Palazzetto dell'Anguillara**, with its corner tower, the last of many which once guarded Trastevere. The picturesque courtyard is a modern reconstruction using ancient material. The building is now the Casa di Dante (marked by a plaque), where readings from *La Divina Commedia* have been given by leading Italian men of letters since 1914 (now Nov–mid-Mar on Sun 11.00–12.00). The library has the best collection in Italy of works relating to the poet.

The Tiber

The Tiber or Tevere (418km) is the most famous though not the longest of the rivers of Italy. It is said originally to have been called Albula and to have received the name Tiberis from Tiberinus, king of Alba Longa, who was drowned in its waters. It rises in the Tuscan Apennines, north-east of Arezzo and is fed by numerous mountain streams. Its swift waters are discoloured with yellow mud, even far from its source: hence the epithet *flavus* (fair or tawny) given to it by the Roman poets. The Roman Via Aurelia (the present Via Lungaretta and Via della Lungarina) had to be raised on a viaduct in order to avoid the waters of the Tiber in flood. The present embankments and Lungotevere roads were built in the late 19C to avoid floods in the city. There are long-term plans to clean its polluted waters.

San Crisogono

In the adjoining Piazza Sonnino is the church of San Crisogono (**Map 8**; **2**), one of the most interesting but least visited churches in Rome. Open daily 07.30–

11.30 and 16.00–19.30. Remains of the early Christian church are open at the same time.

History of San Crisogono

Founded in the 5C, it was rebuilt by Cardinal Giovanni da Crema (work was finished by 1129). The church was reconstructed by Giovanni Battista Soria in 1623 for Scipione Caffarelli Borghese, nephew of Cardinal Camillo Borghese who became Pope Paul V in 1605, and restored in 1866. The campanile survives from 1123. The façade and portico date from the 17C. The earliest religious house and first 5C basilica on the site are preserved below the present church.

The church is dedicated to St Chrysogonus who was martyred in Aquileia around 304 under the Emperor Diocletian. His relics were taken from there to Zara on the Dalmatian coast and in 1202 during the Fourth Crusade were stolen by the Venetians for the church of San Trovaso in Venice. In 1240 they were returned to Zara but were brought here at the end of the 15C or beginning of the 16C.

Important titular cardinals of this church included Giovanni da Crema (or John of Crema) who rebuilt the church and who is buried here. As pontifical legate he was sent all over Europe during the investiture controversy between the Pope and the Emperor in the early 12C. Another cardinal of the church was the Englishman Stephen Langton (1150–1228), who was a famous theologian educated in Paris. He was nominated cardinal and archbishop of Canterbury in 1207 by his friend Innocent III, but because of the hostility of King John was unable to take possession of that see until 1213. He then supported the feudal barons in drawing up the Magna Carta in 1215, which led to the first constitutional struggle in English history.

The plan of the lovely **interior** is typical of the early Christian basilicas in Rome. Twenty-two ancient Roman columns separate the nave from the aisles; the large Ionic capitals were made of stucco in the 17C. The triumphal arch is supported by two huge monolithic porphyry columns. The magnificent 13C Cosmatesque pavement is one of the most beautiful and best-preserved in Rome; when it was restored in the 17C the Borghese crest of a dragon in polychrome stone was substituted for some of the porphyry discs in the paving near the sanctuary. The gilded wood ceiling was also added in the 17C; in the centre is a copy of a painting by Guercino of *St Chrysogonus in Glory* (the original was removed in 1808).

In the **south aisle**, the highly venerated *Madonna and Child* was painted by Giovanni Battista Conti in 1944 as a votive offering for the salvation of Rome during the Second World War. The other altarpieces date from the 17C and include *Three Archangels* by Giovanni da San Giovanni and two works by Paolo Guidotti and his school. The chapel to the right of the sanctuary was apparently redesigned by Bernini (1677–80) and the two Poli family monuments here have fine marble busts by his pupils.

The **baldacchino**, by Giovanni Battista Soria, rests on four ancient columns of yellow alabaster. The high altar encloses the 12C reliquary of St Chrysogonus. On the wall of the apse is a lovely mosaic, placed here by Soria when it was given its square frame, which depicts the *Madonna and Child between St James and St Chrysogonus*. Made for the church, it is usually attributed to the school of Pietro

Cavallini, although some scholars believe it to be one of the earliest works in Rome by the master himself. The handsome carved wood choir stalls date from 1865.

Near the sacristy door in the **north aisle** are inscriptions relating to the history of the church including one recording the work carried out by Giovanni da Crema (1129), and an exquisite little Cosmatesque wall tabernacle from the earlier church. Off the aisle is the chapel of the Blessed Anna Maria Taigi (1769–1837) who was beatified in 1920. Although she was born in Siena she lived most of her life in Rome and had seven children: she was venerated for her maternal qualities as well as her great faith. She is buried here, and another chapel preserves mementoes.

Remains of the **early Christian church** beneath the present church are entered through the sacristy in the north aisle (see above), and approached down a new iron staircase. A *domus ecclesiae* or religious house used by a very early Christian community existed here in the 3C: its brick masonry still exists in part. In the early 5C (mentioned in 499) this was enlarged into a basilican church, considerable remains of which survive. In the 8C Pope Gregory III added an annular crypt. Excavations were first carried out in 1908–28, and have been continued since 1993.

At the bottom of the stairs is the **apse** of the church and remains of the walls of the crypt built to give access to the martyrs' shrine beneath the altar. In the central corridor is a worn fresco of three saints, showing St Chrysogonus in the centre, and at the sides the two companions supposedly martryed with him, St Anastasia and a certain St Rufo. The church was orientated towards the west: looking at the apse, to the left (or south) behind a closed gate is a small room which was a **baptistery**, in which numerous Roman fragments found during the excavations are kept. A few marble steps lead up beside the **south wall** of the church, with traces of frescoes dating from the 6C–7C and 8C (including a roundel with a pope, thought to be Sixtus II). Half-way along the wall can be seen a change in the masonry which distinguishes the earliest building (in brick) from the later basilica. There are two pagan sarcophagi here: the one beautifully carved with the Muses, found in the baptistery, might have been used as a font. On the other side of the apse is another small room, known as the **Secretarium**, traditionally thought to have been used for the storage of vestments. It has interesting traces of its original 6C–7C pavement in white marble tesserae and green serpentine marble discs. The pagan sarcophagus (3C) with marine scenes with tritons and nereids was found here; it was reused in the Middle Ages. On the **north wall** of the church can be seen more traces of frescoes dating from the 8C and 10C: the best-preserved are those from a 10C cycle showing the life of St Benedict, with a scene of the saint in a hood healing a leper covered with spots. The opposite wall, which blocks the centre of the basilican church, was built to support the upper church. At the end is an area still closed off while excavations continue of the east end of the church, with the site of its façade and narthex.

The old Via della Lungaretta, on the line of the last stretch of the ancient Roman Via Aurelia, leads past the façade of Sant'Agata and on the left, in Via San Gallicano, the huge **hospital of San Gallicano**, a remarkable utilitarian building by Filippo Raguzzini (1724). The handsome, long, low façade, with the two floors divided by a balcony, incorporates a church in the centre.

Via della Lungaretta continues straight on to the delightful **Piazza di Santa**

Maria in Trastevere (Map 8; 2), the characteristic centre of Trastevere. The handsome **fountain**, of Roman origin, is said to be on the site of a fountain of pure oil. As the inscriptions record it was restored over the centuries by Donato Bramante, Giacomo della Porta, Bernini and Carlo Fontana (1692). Palazzo di San Calisto on the left of the church, was rebuilt in the 17C by Orazio Torriani.

Santa Maria in Trastevere

The large basilica of Santa Maria in Trastevere (**Map 8; 2**), open daily 07.00–13.00 and 15.30–19.00, dates mainly from the 12C and preserves some beautiful mosaics from that period, and contains some important works of art. The church was constructed by Julius I (337–52), and was probably the first church in Rome dedicated to the Virgin. According to legend a hostel for veteran soldiers existed near the site, and some sort of Christian foundation is known to have existed here under St Calixtus (pope, 217–22). The great basilica of Julius I was rebuilt by Innocent II in 1140, and slightly modified later.

The campanile is Romanesque. The **façade** bears a 12C–13C mosaic of the *Madonna* surrounded by ten female figures with lamps (two of which are extinguished), of uncertain significance. The portico added by Carlo Fontana in 1702 contains an interesting lapidary collection, including Roman and medieval fragments, many of them with Christian symbols, such as the dove. The worn frescoes of the *Annunciation* date from the 15C. The three doorways incorporate Roman friezes.

In the splendid 12C **interior** are 21 vast ancient columns from various Roman buildings, some with fine bases and (damaged) capitals. The gilded wooden ceiling was designed by Domenichino (1617), who painted the central *Assumption*. There is also a fine ceiling in the crossing with a high-relief of the same scene (16C). The Cosmatesque pavement (made up from old material), and the decoration on the walls of the nave and triumphal arch was carried out when the church was remodelled by Pius IX in the 19C. The charming tabernacle at the beginning of the south aisle is by Mino del Reame. In the north aisle is the tomb of Innocent II (d. 1143), erected by Pius IX in 1869, and the Avila Chapel, designed by Antonio Gherardi (1680–86), with a remarkable Baroque dome and very unusual altar.

The **choir** is preceded by a marble screen made up of transennae and plutei, many of them remade in the 19C. Near a Paschal candlestick here is the spot on which a miraculous fountain of oil is supposed to have flowed throughout a whole day in the year of Christ's Nativity in the Roman building. The baldacchino over the high altar is by Virginio Vespignani. The ***mosaics** of the triumphal arch and apse (1140) are particularly fine, with exquisite details including fruit and flowers on the soffit of the arch (there is a coin-operated light): on the arch, the Cross with the symbolic Alpha and Omega between the seven candlesticks and the Evangelical emblems; at the sides, *Isaiah* and *Jeremiah*, beside two palm trees, and above them the rare and touching symbol of the caged bird, representing Christ imprisoned because of the sins of man ('*Christus Dominus captus est in peccatis nostris*'; Lamentations of Jeremiah, IV:20). In the semi-dome, *Christ and the Virgin* are shown enthroned beneath the hand of God bearing a wreath and the monogram of Constantine. On the right are *St Peter*, *St Cornelius*, *St Julius* and *St Calepodius*; on the left *St Calixtus* and *St Lawrence*, and *Pope Innocent II* with a model of the church.

Lower down in the apse and on the triumphal arch are six rectangles with mosaic scenes from the **Life of Mary* by Pietro Cavallini (c 1291), and beneath them a mosaic rectangle with *St Peter* and *St Paul* presenting the donor, Bertoldo Stefaneschi, to the Madonna (1290). Beneath the mosaics in the apse are late 16C frescoes by Agostino Ciampelli.

To the right of the choir are the Armellini monument (1524), with sculptures by Michelangelo Senese, and the **Chapel of the Winter Choir**, with decorations after Domenichino's designs. The chapel was restored by Henry Stuart, Duke of York, when he was titular cardinal of the church in 1759–61 (hence the royal arms above the gate). Henry was the youngest son of James III, the Old Pretender, who was nominated cardinal while living at the Jacobite court in Rome: as 'Henry IX' he was the last of the pretenders to the English throne (see p 170).

The huge 16C organ is to be restored. To the left of the choir is the **Altemps Chapel**, decorated with frescoes and stuccoes by Pasquale Cati (1588), including an interesting scene of the Council of Trent. On the altar is a precious painting of the *Madonna della Clemenza*, flanked by angels, a remarkable Byzantine work thought to date from the 8C, or earlier. On the left wall outside the chapel is the tomb of Cardinal Stefaneschi (d. 1417) by Magister Paulus, beside the monument to Cardinal Filippo d'Alençon (d. 1397), which includes his effigy and the relief of the *Dormition of the Virgin*, also attributed to Magister Paulus or a follower of Orcagna. The sacristy, approached by a passage with two exquisite tiny 1C Roman mosaics from Palestrina, one of marsh birds and the other a port scene, contains a very worn *Madonna with St Sebastian and St Roch* of the Umbrian School.

Via della Paglia skirts the north side of the church of Santa Maria in Trastevere. To the right opens Piazza Sant'Egidio, with the **Museo di Roma in Trastevere**, illustrating the 19C and early 20C history of this district. It is open 10.00–20.00; closed Mon. ☎ 06 581 6563. The contents include drawings and engravings of Roman street scenes and views by Bartolomeo Pinelli; paintings of 19C Rome, including works by Ippolito Caffi, Ettore Roesler Franz and Gino Severini (1903); and charming life-size tableaux of Roman scenes by Orazio Amato (1884–1952) based on paintings by Bartolomeo Pinelli; the reconstructed studio of the poet 'Trilussa' (Carlo Alberto Salustri, 1871–1950); and objects from the studio of the musician Maestro Alessandro Vessella (1860–1929).

Via della Scala leads out of the piazza past the ornate church of **Santa Maria della Scala** (1592), containing a painting of *St John the Baptist* by Gerard van Honthorst (over the first altar on the right) and a ciborium over the high altar by Carlo Rainaldi (1647). If closed, the church can sometimes be entered through the Carmelite monastery to the right, which adjoins the Pharmacy of Santa Maria della Scala, administered by the monks. The old 17C pharmacy upstairs can only be seen by appointment; ☎ 06 440 4237, or ring at the door on the left.

Via della Scala ends at **Porta Settimiana** (**Map 6; 8**), incorporated in the 3C Aurelian Walls and rebuilt by Alexander VI (1492–1503). Trastevere was once defended by the walls, which led away from the river here up to Porta San Pancrazio on the Janiculum, where the Via Aurelia left the city. From Porta San Pancrazio the walls, still partly preserved, lead down south-east to rejoin the Tiber at Porta Portese (see p 228). A branch of the Roman Via Aurelia passed through the walls at Porta Settimiana, following the right bank of the Tiber towards the Vatican.

The street to the right, just before the gate, is Via Santa Dorotea. At no. 20 is the medieval **Casa della Fornarina**, the supposed house of Raphael's mistress (see p 235). Other houses of this type may be seen in Vicolo dei Moroni. Via di Ponte Sisto leads to the Tiber, here crossed by the **Ponte Sisto** footbridge (**Map 6; 8**), erected for Sixtus IV (1471–84), probably by Baccio Pontelli, to replace the ancient Pons Janiculensis (or the Pons Antoninus). It was beautifully restored in 2000 and provided with a new balustrade, built of brick and travertine. Here, surrounded by a garden, is a fountain erected by Paul V which was moved here from Via Giulia on the other side of the Tiber in 1898 when the Tiber embankment was constructed. From the bridge there is a view of the three high arches of the Acqua Paola fountain on the skyline above Trastevere (described on p 331).

The attractive Via Garibaldi, with two raised pavements on either side, leads uphill from Porta Settimiana towards the Gianicolo (see Walk 30). At the end of the first straight section of the road, before a sharp turn to the left, is the entrance at no. 27 to the convent of **Santa Maria dei Sette Dolori** (**Map 6; 7, 8**). The church was begun by Francesco Borromini in 1643, and its unfinished façade (1646) can be seen through the gate. The vestibule and interior of the church are entered through the convent, by the door to the right of the façade; admission is sometimes granted on request. The church has an unusual plan: it is oblong with rounded ends, with two apses in the middle of the long sides, and a continuous series of pillars connected by a heavy cornice. The disappointing interior decoration was added later in the 17C.

Porta Settimiana also marks the beginning of **Via della Lungara** (**Map 6; 5, 8**), the longest of the long, straight streets built by the Renaissance popes. It was laid out c 1507 by Julius II to connect Trastevere with the Borgo. On the left is the building that housed the **Museo Torlonia**, founded by Gian Raimondo Torlonia (1754–1829) with sculptures from other Roman collections, to which he later added the yields from excavations on the family estates, including Cerveteri, Vulci and Porto. Considered to be the most important private collection of ancient sculpture in existence, the Museo Torlonia is not open to the public. For years closed 'for restoration', the interior of the museum was converted into flats in the 1970s and the works put in store. In 1977 the palace and collection were officially sequestered, and interminable bureaucratic procedures took place in an attempt by the State to acquire the collection. The museum has never been reopened. For further information apply to the Amministrazione Torlonia, 30 Via della Conciliazione.

There are over 620 pieces of sculpture, some over-restored, including a few Greek originals. The most important works include the *Giustiniani Hestia*, a splendid statue attributed to Kalamis (5C BC), and a bas-relief of *Herakles Liberating Theseus and Peirithöos*, by the school of Pheidias (4C BC). There are numerous Roman copies of works by Greek sculptors, notably Kephisodotos, Polykleitos, Praxiteles and Lysippos. Of the Roman originals perhaps the most striking is a portrait statue of *Lucilla*, daughter of Marcus Aurelius. The Roman iconographic collection contains over one hundred busts of the Imperial era. The valuable Etruscan paintings (4C BC) are from Vulci. There is also a very fine collection of sarcophagi.

Orto Botanico

At no. 24 at the end of Via Corsini, off Via del Lungara to the left, is the Orto

Botanico (**Map 6**; **7**), one of the most important botanical gardens in Italy. It covers some 12 hectares and is beautifully kept (it is a lovely place to picnic). It is particularly famous for its palms and yuccas. Open 09.30–17.30 or 18.30; closed Sun and Mon. ☎ 06 4991 7017.

The gardens were founded on the Gianicolo in 1660, but have been on this site only since 1883 when Tommaso Corsini donated the gardens of Palazzo Corsini (see below), on the slopes of the hill, to the State.

Near the entrance are two tall cedars beneath which are succulents. An **avenue of palms** leads to a fountain installed for the Palazzo Corsini by Ferdinando Fuga in 1750. A path leads uphill left to the **rose garden** (entered up a flight of steps some way along the path, keep left) laid out on the hillside, specialising in the species known to have been cultivated in Rome in the 17C and 18C. The path continues uphill past ferns and bamboo and a **rock garden**. Near an iris garden towards the top of the hill, the top of the fountain of the Acqua Paola can be seen above the trees on the Gianicolo (see p 331). Beyond a lily pond and more irises a path descends past the **Japanese garden** laid out in 1990–94. From here there is a view of the numerous domed churches in the city as well as the Villa Medici on the Pincio, the Torre delle Milizie and the Vittorio Emanuele II monument. Beyond, at the top of the gardens, is a wooded area of ancient oaks and ilex. In this area of the gardens a Baroque staircase survives and outside the fence there is a 17C ornamental fountain. There are several ancient plane trees here. The path continues to the edge of the gardens—from which there is view of the cupola of the Pantheon (above the trees to the left) and the little spire of Sant'Ivo—and then descends past conifers and sequoia to the foot of the monumental staircase, decorated with tubs of azeleas. A signposted path leads left from here down to a greenhouse used for exhibitions and the **physic garden**, where raised brick beds contain some 300 medicinal plants. Near a pond with numerous aquatic species is a low greenhouse of cacti. The fine 19C glasshouse beyond preserves a rare collection of orchids. Near the exit is a garden of aromatic herbs, which can be identified by the blind by their smell or touch.

Palazzo Corsini

In Via della Lungara, just beyond Via Corsini, on the left, is Palazzo Corsini (**Map 6**; **5**, **7**), the residence of the Florentine Corsini family from the 18C up until the end of the 19C. Here their library and art collection was formed and is still preserved as part of the **Galleria Nazionale d'Arte Antica**, which is divided between this palace and Palazzo Barberini (see Walk 16). It is particularly rich in 17C and 18C paintings of the Roman, Neapolitan and Bolognese schools, but also has important works by Fra Angelico, Rubens, Van Dyck, Murillo and Caravaggio.

Opening times

08.30–19.00; closed Mon. ☎ 06 6880 2323. ✉ www.galleriaborghese.it
The present arrangement is extremely crowded, but more rooms may eventually be opened to the public. The pictures are all labelled.

History of Palazzo Corsini and the Corsini collection

The palace was built by Cardinal Domenico Riario in the 15C, and rebuilt by Ferdinando Fuga for Cardinal Neri Maria Corsini, nephew of Clement XII

(Lorenzo Corsini), in 1732–36, when the family moved from Florence to Rome. The palace had been the residence of Queen Christina of Sweden, who died here in 1689 (see p 158). In 1797 General Duphot was killed near here in a skirmish between the French democratic party and the papal dragoons, and in 1800 Madame Letitia Bonaparte, Napoleon I's mother, came to live in the palace.

The Corsini collection of paintings was founded in the 17C by the uncle of Clement XII, and works were added by Clement himself while he was still cardinal, and then by his nephew Cardinal Neri. In 1827 their descendent Tommaso rearranged the collection and opened it to the public, but after his death the family moved back to Florence. In 1883 the palace was sold, and the collection of paintings donated to the State, and together with numerous other works of art became part of the Galleria Nazionale d'Arte Antica. The original Corsini collection can be identified since it carries inventory nos 1–606.

On the first floor is a vestibule with Neo-classical sculptures including works by John Gibson and Pietro Tenerani. **Room I**. Portraits of the Corsini; a bust of *Clement XII Corsini* by Pietro Bracci; and paintings by Pompeo Batoni, Sebastiano Conca and Francesco Trevisani.

Room II. (558.) *Madonna and Child* and *Scenes from the Life of Christ* by Giovanni da Milano; (464.) *Madonna and Child*, one of the finest versions by Bartolomé Murillo of this familiar subject; works by David Teniers the Younger, and Marten van Cleve; (111.) *Madonna and Child* by Van Dyck, probably painted during his stay in Italy; (388.) *St Sebastian Tended by Angels* by Peter Paul Rubens; (350.) *Portrait of a Man*, by Pourbus the Younger; (347.) *Portrait of Bernardo Clesio* by Joos van Cleve; (354.) portrait of *Cardinal Alessandro Farnese* by Perino del Vaga; (318.) *Self-portrait* by Federico Barocci; (140.) *Philip II of Spain* by Titian; (193.) *Adoration of the Shepherds* by Jacopo Bassano; (99.) *Madonna and Child*, and (488.) *Portrait of a Man*, both by Franciabigio; (116.) *Holy Family* by Fra Bartolomeo; (397., 396., 395.) triptych by Fra Angelico; (436.) *St George and the Dragon* by Francesco Francia; (686.) *Baptism of Christ*, a small bronze by Alessandro Algardi.

Room III (ahead). Works by Michelangelo Cerquozzi and Simon Vouet; (441.) *Judith with the Head of Holofernes* by Gerard Seghers; (107.) *Madonna and Child* by Orazio Gentileschi; (433.) *St John the Baptist* by Caravaggio. **Room IV** displays works by Jacques Callot, Jan Frans Van Bloemen and Luca Carlevaris, and landscapes by Gaspard Dughet and Jan de Momper.

Room V survives from the old Palazzo Riario. It was decorated by a follower of the Zuccari brothers. Queen Christina of Sweden is supposed to have died in this room in 1689: her portrait as *Diana* is by Justus van Egmont (c 1656). A terracotta bust of *Alessandro VII Chigi* attributed to Bernini is also exhibited here, as well as works by Jan Miel and Michael Sweerts.

Room VI. In the centre is the Corsini Throne, dating from the 2C or 1C BC and present in the palace since 1700. The paintings include (106.) *Andromeda* by Francesco Furini, and (371.) a portrait of *Cardinal Corsini* by Baciccio.

Room VII has a splendid view of the palm trees in the Orto Botanico (see above), and of the Garibaldi monument on the Gianicolo. Here are displayed paintings by Sassoferrato, Guercino, Donato Creti, Giovanni Lanfranco, and Guido Reni. Room VIII contains works by Salvator Rosa, Mattia Preti and Luca Giordano.

The palace also houses the **Accademia Nazionale dei Lincei**, founded by Prince Federico Cesi in 1603 for the promotion of learning, and said to be the oldest surviving institution of its kind. Galileo was a Lincean. The administrative offices are in the Villa Farnesina (see below). With it are incorporated the **Biblioteca dell'Accademia** (1848), with 100,000 volumes and other publications; the **Biblioteca Corsiniana**, founded in this palace by the Corsini in 1754 and at the time the most important library in Rome, together with that in the Vatican (it has been preserved intact and has a valuable collection of incunabula, manuscripts and autographs); and the Fondazione Caetani, whose object is to promote scientific knowledge of the Muslim world.

Villa Farnesina

Opposite Palazzo Corsini is the entrance to the graceful Renaissance Villa Farnesina (**Map 6; 6**), built by Baldassare Peruzzi (1508–11) as the suburban residence of Agostino Chigi. It is surrounded by a lovely garden, once much larger. It has delightful early 16C frescoes by Raphael and his school. Open Mon–Sat 09.00–13.00; closed Sun. ☎ 06 683 8831.

History of the Villa Farnesina

Here Agostino Chigi 'the Magnificent', the Sienese banker who controlled the markets of the East, entertained in grandeur Pope Leo X, cardinals, ambassadors, artists and men of letters. He was a patron of Raphael, and died on 10 April 1520, just four days after the artist. At a celebrated banquet in a loggia overlooking the Tiber (demolished in the 19C), as a demonstration of Chigi's extravagance silver plates and dishes were thrown into the river after every course (it was later revealed that a net had been in position to recover them). In 1590 the villa passed to Cardinal Alessandro Farnese, and received its present name, and through the Farnese it was inherited by the Bourbons of Naples in 1731. Since 1927 it has been the property of the State, and houses the administrative offices of the Accademia dei Lincei (see above).

The painted decoration in the villa was carried out between 1510 and 1519. On the ground floor is the festive **Loggia of Cupid and Psyche**, which formerly opened directly on to the garden. The ceiling has famous frescoes illustrating the story of Cupid and Psyche in a beautiful painted pergola with festoons of fruit and flowers. The innovative decorative programme was provided by Raphael—who probably also made the preparatory cartoons, since drawings of some of the scenes survive by him—but the paintings were executed by his pupils, Giulio Romano, Francesco Penni, Giovanni da Udine and Raffaellino del Colle in 1517. The loggia was well restored in 1693, and again in 1997.

The story is taken from Apuleius' *Metamorphoses* (or *The Golden Ass*), written in the 2C AD and the only Latin novel which has survived in its entirety. The young girl Psyche incites the jealousy of Venus because of her beauty: Venus therefore imposes almost impossible obstacles in her way before she can finally drink the cup of immortality in order to marry Cupid.

On the short wall towards the Loggia of the Galatea the first pendentive shows *Venus and Cupid*; on the long wall, opposite the garden, is the beautiful group of the *Three Graces with Cupid*; *Venus with Juno and Ceres*; *Venus on her Way to Visit Jove in a chariot*; *Venus Talking to Jove* (identified by an eagle). On the end wall is

Mercury. On the garden wall, *Psyche* (always dressed in green) is shown giving a phial to Venus; the *Kiss between Cupid and Jove*; and finally *Mercury Accompanying Psyche to Olympus*. In between these pendentives are playful cupids, with birds and symbols of the gods. In the centre of the vault are two painted cloths, shown as if draped from the pergola, on which the happy end to the legend is portrayed in two scenes: the *Council of the Gods*, and the *Nuptual Banquet*.

To the right is the **Loggia of the Galatea**. The ceiling was frescoed by Peruzzi with the constellations forming the horoscope of Agostino Chigi. The lunettes, with scenes from Ovid's *Metamorphoses*, are by Sebastiano del Piombo, although the colossal monochrome charcoal head here, a striking work, is now ascribed to Peruzzi. On the walls: the giant *Polyphemus* by Sebastiano del Piombo, and the celebrated **Galatea* by Raphael, a superb composition showing the sea-nymph. The latter interrupts the decorative sequence and seems to have been painted just after the works by Sebastiano. The other scenes were added in the 17C by Gaspard Dughet. A little room off the other side of the loggia, known as the *Sala del Fregio*, contains a beautifully painted little frieze with mythological scenes by Peruzzi.

On the upper floor is the **Sala delle Prospettive**, the drawing-room, with charming trompe l'oeil imaginary views of Rome and mythological subjects by Peruzzi. The bedroom, known as the **Sala delle Nozze di Alessandro e Rossana**, contains *frescoes by Sodoma. The bedroom scene opposite the windows is particularly fine, with the nude figure of Alessandro, and no fewer than 22 playful cupids.

Superb wall-paintings and stuccoes found in a Roman house in the grounds of the villa are kept in the Museo Nazionale Romano (see p 258). On the second floor of the Villa Farnesina is the **Gabinetto Nazionale delle Stampe** with an exceptionally fine collection of prints and drawings (open to students) housed in a series of beautiful rooms. Exhibitions are held here periodically. In 1975 this institute was merged with the Calcografia Nazionale as the Istituto Nazionale per la Grafica, and there are plans to move it to Palazzo Poli in Piazza di Trevi (see p 169). Open Tues–Sat 09.00–13.00; closed Sun, Mon. ☎ 06 699 801.

The northern section of Via della Lungara is much less interesting: it continues along the busy right bank of the Tiber past the Regina Coeli prison (1881–1900) and the 16C Palazzo Salviati to Piazza della Rovere (**Map 6; 3**). The Borgo beyond is described in Walk 31.

In order to see the rest of Trastevere on the other side of Viale di Trastevere, it is necessary to return to the church of San Crisogono (see above). Across the busy Viale di Trastevere, Via Santini leads into Via dei Genovesi with the church of **San Giovanni Battista dei Genovesi** (**Map 9; 1**) (1481; restored). The remarkable 15C cloister, sometimes open in the afternoons, is entered along Via Anicia on the right (ring at no. 12). It has an arcaded lower gallery and a trabeated upper storey, and a beautiful garden of orange trees. The next turning off Via dei Genovesi is Via di Santa Cecilia which leads right into the piazza in front of the church of Santa Cecilia in Trastevere.

Santa Cecilia in Trastevere

Santa Cecilia in Trastevere (**Map 9; 1**) was built on the site of the house of

St Cecilia and her husband St Valerian, whom she converted to Christianity. Open daily 08.00–18.00. Roman remains beneath the church open same hours.

History of Santa Cecilia in Trastevere

St Cecilia, a patrician lady of the gens Cornelia, was martyred in 230, during the reign of Alexander Severus. She was shut up in the calidarium of her own baths (see below) to be scalded to death. Emerging unscathed, she was beheaded in her own house, but the executioner did such a bad job that she lived for three days afterwards. She was buried in the Catacombs of St Calixtus.

This building was adapted to Christian use probably in the 5C, and in 820 the body of St Cecilia was transferred here and a basilica erected by Paschal I (817–24). Her relics were rediscovered in 1599 and she was ceremonially re-interred in the church by Pope Clement VIII, after which she became a particularly revered Roman saint. As the inventor of the organ, she is the patron saint of music: on her feast day on 22 November churches hold musical services in her honour.

The church, radically altered from the 16C onwards, was partly restored to its original form in 1899–1901.

The slightly leaning **campanile** dates from 1120. Beyond an elaborate façade attributed to Ferdinando Fuga (1725) is the **atrium**, with a fountain made from a large antique marble basin for ceremonial ablutions in a little garden. The portico with four antique Ionic columns bearing a frieze of 12C mosaic medallions precedes the Baroque façade of the church.

The **interior** is an aisled 18C hall, whose piers (1823) enclose the original columns. The ceiling fresco of the *Coronation of St Cecilia* is by Sebastiano Conca. On the **west wall**, to the left of the door, is a *monument of *Cardinal Niccolò Forteguerri* (d. 1473), who assisted Pius II and Paul II in their suppression of the great feudal clans—a beautiful work attributed to Mino da Fiesole (restored in 1891). On the other side of the door is the tomb of Cardinal Adam Easton (d. 1398), a distinguished English churchman who was appointed cardinal in 1381, deposed by Urban VI c 1386, and reappointed by Boniface IX in 1389. It bears the arms of England and may be the work of Paolo Taccone.

In the **south aisle**, the first chapel, contains a fresco of the *Crucifixion* (?14C). A corridor, with landscapes by Paul Brill and a marble figure of *St Sebastian* attributed to Lorenzetto, leads to the ancient calidarium, where St Cecilia was to be scalded to death. The steam conduits are still visible. On the altar is the *Beheading of St Cecilia*, and opposite, *St Cecilia and St Valerian* by Guido Reni. Also off the south aisle opens the Cappella dei Ponziani, with ceiling frescoes and, on the walls, *Saints*, all by Antonio Pastura, as well as a Cosmatesque altar. The 18C Cappella delle Reliquie is by Luigi Vanvitelli. The last chapel contains the theatrical tomb (1929) of Cardinal Rampolla, who was responsible for the excavations beneath the church. A small room preceding it contained a tondo of the *Madonna* by Perugino; stolen in 1993, it was later found broken in two pieces, and has been restored. In the chapel at the end of the aisle is a very damaged 12C–13C fresco detached from the portico showing the *Discovery of the Body of St Cecilia*.

In the **sanctuary** is a fine *baldacchino (1293), signed by Arnolfo di Cambio, and a celebrated *statue of *St Cecilia* by Stefano Maderno (restored in 2002).

The body of the saint is represented lying as it was found when her tomb was opened in 1599, on which occasion the sculptor was present. The luminous 9C *mosaic in the apse shows **Christ Blessing by the Greek Rite**, between St Peter, St Valerian and St Cecilia on the right, and St Paul, St Agatha and St Paschal (the last with a square nimbus indicating that he was still living at the time the mosaic was made) on the left; below are the flock of the Faithful and the Holy Cities. In the north aisle, the fourth, third and second altarpieces are by Giovanni Baglione, and the first altarpiece is by Giovanni Ghezzi.

The **Roman edifices** beneath the church are entered from the west end of the north aisle. The excavations have not yet been fully explained, but are generally thought to consist of two Roman houses, possibly including the house of St Cecilia, that were probably amalgamated in the 4C for Christian use. Some scholars also believe there are remains here of an early Christian basilica. In the various rooms there are mosaic pavements and a number of Christian sarcophagi. A 2C room (sometimes closed) with seven huge basins in the floor was probably used as a tannery. Another room, with Republican columns, contains a niche with a relief of Minerva in front of an altar. A frescoed room with an ancient large font for total immersion (not yet open to the public) was discovered in 1991. The crypt is decorated in the Byzantine style by Giovanni Battista Giovenale (1899–1901), with luminous mosaics by Giuseppe Bravi. Behind a grille are the sarcophagi of St Cecilia, St Valerian and his brother St Tiburtius, St Maximus, and the popes Lucius I and Urban I. The statue of St Cecilia is by Cesare Aureli.

In the nuns' choir inside the **convent** can be seen the splendid *fresco of the **Last Judgement** by Pietro Cavallini, a masterpiece of medieval Roman fresco painting (c 1293). This used to be the inside façade of the old church. The convent is also entered from the west end of the north aisle; only open Tues & Thur 10.00–11.30.

In front of the church is the picturesque Piazza dei Mercanti, with fine 15C houses. The lovely old Vicolo di Santa Maria in Cappella runs from here to **Santa Maria in Cappella** (no. 6), dating from 1090, with a contemporary campanile.

In the other direction, Via di San Michele leads past the long, bright orange building of the huge former **Istituto San Michele a Ripa** (Map 8; 3), seat of the *Ministero per i Beni e le attività Culturali* (Cultural Ministry) since 1983, and of the *Istituto Centrale del Restauro* since 1976. The site was purchased in 1686 by Monsignor Tommaso Odescalchi, nephew of Innocent XI, who founded here a hospice and training centre for orphans and vagabond children, built by Carlo Fontana. In 1701 Fontana added a prison building. The façade of the huge building facing the Tiber was completed after Fontana's death by Nicola Michetti. In 1734 Ferdinando Fuga added a women's prison: the prison buildings were in use up to 1870. Numerous artisans' workshops were later installed here, and a renowned tapestry manufactory. The buildings were purchased by the State in 1969. It is also now the headquarters of the *International Center for the Study of the Preservation and Restoration of Cultural Property*, created by UNESCO in 1956, and has been restored as an exhibition and conference centre.

The entrance at 22 Via San Michele leads into a large courtyard with a fountain. To the left is a second courtyard, off which is the **Chiesa Grande**, begun in 1713 on a Greek-cross plan by Carlo Fontana, and finished in 1835 by Luigi Poletti, who added the Neo-classical choir. The statue of the *Saviour* here is by Adamo Tadolini.

At the far end of the building, the Tiber is crossed by **Ponte Aventino** (Map 9; 3) or Ponte Sublicio. The original bridge at this point, the Pons Sublicius, was the first bridge across the Tiber; it is said to have been built by Ancus Marcius, fourth king of Rome, to connect the Janiculum with the city.

From the bridge there is a good view of the excavations in progress of the Roman port lining the opposite bank of the Tiber along Lungotevere Testaccio. In 193–174 BC a market was constructed there, backed by the Porticus Aemilia, a wharf with extensive storehouses some 500m in length.

To the right, on this side of the Tiber, the **Porta Portese**, built by Innocent X (1644–55) replaces the former Porta Portuensis, the southern gate in the 3C Aurelian Walls which protected Trastevere. The famous Porta Portese flea market, the largest second-hand market in Rome, is much further south, near Stazione Trastevere. It is only open Sun 07.00–13.00.

From Via di San Michele (see above), Via della Madonna del Orto leads away from the Tiber to the church of **Santa Maria dell'Orto** (Map 9; 3), which has an unusual façade crowned with obelisks, attributed to Vignola, and an ornate interior containing 17C and 18C works.

Via Anicia continues left to end in Piazza San Francesco d'Assisi, in which stands the church of **San Francesco a Ripa** (Map 8; 4), built in 1231 to replace the old hospice of San Biagio, where St Francis stayed in 1219. Open daily 07.00–12.00 and 16.00–19.00. The last chapel on the left has the famous *statue of the *Blessed Lodovica Albertoni*, showing her in a state of mystical ecstasy. It is a late work by Bernini, displayed effectively by concealed lighting. Above is an altarpiece by Baciccia. The other chapels on the north side have been well restored: adjoining the first is the burial chapel of the painter Giorgio de Chirico (see p 160), and in the second chapel is an early *Annunciation* by Francesco Salviati. Above the sacristy, lined with 17C wood cupboards, is the cell of St Francis (usually shown on request), which contains relics displayed in an ingenious reliquary, and a 13C painting of the saint.

In the other direction Via Anicia leads back past Santa Maria dell'Orto to Piazza in Piscinula (**Map 9; 1**). Here is the small church of **San Benedetto**, with a charming miniature 11C roofed campanile, the smallest in Rome; the bell is dated 1069. If closed, ring at the door to the right of the façade. Inside, on the left of the vestibule, a fine doorway leads into an ancient cross-vaulted cell in which St Benedict is said to have lived. To the left of the entrance door is a detached and restored 13C fresco of the saint. Eight antique columns with diverse capitals divide the nave from the aisles. The old pavement is Cosmatesque. Above the altar is a 15C painting of *St Benedict*, and a damaged fresco of the *Madonna and Child* (15C).

On the opposite side of the piazza is the restored medieval Casa dei Mattei, with a 15C loggia and 14C cross-mullioned windows.

Via della Lungaretta leads back to Viale di Trastevere and the church of San Crisogono through Piazza del Drago. The remains of a **Roman firestation**, or guardroom, can be seen in Via di Monte Fiore. At the time of Augustus the fire brigade in Rome was organised into seven detachments to protect the city. This station was discovered during excavations in 1865–66: interesting graffiti referring to reigning emperors, from Severus to Giordian III, and a bath or nymphaeum survive (the station was built on the site of a 2C private house). The interior can only be seen with special permission, ☎ 06 689 2115. The entrance is at 9 Via della VII Coorte.

15 • The Quirinal Hill

The Quirinal (61m) is one of the highest of the Seven Hills of Rome. The huge palace built here in the 16C as the pope's summer residence is now the official residence of the Italian president. The dignified piazza outside has a fine view of Rome. Close by are two of the most important Baroque churches in Rome, by the two greatest Baroque architects: Sant'Andrea al Quirinale by Gian Lorenzo Bernini, and San Carlo alle Quattro Fontane by Francesco Borromini. On the first day of every month the Casino Pallavicini, just out of the piazza, with a fresco of Aurora by Guido Reni, is open.

The hill received its name either from a Temple of Quirinus, or from Cures, an ancient Sabine town north-east of Rome from where, according to legend, the Sabines under their king Tatius came to settle on the hill. The name of Quirinus was a title of Romulus, after he had been deified; the festival in his honour was called Quirinalia. It was covered with gardens and summer villas in late Republican days and throughout the Empire.

The Quirinal Hill is reached in a few minutes from the Trevi Fountain by Via di San Vincenzo and Via della Dataria, or directly from Piazza Venezia by Via Quattro Novembre and Via Ventiquattro Maggio.

Piazza del Quirinale

The spacious and dignified Piazza del Quirinale (**Map 3; 7**) occupies the summit (beware of fast traffic). It has a balustrade which opens onto a fine panorama across the rooftops of Rome to St Peter's in the distance. In the middle of the square, on a high pedestal flanking the obelisk, are two famous colossal groups, over 5.5m high, of Castor and Pollux, the *Dioscuri*, standing by their horses. They are Roman copies, dating from the Imperial era, of Greek originals of the 5C BC. The two groups were found nearby in the Baths of Constantine and placed here by Domenico Fontana for Sixtus V (1585–90), who was responsible for the recutting of the false inscriptions on the bases, Opus Phidiae and Opus Praxitelis, which probably date from c AD 450. When Maestro Gregorio admired the statues in the late 12C he had not heard of these two Classical Greek sculptors and thought these were the names of two philosophers. The statues, which have stood somewhere in the city ever since the fall of the Empire, appear in numerous representations of Rome from medieval times onwards. They were formerly called the 'Horse-tamers' and the square was named after them, being known as Monte Cavallo.

The **obelisk**, with a shaft 14.5m tall, which originally stood in front of the Mausoleum of Augustus, was brought here by Pius VI in 1786; Pius VII added the great basin of dark grey granite, now a fountain but which until then had been used as a cattle-trough in the Roman Forum.

Also overlooking the square is a part of the **Scuderie Pontificie**, the papal stables, built in 1722 and in 2000 restored by Gae Aulenti as an exhibition space, and the **Palazzo della Consulta**, once the seat of the supreme court of the Papal States (Santa Consulta), since 1955 the seat of the Italian Corte Costituzionale, a supreme court for matters concerning the Constitution. The façade is by Ferdinando Fuga (1739).

Palazzo del Quirinale

Palazzo del Quirinale (**Map 3; 5, 7**) has been the official residence of the president of the Italian Republic since 1948. The stately front of the palace (restored in 2002) projects into the piazza, while its flank, known as the *manica lunga* (long wing), is in Via del Quirinale. Open Sun 08.30–12.30; closed Aug and on the main public holidays. The gardens are open on 2 June. ☎ 06 46991.

History of Palazzo del Quirinale

The building was begun in 1574 by Flaminio Ponzio and Ottaviano Nonni (Il Mascherino) for Gregory XIII, on the site of a villa rented by Cardinal d'Este from the Carafa, and was continued by Domenico Fontana, Carlo Maderno, Bernini (who worked on the *manica lunga*) and Fuga: it was not completed until the time of Clement XII (1730–40). The principal entrance is by Maderno; the tower on the left of it was added in the time of Urban VIII.

From 1592 the Quirinal was the summer residence of the popes, and some conclaves were held here. Sixtus V died in the palace in 1590. Pius VII left the palace as prisoner of Napoleon, and from its balcony Pius IX blessed Italy at the beginning of his pontificate (1846). From 1870 to 1947 it became the residence of the Kings of Italy. Vittorio Emanuele II died here on 9 January 1878.

Most of the furniture, paintings and tapestries in the **interior** belonged to the Italian royal family. The Oriental vases and the Gobelins tapestries were the property of the papacy. The collection of **tapestries**, which are in the process of being restored, is one of the most important in Europe. On the grand staircase is Melozzo da Forlì's magnificent fresco of *Christ in Glory*, with angels, formerly in the church of the Santi Apostoli. At the top of the stairs is the **Sala dei Corazzieri**, decorated in 1616–17, with a frieze designed by Agostino Tassi and executed by Giovanni Lanfranco and Carlo Saraceni. This and the adjoining **Cappella Paolina** are by Carlo Maderno. The chapel, the same size as the Sistine

The president of the Republic

The president is elected for a seven-year term of office by members of the *Camera dei Deputati* and *Senato della Repubblica*, united in a joint session in Palazzo di Montecitorio, together with about three delegates from each region of Italy. Any Italian citizen over the age of 50 is eligible for election, but he or she must have a two-thirds majority in the first three ballots, or a straight majority in subsequent ballots. The president's powers include the nomination of the prime minister, the dissolution of parliament and the calling of elections. The office-holder presides over the *Consiglio Superiore della Magistratura*, the judicial branch of government; and also has the right to refuse to ratify a law voted by parliament (though not if it is returned for approval a second time). In the past few years there have been serious proposals for Constitutional reforms which envisage the direct election of the head of State by Italian citizens, and an increase in the president's powers, along the lines of the French president. The president's guards, who have to be over six feet tall, have splendid crimson-and-blue uniforms, and always accompany the president on official occasions.

Chapel in the Vatican, has fine stucco decoration by Martino Ferrabosco. The **Cappella dell' Annunziata** was decorated between 1609 and 1612—under the direction of Guido Reni, who executed the scenes of the *Life of the Madonna* and the *Prophets* in the pendentives—by Lanfranco, Francesco Albani and Antonio Carracci. The **Sala del Balcone** contains two paintings by Pietro da Cortona. In the **Salottino di San Giovanni** there is a copy, attributed to Giulio Romano, of the *Young St John the Baptist* by Raphael and his workshop in the Uffizi gallery in Florence. The **Gallery of Alexander VII** has frescoes carried out under the direction of Pietro da Cortona (1656–57) by Francesco Grimaldi, Lazzaro Baldi, Ciro Ferri, Francesco Mola (Joseph and his Brothers, which is considered his most successful fresco), Carlo Maratta, Gaspard Dughet, Antonio Carracci and others. The lovely garden was designed in the 16C by Il Mascherino. He also built the Fountain of the Organ which plays two late-16C pieces.

Via del Quirinale skirts the long wing of the palace. On the right, beyond a public garden recently replanted, with an equestrian statue of *King Carlo Alberto of Savoy* by Raffaele Romanelli (1900), rises the church of **Sant'Andrea al Quirinale** (Map 3; 6), a masterpiece by Bernini (1658–70) and his pupil Mattia de Rossi. Open 08.00–12.00 and 16.00–19.00; closed Tues.

The simple **façade**, of a single order, balances the fine domed elliptical **interior**, with columns, pilasters and frames in pink and grey marble, and gilded and stuccoed decorations. Numerous cherubim look down from the lantern. Bernini's Classical architecture is combined with his original lighting effects: each chapel is lit by windows high up behind the altars. The fine 17C altarpieces include *St Francesco Saverio* by Baciccia, in the first chapel on the right, and a *Deposition* by Giacinto Brandi in the second chapel. The high altarpiece, with the *Crucifixion of St Andrew* by Borgognone, is surmounted by a splendid group of angels and cherubim sculpted by Ercole Antonio Raggi. On the left of the high altar is an altarpiece by Maratta. The sacristy (unlocked on request)—off a corridor to the right of the high altar—has a pretty frescoed ceiling by Giovanni de la Borde, approved by Bernini. The lavabo here is attributed to Bernini.

Beyond another public garden, also on the right, is another small oval church, **San Carlo alle Quattro Fontane** (Map 3; 6; San Carlino), a masterpiece by Borromini, which provides an interesting contrast to Bernini's *Sant'Andrea*. Usually open Mon–Fri 09.30–12.30 and 16.00–18.00; closed Sat afternoon and Sun.

The tall curved **façade** (1665–68) is well adapted to the cramped site on the corner of a narrow street. The **interior** (1638) has convex and concave surfaces in a complicated design using triangles in a unifying scheme: the symbolism throughout is of the Holy Trinity. In the chapel to the left of the altar is *Rest on the Flight into Egypt*, attributed to Annibale Carracci or Giovanni Francesco Romanelli. The small cloister, which can be entered from the church, was also designed by Borromini. The crypt is designed in a fantastical play of curves linked by a heavy continuous cornice. It is thought Borromini intended this as the place of his own burial.

At this point Via del Quirinale ends at the carfax known as the **Quattro Fontane** (Map 3; 6), with its four vistas ending in Porta Pia and the obelisks of the Quirinal, Pincio and Esquiline, typical of the Rome of Sixtus V. The four small fountains that give the busy crossroads its name, dating from 1593, personify

Fidelity, Strength, the *Aniene* and the *Tiber.* Via delle Quattro Fontane leads right to Via Nazionale and left to Piazza Barberini (see Walk 16).

South of Piazza del Quirinale

From Piazza del Quirinale (see above), Via Ventiquattro Maggio, which was named to commemorate the day in 1915 on which Italy declared war on Austria, descends to Largo Magnanapoli. It runs between two of the most attractive of Rome's princely residences. On the right is the entrance to Villa Colonna, the garden annexe of Palazzo Colonna (see p 170); behind a high wall on the left, on the site of the Baths of Constantine, is **Palazzo Pallavicini-Rospigliosi** (Map 3; 8). Built in 1613–16, probably by Carlo Maderno, in 1704 it was purchased by the Pallavicini-Rospigliosi family who still live here. In the 19C the beautiful gardens were greatly altered and diminished.

In the charming little hanging garden is the **Casino Pallavicini** (open first day of every month, except 1 Jan, 10.00–12.00 and 15.00–17.00. ☎ 06 482 7224), designed by Giovanni Vesanzio. The fine façade is decorated with numerous good reliefs of mythological subjects from Roman sarcophagi (2C–3C AD). The pavilion contains Guido Reni's celebrated fresco (1613–14) of **Aurora scattering flowers before the chariot of the Sun,* which is escorted by the Hours. It was greatly admired by travellers to Rome in the 19C. On the walls are four frescoes of the *Seasons* by Paul Brill, and two *Triumphs* by Antonio Tempesta. The ceiling frescoes in the two side rooms are by Giovanni Baglione (left) and Passignano (right). A number of 17C paintings and the sinopia of a fresco of the *Allegory of Night* by Giovanni da San Giovanni, from the ballroom of the palace, are hung here.

The **Galleria Pallavicini** on the first floor of the palace is open only with special permission. It contains some important paintings of Italian and foreign schools (15C–18C). The collection was founded by Nicolò Pallavicini—a friend of Rubens—and his son Cardinal Lazzaro, and includes works by Sandro Botticelli, Lorenzo Lotto, Annibale and Ludovico Carracci, Guido Reni, Guercino, Federico Barocci and Rubens (*Christ and the Apostles*).

Further downhill on the right is the entrance to the church of **San Silvestro al Quirinale** (Map 3; 7), on an upper floor. From here the cardinals used to march in procession to shut themselves in the Quirinal when a conclave was held in summer. Open daily 09.00–13.00; ring at no. 10 on the right.

The **interior** was rebuilt in 1524 on a Latin cross. On the north side, the first chapel, with pretty floor tiles, has two fine landscapes by Maturino and Polidoro da Caravaggio, who also painted the *St Catherine* and *Mary Magdalene* flanking the altar. In the vault are frescoes by Cavaliere d'Arpino. The second chapel has a *Nativity* by Marcello Venusti. On the south side, the second chapel has a painting of *Pius V and Cardinal Alessandrino* by Giacinto Gemignani, and in the centre a 13C *Madonna and Child* by a Roman artist. The domed Bandini Chapel at the end of the north transept contains tondi by Domenichino, and statues of *Mary Magdalene* and *St John the Evangelist* by Alessandro Algardi, probably his first Roman commission (1628). The altarpiece of the *Ascension* is by Scipione Pulzone. A door in the north transept admits to a courtyard, off which is an oratory where the poetess Vittoria Colonna, widowed in the early 1520s, used to meet Michelangelo and others.

Largo Magnanapoli (Map 3; 7, 8) is at the beginning of the busy Via Nazionale. In the centre of the square is a little group of palm trees with some remains of the Servian Wall (see also p 253); in the restored ancient Palazzo Antonelli at no. 158 are other remains in several rooms off the courtyard, including an arch for a catapult. Behind the church of **Santa Caterina da Siena**, which has a good Baroque interior, rises the conspicuous Torre delle Milizie, a medieval tower and still one of the highest buildings in the centre of Rome (see p 132).

At the beginning of Via Panisperna, in a fine position high up on the left, is the tall façade of **Santi Domenico e Sisto**, preceded by a theatrical staircase (1654) by Vincenzo della Greca. Ring for admission at the college next door; bell by the gate. Inside is a huge fresco (1674–75) by the Bolognese painter, Domenico Canuti, a sculptured group (*Noli me tangere*) by Antonio Raggi, and a *Madonna and Child* thought to be an early work by Antoniazzo Romano. Via Quattro Novembre descends from Largo Magnanapoli past the entrance to the Markets of Trajan to Piazza Venezia (see Walks 5 and 6).

Via Nazionale (**Map 3; 8, 6**) leads from Largo Magnanapoli towards Piazza della Repubblica and Termini railway station. On the right it passes the high wall of the extensive garden of the **Villa Aldobrandini**, built in the 16C for the Duke of Urbino, acquired by Clement VIII (Ippolito Aldobrandini), and given by him to his nephews. The villa was a famous meeting-place for the Roman aristocracy during the Napoleonic era. Now owned by the State, it contains an international law library. A splendid Roman fresco of a marriage scene found on the Esquiline in 1605 was kept in one of the garden pavilions here until 1838, when it was moved to the Vatican museum, where it is still known as the *Aldobrandini Marriage*. Part of the garden is now a little public park, entered from Via Mazzarino where steps lead up past impressive 2C ruins to the garden with some fine palms.

Further on in Via Mazzarino, to the left, is the church of **Sant'Agata dei Goti**, built by an Arian community in 462–70, but much restored. If closed, ring at no. 16. The Byzantine plan remains despite the disappointing 20C restorations, with antique columns and decorative capitals with pulvins. In the apse is a well-preserved 12C–13C Cosmatesque tabernacle. The picturesque 17C court is hung with ivy. The original fabric of the building can be seen on leaving the church by the door in the right aisle.

Further along Via Nazionale, on the right, is the huge Neo-classical building of the Banca d'Italia by Gaetano Koch (1886–1904), behind a row of palm trees and colossal lamp-posts. On the left is the **Teatro Eliseo**, a small theatre built in 1910–38. Just beyond Via Milano (with a road tunnel on the left), rises the monumental **Palazzo delle Esposizioni** (Map 3; 8), erected in 1878–82 to a design by Pio Piacentini. It has been radically restored as an important exhibition centre.

Beyond the palace, on a much lower level, is the little church of **San Vitale**, dedicated in 416 and several times restored. It has a fine portico with old columns and 17C doors. In the interior (usually closed) is a carved wood ceiling, and the walls are decorated with effective 17C trompe l'oeil frescoes with landscapes by Cavaliere d'Arpino, Dughet, Andrea Pozzo and others.

16 • Palazzo Barberini and the Via Veneto

This area is particularly busy with traffic, which can make it difficult to appreciate Gian Lorenzo Bernini's most remarkable fountain, in the centre of Piazza Barberini. Nearby part of the Galleria Nazionale d'Arte Antica is being rearranged in the grand Palazzo Barberini, which also contains a painted ceiling which is the masterpiece of Pietro da Cortona. Via Veneto still retains in part its fashionable atmosphere from the 1960s, with some grand hotels and cafés.

Piazza Barberini (Map 3; 6) was transformed between the wars into one of the busiest traffic hubs in the city. Here converge Via del Tritone from the Corso, Via Sistina from the Pincio, Via Veneto, Via Barberini which leads up towards the station, and Via Quattro Fontane which leads up to the Quirinal Hill past Palazzo Barberini.

Isolated in the centre of the square in this unpleasant setting is Bernini's masterpiece, the **Fontana del Tritone** (1642–43), with four dolphins supporting a scallop shell on which is seated a Triton (or merman) who blows a single jet of water through a conch shell held up in his hands. Drawings by Bernini which have survived show that he made a careful study of where the water would fall, but since the water pressure is now lower the full effect can no longer be appreciated: the spray was meant to have reached the scallop shell, and from there the water would brim over into the lowest basin. Commissioned by the Barberini pope Urban VIII, it is decorated with the beautifully carved Barberini coat of arms with the emblem of the bee.

On the north side of the square, at the beginning of Via Veneto, is the small, reconstructed **Fontana delle Api**, designed by Bernini a year later, also decorated with the Barberini bee and with an inscription on the scallop shell stating that the water is for the use of the public and their animals. The small marble basin below was designed at the beginning of the 20C when the fountain was moved from its original site on the corner of Via Sistina, and recomposed here.

Palazzo Barberini

A short way out of the square, on the right of Via Barberini, is the new entrance to the **Galleria Nazionale d'Arte Antica** in Palazzo Barberini (Map 3; 6), a national gallery of paintings in one of the grandest palaces in Rome. It is pre-eminent in Italian Baroque (17C) painting, although there are also some good examples from the 15C–16C, and a large selection of foreign works.

Opening times

09.00–19.00; closed Mon. ☎ 06 482 4184, ✉ www.galleria borghese.it. The Barberini apartments are shown every half hour by appointment, t 06 328 101; admission with the same ticket.

The rooms are not numbered, and some may be closed. Work on the gallery is being carried out, and the arrangement is temporary and subject to change. There is a lift to the upper floors.

History of the Palazzo Barberini

The palace was begun by Carlo Maderno for the Barberini pope Urban VIII in 1624. Work was continued on the central block by Bernini, and Francesco

Borromini designed the windows of the top storey, the stairs and some door-ways. Pietro da Cortona was also involved as architect, and he painted the famous ceiling fresco in the huge main hall.

In 1949 the Palazzo Barberini became the property of the State, and one wing houses part of the Galleria Nazionale d'Arte Antica. This important collection of paintings was opened to the public in 1895 in Palazzo Corsini (see p 222), where part of it is still housed. It incorporates some private collections which were acquired over the years by the State. The right wing of the palace has been occupied for years by offices and club rooms of the armed forces: these have been scheduled to be moved out to another building for many years.

At present the Salone and rooms I–IX, with a chronological display of paintings from the 12C to the 17C, are open on the piano nobile (first floor); on the second floor are late 17C–18C paintings and the Barberini apartments.

A second façade, overlooking a garden of palm trees, faces Via delle Quattro Fontane, where there is another entrance (the huge stone pilasters and iron grille were added in the 19C by Francesco Azzurri).

First floor. The monumental flight of stairs was probably designed by Bernini. In the entrance are displayed three busts by Bernini. On the left is the **Salone**, with a magnificent ceiling fresco of the *Triumph of Divine Providence* by Pietro da Cortona, his main work, painted between 1633 and 1639 to celebrate the glory of the papacy of Urban VIII and the Barberini family. It is a tour de force, particularly in the organisation of the space, and the reduction of the composition into the angles. On the walls are hung seven cartoons by the school of Pietro da Cortona showing scenes from the life of Urban VIII, executed for tapestries manufactured in the Barberini workshops (active in Rome 1627–83) and now in the Vatican. There are also four cartoons for mosaics in the Cappella Colonna in St Peter's by Andrea Sacchi, Bernini and Carlo Pellegrini, and Giovanni Lanfranco.

On the right of the hall is the entrance to rooms I–IX, where the chronological display of paintings begins. Beyond room V (see below) the earliest paintings are displayed in **room I**. A 12C *Madonna* by the Roman school; *Birth of St John the Baptist* by the Maestro dell'Incoronazione di Urbino; painted crucifix by 'Simone' and 'Machilone'; *Scenes from the Life of Christ* by Giovanni Baronzio. There are also works by Simone da Bologna, Giovanni da Rimini and Nicolò di Segna di Tura. **Room II**. *Madonna and Child* by Michele Giambono; and works by Girolamo di Benvenuto. In the alcove is a small polychrome terracotta group of the *Pietà* by Francesco di Giorgio Martini (formerly attributed to Giacomo Cozzarelli). **Room III**. *Madonna and Child* and *Annunciation with Donors*, both by Filippo Lippi (1437); *St Nicholas of Tolentino* by Perugino; and *Mary Magdalene* by Piero di Cosimo. **Room IV** contains three works by Antoniazzo Romano. **Room V**. *Vision of the Blessed de Sylva* by Pseudo Bramantino, and works by Callisto Piazza da Lodi, Girolamo Genga and Domenico Puligo.

Room VI. *Holy Family* by Andrea del Sarto; and works by Brescianino and Domenico Beccafumi. The *Portrait of a lady* by Raphael (also attributed to his pupil Giulio Romano) became known as *La Fornarina* when the Romantics identified the sitter with Margherita, daughter of the Sienese baker (or *fornaio*) Francesco Luti, supposed to have been Raphael's mistress. The portrait has many similarities with another superb portrait by Raphael now in the Palatine Gallery in Palazzo Pitti in Florence, known as *La Velata*. Raphael was engaged to be married to Cardinal Bibbiena's niece, Maria, who predeceased him. Also here are works by Sodoma; and a bust of *Ceres* by Baldassare Peruzzi.

Room VII. Works by Garofalo and Niccolò dell'Abate. **Room VIII**. *Portrait of a Man* by Bartolomeo Veneto; *Mystical Marriage of St Catherine* by Lorenzo Lotto; *Christ and the Adulteress* by Jacopo Tintoretto; *Madonna and Child with St Anne and the Young St John the Baptist* by Giovanni Busi (Il Cariani); *Venus and Adonis*, a replica of a painting in the Prado by Titian; *Adoration of the Shepherds* and *Baptism of Christ* by El Greco; and *Portrait of Stefano Colonna* by Bronzino.

Room IX. The monochrome painting of the *Pietà* (derived from a work by Michelangelo) is by the Master of the Manchester Madonna. The painting of *Bathsheba's Bath* by Jacopo Zucchi belonged to the Monte di Pietà in Rome, but was sent to decorate the Italian Embassy in Berlin from 1908 until 1944. It was lost during the Second World War, but returned to the Galleria Nazionale in 1998.

The other rooms and the chapel on the first floor have vaults painted by Andrea Camassei, Andrea Sacchi (1630–33), Giuseppe Chiari and Pietro da Cortona and his pupils, including Francesco Romanelli.

Second floor. In the **corridor** is a portrait of *Giovanni Fagnani Pecori and his Son* by Lavinia Fontana; works by Dionisio Calvaert, Guercino and Pietro da Cortona; and a *Mary Magdalen and Sleeping Putto* (a fresco) by Guido Reni.

The *Portrait of a Lady* (or of a Sibyl) by Guido Reni was traditionally supposed to be a portrait of Beatrice Cenci, the young girl of 22 who was executed in 1599 for having hired assassins, together with her step-mother Lucrezia and brother Jacopo, to kill her father the previous year. Although Beatrice never confessed to parricide even under torture, she was beheaded. Her father was known to have been a very violent man and was also accused of incest. Her story caught the imagination of the Romantics and in 1819 Shelley, while staying in Livorno, wrote his famous verse drama *The Cenci*. He had seen this portrait in Palazzo Colonna when he came to Rome the previous year, and Stendhal, Charles Dickens and Nathaniel Hawthorne all mention the painting, which did much to augment the aura of tragedy which surrounded the figure of Beatrice.

Room 2 at the end of the corridor has works by Lanfranco, Lodovico Cigoli, Francesco Furini and Sassoferrato. There are portraits by Baciccio of *Clement IX* and *Gian Lorenzo Bernini*, as well as a *Pietà* by him. The two paintings by Bernini himself are *David with the Head of Goliath* and *Portrait of Urban VIII*. Steps lead down to **room 3**, which displays two important works by Caravaggio: *Narcissus*, and *Judith with the Head of Holofernes*. The *St Francis in Meditation* is also attributed to him. Works by Bartolomeo Manfredi, Orazio Gentileschi and Carlo Saraceni are also displayed here. **Room 4** displays portraits by Salvator Rosa, a *Mary Magdalene* by Simon Vouet, and works by Mattia Preti, Luca Giordano and Bernardo Strozzi. Beyond **room 5**, with works by Gerard van Honthorst and Valentin de Boulogne, the last room at present open in this wing has Dutch works, including a portrait of *Erasmus* by Quentin Massys and one of *Henry VIII of England* (possibly a replica) by Hans Holbein.

From here you can enter the delightful 18C **Barberini apartments** (for admission see above), nine rooms with well-preserved Rococo decorations (1750–70), where the Barberini family lived up until 1960. They are also interesting for their period furniture. The dining-room is particularly charming. The paintings are by Paolo Monaldi (1763–70). Visitors are usually asked to descend directly to the exit from the palace from the last room of the apartments.

On Via delle Quattro Fontane, opposite the palace, a building once housed the Scots College from 1604 until 1962, when it moved out of the centre of Rome to Via Cassia. The church of St Andrew (1645–76), deconsecrated in 1962, is now incorporated in a building dating from 1869, which is occupied by a bank.

Via Veneto

The broad and tree-lined Via Veneto (**Map 3**; **6, 4**), correctly Via Vittorio Veneto, begins at Piazza Barberini and climbs in two sweeping curves to Porta Pinciana. The street—with its luxury hotels, great mansions and famous cafés—was especially fashionable for its ambience of *la dolce vita* in the 1960s (after the success of Federico Fellini's film of that name in 1959).

History of the Villa Ludovisi and Via Veneto

The Via Vittorio Veneto was opened in 1886 on part of the huge site of the beautiful park, now obliterated, of the Villa Ludovisi, which was acquired from 1621 onwards by Cardinal Ludovico Ludovisi, nephew of Pope Gregory XV. He had bought some 19 hectares of land by the time of his death and designed a garden which was much admired by John Evelyn. Later travellers who mentioned it include Goethe (1787), Stendhal (1828), Hippolyte Taine (1864) and Henry James (1883). His heirs sold the property to the Boncompagni Rospigliosi family: it came to include an area of some 30 hectares from the stretch of walls between Porta Pinciana to Porta Salaria, down to the present Via Boncompagni and all the area to the south-west now occupied by Via Vittorio Veneto as far as Via di Porta Pinciana.

In 1883 the Rospigliosi decided to destroy the gardens and sell off the huge property as building land. Despite an international outcry, work began on felling the trees and laying out new roads in 1885 and most of the buildings had been constructed by 1889. The only survival of the original villa and gardens is the Casino dell'Aurora (see below). Some one hundred pieces of the famous Ludovisi collection of Classical sculpture, founded by Cardinal Ludovico, were bought by the State in 1901: now part of the Museo Nazionale Romano, they are exhibited in Palazzo Altemps (see p 189). The name Ludovisi is now often used for this aristocratic district of the city.

On the right is the church of the Cappuccini or **Santa Maria della Concezione** (**Map 3**; **6**), architecturally simple and unpretentious in accordance with Franciscan ideals and in strong contrast to the Baroque works of the time (1626). Its founder was Cardinal Antonio Barberini. In the very dark interior all the pictures are labelled.

In the **interior** the first chapel on the south side has *St Michael* by Reni, and to the left, Honthorst's *Mocking of Christ*. The third chapel contains St Francis in Ecstasy and Death of St Francis by Domenichino; and the fifth chapel, Andrea Sacchi's *St Anthony Raising a Dead Man*. An inscription on the pavement in front of the high altar, which reads *hic jacet pulvis, cinis et nihil* ('here lies nothing but dust and ashes'), marks the grave of Cardinal Barberini. On the north side, the fifth chapel contains the *Virgin and St Bonaventure* by Andrea

Sacchi and the first chapel Pietro da Cortona's *St Paul Having his Sight Restored*. A cemetery (entered down the stairs to the right of the church) has five subterranean chapels decorated from the 17C onwards with the bones and skeletons of over 4000 Capuchins, arranged in patterns.

Opposite the church, a street with steps ascends to **Sant'Isidoro** by Antonio Casoni (1620), with a pink façade by Carlo Bizzaccheri (1704). Open Sun at 10.00. The church was attached to a college for Irish students founded by Luke Wadding (1588–1657), the distinguished Irish Franciscan who instigated the Irish rebellion of 1641 against the confiscation of Ulster. His tomb is in the church, which contains several works by Carlo Maratta, and a chapel designed by Gian Lorenzo Bernini with sculptures attributed to his son Paolo.

Further up Via Veneto on the right, by its second curve, is Palazzo Piombino or Palazzo Margherita, a huge building by Gaetano Koch (1886–90), standing in a garden, and now the United States Embassy. Queen Margherita lived here after the death of Umberto I in 1900.

Further on, Via Lombardia leads left from Via Veneto to the **Casino dell'Aurora** at no. 46 (no admission), a relic of the famous Villa Ludovisi. It was the only edifice in the Villa which escaped demolition in 1883. The first Roman scene in Henry James's novel *Roderick Hudson* takes place in the gardens here. The garden-house contains a fine ceiling-painting of *Aurora and Fame* by Guercino (1621).

Via Veneto ends at **Porta Pinciana** (Map 3; 4), a handsome fortified gateway erected by Honorius c 403 and since enlarged. On either side can be seen a long stretch of the Aurelian Walls (272–79) with 18 turrets. Outside the gate is the park of Villa Borghese (see Walk 17).

17 • Villa Borghese and the Galleria Borghese

The magnificent Villa Borghese (Map 3; 1, 2 and 12; 7, 8) is Rome's most famous public park, and the most extensive in the centre of the city, with a circumference of 6km and an area of 688 hectares. It is connected with the Pincio and the Villa Giulia, so that the three form one great park, intersected in every direction by avenues and paths, with fine oaks, giant ilexes, umbrella pines and other trees, as well as statues, fountains and terraces. It also contains the suburban villa that houses the famous Museo e Galleria Borghese, with a very fine collection of paintings and sculptures, including numerous masterpieces by Gian Lorenzo Bernini, Antonio Canova, Raphael, Titian and Caravaggio. However, this is the only museum in Rome where it is obligatory to book a visit in advance.

History of the park of Villa Borghese

The Villa owes its origin, in the 17C, to Cardinal Scipione Borghese, Paul V's nephew. In the 18C Prince Marcantonio Borghese, the father of Prince Camillo Borghese who married Pauline Bonaparte, employed Jacob More from Edinburgh to design the gardens. Early in the 19C the property was enlarged by the addition of the Giustiniani Gardens. In 1902 it was bought by the State, then handed over to the city of Rome, and opened to the public.

Getting there

On foot the Villa Borghese is best approached from Porta Pinciana at the top of Via Veneto, or from the bridge over Viale del Muro Torto, which is reached through the gardens on the Pincio. The park can also be reached from the north by the scenic flight of steps in front of the Galleria Nazionale d'Arte Moderna. A monumental entrance to the park was erected from Piazzale Flaminio, just outside Porta del Popolo. Traffic is excluded from the main area of the park, which is traversed by the electric bus No. 116.

Outside Porta Pinciana (**Map 3; 4**) is Piazzale Brasile, with a monument in Carrara marble to Lord Byron after Bertel Thorvaldsen (1959). From here, Viale del Museo Borghese leads straight for some 600 metres to the Museo e Galleria Borghese.

Museo e Galleria Borghese

The Palazzina or Casino Borghese (**Map 3; 2**) houses the Museo and Galleria Borghese, an impressive collection of paintings and sculpture founded by Cardinal Scipione Borghese, which includes Classical works as well as masterpieces by Bernini, Canova, Raphael and Caravaggio. At the rear of the building is a beautiful formal garden.

Opening times

Although the museum is open 09.00–19.00; closed Mon, it is obligatory to book the visit in advance; ☎ 06 328 101, ✉ www. galleriaborghese.it. Entrance is allowed only every two hours, at 09.00, 11.00, 13.00, 15.00 and 17.00. Unfortunately, the visits are strictly timed and the staff can be rather officious and bossy. The ticket office, information desk, bookshop, bar and toilets are on the lower ground level, which is often unpleasantly crowded. The works are well-labelled, except for the classical sculpture.

History of the Museo e Galleria Borghese

The Casino Borghese was begun for the Borghese in 1608 by Flaminio Ponzio, Paul V's architect, and continued after his death in 1613 by Jan van Santen (Giovanni Vesanzio). It was altered for Marcantonio IV Borghese by Antonio Asprucci and Christopher Unterberger in 1775–90, when the splendid interior decoration was carried out.

Cardinal Scipione Borghese acquired numerous works of art through the good offices of his uncle Paul V, including Raphael's *Deposition*, which he carried off from the church of San Francesco in Perugia. The collection was added to by later members of the family, but much of the sculpture was sold in 1807 to Napoleon I by his brother-in-law Camillo Borghese, and is now in the Louvre. For nearly two centuries the paintings were housed in Palazzo Borghese near the Tiber (see p 154); they were brought here in 1891. The collections were acquired by the State in 1902, and the building had to undergo radical structural repairs at the end of the 20C.

Ground floor. Unless it is raining, the entrance to the ground floor is through the doors under the central portico, with fragments of a triumphal frieze of Trajan. (If it is raining, the entrance is from the lower ground level up a spiral staircase.) The **Salone** has a fine ceiling fresco by Mariano Rossi (1775–78); on the pavement are five fragments of a Roman mosaic (AD 320) with gladiators and wild beasts, found in 1834 at Torrenova, near Rome. Here are displayed *Truth* by Bernini, sculpted in 1645 for the vestibule of his palace on Via del Corso but left unfinished; and a

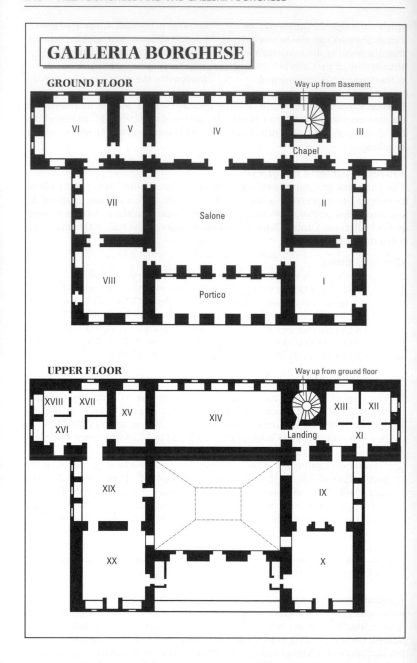

GALLERIA BORGHESE

GROUND FLOOR

Way up from Basement

VI | V | IV | Chapel | III

VII | Salone | II

VIII | Portico | I

UPPER FLOOR

Way up from ground floor

XVIII | XVII | XV | XIV | XIII | XII

XVI | | | Landing | XI

XIX | | IX

XX | | X

fragment found in Rome in 1980 and thought by some scholars to be Michelangelo's first version of the head of Christ for the Rondanini Pietà now in Milan. The Classical sculpture includes the colossal figure of a *Satyr*, colossal heads of **Hadrian** and **Antonius Pius** and statues of **Augustus** and **Bacchus**. Most of the other ceilings on this floor were decorated at the time of Marcantonio Borghese (c 1750–60) by Giovanni Battista Marchetti and numerous assistants.

Room I. The sculpture of **Pauline Borghese* by Canova is justly one of his best-known works (1805–08). Napoleon's sister, who lived in Rome as the wife of Camillo Borghese, is depicted as Venus Victrix. The other sculpture here includes a *Herm of Bacchus* by Luigi Valadier (1773); *Cupid Riding an Eagle* attributed to Pietro Bernini (c 1618); and a portrait of *Pope Clement XII* by Pietro Bracci.

Room II. Here is displayed **David*, a very fine statue carved at the age of 25 (1623–24) by Bernini (the face is a self-portrait). The sarcophagus with the Labours of Hercules on two sides dates from AD 160. Paintings here include *Samson in Prison* by Annibale Carracci (c 1595); *Andromeda Liberated by Perseus* by Rutilio Manetti; *David with the Head of Goliath* by Battistello Caracciolo (1612); and a *Still-life with Birds* by the school of Caravaggio (1602–07).

Room III. **Apollo and Daphne* is another fine sculpture by Bernini (1624), in which the dramatic moment of capture is well portrayed. Over the doors are two landscapes by Paul Brill (c 1595). The Chapel is frescoed by Claude Deruet (d. 1660).

Room IV. The decoration of the room is a notable example of 18C skill and taste in the ornamental arrangement of a great variety of precious marbles, and the incorporation of bas-reliefs and paintings into the design. The busts of Roman emperors, in porphyry and alabaster, were carved in the 17C, and the vases in marble from Luni, with the Seasons are the work of Maximilian Laboureur. The *Rape of Proserpine* is another early masterpiece by Bernini (formerly in the Villa Ludovisi), and the *bozzetto* in bronze of *Neptune* was made by him for a fountain group now in the Victoria and Albert Museum, London. Also here is a bronze replica by Antonio Susini of the antique *Farnese Bull* found in the Baths of Caracalla and taken to Naples in the 18C.

Room V. The *Hermaphrodite* is a replica of a famous Hellenistic prototype; above it is an alabaster vase on a red porphyry base. Also here are a bust of *Agrippa the Elder* (1C AD), and a head of *Aphrodite*. On the floor is a Roman mosaic of a fishing scene (3C BC), and above the doors are more landscapes by Brill.

Room VI. The sculptural group of **Aeneas and Anchises* was carved by Bernini when he was only 15 years old (in 1613), with the help of his father, Pietro Bernini. The paintings here include *Cupid and Psyche* by Jacopo Zucchi (1589), and the *Death of the Virgin*, a preliminary sketch for the church of Santa Maria della Pace by G.M. Morandi.

Room VII has paintings by Tommaso Conca representing the gods and religions of ancient Egypt. Among the sculpture is a *Satyr on a Dolphin* (1C AD), a copy of an original from Taranto (the head was recarved in the 16C).

Room VIII. The **Dancing Satyr* is a 2C AD copy of an original by Lysippus, discovered in 1824 at Monte Cavo and restored under the direction of Thorwaldsen. Here are displayed some masterpieces by Caravaggio: *Boy Crowned with Ivy*, also called *Il Bacchino Malato* (1592–95); *Boy with a Basket of Fruit* (1595); **Madonna of the Palafrenieri* (1605); **St Jerome* (1605–06); *St John the Baptist* (1609–10); and **David with the Head of Goliath* (1609–10).

Other early 17C paintings here include: *Capture of Christ* and *Rape of Europa* by Cavalier d'Arpino; *Joseph and Potiphar's Wife* by Lodovico Cigoli; and *Judith with the Head of Holofernes* by Giovanni Baglione. From room IV a spiral staircase leads up to the first floor.

First floor. On the landing up to the first floor is a bust of *Paul V* by Ludovico Leone. **Room IX** has beautiful paintings by Raphael: the **Deposition* (1507); **Portrait of a Lady with a Unicorn*, possibly the portrait of Maddalena Strozzi (1506); **Portrait of a Man* (1502–04); and a portrait of *Pope Julius II*. The other paintings include: *Holy Family with the Infant St John the Baptist* by Perino del Vaga (1511); *Madonna and Child*, and *St Sebastian* by Perugino, (1490); and the *Madonna and Child with the Infant St John the Baptist and Angels* by Botticelli and assistants (1488).

Room X displays early 16C works by Andrea del Sarto (**Madonna and Child with the Infant St John the Baptist*); Correggio (**Danaë*); Parmigianino (*Portrait of a Man*); Bronzino (**St John the Baptist*); and Lucas Cranach the Elder (*Venus and Cupid with a Honeycomb*).

Room XI has *Madonna*s by Garofalo, and a *Deposition* by Ortolano.

Room XII. *Holy Family* and *Pietà* by Sodoma; *Venus* by Baldassare Peruzzi; portrait of *Mercurio Bua* by Lorenzo Lotto; and an early 16C copy of Leonardo's *Leda and the Swan*.

Room XIII. *St Francis*, *Madonna and Child*, and *St Stephen*, all by Francesco Francia; *Madonna and Child with St Joseph and the Infant St John the Baptist* by the Kress Master of Landscapes; and *Scourging of Christ* by Lorenzo Costa.

Room XIV. Here is displayed Bernini's earliest work, The *Goat Almathea* (c 1615), with Zeus as a child and a small faun at play. It shows the influence of Classical Hellenistic sculpture on this great Baroque sculptor. He also carved the two marble portrait busts here of **Cardinal Scipione Borghese** (c 1632), and the terracotta model for the equestrian statue of Louis XIV (1669–70). The black marble putto, called *Il Sonno* (Sleep) is by Alessandro Algardi. The paintings here include two self-portraits by Bernini, one dating from around 1623 and the other from about ten years later. The *Portrait of a boy* is also by him. *Moses with the Tables of the Law* is by Guido Reni, and the *Prodigal Son* by Guercino.

Room XV. Paintings from the mid 16C: *Last Supper*, and *Sheep and Lamb* by Jacopo Bassano; *St Cosmas and St Damian* by Dosso Dossi, and **Tobias and the Angel* by Giovanni Girolamo Savoldo.

Room XVI. *Adoration of the Christ Child* by Pellegrino Tibaldi; *Nativity* by Giorgio Vasari; and *Allegory of the Creation* by Jacopo Zucchi.

Room XVII. *Madonna*s by Sassoferrato and Pompeo Batoni. **Room XVIII**. **Deposition*, a very fine work by Peter Paul Rubens (c 1602) and *Entombment of Christ* by Sisto Badalocchio. **Room XIX** displays two works by Domenichino: *Diana*, and a *Sybil*.

Room XX. An early masterpiece by Titian **Sacred and Profane Love* (1514) is displayed here. The three other works here by him were probably painted in the 1560s (*Venus Blinding Cupid*, *St Dominic*, and *Scourging of Christ*). The *Portrait of a Young Man* by Antonello da Messina dates from around 1475. Venetian masters represented here include: Lotto (*Madonna and Child with Saints*); Palma Vecchio (*Portrait of a Young Man*); and Giovanni Bellini (*Madonna and Child*).

From the Galleria Borghese Viale dell'Uccelliera leads north-west to Viale del Giardino Zoologico, in which is the entrance to the zoological gardens (**Map 12; 6**), now called the **Bioparco**. Open daily 09.00–17.30.

The zoo was first opened in 1911 and enlarged in 1935: it now has an area of about 17 hectares and more than 1000 animals, all of them born in captivity. The collection is strong in bears and large cats. In Via Ulisse Aldovrandi, on the north side of the zoo and accessible from it, is the **Museo Civico di Zoologia**. The original nucleus of this zoological museum was the 19C study collections of the university, and the civic museum was founded in 1932. It is in the process of modernisation, and includes sections devoted to the fauna which used to inhabit the Roman Campagna, vertebrates, Italian birds, insects and shells. Open 09.00–17.00; closed Mon; combined ticket with the Bioparco.

Villa Borghese

From the Galleria Borghese numerous paths lead into the huge park of Villa Borghese. From Viale dell'Uccelliera, Viale dei Pupazzi (first left) leads past the Fontana dei Cavalli Marini and the attractive **Piazza di Siena**, a rustic amphitheatre with tall pine trees, created by Mario and Antonio Asprucci c 1792, where important equestrian events are held, and opera performances sometimes take place in summer. On the opposite side of the viale is a monument to *Umberto I* by Davide Calandra. At the end of the viale is the Tempietto di Diana attributed to Mario Asprucci (1789).

On Viale Goethe is a monument to *Goethe* by Gustav Eberlein, and the 17C Casina delle Rose. Between the Tempietto di Diana and Piazza di Siena is the so-called Casina di Raffaello (**Map 3; 1**), reconstructed by Antonio Asprucci in 1792. There are long term plans to use the interior, which has decorations by Felice Cinni, as a museum of restored sculptures from the gardens.

Paths lead north to Viale Pietro Canonica, which leads right to La Fortezzuola which dates from the 16C; the crenellations were added in the 19C. In 1926 it became the studio of the sculptor and musician Pietro Canonica (1869–1959) who lived here until his death. He left the house and a large collection of his sculpture to the Commune of Rome as the **Museo Canonica** (**Map 3; 1**). Open 09.00–19.00; closed Mon. ☎ 06 884 2279. The first room contains a portrait sculpture of *Donna Franca Florio* (1903), a bust of *Princess Emily Doria Pamphilj* (1901), and *Dopo il Voto* (*After the Vow*), a statue of a young nun, exhibited in Paris in 1893. **Room II** has the model for a monument to Alexander II of Russia, which was destroyed in the Revolution of 1917. **Room III** contains plaster casts of equestrian statues of *Simon Bolivar* (1954) and *King Feysal I of Iraq* (1933), and several war memorials. The gallery at the right of the entrance contains original models of portraits, notably those of *Lyda Borelli* (1920), *Alexander II of Russia* (1913), *Luigi Einaudi* (1948), the *Duke of Portland* (1896) and *Margaret of Savoy* (1903), and casts of portraits of the English royal family made between 1902 and 1922. The house and small studio are also open, with some fine works of art collected by Canonica, some from Palazzo Reale in Turin.

At the end of the avenue is a reproduction of the Temple of Faustina. The area to the north of Viale Canonica is called the **Giardino del Lago** (**Map 3; 1**), with hedged walks and arbours, laid out in 1785 by Jacob More and Cristoforo Unterberger, 'all'inglese'. On an island in the little lake is a Temple of Aesculapius

Villa Borghese

by Antonio and Mario Asprucci. Seven statues by Vincenzo Pacetti (partly Roman) have been replaced by copies.

Via Esculapio leads west and ends in Piazzale del Fiocco near Canina's **Fountain of Aesculapius** (Fontana di Esculapio) (1830–34), with a Roman statue and on the left the **Portico Egiziano**, built as an imposing entrance to the gardens in the form of pylons. Beyond it is Viale La Guardia, which passes a monument to Victor Hugo (1905), presented by the Franco-Italian League. Paths lead west to Piazzale dei Martiri and the bridge across the Viale del Muro Torto which leads into the Pincio Gardens (**Map 3**; **1**; see p 167). Viale Washington descends from Piazza del Fiocco to a Classical main gateway on Piazzale Flaminio (**Map 12**; **7**), outside Piazza del Popolo, designed as the main entrance to Villa Borghese by Luigi Canina in 1835. From Piazzale del Fiocco, Via Bernadotte leads to the monumental flight of steps which descends to Viale delle Belle Arti in front of the Galleria Nazionale d'Arte Moderna (**Map 12**; **7**; see Walk 18).

18 • Galleria d'Arte Moderna and Museo Etrusco

Although they are some way from the centre of Rome, these two important museums can be reached on foot by taking a pretty walk through the Villa Borghese public gardens. Public transport in this district is not very good, although trams 3 and 19 serve both museums. The Galleria Nazionale d'Arte Moderna, in a purpose-built palace dating from 1911, contains a very fine collection of modern Italian art. The Museo di Villa Giulia, recently modernised and housed in a lovely 16C villa, has extremely interesting Etruscan material from Lazio.

Galleria Nazionale d'Arte Moderna

Just to the north of the huge park of Villa Borghese (see Walk 17) is the Galleria Nazionale d'Arte Moderna (**Map 12**; **7**). Housed in **Palazzo delle Belle Arti**, purpose built for it in 1911 by Cesare Bazzani, this is the most important collection in existence of Italian 19C and early 20C art.

The collection, founded in 1883, was first exhibited in Palazzo delle Esposizioni. It was moved here in 1911, and, as the collection expanded, the building was enlarged at the back in 1934. The 19C art was re-arranged in 1998 in the original gallery as it was when the museum first opened in 1911. Early 20C art up until the 1960s is displayed in the extension wings of 1934. The museum is beautifully kept. A new building in the Flaminio district is to be begun by Zaha M. Hadid to house the gallery's collection of works from after the 1960s and contemporary art. Exhibitions are frequently held here in the central halls of the building.

The works are divided broadly into four sections: left wing: works dating from 1780–1883; right wing: works dating from 1883–1910; upper right wing: works dating from 1910–50; upper left wing: works dating from the 1950s and 1960s. They are well labelled and a description in English is available in each room. However, most of the rooms are un-numbered, so for clarity in the following description, numbers have been given corresponding to the key on the plan on p 246.

Opening times

08.30–19.30; closed Mon. ☎ 06 322 981. There is a pleasant café in the building, as well as a restaurant (booking is advisable, ☎ 06 3229 8223).

The first part of the 19C collection is in the **left wing**, with works dating from 1780–1880. **Room 1** (**Sala della Psiche**) displays a statue of *Psyche* and other works by Pietro Tenerani, a portrait by Andrea Appiani, and *Views of Rome* by Ippolito Caffi and other painters of the Roman school. **Room 2** (**Sala della Saffo**) has Tuscan sculptures, including a marble statue of *Sappho* by Giovanni Duprè, and works by Lorenzo Bartolini and Hiram Powers. The Macchiaioli school of painters is well represented by Giuseppe Abbati, Odoardo Borrani, Antonio Puccinelli (**Portrait of Nerina Badioli*), Stefano Ussi, Giovanni Fattori (Portrait of his first wife), Silvestro Lega (**The Visit*, 1868), Adriano Cecioni and Vincenzo Cabianca. **Room 3** (**Sala dello Jenner**) displays a statue by Giulio Monteverde of *Edward Jenner*, the English physician who discovered vaccination in 1796. Paintings here include *The Bather* by Francesco Hayez, portraits by Il Piccio, and works by Antonio Fontanesi and Domenico Induno.

The central **room 4** (**Sala dell'Ercole**) is named after the colossal statue of *Hercules* made in 1815 by Antonio Canova, and there is a collection of Neo-classical statues from the Torlonia collection here. The historical paintings, many dating from the 1870s, include works by Michele Rapisardi, Tranquillo Cremona (*Marco Polo*), Francesco Hayez (**Sicilian Vespers*, his masterpiece, and arguably the most important work in the entire gallery), and Stefano Ussi (*Prayer in the Desert*). **Room 5** (**Sala Palizzi**) contains numerous paintings donated by the Neapolitan painter Filippo Palizzi (1818–99), including studies of costumes, animals and landscapes, and a large painting of the *Forest of Fontainebleau* by his brother Giuseppe, and works by Edoardo Dalbono. **Room 6** (**Sala Morelli**) is dedicated to another Neapolitan painter, Domenico Morelli, whose fine works here include *Tasso* and *Eleonora d'Este*, the *Temptation of St Anthony*, portraits, the *Assumption*, and the *Entombment of Christ*. **Room 7** (**Sala della Cleopatra**) is named after a marble sculpture by Alfonso Balzico. Here, works by artists from southern Italy include a terracotta statuette of *Brutus* and a bust of a *Philosopher*, both by Vincenzo Gemito , and works by Gioacchino Toma.

The second part of the 19C collection is displayed in the **right wing**, with works dating from c 1880 1910. **Room 1** (**Sala del Voto**) is named after a huge sculpture by Francesco Paolo Michetti (1883). Here also are works by southern Italian painters including Antonio Mancini. **Room 2** (**Sala della Madre**) has a marble statue of a *Mother and Child* by Adriano Cecioni. The paintings by Tuscan artists include works by Stefano Ussi, Egisto Ferroni and Giovanni Fattori, and scenes of Florence and Ravenna by Telemaco Signorini. **Room 3** (**Sala dei Veneti**) contains Venetian scenes and works by Giacomo Favretto and Ettore Tito.

In the large, central **Room 4** (**Sala di Giordano Bruno**) is the plaster model for the monument to *Giordano Bruno* by Ettore Ferrari in the Campo dei Fiori. The paintings include large battle scenes by Michele Cammarano and Giovanni Fattori (*Battle of Custoza*). **Room 5** (**Sala del Giardiniere**) is named after Van Gogh's painting of *The Gardener*, which is hung here together with his *L'Arlésienne*, and works by Cézanne, Monet and Degas. Also here are **Bois de Boulogne*, a triptych of 1881 by Giuseppe de Nittis, **Sogni* by Vittorio Corcos, and a portrait of *Giuseppe Verdi* by Giovanni Boldini. In the centre are sculptures by Medardo Rosso. **Room 6** (**Sala della Stanga**) contains a bronze sculpture (*The Plough*) by David Calandra, and works by Lombard and Piedmontese artists. **Room 7** (**Sala Previati**) is named after Gaetano Previati (1852–1920) whose works are hung here, and there are more sculptures by Medardo Rosso. **Rooms 8**, **9** and **10** at the end contain sculptures by Auguste Rodin (*Bronze Age*), Ettore Ximenes (*Rinascita*), and Domenico Trentacoste, and paintings by Gustav Klimt (*The Three Ages of Man*, 1905), Giulio Aristide Sartorio, Dante Gabriele Rossetti (*Mrs William Morris*) and Frederic Leighton.

Very fine works from 1911–1950 are displayed in the **upper right wing**. The first room has works by artists represented in the 1911 exhibition of Italian art. In **room 2** are exhibited *Le tre Età* by Gustav Klimt, (1905) and *Le Vecchie* by Felice Casorati, (1909). **Room 3** illustrates the beginning of Divisionism, with early works by Giacomo Balla; (including *Villa Borghese, Parco dei Daini*, 1910), Felice Carena, and Duilio Cambellotti. The small **room 4** has portraits by Giovanni Boldini and Paolo Troubetzkoy. There are more works of 1910–20 on the mezzanine above. In **room 5** are works by Amedeo Modigliani, and the Futurists Umberto Boccioni, Giacomo Balla, and Piet Mondrian. **Room 6** illustrates the 1930s with works by Carlo Carrà, Giorgio Morandi, Ardengo

Soffici, and Ottone Rosai. **Room 7** exhibits works by Virgilio Guidi (*In the tram*), Antonio Donghi and Felice Casorati. **Room 8** is devoted to De Chirico, and his brother Alberto Savinio as well as Filippo De Pisis. The large **room 9** has fine works by Felice Casorati (portraits), Mario Sironi (*Solitudine*), Giuseppe Capogrossi (*Il Temporale*), Carlo Levi, Gino Severini, Scipione, Emanuele Cavalli (*La Sposa*, and a portrait), and Massimo Campigli. **Room 10** is devoted to Renato Guttuso, and the last two rooms (**11** and **12**) to the post War period.

A corridor with sculptures by Henry Moore, Libero Andreotti, Arturo Martini, Francesco Messina, Adolfo Wildt, Bruno Innocenti and Giacomo Manzù connects this wing with the last wing, which has the most recent works in the gallery.

The second part of the 20C collection is exhibited in the **upper left wing**, with works from the 1950s and 1960s, mostly donated by the artists or their descendents. **Room 1** is dedicated to Alberto Burri. **Room 2** has works by Jackson Pollock, Antonio Tàpies, Karel Appel, Alberto Giacometti and Alexander Calder. **Room 3** has works by Giuseppe Capogrossi and Ettore Colla. In the central **room 4** are works by Lucio Fontana, Emilio Vedova, Afro, Giulio Turcato, Cy Twombly, Arnaldo and Giò Pomodoro and Pietro Consagra. **Rooms 5–7** exhibit works from the 1960s, including pieces by Enrico Baj and Mario Schifano. On a mezzanine floor is the collection which belonged to Palma Bucarelli, who was director of the gallery from 1935 to 1975.

Outside the gallery, Viale delle Belle Arti widens into Piazza Thorvaldsen, in which, on the right, is a copy of Bertel Thorvaldsen's *Jason*, a gift from the city of Copenhagen. Above the steps is a statue of *Simon Bolivar* (1934). On the hill above, in Via Antonio Gramsci, is the **British School at Rome (Map 12; 5)**, established in 1901 as a School of Archaeology. After the 1911 International Exhibition of Fine Arts in Rome, the site where the British Pavilion had stood was offered to the School by the Comune of Rome. The pavilion, designed by Sir Edwin Lutyens, with a façade based on the west front of St Paul's Cathedral, was reproduced in permanent materials. In 1912, the School widened its scope to the study of the fine arts, literature and history of Italy. Scholarships are awarded, and an annual exhibition is held in June of the artists' work. The researches of the School are published annually in 'The Papers of the British School'.

This district, known as the Valle Giulia, was laid out at the beginning of the century after Viale delle Belle Arti had been opened. Numerous foreign academies and cultural institutes have been established here: near Piazza Thorvaldsen are the Belgian, Dutch and Romanian Academies; in Via Gramsci beyond the British School, are the Faculty of Architecture of Rome University and the Austrian Academy.

Museo Etrusco di Villa Giulia

Further along Viale delle Belle Arti stands Villa Giulia (**Map 12; 5**), a charming 16C suburban villa which houses the important Museo Nazionale Etrusco di Villa Giulia devoted mainly to pre-Roman works found in Lazio, Umbria and southern Etruria. Material from excavations in progress at the Etruscan sites of northern Lazio is also exhibited here. Open 08.30–19.00; closed Mon. ☎ 06 322 6571. There is a café in the garden.

History of Villa Giulia and the Etruscan Museum

The villa was built in 1550–55 for Pope Julius III by Vignola, Vasari and Bartolomeo Ammannati, with some help from Michelangelo. Its correct name is Villa di Papa Giulio. In the 17C the villa was used to house guests of the Vatican, including Queen Christina of Sweden in 1665. The villa was once decorated with numerous pieces of ancient sculpture but these were later taken to the Vatican.

Since 1889 the Villa Giulia has been the home of the Museo Nazionale Etrusco di Villa Giulia. In 1908 the Barberini collection was donated to the museum, and later acquisitions include the Castellani and Pesciotti collections (in 1919 and 1972). The museum was arranged in galleries flanking the garden in 1960, and has been renovated recently. In a park in front of the villa, Villa Poniatowsky, built in the late 16C by Vignola, and altered by Giuseppe Valadier in the early 19C, is being restored to enlarge the museum (at present a garden wing, used as a tannery in the 19C, is used for exhibitions of works recently excavated).

The beautifully designed villa has a **façade** of two orders: Tuscan on the ground floor and Composite above. The porch, in rusticated masonry, leads to an atrium with Corinthian columns and niches for statues. On the left is the library, with frescoes attributed to Taddeo Zuccari and Prospero Fontana. The atrium opens into a semicircular **portico**, with Ionic columns and arches. The delightful vaulted ceiling is painted with vine trellises, birds and putti, and the wall-panels are painted in the Pompeian style (attributed to Paolo Venale). The courtyard is enclosed by walls with Ionic columns, niches and reliefs.

Some of the delicate stucco decorations by Ammannati on the **loggia** survive. Two curved staircases lead down from the loggia to the first level of the **nymphaeum**, an architectural element which was frequently copied in later 16C Italian villas. Although it has lost much of its original decoration, the fountains are adorned with statues symbolising the Tiber and the Arno. On the lower level are a ceiling relief of the miraculous finding of the Acqua Vergine and four marble caryatids. Behind the portico is an aedicula or shrine, with a statue of Hygieia, a Roman copy of a 5C Greek original.

The garden extends on either side of the courtyard. On the right is a reconstruction of the **Temple of Aletrium** (Alatri) by Count Adolfo Cozza (1891), according to the account of Vitruvius and the evidence of the remains (see below).

The **entrance** to the museum is on the left of the semicircular portico.

Ground floor, left wing. Rooms 1–5 contain finds from the necropolis of Vulci, where some 15,000 tombs were discovered, mostly dating from the 9C–5C BC. **Room 1**. The two stone sculptures, of a *Man Astride a Sea-horse* and a *Centaur* (showing Greek influence), were found at the tomb entrances.

Room 2. Fine bronze objects, a statuette of a *Warrior in Prayer* with a pointed helmet, large shield and long plaits (9C from Sardinia), and an *urn in the shape of a hut (mid-7C BC).

Rooms 3 and **4**. Attic red- and black-figure vases imported from Greece, and local Etruscan-Corinthian ware, including a large amphora by the Painter of the Bearded Sphinx, and a black-figure hydria showing women at a fountain.

Room 5. Three terracotta models of a temple, a stoa and a tower, terracotta

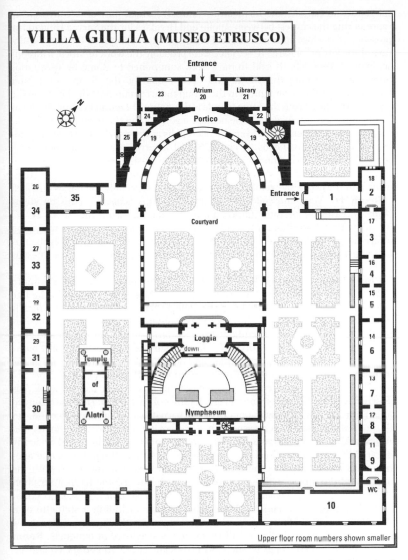

VILLA GIULIA (MUSEO ETRUSCO)

heads, seated figures of children, and figurines from Hellenistic Vulci. Stairs lead down to a reconstructed *tomb from the necropolis at Cerveteri, the ancient Caere, with two chambers, containing beds and the belongings of the dead.

Room 6. Tomb furniture from the Villanovan and Archaic necropolis of Bisenzio-Vesentium, including 8C geometric pottery, and a small bronze rustic chariot decorated with figurines which was used as an incense-burner (late 8C).

Room 7. Finds from the sanctuary of Portonaccio at Veio discovered in 1916 and 1939, including the celebrated group of *Apollo and Herakles*. These colossal statues in polychrome terracotta (restored) formed part of a votive group representing the contest between Apollo and Herakles for the Sacred Hind in the presence of Hermes and Artemis, and are a splendid example of Etruscan sculpture of the late 6C or early 5C BC. They were probably the work of Vulca, a famous sculptor of Veio, who is said to have been summoned to Rome by Tarquinius Superbus to execute the statue and decorations for the Temple of Jupiter Capitolinus. Of the other figures in the group there remain only the hind and the *head of Hermes. From the same temple is the statue of *Latona* holding Apollo as a child, and the antefixes with the head of a gorgon and the head of a maenad.

Rooms 8–10 house finds from the necropolis at Cerveteri (7C–1C BC), including terracotta votive heads in **room 8** and a terracotta *sarcophagus (6C), representing a husband and wife on a couch at a feast, in **room 9**; this remarkable and rare sculpture shows the extraordinary skill of the Etruscan artists, evident in the expressive rendering of the features, especially the hands and feet.

Room 10. Very fine collection of drinking cups (*skyphoi*), cups on stems (*kylixes*), vases for perfume (*aryballoi*), and amphorae from the 7C to 2C BC, including Protocorinthian ware with geometric decoration, Bucchero ware, and a rare Attic kylix with lively figures of satyrs dancing, the story of Polyphemus and vine motifs, and a small red-figured kylix showing two exploits of Theseus and a young cithara player.

Upper floor, left wing. **Room 11** has a display of inscriptions relating to public dignatories. **Rooms 12–16** display the Antiquarium formed in the late 17C by Father Anastasius Kircher in the Collegio dei Gesuiti and part of which is now incorporated in the Prehistoric and Ethnographic Museum in EUR (see p 434). In **room 12** is the splendid *Cista Ficoroni*, which is the largest and most beautiful of the *cistae*, or beauty cases, to have survived. These were toilet boxes made for the mirrors, strigils, spatulae and other implements for the care of the body, and virtually unique to Praeneste (modern Palestrina). The *cistae* are usually cylindrical, with engraved decoration in repoussé or pierced work, lids adorned with small figures, and feet and handles of cast metal. This one is named after Francesco Ficoroni who bought it and gave it to the Kircher collection. On the body of the *cista* is a representation of the boxing match between Pollux and Amykos, king of the Bebryces, an elaborate design pure in its lines and evidently inspired by some large Greek composition, possibly a wall-painting contemporary with those Mikon in the Stoa Poikile at Athens. The names of both the maker and the buyer of the *cista* are recorded in an archaic Latin inscription (*Novios Plautios med Romai fecit, dindia Macolmia fileai dedit*); it was no doubt a wedding present. In **room 13** are small bronzes including a statuette of a *Ploughman* at work, found at Arezzo, and elongated votive figurines. **Room 14** has more bronzes, including candlesticks and objects used at banquets. **Room 15** has more domestic objects, such as mirrors and cistae. In **rooms 16** and **17** are displayed ceramics including the *Chigi Vase* found at Formello (Veio), of exquisite workmanship and the finest extant example of the Protocorinthian style (first half of the 7C BC); among the subjects depicted are a lion-hunt, a hare-hunt, a troop of soldiers and the Judgement of Paris.

Room 18 displays the Pesciotto collection, with vases from the Villanovan and Archaic periods (8C–6C BC), including incised bucchero ware and bronzes of vases.

Stairs lead up to the hemicycle (**room 19**) with the **Castellani collection** of ceramics, many of them from Cerveteri, amassed in the 19C by Augusto Castellani, a member of a renowned firm of goldsmiths. It includes alabaster vases imported from Greece and Cyprus, Etruscan vases showing Oriental influence, black- and red-figure Attic vases, two amphorae (in case 5) signed by Nikosthenes (540–510 BC), miniature kylixes, amphorae, and examples of Faliscan, Campanian and Apulian ware. The rooms have a good view of the courtyard and garden of the villa. In the centre of the hemicycle is the entrance to **room 20** with the Castellani jewellery collection, one of the finest collections of antique jewellery in existence, with Minoan, Hellenistic, Roman and Oriental pieces. There are also copies or reworkings made by the Castellani jewellers in the 19C. On the right are **rooms 21** and **22** with **finds from Pyrgi**, the Etruscan port of Cerveteri, where excavations were begun in 1957. In the first room are are sculptural fragments and a remarkable temple relief (470–460 BC) illustrating the myth of the Seven against Thebes. In **room 22** are displayed three gold-leaf plaques dating from the 5C BC, two of them with inscriptions in Etruscan and one in Phoenician referring to the dedication of the sanctuary to the Phoenician 'Astarte' and the Etruscan 'Uni'. These are important as they are the oldest historical inscriptions known from pre-Roman Italy. On the other side of **room 20, rooms 23–25** have an interesting display illustrating the history of the museum, including plans and models.

We now return to the **hemicycle**, in the second part of which are bronzes from the Castellani collection. Stairs lead up to the right wing.

Rooms 26–31 are on the **upper floor of the right wing**. They exhibit material from the Ager Faliscus, the area between Lake Bracciano and the Tiber. The Falisci were an Italic people akin to the Latins but much influenced by their Etruscan neighbours. **Room 26**. 8C–7C BC finds from Capena (on the Tiber south of Monte Soratte), including an Etrusco-Campanian *dish with a war elephant and her baby, evidence of the impression made in Italy by the elephants of Pyrrhus. Material from Nepi and Vignanello is also shown here.

Room 27. Finds from Narce, the main centre in the southern part of the Ager Faliscus, which was extensively excavated at the end of the 19C and early 20C. This collection of grave goods, vases, gold jewellery and objects in bronze formed the original nucleus of the museum (which was at first called the Museo Falisco).

Rooms 28 and **29**. Fine collection of black- and red-figure vases from the necropolis of Falerii Veteres (Civita Castellana), which was the main centre of the Faliscans: a bronze urn in the shape of a hut; two bowls with Dionysos and Ariadne and a Faliscan inscription (resembling Latin): 'Today I drink wine, tomorrow I shall have none'; an amphora with volutes, showing Eos and Kephalos and Boreas and Orithyia; interesting *stamnoi*; *rhytons (drinking-horns), masterpieces of Greek ceramic art of the first half of the 5C BC, one shaped like a knuckle-bone and signed by Syriskos, and another in the form of a dog's head and attributed to Brygos; a large *krater (mid-5C) with girls dancing, and two other red-figured 6C–5C *kraters with Herakles and the Nemean lion, and Herakles being received into Olympos.

Room 30 (on two levels). Sculptures and architectonic terracottas from temples (5C–2C BC) near Falerii Veteres, with good antefixes of Persian Artemis and a winged genius. Below are large figured terracottas from the pediments, including a bust of *Apollo*, a head of *Mercury*, and a female head, showing the influence of Greek sculpture. In the glass cases are excellent examples of temple decoration and cult statues: antefixes with heads of maenads and of *Silenus*, and part of an ornament from a temple pediment with two warriors, from Sassi Caduti (early 5C); votive portraits from the Temple at Vignale, and the acropolis of Falerii Veteres; a female head in peperino, crowned in bronze-leaf, from Celle; and a head of *Zeus* from Scasato.

On the **ground floor of the right wing room 31** continues the exhibition of material from Falerii, including a 4C temple. **Room 32**. Coffin formed from the trunk of an oak-tree (from Gabii); an antefix with a maenad's head, from Lanuvium; and a terracotta model, perhaps of a temple, from Velletri. **Room 33** displays the collection from the Tomba delle Ambre, at Satricum in the territory of the Volsci, including sculptures from the temple of Mater Matuta (6C BC), and a collection of votive objects dating from the 7C BC.

At the end of this wing is **room 34**, with works from Palestrina, the ancient Praeneste, a flourishing centre of Latin and Volscian civilisation. Since the trade and industry of Etruria and Latium were derived from the same sources, the culture here naturally had much in common with the Etruscans. The material includes finds from the Barberini and Bernardini tombs, two important examples of the Oriental period (7C BC), in which objects in gold and silver, as well as bronzes and ivories, show the influence of Egyptian, Assyrian and Greek art. The *Barberini collection was formed of the finds unearthed between 1855 and 1866 from tombs in the locality of Colombella, just south of the town of Palestrina. It was acquired by the State in 1908, and includes the contents of a large tomb covered with marble slabs of the Oriental period (7C BC), and the contents of deep-laid tombs of the 4C–2C BC. The ***Bernardini Tomb**, discovered in 1876, a trench-tomb lined with tufa and covered by a tumulus, exactly corresponds with the style of the Barberini tombs and with that of the Regolini-Galassi tomb in the Vatican.

Notable among the goldsmith's work are two *pectorals, or large buckles, of gold granulated work, decorated with cats' heads, chimaeras and sphinxes; a *patera* (libation cup) in silver-gilt with a pharaoh in triumph, horses and an Assyrian royal hunt; *caldaia*, for heating or cooling water, in silver-gilt, with six serpents on the brim, and decorated with horsemen, foot-soldiers, farmers and sheep being attacked by lions. The ivories include cups; a lion with a dead man on his back; and mirror-handles (?) shaped like arms. Among the bronzes are a conical vase-stand with fantastic animals in repoussé; and a throne in sheet-bronze, with ornamental bands and figures of men and animals. The contents of the 4C–2C tombs include a full collection of bronze mirrors and *cistae*, see p 250.

The last room, around the corner to the right, is **room 35**, which contains works from centres inhabited by the Umbri. Finds include goldsmith's work and a bronze helmet inlaid with silver from Todi, and an Attic *bowl signed by Pampheios, showing Odysseus evading Polyphemos.

Villa Poniatowski, nearby (see above) is being restored to house more of the collection.

19 • The Museo Nazionale Romano and district

On the huge and busy Piazza dei Cinquecento opposite Termini station are two very important museums of ancient Roman art, both part of the Museo Nazionale Romano (formerly exhibited in the Baths of Diocletian). Palazzo Massimo alle Terme (opened in 1998) contains one of the finest collections in the world of Classical sculpture, as well as superb ancient Roman wall-paintings, stuccoes and mosaics. Across the square new halls were opened in 2001 on the site of the former convent built in the 16C on part of the ruins of the Baths of Diocletian to display the museum's remarkable collection of epigraphs, one of the most important in the world. A beautiful octagonal hall of these baths survives and is used to display some remarkable sculptures from the collection. It is entered from Piazza della Repubblica, beside the huge central hall of the baths which was converted into the church of Santa Maria degli Angeli in the 16C. Nearby is the fine Baroque church of Santa Maria della Vittoria contains an important sculpture of St Theresa by Gian Lorenzo Bernini.

The vast **Piazza dei Cinquecento** (Map 4; 3), by far the largest square in Rome, is the terminus or junction of many bus services, and is always busy with traffic. In winter hundreds of thousands of starlings come to roost here at dusk. At one end stands **Stazione Termini**, one of the largest railway stations in Europe. The two underground lines intersect here. Its reconstruction, begun in 1938, was delayed by the Second World War, and it was not opened until 1950; it was modernised in 2000. A gigantic quasi-cantilever construction, sweeping upwards and outwards, serves as a portico. The station was named after the Baths (Termini) of Diocletian which are close by (see below). In the right wing of the station, entered at 34 Via Giolitti, is an exhibition of works dating from the 1980s which belong to the Galleria Nazionale d'Arte Moderna, see p 244.

In front of the station, on the left, is the best-preserved fragment of the **Servian Wall**, formed of massive blocks of tufa. This wall, some 11km long, was traditionally attributed to Servius Tullius, sixth king of Rome; it is now thought that the wall dates from about 378 BC, although sections of an earlier earthen bank (*agger*) which may be the work of Servius have been identified. There were 12 gates (see the plan on p 64). Further fragments of the wall were unearthed during the reconstruction of the station. Beneath the station remains were found of a private house and of baths, with good mosaics, dating from the 2C AD (not at present open to the public).

Palazzo Massimo alle Terme

On the south side of Piazza dei Cinquecento is Palazzo Massimo alle Terme (**Map 4; 5**) which houses the most important part of the Museo Nazionale Romano. The vast State collections of ancient Roman art, known collectively as the Museo Nazionale Romano, one of the great museums of the world, with numerous masterpieces of Classical art are now divided into four museums in the city: the most important section is in this building; the epigraphic collection is displayed across the road in modern halls on part of the site of the Baths of Diocletian, and sculptures found in ancient Roman baths exhibited in an octagonal hall of the Baths, both described below. The Ludovisi collection is now kept in Palazzo

Altemps (see p 188), and Roman remains of a theatre and adjoining cryptoporticus, together with medieval finds from the city are housed in the Crypta Balbi (described on p 200).

History of the Museo Nazionale Romano

The museum was founded in 1889 in the Baths of Diocletian for the archaeological finds made in Rome since 1870, together with some private collections, including part of the Kircher collection. After years of partial closure the most important part of the collection was reopened in Palazzo Massimo in 1998. This building was erected in 1883–87 by Camillo Pistrucci to house the Jesuit Collegio Massimiliano Massimo. It was restored in 1995–98 as the main seat of the Museo Nazionale Romano, and renamed Palazzo Massimo alle Terme.

The severe modern arrangement in this cold 19C building has taken some of the 'character' away from these splendid works, which were seen to much greater advantage when displayed in the ancient halls of the Baths of Diocletian across the square, although some important sculptures from the collection are still exhibited in the splendid Octagonal Hall of the Baths.

Opening times
09.00–19.45; closed Mon. ☎ 06 4890 3500. For the *Archaeological Card*, see p 41.

To visit the superb frescoes and stuccoes on the second floor—which are excellently displayed with all the latest methods of conservation and clear lighting—it is necessary to book an accompanied visit (about 45mins) when buying your ticket; the booking service is well organised.

Note. Some extremely important sculptures from the collection are exhibited in the splendid Octagonal Hall of the Baths of Diocletian, described on p 264. This is only open 09.00–14.00; fest. 09.00–13.00; closed Mon, and entrance is free.

Throughout the museum the labelling (also in English) is excellent.

The chronological display starts on the **ground floor** and illustrates Roman Republican sculpture from the time of Sulla to Augustus, including many portraits, and some Greek originals. Near the entrance is a colossal statue of **Minerva** in pink alabaster, basalt and marble (late 1C BC–early 1C AD), found in Piazza dell'Emporio at the foot of the Aventine Hill; the head is a cast. Portrait heads are displayed in the corridor and in the interior courtyard are two reliefs of female figures (thought to represent the Roman provinces of Thrace and Egypt) dating from the 2C AD. After being found in the Campo Marzio in the 17C they were restored and kept in Palazzo Odescalchi.

Room I. Fragments of a calendar showing holidays, and a list of magistrates who held office between 173 and 67 BC, found in Nero's Villa at Anzio (84–55 BC); male portrait heads from Palestrina and Mentana (1C BC), and a head once thought to be a portrait of Caesar, from the von Bergen collection, dated 50–40 BC. The statue displayed here may be the portrait of a general: it was found in the Sanctuary of Herculus Victor at Tivoli. Dating from the 1C BC, it is thought to be by a Greek sculptor.

Room II. Stele and portraits dating from the late 1C BC. One stele shows a citizen in a toga; the funerary relief of the Rabirii comes from the Via Appia Antica; and the three male portrait heads from Priverno. In the corridor is a mosaic pavement (1C BC), with the *Rape of Hylas* made from tiny tesserae (2C BC) in a small quadrangle in the centre. Room III (to the right of room IV) is at present closed.

Room IV. Portraits of Romans close to Augustus or members of his family. The early portrait of *Octavian* (from 44 BC–27 BC) shows the Emperor before he received the honorific title of Augustus. Here, too, are a supposed portrait of his sister *Octavia* and two portraits of his wife *Livia*; portraits of the two men whom he designated his successors, *Germanicus* (in bronze), found in Mentana, and *Drusus Major*, found in Lanuvio; as well as one of his actual successor, *Tiberius*. Portraits of private citizens include a bronze head of a man called *Cornelius Pusio*, and a statue with a fine portrait head of a woman represented as *Artemis*, from Ostia.

Room V, also dedicated to Augustus, contains a celebrated statue of *Augustus, one of the finest portraits known of the Emperor, found in the Via Labicana. He is portrayed in a toga which also covers his head, as *pontifex maximus* or high priest, a demonstration of his piety. The *frescoes from the Columbarium on the Esquiline date from the time of Caesar, and an *altar from Ostia, with reliefs of the origins of Rome (including Romulus and Remus suckled by the She-wolf) is dated 1 October AD 124.

In the corridor is a mosaic dating from the 1C BC, with two ducks and a wild cat attacking a bird. **Room VI**. Terracottas found during excavations beneath the so-called Domus Tiberiana on the northern slopes of the Palatine Hill in the 1980s.

Room VII. Three beautiful Greek sculptures found in the Gardens of Sallust (see below). The *Daughter of Niobe is a Greek original of the 5C BC by the school of Kresilas. Made for the pediment of a Greek temple, it was part of a statuary group which illustrated the legend of Niobe, who was famous for having borne numerous children. When she dared to boast that this made her at least equal to Leto who had had only two children (Apollo and Artemis), her own children (known as Niobids) were all killed. The girl depicted in the statue is shown dying as she tries to extract an arrow from her back. The headless statue of a girl in a peplos, known as the Peplophoros, was found in Piazza Barberini. It is also probably a Greek original of the first half of the 5C BC. The Pedagogue probably portrays the attendant of one of the youngest of Niobe's children: it may be a 2C AD copy of a 4C bc Greek original.

Room VIII. Neo-Attic works including sculptures of *Athena*, found on the Celian Hill; *Aphrodite*, a copy of the *Cnidian Aphrodite* by Praxiteles, signed by the Greek artist Menofantou and a *Muse* who once held a tragic mask, the replica of a Hellenistic original. Also here are decorative reliefs, including a base with dancing maenads, and a fountain basin with a frieze of marine figures.

On the **first floor** are sculptures dating from the period of the Emperors (1–4C AD), many of them modelled on Classical Greek works, are exhibited here.

Room I. Portraits of the Flavian emperors, including three of *Vespasian* and two of *Nerva*. In the centre is one of the few surviving portraits of *Domitian*; after he was killed all statues and busts of him were ordered to be destroyed. The statue of *Julia*, Titus' daughter, has a beautiful head.

Room II. Portraits of *Trajan* and *Hadrian*. A statue of *Trajan* shown as Hercules is exhibited next to a portrait of his wife *Plotina*, found in Ostia. On the opposite wall is a portrait of *Hadrian* beside two busts of his wife *Sabina* and one of his lover *Antinous*. **Room III** contains portraits of *Antoninus Pius*, including

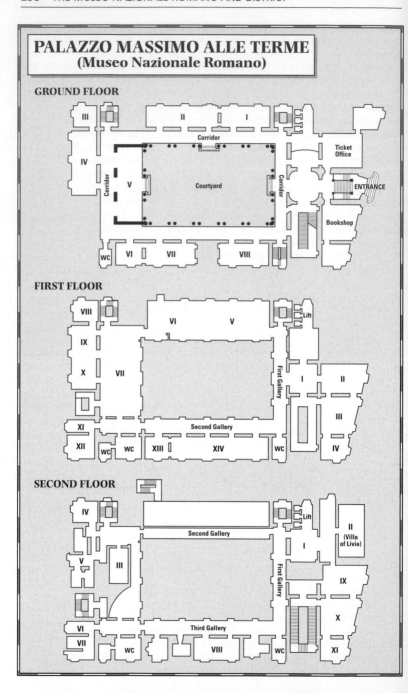

a fine statue found in Terracina, and of his wife and daughter. **Room IV** displays portraits of the Antonines—*Marcus Aurelius*, *Lucius Verus* and *Commodus*.

The **first gallery** displays portraits found in Hadrian's villa in Tivoli. The heads of a woman and of a barbarian date from Hadrian's time, and the others, including portraits of *Antoninus Pius* and *Marcus Aurelius*, are later. The head of a young girl is thought to represent Crispina, the wife of Commodus.

Room V displays sculptures found in the Imperial villas outside Rome, including Hadrian's villa in Tivoli and Nero's villas at Subiaco and Anzio. The headless **Ephebus of Subiaco*, a Roman copy of an original of the 4C BC (probably of one of the Niobids), and the head of a *Young Girl Sleeping* (possibly representing another dying Niobid), both come from Nero's villa at Subiaco. The so-called **Maiden of Anzio*, a masterpiece of Greek art dating from the end of the 4C or beginning of the 3C BC, is by a sculptor from the school of Lysippos, also showing the influence of Praxiteles. It represents a young girl approaching an altar and carrying a tray with implements for a sacrifice, and was discovered in Nero's villa at Anzio in 1878. The statue of *Apollo* (1C AD), modelled on a work by an unknown Attic predecessor of Praxiteles, was also found in Anzio. The works from Hadrian's villa at Tivoli, which are replicas of Hellenistic works, include a beautiful statue of *Aphrodite*, crouching, and the so-called *Dancer of Tivoli*.

At the end of room V the statue of *Apollo*, found in the Tiber, is a copy of an original by the school of Phidias, or by Kalamos. In **room VI** are two copies of the statue of the **Discobolo* (Discus-thrower). This famous statue by Myron, made in bronze c 450 BC, and described by Pliny the Younger, was praised for its virtuosity in portraying the human figure in motion. It was one of the most frequently copied Greek masterpieces. The finest and best-preserved replica is the one from the Lancelotti collection displayed here, which dates from the 2C AD: it was restored in the 18C and sold to Hitler in 1938, but recovered ten years later. The other copy (without a head) was found at Castelporziano in 1906 and has been repaired. The heads of athletes here are also copies from 5C and 4C BC works.

Room VII. Statues of deities including a bronze statue of *Dionysus* and a marble statue of *Hermaphroditus Asleep* (both dating from the 2C AD). At the end of the room are two statues found in Castel Gandolfo: the head of the *Bearded Dionysus* was added by order of Mussolini when he donated it to the German nation in 1943 (it was returned to Italy in 1991).

Room VIII. *Torso of the Minotaur*, and *Achilles with a Wounded Amazon*. **Room IX**. Works connected with the theatre, including a statue of an *Actor*. At the far end, in **room X**, are the bronzes from the ships which were built by Caligula (AD 37–41) to transport visitors across the Lago di Nemi for the festival of Diana. They were sunk at the time of Claudius, and were salvaged in 1932 and put on display in a museum on the lakeside; when this was burnt down by German soldiers in 1944, only these bronzes survived the fire.

Room XI. Relief showing a temple pediment and columns from San Lorenzo in Miranda in the Roman Forum. **Room XII**. Sarcophagus from Portonaccio, carved with a scene of a battle between Romans and Barbarians, probably representing a military campaign at the time of Marcus Aurelius.

Room XIII. Bust of *Septimius Severus*. **Room XIV** displays some fine sarcophagi made in the 3C AD. The one found in the 15C, which was part of the Mattei collection, is decorated with figures of the Muses in niches holding masks. Another, from Acilia, has a finely carved procession of Roman dignitaries wearing togas celebrating the investiture of a consul. Another sarcophagus was commissioned by a prefect in charge of the office of the *anonna*, the organisation in Ostia which supplied produce, mainly grain, to the capital (see Chapter 39). The prefect and his wife are shown in the centre of the relief and on either side are female figures personifying the port of Ostia, Abundance and Africa (from where most of the produce was shipped). A sarcophagus dating from the time of Constantine (315 AD) has Christian scenes from the Old and New Testaments. In the second gallery there is a fine display of female portraits (3C–4C AD).

The **second floor** (for admission, see above) has a superb display of *wall-paintings, *stuccoes and *mosaics which used to decorate Roman buildings from the Republican era onwards. **Room I**. Fragment of a fresco with a scene from the *Odyssey*, showing Ulysses and the Sirens, found in a late-Republican house on the Esquiline.

A rectangular room, probably a triclinium, from the Villa of Livia (wife of Augustus) at Prima Porta, has been reconstructed in **room II**; its walls were decorated with splendid *frescoes of trees, an orchard with pomegranates and quinces and a flower garden, which constitute the masterpiece of naturalistic decoration of the second style of Roman painting. Detached and restored in 1952–53, the frescoes were saved just in time from complete decay, and are one of the most remarkable examples known of Roman art.

In the **first** and **third galleries** are displayed some fine mosaic pavements (2C BC–4C AD).

The second gallery and rooms III–V contain the *stuccoes and the *frescoes which decorated numerous rooms in a building of the Augustan age, discovered in 1879 in the grounds of the Renaissance Villa Farnesina near the banks of the Tiber (see p 225). The exquisite frescoes are on black, red or white grounds. The **second gallery** has the frescoes from the cyptoporticus, on a white ground, and **room III** frescoes with theatrical masks, scenes of judgement, naval battles and mythological figures. **Room IV** displays the only mosaic floors that were found in the villa, which are decorated in geometric designs. **Room V** exhibits paintings and stucco decoration from the small bedrooms. Masterpieces of their kind, they have friezes decorated with festoons and cupids, interspersed with landscapes and mythological scenes.

Room VI–VII display more beautiful wall-paintings from a villa at Castel di Guido, thought to have belonged to Antoninus Pius.

Room VIII contains an ornamental wall-fountain decorated with mosaics and shells found in Nero's villa at Anzio. Also here are frescoes from a building near a port on the Tiber, with scenes of boats and fishing, including numerous delightful fish, and stucco decoration from the hypogeum of Aguzzano. **Room IX** has mosaics from the Villa of Septimius Severus at Baccano, including four quadrangles showing four charioteers holding their horses. **Room X** has frescoes dating from the 3C–4C AD, including one of Venus, known as the Dea Barberini, found near the baptistery of San Giovanni in Laterano in the 17C, when it was restored as the Dea Roma.

The last **room XI** has superb polychrome marble intarsia *panels in opus sectile. The two panels from the basilica of Giunio Basso on the Esquiline (early 4C AD) show a mythological scene with Hylas, and the start of a chariot race. The head of the sun god Helios-Sol was found in the Mithraeum beneath Santa Prisca on the Aventine.

The vaults in the **basement** house the treasury, with valuable jewellery and coins. The first room has a display illustrating Diocletian's edict of AD 301, which attempted to combat inflation. It is known from some 132 marble fragments found all over the Empire from 1709 onwards and is of fundamental importance to scholars for the understanding of the Roman economy. Another room has a fine exhibit of gold jewellery, two alabaster cinerary urns, and a sarcophagus found on the Via Cassia with the well-preserved mummy of an eight-year-old girl.

The large main hall (entered through armoured doors) houses the most important **numismatic collection** in Italy, covering all periods of its history. The exhibits come from the Gnecchi collection of Roman and Byzantine coins, the Kircher collections acquired by the State in 1913, and the collection of King Vittorio Emanuele III. The superb display, divided into eleven sections, includes some 1800 pieces

The first section is dedicated to the goddess Juno Moneta and the mint on the Capitoline Hill, the Santa Marinella hoard of bronze ingots, and the earliest coined metal (4C–3C BC). The second section illustrates coins in the Republican era, and the third and fourth sections the Imperial period. Sections five to eight cover the Goths, Byzantines, Lombards, Franks and Normans. A circular area is dedicated to pontifical coinage. Sections nine and ten display late medieval and Renaissance coins, and the last section has 19C coins up to the Unification of Italy, and those minted during the reign of Vittorio Emanuele III. There is also an important study collection open to scholars.

The Baths of Diocletian

Opposite Palazzo Massimo alle Terme, across Viale Einaudi, are the Baths of Diocletian (Terme di Diocleziano). The splendid vaulted rooms of the Baths once provided a superb setting for the collections of the Museo Nazionale Romano, founded here in 1889. Most of the museum has been moved to Palazzo Massimo alle Terme (see above), and the massive Roman buildings are closed indefinitely for restoration, with the exception of the Octagonal Hall (see p 264). However in 2001 the huge collection of epigraphs belonging to the museum was rearranged here in modern halls on the site of a Carthusian monastery built into the ruins in the 16C, and a prehistoric section opened on the first floor of the large cloister.

History of the Baths of Diocletian

Begun in 299 the baths were completed in less than eight years by Diocletian and Maximian. They were the largest of all the ancient Roman baths, and could accommodate over 3000 people at once. They covered a rectangular area, c 380m by 370m, corresponding to that now bounded on the south-east by Piazza dei Cinquecento, on the south-west by Via Torino, on the north-west by Via Venti Settembre, and on the north-east by Via Volturno. The main buildings included a calidarium, tepidarium and frigidarium. The calidarium, which survived into the late 17C, occupied part of Piazza della Repubblica. The tepidarium and the huge central hall of the baths are now occupied by the church of Santa Maria degli Angeli (see below). The frigidarium was an open-air bath behind this hall. Numerous large and small halls, nymphaea and exedrae were located within the precincts. In the 16C a Carthusian convent was built in the ruins. The baths were plundered for their building materials in the 16C–19C.

The only entrance to the baths was on the north-east side, near the present Via Volturno. On the south-west side the closed exedra was flanked by two circular halls: one of these is now the church of San Bernardo alle Terme, the other was at the corner of Via Viminale and Via delle Terme. A third, octagonal hall, on the corner of Via Parigi at the north-west angle of the main complex, is open to the public, described on p 264.

The **entrance** to the Baths of Diocletian is at present through the garden in front of the railway station. Open 09.00–19.00; closed Mon. ☎ 06 488 0530.

The collection of about 10,000 inscriptions in Latin is one of the most important of its kind in the world. Many of the exhibits come from excavations during building work in the capital after Italian Unification, and others from collections formed by Kircher and Gorga. Some of the inscriptions are from tombs along the consular roads leading out of the city, dating mostly from the end of the Republican era to the end of the 2C AD, and others are from Roman centres in Lazio. The present arrangement, which includes some 900 pieces on three floors, seeks to provide a documentation of Rome, from a social, political, administrative, economic and religious aspect.

Although at first sight epigraphs may seem less interesting and less easy to appreciate than, say, ancient Roman sculpture, they are fascinating documents of the ancient Roman world. This new arrangement allows the non expert, perhaps for the first time, to appreciate their significance, although it is necessary to dedicate a lot of time to the visit in order to read the translations, and history of each piece (labelled also in English).

In the **garden** are stelae and altars arranged according to provenence, including a group of stelae dedicated to praetorian guards found in a small cemetery near Ponte Milvio. Beyond the ticket office and book shop, there is a **corridor** with a few Roman sculptures, mostly dating from the 2C–3C AD (including busts, statues, and sarcophagi), as well as a delicately carved funerary altar found in Via di Porta San Sebastiano (1C AD). Off this corridor are the entrances to the Epigraph collection, and the stairs up to the Protohistoric collection (both described below).

At the end of the corridor is the **great cloister** of 1565, traditionally ascribed to Michelangelo, although he died the year before. The arcades, 80 metres long on each side, are supported by 100 travertine columns, and the original pale blue colour of the plaster was restored in 2000. The peaceful, overgrown garden, with a few palm trees, has very worn Roman sculptural fragments scattered among the borders, and it is the home of numerous birds. The fountain dates from 1695 and it is surrounded by seven colossal heads of animals (probably from the Forum of Trajan); it is shaded by four cypresses, one of which, now propped up, is centuries old. Roman sculptures recently cleaned, but many of them damaged, are arranged in the walks of the cloister. They include statues, sarcophagi, and altars, mostly dating from the 1–2C AD, and all of them are well labelled. The amusing trompe l'oeil of a Carthusian monk dates from the 19C.

The entrance to the **Epigraph Collection** is off the corridor (see above). A small room with an introductory display traces the history of epigraphs, and there is a representative selection of artefacts which bear inscriptions.

In the **round hall** beyond is a display of **Archaic finds** (8C–5C BC). In the central case is the oldest testimony of the Greek alphabet so far found in Italy: it is on a simple vase found in Gabii in Lazio, traditionally dated around 770 BC, but now thought to be even older (late 9C). Next to it the *aryballus*, a vessel with a globular body and narrow neck in black terracotta (*bucchero*), bears a votive inscription in Etruscan. Found near Veio, it is dated to the late 7C BC. There are also other 7C inscriptions and more finds from Gabii. Exhibited in a wall case on the left is a reproduction of the golden brooch known as the '*fibula prenestina*', famous in the late 20C when most scholars decided it was a fake: if it is, instead, original it would provide the earliest known example of a Latin inscription (early 7C BC). Also on this wall is a display of ceramics, with inscriptions, found in a votive deposit beneath the Lapis Niger (see p 97) in the Roman Forum (a cast of which is exhibited here). A fragment of a cup in bucchero ware found in the Regia in the Forum bears the owner's name, Rex, thought to refer to one of the last kings of Rome. Architectural fragments of the late 7C and early 6C BC from the Regia are also exhibited here. Displayed on its own is an inscription in tufa from Tivoli, which may refer to Publius Valerius, the first Republican consul of Rome (509 BC).

Other cases in the centre display finds from recent excavations on the slopes of the Palatine, some of which bear the letter V which seems to refer to the cult of Juno Sospita (6C–5C BC).

In the wall cases on the right are displayed finds from a sanctuary in Lavinium in Lazio (see below) including a bronze inscription of the late 6C BC, with a dedication to the twin heroes Castor and Pollux, the earliest reference so far found in Lazio to the Greek cult of the Dioscuri, taken to be the sons of Zeus and brothers of Helen. There are other stone inscriptions to divinities dating from the 6C BC, including one in tufa from Tivoli.

The **main hall** displays works from the **early Republican period** (4C–3C BC) In the first case on the right are black varnish ceramics with inscriptions dating from the 3C BC found in the Tiber in Rome. Some of these, including ex votoes, belonged to the sanctuary of Aesculapius erected in 289 BC on the Isola Tiberina (see p 328). A large marble basin with a dedication to Hercules from a sacred font dating from the 3C BC is the oldest known example of an inscription with metal lettering. Other finds come from sanctuaries in Roman cities in Lazio, including Lanuvium, an ancient city famous for its sanctuary of Juno Sospita, the site of which has been found in the Colli Albani near Genzano. Against the wall are four large cippi (late 4C and early 3C BC) from Lavinium excavated at Pratica di Mare near the sea, which, according to an ancient legend, was the town founded by Aeneas, after his escape from Troy, and named after his wife. Numerous ancient Roman historians, as well as Virgil, upheld this myth, and as early as 300 BC a tradition existed at Lavinium itself which attributed its foundation to the Trojan hero. A tomb sanctuary dedicated to him, in the form of a tumulus burial chamber, restored in the 4C BC, was found nearby, and the cippi come from here.

Displayed on their own at the end of the room are seven remarkable sculptures from a sanctuary dating from the late 4C or early 3C BC found at Ariccia: these include busts of **Demeter** (or Ceres), and her daughter **Kore** (or Persephone), and three seated female statues in terracotta.

On the left side of the room are ceramics bearing the names of members of the Rabirii family whose tomb was unearthed at Tusculum, near Frascati, another important Roman centre. A bronze inscription and finds from a temple at Norba (present day Norma) dating from the late 3C BC are also displayed here. In the last case are objects from Praeneste (Palestrina), one of the oldest towns of Lazio, which was thriving as early as the 7C BC, and which for long remained independent of Rome. It was famous for its cult of Fortuna Primigenia, especially after about 130 BC when a huge Temple of Fortune was built in the town, the most grandiose Hellensitic edifice in Italy. The very unusual 'crown' exhibited here is decorated with acanthus leaves and bears an inscription to Fortuna Primigenia, and next to it is a little cippus in the form of a pine cone, with the name of a dead man.

In the **room to the left** are displayed inscriptions dating from the **late Republican period** (2C–1C BC). These include several with names of slaves, and one found recently near the Meta Sudans (see p 126) relating to a company of singers and actors which gave performances of Greek plays. There are also inscribed statue bases, and inscribed stone panels announcing public works. The funerary inscriptions set up by artisans in the city, include that of Atistia, the wife of the baker whose grand travertine tomb still stands beside the Porta Maggiore (see p 298). A fragment of an inscription in handsome lettering records the funerary oration of a husband to his wife, pronounced between 8 and 2 BC. A group of terracotta pots, found in Via di Porta Sebastiano bear inscriptions with a name and date, probably referring to the cremated person to whom the small piece of bone found inside belonged.

In the smaller area at the end of the main hall there is a dedication in bronze originally set up by a group of players of wind instruments, beneath a bronze statue of Tiberius, dating from 7 BC which was found on the slopes of the Palatine in 1992–93. On the same site a large statue base in marble was unearthed with handsome inscriptions, ordered by the same group of musicians, relating to four statues of *Augustus*, *Nero*, *Claudius*, and *Agrippina*, mother of Nero. Three fragments of Luni marble were part of a calendar with a list of magistrates who held office in Rome between 43 BC and 3 AD.

A circular stair leads to the **second floor** where a very fine display of epigraphs illustrate the social structure of the Roman empire, and other aspects of Roman life. On the left balcony are exhibited numerous epigraphs from a dynastic monument belonging to the Claudia family in the Campo Marzio in the centre of Rome. A fragment with beautiful lettering found outside Porta Pia is now thought to belong to an inscription recording the historian Tacitus who died around 120 AD. In the room at the end are two sarcophagi, with inscriptions on their covers, and funerary stele. On the right balcony are more inscriptions, some relating to public officials and others, military dedications, and on the wall at the end is a dedicatory inscription, which survives in eight fragments, announcing the completion of the Terme di Diocleziano (the baths were begun in 299 AD and completed just eight years later). In a side room are inscriptions relating to members of political and administrative institutions, often specifying the precise social standing of the person in question. Also here is a fragment of red intonaco which bears graffiti made by Roman firemen and found in their guardroom in Trastevere (3C AD; see p 228).

On the **third floor** a side room has a display of epigraphs relating to the economic life of the city during the Empire. On the balcony are inscriptions from religious sanctuaries, including private domestic altars, official religious edicts, and very early references to the Christian religion. At the end, a small room has a display of fakes, and an illustration of how epigraphs were carved. The room beyond displays objects relating to oriental cults, including a relief of Mithras, still with traces of colour, found in the Mithreum below Santo Stefano Rotondo.

From here there is access to the two upper wings of the large cloister where part of the well-labelled **Protostoric collection** is displayed. The finds from Lazio (11C–6C BC) include the contents of numerous tombs found in the necropolis of Osteria dell'Osa at Gabii.

In the gardens on Viale Einaudi there is monument by Francesco Azzurri, erected in memory of 548 Italian soldiers ambushed at Dogali, Eritrea, in 1887. It incorporates an Egyptian **obelisk** found in the Isaeum Campense (see p 178), inscribed with hieroglyphs recording the glories of Rameses the Great or Sesostris, the pharaoh of the time of Moses. Its companion is in Florence. The monument, first erected in front of the old railway station, was moved here in 1924; in 1936–44 it was decorated with the Lion of Judah plundered from Addis Ababa.

Santa Maria degli Angeli (Map 4; 3) occupies the great central hall of the Baths of Diocletian, converted into the church of the Carthusian convent. Open daily 07.30–12.30 and 16.00–18.30. The work of adaptation was carried out in 1563–66 for Pius IV to a design by Michelangelo, who may also have designed the cloisters and other conventual buildings. Michelangelo placed the entrance of the church at the short south-east side of the rectangle and thus had at his disposal a nave of vast proportions. The effect was spoiled by Vanvitelli who, instructed by the Carthusian fathers in 1749, altered the orientation. He made the entrance in the long south-west side and so converted the nave into a transept. To compensate for the loss of length, he built out on the north-east side an apsidal choir, which broke into the monumental south-west wall of the frigidarium The façade on Piazza della Repubblica, with Vanvitelli's doorway, incorporates an apsidal wall, all that is left of the calidarium.

In the disappointing **interior**, the circular vestibule stands on the site of the tepidarium. Here are the tombs of Carlo Maratta (d. 1713), on the right, and Salvator Rosa (d. 1673), on the left. By the entrance into the transept, on the right, stands a fine colossal statue of *St Bruno* by Jean-Antoine Houdon (1766). The vast **transept** is nearly 100m long, 27m wide and 28m high. The eight monolithic columns of red granite, nearly 14m high and 1.5m in diameter, are original; the others, in brick, were added when the building was remodelled. To the right, in the pavement, are a meridian dating from 1703; and the tomb by Antonio Muñoz of Marshal Armando Diaz (d. 1928), Italian commander in-chief in the First World War. The huge paintings include the *Mass of St Basil* by Pierre Subleyras on the left; and the *Fall of Simon Magus* by Pompeo Batoni. In the choir are is the *Presentation in the Temple* by Giovanni Romanelli and the *Martyrdom of St Sebastian* by Domenichino (both on the right), and *Death of Ananias and Sapphira* (painted on slate) by Pomarancio and *Baptism of Christ* by Carlo Maratta (both on the left). In the apse, on the left, is a monument to Pius IV, based on a design by Michelangelo, which also inspired the monument to Cardinal Serbelloni opposite. The door to the sacristy in the left transept leads to a room with impressive remains of the frigidarium of the Baths of Diocletian, and a display explaining the history of the building.

The church faces the large circular **Piazza della Repubblica** (Map 4; 3), formerly called Piazza dell'Esedra from the exedra of the Baths of Diocletian, which is at the end of the busy Via Nazionale. The semicircular porticoed fronts of the palazzi on either side of the entrance to the piazza by Gaetano Koch (1896–1902) follow the line of the exedra. The abundant waters of the Fountain of the Naiads (1870) are supplied by the **Acqua Marcia**, which terminates here.

This aqueduct, built from Tivoli to Rome in 144 BC, was one of the most important and longest of the Roman aqueducts. The same springs were tapped for a new aqueduct, built in part of cast-iron by a private Anglo-Italian company for the Papal States, called the Pia Marcia and inaugurated in 1870 by Pius X. The four groups of erotic reclining nymphs, symbolising the spirits of rivers and springs, and the central Glaucus, were sculpted by Mario Rutelli (1901–11).

Along the modern Via Parigi stand conspicuous remains of buildings demolished to make way for the Baths of Diocletian. At the beginning of the street is a Roman column, a gift from the city of Paris (1961). On the corner of Via Parigi is the **Octagonal Hall**, or Aula Ottagonale, which provides a splendid setting for some Roman sculptures from the Museo Nazionale Romano. Open free 09.00–14.00; fest. 09.00–13.00; closed Mon. ☎ 06 488 0530.

The rectangular exterior hides a domed octagonal interior, a beautiful Roman architectural work. The hall is thought to have connected the open-air gymnasium and gardens of the Baths of Diocletian with the heated calidarium. Roman foundations can be seen through the glass panel in the centre of the hall.

Displayed here are Roman statues and busts, many of them found in the Baths of Caracalla, Diocletian and Trajan, including two famous bronzes: the **Boxer Resting*, a magnificent work signed by Apollonius, dating from the 1C BC; and the so-called **Prince*, a Hellenistic work of the early 2C BC, which depicts a young man, perhaps one of the Seleucids, leaning on a lance in a pose identical to that of the Alexander the Great by Lysippos. Also here is the marble **Aphrodite*, an original Greek work of the 4C BC, possibly by a predecessor of Praxiteles, representing the goddess just risen from the sea; near her right leg is her cloak, supported by a dolphin; the head and arms are missing. The statue was found in the baths at Cyrene.

Along Via Venti Settembre

The short Via Orlando continues past the *Grand Hotel* opened in 1894—when it was the first hotel in Italy with electric light—to the busy Piazza San Bernardo, with its fountain and three churches, which is really just a widening of Via Venti Settembre. The **Fontana dell'Acqua Felice** is the terminal of an aqueduct built in 1585 by Domenico Fontana for Sixtus V, from Colonna in the Alban Hills. The fountain, also by Fontana, has an unsuccessful figure of *Moses* attributed to Prospero Antichi or Leonardo Sormani. The bas-relief of *Aaron* is by Giovanni Battista della Porta, and that of *Gideon* by Flaminio Vacca and Pier Paolo Olivieri; the four lions are copies of ancient Egyptian works removed by Gregory XVI to the Egyptian Museum founded by him in the Vatican.

Across Via Venti Settembre is the church of **Santa Maria della Vittoria** (Map 4: 3), a fine edifice by Carlo Maderno (1620), with a façade by Giovanni Battista Soria. Open daily 07.00–12.00 and 16.00–19.00. Originally dedicated to St Paul, it was renamed from an image of the Virgin (burned in 1833) that gave victory to the Catholic army over the Protestants at the Battle of the White Mountain, near Prague, on 8 November 1620, during the Thirty Years War.

The well-proportioned **interior** is considered one of the most complete examples of Baroque decoration in Rome, rich in colour and glowing with marbles. It has good stuccowork and a fine organ and cantoria by a pupil of Bernini, Mattia de Rossi. The frescoes are by Giovanni Domenico Cerrini.

The second south chapel has an altarpiece of the *Madonna and St Francis* by Domenichino. The fourth chapel on the north side is the Cornaro Chapel by Bernini, a splendid architectural achievement, using the shallow space to great effect. Over the altar is his famous sculptured group, the **Ecstasy of St Teresa*, and below is a gilt-bronze relief of the *Last Supper*. At the sides are expressive portraits of the Venetian family of Cornaro, by pupils and followers of Bernini. The last, half-hidden figure on the left is said to be a portrait of *Bernini* himself. The fresco, by Luigi Serra (1885), in the apse of the church commemorates the *Triumphal Entry of the Catholic Army into Prague*.

In Via Venti Settembre are several huge ministry buildings, including the Ministry of Defence, the Ministry of Agriculture and Forests (1902) and the colossal Treasury building by Raffaele Canevari (1870), containing a **Numismatic Museum**. It includes examples of coins minted from the 13C to the present time (with some foreign works), a collection from the pontifical mint, and an interesting collection of wax seals by Benedetto Pistrucci, who designed the St George and dragon on the English sovereign. Open Tues–Sat 09.00–12.30; closed Mon and fest. ☎ 06 4761 3317. A document giving proof of identity is required.

The short Via Servio Tullio, opposite, leads north to Piazza Sallustio where, behind Villa Maccari on the right, is a considerable fragment of a villa which used to stand in the **Gardens of Sallust** (*Horti Sallustiani*) laid out in 40 BC, on which the historian Gaius Sallustius Crispus lavished the wealth he had accumulated during his African governorship. They had formerly been owned by Julius Caesar. Here, too, are the foundations of the Trinità dei Monti obelisk, showing where it stood in the Middle Ages.

Adjoining Piazza San Bernardo (see above) is the Largo Santa Susanna, another traffic hub with the church of **Santa Susanna** (Map 4; 3), a Paulist church, probably dating from the 4C, restored in 795 and remodelled in the 15C and 16C. It is now the American National church. Open daily 17.00–19.00; fest. 10.00–12.00 and 16.30–19.00. The façade by Carlo Maderno (1603) is considered by many to be his masterpiece; in the good late Mannerist interior (1595) are large frescoes by Baldassare Croce.

Opposite, at the beginning of Via Torino, is the round church of **San Bernardo alle Terme** (in an unattractive colour), built into one of the two circular halls flanking the exedra of the Baths of Diocletian in the 16C. The domed interior contains eight colossal stucco statues of saints by Camillo Mariani (c 1600–05), and a Neo-classical monument to the sculptor Carlo Finelli (d. 1853) by Rinaldo Rinaldi.

Largo Santa Susanna is dominated by the building of the Ufficio Geologico by Raffaele Canevari (1873), containing a collection of minerals, marbles (archaeological and modern) and fossils. Via Barberini, opened in 1926, descends from here to Piazza Barberini. On the right, in a side street called after it, is the church of **San Nicola da Tolentino** (closed indefinitely), rebuilt in 1620 by Carlo Buti, and finished by Martino Longhi the Younger and Giovan Maria Baratta, who built the façade in 1670. The high altar was designed by Alessandro Algardi. It contains a chapel thought to be the last work of Pietro da Cortona (1668), with sculptures by Ercole Ferrata, Cosimo Fancelli and Ercole Antonio Raggi.

Via Barberini ends in Piazza Barberini (see Walk 16).

20 • Around Santa Maria Maggiore

The basilica of Santa Maria Maggiore is one of the four most important churches in Rome: it retains its 5C plan and contains important mosaics and elaborate tombs and sumptuous chapels erected by the popes in the 16C and 17C. Santa Prassede also has important mosaics in the choir and in the exquisite little chapel of St Zeno. Santa Pudenziana, dedicated to St Praxedes' sister, has the earliest known Christian mosaic in a church in Rome. Other churches described in this chapter, both of them, however, in rather unattractive parts of the city, are the American Episcopal church of St Paul's, which has 19C mosaics by Edward Burne-Jones, and Santa Bibiana, where there is a statue by Gian Lorenzo Bernini.

Via Cavour leads from the station and Piazza dei Cinquecento (see Walk 19) to Piazza dell'Esquilino, which is overlooked by the apse of Santa Maria Maggiore, approached by steps. The **obelisk** here, nearly 15m high, was set up by Sixtus V in 1587. Like its twin in Piazza del Quirinale it once stood outside the entrance to the Mausoleum of Augustus. The façade of the huge church faces **Piazza Santa Maria Maggiore** (Map 4; 7), which occupies the highest point of the Cispian summit (55m) of the Esquiline Hill. In this square rises a fluted cipollino **column** 14.5m high, from the Basilica of Maxentius. It was set up here in 1613 for Paul V by Carlo Maderno and crowned with a statue of the Virgin. Maderno also designed the fountain at its base decorated with dragons and masks in travertine.

Santa Maria Maggiore

The church of Santa Maria Maggiore (**Map 4; 5**) retains its original interior magnificence more completely than any other of the four patriarchal basilicas. Open daily 07.00–18.00 or 19.00. A museum is open 09.30–18.30, and here you can request to see the Loggia delle Benedizioni, with its 13C mosaics.

Two important ceremonies are held in the basilica annually. On 5 August the legend of the miraculous fall of snow is commemorated in a pontifical mass in the Borghese Chapel; and on Christmas morning there is a procession in honour of the Santa Culla (Holy Crib), which culminates in the exposure of the relic on the high altar. Santa Maria Maggiore has the privilege of extraterritoriality.

History of Santa Maria Maggiore

According to a 13C legend, the Virgin Mary appeared on the night of 4–5 August c 358 to Pope Liberius (352–66) and to John, a patrician of Rome, telling them to build a church on the Esquiline. In the morning they would find a patch of snow covering the exact area to be built over. The prediction fulfilled, Liberius drew up the plans and John built the church at his own expense. The original title was therefore Santa Maria della Neve (of the Snow). The church was afterwards called Santa Maria del Presepe, after a precious relic of the crib of the Infant Jesus.

A basilica was indeed built here by Pope Liberius on the site of a Roman edifice, and was called the Basilica Liberiana. In 366 supporters of the antipope Ursinus barricaded themselves in the church and surrendered only when the partisans of Pope Damasus I (366–84) took off the roof and pelted them with tiles. Damasus reconstructed the church, as did Sixtus III (432–40), from whose time the present church almost certainly dates. In 1075 Gregory VII (Hildebrand) was seized during Mass by the rebel Cencio, but was rescued next day by his supporters. Nicholas IV (1288–92) added the polygonal apse and transepts. In 1347 Cola di Rienzo was crowned here as Tribune of Rome. Clement X (1670–76) rebuilt the apse, and Benedict XIV ordered Ferdinando Fuga to carry out further alterations and add the main façade.

The fine **campanile**, the highest in Rome, was given its present form in 1377 by Gregory XI, and it has restored polychrome decoration. The **apsidal façade**, completed c 1673, is approached by an imposing flight of steps from Piazza dell'Esquilino. The right-hand section, with its dome, is by Flaminio Ponzio; the central and left sections by Carlo Rainaldi; the left-hand dome by Domenico Fontana. The **main façade**, on Piazza Santa Maria Maggiore, masking one of the 12C, was designed by Fuga (1743); it is approached by steps and is flanked by two grandiose wings. The portico is surmounted by a loggia of three arches (for admission ask at the museum, see below), and contains a bronze statue of *Philip IV of Spain*, on a model by Bernini.

The vast but well-proportioned **interior** (86m long), which still preserves its basilican form, is divided into nave and aisles by 36 columns of shining Hymettian marble and four of granite, all with Ionic capitals supporting an architrave, the whole discreetly rearranged and regularised by Ferdinando Fuga. Over the triumphal arch and in the nave are **mosaics* dating from the time of Sixtus III (432–40), the most important mosaic cycle in Rome of this period; of exquisite workmanship, they are in the classical tradition. The small rectangular biblical scenes high up above the architrave in the nave are difficult to see with the naked eye. On the left are scenes from the *Life of Abraham, Jacob* and *Isaac*; on the right, scenes from the *Life of Moses* and *Joshua* (restored, in part painted); over the triumphal arch, scenes from the early *Life of Christ*. The coffered ceiling, attributed to Giuliano da Sangallo, was traditionally thought to have been gilded with the first gold brought from America by Columbus, presented to Alexander VI by King Ferdinand of Aragon and his wife Isabella, Queen of Castile. The Borgia emblems of rosettes and bulls are prominent. The fine Cosmatesque pavement dates from c 1150. At the **west end** (A) is the monument of *Clement IX* (1670), designed by Carlo Rainaldi, with a statue of the *Pope* by Domenico Guidi and statues of *Faith* and *Charity* by Cosimo Fancelli and Ercole Ferrata. The tomb (B) of Nicholas IV (1574), with sculptures by Leonardo Sormani da Sarzana, was designed by Domenico Fontana.

In the **south aisle**, the baptistery (C), with a high-relief of the *Assumption* by Pietro Bernini, leads to the entrance to the sacristy (D; no admission); both were designed in the early 17C by Flaminio Ponzio. By the entrance, the Santarelli monument has a bust by Alessandro Algardi. In the vault of the Cappella San Michele (E; usually closed), by a side door, are traces of 15C frescoes including two *Evangelists* by the circle of Piero della Francesca and a *Pietà* attributed to Benozzo Gozzoli. A column in the adjoining courtyard celebrates the conversion

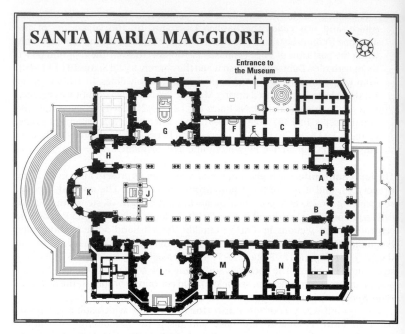

of Henry IV of France. Here is the entrance to the museum, described below. The Cappella delle Reliquie (**F**), designed by Fuga, has ten red porphyry columns, and a 15C wooden crucifix.

The **Sistina Chapel** (**G**), on a domed Greek-cross plan, is a work of extraordinary magnificence carried out for Sixtus V by Domenico Fontana (1585). It is a veritable church in itself, decorated with statues, stuccoes by Ambrogio Buonvicino, and late 16C Mannerist frescoes by Cesare Nebbia, Giovanni Battista Pozzo, Paris Nogari, Lattanzio Mainardi and Giacomo Stella. The marble decoration was brought from the Septizodium on the Palatine (demolished by Sixtus V) and set up here by Carlo Maderno. The sumptuous tomb of Sixtus V on the right has a statue by Leonardo Valsoldo, and the tomb of Pius V on the left a statue by Leonardo Sormani da Sarzana. The temple-like baldacchino, with four gilt-bronze angels by Sebastiano Torrigiani, covers the original little Cosmatesque Chapel of the Relics (for admission, ask at the museum), redesigned by Arnolfo di Cambio (late 13C), with figures of the crêche by his assistants. By the two sanctuary steps is the simple pavement tomb of the Bernini family, including Gian Lorenzo. In the chapel at the end of the aisle (**H**) is the beautiful *tomb of Cardinal Consalvo Rodriguez (d. 1299), a masterpiece by Giovanni Cosmati, showing the influence of Arnolfo di Cambio. The mosaic of the *Madonna Enthroned with Saints* fits well with the architectonic lines of the tomb, which was completed by the beginning of the 14C.

The **confessio** (**J**), reconstructed in the 19C by Virginio Vespignani, contains a colossal kneeling statue of *Pius IX* by Ignazio Jacometti. The baldacchino over the high altar, with four porphyry columns, is by Ferdinando Fuga; a porphyry sarcophagus which contains the relics of St Matthew and other martyrs serves as the high altar; the fragment of the crib of the Infant Jesus is kept below in the confessio in a reliquary adorned with reliefs and silver statuettes.

The ***mosaic of the apse** (K), dating from the time of Nicholas IV (1288–94), is signed by Iacopo Torriti (1290–95) and represents the *Coronation of the Virgin*, with angels, saints, Nicholas IV, Cardinal Iacopo Colonna and others. It is the culminating point of all the mosaics in the church, which commemorate the declaration at the Council of Ephesus (5C) that the Virgin was the Mother of God (Theotókos). The Virgin is seated on the same throne as Christ, a composition probably derived from the 12C mosaic in the apse of Santa Maria in Trastevere (see p 219). Below, between the windows, are more mosaics by Torriti depicting the *Life of the Virgin*, notably, in the centre, the *Dormition*. The four reliefs below the windows are from the old ciborium by Mino del Reame.

In the **north aisle**, balancing the Sistina Chapel, is the even more sumptuous **Borghese Chapel** or Cappella Paolina (L). This chapel, erected by Paul V, was designed by Flaminio Ponzio (1611). The best-known contemporary artists were employed to decorate it, including Lodovico Cigoli, Cavaliere d'Arpino, Guido Reni, Giovanni Baglioni and Passignano, and the sculptors Stefano Maderno, Francesco Mochi and Nicolas Cordier. On the altar, surrounded with lapis lazuli and agate, is a *Madonna and Child with Crossed Hands*, now thought to date from the 12C–13C, although it has also been attributed to a Byzantine artist working before the 10C. The tombs of Clement VIII and Paul V, with statues by Silla Longhi, are on either side. The Sforza Chapel (M), usually kept locked, erected by Giacomo della Porta to a design by Michelangelo, contains an *Assumption* by Sermoneta and the tombs of Cardinal Guido Ascanio, grandson of Paul III, and his brother Cardinal Alessio. In the beautifully restored Cesi Chapel (N), probably designed by Guidetto Guidetti (c 1550), are two Cesi tombs by Guglielmo della Porta and an altarpiece of the *Martyrdom of St Catherine* by Sermoneta. The tomb, in the style of Giovanni Dalmata, of Cardinal Philippe de Levis de Quelus and his younger brother Archbishop Eustache (1489) is above the Porta Santa, installed in 2000 (P).

The **museum** (for opening times, see above) is entered off the south aisle. It was arranged in 2001 in underground rooms where excavations were carried out in 1967–72 of a large Roman building with remains of frescoes, including a remarkable rural calendar dating from the 2C AD, with illustrations for each month. The church silver and liturgical objects date mostly from the 17C and 18C. The paintings include a tondo of the *Madonna* by Beccafumi, *Christ carrying the Cross* by Sodoma, and *Christ crowned with thorns* by Paris Bordone.

Here you can ask to visit the **upper loggia** (Loggia delle Benedizioni) of the main façade. From the portico a monumental staircase leads up past a bronze statue of *Pope Paul V* by Paolo Sanquirico (1605) to the open loggia, from which there is a good view which includes the basilica of San Giovanni in Laterano at the end of the long, straight Via Merulana on the right. The mosaics on the earlier façade, dating from the time of Nicholas IV (1294–1308), can be seen from the loggia. The upper part, signed by Filippo Rusuti, depicts *Christ Pantocrator with Angels and Saints*. The four scenes below, illustrating the *Legend of the Snow*, were probably completed by assistants. The four 18C statues of angels by Pietro Bracci were originally over the high altar of the church.

Santa Prassede

Just off Piazza Santa Maria Maggiore, Via Santa Prassede leads to the inconspicuous side entrance of the church of Santa Prassede (**Map 4**; **7**), built by
St Paschal I in 822 and still enveloped on all sides by medieval and later buildings. Open daily 07.30–12.00 and 16.00–18.30.

History of Santa Prassede

The building is dedicated to Praxedes, sister of Pudentiana and daughter of
Pudens, in whose house St Peter is traditionally supposed to have first found
hospitality at Rome (see below). An oratory is said to have been erected here
about AD 150 by St Pius I, and a church is known to have been in existence
on this site at the end of the 5C. Paschal's 9C church was restored in 1450,
1564, 1832 and 1869. Here in 1118 the Frangipani attacked Pope Gelasius
II with arrows and stones, driving him to exile in France, where he died.

Browning's poem, *The Bishop Orders his Tomb at Saint Praxed's Church,
Rome, 15—*, is set in this church.

The main west entrance, on the old Via San Martino ai Monti, is kept locked: it is
preceded by a medieval **porch** with two reversed Doric capitals. The only part of
the exterior visible is the Zeno Chapel, beside the south entrance.

The **nave** has 16 granite columns and six piers supporting an architrave made
up from ancient Roman fragments. The effective trompe l'oeil frescoes date from
the late 16C and are by Paris Nogari, Baldassare Croce, Agostino Ciampelli and
others. In the pavement in the nave, remade in 1919, a large porphyry disc with
an inscription indicates the well where St Praxedes is supposed to have hidden
the bones of Christian martyrs.

The **choir** is approached by steps of rosso antico. The fine Baroque
baldacchino by Francesco Ferrari (1730) partially hides the splendid 9C
*mosaics (there is a coin-operated light on the right). On the entrance-arch are
depicted (outer face) the *New Jerusalem*, whose doors are guarded by angels, and
(inner face) *Christ and Saints*. The apse-arch shows the *Lamb of God* with the
seven golden candlesticks, the symbols of the Evangelists, and 24 Elders. The
semi-dome has *Christ between* (right) *St Peter*, *St Pudentiana* and *St Zeno* and
(left) *St Paul*, *St Praxedes* and *St Paschal* (the latter's square nimbus indicates he
was still alive when the mosaic was executed); below them are shown the Lamb,
the flock of the Faithful and a dedicatory inscription; above, the monogram of
Paschal I. On the left and right of the sanctuary are six Roman *columns of very
unusual design incorporating the form of acanthus and laurel leaves.

In the **crypt** beneath are four early Christian sarcophagi, including one with
the remains of St Praxedes and St Pudentiana, and a 13C Cosmatesque altar
with a very damaged fresco above depicting the Madonna between St Praxedes
and St Pudentiana.

In the **south aisle** is the Byzantine **Chapel of St Zeno** (there is a coin-operated light on the left). The most important work of this date in Rome, it was built
in 817–24 by St Paschal as a mausoleum for his mother, Theodora. The entrance
is flanked by two ancient porphyry columns with 9C Ionic capitals which support
a rich 1C architrave from a pagan temple, elaborately sculptured; on this rests a
Roman marble urn (3C). Above is a double row of 9C mosaic busts: in the inner
row, the *Virgin and Child*, *St Praxedes* and *St Pudentiana*, and other saints; in

the outer, *Christ and the Apostles*, and four saints (the lowest two perhaps added in the 13C). The exquisite vaulted interior, the only chapel in Rome entirely covered with *mosaics, was known as the *Garden of Paradise*. The pavement is perhaps the oldest known example of opus sectile. Over the door, *St Peter* and *St Paul* uphold the throne of God; on the right are *St John the Evangelist*, *St Andrew* and *St James*, and *Christ between St Paschal and St Valentine* (?); inside the altar-niche, are the *Madonna and Child between St Praxedes and St Pudentiana*; on the left, *St Praxedes*, *St Pudentiana* and *St Agnes*, and four half-length female figures including *Theodora* (with the square nimbus). In the vault are *Christ and Four Angels*. The bases of the four supporting columns date from the 9C, except for the one on the right of the altar which is a fine 5C Roman work. In a niche on the right are fragments of a column brought from Jerusalem after the Sixth Crusade (1228), and said to be that at which Christ was scourged.

In the adjoining funerary chapel is the *tomb of Cardinal Alain Coëtivy (1474) by Andrea Bregno. Outside, on a nave pillar, is the tomb of Giovanni Battista Santoni (d. 1592), one of the earliest works of Gian Lorenzo Bernini. At the east end of the aisle, a chapel contains the tomb of Cardinal Pantaleon of Troyes (d. 1286), with Cosmatesque fragments attributed to Arnolfo di Cambio, marble architectural fragments and a 16C crucifix. In the second chapel in the south aisle are two paintings by Ciro Ferri and ceiling frescoes by Borgognone.

In the **north aisle**, the first chapel contains an altarpiece by Giuseppe Severoni; and the second chapel, *St Charles Borromeo* by Stefano Parrocel and two paintings on the side walls by Ludovico Stern. The chair used by St Charles Borromeo is also preserved here. The third chapel has *frescoes by Cavaliere d'Arpino, and an altarpiece of *Christ Bearing the Cross* by Federico Zuccari. Against the left wall, in a frame, is the top of the table used by St Charles Borromeo. The fourth chapel was decorated with frescoes and mosaics in 1933. In the sacristy, the altarpiece is by Ciampelli. On the right wall is a good painting of the *Flagellation*, attributed to Giulio Romano, and a *Deposition* by Giovanni de Vecchi. To the right, a spiral staircase (admission only with written permission) leads up to the campanile with 9C wall-paintings.

East of Santa Maria Maggiore

Via San Prassede ends in Via San Martino al Monte. To the left, across the busy Via Merulana, Via San Vito leads to the 4C church of **Santi Vito e Modesto** (open only at 10.00), restored in the 20C. It contains frescoes by Antoniazzo Romano, and excavations have revealed traces of the Servian Wall and a Roman aqueduct.

Outside the church is the **Arch of Gallienus**, the middle arch of a triple gate erected in the time of Augustus and dedicated in AD 262 in honour of Gallienus and his consort Salonina by the city prefect Aurelius Victor; it occupies the site of the Porta Esquilina of the Servian Wall.

To the north, across Via Carlo Alberto is **Sant'Antonio Abate**, with a doorway attributed to the Vassalletto family of sculptors (1262–66). The interior was redesigned c 1730. Services on Sundays at 10.00, with Russian-Byzantine rites.

Via Carlo Alberto connects Piazza Santa Maria Maggiore with the huge 19C **Piazza Vittorio Emanuele** (Map 4; 8), which is surrounded by porticoes and planted with fine palms and plane trees, cedars of Lebanon and oleanders. Although the centre of the square has been pretentiously redesigned in recent years, it is very poorly kept. The impressive ruins of a fountain here, known as the **Trofei di Mario**, date from the time of Alexander Severus. This was formerly the terminal of an aqueduct (either the Acqua Claudia or the Aniene Nuovo), and the marble panoplies known as the Trophies of Marius were removed from here to the balustrade of Piazza del Campidoglio in the 16C. Beside it (protected by a fence) is the curious **Porta Magica** or **Porta Ermetica**, with an alchemist's prescription for making gold, dating from 1680. This was moved here in the 20C from the villa of Massimiliano Palombara. Until a few years ago there was a daily food market in the piazza, noted for its abundance of North African, Middle Eastern and Chinese products, but this has been moved to a covered market building nearby (open in the mornings). However, the area, with its crowded streets, is still full of multi-ethnic shops and restaurants.

In the north corner of the square is the church of **Sant'Eusebio** (only open at 06.30 and 18.30), founded in the 4C and rebuilt in 1711 and 1750. The ceiling painting of the *Triumph of St Eusebius* is by Raphael Mengs; in the apse are fine, elaborately carved 16C stalls. In the sacristy, in the right aisle, is the carved top of the tomb of St Eusebius (15C) from the earlier church.

Via Napoleone III leads out of Piazza Vittorio Emanuele to Via Rattazzi in which, on the right, surrounded by a garden with remains of the Servian Walls, is the former **Acquario Romano**, built in 1887 as an aquarium by Ettore Bernich, with an interesting interior in Pompeian style, recently restored as an exhibition space and for theatrical productions.

Via Giovanni Giolitti skirts the huge building of Stazione Termini: to the right it passes **Santa Bibiana** (**Map 5**; **7**). This 5C church was rebuilt by Bernini in 1625, and it was his first architectural work. It contains eight columns from pagan temples, including, to the left of the entrance, that at which St Bibiana (Viviana) was supposed to have been flogged to death. On the architrave are frescoes by Agostino Ciampelli (on the right) and Pietro da Cortona (on the left). The *statue of the saint, set in an aedicula above the altar, is a fine early work by Bernini.

Just beyond, on the left, is Piazza Guglielmo Pepe, in which are six arches of an ancient aqueduct. Via Santa Bibiana, the underpass beneath the railway, leads to **Porta San Lorenzo** (**Map 5**; **7**). Immediately north, in the Aurelian Wall, is Porta Tiburtina, built by Augustus and restored by Honorius in 403. The triple attic carried the waters of the Acquae Marcia, Tepula and Julia (see p 432). Further north, in Piazzale Sisto V, is an arch formed out of a section of the Aurelian Wall by Pius V and Sixtus V at the end of the 16C to carry the waters of the Acqua Felice.

Santa Pudenziana

From Piazza dell'Esquilino, opposite the apse of Santa Maria Maggiore, Via Agostino Depretis runs north-west. The first turning on the left, Via Urbana, leads in a few metres to Santa Pudenziana (**Map 4**; **5**). Open daily 08.00–12.00 and 16.00–18.00. One of the oldest churches in Rome, it is thought to have been built c 390 above a Roman thermal hall of the 2C. It was rebuilt several times later, notably in 1589. The church is dedicated to Pudentiana, sister of Praxedes (see above), and daughter of the Roman senator Pudens, a legendary figure who is supposed to have given hospitality to St Peter in his house on this site. The church is now well below the level of the modern street.

The façade was rebuilt and decorated in the 19C; the fine **campanile** probably dates from the late 12C. The good doorway preserves a medieval frieze in relief.

In the disappointing **interior** the nave and aisles are divided by Roman columns built up into piers. The dome was painted by Pomarancio. The precious *apse mosaic, the earliest of its kind in Rome, dates from 390. It was damaged by a 16C restoration, which removed the two outermost Apostles at each end and cut the others in half. It shows *Christ Enthroned* and holding an open book, between the Apostles and two female figures representing the converted Jews and the converted pagans (or Gentiles), crowning St Peter and St Paul. The Roman character of the figures is marked; the magisterial air of Christ recalls the representations of Jupiter, and the Apostles, in their togas, resemble senators. Above is a jewelled Cross and the symbols of the Evangelists, and buildings (including houses, thermae and a basilica) representing Jerusalem and Golgotha.

In the chapel at the end of the **north aisle** an altar, presented by Cardinal Wiseman, encloses part of the legendary communion-table of St Peter; the rest of it is in San Giovanni in Laterano. The marble group of *Christ Entrusting the Keys to St Peter* is by Giovanni Battista della Porta. The Cappella Caetani, opening off the aisle, is a rich Baroque work by Francesco da Volterra, finished by Carlo Maderno. The altar relief is by Pietro Paolo Olivieri. Behind the apse are fragments of frescoes and a statuette of the *Good Shepherd*.

The interesting buildings off the courtyard (approached through a door in the left aisle) have been closed indefinitely. These include part of 2C baths and the **Oratorium Marianum**, containing 11C frescoes and brick stamps of Hadrian's time. The building incorporates part of the baths said to have been erected by Novatian and Timotheus, the brothers of Pudentiana and Praxedes, above the so-called house of Pudens. The baths extend on to the pavement in Via Balbo; the frescoes are also visible from here.

Via Urbana continues to the undulating Via Panisperna, in which the church of **San Lorenzo in Panisperna** (Map 1; 5) stands on the traditional site of the martyrdom of St Lawrence. It is in a delightful court of old houses with a villa to the left (part of the Ministry of the Interior, see below). The church contains a vast fresco of the martyrdom by Pasquale Cati.

The huge **Palazzo del Viminale** (1920), now the Ministry of the Interior, fronts Piazza del Viminale on Via Agostino Depretis. On the parallel Via Napoli, on the corner of Via Nazionale, is the American Episcopal church of **St Paul's** (**Map 4; 3**) 'within the Walls', an interesting building by George Edmund Street (1879). Open only for services: at 10.30 on Thur; and at 08.30 and 10.30, and 18.00 or 19.30 on fest.

The conspicuous red-and-white exterior, in travertine and red brick, is in a Romanesque style (the mosaics are by George Breck, former director of the American Academy in Rome). In the **interior** the *mosaics in the large apse and choir are by Edward Burne-Jones. The figures in the lower register include portraits of *J.P. Morgan*, *Archbishop Tait*, *General Grant*, *Garibaldi* and *Abraham Lincoln*. On both walls of the nave are ceramic tiles designed by William Morris. The stained-glass windows were made by the English firm of Clayton and Bell.

In Via Viminale is the **Teatro dell'Opera**, built in 1880 by Achille Sfondrini for Domenico Costanzi. The Roman première of Verdi's *Falstaff* was performed here in 1893. The theatre was acquired by the Comune of Rome in 1926, and restored and enlarged by Marcello Piacentini in 1959–60. It is the most important lyric theatre in Rome.

21 • The Esquiline Hill and San Pietro in Vincoli

The Esquiline (65m), the highest and most extensive of the Seven Hills of Rome, has four summits. Most of the Oppius or Oppian Hill is covered by a park (the Parco Oppio), on the site of the Baths of Titus and of Trajan and Nero's Domus Aurea (described in Walk 22). The Cispius, extending to the north-east, is crowned by the basilica of Santa Maria Maggiore (see Walk 20). The other two summits are the Subura, above the low-lying district of that name, and the Fagutalis, named from a beech grove. This chapter also describes the basilica of San Pietro in Vincoli, which contains the unfinished tomb of Julius II begun by Michelangelo, with his statue of Moses; and the Museo Nazionale di Arte Orientale, the most important collection of Oriental art in Italy.

History of the Esquiline Hill

The four summits of the Esquiline, together with the three of the Palatine, formed the early city of the Septimontium. According to the erudite Varro, the name Esquiline was derived from the word *excultus*, which referred to the ornamental groves planted on the hill by Servius Tullius, including the *Querquetulanus* (oak grove) and *Fagutalis* (beech grove).

Formerly a place of vineyards and gardens, most of the hill was considered an unhealthy place to live, but the area between the modern Via Cavour and the slopes of the Oppian Hill, called the Carinoe, was a fashionable residential district. Pompey lived here, in a small but famous house that was occupied after his death by Antony. The fabulously rich Maecenas (c 70–8 BC) also had a villa here (a garden building of which survives, see below) which he left to his close friend Augustus. The remarkable Roman statues unearthed here are exhibited in the Centrale Montemartini (see p 411). His fame as a generous patron of the arts (he was particularly praised for this quality by Horace who may also have had a house here) survives to this day as his name is still used in modern parlance to describe a great patron. The poets Virgil and Propertius, who were praised by Maecenas, also lived on the hill. The villa of Maecenas was eventually acquired by Nero, who incorporated it in his famous Domus Aurea, and the site was afterwards occupied by the Baths of Titus.

Via Cavour (Map 7; 6 and 4; 7, 5), opened in 1890 and now an important traffic artery of the city, runs from Via dei Fori Imperiali (see Walk 5) to Piazza dei Cinquecento and Termini station. At its southern end, on the left, is the base of the massive **Torre dei Conti**, all that remains of a great tower erected after 1198 by Riccardo dei Conti, brother of Innocent III. It was damaged by an earthquake in 1348 and reduced to its present state by Urban VIII in the 17C. Via Cavour now passes through the ancient Subura, of which the scarcely noticeable hill was one of the four summits of the Esquiline. The district was connected via the Forum of Nerva to the Roman Forum by the ancient road called the Argiletum (see p 134).

At the first important crossroads, Via degli Annibaldi provides an interesting glimpse of the Colosseum to the right, and Via dei Serpenti leads left to the **Madonna dei Monti** (Map 7; 6), a fine church by Giacomo della Porta, who also designed the fountain nearby. The 17C **interior** contains stuccoes by

Ambrogio Buonvicino and frescoes by Cristoforo Casolani. On the south side the first chapel has frescoes by Giovanni da San Giovanni, and the third chapel **Christ Carrying the Cross** by Paris Nogari. The dome was decorated in 1599–1600 by Cesare Nebbia, Orazio Gentileschi and others. In the chapels on the north side are the *Adoration of the Shepherds* by Girolamo Muziano; two paintings by Cesare Nebbia; and an **Annunciation** by Durante Alberti.

On Via Cavour, at the end of a high wall, there is a flight of steps on the right called Via San Francesco di Paola. This is on the site of the ancient Via Scelerata, which apparently received its name, meaning a site where a crime was committed, from the impious act of Tullia, who here drove her chariot over the dead body of her royal father Servius Tullius. According to legend she was responsible for ordering her brother-in-law Tarquinius Superbius to murder both her husband and her father, so that he would become king and she could marry him.

On the right is the base of a medieval tower, with bands of black and white stone. In the little Piazza San Francesco di Paola a large 17C palace houses the administrative offices of the **Istituto Centrale del Restauro** (a State restoration centre), which now has its main laboratories in the former **Istituto di San Michele** (see p 227). The steps pass beneath an archway above which is an attractive Doric loggia (being restored in 2002), once part of the house of Vannozza Catanei (1442–1518), the beautiful mistress of Pope Alexander VI, and mother of four of his children, including Lucrezia and Cesare Borgia.

San Pietro in Vincoli

At the top of the steps is the piazza in front of the basilica of San Pietro in Vincoli (**Map 4; 7**). Open daily 07.00–12.30 and 15.30–18.00.

History of San Pietro in Vincoli

The two chains with which St Peter was supposed to have been fettered in the Tullianum (see p 133) are said to have been taken to Constantinople. In 439 Juvenal, Bishop of Jerusalem, gave them to the Empress Eudoxia, wife of Theodosius the Younger. She placed one of them in the basilica of the Apostles at Constantinople, and sent the other to Rome for her daughter Eudoxia, wife of Valentinian III. In 442 the younger Eudoxia gave the chain to St Leo I (pope 440–61) and built the church of San Pietro in Vincoli (also called the Basilica Eudoxiana) for its reception. Later the second chain was sent to Rome. On being brought together, the two chains miraculously united.

The church was restored in 1475 under Sixtus IV by Meo del Caprina, who was responsible for the façade, with its beautiful colonnaded portico.

The basilican **interior**, much affected by restoration, preserves its 20 ancient columns with Doric capitals (the Ionic bases were added in the 17C). The nave, almost four times as wide as the aisles, has a ceiling painting by Giovanni Battista Parodi, representing the cure of a person possessed by an evil spirit through the touch of the holy chains.

In the **south aisle**, the first altarpiece of *St Augustine* is by Guercino. The tomb on the left was designed by Domenichino, who painted the portrait above; the second altarpiece is a copy of his **Deliverance of St Peter**, now in the sacristy. At the end of the aisle is the **tomb of Julius II** (being restored, but still visible, partly from the scaffolding), the famous unfinished masterpiece of Michelangelo, who was so harassed while working on the monument that he called it the 'tragedy of a sepulchre'. Hindered by his quarrels with Julius II and by the jealousy of that pope's successors, Michelangelo finally abandoned work on the tomb, and the great pontiff, who had contemplated for himself the most splendid monument in the world, lies uncommemorated in St Peter's. Some 40 statues were to have decorated the tomb, including the two slaves now in the Louvre, and the four unfinished slaves in the Accademia gallery in Florence. No idea of the original design of the monument (for which many drawings survive) can be gained from this very unsatisfactory grouping of statues and niches.

Only a few magnificent fragments remain here, notably the powerful figure of *Moses, Michelangelo's most strongly individualised work, in whose majestic glance is seen the prophet who spoke with God. The satyr-like horns represent beams of light, a traditional attribute of the prophet in medieval iconography. The beautiful figures of *Leah and *Rachel on either side—symbols of the active and contemplative life (see Dante, *La Divina Commedia*, Purgatorio, xxvii, 108)— are also by Michelangelo. The rest is his pupils' work, although the effigy of the pope, for long thought to be by Maso del Bosco, was attributed by some scholars to Michelangelo himself during restoration work on the statue in 1999. The *Madonna* is by Alessandro Scherano, and the *Prophet* and *Sibyl* by Raffaello da Montelupo.

The east end of the church is closed for restoration. The sacristy has a pretty 16C frescoed vault by Paris Nogari and a small 15C marble bas-relief of the *Madonna and Child*. In the vestibule is the original painting of the *Deliverance of St Peter* by Domenichino. In the last chapel of this aisle is *St Margaret by Guercino. The bishop's throne in the apse is a marble chair brought from a Roman bath. The frescoes are by Giacomo Coppi. The baldacchino over the high altar is by Virginio Vespignani (19C). In the confessio below are the Chains of St Peter, displayed in a tabernacle with beautiful bronze *doors attributed to Caradosso (1477). Stairs lead down to a tiny crypt (closed), in which there is a fine late 4C Roman sarcophagus with figures representing scenes from the New Testament, supposed to contain the relics of the seven Jewish Maccabee brothers (1C BC).

In the **north aisle**, the second altar has a well-preserved 7C mosaic icon of the bearded *St Sebastian (coin-operated light, on the right); and the first altarpiece of the *Descent from the Cross* is by Pomarancio. Near the west wall, the tomb of Cardinal de Cusa has a good coloured relief (1465), attributed to Andrea Bregno. On the end wall to the right of the entrance door is the little tomb of the artist brothers Antonio and Piero Pollaiolo with two expressive portrait busts attributed to Luigi Capponi. Above is a very worn fresco of the plague of 1476 by an unknown 15C artist, and to the left, an early fresco of the *Head of Christ* (behind glass).

The **cloister**—entered at 16 Via Eudossiana on the right, now the University Faculty of Engineering—is attributed to Giuliano da Sangallo. The lovely well-head is by Simone Mosca.

The narrow and pretty Via delle Sette Sale leads out of the piazza on the left of San Pietro in Vincoli. This unexpectedly rural street passes between two of the summits of the Esquiline, the Cispius on the left and the Oppius on the right. The park which now covers the Oppian Hill is described in Walk 22.

At the end of Via delle Sette Sale, by its junction with Viale del Monte Oppio, is the church of **San Martino ai Monti** (Map 4; 7), the church of the Carmelites. Built c 500 by St Symmachus and dedicated to St Sylvester and St Martin, it replaced an older church founded in the 4C by Pope St Sylvester I, who came from Mount Soracte to cure Constantine of an illness. It was rebuilt in the 9C and given its present appearance c 1650 by Filippo Gagliardi. In this church, the decisions of the Council of Nicaea (325), which recognised that Christ and God were of the same substance, were proclaimed in the presence of Constantine, and the heretical books of Arius, Sabellius and Victorinus were burnt.

In the **interior** the broad nave is divided from the aisles by 24 ancient Corinthian columns which support an architrave, and the presbytery is raised above the crypt. The fine 17C decoration, with statues, stucco medallions and frescoes, is by Paolo Naldini and Filippo Gagliardi. In the lower side aisles are frescoes of the *Life of Elijah* and landscapes of the Roman Campagna by Gaspard Dughet, and in the left aisle there are interesting views of the interiors of San Giovanni in Laterano and St Peter's before reconstruction, by Filippo Gagliardi. The *Council of Pope Sylvester* is by Galeazzo Leoncino.

The tribune, with a double staircase, leading to the high altar, and the taber-nacle are by Gagliardi, who also designed the elaborate stucco decoration of the **crypt**. Here, on the left, a door (key in the sacristy) leads to stairs which descend to a private chapel of the 3C, with traces of frescoes and mosaics, incorporated in eight large halls of a Roman building. In the left aisle, on the second altar, is *St Albert* by Girolamo Muziano, and on the first altar, *Vision of St Angelo* by Pietro Testa.

Behind the church are two heavily restored medieval towers. Viale del Monte Oppio ends at the Largo Brancaccio, on the busy 19C Via Merulana.

Here on the right is **Palazzo Brancaccio** built for Mary Elizabeth Bradhurst Field by Gaetano Koch in 1879, and enlarged by Luca Carimini. The interior has decorations in the neo-Baroque style by Francesco Gai. It now houses the *Istituto Italiano per il Medio ed Estremo Oriente*, and, on the second floor, the **Museo Nazionale di Arte Orientale**, founded in 1957 and the most important collec-tion of Oriental art in Italy. Open daily 08.30–14.00; Sun, Tues, & Thur 08.30–19.30; closed first and third Mon of the month. ☎ 06 487 4415. Handsheets are available.

Rooms II and **III**. Pre-Islamic Iran, including finds from the urban site of Shahr i Sokhta, dating from 3200 1800 BC, and from Swat in north-east Pakistan, with artefacts from a necropolis dated 1500–500 BC. These include accountants' implements, seals, coins, examples of cuneiform writing, terra-cotta figures and vases and ceramics, bone and metal utensils, fragments of fabric, and jewellery. There are also Luristan bronzes, weapons and horsebits.

Rooms IV and **V**. Tibet, Nepal and Gandhara, including architectural fragments in wood, and jewellery. **Room VI** displays Islamic art, **room VII** Japanese art including screen paintings, bronzes and ceramics, **room IX** finds from south-east Asia, and **room X** the Indian collection.

Rooms XI–XIV. China: funerary statues, ritual objects and masks, sculptures of Buddha, bronze mirrors, ceramic and porcelain figures, and Imperial warm-ing plates.

To the south, in Largo Leopardi, is the so-called **Auditorium of Maecenas**. Open 09.00–13.30; fest 09.00–13.00; Apr–Sept also Tues, Thur and Sat

16.00–19.00; closed Mon. ☎ 06 487 3262. An Augustan apsidal building, this was in the gardens of Maecenas (see above), and may have been a nymphaeum. The unusual apse has tiered seats in a semicircle. Although it has been restored, the traces of red landscape paintings in the apse and wall niches have all but disappeared. The building is adjoined by a stretch of the Servian Wall.

The rest of the Esquiline hill is described in Walk 22.

22 • The Domus Aurea and the Oppian Hill

The Oppian Hill (Map 10; 1, 2), just north-east of the Colosseum, is one of the four summits of the Esquiline (see Walk 21) and was one of the Seven Hills (Septimontium) of primitive Rome. On its slopes is the Parco Oppio, a public garden that has recently been replanted, which contains the famous Domus Aurea, built by Nero, extremely important for its architecture as well as the remains of its fresco and stucco decorations. San Clemente is a well-preserved basilica with 12C mosaics and a chapel with 15C frescoes by Masolino. The lower church has early frescoes and interesting Roman remains. The church of Santi Quattro Coronati nearby has a 13C fresco cycle and a charming little cloister.

The Domus Aurea

Above Via Labicana, at the north-east corner of the Colosseum, Viale Domus Aurea leads up to the entrance on the left of the extensive ruins of a wing of the Domus Aurea, Nero's Golden House (**Map 10**; **2**).

Opening times

09.00–19.45; closed Tues. Accompanied visits enter every quarter of an hour, and the tour takes about half an hour.

Note. It is necessary to book a visit: often the best way is to do so on the spot at the entrance; visitors not in a group can often go in directly or shortly afterwards. Otherwise, ☎ 06 3996 7700

Audio guides are available, but the staff themselves are well informed. The numbers of the rooms given in the text below are those found in situ and on the plan of the site on p 280.

History of the Domus Aurea

Nero already had one palace, the Domus Transitoria on the Palatine, which was destroyed in the fire of AD 64. Even before its destruction he had planned to build another, the Domus Aurea, in the heart of the city. With its outbuildings and gardens, it was to extend over part or all of the Palatine, much of the Celian and part of the Oppian hills, an area of about 50 hectares. When it was completed Nero is reputed to have commented that at last he was beginning to be housed like a human being.

He employed Severus as architect and Fabullus as painter, and produced what has been called the first expression of the Roman revolution in architecture. The understanding and use of vaulted spaces in the palace was quite new. It is thought that nearly all the rooms were vaulted, although some of the ceilings in the wing that survives are no longer intact. The atrium or vestibule, with the colossal statue of the Emperor (see p 126), was on the summit of the Velia; the main part of the palace was on the site of the so-called Domus Tiberiana on the Palatine; the gardens, with their lake, were in the valley now occupied by the Colosseum.

This grandiose edifice did not long survive the tyrant's death in 68, and his successors hastily demolished or covered up his buildings, and restored to the city the huge area they had occupied. In 72 Vespasian obliterated the lake to build the Colosseum; Domitian (81–96) buried the constructions on the Palatine—except the cryptoporticus—to make room for the Flavian palaces. Trajan (98–117) destroyed the houses on the Oppian to build his baths; and Hadrian (117–38) built his Temple of Venus and Roma on the site of the atrium, and moved the statue.

When the rooms with their stuccoed and painted walls and vaults were first discovered underground in the 1490s they at once became famous, and their decorations were called 'grotesques' (from grotto, underground room). This delicate type of decoration, normally on a light ground, is characterised by fantastical motifs with intricate patterns of volutes, festoons, garlands, and borders of twisted vegetation and flowers interspersed with small winged human or animal figures, birds, masques, griffins, and sphynxes. Renaissance artists came to see and study the rooms—some left their names scratched on the walls—and this type of decoration became very fashionable and was widely copied: it clearly inspired Raphael when decorating his Loggia in the Vatican.

The Domus Aurea was reopened to the public in 1999 after 15 years' closure.

During the visit it is difficult to obtain a clear idea of the layout from the buildings uncovered, which formed only a small part of the vast palace complex. A further difficulty is created by the intrusion of the Baths of Trajan at many points. However, it may help if you consider that the rooms which can at present be seen probably formed **three main areas**, and that the design of each of these groups of rooms appears to have been more important to the architect than the way they were joined together. These areas, as shown on the plan are: an internal peristyle (not shown on the tour), where the great porphyry vase now in the Circular Hall of the Vatican was found, which would have included in its design the nymphaeum (**45**); the rooms around the large Room of the Gilded Vault (**80**) and the five-sided court to the south; and the complex of rooms around the Octagonal Hall (**128**). The area of the palace to the west of the present entrance, which included the Imperial bedrooms, and a triclinium which opened onto the peristyle, as well as another cryptoporticus to the north, is at present closed. The rooms between these main areas tend to have less intricate designs and are often connecting corridors or subsidiary service rooms.

The **entrance** is through the semicircular wall of the great exedra of the Baths of Trajan. The entrance corridor, with a fine barrel vault, also part of the Baths of Trajan, leads into a series of rooms (**36, 35, 37, 47** and **49**) which once bordered the peristyle. The remains of Republican houses excavated in the 20C can also be seen here. The **Corridor of the Eagles** (**50**) is named after the very worn frescoes of eagles in the vault. Beyond is the **nymphaeum** (**45**). This has an interesting vault mosaic, the only one surviving in the rooms of the palace so far excavated, and the earliest one known, depicting *Ulysses and Polyphemus*. On the walls are the remains of a shell decoration and artificial stalactites; an opening in the east wall provided for a cascade of water. This formed part of the

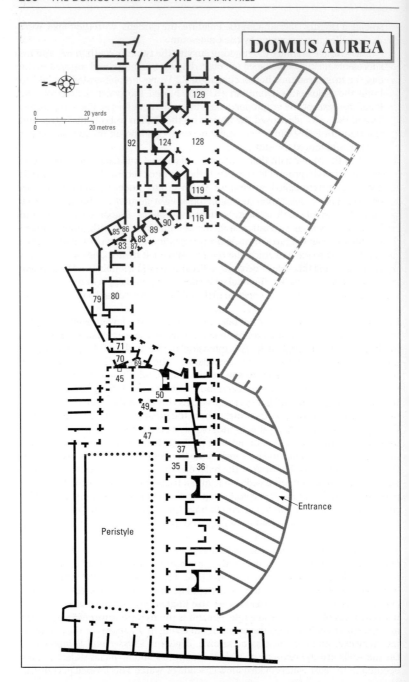

DOMUS AUREA

N

0 — 20 yards
0 — 20 metres

129

124   128

92

119

116

85 86
83 87 88 89 90
79 80

71
70 69
45
50
49
47
37
35 36

Peristyle

Entrance

peristyle, or interior court, to the west (see plan). A room with very worn frescoes by Fabullus (**69**) contains a seated statue of a *Muse* in Pentelic marble, dating from the 1C BC; it was found here and is the only statue remaining in situ. Behind the nymphaeum, an irregularly shaped room (**70**) has well-preserved red and yellow frescoes with restored perspectives; the remains of a warehouse built by Claudius; and, above, an oven which was part of Trajan's Baths. Beyond is a room (**71**) with traces of paintings of birds.

From here we enter the first designed complex of rooms, centred around the large **Room of the Gilded Vault** (**80**). Here a huge mound of rubble excavated during the construction of Trajan's Baths can be seen blocking the open court-yard to the south, which would have looked on to an extensive garden with a view down to the lake in the valley where the Colosseum now stands. The beautiful decoration of the barrel vault in stucco and paint has almost completely disappeared: the paintings are attributed to Fabullus and the stucco work was covered with gold-leaf. In the Renaissance, when it was much better preserved, numerous artists studied this vault and were able to see it at close quarters by letting themselves down through the holes still visible, and standing on the rubble which then filled the room almost up to the ceiling. Some of their signatures can be seen here. Behind is a corridor (**79**) with more frescoes, including eagles in the vault and on the walls (recently restored). These include friezes of animals and birds and a small 'picture' with a still-life of fish and bread.

Beyond a room with a painted false window (**85**) and another with landscapes against a white ground (**86**) is the well-preserved long **cryptoporticus** (**92**), which has remarkably effective lighting provided by a series of windows high up on the left wall, through which the natural light is directed onto a second series of lower windows on the right wall. The graceful decoration features grotesques of plants and animals, as well as Egyptian motifs. The signatures of 16C artists (including Giovanni da Udine) on the vault are usually difficult to see because of the damp. The beautiful marble fountain basin is one of just two pieces of sculpture found in the Domus Aurea which have not been removed to a museum.

The visit continues through rooms 83, 87, 88, 89 and 90 before reaching what was probably a service room (**116**): it preserves its black-and-white geometric mosaic floor, and black and red walls. A room near here which faced the pentagonal courtyard, once decorated with stuccoes and frescoes of which very little remains, has a fresco which is thought to represent the courtyard itself. The **Room of Achilles at Scyros** (**119**) has, together with room **129**, the best-preserved decoration of all the rooms in the palace so far discovered (it was found in the 20C). The barrel vault has exquisite stucco and painted decoration, probably the work of Fabullus. In the centre is a well-preserved scene of *Achilles at Scyros*, surrounded by refined decorations. The **Octagonal Hall** (**128**) was the most important part of this whole wing of the Domus Aurea and has an entirely original design and structure. The light effect is masterly both from the wide central opening in the dome, and from the side rooms. There is an opening for a cascade (**124**) and some painted stucco decoration just survives in places. The **Room of Hector and Andromache** (**129**), which balances room **119**, has more extremely well-preserved and delicately painted friezes of Homeric subjects on the vault.

You now retrace your steps back to the entrance.

In the rest of the Parco Oppio are more scattered remains of the huge **Baths of Trajan**, built after a fire in 104 by Apollodorus of Damascus and inaugurated in 109. Their design was taken as a model by later builders of Imperial baths. Beneath a building thought to have been a library a remarkable Roman fresco of a city was discovered in 1998 (not yet open to the public). The conspicuous ruins include an exedra which was decorated as a nymphaeum, and a hall with two apses. Between Via Terme di Traiano and Viale del Monte Oppio (well below ground-level) is a nymphaeum on a basilican plan, probably part of Nero's Domus Aurea, restored by Trajan.

At 2 Via Terme di Traiano is the entrance (for admission by previous appointment, ☎ 06 6710 2070) to the so-called **Sette Sale**, a remarkable large vaulted building with nine sections, in fact the reservoir of the Baths of Trajan. Excavations have shown that a house was built above the reservoir in the 4C. The famous *Laocoön*, now in the Vatican museums, was discovered in 1506 in a vineyard near the Sette Sale. Of the smaller **Baths of Titus**, which occupied the south-west corner of the Oppian Hill, hardly anything remains.

At the bottom of the hill, on the east side of the Colosseum and between Via Labicana and Via San Giovanni in Laterano (**Map 10**; **1**, **2**) are remains of the **Ludus Magnus**, the principal training-school for gladiators, constructed by Domitian. Part of the curved wall of a miniature amphitheatre used for training can be seen.

San Clemente

Via San Giovanni in Laterano leads away from the Colosseum past a new office block, beneath which were found remains of houses before AD 64 with fine mosaics, to San Clemente (**Map 10**; **2**), dedicated to St Clement, the fourth pope. One of the best-preserved and oldest of the medieval basilicas in Rome, it consists of two churches superimposed, raised above a large early Imperial building.

Opening times

Daily 09.00–12.30 and 15.00–18.00; fest. 10.00–12.30 and 15.00–18.00. There is an entrance fee to visit the lower church. The letters in the text below refer to the plans on pp 283 and 285.

History of San Clemente

The lower church, mentioned by St Jerome in 392, was the scene of papal councils under St Zosimus in 417 and under St Symmachus in 499. Restored in the 8C and 9C, it was destroyed in 1084 during the sack of Rome by the soldiers of Robert Guiscard. Eight centuries later, in 1857, it was rediscovered by Father Mullooly, prior of the adjoining convent of Irish Dominicans, and was excavated in 1861.

The upper church was begun in 1108 by Paschal II, who used the decorative marbles from the ruins of the old church. In the 18C it was restored by Carlo Stefano Fontana for Clement XI. The convent still houses ten Irish Dominicans.

The **upper church** is entered by the side door in Via San Giovanni in Laterano (**B**). The façade (**A**) is turned towards the east and looks onto an atrium with Ionic columns surrounding a courtyard with a little fountain, outside which is a gabled porch of four 12C columns.

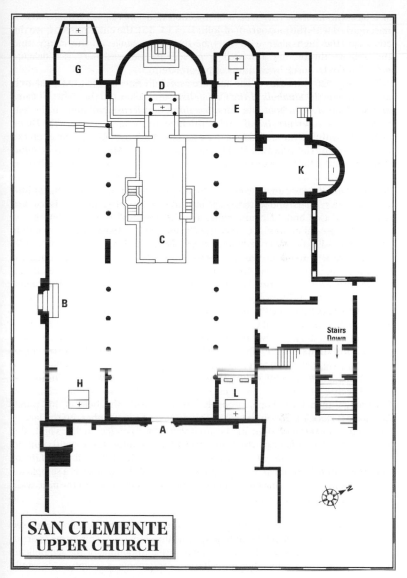

**SAN CLEMENTE
UPPER CHURCH**

The typically basilican interior has a nave with a large apse, aisles separated by two rows of seven columns, and a pre-Cosmatesque pavement. The walls of the nave were decorated with a cycle of paintings in 1713–19 under the direction of Giuseppe Chiari, who also executed the *Triumph of St Clement* on the ceiling. The **Schola Cantorum** (C), from the lower church, contains two ambones, candelabrum and a reading-desk, all characteristic elements in the arrangement of a basilican interior. The *screen of the choir and sanctuary, with its transennae, marked with the monogram of John II (533–35), the choir raised above the confessio, the high altar with its tabernacle, the stalls of the clergy, and the bishop's throne, are also well preserved. In the presbytery is a delicate baldacchino (**D**) borne by columns of pavonazzetto.

The early 12C *mosaics in the apse are especially fine; on the triumphal arch are *Christ and the Symbols of the Evangelists*, and below (on the right), *St Peter* and *St Clement*, with boat and oars, *Jeremiah* and *Jerusalem*, and on the left, *St Paul* and *St Lawrence*, *Isaiah* and *Bethlehem*. In the apse-vault are the *Dome of Heaven* with the Hand of God above Christ on the Cross. The 12 doves on the Cross represent the Apostles. Beside the Cross are the *Madonna and St John*. From the foot of the Cross springs a vine with acanthus leaves, encircling figures of St John the Baptist, the Doctors of the Church and other saints, while the rivers of Paradise flow down from the Cross, quenching the thirst of the faithful (represented by stags) and watering the pastures of the Christian flock. Below are the Lamb of God and 12 companions. On the apse wall below are impressive large 14C frescoed figures of *Christ*, the *Virgin* and the *Apostles*. To the right is a beautiful wall-tabernacle, probably by Arnolfo di Cambio.

In the **south aisle** (**E**) are the tombs of Archbishop Giovanni Francesco Brusati by Luigi Capponi (1485), and of *Cardinal Bartolomeo Roverella by Andrea Bregno and Giovanni Dalmata (1476). The Chapel of St John the Baptist (**F**) contains late 16C frescoes attributed to Jacopo Zucchi and a 16C statue of *St John the Baptist*; in the Chapel of St Cyril (**K**) there is a *Madonna* attributed to Sassoferrato (one of several versions). In the chapel by the west door (L) are three paintings of scenes from the *Life of St Dominic*, attributed to Sebastiano Conca.

In the **north aisle**, the chapel to the left of the presbytery (**G**) has *Our Lady of the Rosary* by Sebastiano Conca and the tomb of Cardinal Antonio Venier (d. 1479), incorporating columns from a 6C tabernacle. The **Chapel of St Catherine** (**H**) contains *frescoes by Masolino da Panicale, commissioned by Cardinal Branda Castiglione, probably executed with the help of his pupil, Masaccio (before 1430): on the left entrance pier, *St Christopher*; on the face of the arch, the *Annunciation*; in the archivolt, the *Apostles*; in the vault, the *Evangelists* and F*athers of the Church*; behind the altar, the *Crucifixion*; on the right wall, the *Life of St Ambrose*; and on the left wall, the *Life of St Catherine of Alexandria*. To the right above, outside the chapel, is a sinopia for the *Beheading of St Catherine* (found during restoration) and, on the aisle wall, the sinopia for the *Crucifixion*.

Off the south aisle is the entrance to the **lower church** (for admission, see above), the apse of which was built above a Mithraeum (3C). This formed part of a late 1C apartment house. Below this again are foundations of the Republican period. The staircase, which has miscellaneous fragments of sculpture, descends to the frescoed **narthex**.

At the foot of the steps a catacomb (see below) can be seen through a grate in the floor. On the right wall is a *fresco (late 11C) of the *Legend of St Clement* (**A**), who was banished to the Crimea and there executed by drowning in the Black Sea. The scenes include the miracle of a child found alive in a church at the bottom of a sea full of fish. Below are St Clement and the donor of the fresco. Further on is the *Translation of St Cyril's Body* (**B**) from the Vatican to San Clemente (11C). An

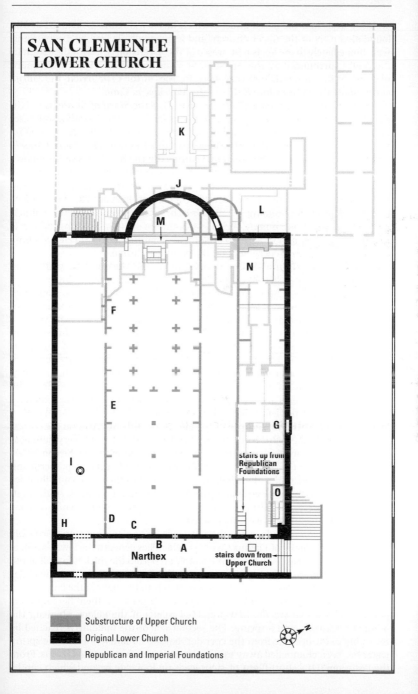

SAN CLEMENTE
LOWER CHURCH

K

J

L

M

N

F

E

G

I

stairs up from
Republican
Foundations

O

H

D

C

B   A

Narthex

stairs down from
Upper Church

Substructure of Upper Church

Original Lower Church

Republican and Imperial Foundations

archway leads into the aisled church which has a wide nave obstructed by the foundation piers of the upper church, and is unequally divided by a supporting wall. Immediately to the left is a 9C fresco of the *Ascension* (C), with the Virgin in the centre surrounded by the Apostles, St Vitus and St Leo IV (with a square nimbus). In the corner (D) are very worn frescoes of the *Crucifixion*, the *Marys at the Tomb*, the *Descent into Hell* and the *Marriage at Cana*.

Further along, on the left wall of the nave (E), is the *Story of St Alexis* (11C): the saint returns home unrecognised and lives for 17 years beneath a staircase; before dying he sends the story of his life to the pope, and is thus recognised by his wife and father. Above this is the lower part of a fresco of *Christ amid Angels and Saints*. Further on is the *Story of Sisinius* (F): the heathen Sisinius follows his Christian wife in secret, in that way hoping to capture the pope, but he is inflicted with a sudden blindness; below, Sisinius orders his servants to seize the pope, but they, also struck blind, carry off a column instead. This fresco more probably depicts the building of the church, as is explained by the painted inscriptions, which are among the oldest examples of Italian writing. Above is the surviving lower part of a fresco of *St Clement enthroned by St Peter, St Linus and St Anacletus*, his predecessors on the pontifical throne.

In a niche in the **right aisle** is a 5C or 6C Byzantine *Madonna* (G), which may have been originally a portrait of the Empress Theodora; *Female Saints* with the crown of martyrdom; and a beardless *Christ*. The frescoes, much damaged, probably depict the *Council of Zosimus*, the *Story of Tobias*, and the *Martyrdom of St Catherine*. At the end are a sarcophagus of the 1C AD with the story of Phaedra and Hippolytus, and a Byzantine figure of *Christ* (7C or 8C), almost totally obliterated. In the left aisle are some extremely faded frescoes (H) of uncertain subjects. In the floor (I) is a circular recess, once thought to be an early baptismal piscina, but which some scholars now think could be the remains of a bell foundry. At the end beyond remains of a tomb, perhaps that of St Cyril, the apostle of the Slavs (869), excavations are in progress of an area where a font has been found.

From the end of the left aisle, a 4C staircase descends to the 1C level with a 'palazzo', and a **Mithraic temple** of the late 2C or early 3C. Around the corner at the bottom, to the right, is the pronaos of the temple (J), with very damaged stucco ceiling ornaments; opposite is the triclinium (K) with benches on either side and an altar in the centre showing Mithras, in his Phrygian cap, sacrificing a bull to Apollo, and in the niche behind is a statue of Mithras; the vault imitates the roof of a cavern. At the far end of the corridor, to the right and seen through a gate, is the presumed Mithraic school (L) with a mosaic floor and stuccoed vault, where catechumens were instructed.

From the pronaos, a door on the left leads to the 1C '**palazzo**', probably belonging to the family of Flavius Clemens, which lies beneath the lower basilica. A long narrow passage (M) divides the temple area from the thick tufa wall of the building constructed, after Nero's fire, on Republican foundations. Only two sides of this building have been excavated. Immediately to the right at the bottom of a short flight of steps is a series of rooms which preserve their herring-bone paving; the last two are the best-preserved rooms of the palace, showing the original brickwork, and a spring. The second side of the building is reached by returning to the opening from the corridor; beyond a room (N) where the spring water has been channelled away by tunnels are seven more vaulted rooms. From the last room (O) a short flight of steps leads up to a gate beyond which can be seen a small catacomb, which was probably used in the 5C or 6C, as it was within the city walls. A staircase on the right leads up to the lower church and exit.

Santi Quattro Coronati

Opposite San Clemente is Via dei Querceti, at the foot of the high wall of the fortified 12C monastery and church of Santi Quattro Coronati (**Map 10; 2**). The steep Via dei Santi Quattro on the left, an unexpectedly rural street, leads up to the entrance of this remarkable castellated building of the Middle Ages. The church, Chapel of St Sylvester and cloister are usually open 09.30–12.00 and 15.30–18.00; fest. 09.30–10.45 and 16.00–17.45, although—since it belongs to a convent—the opening hours are subject to change.

History of Santi Quattro Coronati

The original 4C or 5C foundation, on a huge scale, was destroyed by Norman soldiers in 1084, and the present church was erected on a smaller scale in 1110 by Paschal II, making it, together with San Clemente, one of the oldest churches in Rome. It was well restored in 1914 by Antonio Muñoz. The church is dedicated to the four crowned martyrs—Claudius, Nicostratus, Symphorian and Castorius—who were a group of sculptors from the Roman province of Pannonia (near the Danube) martyred by Diocletian because they had refused to make a statue of Aesculapius. The church is therefore specially venerated by sculptors and marble masons. Extremely interesting frescoes of the **Twelve Months of the Year** were discovered in a hall of the monastery in 1999 and attributed to the 13C Roman School.

The entrance gate passes beneath the unusual **campanile**, dating from the 9C. This squat fortified tower is the oldest bell tower to survive in the city. The small court which succeeds the 5C atrium has a portico with 16C frescoes, and beyond is a second court, once part of the nave, whose columns have survived. On the right of the portico is the **Chapel of St Sylvester** (ring for the key at the monastery of the closed order of Augustinian nuns, first door on the right). It was built in 1246, and contains a delightful and particularly well preserved *fresco cycle of the same date, illustrating the story of the *Life of Constantine*. It is probably the work of artists from the Veneto, working in the Byzantine style. The first scene in the narrative begins on the left wall: Constantine catches leprosy; the sick Emperor, asleep, dreams of St Peter and St Paul who suggest he tries to get help from Pope Sylvester; three mounted messengers ride towards Mount Soratte in seach of the Pope. The messengers climb the mountain to reach the Pope's hermitage; the Pope returns to Rome and shows the Emperor the effigies of St Peter and St Paul; Constantine is baptised by total immersion; Contantine, cured of leprosy, presents his Imperial tiara to the Pope; the Pope rides off wearing it, led by Constantine; the Pope brings back to life a wild bull; the finding of the True Cross; the Pope liberates the Romans from a dragon.

The floor is Cosmatesque, and the 16C frescoes in the presbytery are attributed to Raffaellino da Reggio.

At the back of the second court is the entrance to the **church**. The aisled interior has a disproportionately wide apse and a 12C matroneum, or women's gallery. The 12C pavement is in opus alexandrinum, and the fine wooden ceiling dates from the 16C. On the west wall and that of the south aisle are remains of

14C frescoes. In the south aisle is an altarpiece of the *Adoration of the Shepherds* by the 16C Flemish school; in the north aisle an altarpiece of *St Sebastian Tended by Holy Women* by Giovanni Baglione; and (at the west end) an *Annunciation* by Giovanni da San Giovanni. Against the north pillar of the apse is a beautiful 15C tabernacle attributed to Andrea Bregno or Luigi Capponi. The apse is decorated with good frescoes by Giovanni da San Giovanni (1630), depicting the history of the Quattro Coronati and the glory of all saints. The tomb of the four martyrs is in the 9C crypt (usually closed). From the north aisle is the entrance to the delightful tiny cloister (ring for admission) of the early 13C, with a 12C fountain and lovely garden. It is one of the most secluded spots in Rome. On the left is the 9C Chapel of Santa Barbara, interesting for its architecture and fine corbels made from Roman capitals, and with remains of medieval frescoes in the vault.

The church and convent are on the edge of the Celian Hill, which is described in Walk 25.

23 • Around San Giovanni in Laterano

The basilica of San Giovanni in Laterano was the first church to be built in Rome, but it now has a 17C appearance. It is interesting for its sumptuous decorations, papal tombs and charming cloister. In the separate baptistery are lovely early mosaics, and in front of the basilica is the oldest obelisk in Rome. The Lateran palace, once the residence of the popes, contains an historical museum. The Scala Santa and Sancta Sanctorum, both important Christian monuments, are close by. Cars are banned from the huge Piazza di Porta San Giovanni when it is used for political demonstrations or popular concerts.

The public gardens between San Giovanni and Santa Croce in Gerusalemme were restored in 2000 and have greatly improved the district. Santa Croce is another historic basilica, but it was rebuilt in the 18C. Nearby is a good museum of musical instruments.

Porta Maggiore, now in a decidedly unattractive traffic-ridden area, is interesting as it incorporates several Roman aqueducts, and beside it is an unusual Roman tomb.

Getting there

On foot, the pleasantest approaches to San Giovanni in Laterano are by Via di San Giovanni in Laterano from the Colosseum (see p 282), or by Via di Santo Stefano Rotondo from the Celio hill, otherwise the monuments are best reached by public transport, since the district is not particularly attractive. San Giovanni in Laterano is also served by the *ATAC* bus *Basiliche City Tour*.

On the edge of the Celian Hill (see p 303), around the busy **Piazza di San Giovanni in Laterano (Map 11; 3)**, are assembled some of the most important monuments in Christian history, including the first church of Rome. For centuries the popes exhibited masterpieces of Classical sculpture here, symbolising the power of ancient Rome, including the equestrian statue of *Marcus Aurelius*, the *She-wolf*, and the *Spinario* (all of them now in the Capitoline museums). Here in 1588, on a line with Via di San Giovanni and Via Merulana, Domenico Fontana set up the red granite **obelisk**, the oldest in the city. It had been erected by Thothmes IV in front of the Temple of Ammon at Thebes (15C BC), and was brought to Rome by Constantius II (357) to decorate the Circus Maximus, where it was discovered in three pieces in 1587. It is the tallest obelisk in existence (31m high, 47m with the pedestal), even though one metre had to be sawn off during its reconstruction.

Egyptian obelisks

There are thirteen obelisks in Rome: only five are left in Egypt itself. These monolithic tapered shafts were constructed by the Egyptians to symbolise the sun. They were often set up in pairs to decorate the entrance to temples, and incised with inscriptions in hieroglyphs. After Egypt was annexed as a Roman province in 30 BC, Egyptian art exerted an important influence on the Romans, and an Egyptian Temple of Isis was erected in the city (see p 178). There was a vogue for Egyptian works of art, many of which were transported to Rome, including obelisks which were often dedicated to Apollo or the sun. The obelisks were reused in the 16C in papal urban-planning schemes to decorate piazze and gardens, and to create vistas at the end of new streets. Others were discovered either abandoned or buried in the 17C and 18C and were reerected in the city. Bernini set up one as the crowning point of his splendid fountain in Piazza Navona, and obelisks also decorate the fountains in Piazza della Rotonda and Piazza del Popolo. Bernini placed another, from the Temple of Isis, squarely on the back of a delightful elephant outside the church of Santa Maria sopra Minerva. In the 18C the obelisks in Piazza della Trinità dei Monti and Piazza del Quirinale were set up. The latter used to form a pair with that in Piazza dell'Esquilino, which were originally used by Augustus to flank the entrance to his Mausoleum. The obelisk in Piazza di Montecitorio, formerly the gnomon of a huge sundial in Campus Martius, was only rediscovered in the 18C, when it was erected outside the Italian parliament. There are also two obelisks in the Pincio gardens and the park of Villa Celimontana (this one used to form a pair with the obelisk in Piazza della Rotonda). They all bear Egyptian hieroglyphs, with the exception of the one in Piazza San Pietro outside St Peter's which has no inscription; the two in Piazza Trinità dei Monti and Piazza Navona had their hieroglyphs recut by the Romans. There is yet another Egyptian obelisk in Piazza dei Cinquecento, this time incorporated into a monument commemorating a battle in Eritrea in 1887.

On the west side of the square is the Ospedale di San Giovanni, the main hospital in Rome for emergencies. Excavations in 1959–64 beneath the hospital revealed remains of a villa, thought to be that of Domizia Lucilla, mother of Marcus Aurelius.

San Giovanni in Laterano

The church of San Giovanni in Laterano (**Map 11; 3**) is the cathedral of Rome and of the world (*Omnium urbis et orbis Ecclesiarum Mater et Caput*). Open daily 07.00–18.00; 07.00–19.00 in summer. Cloisters open Sun only.

History of San Giovanni in Laterano

The basilica derives its name from the rich patrician family of Plautius Lateranus, who, having been implicated in the conspiracy of the Pisoni, was deprived of his property and put to death by Nero. Excavations in the 20C in the neighbouring Via Aradam revealed a large Roman building thought to be the house of the Pisoni and Laterani expropriated by Nero. The property afterwards passed to Constantine as the dowry of his wife Fausta. In this Domus Faustae, church meetings were probably held as early as 313. The Emperor presented it, together with the land occupied by barracks (excavated in 1934–38 beneath the nave of the present basilica) built in the 2C for his private horseguards, the *Equites Singulares*, to St Melchiades (pope 311–14), for the purpose of building a church for the see of Rome.

It was the first Christian basilica to be constructed in Rome. The original five-aisled church with an apse, on a basilican plan, was probably built between 314 and 318, and was dedicated to the Redeemer and later to St John the Baptist and St John the Evangelist. It served as a model for all subsequent Christian churches. Partly ruined by the Vandals, it was restored by St Leo the Great (440–61) and Hadrian I (772–95) and, after the earthquake of 896, by Sergius III (904–11). Nicholas IV (1288–92) enlarged and embellished the building to such an extent that it was considered the wonder of the age; Dante described it with admiration when Boniface VIII proclaimed the first Holy Year in 1300 from the loggia of the east façade.

The church was destroyed by fire in 1308 and rebuilt by Clement V (1305–14) soon afterwards; it was decorated by Giotto. In 1360 it was burnt down again and its ruin was lamented by Petrarch. Under Urban V (1362–70) and Gregory XI (1370–78) it was entirely rebuilt by the Sienese artist Giovanni di Stefano. Martin V (1417–31), Eugenius IV (1431–47) and their successors added to its splendour (Sixtus V employing Domenico Fontana, and Clement VIII, Giacomo della Porta). In 1646–49 Innocent X commissioned Francesco Borromini to rebuild the church yet again, and in 1734 Clement XII added the east façade. The ancient apse was entirely reconstructed in 1875–85 and the mosaics reset following the original designs.

Until 1870 the popes were crowned here, and it was the seat of five General Councils of the church, in 1123, 1139, 1179, 1215 and 1512. Under the Lateran Treaty of 11 February 1929, this basilica, with those of San Paolo fuori le Mura and Santa Maria Maggiore, was accorded the privilege of extraterritoriality. After the ratification of the treaty the pope left the seclusion of the Vatican for the first time since 1870. On 24 June 1929, Pius XI officiated at San Giovanni in Laterano, and the annual ceremony of blessing the people from the loggia was later resumed. The pope traditionally attends the Maundy Thursday celebrations in the basilica.

The **north front**, on Piazza di San Giovanni in Laterano, built by Domenico Fontana in 1586, has a portico of two tiers. It had to be restored after damage from an explosion in 1993 caused by a car bomb placed by the Mafia. Beneath it, on the left, is a statue of *Henry IV of France* by Nicolas Cordier (c 1610), erected in gratitude for his gifts to the chapter. The two towers behind date from the time of Pius IV (1560). The principal or **east front**, overlooking the vast Piazza di Porta San Giovanni, is a theatrical composition by Alessandro Galilei (1734–36).

It consists of a two-storeyed portico surmounted by an attic with 16 colossal statues of *Christ with the Apostles and Saints*. On Maundy Thursday the pope gives his benediction from the central loggia. Beneath the portico, the central portal has the ancient bronze doors of the Curia in the Roman Forum (see p 96), moved here in the 17C by Alexander VII. On the left (A) is a statue of *Constantine*, from his baths on the Quirinal. On the right is the entrance to the Museo Storico Vaticano in the Lateran palace (see below).

The **interior**, 130m long, with two aisles on either side of the nave, preserves in part its original 4C proportions, although it was entirely remodelled by Borromini in 1646–49. In the niches of the massive piers which encase the verde antico pillars are colossal statues of the *Apostles* made in the early 18C by Lorenzo Ottoni, Camillo Rusconi, Giuseppe Mazzuoli, Pierre Legros, Pierre Monnot, Angelo de Rossi and Francesco Moratti. Above them are stuccoes designed by Alessandro Algardi with *Scenes from the Old and New Testaments*. Higher still are paintings of prophets (1718) by Domenico Maria Muratori, Marco Benefial, Giuseppe Nicola Nasini, Giovanni Odazzi, Giovanni Paolo Melchiorri, Sebastiano Conca, Benedetto Luti, Francesco Trevisani, Andrea Procaccini, Luigi Garzi, Giuseppe Chiari and Pierleone Ghezzi. The rich ceiling is by Flaminio Boulanger and Vico de Raffaele, and the marble pavement is of Cosmatesque design.The outer aisles were also decorated by Borromini, and the funerary monuments reconstructed and enclosed in elegant Baroque frames.

Right aisles. Inner aisle. On the first nave pier (B) there is a very interesting fragment of a fresco detached from the exterior loggia showing *Boniface VIII proclaiming the Jubilee of 1300*, which for long was considered to be by the school of Giotto, but which most scholars now consider to be by the hand of the master himself. Beyond is the cenotaph (C) of Sylvester II (d. 1003), by the Hungarian sculptor William Fraknoi (1909)—beneath is a medieval memorial slab to the same pope. On the following piers are the tombs of Alexander III, the pope of the Lombard League (D); of Sergius IV (E); and of Cardinal Ranuccio Farnese (F), by Vignola. In the outer aisle, enclosed in Borromini's Baroque frames, are a tomb of Cardinal Antonio de Chaves (1447) attributed to Isaia da Pisa (J), and the tomb of Cardinal Casati (1290), by the Cosmati family (H). Over the window-screen outside the Cappella Massimo is a fragment of the original altar with a statuette of *St James*, attributed to Andrea Bregno (I). The Cappella Torlonia (K), richly decorated by Quintiliano Raimondi (1850), is closed by a fine iron balustrade, and has a sculptured altarpiece (*Descent from the Cross*) by Pietro Tenerani. Beyond is the tomb of Giulio Acquaviva (1574), made cardinal at the age of 20 by Pius V. The tomb of Paolo Mellini (1527) is in the embrasure of the Porta Santa, which is opened only in Holy Years, with a damaged fresco (M).

In the **left aisles**, at the beginning of the outer aisle is a sarcophagus with the cast of a recumbent figure of Cardinal Riccardo degli Annibaldi (1276) by Arnolfo di Cambio; the original is now exhibited in the cloisters (see below). The **Cappella Corsini** (L), a graceful early 18C structure by Alessandro Galilei, contains above its altar a mosaic copy of Guido Reni's painting of *St Andrea Corsini*. To the left is the tomb of Clement XII (Lorenzo Corsini, died 1740), a porphyry sarcophagus from the Pantheon, and a beautiful figure of *Temperance* by Filippo della Valle. In the vault below is a *Pietà* by Antonio Montauti. In the aisle are tombs of (U) the Archpriest Gerardo da Parma (1061) and of (V) Cardinal Bernardo Caracciolo (d. 1255); at the end, beyond the pretty Cappella

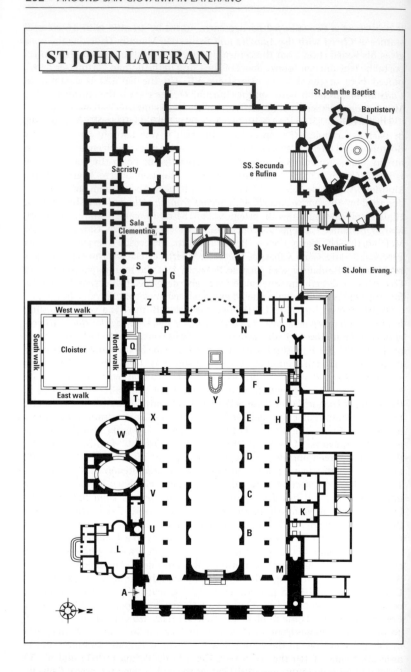

ST JOHN LATERAN

St John the Baptist

Baptistery

Sacristy

SS. Secunda
e Rufina

Sala
Clementina

St Venantius

St John Evang.

S

G

Z

West walk

North walk

South walk

Cloister

P

N

O

Q

East walk

T

Y

F

J

X

E

H

W

D

V

C

I

K

U

B

L

M

A

N

Lancellotti (W), by Francesco da Volterra (1585–90, rebuilt 1675 by Giovanni Antonio de' Rossi, is (X) the tomb of Cardinal Casanate (1707).

The **transepts** were built during the papacy of Clement VIII (1592–1605) by Giacomo della Porta, and the large frescoes depicting the *Conversion of Constantine*, *His gift to the pope*, and the *Building of the basilica*, completed in 1600 under the direction of Cavaliere d'Arpino by Giovanni Battista Ricci, Paris Nogari, Cristoforo Roncalli, Orazio Gentileschi, Cesare Nebbia, Giovanni Baglione and Bernardo Cesari. In the central space is the papal altar, reconstructed by Pius IX, containing many relics, including the heads of St Peter and St Paul, and part of St Peter's wooden altar-table. Above Is the Gothic *baldacchino by Giovanni di Stefano (1367), frescoed by Barna da Siena. In the enclosure in front of the confessio (Y) is the *tomb-slab of Martin V (d. 1431), by Simone Ghini.

In the **right transept** are the great organ by Luca Blasi (1598), supported by two columns of giallo antico, and the tomb (N) of Innocent III (d. 1216) by Giuseppe Lucchetti (1891), erected when Leo XIII brought the ashes of his great predecessor from Perugia. In the corner in the little Cappella del Crocifisso (O) is a Cosmatesque kneeling statue of Boniface IX (late 14C).

In the **left transept** is the tomb of Leo XIII (P), by Giulio Tadolini (1907). At the end is the Altar of the Holy Sacrament (Q), by Pier Paolo Olivieri (from the time of Clement VIII), flanked by four antique bronze columns. On the right is the Cappella del Coro (Z), with fine stalls of c 1625.

The **apse** was reconstructed, at the expense of Leo XIII, by Virginio and Francesco Vespignani in 1885 when the fine apse mosaics were destroyed and replaced by a copy. The original mosaics were designed by Iacopo Torriti and Iacopo da Camerino (1288–94) from an antique model. Beneath the *Head of Christ* (the copy of a mosaic fabled to have appeared miraculously at the consecration of the church) the Dove descends on the bejewelled Cross. From the hill on which it stands four rivers flow to quench the thirst of the faithful. On the left are the *Virgin with Nicholas IV* and *St Peter* and *St Paul*, and on the right *St John the Baptist*, *St John the Evangelist* and *St Andrew*; the figures of *St Francis of Assisi* (left) and *St Anthony of Padua* (right) were added by *Nicholas IV*. At their feet flows the Jordan. Kneeling at the feet of the Apostles in the frieze below are the tiny figures of Torriti and Camerino.

The doorway beneath Leo XIII's tomb admits to a corridor (G), normally closed to visitors, which contains the tombs of Andrea Sacchi and the Cavaliere d'Arpino, and (behind the apse) two fine statues of *St Peter* and *St Paul* by Deodato di Cosma. On the left is the old sacristy (S), with a beautiful *Annunciation* by Marcello Venusti, after Michelangelo.

In the left aisle (T) is the entrance to the peaceful *cloister (only open

Detail of the cloister in San Giovanni in Laterano

on Sunday), the masterpiece of Iacopo and Pietro Vassalletto (c 1222–32), a magnificent example of Cosmatesque art. The columns, some plain and some twisted, are adorned with mosaics and have fine capitals. The frieze is exquisite. In the centre is a well-head dating from the 9C. Many interesting fragments from the ancient basilica are displayed around the cloister walls.

East walk: (**27.**) large marble inscription (1072) recording the restoration of the basilica by Pope Alexander II; (**38.**) papal throne, an antique marble chair with Cosmati decorations from the time of Pope Nicholas IV. A door from this walk leads into the little **museum** which contains two Florentine tapestries (1595–1608), an early 16C ex-voto of Tommaso Inghirami, numerous gifts, including a French cope, given to Pius IX, the *cope of Boniface VIII (13C English workmanship), and a model of the Colonna dell'Immacolata (1854) in Piazza di Spagna. At the end of the east side (**66.**) is the tomb effigy of Giovanni Cardelli (d. 1465).

South walk: (**73.**) 6C head of a Byzantine empress (on a 2C Roman bust; removed); (**84.**) inscription recording the papal bull of Sixtus IV (1475); (**81.**) two half-columns decorated with palm leaves; *tomb of Cardinal Riccardo Annibaldi, the first important work of Arnolfo di Cambio in Rome (c 1276), reconstructed from fragments, which include reliefs and the recumbent statue; (**103.**) Roman sarcophagus, with four portraits; various pavement tomb-slabs, carved in relief. **West walk**: (**167–168.**) four small columns supporting a marble slab, taken in the Middle Ages to represent the height of Christ; (**188.**) head from the tomb of Lorenzo Valla (d. 1465); bronze door with an inscription of 1196. **North walk**: (**201.**) Roman cippus, reused in the 16C; (**229.**) circular altar dating from the 5C AD; various pieces of Cosmati work.

Beside the north front of the basilica, in the south-west corner of Piazza di San Giovanni in Laterano, is the **Baptistery of San Giovanni**, or San Giovanni in Fonte. Open Sun–Thur 09.00–13.00 and 17.00–19.00; 09.00–13.00 and 16.00–18.00 winter, but closed Thur; Fri, Sat 09.00–13.00. It was built by Constantine c 315–24, but was not, as legend states, the scene of his baptism as the first Christian emperor (337). It is a centrally planned octagonal building, although the original baptistery, designed for total immersion and derived from Classical models, may have been circular. It was remodelled by Sixtus III (432–40), and its design was copied in many subsequent baptisteries. It was restored again by Hadrian III in 884.

In the **interior** are eight columns of porphyry erected by Sixtus III; they support an architrave which bears eight smaller white marble columns. In the centre is the green basalt font. The 17C decorations were added by Urban VIII, and the harsh frescoes of scenes from the *Life of St John the Baptist* on the drum of the cupola are modern copies of works by Andrea Sacchi.

The interesting chapels are kept unlocked but you have to push the doors open. The **Chapel of St John the Baptist** was founded by the martyred pope, St Hilarius (461–68). It preserves its original doors (once thought to come from the Baths of Caracalla), which resound musically when opened. The **Chapel of St Cyprian and St Justina** (or St Secunda and St Rufina) occupied the narthex of Sixtus III, altered to its present form in 1154. Over the door is a relief of the *Crucifixion* after Andrea Bregno (1492). High up on the wall can be seen a fragment of the original marble intarsia decoration of the baptistery. In the north apse is a beautiful 5C *mosaic with vine tendrils on a brilliant blue ground. A door leads out into a courtyard from where the outer face of the narthex with two beautiful, huge antique columns supporting a fine Roman architrave can be seen.

The **Chapel of St Venantius**, added by Pope John IV in 640, contains mosaics commissioned by Pope Theodore I (642–49): in the apse, the *Head of Christ flanked by angels* and the *Madonna with Saints and Pope Theodore*, and on the triumphal arch, the *Martyrs* whose relics Pope John brought from Dalmatia and (high up) views of Jerusalem and Bethlehem. Remains of 2C Roman baths built above a 1C villa, with a mosaic pavement, may also be seen here. The structure of the original baptistery is visible in the walls and beneath the apse. The **Chapel of St John the Evangelist**, dedicated by St Hilarius, with bronze doors of 1196, is decorated with a vault mosaic (5C) of the *Lamb surrounded by symbolic birds and flowers. The altar has alabaster columns. On the left is Luigi Capponi's *St Leo Praying to St John*.

Adjoining the basilica, and facing Piazza di Porta San Giovanni, is **Palazzo Lateranense**, the Lateran Palace (**Map 11; 3**), used by the popes before the move to Avignon in 1309.

History of the Lateran Palace

The old palace, which dated from the time of Constantine, was almost destroyed in the fire of 1308 which devastated San Giovanni in Laterano. On the return from Avignon in 1377 the Holy See was transferred to the Vatican. In 1586 Sixtus V demolished or displaced what the fire had left and ordered Domenico Fontana to carry out a complete reconstruction. The new Lateran was intended to be a summer palace for the popes, but they used the Quirinal instead. The interior was restored in 1838. Under the Lateran Treaty of 1929, the palace was recognised as an integral part of the Vatican City. It is now the seat of the Rome Vicariate and offices of the Rome diocese, and, since 1991 the Historical Museum of the Vatican has been housed here.

The **Museo Storico del Vaticano** is open at 09.30, 11.00 and 12.15 on Saturdays, and on the first Sun of month.

The entrance is from the portico at the main (east) façade of the basilica of San Giovanni in Laterano. The Papal Apartments, with late Mannerist frescoes by Giovanni Guerra and others and some good ceilings, contain interesting 17C and 18C tapestries, Gobelins and Roman works made in the San Michele workshops. The well-labelled historical museum is displayed on three sides of a loggia. It illustrates the history of the papacy from the 16C to the present day; papal ceremonies of the past; and the Papal Guards disbanded by Paul VI in 1970.

On the east side of Piazza di San Giovanni are three survivals from the old Lateran palace: the **Scala Santa**, the Sancta Sanctorum and the Tribune. The building that houses the Scala Santa and chapel of the Sancta Sanctorum was designed by Domenico Fontana, architect of the new Lateran Palace, in 1589. Open daily 06.15–12.15 and 15.00–18.30; summer 15.00–19.00. In the 15C the staircase from the old Lateran palace was declared to be that from Pilate's house which Christ descended after his condemnation: a legend related how it had been brought from Jerusalem to Rome by St Helena, mother of Constantine. The 28 Tyrian marble steps are protected by boards and only worshippers on their knees are allowed to ascend them. In the vestibule are 19C sculptures by Ignazio Jacometti. The vault and walls of the Scala Santa and the side staircases were decorated at the end of the 16C under the direction of Giovanni Guerra and Cesare Nebbia.

At the top is the chapel of the **Sancta Sanctorum** or chapel of St Lawrence, the private chapel of the pope, which preserved the most sacred relics removed from the old Lateran palace. Mentioned in the *Liber Pontificalis* in the 8C, it was rebuilt in 1278 and is never open, though partly visible through the grating. It contains frescoes and mosaics carried out for Pope Nicholas III (1277–80), restored for the first time in 1995. Protected by a silver tabernacle presented by Innocent III is the relic which gives the chapel its particular sanctity. This is an ancient painting on wood of Christ, which could date from as early as the 5C although it has been many times repainted and restored. It is said to have been begun by St Luke and an angel: hence its name *Acheiropoeton* (the picture made without hands). The precious relics and their reliquaries are now exhibited in the Vatican Museums. The chapel has a beautiful Cosmatesque pavement. The other rooms in the building have been occupied by a Passionist convent since 1953.

To the east of the Scala Santa is the **Tribune**, erected by Ferdinando Fuga for Benedict XIV in 1743 and decorated with good copies of the mosaics from the Triclinium of Leo III, the banqueting hall of the old Lateran Palace. In the centre is Christ Sending the Apostles to Preach the Gospel; on the left, Christ gives the keys to St Sylvester and the labarum, or standard of the Cross, to Constantine; on the right, St Peter gives the papal stole to Leo III and the banner of Christianity to Charlemagne. A fragment of the original mosaic is in the Museum of Christian Art in the Vatican.

The huge **Piazza di Porta San Giovanni** is often used for political demonstrations, or concerts of popular music, and here the festival of San Giovanni is celebrated with a traditional fair on the night of 23–24 June. **Porta San Giovanni** (**Map 11; 3**), built in 1574 by Giacomo del Duca, superseded the ancient Porta Asinaria, on the site of the Porta Coelimontana of the Servian Wall. The old gate, with its vantage-court, can be seen between two fine towers to the west of the modern gateway.

Outside the gate the busy Via Appia Nuova (see p 431) leads out of the city through the extensive southern suburbs towards the Alban Hills.

From Piazza di Porta San Giovanni, Viale Carlo Felice leads east to Piazza di Santa Croce in Gerusalemme, parallel to a stretch of the Aurelian Walls. The public gardens laid out in 1926 by Raffaello De Vico on the site of a park created by the Cistercian monks of Santa Croce, who planted avenues of over 500 mulberry trees and elms here in 1744 were restored in 2000. They have made this busy traffic artery a more attractive part of the city.

Santa Croce in Gerusalemme

The church of Santa Croce in Gerusalemme (**Map 11; 2**), one of the 'Seven Churches' of Rome (see p 48), has been occupied by Cistercians since 1561. Open daily 08.00–19.00.

History of Santa Croce in Gerusalemme

According to tradition, this church was founded by Constantine's mother, St Helena. It was in fact probably built some time after 326 within part of the large Imperial palace erected for St Helena in the early 3C on the south-west extremity of the city. The principal edifice was known as the Sessorium, and the church took the name of Basilica Sessoriana. Here was enshrined a relic of the True Cross saved in Jerusalem by St Helena. It was rebuilt in 1144 by Lucius II, who added the campanile, and completely modernised by Benedict XIV in 1743–44.

The impressive theatrical **façade** and oval **vestibule** were built to a very original design by Domenico Gregorini and Pietro Passalacqua in 1744. The 18C **interior** has the nave and aisles separated by granite columns, some of them boxed in pilasters. The Cosmatesque pavement was restored in 1933. The vault paintings of *St Helena in Glory* and the *Apparition of the Cross* towards the east end are by Corrado Giaquinto (1744). Near the west door, to the right, is the long epitaph of Benedict VII (d. 983), who is buried here. The second south altarpiece of *St Bernard introducing Vittore IV to Innocent II* is by Carlo Maratta. Above the high altar, with the basalt tomb which encloses the remains of St Caesarius and St Anastasius, is a graceful 18C baldacchino. In the apse is a large fresco cycle of the *Invention of the Cross* attributed to Antoniazzo Romano. The tomb on the east wall, of Cardinal Quiñones (d. 1540), is by Jacopo Sansovino.

A stairway at the end of the south aisle leads down to the **Chapel of St Helena**. It contains a statue of the saint, originally a figure of Juno found at Ostia, copied from the Barberini statue now in the Vatican. The altar is reserved for the pope and the titular cardinal of the basilica. The vault mosaic, the original design of which is probably by Melozzo da Forlì (c 1480), was restored by Baldassare Peruzzi and later by Francesco Zucchi. It represents *Christ and the Evangelists, with St Peter and St Paul, St Sylvester* (who died here at Mass), *St Helena and Cardinal Carvajal*. The Gregorian Chapel, built by Cardinal Carvajal in 1523, has an early 17C Roman bas-relief of the *Pietà*.

At the end of the north aisle in the **Chapel of the Relics**, by Florestano di Fausto (1930), are preserved the pieces of the True Cross, together with other greatly venerated relics. There are long-term plans to open a small museum in the convent to exhibit fragments of 12C frescoes detached from the roof of the nave, a 14C fresco of the *Crucifixion* from the Chapel of the Crucifix, and French 14C statues of *St Peter* and *St Paul* formerly in the Gregorian Chapel.

On the right of the basilica are remains of the **Amphitheatrum Castrense** (no admission), a graceful edifice built of brick by Elagabalus or Alexander Severus for amusements of the Imperial court, incorporated with the Aurelian Wall by Honorius. To the left of the basilica, in the gardens of the former Caserma dei Granatieri, rises a large ruined apsidal hall known since the Renaissance as the **Temple of Venus and Cupid**. It was built in the early 4C by Maxentius or Constantine.

In the barracks here are two military museums, and the fine **Museo Nazionale di Strumenti Musicali**, with a remarkably representative display dating from Roman times to the 19C, most of it collected by the tenor Evangelista Gorga (1865–1957). Open 08.30–19.30; closed Mon. ☎ 06 701 4796. The attractive building of c 1903, in the Art Nouveau style, looks north to a section of the Aurelian Wall. On the other side of the building, near the basilica, are more Roman ruins. The collection is beautifully displayed in rooms on the first floor (some of which can be closed because of lack of custodians).

Room 1. Archaeological material, including Roman works in terracotta and bronze. **Room 3**. Exotic instruments from the Far East, America, Africa and Oceania. **Room 4**. Instruments used for folk-dances and folk-songs made in Naples, Russia, Spain, and elsewhere. **Room 5**. In the centre is the pianoforte built by Bartolomeo Cristofori in 1722. Also displayed here are other 18C pianos, and a late 17C German clavichord. **Room 6**. Military instruments and instruments used by street musicians; hunting horns; 19C walking sticks which could become violins and flutes; a portable 18C harpsichord; 19C processional organs; hurdy-gurdies; Aeolian harps; and accordions. **Room 7**. Church music, with an organ, bells and a 'marina' trumpet. **Room 9**. A unique organ built by Montesanti, with pipes and reeds of 1777; a glass harmonica; spinets, and lutes. Rooms 11–15 are arranged in roughly chronological order with instruments from the 11C to 18C. **Room 11**. The oldest known German harpsichord, made in 1537 by Mueller. **Room 13**. The elaborate Barberini harp. **Rooms 16–18**. Mechanical instruments, including musical boxes.

To the east of the barracks, across Viale Castrense and outside the Aurelian Wall, are the well-preserved remains of the extensive **Circus Varianus**, dating from the reign of Elagabalus (218–22). From Piazza di Santa Croce, Via di Santa Croce leads north-west towards Via Conte Verde and Piazza Vittorio Emanuele. On the left it passes the end of the Villa Wolkonsky, formerly the German Embassy, and now the residence of the British ambassador. Via Statilia, skirting the north side of the villa, runs parallel to a fine series of arches of the **Aqueduct of Nero**, an extension of the Acqua Claudia (see below) built by Nero to provide water for his various constructions on the Palatine and Oppian Hills.

Around Porta Maggiore

The ugly Via Eleniana leads north from Piazza di Santa Croce to the large and busy Piazza di Porta Maggiore, in an unattractive part of the city. On the west side of this square is the beginning of Via Statilia, with some arches of the Acqua Claudia (see p 432), restored to carry the Acqua Marcia (1923). On the east side is the **Porta Maggiore**, or Porta Prenestina (**Map 11; 2**), built by Claudius in AD 52, and formed by the archways carrying the Acqua Claudia and the Anio Novus over the Via Prenestina and the Via Casilina.

The Porta Prenestina was a gate in Aurelian's Wall; it was restored by Honorius in 405. The ancient Via Prenestina and Via Labicana which pass under the arches can still be seen. Also here are the foundations of a guardhouse added by Honorius. On the outside of the gate is the unusual **Tomb of the Baker** Marcus Virgilius Eurysaces, a public contractor, and his wife Atistia. This pretentious monument, built entirely of travertine, dates from c 30 BC. The circular openings represent the mouths of a baker's oven; above is a frieze illustrating the stages of bread-making.

In Via Giolitti, which runs beside Termini station, is the so-called **Temple of Minerva Medica** (**Map 5; 7**), now surrounded by ugly buildings. This large, ten-sided domed hall is a remarkable survival from the 4C (the ruin is conspicuous on the approach to Rome by train, just before it reaches Termini station). It was probably the nymphaeum of the Gardens of Licinius, but was given its present name after the discovery inside it of a statue of Minerva with a serpent, which probably occupied one of the nine niches round its walls. The cupola, which collapsed in 1828, served as a model for many Classical buildings. The church of Santa Bibiana (described on p 272) is a short way further north-west in Via Giolitti.

Beyond the temple, Viale Manzoni leads left past the end of Via di Porta Maggiore. Near Via Luzzatti is the **Hypogeum of the Aureli**, an early Christian tomb which belonged to the freedmen of the gens Aurelia, with mosaics and well preserved wall-paintings (AD 200–250), suggesting a mixture of Christian and gnostic beliefs. It was discovered in 1919, but is open only by special permision: enquire at the Pontificia Commissione di Archeologia Sacra, ☎ 06 446 5610.

Outside Porta Maggiore

Outside Porta Maggiore as you face east are two main roads, the Via Prenestina on the left, and the Via Casilina on the right.

About 130m from the gate, at no. 17 Via Prenestina, which leads to Praeneste (now Palestrina), is the entrance to the **Basilica di Porta Maggiore**, a remarkable and very well preserved building of the 1C AD that was unearthed in 1916. It is approached by a modern staircase beneath the railway. It has the rudimentary form of a cult building, with a central porch, an apse at the east end, a nave and two arched aisles with no clerestory. This became the basic plan of the Christian church. The ceiling and walls are covered with exquisite stuccoes representing landscapes, mythological subjects, and scenes of early childhood; the principal design of the apse is thought to depict the death of Sappho. The purpose for which it was built is still under discussion: it may have been a type of funerary hall, or have been used by a mystical sect, perhaps the Pythagoreans. Admission only by special permission; write giving your local telephone number and days of availability to the *Ripartizione X del Comune di Rome*, 29 Via Portico d'Ottavia, 00100 Rome. ☎ 06 6710 3819, ▤ 06 689 2115.

Farther on is the **Parco dei Giordiani**, a public park surrounding the remains of the 3C Villa dei Giordiani, one of the largest suburban Roman villas, including an octagonal hall and a circular mausoleum known as the Tor de'Schiavi. Beyond **Ponte di Nona** (at the ninth Roman milestone, about 11km from Porta Maggiore) are the ruins of **Gabii**, an important Latin town in the 7C–6C BC, and half-way between Rome and Palestrina. A legend relates that Romulus and Remus were sent to Gabii to study Greek, and the town was supposed to have been captured by Tarquinius Superbus. Here are the remains (with its altar) of a temple known as the Temple of Juno—probably actually dedicated to Fortune—reconstructed in the mid-2C BC. A vast number of bronze statuettes were found in a sanctuary on the site, which is not yet open to the public while excavations continue. In the neighbourhood are the stone quarries from which parts of Rome were built.

Via Casilina, the ancient Via Labicana, traverses ugly suburbs. Five kilometres from the Porta Maggiore are the ruins known as the **Tor Pignattara**. This was the mausoleum of St Helena, the mother of Constantine, who died c 330. It was circular outside and octagonal within and had terracotta amphorae (*pignatte*) in the vault to diminish the load. It is now in a courtyard near a church built in 1922.

24 • San Lorenzo fuori le Mura

The basilica of San Lorenzo fuori le Mura (Map 5; 4) is one of the seven pilgrim-age churches of Rome. It has remarkable architectural features, including two storeys of ancient columns in the presbytery, superb Cosmati work, and exten-sive catacombs off the lovely cloister. Despite serious war damage it retains its venerable character. It is a much more peaceful and friendly church to visit than some of the other major basilicas such as San Paolo fuori le Mura and San Giovanni in Laterano.

Opening times

Daily 08.00–12.30 and 15.00–19.20. It stands in Piazza San Lorenzo, not a very attractive part of the city, next to the huge cemetery, and is best reached by public transport. Numerous buses and trams run from the centre of the city, including bus No. 71 from Piazza San Silvestro, and trams 19 and 3.

The catacombs are shown on request.

Note. It is best to visit the church in the afternoon since funerals are often held at 09.30, 10.15, 11.00 and 11.45.

History of San Lorenzo fuori le Mura

St Lawrence is thought to have been a deacon under Pope Sixtus II, and despite the tradition that he was roasted alive on a gridiron (and the numerous paintings and sculptures which show the scene), he was probably in fact beheaded when he was martyred in 258. He was buried here in the Campo Verano (see below). He has always been venerated as one of the most important early Roman martyrs, and by the 4C was considered one of the patron saints of the city, together with St Peter and St Paul.

The basilica consists of two churches placed end to end. Parallel to the 4C covered cemetery basilica built by Constantine in honour of St Lawrence, Pelagius II built a new church in 579. In 1216 Honorius III demolished the apse of the 6C church and built onto it another church, with a different orientation (placing the entrance at the opposite end). The churches were skilfully restored in 1864–70 by Virginio Vespignani.

San Lorenzo was the only church in Rome to suffer serious damage during the Second World War, when it was partly destroyed by Allied bombs on 19 July 1943 (the target was meant to have been Tiburtina railway station close by): the façade and the south wall were carefully rebuilt in 1949.

On the right of the church is the entrance to the **monastery**, owned by Franciscan Cappuchin friars since 1857, with four wide arches supported by Roman columns and a charming gallery above.

The simple Romanesque **campanile** dates from the 12C. The reconstructed 13C **narthex** of six antique Ionic columns has a carved cornice and a mosaic frieze. This is thought to be the work of Vassalletto. Inside are three Roman sarcophagi (the one with vintage scenes is particularly interesting), a plaque of 1948 commemorating repairs ordered by Pius XII after war damage, and a monument (1954) by Giacomo Manzù to the statesman Alcide De Gasperi, the Christian Democrat who dominated Italian politics between 1943 and 1953. The 13C frescoes (restored in the 19C and again after war damage) depict the *Lives of St Lawrence* and *St Stephen*.

The lovely light basilican **interior**, with a raised chancel and no transept, retains its 13C appearance. Twenty-two Ionic columns of granite support an architrave, and the floor is paved with a 12C Cosmatesque mosaic. Near the entrance is the tomb of Cardinal Fieschi, a large Roman sarcophagus with a splendid relief of a marriage scene, converted to its present use in 1256; it was rebuilt from the original fragments after the bombardment. In the **nave** on the right is a beautiful Cosmatesque ambone, extremely well preserved, with exquisite carvings and marble inlay, which incorporates a paschal candlestick with a twisted stem. Three fresco fragments remain on the south wall of the nave. The frescoes on the outer face of the triumphal arch are by Cesare Fracassini (1838–68).

The lovely baldacchino in the **choir** is signed by Giovanni, Pietro, Angelo and Sasso, sons of the mastermason Paolo (1147); the upper part was restored in the 19C. It has porphyry columns with exquisitely carved bases, surrounded by a miniature Cosmati pavement. Beneath are preserved the relics of St Lawrence and other martyrs. Steps lead up to the beautiful raised chancel which incorporates the 6C church (except for its apse, which was demolished), which is on a slightly different axis. The Corinthian columns with magnificent huge capitals support a charming entablature constructed out of miscellaneous antique fragments mostly dating from the 1C AD and, above, a delicate arcaded gallery, with smaller columns, and windows with transennae. The two large antique capitals at the west end of the chancel are decorated with trophies and winged Victories. From here can be seen the inner face of the triumphal arch, which bears a remarkable 6C **mosaic** (reset during the Byzantine revival) of *Christ Seated on a Globe flanked by St Peter, St Paul, St Stephen, St Lawrence* and *St Hippolytus*, and *Pope Pelagius II* offering a model of the church. Beneath the two latticed windows are representations of Bethlehem and Jerusalem. On the arch is a beautiful mosaic inscription, and, on the soffit, a ribbon charmingly decorated with fruit and flowers.

There are two long marble benches and at the east end the handsome 13C episcopal throne with a 13C Cosmati screen.

The remains of the earliest church, cloister and catacombs are all shown on request at the sacristy. The lower level has some remains of the **earliest basilica**, including some of the original pillars, and in its narthex is the mausoleum of Pius IX (d. 1878), rebuilt by Raffaele Cattaneo in 1881 and decorated with mosaics by Ludovico Seitz. Beneath the chancel St Lawrence and two companions are buried.

The charming **cloister** with two storeys overlooking a little garden dates from 1187–91. Here is the entrance to the extensive **Catacombs of St Cyriaca** where the body of St Lawrence is said to have been placed after his death in 258. They are on five levels, although only the middle one can be visited. Although lights have been installed, it is sometimes possible (on request) to visit them by candle-light. The catacombs, which have been known since earliest times, are now devoid of paintings and have only a few inscriptions; all the others have been removed and are now exhibited on the walls of the cloisters.

To the right of the church is the entrance to the huge municipal cemetery called **Campo Verano** (Map 5; 6), on the site of the estate of the Emperor Lucius Verus. It was designed by Giuseppe Valadier in 1807–12, with a chapel and quadriporticus by Virginio Vespignani. The four colossal allegorical figures at the entrance date from 1878. Among the tombs, in the first avenue to the left, is that of Goffredo Mameli, the soldier-poet (d. 1849). On the high ground beside Via Tiburtina is a memorial of the Battle of Mentana (1867). In the zone of the new plots is a First World War memorial by Raffaello de Vico.

Piazza San Lorenzo, a busy traffic hub and bus and tram terminus, is traversed by Via Tiburtina, on the site of the ancient Roman road to Tibur (now Tivoli). Viale Regina Elena leads north-west between the Istituto Superiore di Sanità, with a research centre for chemical microbiology, and the **Città Universitaria** (**Map 5**; **3**, **4**) on the left, an interesting example of Fascist architecture. The faculty buildings and chapel were designed on a monumental scale by Marcello Piacentini and completed in 1935, in which year the seat of the University of Rome was transferred here from Palazzo della Sapienza. Numerous other buildings have been built in this century (some by Giovanni Michelucci) as the university has expanded. The entrance is in Piazzale Aldo Moro, near a bronze statue of Minerva by Arturo Martini. In the Rector's Palace there is a fresco by Mario Sironi. The University Library was founded by Alexander VII and now has more than a million volumes. In the Faculty of Letters are three **study collections** open by appointment: the Museo delle Origini (founded in 1942), which illustrates the prehistory of Italy (☎ 06 4991 3924); the Museo delle Antichità Etrusche e Italiche (☎ 06 4991 3315); and the Museo dell'Arte Classica (formerly the Museo dei Gessi), with more than 1000 casts of Greek and Hellenistic statuary (☎ 06 4991 3960). The Botanical Institute has an important herbarium (☎ 06 4991 2410).

The **Policlinico** (**Map 5**; **3**) is a large teaching hospital, designed by Giulio Podesti in 1893. To the west, with an entrance on Viale Castro Pretorio, are the buildings of the **Biblioteca Nazionale Centrale Vittorio Emanuele II** (**Map 5**; **3**), opened in 1975. The National Library, the largest in Italy, was founded in 1877 with the contents of the library of the Jesuit Collegio Romano, its former seat, and later enriched with the books from 70 monastic libraries. It now has about 4,500,000 volumes (a copy of every book published in Italy has to be sent here), 1935 incunabula, and 6500 manuscripts. Open Mon–Fri 09.00–18.30; Sat 09.00–13.30; closed Sun.

The library stands on the site of the **Castra Pretoria**, the huge Roman barracks of the Praetorian Guard. The *Praetoriae Cohortes*, or emperor's bodyguard, originally nine or ten cohorts (9000–10,000 men), were instituted by Augustus and concentrated into a permanent camp here by Sejanus, minister of Tiberius, in AD 23; some portions of his building survive. In later Imperial times the Praetorian Guard acquired undue influence in the conduct of affairs of state. Many an emperor had to bribe them on his accession with a 'donative'. On one occasion, after the death of Pertinax in 193, they put up the Roman Empire itself for sale by auction; it was bought by Didius Julianus, who enjoyed his purchase for 66 days. Centuries later the Castra Pretoria passed into the hands of the Jesuits, who renamed it Macao after their most successful foreign mission. It was again used as barracks in the 20C.

Via San Martino della Battaglia leads south-west to **Piazza dell' Indipendenza** (**Map 4**; **4**), on the site of the Campus Sceleratus, where Vestals who had forgotten their vows of chastity were buried alive. Via Solferino continues to Piazza dei Cinquecento in front of Termini station (see Walk 19).

25 • The Celian Hill

The Celio or Celian Hill (51m), now separated from the Palatine by Via di San Gregorio, is, together with the Aventine, the southernmost of the Seven Hills of Rome and the most extensive after the Esquiline. It is easily reached on foot by Via Claudia from the Colosseum, or the prettier Clivo di Scauro from Via di San Gregorio. Isolated from the busy area which surrounds it below, it is a peaceful little district. The picturesque church of Santi Giovanni e Paolo, in a quiet corner of the hill, covers Roman remains, and Santa Maria in Domnica on top of the hill has a fine 9C mosaic and a Roman stone boat outside, used as a fountain. Villa Celimontana is now a delightful public park. Santo Stefano Rotondo is a remarkable large circular church. On the lower slopes of the hill are the 17C church of San Gregorio Magno, with interesting chapels outside, and a building which is being restored to house part of the extremely important collection of Roman objects found during excavations in the city, known as the Antiquarium Comunale.

History of the Celian Hill

The Celian Hill is supposed originally to have been called *Mons Querquetulanus* from the oak forests which covered its slopes. It received its name of *Mons Coelius* from Caelius (or Coelius) Vibenna, an Etruscan who is said to have helped Romulus in his war against the Sabine king Tatius, and to have settled here afterwards. Tullus Hostilius lived on the hill and transferred to it the Latin population of Alba Longa. It became an aristocratic district in Imperial times. Devastated by Robert Guiscard in 1084, it remained almost uninhabited for centuries, and even today it is sparsely populated.

The tree-lined Via di San Gregorio (**Map 10**; **1**, **3**) is a busy road with fast traffic in the declivity between the Celian and Palatine hills south of the Colosseum. It follows the line of the ancient Via Triumphalis. About half-way along it the narrow and pretty **Clivo di Scauro**, the ancient Clivus Scauri, probably opened in the 1C BC, ascends the Celian Hill.

San Gregorio Magno and Santi Giovanni e Paolo
At the beginning of the Clivo di Scauro a short road on the right leads up to the church of **San Gregorio Magno** (**Map 10**; **3**), a medieval church altered and restored in the 17C and 18C (open 09.00–12.30, 15.30–18.00; closed Sat).

The staircase, façade and atrium are by Giovanni Battista Soria (1633) and are considered his masterpiece. In the **atrium** are several fine tombs, including (near the entrance) that of Sir Robert Peckham (d. 1569), a self-exiled English Catholic. There is a memorial to Sir Edward Carne (d. 1561), another English Catholic and an envoy of Henry VIII and Mary I. Beyond the gate into a garden are the tombs of Canon Guidiccioni (1643) and, on the right, beside the convent door, the brothers Bonsi (1481), the latter by Luigi Capponi.

For admission to the **interior** of the church ring at the door of the convent on the right in the atrium. It has 16 antique columns and a restored mosaic pavement; it was rebuilt in 1725–34 by Francesco Ferrari. At the end of the south aisle is the **Chapel of St Gregory**, with a fine altar-frontal sculptured by Luigi Capponi, and an altarpiece of the Saint painted by Sisto Badalocchio. The marble chair dating from the 1C BC is known as the Throne of St Gregory.

In the sanctuary are two 15C–16C statues of *St Andrew* and *St Gregory*. Off the north aisle is the **Salviati Chapel**, by Francesco da Volterra and Carlo Maderno: on the right is an ancient fresco of the *Madonna* (repainted in the 14C or 15C) which is supposed to have spoken to St Gregory; on the left is a fine tabernacle by the school of Andrea Bregno (1469). The altarpieces in the nave date from the 18C.

On the left of the church are the three **oratories of Santa Barbara, Sant'Andrea** and **Santa Silvia**, surrounded by ancient cypresses, open 09.30–13.00, 15.30–19.00, closed Mon morning. The oratories of Santa Barbara and Sant'Andrea survive from a monastery founded by St Gregory the Great (590–604) on the site of his father's house, and dedicated to St Andrew. It was in this convent in 596 that St Augustine received St Gregory's blessing before setting out with 40 other monks on his mission to convert the English to Christianity. The rest of the monastery was demolished in 1573 and the two chapels were restored in 1602. In the centre is the **chapel of Sant'Andrea**, preceded by a portico with four antique cipollino columns. Inside on the right is a **Flagellation of St Andrew* by Domenichino, and on the left S*t Andrew on the Way to his Martyrdom* by Guido Reni. On the entrance wall are depictions of St Silvia and St Gregory by Giovanni Lanfranco. The altarpiece of the *Madonna in Glory between St Andrew and St Gregory* is by Pomarancio. Above the altar, in the space between the original roof and the lower Renaissance wooden ceiling, there is an 11C mural (but it is not visible).

The chapel on the left, dedicated to **Santa Barbara**, contains a statue of *St Gregory* by Nicolas Cordier. The 3C table is supposed to be the one at which St Gregory served twelve paupers daily with his own hands, among whom an angel once appeared as a thirteenth; this legend gave the alternative name to the chapel, the Triclinium Pauperum. A fresco on the left, by Antonio Viviani (1602), commemorates the famous incident of the fair-haired English children, *non Angli sed Angeli* ('not Angles but Angels'), which culminated in St Augustine's mission.

The chapel on the right was built in 1603 and dedicated to **Santa Silvia**, mother of Gregory. It contains her statue by Nicolas Cordier, and a fresco of an **Angel Choir* by Guido Reni.

Also here are remains of a 6C basilican hall of the **Library** erected by Pope St Agapitus I to contain Christian texts. Through a window can be seen the Roman masonry in the foundations of the chapels. The 17C portal (which provided access from the Clivo di Scauro) bears a fresco of the *Ecce Homo* by Sisto Badalocchio. In the little garden here are walls dating from the Republican period.

On the other side of the Clivo di Scauro, Viale del Parco del Celio (beware of trams) leads up to the Casina dei Salvi, where part of the **Antiquarium Comunale**, also known as the Antiquarium del Celio, is housed, but it has been closed for restoration for several years; ☎ 06 700 1569.

The antiquarium was founded in 1885 for objects found during excavations in Rome, and illustrates the everyday life of the city from earliest times to the end of the Empire. This extremely important archaeological collection, with some 60,000 works, was first exhibited here in 1894, but much of it, housed in Palazzo Caffarelli on the Capitoline Hill, has remained inaccessible to the public for decades. It includes material dating from the 9C–6C BC from the Esquiline necropolis, finds from excavations near Sant'Omobono and on the Capitoline.

In the garden outside are architectural fragments, tombs, reliefs and inscriptions. The small collection arranged here a few years ago has finds dating from the Imperial period, including frescoes from Roman houses, bronze waterspouts and valves dating from the late Empire and an interesting model of a water pump, a mosaic with the scene of a port found in the gardens of Palazzo Rospigliosi in 1878 during the construction of Via Nazionale, household items in brass and glass, jewellery, bronze and terracotta cooking and eating utensils, bone, ivory, bronze and iron hand-tools for working wood and marble, instruments for measuring liquids, solids and distances, and heavy farming tools.

The picturesque Clivo di Scauro ascends from Via di San Gregorio past an orchard in front of two Roman *tabernae* (shops), past the 17C portal in front of the Library of Agapitus I (see above). It continues uphill beneath the medieval buttresses which span the road of the church of Santi Giovanni e Paolo past its fine apse, a rare example of Lombard work in Rome, dating from 1216. The tall façade of a Roman house is incorporated in the left wall of the church and here is the new entrance to the **Roman Houses beneath the church of Santi Giovanni e Paolo** (open 10.00–13.00, 16.00–19.00, closed Tues & Wed, ☎ 06 045 4544). These were restored in 2000 when a small antiquarium was also redisplayed in a circular room adjoining the archaeological area. The Roman remains are particularly interesting for their wall paintings.

According to tradition this was the site of the house of two court dignitaries under Constantine II, named John and Paul, who were martyred by Julian the Apostate and were buried here. Excavations were begun at the end of the 19C and at least four phases of habitation were found from the 1C–5C AD including two Roman apartment houses with shops (2C–3C AD), a Roman *domus*, and a Christian house and an oratory founded before 410 by the senator Byzantius and his son Pammachius, a friend of St Jerome.

In the first room are explanatory panels, and straight ahead is a room with delightful wall paintings of youths bearing garlands and a great variety of birds beneath putti amongst vines and more birds. The rooms to the right have architectural frescoes with painted imitation marble, and figures of philosophers, goats, and masques. In the little medieval oratory (near the road) are 9C frescoes including a rare representation of the *Crucifixion* with Christ robed. In another area there is a nymphaeum with a striking fresco of Proserpine and a nereid, and boats manned by cupids. An iron staircase leads up to the confessio, decorated with 4C frescoes the significance of which is not entirely clear: on the end wall is a praying figure, perhaps one of the martyrs, between drawn curtains, at whose feet are two other figures. On the right are *St Priscus*, *St Priscillian* and *St Benedicta* (who tried to find the remains of the martyrs and were themselves killed), awaiting execution with eyes bound; this is probably the oldest existing painting of a martyrdom. The **antiquarium**, beautifully displayed, exhibits Roman and medieval finds, including sculptural fragments, ceramics dating from the 3C–4C AD, terracotta and glass (1C BC–1C AD), 12C Islamic ceramic plates removed from the campanile in 1951, a 12C fresco detached in 1955 from the Oratory perhaps covering an 8C work, roof tiles, architectural fragments, opus sectile decorations, and amphorae.

The church of **Santi Giovanni e Paolo** (Map 10; 3) stands beside the 12C convent built above remains of the Temple of Claudius (see below). Open Mon–Sat 08.30–12.00 and 15.30–18.00, closed Sun morning.

History of Santi Giovanni e Paolo

The church was built above Roman houses and an early Christian oratory (described above). This was demolished by Robert Guiscard in 1084, and rebuilding was begun by Paschal II (1099–1118) and continued by Hadrian IV (Nicholas Breakspeare, the only English pope; 1154–59), who was responsible for the apse and the campanile. Excavations carried out in 1949 revealed the early Christian façade and some of the ancient constructions beneath the convent.

The travertine blocks of the temple are clearly visible in the base of the beautiful tall **campanile** (45m), the first two storeys of which were begun in 1099–1118, and the five upper storeys completed by the middle of the 12C. The Islamic ceramic plates inserted into the masonry are copies of the originals now displayed in the antiquarium (see above).

The 12C Ionic **portico** has eight antique columns and is closed by an iron grille (1704). Above is a 13C gallery and the early Christian façade with five arches. The 13C Cosmatesque doorway is flanked by two lions. The **interior** (frequently used for weddings), hung with chandeliers, with granite piers and columns, was restored in 1718 by Antonio Canevari. The ceiling dates from 1598 and the floor, in opus alexandrinum, was restored in 1911. A tomb-slab in the nave, protected by a railing, commemorates the burial place of the two martyrs to whom the church is dedicated. Their relics are preserved in a porphyry urn under the high altar. In the third south chapel designed by Filippo Martinucci (1857–80), is the altar-tomb of

Santi Giovanni e Paolo

St Paul of the Cross (1694–1775), founder of the Passionists, whose convent adjoins the church. The apse has frescoes by Pomarancio. In a storeroom (unlocked by the sacristan) on the left of the high altar can be seen a remarkable fresco of *Christ and the Apostles* dated 1255 by a painter of the Roman school showing the influence of Byzantine art. The Sacristy contains a painting of the *Madonna and Child with Saints* attributed to a late 15C Umbrian master.

Outside the church, beyond a door beside the Campanile, can be seen remains of the 'Claudianum', two storeys of a huge Roman portico connected with the Temple of Claudius (see below). In the piazza are some arches of Roman shops dating from the 3C AD. Here a gates leads to the delightful public park of the Villa Celimontana (described below).

Santa Maria in Domnica and Santo Stefano Rotondo

The picturesque Via di San Paolo della Croce, which runs between two garden walls above which can be seen orange trees, continues to the **Arco di Dolabella e Silanus** (AD 10), a single archway that Nero afterwards used for his aqueduct to the Palatine.

Here is the entrance to the former hospice of the Trinitarian church of **San Tomaso in Formis** (open only on Sundays at 10.30). St John of Matha died here in 1213: he founded the order of Trinitarians for the redemption of slaves, and above the doorway is a mosaic (c 1218) of *Christ between Two Christian Slaves*, one white, the other black.

Outside the arch, in Via della Navicella to the right, on the summit of the hill, is the church of **Santa Maria in Domnica** (**Map 10; 3, 4**), or della Navicella, of ancient foundation. Open 09.00–12.00 and 15.30 18.00. Its title is a corruption of *Dominica* (Chief). The alternative name is derived from the Roman stone boat that Leo X had made into a fountain in front of the church. The boat was probably a votive offering from the Castra Peregrina, a camp for non Italian soldiers, situated between Via Santo Stefano and Via Navicella.

The present church, restored by St Paschal I (pope, 817–24), and practically rebuilt in the 16C by Cardinal Giovanni de' Medici (later Leo X) from the designs of Andrea Sansovino, has a graceful portico.

In the lovely **interior** the nave contains 18 granite columns; over the windows is a frieze by Perino del Vaga from designs by Giulio Romano. On the triumphal arch, flanked by two porphyry columns, is a beautifully coloured 9C mosaic of *Christ with Two Angels and the Apostles*, and the larger figures of *Moses and Elijah* below; in the semi-dome, *St Paschal kisses the foot of the Madonna and Child* surrounded by a throng of angels. The crypt contains interesting Roman sarcophagi, fragments of 9C plutei, and a 17C altar.

On the left of the church is the main entrance to the public park of the **Villa Celimontana** or **Villa Mattei** (**Map 10; 3**). Built for Ciriaco Mattei in 1582, it now houses the Società Geografica Italiana, with the best library of maps in Italy. It was once celebrated for its splendid gardens; some fine palms, umbrella pines, and plane trees survive here, together with a few fountains, and the park is well kept (there is a children's playground in one corner). Open 07.00–dusk, free jazz concerts are held here at night in summer.

Some of the ancient marble fragments which used to decorate the gardens were removed to the courtyard of Palazzo Altemps in 1996 for protection, and some have been replaced here by copies. From the ilex wood to the left of the villa there is a good view over trees towards the Baths of Caracalla. Here is a neglected granite Roman **obelisk**, probably from the Temple of Isis Capitolina, presented by the Senate to Mattei in 1582. It formed a pair with that in Piazza della Rotonda. It was surrounded by antique statuary and a circle of trees, only a few of which now survive, and it has had to be propped up with scaffolding.

On the other side of Via della Navicella, near a conspicuous survival of the Claudian aqueduct, Via di Santo Stefano Rotondo leads to the church of **Santo Stefano Rotondo** (Map 10; 4), one of the largest and oldest circular churches in existence. Open Tues–Sat 09.00–13.00 and 13.50–16.20; Mon 13.50–16.20; closed fest. The entrance is at no. 7.

History of Santo Stefano Rotondo

The church dates from the time of Pope St Simplicius (468–83). The original plan included three concentric rings, the largest 65m in diameter, intersected by the four arms of a Greek Cross. This complex design was almost certainly taken from eastern models, perhaps the church of the Holy Sepulchre in Jerusalem, as well as ancient Roman buildings. The outer ring and three of the arms were pulled down by Nicholas V in 1450, so that the diameter was reduced to 40m. The vestibule is formed by the one remaining arm of the Greek Cross. A Mithraeum of the 2C–3C AD and part of the barracks of the Castra Peregrina were found beneath the floor in 1973, and can sometimes be seen on Saturdays at 11.00 (☎ 06 3996 7700).

The circular **nave** has a double ring of antique granite and marble columns, 34 in the outer and 22 in the inner series, while two Corinthian columns in the centre and two pillars support three arches covered in 1998 with bright white plaster. An incongruous wooden floor was laid during restoration work in the 1990s. On the left of the entrance is an antique Roman throne, said to be that of St Gregory the Great. In the first chapel on the left is a small 7C mosaic showing Greek influence, depicting *Christ above the jewelled Cross with St Primus and St Felician*. Outside the second chapel is a fine 16C tomb. The Renaissance altar by Bernardo Rossellino was reconstructed in the centre of the church in 1990. At the height of the Counter Reformation, the walls were covered with frescoes—with vivid scenes of martyrdom in chronological order—by Antonio Tempesta and Pomarancio on the orders of Gregory XIII. Some of these were repainted in the 19C.

Via della Navicella leads northwards into Piazza Celimontana in front of the huge 19C Ospedale del Celio, a military hospital. In 1991, traces of Roman insulae were excavated in the square, and work on new pavilions for the hospital in the extensive gardens revealed remains of an ancient Roman domus, thought to be that of the Simmachi. On the left of Via Claudia, which descends from here to the Colosseum, are remains of the **Temple of Claudius**, built by Nero's mother Agrippina, fourth wife of Claudius, to whom she dedicated the temple (AD 54). Nero converted it into a nymphaeum for his Domus Aurea, and Vespasian rebuilt it in 69.

26 • The Circus Maximus and Baths of Caracalla

The very fine Baths of Caracalla are among the most imposing Roman remains in the city. Only the shape of the Circus Maximus, the largest circus in ancient Rome, survives, but it is impressive for all that, and can be enjoyed as a public park from which there is a very fine view of the monumental ruined Roman buildings at the southern end of the Palatine. Via di Porta San Sebastiano is an attractive old road which passes San Cesareo, with exquisite Cosmati work, the House of Cardinal Bessarion and the Tomb of the Scipios (but these last two are at present closed to the public). Porta San Sebastiano is a well-preserved gateway in the Aurelian Walls, a stretch of which can be explored from here through the Museo delle Mura.

Getting there

Public transport in this area is unreliable and subject to change, so it is sometimes best to walk from the Circus Maximus to the Baths of Caracalla, and from there along the more peaceful Via di San Sebastiano to the Museo delle Mura. Bus 628 runs from Torre Argentina to the Circus Maximus and Baths of Caracalla. The *Archeobus* (see p 417) for the Via Appia Antica has stops for the Baths of Caracalla and Porta San Sebastiano.

Circus Maximus

The Circus Maximus or Circo Massimo (**Map 9; 4**) lies in the Valle Murcia, between the Palatine and the Aventine hills; now planted with grass, it is used as a public park (and now sometimes also for important political demonstrations).

History of the Circus Maximus

The circus was the first and largest in Rome. According to Livy, it dates from the time of Tarquinius Priscus (c 600 BC), who is said to have inaugurated a display of races and boxing matches here after a victory over the Latins; but the first factual reference to the circus is in 329 BC. The circus was altered and enlarged on several occasions.

In the time of Julius Caesar its length was three *stadia* (1875 Roman feet) and its width one *stadium*. The resultant oblong was rounded at one end and straight at the other. Tiers of seats were provided all round except at the straight end; here were the *carceres*, or stalls for horses and chariots. In the centre, running lengthwise, was the *spina*, a low wall terminating at either end in a *meta*, or conical pillar, denoting the turnings of the course. The length of a race was seven circuits of the *spina*. Though primarily adapted for chariot races, the circus was also used for athletic contests, wild-beast fights, and (by flooding the arena) mock sea-battles. It could accommodate from 150,000 to 385,000 spectators; its capacity varied from one reconstruction to the next.

The circus was destroyed by fire under Nero (AD 64) and again in the time of Domitian. A new circus was built by Trajan; Caracalla enlarged it and Constantine restored it after a partial collapse. The last games were held under the Ostrogothic king Totila in AD 549.

The extant remains belong to the Imperial period. Some seats and part of the substructure of the stairways can be seen at the curved east end, around the medieval Torre di Moletta near Piazza di Porta Capena, as well as the walls of some ancient taverns. In the centre of this curve was the entrance gate: this was a triumphal arch commemorating Titus's conquest of Jerusalem in AD 80–81, and a few fragments of its decorative columns survive. Excavations have been carried out here since 1984. The obelisks now in Piazza del Popolo and outside San Giovanni in Laterano once stood in the circus. At the west end of the circus, on Via dell'Ara Massima di Ercole, are remains of a large Roman public building (2C AD) with a 3C Mithraeum beneath.

Via dei Cerchi skirts the north-east side of the Circus Maximus and gives a good view from below of the ancient buildings on the south slopes of the Palatine (see Walk 3); Via del Circo Massimo borders its south-west side, at the foot of the Aventine Hill. In Piazzale Ugo La Malfa is a seated bronze statue of *Giuseppe Mazzini* by Ettore Ferrari, unveiled at the centenary of the Roman Republic in 1949.

At the circus's east end is **Piazza di Porta Capena** (Map 9; 4), a busy road junction at the beginning of Via di San Gregorio, which leads to the Colosseum (see p 303). It occupies the site of the Porta Capena, a gate in the Servian Wall which was the original starting-point of the Via Appia (see p 416). After Aurelian had built his much more extensive walls, the stretch of the road between Porta Capena and Porta Appia (now Porta San Sebastiano) became known as the 'urban section' of the Via Appia. This part of the Via Appia is now called Via delle Terme di Caracalla as far as Piazzale Numa Pompilio, and, beyond that square, Via di Porta San Sebastiano.

On the north-east side of Piazza di Porta Capena is the **Vignola**, a charming little 16C palace moved here from near Via Santa Balbina in 1911 and reconstructed using the original masonry. The 4C **Stele of Axum** was stolen from the ancient capital of Ethiopia by Mussolini during the Italian occupation in 1935–36 and erected here in 1937. Despite the peace treaty of 1947 and numerous international protests, the monument has never been returned, although the project is now again under discussion. On the modern Viale Aventino, which runs south-west from the square, rises the huge building begun in 1938 by Mario Ridolfi and Vittorio Cafiero to house the Ministero per l'Africa Italiano. Since 1951 it has been the seat of the *United Nations Food and Agriculture Organization (FAO)*.

Viale Guido Baccelli leads through the Parco di Porta Capena, opened in 1910. There is an open-air sports stadium here. At the junction of this road with Via Santa Balbina is the church of **Santa Balbina** (Map 9; 6), entered through the former convent on the right of the portico. Open daily 09.00–12.00 and 15.00–17.00. Founded in the 5C, the church has been rebuilt, and was restored in 1930. The pleasant **interior** has a wooden ceiling bearing the name of Cardinal Marco Barbo (1489). The transennae in the pretty windows, and the schola cantorum, were installed in 1931. In the floor are set numerous good Roman black-and-white mosaics (1C AD) found in Rome in 1939. The 13C Cosmatesque episcopal chair in the apse is in excellent condition. The apse fresco of the *Glory of Christ* is by Anastasio Fontebuoni (1523). The fresco fragments include a good *Madonna Enthroned with four Saints* and the *Redeemer* above, attributed to the school of Pietro Cavallini. The bas-relief of the *Crucifixion*

(1460) is attributed to Mino da Fiesole and Giovanni Dalmata, and the *tomb of Stefanus de Surdis (1303) is by Giovanni Cosmati.

Baths of Caracalla

In Via delle Terme di Caracalla is the entrance to the huge Baths of Caracalla (*Terme di Caracalla*), or *Thermae Antoninianae* (**Map 10; 5**), the best-preserved and most splendid of the Imperial Roman baths in the city. The romantic sun-baked ruins, free of modern buildings, are on a vast scale and are an architectural masterpiece. Their remarkably complex design included huge vaulted rooms, domed octagons, exedrae and porticoes. Beneath ground-level there is an intricate heating system and hydraulic plant, which may be restored and opened to the public. Of the elaborate decoration only a few architectural fragments and some floor-mosaics remain, revealing the baroque taste of the 3C in the introduction of divinities on the fine Composite capitals. The walls were once lined with marble and stucco. Open Tues–Sat 09.00–dusk; Mon 09.00–13.00. ☎ 06 575 8626.

History of the Baths of Caracalla

Begun by Antoninus Caracalla in 212, the baths were opened in 217 and finished under Elagabalus and Alexander Severus. The baths were fed by a branch of the Acqua Marcia, an aqueduct built specially for this purpose in 212–17. After a restoration by Aurelian they remained in use until the 6C, when the Goths who invaded the city damaged the aqueducts.

Roman citizens had free access to the baths, which could accommodate some 1600 bathers at one time: men and women bathed nude, but separately and at different times of the day. The bathers first went through a series of exercises or sports (including wrestling) in the open or covered gymnasiums then entered a sequence of baths of varying temperatures. They might then be rubbed down with oil, using a strigil, and massaged. Entertainment and libraries were also provided. The Romans were the first to give importance to the refreshing combination of exercise and cleanliness for the body.

The baths, built on an artificial platform, have always been above ground, but excavations in the 20C greatly enlarged the area accessible to the public. In the 16C–17C, the *Belvedere Torso* (now in the Vatican museums), the *Farnese Hercules*, *Farnese Bull* and *Farnese Flora* (now in Naples), and many other statues were found among the ruins. The two huge bath tubs now used as fountains in Piazza Farnese and the mosaic of the athletes now in the Vatican also came from here. Shelley composed a large part of his *Prometheus Unbound* in this romantic setting. From 1937 to 1993 opera performances were given here in summer.

An enclosed **garden**, now planted with pines, laurels and cypresses, surrounds the main buildings of the baths, although part of it is closed. Along the boundary wall were two huge exedrae with an apsidal central hall (**a, b**), and in the middle of the south side a shallow exedra in the form of a stadium (**c**) with tiers of seats concealing the huge water cisterns, which held 80,000 litres each. On either side were two halls (**d, e**), probably libraries. The present entrance skirts the boundary wall on the west side past remains of one of the exedrae (**a**), and older buildings below ground-level, including a **Mithreum** (**f**), the largest discovered in Rome (no admission). Excavations and restorations (including conspicuous reconstructions) have been carried out in the area of the stadium and one of the libraries, and on the east side of the garden, where a house and triclinium of the time of Hadrian have been discovered. This area is fenced off.

The main buildings of the baths (220m by 114m) are symmetrically arranged around the huge central hall (**q**) and the piscina (see below). The bathers normally entered through a **vestibule** (**g**) to reach the **apodyteria** (**h**) or dressing-rooms. The vestibule on the west side has a 15C fresco, from a church on this site. The mosaic on the floor of the apodyteria on the eastern side, with a pattern representing waves, is clearly seen from the far end of the baths. The two **palestrae** (**j**), for sports and exercises before bathing, consisted of an open courtyard with porticoes on three sides and a huge hemicycle opposite five smaller rooms. The pavement here has remains of fine polychrome geometric mosaics. The series of rooms to the south (**k**, **l**, **m**, **n**), which may have

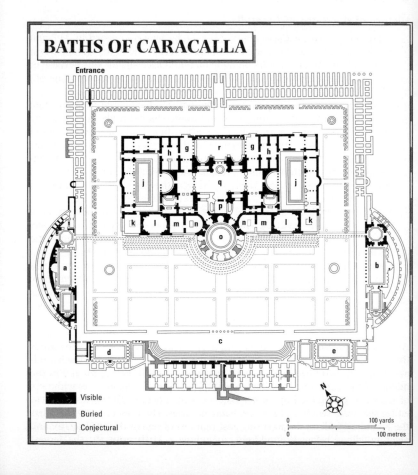

BATHS OF CARACALLA

Entrance

Visible
Buried
Conjectural

N

0 100 yards
0 100 metres

included a Turkish bath or **laconicum** (l) led to the circular **calidarium** (o), 34m across, only part of one side of which remains. It had high windows on two levels designed to admit the sun's rays for many hours of the day, and was formerly covered with a dome. From here the bathers passed into the **tepidarium** (p) and the large vaulted central hall (q). Beyond is the **natatio** or swimming pool (r) with an open-air piscina. This has niches on two levels for statues, and two hemicycles.

Opposite the baths, in Piazzale Numa Pompilio, is the church of **Santi Nereo ed Achilleo** (Map 10; 5). The church stands on the site of the 4C Oratory of the Fasciola, which was named from the bandage which is supposed to have fallen from the wounds of St Peter after his escape from the Mamertine prison. In 524 the oratory was enlarged into a church by John I, when he brought here the bodies of Nereus and Achilleus, the Christian servants of Flavia Domitilla, niece of the Emperor Domitian, who had been martyred at Terracina. The church was enlarged by Leo III c 800 and again by Pope Sixtus IV (1471–84), and was rebuilt by Cardinal Baronius in 1597.

The aisled **interior** has frescoes by Pomarancio. The ancient ambo and the 15C candelabrum come from other churches; the fine plutei and the high altar, which covers the body of St Domitilla, are of 13C Cosmati work. The mosaic on the choir-arch, of the time of Leo III (815–16), shows the *Transfiguration*, with a *Madonna* and an *Annunciation* at the sides. The bishop's throne in the apse is carved with a fragment of St Gregory's 28th homily, which he delivered from this throne when it stood in the first church dedicated to St Nereus and St Achilleus in Via Ardeatina.

On the other side of the piazza is the rebuilt church of **San Sisto Vecchio**, with its convent, the residence in Rome of St Dominic (1170–1221). The campanile dates from the 13C. The façade and interior were designed by Filippo Raguzzini in 1725–27. It contains remains of a fresco cycle of the 13C–14C. Remains of the 13C church are visible in the cloister.

Via di Porta San Sebastiano

From Piazzale Numa Pompilio, roads lead to four of the gates in the Aurelian Wall: Via Druso north-northeast to Porta Metronia, Via di Porta Latina south-east to Porta Latina, Via di Porta San Sebastiano south-southeast to Porta San Sebastiano, and the continuation of Via delle Terme di Caracalla south to Porta Ardeatina, adjoining the Bastione del Sangallo.

Via di Porta San Sebastiano (Map 10; 8), on the line of the urban section of the Via Appia, is a beautiful road which runs between high walls behind which are fine trees and gardens; it is, however, disturbed by the occasional fast car. On the right, beyond a walled public garden, is the ancient church of **San Cesareo** (Map 10; 6) rebuilt at the end of the 16C, with a façade attributed to Giacomo della Porta. Open Sun 10.00–13.00 or by request; for admission ring at no. 4 or ☎ 06 700 9016. **Inside** is some fine *Cosmati work, including the high altar, the bishop's throne, the transennae, the candelabrum, the ambo and the fronts of the side-altars. The two angels beneath the high altar are probably from a 15C tomb by Paolo Romano. The beautiful wooden ceiling, gilded on a blue ground, bears the arms of the Aldobrandini pope, Clement VIII (1592–1605), who restored the church in 1600. The apse mosaic of the *Eternal Father* was designed by Cavaliere d'Arpino, who also painted the frescoes. The baldacchino dates from the time of Clement VIII.

Below the church (and closed indefinitely for restoration), is a large black-and-white *mosaic of the 2C AD, suffering from humidity. The fantastic sea-monsters, animals and figures may have decorated the floor of Roman baths. Two apses and the base of a large column, dividing the excavated area, suggest that the first part was later adapted as a church.

Beyond the church, at no. 8 on the right, the garden of the 15C **House of Cardinal Bessarion**, a native of Trebizond and a monk who became a famous Humanist scholar (1389–1472), can be seen. He was a candidate to succeed Nicholas V as pope in 1455. He bequeathed his remarkable collection of Greek and Latin manuscripts to the Biblioteca Marciana in Venice in 1468. The delightful house and garden are a good example of a 15C summer home. The house contains 15C frescoes and wall-paintings of garlands and ribbons which cast painted shadows, and overall patterns of acanthus leaves and pomegranates. The house is now often used for receptions held by the Comune of Rome and can be seen only by appointment; for admission, apply to the *Comune di Roma,* ☎ 06 6710 3833.

About 500m further along the road, at no. 9 on the left, beside two old columns and a little fountain, can be seen the charming entrance into a garden in front of the **Tomb of the Scipios**. The tomb, one of the first to be built on the Via Appia, was discovered in 1780. It was built for Lucius Cornelius Scipio Barbatus, consul in 298 BC, and great-grandfather of Scipio Africanus. Many other members of the gens Cornelia were buried here, up to the middle of the 2C BC, although Scipio Africanus was buried at Liternum (Patria, near Naples), where he died. The sarcophagus of Scipio Barbatus and the funerary inscriptions found here were replaced by copies when they were removed to the Vatican. The other tombs include those of his son, Lucius Scipio (consul 259 BC), the conqueror of Corsica; of Cornelius Scipio Asiaticus; of Gneus Scipio Hispanus (*praetor* 139 BC) and Aula Cornelia his wife; and an inscription to Publius, possibly the son of Scipio Africanus. Also here are a three-storeyed house of the 3C which retains traces of paintings and mosaics, and an underground columbarium. The tomb was closed many years ago for restoration; for admission information enquire at the Museo delle Mura (see below).

Beside the tomb is an attractive little public park called the Parco degli Scipioni, with lovely trees and particularly peaceful. Here, too, is the **Columbarium of Pomponius Hylas**, one of the best-preserved burial places of its kind in existence. It is an underground chamber with niches that contain urns where the ashes of the dead were kept. The steep original staircase, with a small mosaic inscription giving the name of the founder and his wife Pomponia Vitalis, leads down to the 1C burial chamber which preserves its niches and funerary urns, and stucco and painting decoration. It is kept locked; for information, ☎ 06 6710 3833.

Nearby, at no. 13 Via di Porta San Sebastiano, are other interesting columbaria discovered in the 19C in the **Vigna Codini**, now private property (no admission). The largest had room for some 500 urns, another in the form of a horseshoe has vaulted galleries decorated with stuccoes and paintings. For admission enquire at the Museo delle Mura (see below).

A gate leads out of the park into the pretty rural Via di Porta Latina where, in a quiet cul-de-sac to the left, with a large cedar and ancient well, is the picturesque church of **San Giovanni a Porta Latina**. It has a narthex of four Roman columns, and a beautiful 12C campanile. The church, founded in the 5C, was rebuilt by Hadrian I in 772, and restored several times, but the interior retains its beautiful 11C basilican form. It contains 12C frescoes restored in 1940. The apse has three lovely windows of selenite, and a fine marble pavement in opus sectile.

In the other direction Via di Porta Latina leads to the gate in the walls, past the little octagonal chapel of **San Giovanni in Oleo**, traditionally marking the spot where St John the Evangelist stepped unharmed from a cauldron of boiling oil. Rebuilt in the early 16C during the reign of Julius II, it has an interesting design, formerly attributed to Donato Bramante, but now usually thought to be by Antonio da Sangallo the Younger or Baldassare Peruzzi. It was restored in 1658 by Francesco Borromini, who added the frieze. The interior (ring at no. 17) contains stuccoes and paintings by Lazzaro Baldi.

Porta Latina is an opening in the Aurelian Wall (see below) with two towers built by Belisarius, the 6C Byzantine general. Outside the gate, Viale delle Mura Latine skirts the wall to Porta San Sebastiano.

Near the end of Via di Porta San Sebastiano is the so-called triumphal **Arco di Druso**, in fact the arch that carried the aqueduct for the Baths of Caracalla over the Via Appia. Only the central of three openings survives; it is decorated with Composite columns of giallo antico.

Porta San Sebastiano (Map 10; 8), the Porta Appia of ancient Rome, is the largest and best-preserved gateway in the Aurelian Wall. It was rebuilt in the 5C by Honorius and restored in the 6C by Belisarius. The two medieval towers at the sides rest on basements of marble blocks. It was at the Porta San Sebastiano that the senate and people of Rome received in state the last triumphal procession to enter the city by the Via Appia, that of Marcantonio Colonna II after the victory of Lepanto in 1571. The interior has been restored as the **Museo delle Mura** (Museum of the Walls). Open Tues–Sun 09.00–19.00; fest. 09.00–17.00 in winter; closed Mon. ☎ 06 7047 5284.

History of the Aurelian Walls

The Aurelian Walls were built by the emperors Aurelian (270–75) and Probus (276–82) and most of them survive to this day; some stretches are at present being restored. The walls were raised to almost twice their height by Maxentius (306–12), and then restored by Honorius and Arcadius in AD 403.

The enceinte took in all seven hills, the Campus Martius, and the previously fortified area of Trastevere. It was about 19km round and had 18 main gates and 381 towers (see the plan on p 64). The area within the walls was roughly 3391 acres, or 5.3 square miles. The walls continued to be the defence of Rome until 1870, when the army of the Kingdom of Italy breached them with modern artillery, north-west of the Porta Pia. Many of the gates are still in use under their modern names. The buildings of the city were contained within the area enclosed by the walls up until the 19C: outside them, travellers would approach the city across many miles of desolate *campagna*.

The museum is arranged in the rooms on two levels above the gate, and in the two towers. It contains prints and models illustrating the history of the walls. The terrace at the top of the gate is also open, from which there is a fine view. The ramparts along the inner face of the walls, traversing nine defensive towers, are open for some 400 metres, as far as Via Cristoforo Colombo (**Map 10; 8**). They provide a very unusual view of rural Rome, bordering overgrown fields and woods. The Bastione del Sangallo, a formidable structure built for Paul III in 1537 by Antonio da Sangallo the Younger, which is beyond Via Cristoforo Colombo, is not yet accessible.

The next stretch of the Via Appia outside the gate is described in Walk 36.

27 • The Aventine Hill

The Aventine Hill (Map 9; 3, 5) rises on the south-west side of the Circus Maximus (see Walk 26). It has two summits: the Aventine of ancient Rome (40m), which extends south-west of Via del Circo Massimo in the direction of the Tiber, and the Piccolo Aventino, to the south. These are now divided by the busy Viale Aventino, which runs south-west from Piazzale Porta Capena towards Testaccio.

A very small, secluded residential area with beautiful trees and gardens, one or two simple hotels, but no bars, cafés, restaurants, or shops, the Aventine is one of the most peaceful places in the centre of Rome. It remained remarkably unchanged in the 20C. There are fine views of Rome across the Tiber to the north-west from the little public gardens next to Santa Sabina, one of the loveliest churches in Rome, and there is a famous view of the dome of St Peter's through the keyhole of the garden of the Knights of Malta, which can now be visited.

History of the Aventine Hill

The Aventine is the southernmost of the Seven Hills of Rome, and was not at first included within the precincts of the city, remaining outside the *pomoerium*, or line of the walls, throughout the Republican era. For centuries it was sparsely populated. In the Imperial era the Aventine became an aristocratic district, and in the early Middle Ages it was already covered with elegant mansions.

It was to the Temple of Diana on the Aventine that Gaius Gracchus, after failing to obtain his re-election as tribune for the third time in 121 BC, withdrew with his colleague Fulvius Flaccus for their last stand against the Senate. Aventino is still a current political term used when the opposition party decide to abstain from participation in the affairs of parliament and abandon the Chamber of Deputies.

From the Circus Maximus, Clivo dei Publicii and Via di Valle Murcia both mount the hill to Via di Santa Sabina (**Map 9; 3**). In Via di Valle Murcia there is a **rose garden**, the Roseto, created here in 1950, which now has some 200 varieties of roses. Open to the public daily in May and June 08.00–19.30. ☎ 06 574 6810. This was the site of the Jewish cemetery from 1645 to 1895 (moved in 1934 to the cemetery of Campo Verano).

A more direct approach to the Aventine for those on foot is from the Lungotevere Aventino by the Clivo di Rocca Savelli, an attractive lane which leads up past the wall of the 12C Savelli castle, and has steps up into the pretty little walled garden known as the **Parco Savello** or **Giardino degli Aranci**, planted with orange trees (open to the public; the main entrance is on Via di Santa Sabina). It has a superb view of Rome to the north and north-west: visible on the right is the brick Torre delle Milizie, with the tower of Santa Maria in Cosmedin in the foreground. Next comes the tower of Palazzo Senatorio on the Capitoline Hill, and the Vittorio Emanuele II monument. On the skyline the bright Villa Medici, with its two towers, can be seen in the trees. Beyond the dome of San Carlo al Corso is the dome of the Synagogue and on the right of it can be seen part of the dome of the Pantheon. On the left is the Rococo spire of Sant'Ivo and the dome of Sant'Andrea della Valle. Straight ahead the dome of St Peter's is prominent and the green hill of the Gianicolo. A door in the wall leads into Piazza Pietro d'Illiria, with a splendid wall-fountain, beside the church of Santa Sabina.

Santa Sabina

The church of Santa Sabina (**Map 9; 3**) is perhaps the most beautiful basilica in Rome to have survived from the early Christian period. Open daily 06.30–12.45 and 15.30–19.00. It was built by Peter of Illyria (422–32), a priest from Dalmatia, on the legendary site of the house of the Roman matron Sabina—who was later canonised—and near a temple of Juno. It was restored in 824 and in 1216. In 1219 Honorius III gave it to St Dominic for his new order. It was disfigured in 1587 by Domenico Fontana and skilfully restored by Antonio Muñoz in 1919 and 1937.

The church is preceded by a small 15C **portico**. The entrance is from the vestibule, to the left, through the far door, which has 18 remarkable wooden panels carved in the early 5C with scriptural scenes; they include one of the oldest representations of the Crucifixion in existence (the panels are probably not in their original order).

The beautifully proportioned Classical **interior** is modelled on the basilicas of Ravenna. Of its mosaic decoration, which formerly covered the nave walls and apse, only one section above the doorway remains, showing seven hexameters in classical gold lettering on a blue ground, with the founder's name (Celestino I) and the date 430, and, at the sides, two female figures which personify the converted Jews (*ex-circumcisione*) and the converted pagans or Gentiles (*ex-gentibus*). The wide and tall nave is divided from the aisles by 24 beautiful fluted **Corinthian columns** from a neighbouring 2C building. The spandrels of the arcades are decorated with a splendid 5C marble inlay in opus sectile, and the handsome large windows, 34 in all, have transennae of varied design based on original fragments.

In the centre of the nave is the tombstone, with a mosaic effigy, of Fra'Muñoz de Zamora (d. 1300), perhaps by Iacopo Torriti. The schola cantorum, ambones and bishop's throne in the choir have been reconstructed from ancient fragments. The unattractive apse fresco by Taddeo Zuccari was repainted by Vincenzo Camuccini in 1836. Below the right aisle an ancient column, older than the church, can be seen. Adjacent to it, the chapel of St Hyacinth was frescoed by the Zuccari; and at the end of the aisle is the tomb of Cardinal Auxias de Podio (1485), by the school of Andrea Bregno. Beneath the nave, excavations have revealed remains of a small temple and an edifice of the early Imperial period with a fine marble pavement. Over the altar of the Baroque Elci Chapel, in the left aisle, is the *Madonna of the Rosary with St Dominic and St Catherine* by Sassoferrato. In the convent is **St Dominic's room**, now a chapel, where the saint lived and had a meeting with St Francis. The beautiful, partly restored **cloister** of 1216–25, with 103 columns, is entered from the end of the vestibule (for admission ask at the Dominican convent). The peaceful little garden has cypresses and box hedges.

Beyond the convent is another little public garden with orange trees, pine trees, a palm tree and bougainvillea, which is usually even more peaceful than the Parco Savello. From the parapet, the view (now somewhat hidden by the trees) over Rome includes the long, orange façade of the former Istituto di San Michele in the foreground; straight ahead, St Peter's, with the trees of the Gianicolo on the skyline to the left; and to the right the domes of Sant'Andrea della Valle and San Giovanni dei Fiorentini, the little spiral tower of Sant'Ivo, the dome of the Pantheon, the Synagogue, the Villa Medici with its two turrets on the skyline, the Vittorio Emanuele II monument, the Capitoline Hill and the Torre delle Milizie, just behind the tree on the extreme right.

The church of **Sant'Alessio** (Map 9; 3), until 1217 dedicated to San Bonifacio and near which the powerful Roman family of Crescentii built a convent in the 10C, is preceded by an attractive courtyard and retains its fine Romanesque campanile. Open daily 08.30–12.30 and 15.30–17.00 or 18.20. The interior of the church was modernised by Tommaso de Marchis in 1750, but two tiny exquisite mosaic columns remain on either side of the wooden bishop's throne in the apse, as well as part of the Cosmati pavement and frieze around the main portal. At the west end of the left aisle, set in an altar of 1700 by Andrea Bergondi, is a portion of the wooden staircase beneath which St Alexis is supposed to have lived and died in poverty, unrecognised by his wealthy family.

Via di Santa Sabina ends at the delightful **Piazza dei Cavalieri di Malta**, with elaborate decorations by Giovanni Battista Piranesi, seen against a background of cypresses and palms. Piranesi also designed the monumental entrance in the square to the **Priorato di Malta** (Map 8; 5), the residence of the Grand Master of the Knights of Malta, and the seat of the order's embassies to Italy and the Vatican. There is a remarkable view of the dome of St Peter's at the end of an avenue in the gardens, through the keyhole in the doorway. The garden and church are open on Saturdays at 10.00 and 11.00 (ring at no. 4); for information, ☎ 06 6758 1234, Mon–Fri 09.00–13.00. The Order of the Knights of St John of Jerusalem (or Knights Hospitallers) was founded by a certain Gerard in 1113 to assist pilgrims to the Holy Land. The order was based on the island of Rhodes from 1310 to 1522, and then on Malta until 1798. Their headquarters are now in Rome, at 68 Via Condotti, and the knights continue to carry out charitable work. The Military Order of Malta is the smallest sovereign state in the world.

The charming little **garden**, planted with roses and baytrees, has a magnificent high double hedge formed by a variety of evergreen plants including laurel, laurustinus, viburnum, box, myrtle and prunus which frames the view of the dome of St Peter's. From the terrace there is a view over the Tiber towards Monte Mario. The Renaissance parterres were restored by Charles R. Sutton in the early 20C.

On the left, a drive leads to the back of the villa and the church of **Santa Maria del Priorato**, or Aventinense, a Benedictine foundation once incorporated in the residence of the patrician senator Alberic, who was the virtual ruler of Rome from 932 to 954. It passed into the hands of the Templars, and from them to the Knights of Malta. It was rebuilt in 1765 by Piranesi, his only architectural work. Behind six palm trees the fine façade of a single order crowned with a tympanum has rich decorative details. The harmonious interior is striking, with fine stucco decoration; the Rococo high altar by Tommaso Righi is cleverly lit. It contains 15C tombs and a statue of Piranesi by Giuseppe Angelini. The villa (admission rarely granted) contains a Chapter Hall with portraits of all the Grand Masters, and an altarpiece from the church by Andrea Sacchi.

On the west side of the Priorato, facing Via della Marmorata, is the ancient brick **Arco di San Lazzaro**, which may have had some connection with the storehouses (*emporia*) in this neighbourhood. A large Benedictine seminary (1892–96) stands next to the church of Sant'Anselmo, built in 1900 in the Lombard Romanesque style. Mass with Gregorian chant is held here on Sundays at 09.30.

Via Porta Lavernale, Via di Sant'Anselmo and Via Icilio (turn left) lead towards Santa Prisca on the other side of the hill. The church of **Santa Prisca** (Map 9; 4), possibly dating from the 4C, is said to occupy the site of the house of Aquila and Prisca, friends of St Peter. In the interior (open only for services) the pretty frescoes in the nave are by Anastasio Fontebuoni. Beneath the church are a **Mithraeum** (not open to the public), with frescoes and a statue of *Mithras Slaying the Bull* and the recumbent figure of *Saturn*, and a nymphaeum.

Via di Santa Prisca continues down to the wide and busy Viale Aventino. In Piazza Albania on the right are extensive remains of the Servian Wall (c 87 BC). Across the square, Via San Saba leads up to the Piccolo Aventino and the steps preceding the church of **San Saba** (Map 9; 6) with a little porch and walled forecourt. Open daily 08.00–12.00 and 13.00–19.00. Beneath the church were found fragments of frescoes (now exhibited in the sacristy corridor) belonging to the first church founded in the 7C by Palestinian monks escaping from the Eastern invasions. The present church may date from c 900, although it has been rebuilt several times and was restored in 1943. In 1463, under Cardinal Piccolomini, the loggia was added above the portico and the four original windows were bricked in.

In the portico are sculptural fragments, some Oriental in character (including a knight and falcon), and a large Roman sarcophagus with figures of a bridegroom and Juno Pronuba. The fine Cosmatesque doorway is by Giacomo, the father of Cosma, who also probably designed the floor. In the **interior**, the right aisle has remains of a schola cantorum, a patchwork of Cosmatesque work. On the left-hand side of the church is a short fourth aisle, with remains of 13C frescoes. High up on the arch over the apse is an *Annunciation*, another addition for Cardinal Piccolomini. In the apse, above the bishop's throne is a fine Cosmatesque marble disc and a 14C fresco of the *Crucifixion*.

Porta San Paolo and the area further south are described in Walk 35.

28 • Piazza della Bocca della Verità and district

Piazza della Bocca della Verità is an open space with a picturesque group of buildings, now sadly disturbed on all sides by busy traffic. In a little garden beside a fountain there are two ancient Roman temples. Santa Maria in Cosmedin is an important medieval church, but it has lost much of its atmosphere in recent years and is often hurriedly visited by tour groups whose buses can park directly outside. The huge carved human face in the portico of the church, from which the piazza takes its name, is now a well-known tourist attraction. The church is not looked after as well as it might be. In contrast, the lovely church of San Giorgio in Velabro, in a quiet cul-de-sac close by, beside two ancient Roman arches, is one of the most memorable medieval buildings in Rome. The churches of San Teodoro and San Nicola in Carcere, which both incorporate Roman buildings, are also described in this Walk.

Piazza della Bocca della Verità (**Map 7; 7**) occupies part of the site of the Forum Boarium, or cattle-market, the oldest market of ancient Rome. The **Temple of Portunus**, the god of harbours, was formerly thought to be dedicated to Fortuna Virilis. This pseudoperipteral temple, which dates from the end of the 2C BC, has four fluted Ionic columns in front of the portico and two at the sides: it is one of the most precious examples to have survived of the Graeco-Italian temples of the Republican age. In 872 it was consecrated as the church of Santa Maria Egiziaca.

The little round **Temple of Hercules Victor**, was for long thought to be dedicated to Vesta, but an inscription from the base of a cult statue found here confirmed its dedication to Hercules Victor. It also dates from the end of the 2C BC and is the oldest marble edifice to survive in Rome. A charming little building, it consists of a circular cella of solid marble, surrounded by 20 fluted columns. The original ones are those in Greek marble; after severe damage in the 1C AD the temple was restored under Tiberius and some of the columns and capitals replaced, using Luni marble. One of the columns is missing on the north side but its base remains. The exquisite capitals were restored in 1991. In the Middle Ages the temple became the church of Santo Stefano delle Carrozze and later Santa Maria del Sole. The original roof and ancient entablature have not survived.

The fine **fountain** is by Carlo Bizzaccheri (1717). The entrance to a side conduit of the Cloaca Maxima (see below) can be seen here under a travertine lid.

Santa Maria in Cosmedin
Santa Maria in Cosmedin (**Map 7; 7**) is a fine example of a Roman medieval church, preceded by a little gabled porch and arcaded narthex. Open 10.00–13.00 and 14.30–18.30. Sung mass on Sunday at 10.30.

History of Santa Maria in Cosmedin
The building incorporates two earlier structures, the arcaded colonnade of the Imperial Roman *Statio Annonae*, or market inspector's office, and the side-walls of a porticoed hall, part of an early Christian welfare centre, or *diaconia* (c 600). Nearby were a monumental altar and a temple, both dedicated to Hercules, the latter restored by Pompey. The oratory was enlarged into a basilican church by Hadrian I (772–95); assigned to Greek refugees driven from Constantinople by the iconoclastic persecutions, it became known as

the Schola Graeca. Its other name, 'in Cosmedin', probably comes from a Greek word meaning decoration, referring to the embellishments of Hadrian. At that period it had a matroneum and three apses. Cardinal Alfano, chamberlain of Calixtus II, rebuilt the church c 1123, closed the galleries, and added the schola cantorum. The church was over-restored and the pretty 18C façade torn down in 1894–99; it has again been restored recently.

The fine tall **campanile** of seven storeys also dates from the 12C. Beneath the portico, to the left, is the so-called **Bocca della Verità** (Mouth of Truth), a large cracked marble disc representing a human face, the open mouth of which was believed to close on the hand of any perjurer who faced the ordeal of placing it there. It is in fact a slab that once closed an ancient drain, and was put here in 1632. Also here is the tomb of Cardinal Alfano (see above). The principal doorway is the work of Johannes de Venetia (11C).

The fine **interior**, with a nave and two aisles each ending in an apse, closely reproduces the 8C basilica with some 12C additions. The arcades are supported on antique columns with good capitals grouped in threes between piers. In the first part of the nave remains of the arcaded colonnade and side walls of the *Statio Annonae* and *diaconia* can be seen. High up on the walls are the remains of 11C frescoes. The schola cantorum, screen, paschal candelabrum, episcopal throne and beautiful pavement (1123) are the *work of the Cosmati family of marble sculptors. The baldacchino over the high altar (an antique porphyry bath) is by Deodatus, third son of the younger Cosma (1294). The paintings in the apses are restored. Off the south side is a chapel with a *Madonna and Child*, attributed to the late 15C Roman school, over the altar. To the right the former sacristy (now a souvenir shop) contains a precious mosaic of 706 on a gold ground, representing a fragment of the *Adoration of the Magi*, formerly in the oratory of John VII at St Peter's. The tiny crypt (no admission) was built into part of the altar dedicated to Hercules, the columns of which remain.

Santa Maria in Cosmedin and Piazza della Bocca della Verità

To the left of the church, across the busy Via dei Cerchi, the peaceful Via del Velabro (**Map 7; 7. 8**) leads out of the piazza. Its name perpetuates that of this ancient district of Rome, the Velabrum, the derivation of which is uncertain. This was once a stagnant marsh left by the inundations of the Tiber, which extended between the river and the Palatine, and included the Forum Boarium. The Velabrum is famous in legend as the spot where the shepherd Faustulus found the twins Romulus and Remus. It was drained by the **Cloaca Maxima**, which was an extensive hydraulic system serving the valleys between the Esquiline, Viminal and Quirinal hills, as well as the Roman Forum. At first a natural watercourse to the Tiber, it was canalised by Tarquinius the Elder and Servius Tullius (c 616–535 BC), and arched over in c 200 BC. It is still in use: part of it can be seen through a gate opposite the church of San Giorgio in Velabro; for admission, ☎ 06 6710 3819. The mouth of the drain in the left bank of the Tiber can be seen from Ponte Palatino.

The massive four-sided **Arco di Janus** formed a covered passage at a cross-roads (*quadrivium*) and provided shelter for the cattle-dealers of the Forum Boarium. Poorly proportioned, it is a work of the decadence, dating perhaps from the reign of Constantine, and is built partly of ancient fragments, with numerous niches for statues.

To the left, in a peaceful spot, is **San Giorgio in Velabro** (Map 7; 7. 8), an ancient church probably dating from the 9C or earlier, built over a *diaconia* established here c 600. The **campanile** dates from the 12C. The church was well restored to its medieval appearance in 1926 by Antonio Muñoz. It was severely damaged in a bomb explosion in 1993 (the work of the Mafia), which destroyed the 9C–12C Ionic **portico**, but it has been carefully reconstructed and the church restored. Open 10.00–13.00 and 15.00–18.30; the church is often used for weddings at the weekends.

The beautiful plain **interior** is basilican, with nave and aisles separated by 16 ancient columns of granite and pavonazzetto. The pretty windows were restored in the 20C. The irregularity of the plan, which can be seen from the wooden ceiling, suggests an earlier construction was incorporated in the 9C building. In the apse is a fresco of *Christ with the Madonna and St Peter, St Sebastian and St George* attributed to Pietro Cavallini (c 1296; repainted in the 16C). The altar, with some Cosmatesque decoration, and the canopy date from the 13C.

To the left of the church is the ornate little **Arcus Argentariorum** (AD 204), which was erected by the money-changers (*argentarii*) and cattle-dealers in honour of the Emperor Septimius Severus, his second wife Julia Domna, and their children, Caracalla and Geta. The portrait and name of Geta were effaced as a mark of his disgrace after his assassination by his brother in 212.

To the left of the arch, a quiet street leads to the church of **San Giovanni Decollato**, with an interesting 16C interior. Open on 22 June, or by appointment, ☎ 06 679 4572. The interior has fine stucco and fresco decoration dating from 1580–90. The altarpiece of the *Decapitation of St John* is by Giorgio Vasari. In front of the west door is the entrance to the oratory with remarkable *frescoes by the 16C Roman Mannerists, Jacopino del Conte, Francesco Salviati, Pirro Ligorio and others. There is also a 16C cloister.

On the other side of the road, reached by a raised pavement, is **Sant'Eligio dei Ferrari**, which has a Baroque interior, open for services on Sundays.

Santa Maria della Consolazione and San Teodoro

Via San Giovanni Decollato ends in Piazza della Consolazione in front of the church of **Santa Maria della Consolazione**. Open daily 06.00–12.00 and 15.30–18.00 or 18.30. The façade is by Martino Longhi the Elder (1583–1606); the upper part was added in the same style in the 19C. In the first chapel to the right are frescoes by Taddeo Zuccari (1556) of the *Life of Christ* (including the *Flagellation*) and the *Crucifixion*. In the sanctuary, the *Birth of Mary* and the *Assumption* are by Pomarancio, and over the altar is the *Madonna della Consolazione*, a 14C fresco repainted by Antoniazzo Romano. In the first chapel on the left, is a marble relief of the *Marriage of St Catherine* by Raffaello da Montelupo (1530). The cliff above the church, on the Capitoline Hill, is thought to be the Tarpeian Rock (see p 90).

From here, Via dei Fienili leads to Via di San Teodoro, which corresponds to the ancient Vicus Tuscus, skirting the western foot of the Palatine, the ancient buildings of which are clearly seen from here. On the left, well below the level of the road, is the small round domed church of **San Teodoro** (Map 7; 8). The first church was built on part of the site of the great granary warehouse known as the Horrea Agrippiana, which had been used as an early Christian *diaconia*. The present church dates from the time of Nicholas V (c 1453).

St Theodore Stratelates (or Tyro) was martyred around AD 311 in Turkey. The famous Roman bronze she-wolf now in the Capitoline museums (see p 85) was found beside the church.

The church is preceded by a delightful courtyard designed by Carlo Fontana in 1642–45, which surrounds a pagan altar. The **interior** preserves the apse of the 6C oratory with its original, though much-restored, mosaic (c 600) showing *Christ Blessing* and saints, including Peter, Paul and Theodore. The angels and frame below the mosaic are by Carlo Fontana (1704). The altarpiece on the right is by Giuseppe Ghezzi (1707) and that on the left by Francesco Manno (1809). Remains of earlier buildings, including the Roman structures, have been found beneath the foundations and are shown on the first and third Sunday of the month at 11.30.

Some way along Via di San Teodoro on the right is the church of **Sant'Anastasia** (closed), dating from 492 and several times restored. The Classical façade is by Luigi Arrigucci. Inside, under the high altar, is a recumbent statue of St Anastasia, begun by Francesco Aprile and finished by Ercole Ferrata. Beneath the church are remains of an Imperial building.

Sant'Omobono and San Nicola in Carcere

From Piazza della Consolazione (see above) Vico Jugario, a road on the site of the Roman road that connected the Forum Holitorium the vegetable and oil market which extended from the Capitoline Hill to the Tiber with the Roman Forum, skirts the foot of the Capitoline Hill: on the right the arcades of a portico built of peperino in the Republican era can be seen. On the left is the church of **Sant'Omobono**, with a 16C façade. Open only on the first Sunday of the month at 11.00. It contains a 17C lunette showing God as divine tailor putting a fur coat on Adam.

Surrounding the church is the **Area Sacra di Sant'Omobono** (Map 7; 7), which is closed but partly visible through the railings, where excavations have revealed traces of habitation as early as the 9C BC. Excavations begun in 1937, continued in the 1960s and still not completed, have revealed interesting remains on seven different levels, the oldest dating from c 1500 BC. Traces of hut dwellings of the 9C–8C BC, similar to those on the Palatine, have also been found. The archaeological evidence has thrown new light on the origins of Rome and the presence of the Etruscans here in the 7C and 6C BC. Two archaic temples (mid-6C BC), dedicated to Fortuna and Mater Matuta and traditionally founded by Servius Tullius, rest on an artificial mound c 6m high in which were found Bronze Age and Iron Age shards and imported Greek pottery of the 8C BC. In front of the temples are two archaic altars, possibly dedicated to Carmenta. The most conspicuous remains mostly date from after 213 BC when the temples were reconstructed. The material found on the site, including a terracotta group of *Hercules and Minerva* from one of the temples, is kept in the Antiquarium Comunale (see p 304).

Vico Jugario ends beside a medieval fortified mansion which has been over-restored, and a path with steps, called Via di Monte Caprino, which climbs up the Capitoline Hill. On the other side of the wide and busy Via del Teatro di Marcello is **San Nicola in Carcere** (**Map 7**; **7**). Open daily 07.30–12.00 and 16.30–19.00; fest. 10.30–13.00. This 11C church, probably on the site of an older sanctuary, was reconstructed and consecrated in 1128. It was remodelled in 1599 by Giacomo della Porta, who designed the façade using three columns from a Roman temple, and detached from the surrounding buildings in 1932.

The church occupies the site of three Republican temples in the Forum Holitorium, which are thought to have been dedicated to Janus, Juno Sospita and Spes. The first, to the right of the church, was Ionic hexastyle, with columns on three sides only, the remains of which can be seen incorporated in the south wall of the church; the second, now incorporated in the church, was Ionic hexastyle peripteral; the third, on the left of the church, was Doric hexastyle peripteral.

Major excavations have been carried out on either side of the church. The **interior** has fine antique columns from the temples with diverse capitals, and a beautiful ancient urn in green porphyry beneath the high altar and baldacchino. At the end of the left aisle is an altarpiece of the *Ascension* by Lorenzo Costa. The apse frescoes date from 1865. The Roman remains beneath the church can sometimes be visited.

The Teatro di Marcello, Ghetto and Tiber island are all described in Walk 29.

Via Petroselli leads back towards Piazza Bocca della Verità past ugly municipal public offices set up by the Fascist regime in 1936–37, and the eccentric **Casa dei Crescenzi** (no admission), a unique example of a mansion built by a wealthy Roman in the Middle Ages. Formerly a tower guarding the river, it dates from c 1100 and the inscription over the door states that it was erected by one Nicolaus, son or descendant of Crescentius and Theodora, probably members of the Alberic family, the most powerful clan in Rome at the end of the 10C. It is constructed mainly from fragments of Classical buildings or medieval copies of Roman works. The bricks of the lower storey are formed into half-columns, with rudimentary capitals. A fragment of the upper storey and its arcaded loggia survives. It is now used by the Centro Studi per la Storia dell'Architettura, and concerts are occasionally held here.

Via di Ponte Rotto leads to the iron **Ponte Palatino** on the Tiber. In the bed of the river, upstream, is a single arch of the **Pons Aemilius**, the first stone bridge over the Tiber, the piers of which were built in 179 BC, and were connected by arches in 142 BC. From the 13C onwards it was repaired numerous times, and has been known as the Ponte Rotto since its final collapse in 1598. From the parapet of the Ponte Palatino the mouth of the Cloaca Maxima (see above) may be seen under the quay of the left bank when the river is low.

29 • Teatro di Marcello, Ghetto and Isola Tiberina

This area immediately west of the Capitoline Hill, although in the very centre of Rome, includes some unexpectedly peaceful narrow streets around Piazza di Santa Maria in Campitelli, Piazza Mattei and Piazza Margana which preserve much of the character of old Rome. The small piazze are decorated with fountains, palaces and churches, and the characteristic *sanpietrini* paving and a few old-fashioned shops survive. In the interesting area of the Ghetto are some Roman remains, including the over-restored Teatro di Marcello. The Isola Tiberina is the only island in the Tiber: there are very picturesque views of it from the Tiber embankments and the two Roman bridges which connect it to either bank, although most of it is occupied by public buildings not generally open to visitors.

From the foot of the steps up to the Capitoline Hill (see p 75) the broad and traffic-ridden Via del Teatro di Marcello (**Map 7; 5, 7**), which was opened in 1933, skirts the western base of the hill. It descends past the severe façade of the **Monastero di Tor de' Specchi** on the right, founded in 1425 by St Francesca Romana. The Oratory was decorated by Antoniazzo Romano, but is only open to visitors once a year on 9 March.

Beyond rises the cavea of the **Teatro di Marcello** (Map 7; 7). The theatre, together with remains of two temples, is now surrounded by a fence, and admission is restricted during current restoration work; for information, ask at the archaeological offices of the Comune di Roma just beside the theatre, at 29 Via Portico d'Ottavia, Mon–Sat 09.00–18.00, or ☎ 06 6710 3819.

History of the Teatro di Marcello

The theatre, planned by Julius Caesar, was dedicated in 13 or 11 BC by Augustus to the memory of his nephew (Octavia's son) and son-in-law, Marcellus, who had died in 23 BC at the age of 19. It was restored by Vespasian and Alexander Severus. The building was pillaged in the 4C for the restoration of Ponte Cestio. It was fortified in the early Middle Ages and made into a stronghold by the Savelli and Orsini families. Renaissance architects frequently studied the theatre. In the 16C it was converted into a palace for the Savelli by Baldassare Peruzzi who built the façade into the curved exterior of the cavea. The theatre was restored in 1932, when numerous houses and shops on the site were demolished.

The cavea originally had at least two tiers of 41 arches, the first with Doric and the second with Ionic engaged columns probably crowned by an attic of the Corinthian order. Only 12 arches in each of the first two tiers survive; the upper stage has disappeared in the course of various alterations. The theatre could probably have held some 15,000 spectators.

Beside the theatre are three conspicuous columns which belonged to the **Temple of Apollo Medico**, built in 433 BC and restored by the consul Caius Sosius in 33 BC. Nearby are the ruins of the Temple of Bellona, built in 296 BC.

Via Montanara leads away from Via del Teatro di Marcello past the pretty deconsecrated church of **Santa Rita** by Carlo Fontana, moved here in 1937 from the foot of the Capitoline Hill, below Santa Maria in Aracoeli. It has an interesting oval interior, used for exhibitions.

Beyond opens the handsome Piazza Campitelli, which is unexpectedly peaceful. The lovely **fountain** (1589) was designed by Giacomo della Porta. Beneath the pretty upper marble bowl is a delicately carved Classical decoration with garlands of fruit. On the lower travertine basin are shields with the coats of arms of the Roman families who lived nearby and helped pay for the erection of the fountain, as well as the initials SPQR representing the municipality. Facing the church are three fine palaces: the 16C Palazzo Cavalletti at no. 1, and Palazzo Albertoni and Palazzo Capizucchi at nos 2 and 3, both dating from the late 16C and attributed to Giacomo della Porta.

The charming façade of **Santa Maria in Campitelli** (Map 7; 5, 7) was erected by Carlo Rainaldi when the church was rebuilt (1662–67) in honour of a tiny, miraculous image of the *Madonna*, which was believed to have halted an outbreak of pestilence. Open daily 07.00–12.00 and 16.00–19.00. The fine **interior** has an intricate perspective effect using numerous arches, columns and a heavy cornice. In the second chapel on the right is an altarpiece of *St Anne, St Joachim and the Virgin* by Luca Giordano (there is a light on the right). Here also is the cast of an altar dedicated to Santa Maria in Portico by Pope Gregory VII in 1073. On it has been placed a reproduction of the image of the *Madonna*, a small work in gilded bronze and enamel, perhaps dating from the 11C, the original of which is preserved at the east end above the altar, surrounded by an elaborate Baroque gold frame. In the first chapel on the left are two tombs of the Altieri family; in the left transept, the *Birth of St John the Baptist* is by Baciccia.

Via Cavalletti and Via de'Delfini lead east out of the piazza to the picturesque **Piazza Margana**, where several houses are hung with old vines. At no. 19 Palazzo Maccarani-Odescalchi, with a pretty courtyard, dates from the 17C.

Via de'Funari, named from the rope-makers who used to live here, leads out of the north side of Piazza Campitelli, through an area of charming old streets, to **Santa Caterina dei Funari** (Map 7; 5), a church built in 1560–64 by Cardinal Federico Cesi. It has a fine façade, in need of cleaning, by Guidetto Guidetti (1564) and an original campanile. The interior contains 16C paintings by Girolamo Muziano, Scipione Pulzone, Livio Agresti, Federico Zuccari and Marcello Venusti, and a fine stuccoed and painted *chapel by Vignola.

Across Via Caetani (see p 202) is the huge **Palazzo Mattei**, which comprises five palaces of the 16C and 17C. The fine façades in Via dei Funari and Via Michelangelo are by Carlo Maderno. In the little Piazza Mattei, nos 19 and 17 open onto courts, and a third door at no. 31 Via dei Funari gives access to a fine courtyard and a staircase beautifully decorated with 17C stuccoes surrounding antique reliefs. Inside are frescoes by Domenichino, Giovanni Lanfranco and Francesco Albani. Parts of the buildings, now owned by the State, are used by the *Centro Italiano di Studi Americani*.

The charming **Fontana delle Tartarughe** in Piazza Mattei, by Taddeo Landini (1584) to a design by Giacomo della Porta, was restored in 1658, perhaps by Bernini, when the tortoises were added; these have now been replaced by copies. At the south-west angle of the piazza is Palazzo Costaguti (no admission), with ceilings on the first floor painted by Albani, Domenichino, Guercino, Lanfranco and others.

The Ghetto

Via della Reginella, a survival from the old Ghetto, leads out of Piazza Mattei to emerge on Via del Portico d'Ottavio, in an area formerly occupied by the Ghetto.

History of the Ghetto

From 1556 onwards the Jews of Rome were segregated and subject to various restrictions on their personal freedom, although to a lesser degree than in other European countries. Even so, Pope Paul IV forced them to wear distinctive yellow hats and to sell their property to Christians. The walls of the Ghetto were torn down only in 1848, and the houses demolished in 1888 before the area south of Via del Portico d'Ottavia was reconstructed around the new synagogue. Many Jewish people still live in the area between Lungotevere Cenci, Via Catalana and Via del Portico d'Ottavia.

In the wide Via del Portico d'Ottavia, on the right at no. 1 is the **Casa di Lorenzo Manilio**, with a handsome long inscription in fine marble lettering dating the house in the ancient Roman manner, to 2221 years after the foundation of Rome (i.e. 1468), and decorated with ancient Roman sculptural fragments. On the façade facing Piazza Costaguti, the patriotic invocation *Have Roma* ('Hail Rome!') can be seen above three of the first-floor windows, which also date from the time of Manilio. Also here is a charming little 18C portico, once belonging to a chapel but now in very poor condition, next to a picturesque passageway.

On the other side of Via del Portico d'Ottavio is the ugly Piazza delle Cinque Scole, laid out in the 19C when the Ghetto was demolished, with a fountain from Piazza Giudea by Giacomo della Porta. The name of the piazza recalls the five synagogues which once occupied a building here. **Palazzo Cenci**, restored in the 16C, belonged to the family of Beatrice Cenci who was beheaded for parricide in 1599 (see p 236). At the end is Monte de Cenci, an artificial mound—probably on Roman remains—with a pretty little piazza between Palazzo Cenci and the church of **San Tommaso dei Cenci**. An antique altar is incorporated into its façade. It contains a chapel frescoed by Sermoneta (1575) and two carved Roman brackets supporting a side altar. The church is sometimes open on Sunday at 10.30.

Via del Portico d'Ottavio leads back towards the Teatro di Marcello past several medieval houses, including no. 13 (in very poor repair), with a fine court with *loggie*, and a number of restaurants. At the end, the shop at no. 25 has an ancient Roman architrave framing the door. Here is the church of **Sant'Angelo in Pescheria**, founded in 755 inside the ancient Roman **Portico of Octavia** (Map 3; 8).

History of the Portico of Octavia

This was once a huge rectangular portico (c 119m by 132m) with about 300 columns, which enclosed two temples dedicated to Jupiter and Juno. Erected by Quinto Cecilio Metello in 146 BC, it was reconstructed by Augustus in honour of his sister Octavia c 23 BC, and restored by Septimius Severus in AD 203. The southern extremities of the area of the portico have been exposed, and remains of columns to the west and the stylobate to the east can also be seen.

The entrances consisted of two propylaea with eight columns and four piers; the one on the south-west survives and now serves as a monumental entrance to the church. The portico was used from the 12C as a fish market (hence the name of the church, in Pescheria) up until the destruction of the Ghetto in 1888. An arch was added, and the pediment repaired in the Middle Ages.

The **church** of Sant'Angelo in Pescheria was rebuilt in the 16C and contains a fresco of the *Madonna Enthroned with Angels* attributed to Benozzo Gozzoli or his school, and an early 12C *Madonna and Child*. Open Wed at 17.30 and Sat at 17.00. From this church Cola di Rienzo and his followers set out to seize the

Capitoline on the night of Pentecost, 1347. Here from 1584 until the 19C papacy of Pius IX, the Jews were forced to listen to a Christian sermon every Saturday. Excavations of the portico in front of the church, surrounded by an ugly fence, appear to have been abandoned: remains of the portico can also be seen on the right of the church, beyond which rises the Teatro di Marcello and the three tall columns of the temple of Apollo Medico.

On the wall of the little 'medieval' house here (now the headquarters of the antique monuments and archaeological excavations office of the Comune di Roma) a plaque commemorates the 2091 Roman Jews who died in concentration camps in the Second World War (along with 6000 other Italian Jews). The area roughly occupied by the old Ghetto, from here to Via Arenula, and between Via del Portico d'Ottavia and the Tiber, is now recognised as the site of the Circus of Flaminius (221 BC).

The monumental **Synagogue** (**Map 7**; 7) was built on Lungotevere dei Cenci by Vincenzo Costa and Osvaldo Armanni in 1899–1904. It contains a **Museum of Jewish Art**, illustrating the history of the community in the city. Open Mon–Thur 09.00–16.30; Fri 09.00–13.30; Sun 09.00–12.00; closed Sat. ☎ 06 6840 0661. A Holy Ark in marble dating from 1523, but incorporating some Roman fragments, which was demolished in 1908–10, has been reconstructed and temporarily exhibited in the vaults of the synagogue.

From the left side of Sant'Angelo in Pescheria the narrow old Via della Tribuna di Campitelli leads back past a harshly restored old house with Ionic columns set into its façade, to Piazza Campitelli (see above).

Isola Tiberina

Lungotevere dei Cenci faces the Isola Tiberina (**Map 7**; 7), a pretty little island in the Tiber, reached by **Ponte Fabricio**, the oldest Roman bridge to have survived in the city and still in use for pedestrians. The inscription over the fine arches records the name of the builder, Lucius Fabricius, and the date, 62 BC. The bridge is also known as the Ponte dei Quattro Capi from the two herms of the four-headed Janus on the parapet. Remains of the 'Ponte Rotto' (see p 324) can be seen downstream.

History of the Isola Tiberina

The island, which provides an easy crossing-place on the Tiber, is thought to have been settled early in the history of Rome. During a plague in the city in 293 BC the Sybelline books were consulted and ambassadors were sent to the famous sanctuary of Asklepios, the god of healing, at Epidauros in Greece. They returned with his symbol, the sacred serpent, which escaped from its basket and was found on this island, so it was decided that here a temple to the god, called by the Romans Aesculapius, should be erected: the building was dedicated in 289 BC. Ever since, the island has been associated with the work of healing. It is now largely occupied by the hospital of the Fatebenefratelli, founded in 1548 and modernised by Cesare Bazzani in 1930–34. The island was formerly encircled with a facing of travertine, a portion of which still remains at the extremity. It is in the form of a ship with the serpent of Aesculapius carved on it in relief.

On the right is the church of **San Giovanni Calibita** founded in the 11C and reconstructed in 1640. In the 18C interior is a ceiling painting by Corrado Giaquinto. On the left is a tall medieval tower, formerly part of an 11C fortress, and Piazza San Bartolomeo.

The church of **San Bartolomeo**, on the site of the Temple of Aesculapius, was built in the 10C in honour of St Adalbert, Bishop of Prague, and several times restored, notably by Orazio Torriani in 1624. The tower is Romanesque, and the interior contains 14 antique columns, and an interesting sculptured well-head on the chancel steps, probably from the original church. There is a hall crypt beneath the transept.

The south side of the island is joined to Trastevere (see Walk 14) by the **Ponte Cestio**, probably built by Lucius Cestius in 46 BC, restored in AD 370, and rebuilt in 1892, the central arch to its original design and measurements.

30 • The Janiculum Hill

The Janiculum (Map 6; 5, 7) or Gianicolo, though not counted as one of the Seven Hills of Rome, is a ridge rising steeply from the Tiber and approximately parallel to its course for the whole of its length. The hill's highest point, to the south, is Porta San Pancrazio (82m); to the north it reaches almost as far as Piazza San Pietro. It is now mostly covered with parks and gardens, and offers wonderful views from the ridge. It has two important churches: at its southern end, San Pietro in Montorio, with a superb fresco by Sebastiano del Piombo and the celebrated Tempietto by Bramante in its courtyard; and to the north, Sant'Onofrio. Some way further west, outside Porta San Pancrazio, is the huge public park of Villa Doria Pamphilj.

The Janiculum is crossed by bus No. 870 (infrequent service) from Corso Vittorio Emanuele II (Via Paola), near the Tiber (Map 6; 3). By foot the prettiest approach is from Trastevere, taking Via Garibaldi or Vicolo del Cedro behind Piazza Sant'Egidio (see Walk 14).

History of the Janiculum Hill

The hill's ancient name was *Mons Aureus*, which referred to the yellow sand which covers its surface. The name of *Mons Janiculus* is derived from the old Italian deity Janus, who, according to legend, founded a city on the hill; his temple was in the Roman Forum. Numa Pompilius, the Sabine successor of Romulus, was buried on the Janiculum, and Ancus Marcius, the fourth king, is said to have built the Pons Sublicius over the Tiber to connect the Janiculum with the city of Rome. The hill provided a natural defence against the Etruscans, but it does not appear to have been fortified until after 87 BC, during a period of civil strife between Marius and Sulla, when a wall was built from Pons Aemilius to the Porta Aurelia (Porta San Pancrazio).

Part of the Janiculum was included within the Aurelian Walls, and it was completely surrounded by Urban VIII when he built his wall in 1642. It was the scene of Garibaldi's heroic stand in defence of the Roman Republic against French troops commanded by Nicolas Oudinot in 1849.

Via Garibaldi (**Map 6; 8**) mounts the hill from Trastevere. Above the church of Santa Maria dei Sette Dolori (see p 221), on the right, is the former entrance gate to the Bosco Parrasio, where in 1725 the academy of **Arcadia** was established. It was founded in 1690 to carry on the work of the academy inaugurated by Queen Christina of Sweden ten years before for the discussion of literary and political topics. The object of Arcadia was to eliminate bad literary taste and to purify the Italian language, and it exercised a profound influence on Italian literature during the 18C. In 1786 Goethe was admitted as a 'distinguished shepherd'. Later its importance waned and in 1926 it was absorbed into the *Accademia Letteraria Italiana*.

The paintings which belong to the academy are at present kept at the Museo di Roma (see p 204). The garden can sometimes be seen on request at 32 Via di Porta San Pancrazio. Beyond a lovely circular dining-room with a dome (1725) by Antonio Canevari is an amphitheatre, from which steps wind down through a small wood, circling a giant Roman pine.

San Pietro in Montorio

Via Garibaldi continues to mount in sweeping curves (if you are on foot you can take a short cut via steps to the right of the road), until it reaches a terrace. Here is the church of San Pietro in Montorio (**Map 6**; **7**), built on a site wrongly presumed to have been the scene of St Peter's crucifixion. Open daily 07.30–12.00 and 16.00–18.30. There are press-button lights in some of the chapels.

History of San Pietro in Montorio

Mentioned in the 9C, the church was rebuilt in the late 15C at the expense of King Ferdinand of Aragon and his wife Isabella, Queen of Castile. The apse and campanile, damaged in the siege of 1849, were restored in 1851. Raphael's *Transfiguration* (now in the Vatican Pinacoteca) adorned the apse from 1523 to 1809. The church is the burial place of Beatrice Cenci, beheaded as a parricide at Ponte Sant' Angelo in 1599 (see p 236), and Hugh O'Neill of Tyrone and Roderick O'Donnell of Tyrconnel (1608), leaders in the Irish revolt against James I.

In front of the fine travertine **façade** attributed to the school of Andrea Bregno is a group of palm trees and a terrace with a view (partly blocked by trees) of a number of domed churches and the Vittorio Emanuele II monument and, in the distance among the trees of its garden, the Villa Medici.

In the **interior** on the **south side**, the first chapel contains the **Flagellation*, a superb work by Sebastiano del Piombo from designs by Michelangelo. Commissioned by the Florentine banker Pierfrancesco Borgherini in 1521, it is one of the most remarkable frescoes in Rome outside the Vatican. The frescoes in the vault of the *Transfiguration* and saints and prophets are by the same artist. In the second chapel the *Madonna della Lettera* is a detached fresco fragment attributed to Giovanni Battista Lombardelli; above are the **Coronation of the Virgin and four Virtues* attributed to Baldassare Peruzzi. The fifth chapel has an altarpiece of the *Conversion of St Paul* by Giorgio Vasari, and a balustrade and two tombs by Bartolomeo Ammannati. The apse is decorated with a copy of Guido Reni's *Crucifixion of St Peter* now in the Vatican.

On the **north side**, the fifth chapel, designed by Daniele da Volterra, contains a *Baptism of Christ* attributed to Giulio Mazzoni. The fourth chapel, designed by Carlo Maderno, has pretty stuccowork also attributed to Mazzoni; and three paintings by a Flemish artist, probably Dirk Baburen (1617), a pupil of Caravaggio. The third chapel has an altarpiece after Antoniazzo Romano. The second, the Raimondi chapel, has an early work by Bernini, with an unusual relief of the *Ecstasy of St Francis* executed by his pupils Francesco Baratta and Andrea Bolgi. The first chapel contains *St Francis Receiving the Stigmata* by Giovanni de Vecchi. Near the west door is the tomb of Giuliano da Volterra (d. 1510), by a follower of Andrea Bregno.

The second door on the right of the church, flanked by two oleander bushes, gives access to a courtyard with the *Tempietto, an extremely important Renaissance work by Donato Bramante that is usually dated 1499–1502 or 1508–12. Erected on the supposed exact site of St Peter's martyrdom, it is a miniature circular building with 16 Doric columns of granite, which combines all the grace of the 15C with the full splendour of the 16C. It can be seen from the gate, but to see the interior ring at the convent, 08.00–12.00 and 16.00–19.00. Stairs designed by Bernini lead down to a crypt with pretty stuccoes by Giovanni Francesco Rossi. To the right of the court is the Spanish Academy.

Bramante's Tempietto

Porta San Pancrazio and Villa Doria Pamphilj

Via Garibaldi continues to a monument by Giovanni Jacobucci (1941), which commemorates the defenders and deliverers of Rome in 1849–70, and incorporates the tomb of Goffredo Mameli (1827–49), the patriot, poet and author of *Fratelli d'Italia*, the Italian national anthem. Further on is the fountain of the **Acqua Paola**, constructed—as the handsome inscription states—for Paul V, by Giovanni Fontana and Flaminio Ponzio (1612), using marble from the Roman Forum. The water, which flows abundantly from the subterranean Aqueduct of Trajan, itself fed by springs near Lake Bracciano about 48km north-west of Rome, falls into a large granite basin added by Carlo Fontana in 1690, beneath six columns, four of which are from the façade of Old St Peter's. The building now unexpectedly houses a small theatre with some 100 seats, run by a theatre club. The Rome water company turns off the fountain for two hours when performances are being held. When the club is open you can ask to go up to the roof above the fountain, from where there is a splendid view. A plaque set up in 1726 records the owners of each of the conduits served by the aqueduct. The charming little garden with bougainvillea and vines has some Classical fragments.

On the right of the road is a subsidiary entrance to the Passeggiata del Gianicolo (see below). At the top of the hill is the **Porta San Pancrazio** (Map 6; 7), built by Urban VIII, and rebuilt by Virginio Vespignani in 1857 after the decisive battle here between the French forces and Garibaldi in 1849. This gate, once known as the Porta Aurelia, was the starting-point of the Via Aurelia.

To the right of the gate is the Villa Aurelia (also rebuilt after 1849), acquired by the **American Academy in Rome** in 1911 (the main seat of the Academy, with the library, is now a short way further south, entered from Via Masina). Viale delle Mura Gianicolensi leads south to the **Villa Sciarra** (Map 8; 3), with a beautiful garden laid out in 1902–30 by George Wurts. Open daily 07.00–dusk.

It has particularly fine wisteria which flowers in early spring. Beyond is the residential district of Monteverde.

In front of Porta San Pancrazio, Via di San Pancrazio leads south-west past Via Giacinto Carini in which a plaque set up in 2000 marks the house (no. 45) where the writer Pier Paolo Pasolini lived from 1959 to 1963. In Via di San Pancrazio are the ruins of the Vascello, a Baroque villa where Goffredo Mameli and Luciano Manara were killed in a last sally in 1849. Further on is an entrance to the **Villa Doria Pamphilj** or Belrespiro, by far the largest park in Rome (9km round). It was laid out in 1644–52 for Prince Camillo Pamphilj, nephew of Innocent X. The beautiful park is owned partly by the State and partly by the Comune of Rome and is open to the public daily, sunrise to sunset. The historic gardens within the park were restored in 2000. The views take in the environs of Rome (including stretches of the open countryside of the Roman Campagna) as well as the city, and the splendid umbrella pines are a special feature of the park. The grounds were cut in two in 1960 by the Via Olimpica.

The **Casino del Bel Respiro** in the park, a splendid Baroque building, is the most important architectural work of Alessandro Algardi dating from 1644–52. He was assisted by Giovanni Francesco Grimaldi, and possibly also Bernini. Algardi was responsible for the stuccoes (1646). Surrounded by a formal garden it is sometimes used for receptions by the Italian State, and is not normally open to the public.

On the northern edge of the park, approached from Via Aurelia Antica at no. 183 is the **Villa Vecchia**, decorated with exquisite stuccoes by Francesco Nicoletti in 1749–51.

Via di San Pancrazio (see above) passes the basilica of **San Pancrazio**, on the site of the tomb of St Pancras who—according to Christian tradition—was martyred under Diocletian in 304. A Christian cemetery and 5C oratory existed here, and the present large basilica was built by Honorius I in 630, and remodelled in the 17C. The Baroque interior, which has been undergoing restoration for many years, incorporates the apse, part of the transept and the annular crypt of the 7C church. The 4C Catacombs of San Pancrazio contain Oriental inscriptions. Admission from the church, Mon–Sat.

The Passeggiata di Gianicolo

Beyond Porta San Pancrazio is the beginning of the Passeggiata di Gianicolo (**Map 6**; **7**), a wide avenue with fine pine trees laid out in 1884 across the former grounds of the Villa Corsini, above the fortifications of Urban VIII. At Piazzale del Gianicolo, where there is a panoramic terrace, the road is joined by that from the Acqua Paola (see above). The conspicuous **equestrian statue of Garibaldi** by Emilio Gallori, erected in 1895 on the site of the hero's exploits of 1849, stands here. Around the base are four bronze groups: in front, *Charge of Manara's Bersaglieri* (Rome, 1849); behind, *Battle of Calatafimi* (Sicily, 1860); at the sides, *Europe* and *America*. The statue itself is 7m high. Every day a cannon is wheeled out of the storeroom below the terrace by a small group of soldiers and a blank shot is fired at 12 noon, which can be heard all over the centre of the city.

The Passeggiata now goes downhill. On the right is the **Villa Lante**, built by Giulio Romano in 1518–27, and owned by Finland since 1950. On the left is the bronze equestrian statue of *Anita Garibaldi*, Garibaldi's wife, by Mario Rutelli, presented by the Brazilian Government in 1935 to honour her Brazilian origin, and incorporating her tomb. Further on is a memorial tower by Manfredo Manfredi, presented to Rome in 1911 by Italian residents in Argentina.

From this point there is an especially fine **view** of Rome, even better (because it is clear of trees) than that from Piazzale del Gianicolo. On the extreme left is the dome of St Peter's, then Castel Sant'Angelo, San Giovanni dei Fiorentini, Palazzo di Giustizia and the modern Prati district, with the green slopes of the Villa Borghese, the Pincio and the gardens of the Villa Medici behind, among which the French Academy and the Trinità dei Monti stand out. To the right is the façade of Montecitorio with its clock. Below the hill is the prison of Regina Coeli, and beyond the river the little spire of the church of Sant'Ivo, the dome of the Pantheon, and the Quirinal palace. Further to the right is Sant'Andrea and, in the distance, the bell-tower and domes of Santa Maria Maggiore. Then come the Torre delle Milizie, the triple-arched loggia of the Palazzo Farnese, the Vittorio Emanuele II monument, the bell-tower of Palazzo Senatorio on the Capitoline Hill, and the dome of the Synagogue. Behind them are the statues crowning the façade of San Giovanni in Laterano. Among the trees of the Gianicolo, on the extreme right, is the Acqua Paola. The Alban, Tiburtine and Praenestine hills fall away gradually on the right.

The avenue continues downhill and a short flight of steps leads up to the little Piazzale di Sant'Onofrio, with ilex trees and a fountain. Here is the church of **Sant'Onofrio** (Map 6; 5), founded by Blessed Nicolò da Forca Palena in 1419 and restored by Pius IX in 1857. Open Sun 09.00–13.00, or by appointment. ☎ 06 686 4498.

A graceful L-shaped Renaissance portico connects the church and monastery. In the lunettes beneath the portico are three frescoes from the *Life of St Jerome* (his baptism, chastisement for reading Cicero and temptation) by Domenichino, and over the door, a *Madonna* by Claudio Ridolfi. By the convent entrance is the tomb of the founder.

The dark **interior** is paved with numerous tombstones. On the left, the first chapel contains a monument by Giuseppe de Fabris (1857) to the poet Torquato Tasso (see below), and the third chapel, the tombstone of Cardinal Mezzofanti (d. 1849), who could speak 50 or 60 languages. In the pretty apse over the main altar are repainted frescoes by the school of Pinturicchio. The fresco of *St Anne Teaching the Virgin to Read*, on the right above the monument of Giovanni Sacco (d. 1505), is by a pupil of Andrea Bregno. The second chapel on the right contains a *Madonna di Loreto* attributed to Annibale Carracci or his school; in the vault pendentives above the altar in the first chapel, the *Annunciation* is by Antoniazzo Romano (there is a light).

The **monastery**, now occupied by American friars of the Atonement, has a charming 15C cloister with frescoes of the *Life of St Onophrius* by Cavaliere d'Arpino, Sebastiano Strada and Claudio Ridolfi. In the atrium is a monument to the 'Arcadian' poet, Alessandro Guidi (d. 1712). In the upper corridor, above a glazed terracotta Della Robbia frieze, is a much-repainted fresco of the *Virgin with a Donor* attributed to Giovanni Antonio Boltraffio. The epic poet Torquato Tasso (1544–95) spent his last days and died here. The Museo Tassiano contains the poet's death mask, mementoes, manuscripts and editions and translations of his works. Admission only by appointment with the Cavalieri del Santo Sepolcro, 33 Via della Conciliazione.

The steep Salita di Sant'Onofrio leads down to the Tiber at Piazza della Rovere

(**Map** 6; 3), where Via della Lungara also terminates. A gentler descent is by the road to the left, which passes the buildings of the pontifical North American College. **Ponte Principe Amedeo** (1942) crosses the Tiber, and on the left is the road tunnel known as the Traforo Principe Amedeo, which leads under the Janiculum to Largo di Porta Cavalleggeri. In 2000 a huge six-storey underground car park was built here by the Vatican to house as many as 100 tour coaches and about 800 cars (with escalators up to the Audience Hall in Vatican City and numerous facilities for tour groups). Despite the fact it is on land which belongs to the Vatican, half of the funding was supplied by the Italian State. During construction of the access ramp in 1999 some frescoed rooms of a Roman *domus* of c 1C–2C AD were found. After a public outcry and protests from numerous scholars it was decided to detach the frescoes and go ahead with excavations but at the same time complete the car park and its three entrances. The creation of the car park has also entailed the destruction of a fragment of the Leonine wall built to defend the Borgo in the 9C and the damage of a bastion built by Antonio da Sangallo the Younger in 1543. The Porta Santo Spirito, an unfinished gateway begun in 1540 by Antonio da Sangallo leads by Via dei Penitenzieri into the Città Leonina, or rione of the Borgo (see Walk 31).

31 • The Borgo and Castel Sant'Angelo

The Borgo (Map 6; 3, 1), a district on the right bank of the Tiber, has always been associated with the Catholic Church, since it was here that St Peter was buried and the first church of St Peter's built on the site of his tomb. It was the stronghold of the papacy from 850 until 1586, when it was formally incorporated in the city of Rome. Five streets in the district still have the prefix Borgo. Borgo Sant'Angelo and Borgo Santo Spirito run respectively north and south of Via della Conciliazione (in the construction of which the original Borgo Nuovo and Borgo Vecchio were destroyed). The Borghi Angelico, Vittorio and Pio survive between the Castel Sant'Angelo and the Vatican.

This chapter describes Castel Sant'Angelo, first built as a mausoleum by the Emperor Hadrian but later adapted by the popes as a fortress. It is a massive edifice, and most of the interesting interior is open as a museum. It is approached across the Tiber by Bernini's Ponte Sant'Angelo. Vatican City and St Peter's, in the main part of the Borgo, are described in Walks 32–34.

History of the Borgo

The Borgo was known in ancient Rome as *Ager Vaticanus*. It was chosen by Caligula (AD 37–41) for his circus, which was enlarged by Nero (54–68). (The site of the Circus of Nero, just south of the basilica of St Peter's, was identified during excavations in the 20C.) In the adjoining gardens many Christians were martyred under Nero in AD 65, including St Peter, who was buried in a pagan cemetery nearby. Over his grave the first church of St Peter's was built (c AD 90) to commemorate his martyrdom. Also within the Ager Vaticanus, Hadrian built his mausoleum (now Castel Sant'Angelo) in 135.

Inscriptions found on the temples of Cybele and Mithras suggest that paganism retained its hold with great tenacity here up until the late 4C. Despite this tendency, churches, chapels and convents were built round the first church of St Peter, and the district attracted Saxon, Frank and Lombard pilgrims. Around this time it came to be called the Borgo (borough), a name of Germanic origin from *borgus*, meaning a small fortified settlement. In 850 Leo IV (847–55) surrounded the Borgo with walls 12m high, fortified with circular towers, to protect it from the incursions of the Saracens: hence the name Civitas Leonina or Città Leonina. Remnants of Leo IV's wall survive to the west of St Peter's. The Leonine City became the papal citadel: within its walls John VIII was besieged in 878 by the Duke of Spoleto; in 896 Arnulph of Carinthia attacked it and Formosus crowned him emperor. Gregory VII took refuge in the Castel Sant'Angelo from the Emperor Henry IV, and was rescued by Robert Guiscard in 1084. After the coronation in 1167 of Barbarossa in St Peter's, the Romans besieged the Leonine City, and it was attacked again 12 years later.

During the 'Babylonian captivity' (1309–78), when the papacy was in Avignon, the Borgo fell into ruin, but when the popes returned to Rome they chose the Vatican as their residence in place of the Lateran. In the 15C Eugenius IV and Sixtus IV, and early in the 16C Julius II and Leo X, were active in developing and embellishing the Borgo as well as the Vatican. The original area of the Borgo was enlarged to the north of Borgo Angelico. After the Sack of Rome in 1527, however, the Borgo became one of the poorest and least populated districts of Rome, and in 1586 Sixtus V relinquished the papal claim to this area, so that it was united to the city of Rome.

The celebrated **Ponte Sant'Angelo** (Map 6; 3)—pedestrians only—the ancient Pons Aelius or Pons Adrianus, was built by Hadrian (Aelius Hadrianus) in 134 as a fitting approach from the Campus Martius (see p 200) to his mausoleum, known since the Middle Ages as the Castel Sant'Angelo. Although the Roman bridge was decorated with statues, it was transformed by Gian Lorenzo Bernini when he designed the ten statues of *Angels* holding the symbols of the Passion. These were executed in 1688 by his pupils, including Ercole Ferrata, Pietro Paolo Naldini, Cosimo Fancelli and Ercole Antonio Raggi; two of the angels on the balustrade are copies of the originals, which are in the church of Sant'Andrea delle Fratte. At the end towards the castle, the statues of *St Peter* and *St Paul*, by the school of Lorenzetto and Paolo Taccone (1464), were set up by Clement VII in 1534. The three central arches of the bridge are part of the original structure; the end arches were restored and enlarged in 1892–94 during the construction

of the Lungotevere embankments.

Upstream is **Ponte Vittorio Emanuele** (1911), decorated with monumental sculptures in travertine, and bronze Victories.

Ponte Sant'Angelo

Castel Sant'Angelo

Facing the bridge is Castel Sant'Angelo (**Map 6; 1, 3**), an enormous circular structure begun by Hadrian as a mausoleum for himself and his family. In the early Middle Ages the tomb was surrounded with ramparts and became the citadel of Rome. In its general plan, the castle follows the shape of Hadrian's mausoleum, the exact design of which is unknown. The curtain walls of the inner ward, between the medieval bastions, are original; so is the entrance (no longer in use), except that the Roman threshold was lower. The round tower is Hadrian's, without its marble facing and its statues. Above it are additions of the Renaissance and later, such as the arcaded galleries. The central tower was the base of a statue of Hadrian driving a chariot, now replaced by a bronze angel. The pentagonal outer ward, added in the 16C, used to have five bastions; two of them were demolished during the construction of Piazza Pia and of the Lungotevere. The ditch between the two fortifications, planted with trees and covered with lawns, is a public park.

Opening times

09.00–19.00, closed Mon. ☎ 06 681 9111. Some rooms are often closed, and sometimes certain areas of the castle are temporarily inaccessible; the works of art are frequently rearranged.

Guided tours of some parts of the castle not normally open to the public, including the prisons and the covered passageway which connected the castle to the Vatican (but this is temporarily closed in 2002), are usually provided on certain days of the year (often on Sat & Sun): booking is necessary, ☎ 06 681 9111. The interior of the castle is a labyrinth of rooms, staircases, courtyards and terraces, making it easy to get lost, but the various parts are numbered with arabic numerals that correspond to the numbers given in the description below, and the four plans within the text.

There is a **café (60)** in the Gallery of Pius IV. There is also a lift, reserved for staff and the disabled.

History of Castel Sant'Angelo

The mausoleum was begun by Hadrian c 128 and was completed in 139, a year after his death, by his successor Antoninus Pius. Rising to a height of nearly 50m, it consisted of a base 89m square and a circular structure above supporting a central round tower 64m in diameter, of peperino and travertine overlaid with marble. Above this was an earthen tumulus planted with cypress trees. At the top was an altar bearing a bronze quadriga driven by Hadrian, represented as the Sun, ruler of the world. Inside the building, a spiral ramp which is still in existence led to a straight passageway ending in the cella, in which was the Imperial tomb. Hadrian, his wife Sabina and his adopted son Aelius Caesar were buried in the mausoleum, as were succeeding emperors until Septimius Severus (211). When Aurelian built his wall round Rome, he continued it on the left bank of the Tiber opposite the Porta Settimiana. He built the Porta Aurelia Nova on the city side of the Pons Aelius and made Hadrian's mausoleum into a bridgehead on the other side of the river, surrounding it with a wall strengthened with towers.

The mausoleum was gradually transformed into a castle. Theodoric (474–526) used it as a prison and for a time it became known as the Carceri Theodorici. According to legend, while crossing the Pons Aelius at the head of a procession to pray for the cessation of the plague of 590, St Gregory the Great saw an angel sheathing his sword on the top of the fortress. The vision accurately announced the end of the plague and from then onwards the castle bore its present name.

In the following centuries the possession of Castel Sant'Angelo was contested between popes and antipopes, the imperial forces and the Roman barons. In 1084 Gregory VII was rescued from Henry IV's siege by Robert Guiscard. By the late 12C the castle was established as papal property. It was from here that Cola di Rienzo fled to Bohemia on 15 December 1347, at the end of his first period of dictatorship. In 1378 the castle was severely damaged by the citizens of Rome, resentful of foreign domination.

In the reign of Boniface IX rebuilding began. Alexander VI had Antonio da Sangallo the Elder complete the four bastions of the square inner ward which had been begun by Nicholas V. After these improvements it was estimated that the castle could withstand a three-year siege. Julius II built the south loggia, facing the river. When Clement VII and some 1000 followers (including 13 cardinals and 18 bishops) took refuge here in 1527 from the troops of Charles V, Benvenuto Cellini took part in its defence (in his *Autobiography* he gives a colourful description of his valour and marksmanship on this occasion). Paul III built the north loggia and decorated the interior with frescoes. The outer ward, with its defensive ditch, was added by Pius IV. Urban VIII provided the castle with cannon made of bronze taken from the ceiling of the Pantheon portico, and he employed Bernini to remodel the outer defences.

From 1849 to 1870 the castle was occupied by French troops. Under the Italian Government it was used as barracks and as a prison until 1901, when the work of restoration was begun. In 1933–34 the castle was adapted for use as a museum and the surrounding area was cleared.

The castle is particularly interesting for its architecture, and now contains the **Museo Nazionale di Castel Sant'Angelo**, inaugurated in 1925. The 58 rooms, some of which have fine 16C stuccoes and frescoes, contain a collection of paintings, furniture, and tapestries, as well as a military museum (partially closed). The views of Rome and the Tiber are superb.

The castle is entered from the gardens on the east side. A ramp leads down to the **Portone Peruzzi**, an entrance gate to the castle built in 1556 by Giovanni Sallustio Peruzzi for Paul VI. It was adapted in 1628 for the use of barracks built by Urban VIII, but had to be demolished and moved to this side of the castle in 1892 when the Lungotevere was built. Inside the gate a cobbled street leads left between the foot of Hadrian's splendid round tower and the medieval castle walls past two vaulted oil stores (**79**), where architectural and sculptural fragments found in the castle, including Roman and Byzantine pieces, have been arranged. Also displayed here are three models of the castle as it has appeared at three different stages since the 16C. Opposite the main entrance to the castle (now closed), iron stairs lead down to an underground **vestibule** (**1**), with two models of Hadrian's tomb. The shaft (**2**) of a lift built for the infirm Leo X can be seen here, and a niche for a statue of Hadrian. On the right is a **spiral ramp** (**3**), 125.5m long, which rises gently to the sepulchral cella. The ramp, dating from Roman times, is in a remarkable state of preservation; the floor has remains of mosaic decoration. Along it are four vents, one of which was converted into a prison, mentioned by Benvenuto Cellini.

The **Staircase of Alexander VI** (5) cuts diametrically across the circular Roman building. By means of a bridge (6) built in 1822 by Giuseppe Valadier in place of a drawbridge, the staircase passes above the Roman **sepulchral cella** (7), of which only the travertine wall-blocks survive, with some fragments of marble decoration. The urns containing the Imperial ashes were kept here. Hadrian's porphyry sarcophagus was taken by Innocent II (1130–43) for use as his own tomb in San Giovanni in Laterano, where it was destroyed by fire in 1360.

At a landing lit by a round window (9), the Staircase of Alexander VI originally turned to the right. Paul III closed this section and opened one to the left (10), by Antonio da Sangallo the Younger, to give access to the **Courtyard of the Angel** (11), named after the marble statue of an *Angel* (13) by Raffaello da Montelupo, removed here from the terrace at the top of the castle.

At the end of the court are the Staircase of Urban VIII and the façade by Michelangelo of the **Medici Chapel** (12), built c 1514 for Leo X. On the right is a series of rooms on two levels which house a **Museum of Arms and Armour** (14, 15 and II–VII), now partly closed. The collection has material from the Stone Age to the 20C, and includes 15C–18C arms found during excavations within the

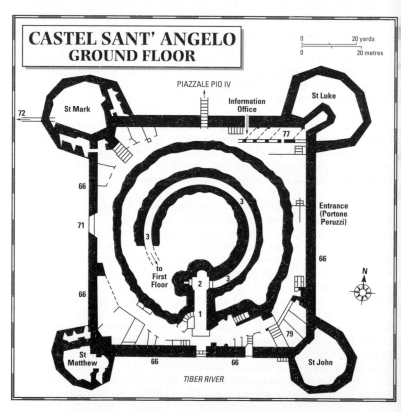

CASTEL SANT' ANGELO
GROUND FLOOR

0   20 yards
0   20 metres

PIAZZALE PIO IV

Information Office

St Mark

St Luke

72

77

66

71

3

3

Entrance
(Portone
Peruzzi)

66

to
First
Floor

2

3

1

79

66

66

St Matthew

St John

N

TIBER RIVER

castle precincts. There is a display of prehistoric weapons, 14C–17C defensive arms, swords, pikes and firearms. The 19C–20C material includes exotic arms from Africa and China, and 19C uniforms. Also off the Court of the Angel are the **Rooms of Clement VIII** (16, 17) and the **Hall of Justice** (18), which are usually open only for exhibitions. The Hall of Justice is so called because it was the seat of the tribunal of the 16C–17C. It was built in Roman times above the sepulchral cella, and has a fresco of Justice attributed to Domenico Zaga.

Another door in the courtyard leads into the **Hall of Apollo** (19), named after the 16C mythological grotesques on the ceiling attributed to Luzio Luzi. On the right is a trapdoor covering a cellar 9m deep; adjacent is the top of the lift-shaft seen from the spiral ramp. On the right is the **Chapel of Leo X** (20), with a relief of the *Madonna and Child* attributed to Raffaello da Montelupo.

Opposite are the **Rooms of Clement VII**. The first room (21) is decorated with a frieze by Giulio Romano, and has a coffered ceiling. Here are displayed detached frescoes by Niccolò l'Alunno; *St Jerome* by Lorenzo Lotto; a polyptych by the

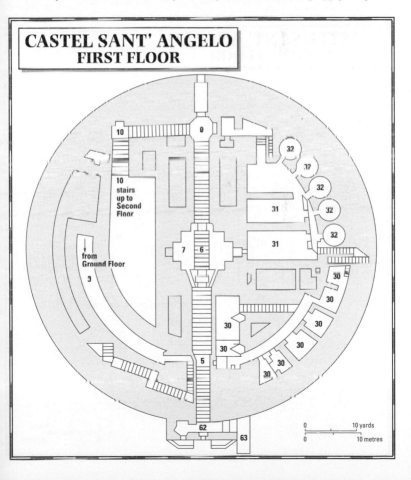

Zavattari brothers; a *Madonna Enthroned* by the 15C Tuscan school; and *Christ Blessing* and *St John the Baptist* by Carlo Crivelli. In the second room (**22**): *Pietà* by Martino Spanzotti; **Madonna and Child* by Bartolomeo Montagna; *Madonna and Saints* by Luca Signorelli; and *Mocking of Christ* by Giampietrino.

A passage (**23**) leads right out of the **Hall of Apollo** into the large **Courtyard of Alexander VI** (**24**), with a fine marble well, stone cannon balls, and catapults. Theatrical performances were given here in the time of Leo X and Pius IV. A small staircase (**26**) leads up to the charming **Bathroom of Clement VII** (**27**) decorated with stuccoes and frescoes attributed to Giovanni da Udine. This room communicates with a small dressing room on the next floor (closed). The **Courtyard of Leo X** (**28**), with a loggia, is also usually closed; below it is a 15C casemate. Adjacent is a small triangular courtyard from which stairs lead to a chamber which had a stove for heating the bath water and the air which circulated between the hollow walls.

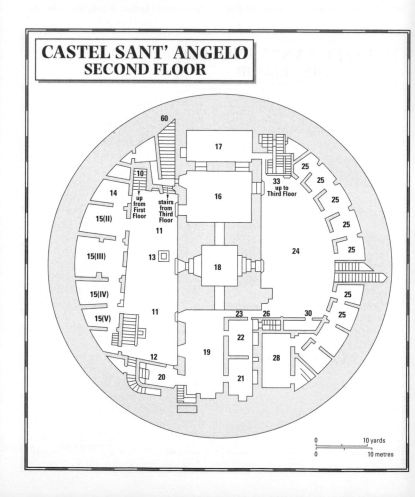

CASTEL SANT' ANGELO
SECOND FLOOR

On the right side of the Courtyard of Alexander VI is a semicircular, two-storeyed building, the rooms of which (25) were formerly used as **prison cells**. In the second room from the right, Benvenuto Cellini was imprisoned during the first period of his captivity. A staircase leads down from the courtyard to the historical prisons (30), which are normally closed but shown on sporadic guided tours (see above). Two large underground oil stores (31) contain 84 jars, with a capacity of c 22,000 litres. The oil not only served to feed the garrison, but also as a defence, since boiling oil could be poured on attackers. The five grain silos (32) were later used as prison cells. Other macabre cells open off a corridor; numerous bones found under the floors indicate that the prisoners were buried where they died. Benvenuto Cellini is said to have passed the second period of his captivity in the last cell.

Stairs lead back up to the Courtyard of Alexander VI, and from there a staircase (33) continues up to the semicircular **Gallery of Pius IV** (35), a terrace with a splendid *view. To the left is the **Loggia of Paul III** (34), with another fine view, built by Antonio Sangallo the Younger and decorated with stuccoes and Mannerist grotesques in 1543–48. In the Gallery of Pius IV a series of small rooms was used originally as quarters for the household of the papal court and later as political and military prison cells. Rooms with the reconstruction of a political prison in the first half of the 19C, and an interesting muster of uniforms, decorations and medals of the various Italian states before the Unification (36–37) are kept closed. The **Loggia of Julius II** (38), on a design by Giuliano da Sangallo, faces south towards the Ponte Sant'Angelo.

A short staircase leads from here to the **Papal Apartments**, decorated for Paul III in 1542–49 and appropriately furnished. The **Sala Paolina** or del Consiglio (39) has *stuccoes by Girolamo da Sermoneta and Baccio da Montelupo. The walls are decorated by Pellegrino Tibaldi, Domenico Zaga, Perino del Vaga, Polidoro da Caravaggio, Giovanni da Udine and others. On the right is an amusing trompe-l'oeil fresco of a courtier entering the room through a painted door. In the floor is the coat of arms of Innocent XIII, who restored the room. The **Camera del Perseo** (40) takes its name from the beautiful frieze by Perino del Vaga and his *bottega*. The carved wooden ceiling dates from the 16C. The tapestries come from State collections and include one showing an episode in the life of Julius Caesar. The painting of *Christ Carrying the Cross* is by Paris Bordone.

The **Camera di Amore e Psiche** (41), seen beyond a railing, has another frieze by Perino del Vaga and his *bottega*, illustrating the story of Cupid and Psyche in 17 episodes. It has a fine carved and gilt 15C ceiling, a large 16C canopied bed, a clavichord, and other furniture. The paintings include *Christ Carrying the Cross* by Sebastiano del Piombo and *Girl with a Unicorn* by a 16C artist. The statuette is attributed to Jacopo della Quercia (1371–1438).

From the Sala Paolina a corridor (43) frescoed in the Pompeian style by Perino del Vaga and his *bottega* leads to the **Hall of the Library** (44), with ceiling frescoes by Luzio Luzi and stuccoes by Sicciolante da Sermoneta (16C). The marble chimneypiece is by Raffaello da Montelupo. The furniture includes four dower chests and a 15C wardrobe. The **Room of the Mausoleum of Hadrian** (45) is named after a frieze by Luzi and his school. Here are hung two paintings depicting Bacchanals, one a copy by Poussin of an original by Giovanni Bellini, and the other by Jordaens. The fine painting of the *Madonna between St Roch and St Sebastian* is a copy from Lorenzo Lotto. A case contains 15C–17C ceramics.

Beyond room 46 a short flight of stairs leads to the **Appartamento Cagliostra** (**47–49**; closed), three 16C rooms decorated with grotteschi by Luzi and containing a collection of majolica including 15C *albarelli* (cylindrical pharmacy jars), floor tiles, Deruta and Faenza ware.

A small vestibule leads out of the Hall of the Library into the central **Room of the Secret Archives**, or of the **Treasury** (**50**). The walnut cupboards in this room were used for the archives inaugurated by Paul III. In the middle are some large chests in which Julius II, Leo X and Sixtus V kept the Vatican treasury. A Roman staircase ascends to the **Round Hall** (**51**), situated beneath the statue of the angel (see below) and above the last room. Formerly used as a political prison, it now contains the iron core of the angel, a cast of the head, and the original sword. A short staircase leads to the **Hall of the Columns**, which is usually closed: this contains a charming 15C polychrome wood group of the *Deposition*, and a wooden model of the *Archangel Michael* attributed to Pietro Bracci. The two adjoining rooms (**52–53**) are only open for exhibitions.

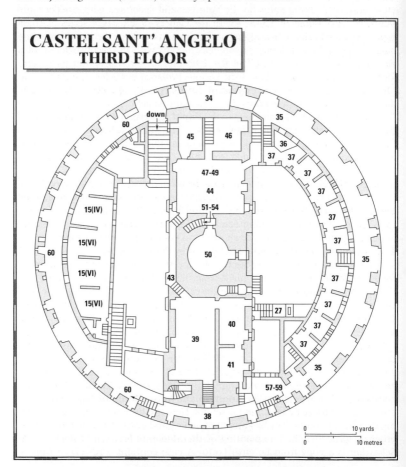

CASTEL SANT' ANGELO
THIRD FLOOR

The staircase continues up to the **terrace** (54) at the top of the castle, scene of the last act of Puccini's opera *Tosca*. Above—on a small, higher terrace—can be seen the huge bronze *Angel* (4m high), shown in the act of sheathing his sword, by Peter Anton Verschaffelt (1752). This commemorates the vision of Gregory the Great after which the castle is named (see pp 336–337). The bell known as the *Campana della Misericordia* used to announce the execution of capital sentences.

The *view* from the terrace is superb. On the left, in the foreground, is the Palace of Justice, with the Villa Medici just visible behind. Further to the left is the Prati district; in the distance, the green park of the Villa Borghese and of the Pincio. Across the Tiber, you can see the Ministry of Finance, with the orange Quirinal building in front; then Palazzo della Consulta, with Santa Maria Maggiore behind it. To the right, on the skyline, stands the Torre delle Milizie, with the cupola of the Pantheon in front. Next comes the Vittorio Emanuele II monument, with San Giovanni in Laterano behind it and the Alban Hills in the distance. Continuing to the right, you can see the bell-tower of Palazzo Senatorio on the Capitoline Hill, and in front, the two cupolas of Sant'Andrea della Valle and San Carlo ai Catinari; then the Aventine, with San Paolo fuori le Mura in the background; and further right, beyond Ponte Sant'Angelo, are Trastevere and the Janiculum, St Peter's and the Vatican, and Monte Mario. Immediately below are Ponte Sant'Angelo and Ponte Vittorio Emanuele, with the Lungotevere.

From the terrace the **descent** is sometimes signposted by a modern staircase which passes three rooms of the Appartamento del Castellano, beyond which stairs continue down to the Gallery of Pius IV and the Courtyard of the Angel. Otherwise you are obliged to return from the terrace down the same staircase to the Hall of the Library, which you cross diagonally to the door on the left of the fireplace. Stairs lead from here to the loggia of Paul III, from which another flight of stairs continues down to the Courtyard of Alexander VI. After this the route follows Paul III's staircase, and Alexander VI's staircase to the exit.

The **ramparts** are traversed by open walkways (66) which encircle the Roman structure and connect the four bastions of the square inner ward; these are signposted to the right from the drawbridge near the entrance (63). The first part of the walkway passes above a terrace with four 15C cannon and piles of marble and stone cannon balls, once part of the castle's ammunition store. Beyond the **Bastion of St Matthew** are the mills (71) used from the time of Pius IV to grind flour for the castle. At the **Bastion of St Mark** is the beginning of the covered way that connects the castle with the Vatican, the **Corridolo** or **Passetto** (72), part of which can usually be visited on guided tours on certain days of the year (see above), although it is at present closed for restoration. This was built in 1277–80 by Nicholas III above Leo IV's 9C defensive wall of the Borgo. It was reconstructed by Alexander VI, who used it as an escape route from the Vatican in 1494. It was again used in 1527 when Clement VII took refuge in the castle from the troops of Charles V.

Between the bastions of St Mark and St Luke is a passageway (closed) leading into the public gardens and Piazzale Pio IV. Just before the **Bastion of St Luke** is the **Chapel of the Crucifix**, or of Clement XII (77), in which condemned criminals had to attend mass before execution. The circuit continues above the reconstructed gate of 1556, the present entrance to the castle, to the **Bastion of St John**, beyond which steps lead down to ground-level.

Beside Castel Sant'Angelo, on the river front, is the huge **Palazzo di Giustizia** (**Map 6**; **2**), the Palace of Justice, known as the Palazzaccio. A colossal ornate building in solid travertine, decorated with sculptures by Enrico Quattrini and Ettore Ximenes, it was built between 1889 and 1910. It was evacuated in 1970 because it was in danger of collapse; although it is still under restoration, it has been partially reopened. New judiciary offices and law courts have been built by Giuseppe Perugini and others in the Città Giudiziaria (**Map 16**; **1**), in Piazzale Clodio.

To the north, beyond Piazza Cavour, an important traffic centre and terminus for buses, are the Prati and Trionfale extensvie residential districts, of marginal interest to visitors. In Via Pompeo Magno is the church of **San Gioacchino** (**Map 2**; **3**), erected by Raffaele Inganni in 1890, with bronze capitals and an aluminium cupola painted inside to represent a star-strewn sky.

About 500m north of the church is Piazza Mazzini. In Viale Mazzini to the right is the church of **Cristo Re**, built in 1930 by Marcello Piacentini, with a sculpture by Arturo Martini over the central door. It contains frescoes by Achille Funi and sculptures by Corrado Vigni and Alfredo Biagini. Next to it is the headquarters of the Italian State-owned radio and television network (*R.A.I.*). About 700m further north, at 31 Lungotevere della Vittoria, is the **Museo dell'Arma del Genio** (**Map 16**; **6**), illustrating Italian military transport, bridge-building and communications. It includes a military aircraft of 1909, and models of historical fortifications and armoury from Roman times to the present day. Open Tues, Thur, Sat 09.30–12.00. ☎ 06 372 5446.

Monte Mario, which rises to the north-west, is described in Walk 38.

Via della Conciliazione

From Castel Sant'Angelo the unattractive, austere **Via della Conciliazione** (**Map 6**; **3**) leads towards St Peter's. The approach to the great basilica was transformed by this broad straight thoroughfare, typical of Fascist urban planning, which was completed in 1937. In its construction two characteristic streets of the Leonine City, the Borgo Nuovo opened in 1499 and the Borgo Vecchio, known as the Spina di Borgo, and the buildings between them were destroyed, except for one palace which was moved (see below). The colonnaded piazza in front of St Peter's was not originally designed to be seen from a distance, and its impact is lessened by this monumental approach.

Via della Conciliazione first passes on the right the Carmelite church of Santa Maria in Traspontina (1566–87). Beyond is **Palazzo Torlonia** (formerly Giraud), a delightful reproduction of the Palazzo della Cancelleria, built by Andrea Bregno in 1495–1504 for Cardinal Adriano Castellesi. The cardinal gave the palace to the English king Henry VII, and Henry VIII then donated it to his papal legate, Cardinal Campeggio. The next palace is **Palazzo dei Convertendi**, built in the second half of the 17C and re-erected in its present position in 1937 when Via della Conciliazione was constructed. It originally occupied the site of a house built by Donato Bramante for Raphael, who died in it in 1520. On the south side of the street is **Palazzo dei Penitenzieri**, probably built by Baccio Pontelli for Cardinal Domenico della Rovere in 1480. It is now occupied by the Penitentiaries who hear confessions in St Peter's. Via della Conciliazione ends in Piazza Pio XII, in front of Piazza San Pietro (see Walk 32).

Parallel to Via della Conciliazione to the north is Borgo Sant'Angelo, which is skirted by the wall that supports the covered way connecting Castel Sant'Angelo with the Vatican (see above). Borgo Pio, one street further north, is the prettiest street to have survived in the Borgo. Partly closed to traffic, it is a local shopping street and has several pizzerie.

On the other side of Via della Conciliazione is Borgo Santo Spirito. Here a flight of steps leads up to the little church of **San Michele e Magno**, founded in the 8C and retaining a 13C campanile. Inside is the tomb of the painter Raphael Mengs (d. 1779). Open Sunday mornings.

On the corner of Via dei Penitenzieri is **Santo Spirito in Sassia** (Map 6; 3), a church founded in 726 for Saxon pilgrims by Ine, king of Wessex, who died in Rome in the same year. The church was rebuilt in 1540 by Antonio da Sangallo the Younger: the design of the façade was probably his, but the work itself was done in 1585 by Ottavio Mascherino. The campanile, entirely Tuscan in character, and attributed to Baccio Pontelli, is one of the most graceful in Rome.

In the **interior** the wooden ceiling dates from 1534–49. On the west wall are two interesting paintings in elaborate frames: the *Visitation* by Francesco Salviati, and the *Conversion of Saul*, attributed to Marco da Siena. On the south side, the first chapel contains the *Pentecost* by Jacopo Zucchi; and the second chapel, the *Assumption* by Livio Agresti. The interesting little porch in front of a side door with two columns has 16C frescoes and a pretty ceiling. It supports the organ of 1546–52. The huge apse was covered with frescoes by Jacopo and Francesco Zucchi in 1583. On the north side, the third chapel has a 16C crucifix and frescoed decorations in Roman style imitating precious marbles with figures in grisaille. On the second altar, the *Coronation* of the Virgin is by Cesare Nebbia.

It was from the ramparts of the Leonine City near here that Benvenuto Cellini, according to his own statement, shot the Constable de Bourbon in 1527; a plaque on the outer wall of the church, however, attributes the deed to Bernardo Passeri, another goldsmith.

Adjoining the church are the buildings of the huge **Ospedale di Santo Spirito**, founded by Innocent III c 1198 as a hospital and hostel, and rebuilt for Sixtus IV by various architects (c 1473–78). The first building, the Palazzo del Commendatore (the house of the director of the hospital), with a spacious courtyard, dates from c 1567. The harmony of the proportions of the main building were spoilt by Alexander VIII, who added a storey, and by Benedict XIV, who blocked up the arches of the portico. The portal is an effective example of the early Renaissance style. The chapel (admission by special permission only) contains an altar with a baldacchino of the time of Clement VIII (1592–1605) and an altarpiece of *Job* by Carlo Maratta. The riverfront, the Lungotevere in Sassia, was rebuilt and extended in 1926 in harmony with the old style.

The hospital contains two institutions devoted to the history of medicine, the **Lancisiana Library**, founded 1711, in the Palazzo del Commendatore and the **Historical Medical Academy**. At no. 3 Lungotevere in Sassia is the **Museo Storico Nazionale dell'Arte Sanitaria**, a museum devoted to the history of medicine, unique in Italy. It includes anatomical drawings by Paolo Mascagni (1752–1815), the collection of the surgeon Giuseppe Flajani (1741–1808), surgical instruments, and reconstructions of a 17C pharmacy and of an alchemist's laboratory. Open Mon, Wed, Fri 10.00–12.00. ☎ 06 6835 2353.

32 • St Peter's

The huge basilica of St Peter's is the most important Roman Catholic church in the world and is one of the most visited places in Rome. It is the composite work of some of the greatest artists of the 16C, and a masterpiece of the Italian High Renaissance. Orientated towards the west and approached through its monumental piazza, the church has its fitting culmination in Michelangelo's dome. St Peter's stands on land now part of the independent Vatican State, the Pope's residence, usually called the Vatican City, on the right bank of the Tiber (see Map 1; 5, 6), which is described in Walk 34. The famous Vatican museums next to St Peter's are described in Walk 33.

Piazza San Pietro

Piazza San Pietro (**Map 1**; **6**), the masterpiece of Gian Lorenzo Bernini (1656–67), is one of the most superb conceptions of its kind in civic architecture, and is a fitting approach to the world's greatest basilica (see plan on p 348). In this piazza on 13 May 1981 a Turk, Mehmet Ali Agca, made an attempt on the life of John Paul II.

Partly enclosed by two semicircular colonnades, the piazza has the form of an ellipse adjoining an almost rectangular quadrilateral. Each of the two colonnades has a quadruple row of Doric columns, forming three parallel covered walks. There are in all 284 columns and 88 pilasters. On the Ionic entablature are 96 statues of saints and martyrs. At the end, above a triple flight of steps, rises St Peter's basilica, with the buildings of the Vatican towering on the right.

In the middle of the piazza, on a tall plinth, is an **obelisk** devoid of hieroglyphics, 25.5m high. It was brought from Alexandria (where it had been set up by Augustus) in AD 37, and it is thought that Caligula placed it in his circus, later called the Circus of Nero. In 1586 Sixtus V ordered its removal from the south of the basilica to its present site and put Domenico Fontana in charge of operations. No fewer than 900 men, 150 horses and 47 cranes were required. In the 18C the delightful story was invented that the pope forbade the spectators, under pain of death, to speak while the obelisk was being raised into position. A sailor called Bresca, seeing that the tension on the ropes had not been correctly assessed and that they were giving way under the strain, transgressed the order, and shouted 'Acqua alle funi!' ('Wet the ropes!'). It is said that the pope rewarded him by granting his family the privilege of supplying St Peter's with palms for Palm Sunday.

Round the foot of the obelisk is a plan of the mariner's compass, giving the names of the winds. The globe which surmounted the obelisk until 1586, when it was replaced by a cross, is now in the Musei Capitolini.

The two abundant **fountains** are supplied by the Acqua Paola. The one on the right was designed by Carlo Maderno (1614): a similar fountain had existed in the piazza since 1490. It was moved to its present site and slightly modified by Bernini in 1667, when the second fountain was begun. Between the obelisk and each fountain is a round porphyry slab from which you have the illusion that each of the colonnades has only a single row of columns.

Covered galleries, also decorated with statues, unite the colonnades with the portico of St Peter's. The gallery on the right, known as the **Corridore del Bernini** and leading to the Scala Regia, is closed by the **Portone di Bronzo**. A great staircase of three flights leads up to the portico of the basilica. At the foot are colossal statues of *St Peter* (by Giuseppe de Fabris) and *St Paul* (by Adamo Tadolini), set up here by Pius IX.

St Peter's

St Peter's or the **Basilica di San Pietro in Vaticano** (Map 1; 5, 6), on a vast scale, is perhaps the world's most imposing church. It is built on the site of a basilica begun by Constantine, the first Christian Emperor, and also where the great apostle St Peter was buried after his martyrdom close by. This splendid church was famous throughout Europe for centuries, but in the mid-15C it was decided to rebuild it on an even grander scale: this herculean task, carried out by the leading architects of the time, was not completed until the early 17C.

Opening times

The **basilica** is open daily 07.00–19.00; Oct–Mar 07.00–18.00.

The **treasury** is open daily 09.00–18.30; Oct–Mar 09.00–17.30.

The **dome** can be ascended 08.00–one hour before the basilica closes; closed Christmas Day and Easter Day, and when the pope is in the basilica (often Wednesday morning).

The **Vatican Grottoes** or **Tombe dei Papi** are open Mon–Fri 07.00–one hour before the basilica closes, except when the pope is in the basilica. Group tours of the **necropolis and tomb of St Peter** (described on p 362) are conducted most days 09.00–12.00 and 14.00–17.00; the visit takes about 1hr and groups are limited to 15 people. Apply in writing or in person to the Ufficio Scavi (beneath the Arco della Campana, left of St Peter's) Mon–Fri 09.00–17.00. ☎ 06 6988 5318.

Dress

You are not allowed inside St Peter's or the Vatican City wearing shorts or mini-skirts, or with bare shoulders.

Services

Mass is held on Sunday at 07.00, 08.00, 09.00 and 10.00, with Sung Mass at 10.30, and frequently during the week. Holy Communion can be taken in the Cappella del Santissimo Sacramento throughout the day on Sunday. For information on services, ☎ 06 6988 5318.

Papal audiences

General audiences usually take place at 10.00 or 11.00 on Wednesday mornings in the New Audience Hall, or in the Piazza (when the Pope is transported by jeep). The New Audience Hall is reached under the colonnade to the left of the façade of St Peter's. A special section is set aside for newly married couples. Audiences are now also sometimes held in St Peter's.

Application to attend an audience can be made in writing to the Prefetto della Casa Pontificia, Città del Vaticano, 00120 Rome. ☎ 06 6988 3017; 🖷 06 6988 5863. Otherwise you can apply in person at the Portone di Bronzo, in the colonnade to the right of St Peter's, 09.00–13.00. At the far end of the Corridore del Bernini (see above) is the Scala Regia, the staircase leading to the Sala Regia. At a table at the entrance you are asked to fill in a form and take it to the office of the Prefettura on the first floor, reached by the Scala Pia.

Information office

In Piazza San Pietro, to the left of the façade of the basilica. Open Mon–Sat 08.30–19.00 (closed Wed, when papal audiences are being held in the Piazza). ☎ 06 6988 2019. 🖾 www.vatican.va

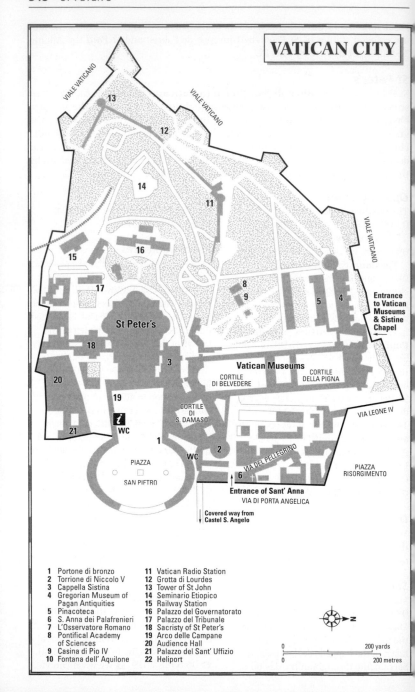

VATICAN CITY

1 Portone di bronzo
2 Torrione di Niccolo V
3 Cappella Sistina
4 Gregorian Museum of
  Pagan Antiquities
5 Pinacoteca
6 S. Anna dei Palafrenieri
7 L'Osservatore Romano
8 Pontifical Academy
  of Sciences
9 Casina di Pio IV
10 Fontana dell' Aquilone
11 Vatican Radio Station
12 Grotta di Lourdes
13 Tower of St John
14 Seminario Etiopico
15 Railway Station
16 Palazzo del Governatorato
17 Palazzo del Tribunale
18 Sacristy of St Peter's
19 Arco delle Campane
20 Audience Hall
21 Palazzo del Sant' Uffizio
22 Heliport

0   200 yards
0   200 metres

History of St Peter's

According to the *Liber Pontificalis*, c AD 90 Pope St Anacletus built an oratory over the tomb of St Peter, close to the Circus of Nero, near which he had been martyred. It is now thought that there may have been a confusion of names, and that Pope St Anicetus (155–66) was probably responsible for the oratory.

At the request of Pope St Sylvester I the Emperor Constantine began a basilica on the site of this oratory c 319–22. It was consecrated on 18 November 326. This basilica was 120m long and 65m wide, about half the size of the present edifice. It was preceded by a great quadrangular colonnaded portico. The nave and double aisles were divided by 86 marble columns, some of which were said to have been taken from the Septizodium on the Palatine (if so, this was long before the demolition of that building by Sixtus V). It contained numerous monuments to popes and emperors, was decorated with frescoes and mosaics, and was visited by pilgrims from all over Europe. Charlemagne was crowned here by Leo III in 800. Some of its relics are preserved (see below). Its façade is shown in Raphael's fresco of the *Incendio di Borgo* in the Stanze in the Vatican.

In the middle of the 15C the old basilica showed signs of collapse, and Nicholas V, recognising its importance to the prestige of the Roman Catholic faith, decided to rebuild it. He entrusted the work to Bernardo Rossellino, Leon Battista Alberti and Giuliano da Sangallo, but on Nicholas's death in 1455, building work was virtually suspended for half a century. Julius II decided on a complete reconstruction and employed for the purpose Donato Bramante, who started work in 1506. Most of the old church was dismantled, and much was destroyed which could have been preserved: Bramante was nicknamed 'Bramante Ruinante'. The new basilica was on a Greek-cross plan surmounted by a gigantic central dome and flanked by four smaller cupolas. By the time of Bramante's death in 1514, the four central piers and the arches of the dome had been completed.

Leo X employed Raphael to continue the building, now on a Latin-cross plan, in collaboration with Fra Giocondo (d. 1515) and Giuliano da Sangallo (d. 1516). On Raphael's death in 1520 Baldassare Peruzzi reverted to Bramante's design. Neither Adrian VI, the austere theologian who regarded art as hostile to the Church, nor Clement VII, overwhelmed by political disturbances brought about by the Reformation and culminating in the Sack of Rome (1527), were interested in the completion of the basilica. Under Paul III, however, the work received fresh impetus from Antonio da Sangallo the Younger. In 1539 he made a huge wooden model of the basilica, readopting the Latin-cross plan: this remarkable work, 736cm by 602cm and 468cm high, survives, although it is not at present on display. At Sangallo's death in 1546, Michelangelo, then 72 years old, was summoned by Paul III. Michelangelo decided on the original Greek-cross plan, and developed Bramante's idea with even greater audacity. He took as his model Brunelleschi's cupola for the Florentine cathedral, replaced Bramante's piers with new, stronger ones, and completed the dome as far as the drum. His plan for the façade was derived from the Pantheon. Confirmed in his appointment by Paul III's successors, he continued to direct the work until his death in 1564. Vignola and Pirro Ligorio then took over the work, and were followed by Giacomo della Porta (assisted by Carlo Fontana), who completed the dome in 1590, adding the vault and lantern, and added the two smaller domes. Clement VIII covered the vault with strips of lead reinforced with bronze ribs.

In 1605 Paul V demolished what had been left of the old basilica, pulled down the incomplete façade, and directed Carlo Maderno to lengthen the nave towards the old Piazza San Pietro. The present façade and portico are Maderno's work. Thus, after many vicissitudes, the basilica was completed on a Latin-cross plan. On 18 November 1626, the 1300th anniversary of the original consecration, Urban VIII consecrated the new church. Bernini, who succeeded Maderno in 1629 and was commissioned to decorate the interior, wanted to erect two campaniles by the façade, but the one that he completed began to crack on its sinking foundations and was pulled down. Alexander VII kept Bernini as architect of St Peter's, and under him the piazza was begun in 1656. The sacristy was built in the 18C.

In 1940 the ancient cemetery in which St Peter was buried after his crucifixion was discovered beneath the Vatican Grottoes, and on 23 December 1950, the pope announced that the tomb of St Peter had been identified. Despite its importance, St Peter's does not have cathedral status and nor is it the mother church of the Catholic faith (that position is held by San Giovanni in Laterano).

Dimensions

The exterior length of the church, including the portico, is 211.5m; the cross on the dome is 136.5m above the ground. The façade is 115m long and 45.5m high. Inside, the church is 186m long and 137m wide across the transepts. The nave (including the aisles) is 60m across and 44m high; the diameter of the dome is 42m, or 1.5m less than that of the Pantheon. The total area is 49,737 square metres; the area of St Paul's in London is 26,639 square metres.

Exterior

At the top of the triple flight of steps rises the long polychrome **façade** (restored in 1999). Its great size impairs the view of the dome from the piazza. Eight columns and four pilasters support the entablature. A dedicatory inscription on the frieze records its erection in 1612, during the pontificate of Paul V. The attic, almost without ornament, is surmounted by a balustrade on which are statues of *Christ, St John the Baptist* and 11 of the *Apostles* (St Peter's statue is inside) and, near the ends, two clocks by Giuseppe Valadier. Under the left-hand clock are the **six bells** of the basilica, electrically operated since 1931. The oldest bell dates from 1288; the largest (1786) is 7.5m round and weighs 9.75 tonnes. Above the doors and extending beyond them on either side is a row of large windows with balconies. The central balcony is that from which the senior cardinal-deacon proclaims the newly elected pope and from which the new pope gives his blessing. Below the balcony is a relief, by Ambrogio Bonvicino, of *Christ Handing the Keys to St Peter*.

Portico

The portico is prolonged by vestibules at both ends connecting with the covered galleries of the piazza. The pavement was designed by Bernini. The vault is magnificently decorated in stucco by Martino Ferrabosco; in the lunettes below it are 32 statues of canonised popes. Of the five entrances to the church, that on the extreme right is the **Porta Santa**, which is sealed from the inside and opened only in Holy Years (see 351). It was last opened at Christmas 1999 and closed at

Christmas 2000. The panels on the door are by Vico Consorti (1950). The door on the right of the main door is by Venanzio Crocetti (1968). The bronze **central door**, from Old St Peter's, was decorated by Filarete in the 1430s with reliefs of *Christ*, the *Virgin*, *St Peter* and *St Paul* and their martyrdoms, on a commission from Eugenius IV. After 1439 he added the four small panels depicting events in the life of Eugenius, including the Council of Florence. Around them is a frieze of Classical and mythological subjects, animals, fruits and portraits of emperors. The door to the left is by Giacomo Manzù (1963), and has sculptures depicting the deaths of religious figures and abstract themes of death; the door on the extreme left is by Luciano Minguzzi (1977).

High up on the wall between the doors are three framed **inscriptions**: the one on the left commemorating the donation by Gregory II of certain olive trees to provide oil for the lamps over the tomb of St Peter; the Latin epitaph of Hadrian I (772–95), attributed to Charlemagne; and the bull of Boniface VIII proclaiming the first Jubilee or Holy Year (1300). In the tympanum above the central entrance (that is, looking backwards, against the light) is the *Navicella*, a mosaic representing Christ walking on the waters. Commissioned by Boniface VIII's nephew, Cardinal Stefaneschi, in 1297 and executed by Giotto for the quadrangular

---

Holy Years

Throughout the centuries Rome and the papacy have enjoyed huge economic benefits from the number of visitors in the city during Jubilees or Holy Years. The Roman Catholic Church adapted the secular Jewish idea of the jubilee which occurred every 50 years, as described in the book of Leviticus in the Old Testament, when the Jews were required to free slaves and remit debts. The papacy gave the Jubilee an exclusively religious meaning when it allowed the remission of the temporal punishment of sins for those pilgrims who visited Rome during a specific year; in 1500 the Jubilee was renamed Holy Year. For a history of Rome as a centre of pilgrimage, see p 353.

The first Holy Year was proclaimed by Boniface VIII from the balcony of San Giovanni in Laterano on 22 February 1300 (a fresco showing him reading the bull survives inside the church), and it was expected that there would be one every century from then on. In 1343 Clement VI reduced the interval from 100 to 33 years (the lifetime of Christ) and Paul II (1464–71) to 25 years. This quarter-century interval has been maintained, with few exceptions, ever since: there were Holy Years in 1900, 1925, 1950, 1975 and 2000. In addition to the regular celebrations, a Jubilee has occasionally been proclaimed for a special reason, as in 1933, when Pius XI commemorated the 19th centenary of the Crucifixion, or in 1983–84 when John Paul II commemorated the 1950 years since the death and resurrection of Christ.

A Holy Year is usually inaugurated on the preceding Christmas Eve with the opening of the Holy Door (Porta Santa) of St Peter's by the pope. He used to wield a silver hammer and a temporary wall in front of the door would fall inwards (in 1983 Pope John Paul II used a bronze hammer and the Porta Santa was unlocked for him; in 1999 the door, already unlocked, was pushed open by the pope). The Holy Doors of the three other major basilicas are also kept open throughout Holy Years at the end of which (usually at Epiphany of the following year) they are all reclosed.

courtyard of Old St Peter's, this huge mosaic was designed to be seen by pilgrims as they left the church: it symbolised the role of the Church through Christ of bringing help to those in trouble. It has frequently been moved, and has suffered from resetting and restoration; it is now virtually a copy of the original.

The equestrian statue of *Charlemagne* (1), at the left end of the portico, is by Agostino Cornacchini; that on the right, of *Constantine I* (2), is by Bernini.

Interior

The immensity of the interior is disguised by the symmetry of its proportions. The work of Bernini for this majestic church, which begins with the approach to it and his decorations on Ponte Sant'Angelo, and is continued in the piazza, culminates in the magnificent baldacchino and exedra in the tribune. As the shrine of St Peter, the church has a ceremonial air. The gilded coffered ceiling was designed by Bramante. The coloured marble of the walls and pavement is the work of Giacomo della Porta and Bernini.

Nave. The first part of the nave, with its aisles and three side chapels, is Carlo Maderno's extension, which transformed the plan of the church from a Greek to a Latin cross. The round slab of porphyry let into the pavement in front of the central door is that on which the emperors used to kneel for their coronation in front of the altar of the old basilica. Further on are metal lines indicating the lengths of the principal churches of Europe. The nave is separated from the aisles by colossal piers, each decorated with two fluted Corinthian pilasters, supporting great arches. In the niches between the pilasters of the nave and transepts are statues of the founders of the religious orders. The aisles have sumptuous decorations by Bernini. Over the spaces between the piers are elliptical cupolas, three on either side, decorated with elaborate mosaics. In addition to these six minor cupolas there are four circular domes over the corner chapels in the main body of the church.

Four pentagonal **piers** support the arches on which rests the drum of the cupola. The piers are decorated with balconies and niches designed by Bernini. Each balcony has two spiral columns taken from the saint's shrine in the old basilica (another of these, the Colonna Santa, is in the Treasury; see below). The niches are filled with colossal statues that give each of the piers its name: *St Longinus* (3) by Bernini; *St Helena* (4) by Andrea Bolgi; *St Veronica* (5) by Francesco Mochi; and *St Andrew* (6) by François Duquesnoy. On the balconies are reliefs referring to the *Reliquie Maggiori*; these precious relics, which are displayed in Holy Week, are preserved in the podium of the pier of St Veronica. They are the lance of St Longinus, the Roman soldier who pierced the side of Christ on the Cross, acquired by Innocent VIII from the Ottoman sultan Bayezid II; a piece of the True Cross preserved by St Helena; and the cloth of St Veronica, with the miraculous image of Christ's face. The head of St Andrew, St Peter's brother, was presented to Pius II in 1462 by Thomas Paleologos, despot of the Morea, who had saved it from the Turks during their invasion of Greece in 1460. At the end of the 20C it was returned to the Greek Orthodox Church at Patras.

Michelangelo's **dome** is an architectural masterpiece. Simple and dignified, and flooded with light, it rises immediately above the site of St Peter's tomb. The Latin inscription on the frieze of the dome is a continuation of the Greek inscription in the tribune. In the pendentives are huge mosaics of the *Evangelists*: the pen held by St Mark is 1.5m long. On the frieze below the drum is inscribed in letters

Rome as a centre of pilgrimage

As the burial place of St Peter, Rome has always been considered a holy city—a second Jerusalem. A huge quantity of relics (the bones of saints, or objects associated with the life and Passion of Christ), often endowed by popular belief with miraculous powers, were brought to the city from the East, and in the Middle Ages pilgrims from all over Europe travelled down through Italy to see them and the basilica of St Peter's.

The Via Francigena was one of three pilgrimage routes in medieval Europe (the other two lead to Santiago de Campostela and Jerusalem). It was so called from the 9C onwards, because it originated in Frankish territory, then in alliance with the Papacy. Sometimes called the Via Romea by medieval chroniclers, its route across France from Calais traversed Picardy, Champagne and the Ardennes; from Switzerland the Alps were crossed by the Great St Bernard Pass; and from Aosta it passed through northern Italy, entering Tuscany at the Passo della Cisa on the Emilian border and traversing Lazio before reaching Rome. Sigeric, who studied to be a churchman under St Dunstan at the Benedictine abbey of Glastonbury in England, travelled along the Via Francigena to receive the pallium, the symbol of his investiture as archbishop of Canterbury, from the hands of the pope. He described his return journey in 990, with its 80 stopping-places (his manuscript is in the British Museum, London). The journey from England to Rome was usually made in spring and took about two and a half months. Most pilgrims probably did the entire trip by foot carrying a characteristic stave, although prelates such as Sigeric may have travelled on horseback. The road was rough and paved only in places, and was not suitable for wheeled vehicles, but this overland route was considered safer and easier than the trip by sea. Numerous *ospedali* or stopping places grew up along the way to offer help and accommodation to travellers. Apart from pilgrims, the road was used by merchants and traders, and goods as well as works of art were transported along it. Its importance diminished after the 13C when other routes were opened over the Alps. Gradually, the city of Rome became more and more organised for the reception of pilgrims; the hospital and hostel of Santo Spirito in the Borgo, for example, was built for them in the 12C.

Rome was especially busy in Jubilee or Holy Years (see above), when the pope gave a full pardon to those confessed communicants who visited the two major basilicas of St Peter's and San Paolo fuori le Mura 15 times (for foreigners) or 30 times (for Romans) every day for three weeks. Visits to San Giovanni in Laterano and Santa Maria Maggiore were later added. Dante, who visited Rome himself in 1300, the year of the first Jubilee, described the huge number of pilgrims he found in the city. In 1450 Nicholas V celebrated the Jubilee with great splendour, but that year is also remembered for the fact that hundreds of pilgrims died in a suffocating crowd on Ponte Sant'Angelo, then the only way across the Tiber to St Peter's. In 1500 San Lorenzo fuori le Mura, Santa Croce in Gerusalemme and San Sebastiano were added to the four major basilicas to establish the Seven Churches of Rome which were the most important places pilgrims were required to visit. In 1600 it is estimated that some 1,200,000 visitors came to Rome.

nearly 2m high: TU ES PETRUS ET SUPER HANC PETRAM AEDIFICABO ECCLESIAM MEAM ET TIBI DABO CLAVES REGNI CAELORUM ('You are Peter, and upon this rock I will build my church; and I will give you the keys of the kingdom of heaven'). The dome is divided into 16 compartments, corresponding to the windows of the drum, by ribs ornamented with stucco; in these compartments are six bands of mosaic by Cavaliere d'Arpino, representing saints, angels and the company of Heaven; in the lantern above is the Redeemer.

Under a canopy against the pier of St Longinus is the famous bronze statue of *St Peter* (7), seated on a marble throne. It was once believed to date from the 5C or 6C but, since its restoration in 1990, is considered to be the work of Arnolfo di Cambio (c 1296). The extended foot of the statue has been worn away by the kisses of the faithful. The statue is robed on high festivals. Above is a portrait in mosaic of Pius IX (1871).

Over the high altar rises the great **baldacchino** (8), designed by Bernini and unveiled on 28 June 1633 by Urban VIII. This colossal Baroque structure, a combination of architecture and decorative sculpture, is cast from bronze taken from the Pantheon. Four gilt-bronze Solomonic columns rise from their marble plinths, which are decorated with the Barberini bees. The columns resemble in design the Colonna Santa (see below) but are decorated with figures of genii and laurel branches. They support a canopy from which hang festoons and tassels and on which angels by Duquesnoy alternate with children. From the four corners of the canopy ascend ornamental scrolls, which support the globe and cross. Inside the top of the canopy the Holy Spirit is represented as a dove in an aureole.

The **high altar**, at which only the pope may celebrate, is formed of a block of Greek marble found in the Forum of Nerva and consecrated by Clement VIII on 26 June 1594. It covers the altar of Calixtus II (d. 1123) which in turn encloses an altar of Gregory the Great (d. 604). It stands over the space that is recognised as the tomb of St Peter.

In front is the **confessio** (9), built by Maderno and encircled by perpetually burning lamps. It is directly above the ancient Roman necropolis where the Tropaion of Gaius (see below) was found, below the Vatican Grottoes. The mosaic niches and urn mark the burial place of St Peter.

South aisle. Above the Porta Santa in the south aisle is a mosaic of *St Peter* (10), designed by Ciro Ferri (1675). The **Cappella della Pietà** (11) is named after Michelangelo's **Pietà* (1499). The artist made this exquisite work at the age of 25 for the French ambassador, Cardinal Jean de Bilhères de Lagraulas. It is perhaps the most moving of all Michelangelo's sculptures and is the only one inscribed with his name (on the ribbon falling from the left shoulder of the Virgin). The mosaic decorations of the cupola, by Pietro da Cortona and Ciro Ferri, depict the *Passion*. The *Triumph of the Cross* is by Giovanni Lanfranco.

The monument to Queen Christina of Sweden (12) is by Carlo Fontana (1689), and the statue of *Leo XII* (13) by Giuseppe de Fabris (1836). Beneath the latter is the entrance to the small **Cappella del Crocifisso** (14), which has a *Crucifixion* ascribed to Pietro Cavallini; it is usually closed.

The **Cappella di San Sebastiano** (15) has an altar mosaic of the saint's martyrdom, after Domenichino. The monument (16) to Pius XI (d. 1939) is by Francesco Nagni. Opposite is a monument to Pius XII (d. 1958) by Francesco Messina. Under the next arch are a fine Baroque monument (17) to Innocent XII (d. 1700) by Filippo Valle, and one by Bernini of the Countess Matilda of

Tuscany (d. 1115), whose remains were moved here from Mantua in 1635.

The iron grille of the **Cappella del Santissimo Sacramento** (19) was designed by Francesco Borromini. Over the altar is a gilt bronze ciborium by Bernini, modelled on Bramante's Tempietto at San Pietro in Montorio (see p 331). The two angels also form part of this unfinished composition. Behind is the *Trinity* by Pietro da Cortona. Over the altar on the right is a mosaic of the *Ecstasy of St Francis*, after Domenichino.

Under the next arch are the interesting monument (20) to the reformer of the calendar, Gregory XIII (d. 1585), by Camillo Rusconi (1723); and the unfinished tomb (21) of Gregory XIV (d. 1591). Beneath a mosaic of the *Communion of St Jerome* after Domenichino (22) is the tomb of John XXIII who died in 1963 and was greatly beloved by the Italians (his wax effigy is fulled robed). Always affectionately known simply as 'Papa Giovanni' he was beatified in 2000.

The **Cappella Gregoriana** (23) was built for Gregory XIII from designs by Michelangelo. It has a cupola 42m above the floor. The chapel is dedicated to the Madonna del Soccorso, an ancient painting (24) on part of a marble column from the old basilica, placed here in 1578. Beneath the altar is the tomb of St Gregory of Nazianzus, and on the right (25) is that of Gregory XVI (d. 1846) by Luigi Amici (1855). Under the next arch is a mosaic (26) of the *Mass of St Basil* after Pierre Subleyras. Opposite is the tomb of Benedict XIV (27), by Pietro Bracci; the statue of Benedict XIV (d. 1758) shows him proclaiming the Holy Year of 1750.

The **south transept** is reserved for those wishing to make confession. It has three altars decorated with mosaics, depicting *St Wenceslas* (28) after Angelo Caroselli; the *Martyrdom of St Processus and St Martinian, St Peter's gaolers*, after Valentin (29); and the *Martyrdom of St Erasmus* (30), after Nicolas Poussin (1629). The splendid monument of Clement XIII (31) is by Antonio Canova.

Because this part of the church is usually cordoned off, the altars keyed 32–37 on the plan are usually not visible. The **Altar of the Navicella** (32) has a mosaic of *Christ Walking on the Waters* after Lanfranco; the subject is the same as that of Giotto's mosaics in the portico. The **Cappella di San Michele** (33) contains mosaics of *St Michael* (34) after Guido Reni, and of *St Petronilla* (35) after Guercino. To the left (36) is the monument of Clement X (d. 1676) by Mattia de Rossi; opposite (37) is a mosaic of *St Peter Raising Tabitha* after Placido Costanzi.

Two porphyry steps from the old basilica lead to the **tribune**, the most conspicuous object in which is the **Chair of St Peter** (38), an ambitious and theatrical composition by Bernini (1665). This enormous gilt-bronze throne is supported by statues of four Fathers of the Church: *St Augustine* and *St Ambrose* of the Latin Church (in mitres), and *St Athanasius* and *St John Chrysostom* of the Greek Church (bareheaded). It encloses an ancient wooden chair inlaid with ivory, said to have been the episcopal chair of St Peter. A circle of flying angels surrounds a great halo of gilt stucco in the centre of which, providing the focal point of the whole church, is the Dove, set in the window above the throne.

On the right of the Chair of St Peter is the fine monument (39) to Urban VIII (d. 1644), also by Bernini, with statues of the Pope and allegorical figures of *Charity* and *Justice*. The design of the tomb is clearly influenced by the Medici tombs in Florence by Michelangelo. The use of different materials in the sculpture give an effective colour to the monument. On the left (40) is the monument to Paul III (d.

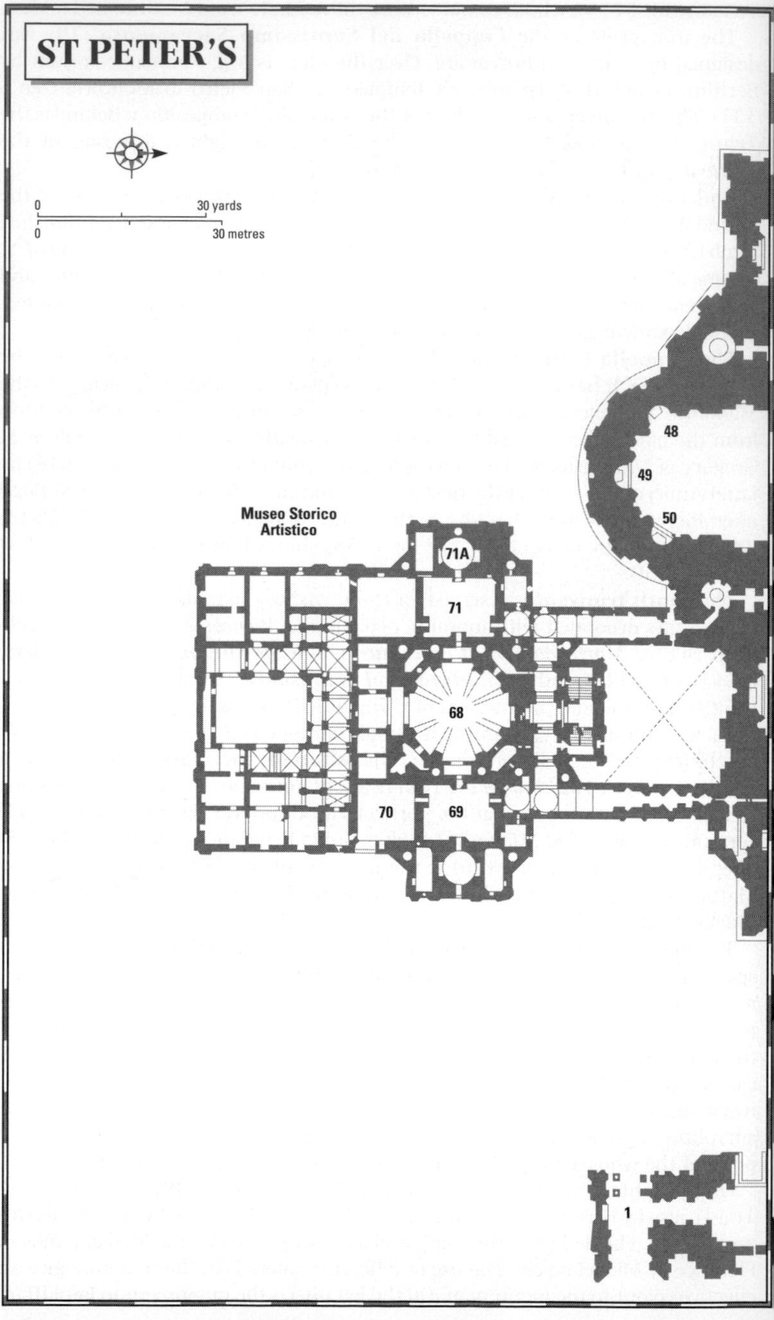

ST PETER'S

0 — 30 yards
0 — 30 metres

Museo Storico Artistico

48

49

50

71A

71

68

70

69

1

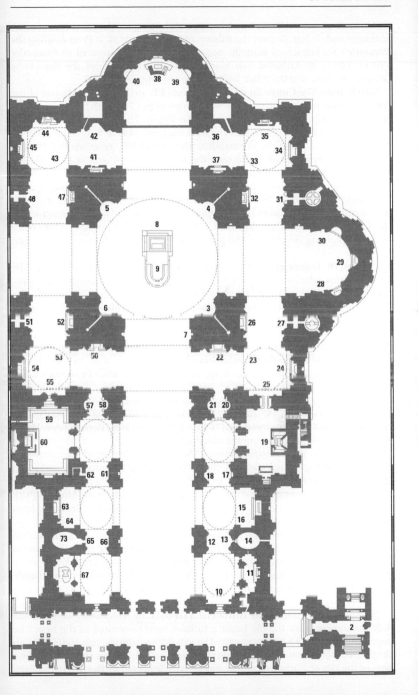

1549) by Guglielmo della Porta, a less successful attempt at the same type of tomb sculpture and design. Beyond the tribune (41) is a mosaic of *St Peter Healing the Paralytic* after Francesco Mancini; opposite (42) is the monument to Alexander VIII (d. 1691) by Arrigo di San Martino; the bronze statue of the Pope is by Giuseppe Bertosi, and the other sculptures are by Angelo de Rossi.

North aisle. The **Cappella della Colonna** (43), in the north aisle, one of the corner chapels with round cupolas, was decorated in 1757 with figures of angels carrying garlands and with symbols of the Virgin. The lunettes have mosaics after Francesco Romanelli. In this chapel is the tomb (44) of St Leo the Great (d. 461); above is a relief by Alessandro Algardi (1650), representing *St Leo Arresting the Progress of Attila* with the help of St Peter and St Paul. On the altar to the left is an ancient and greatly venerated representation of the *Virgin*, painted on a column from the old basilica (45). In the middle of the chapel is the tombstone of Leo XII (d. 1829). The monument (46) of Alexander VII (d. 1667) was Bernini's last work in St Peter's. Opposite is a mosaic (47), the *Apparition of the Sacred Heart* after Carlo Muccioli, set here in 1922 by Benedict XV in place of an oil-painting on slate of the punishment of Simon Magus, by Francesco Vanni.

The **north transept** contains confessionals for foreigners, served by the Penitentiaries, who hear confessions in ten languages. The three altars are decorated with mosaics of *St Thomas* (48), after Vincenzo Camuccini; the *Crucifixion of St Peter* (50), after Guido Reni; and *St Joseph* (49). In front of the central altar is the tomb of the composer Palestrina (1594) by Achille Funi.

Over the door to the sacristy (51) is the Neo-classical monument to Pius VIII (d. 1830) by Pietro Tenerani; opposite (52) is a mosaic of *Ananias and Sapphira* after Pomarancio. The **Cappella Clementina** (53) is the fourth of the corner chapels with round cupolas; the cupola is decorated with mosaics after Pomarancio. The chapel is named after Clement VIII (d. 1605), who ordered Giacomo della Porta to decorate it for the Jubilee of 1600. It contains the tomb of St Gregory the Great (d. 604) beneath the altar (54). Above it is a mosaic of a *Miracle of St Gregory* after Andrea Sacchi. The monument (55) to Pius VII (d. 1823) by Bertel Thorvaldsen, is a Neo-classical work showing the influence of Canova.

The mosaic of the *Transfiguration* (56) is a copy (enlarged four times) of Raphael's painting in the Vatican picture gallery. Opposite, beneath the aisle arch (57), is the *monument of Leo XI, who reigned for only 27 days (d. 1605), by Alessandro Algardi, and that of Innocent XI (d. 1689) by Pierre Monnot (58), the urn of which is decorated with a relief of the *Liberation of Vienna* by John Sobieski.

The **Cappella del Coro** (59) is richly decorated in stucco by Giovanni Battista Ricci from designs by Giacomo della Porta. It has a fine gate with the arms of Clement XIII, elegant classical stalls by Bernini, and two large organs. The altar-piece (60), after a painting by Pietro Bianchi, represents the *Immaculate Conception*. In the pavement is the simple tombstone of Clement XI (d. 1721). The chapel is closed.

The bronze **monument to Innocent VIII** (61), by Antonio Pollaiolo, is the only monument from the old basilica to have been re-created in the new. The pope, who died in 1492, is represented by two bronze statues, one recumbent on the urn, the other seated and holding the spearhead which was supposed to have pierced the side of Christ and which was given to Innocent by Bayezid II. Opposite

(62) is the monument to St Pius X (d. 1914, and canonised in 1954), by Pier Enrico Astorri.

The **Cappella della Presentazione** (63) is named after its altar mosaic of the *Presentation of the Virgin* after Francesco Romanelli; beneath the altar is the tomb of St Pius X. The cupola is decorated with a mosaic after Carlo Maratta, exalting the glory of the Virgin. On the right is a monument to Pope John XXIII (whose tomb is in the south aisle, see 22, above), by Emilio Greco. The monument (64) to Benedict XV (d. 1922) is by Pietro Canonica. Under the next arch are the Stuart monuments: above the door on the right (now used as an exit from the cupola, see below) is the monument (65) to Clementina Sobieska (d. 1735), wife of James Stuart, the Old Pretender (she is here called Queen of Great Britain, France and Ireland), by Filippo Barigioni; on the left is the *monument to the last Stuarts (66), by Canova, with busts of the Old and Young Pretenders (d. 1766 and 1788) and of Henry, Cardinal York (d. 1807). King George IV contributed to the expense of this monument. (For a history of the Jacobites in Italy, see p 170.)

In the **baptistery** (67) the cover of a porphyry sarcophagus, placed upside-down, is used as the font. It formerly covered the tomb of the Emperor Otho II (973–83) in the Grottoes. The present metal cover is by Carlo Fontana. The mosaics reproduce paintings of the *Baptism of Christ* by Carlo Maratta; of *St Peter Baptising the Centurion Cornelius* by Andrea Procaccini; and of *St Peter Baptising his Gaolers St Processus and St Martinian* by Giuseppe Passeri. At the end of the nave can be seen the back of the doors by Giacomo Manzù, with a dedicatory inscription.

Treasury

The Treasury or **Museo Storico Artistico** (for admission see above) is entered by the door under the monument to Pius VIII (51). In the vestibule is a large stone slab with the names of the popes buried in the basilica, from St Peter to John Paul I. A corridor leads to the entrance to the treasury, rearranged in 1975 in dark modern exhibition rooms (the harsh illumination has been justly criticised). The treasury was plundered in 846 by the Saracens, and again during the Sack of Rome by Imperial troops in 1527, and was impoverished by the provisions of the Treaty of Tolentino (1797), which Pius VI was forced to conclude with Napoleon. It still, however, contains objects of great value and interest, including vestments, missals, reliquaries, pyxes, patens, chalices, monstrances, crucifixes and other sacred relics, as well as candelabra and ornaments.

Room I. The *Colonna Santa, a 4C Byzantine spiral column, is one of 12 from the old basilica: eight decorate the balconies of the great piers of the dome in St Peter's, but the remaining three are lost. The column was once thought to be that against which Christ leaned when speaking with the doctors in the Temple of Jerusalem. The gilt-bronze cock (9C) used to decorate the top of the campanile of the old basilica.

Room II (**Sagrestia dei Beneficiati**; 71). The *Vatican Cross, the most ancient possession of the treasury, dating from the 6C, was the gift of the Emperor Justinian II. It is made of bronze and set with jewels. Also here are the so-called *dalmatic of Charlemagne, now usually considered to date from the 11C or the early 15C; a Byzantine case with an enamelled cross; a fragment of a Byzantine diptych in ivory; and a copy (1974) of the ancient Chair of St Peter, now incorporated in Bernini's decoration in the tribune of St Peter's.

Cappella della Sagrestia dei Beneficiati (71A). The beautiful *ciborium by

Donatello (c 1432), from the old basilica, encloses a painting of the *Madonna della Febbre* (the protectress of victims of malaria). Over the chapel altar is *St Peter Receiving the Keys* by Girolamo Muziano. A plaster cast of Michelangelo's *Pietà* in St Peter's is also displayed here.

Room IV. The huge **Monument of Sixtus IV* is a masterpiece in bronze by Antonio Pollaiolo (1493). It can be seen to advantage from the raised platform. This pope is remembered as the builder of the Sistine Chapel (which is named after him), and for opening the Vatican library to the public for the first time. He also donated some important Classical bronzes to the city of Rome.

Room V displays the ceremonial ring of Sixtus IV (1471–84); a reliquary bust of St Luke the Evangelist (13C–14C); and a wooden crucifix probably dating from the 14C. A passage containing illuminated manuscripts, including one from the Giulia choir (1543) and a 17C ivory crucifix, leads to **room VI** with a Cross and candelabra by Sebastiano Torrigiani; a crucifix and six candelabra (1581) made by Antonio Gentili for Cardinal Alessandro Farnese and presented by him to the basilica in 1582; and two huge **candelabra of the 16C, traditionally attributed to Benvenuto Cellini.

Room VII contains a 13C Slavonic icon in a jewelled silver frame, and reliquaries; and model of an angel in clay by Bernini (1673), used for one of the angels flanking the ciborium in the Cappella del Sacramento. **Room VIII**. The gold chalice set with diamonds (18C), was bequeathed to the Vatican by Henry Stuart, Cardinal York. The platinum chalice, presented by Charles III of Spain to Pius VI, is interesting as the first recorded use of platinum for such a purpose. The gilt-bronze tiara was made in the 17C for the seated statue of St Peter in the basilica (see p 354), which on high festivals is attired in full pontificals. In **room IX** is the superbly carved **sarcophagus of Junius Bassus, prefect of Rome in 359, which was was found near St Peter's in 1505.

From the entrance to the museum, a second corridor (not usually open to the public) leads right, off which is the **sacristy** (68), built for Pius VI by Carlo Marchionni (1776–84). It is an octagonal hall with a cupola supported by pilasters of yellow Siena marble and grey marble columns from Hadrian's Villa near Tivoli. To the left, the **Sagrestia dei Canonici** (69) has paintings by Francesco Penni and Giulio Romano. The adjoining **chapter house** (70) contains paintings by Andrea Sacchi.

Dome

Outside the basilica, at the right end of the portico, is the entrance to the **dome** (for admission, see above). A lift or staircase ascends to the roof, from which there is a close-up view of the spring of the dome, with the Cross 92m above. The two side cupolas by Giacomo della Porta are purely decorative and have no opening into the interior of the church. On the roof are buildings once used by the *sanpietrini*, the workmen permanently employed on the fabric of St Peter's. Two stairways lead to a curving corridor from which you can enter the first circular **gallery** around the interior of the drum of the dome: this is 53m above the ground and 67m below the top of the dome. From here there is an impressive view of the pavement far below and of the interior of the dome; the decorative details and mosaics are on a vast scale. The higher circular gallery is closed to the public.

Signs indicate the way on up via a spiral staircase with lancet windows, and a curving narrow stair between the two shells of the dome. The first big window has a view south, with the roof of the huge Audience Hall (1971) directly below.

Iron stairs continue up to the tiny marble stairs which emerge on the loggia around the pretty **lantern**, 537 steps above the pavement of the basilica. There is a *view of the Vatican City and gardens, and beyond, on a clear day, of the whole of Rome and of the Campagna from the Apennines and the Alban hills to the sea. A copper ball 2.5m in diameter, just large enough to hold 16 people, is surmounted by the Cross, 132.5m above the ground. Another staircase leads down and out onto the roof, beside the huge statues on the façade, with a view from the parapet of Piazza San Pietro. The exit is at present inside St Peter's, under the Sobieska monument, next to the baptistery (**65**).

The Tombs of the Popes and the Tomb of St Peter

The entrance signposted *Sepolcro di San Pietro e Tombe dei Papi* is at present by the pier of St Andrea (see Plan on pp 356–357), although one of the entrances at the other three piers is sometimes used. The exit is on the outside of the church, to the right of the portico. For admission, see above.

In the space between the level of the existing basilica (30m above sea-level) and that of the old one (27m), the Renaissance architects built the so-called Sacred Grottoes and placed in them various monuments and architectural fragments from the former church. They were used for the burial of numerous popes. Excavations were carried out below the level of the old basilica from 1940 to 1957.

The Old Grottoes have the form of a nave with aisles (corresponding to Maderno's nave but extending beyond it); on either side are the annexes discovered during the excavations. The New Grottoes are in the form of a horseshoe, with extensions. The centre is immediately below the high altar of St Peter's. Four of the extensions reach to points below the four piers of St Longinus, St Helena, St Veronica and St Andrew.

At present only part of the **Old Grottoes** are open to the public. Stairs lead down from the pier of St Andrea to the west end of the nave, where, behind glass and flanked by two lions and two angels, a mosaic marks the **tomb of St Peter** (**1**), directly below the confessio in the church above. The **Tropaion of Gaius** (**2**, see below) is behind on a lower level, with the foundation of the altar of Calixtus II enclosing that of Gregory I, where the rear wall was breached during the excavations for St Peter's tomb. On the right is a chapel (**3**) with a 15C altar of the Virgin, and the tomb (**4**) of Pius VI (d. 1799) in an early Christian sarcophagus. In the aisle of the Old Grottoes are (**5**) the tomb of Queen Christina of Sweden (d. 1689), and opposite (**6**) the tomb of Queen Charlotte of Cyprus (d. 1487). After a short flight of steps there are more tombs: on the left (**7**) that of Innocent IX (d. 1591), and on the right (**8**) that of Benedict XV (d. 1922), followed by those of (**10**) Marcellus II (d. 1555), and (**11**) John Paul I (d. 1978). The chapel (**12**) beyond has a relief of the *Madonna* attributed to Isaia da Pisa. Here is the plain tomb slab of Paul VI (d. 1978). At the beginning of a corridor here (**13**) four beautiful old mosaics from the old basilica can be seen. In the aisle (**14**) is the unfinished tomb of Paul II (d. 1471) by Mino da Fiesole, Giovanni Dalmata and others, and the tomb of Boniface VIII (**15**). At the west end of the grottoes (**16**) there is a kneeling statue of *Pius VI* by Canova. The present exit is through a corridor with some column bases from Constantine's basilica, and the cenotaph of Calixtus III with good reliefs. The corridor leads out to the portico of St Peter's, beside the equestrian statue of Constantine I.

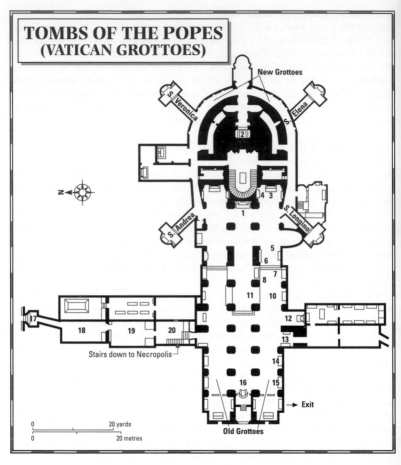

**TOMBS OF THE POPES
(VATICAN GROTTOES)**

New Grottoes

S. Veronica

S. Elena

2

S. Andrea

4 3

1

S. Longino

5

6

7

8

11 10

12

17

18 19 20

13

Stairs down to Necropolis

14

16 15

→ Exit

Old Grottoes

0   20 yards
0   20 metres

The **New Grottoes** (not at present open to the public) are in a horseshoe corridor, lined with fine reliefs of the *Life of St Peter* attributed to Matteo del Pollaiolo, which decorated the tabernacle over the high altar of the old basilica.

For admission to the **Necropolis** and St Peter's Tomb, see p 347.

History of the Necropolis

In 1940 a double row of mausoleums dating from the 1C AD, running from east to west below the level of the old basilica, was discovered. The extreme west series of these is on higher ground and adjoins a graveyard which is immediately beneath the high altar of the present church. Constantine significantly chose to erect his basilica above this necropolis, presumably knowing that it contained the tomb of St Peter. This was a most difficult undertaking because of the slope of the hill; he had to level the terrain and make use of supporting foundation walls.

A baldacchino in the presbytery covered the **Tropaion of Gaius**, a funerary monument in the form of a small aedicule or niche, referred to c 200 and probably built by Pope Anicetus. This monument was discovered during excavations. It backs on to a supporting wall plastered with red, dating from the same period. An empty space beneath it is believed to be the tomb of St Peter. This was probably a mound of earth covered by brick slabs, and it shows signs of the interference which history records. That this was a most revered grave is evident from the number of other graves which crowd in on it, without cutting across the tomb. In front of the red wall, on which a Greek inscription is taken to name the saint, is a later wall, scratched with the names of pilgrims invoking the aid of Peter. Bones, obviously displaced, of an elderly and powerfully built man, were found beneath this second graffiti wall and declared by Paul VI to be those of St Peter. The site of the Circus of Nero, the most likely place of St Peter's martyrdom, lay along the south flank of the basilica, and extended as far as the present Via Sant'Uffizio. The necropolis was in use until Constantine's reign.

To join a tour of the necropolis you are usually asked to enter the Vatican City through the Arco delle Campane, and meet in Piazza dei Protomartiri Romani (see plan on p 348). The visit normally starts at the South Annexe (**17**) of the Old Grottoes (see plan on p 362), and passes through two rooms (**18** and **19**) with 14C–15C tomb slabs and sarcophagi. A third room (**20**) has transennae and architectural fragments of the 4C–9C, and part of the nave foundation wall of the old basilica. There are plans here of the Tropaion of Gaius and the old basilica of St Peter's. From here stairs lead down to the well preserved necropolis.

Among the 18 loculi cleared, the one purely Christian mausoleum provided the most ancient mosaics yet discovered on a Christian subject. Here, on the vault richly decorated with a vine pattern, is Christ as Helios, the sun-god. On the walls are the sinopie remain of mosaics which have become detached from the surface (on the left, Jonah, and ahead, Fishermen). In the other mausoleums Oriental cults and those of Greece and Rome are combined. Christians were also buried in the mausoleum of the Caetenii, with the grave of Aemilia Gorgonia; in the magnificent stuccoed mausoleum of the Valerii, which has reliefs in niches and where, despite the pagan sarcophagus (3C), the inscription of Valerinus Vastulus specifies his Christian burial; and in the so-called Egyptian chamber. The paintings of peacocks in the mausoleum of the family of Aelius Tyrannus, the marble bust of the woman in that of the Valerii, and the remarkable sarcophagus of Marcius Hermes and his wife, mirror the tastes and wealth of the families of freedmen to whom the loculi belonged. Among the many sarcophagi is one for a child, with figures of the mourning parents. One column of the Tropaion of Gaius (see above) survives and you can see where the rear wall was breached during the excavations for St Peter's tomb. Behind is the foundation of the altar of Calixtus II enclosing that of Gregory I.

33 • The Vatican Museums

The extensive buildings and interior courts of the Vatican Palace (Map 1; 3), the largest building in the Vatican City (see p 404), cover an area of 5.5 hectares. Most of the palace is open to the public, as the apartments reserved for the pope and the papal court are contained in a relatively small area. The Vatican Museums contain some of the world's greatest art treasures, and are unique in their scope, quality and abundance. They include the remarkable collections of Greek and Roman sculpture in the Pio-Clementino Museum and the Chiaramonti Museum, as well as the Egyptian and Etruscan collections, and the Museum of Christian Art. The palace also contains the famous Sistine Chapel frescoed by Michelangelo and the Stanze decorated by Raphael, the Vatican picture gallery (the Pinacoteca), the exhibition rooms of the Vatican library, the Borgia Rooms and the Gallery of Modern Religious Art, the Chapel of Nicholas V, the Gallery of Maps, and the Gallery of Tapestries. The Gregorian Museum of Pagan Antiquities, Pio Christian Museum and the Ethnological Missionary Museum are at present closed for restoration.

History of the Vatican Palace and its collections

In the days of Pope St Symmachus (498–514), a house was built beside the first basilica of St Peter. This house was not the residence of the popes who, until the migration to Avignon in 1309, lived in the Lateran Palace; but it was used for state occasions and for the accommodation of foreign sovereigns. Charlemagne stayed here in 800 and Otho II in 980. By the 12C it had fallen into disrepair. Eugenius III (1145–53) was the first of numerous popes to restore and enlarge it. In 1208 Innocent III built a fortified residence here which was added to by his successors. When Gregory XI returned from Avignon in 1378 he found the Lateran uninhabitable and so took up residence in the Vatican. On his death in the same year, the first conclave was held in the Vatican. A covered way (the *Corridoio* or *Passetto*) which connected the Vatican Palace to Castel Sant'Angelo was used in emergencies when some fortified protection was required (see p 343).

Nicholas V transformed the house into a palace, which he built round the Cortile dei Pappagalli. In 1473 Sixtus IV added the Sistine Chapel. Innocent VIII had Giacomo da Pietrasanta build the Belvedere Pavilion on the north summit of the Vatican Hill. The Borgia pope, Alexander VI, decorated a suite of rooms on the first floor of the palace of Nicholas V and these became known as the Appartamento Borgia; he also added the Borgia Tower. Julius II began to form the famous collection of Classical sculpture, which he installed in the Cortile delle Statue, now the octagonal courtyard of the Belvedere. He also commissioned Donato Bramante to unite this area with the palace of Nicholas V by means of long corridors, thus creating the great Courtyard of the Belvedere.

Leo X decorated the east side of the palace with open galleries looking on to the Courtyard of St Damasus, one of which became known as the Loggia of Raphael. Paul III employed Antonio da Sangallo the Younger to build the Cappella Paolina and the Sala Regia. Under Pius IV and Gregory XIII various additions were made by Pirro Ligorio. Sixtus V assigned to Domenico Fontana the construction of the block overlooking Piazza San Pietro and of the great library, which was built at right angles to the long corridors and thus divided the Courtyard of the Belvedere in two. The Scala Regia of Bernini was begun under Urban VIII and completed under Alexander VII. The Museum of Pagan Antiquities was founded by Clement XIII.

Clement XIV converted the Belvedere courtyard into a museum which his successor Pius VI enlarged; hence its name, Pio-Clementino. The architect was Michelangelo Simonetti, who altered the courtyard and added several rooms. Pius VI was also the founder of the picture gallery. Pius VII of the Chiaramonti family founded the sculpture gallery which bears his name and added the New Wing by Raffaele Stern, which paralleled the library. Its construction divided the Courtyard of the Belvedere into three separate courtyards: that nearest the pontifical palace retaining the old name, the Courtyard of the Belvedere; the relatively small Courtyard of the Library; and the Courtyard of the Fir Cone, named after a bronze fir cone (pigna) placed in it by Paul V. Gregory XVI was responsible for the Etruscan and Egyptian Museums. Pius IX closed the fourth side of the Courtyard of St Damasus and built the Scala Pia. Leo XIII restored the Borgia Rooms and reopened them to the public.

Under Pius XI the new picture gallery and a new entrance to the Vatican Museums in the Viale Vaticano were built, both of them dating from 1932. A new building was opened in 1970 by Paul VI to house the former Lateran museums, the Gregorian Museum of Pagan Antiquities and the Pio Christian Museum; in 1973 the Ethnological Missionary Museum was opened beneath. An extensive series of galleries in and around the Borgia apartments were opened in 1973 as a Museum of Modern Religious Art. A grand new entrance of no great architectural distinction was opened in 2000 beside the former entrance on Viale Vaticano (which has now become an exit).

Opening times

March–Oct Mon–Fri 08.45–14.20 (with last exit at 15.45) and Nov–Feb 08.45–12.20 (with last exit at 13.45). Saturdays 08.45–12.20 (with last exit at 13.45). Closed Sun except for the last Sun of the month (unless it is a holiday) when it is open free. Also closed on New Year's Day, 6 Jan, 11 Feb (the anniversary of the founding of the Vatican City State), Easter Mon, 1 May, Ascension Day, Corpus Christi (both usually fall in May or June), 29 June, 15–16 Aug, 1 Nov, 8 Dec, Christmas Day and Boxing Day, and whenever special reasons make it necessary.

Information

☎ 06 6988 3333 or 06 6988 4947.

Admission charges

€ 10,00 (it is frequently increased). There is a reduction (€ 7) for students under the age of 24 in possession of a student card. Children under the age of six are admitted free. All the Vatican museums and collections and areas of the palace described below (including the Sistine Chapel) are covered with this ticket, but only for one single visit. Note that there are different ticket offices for tour groups and individual visitors, and for students.

Plan of visit

Because of the number of different museums the Vatican Palace contains, and the vast extent of the halls and galleries on two floors, it is not practicable to see them all in a single visit. You are strongly recommended not to attempt to see too much, and to plan to return at least two or three times. Saturdays and Mondays, or those following holidays, are usually the most crowded days, and Easter is always the busiest time of the year (see below). It is sometimes wise to plan a visit at the end of the morning (at 12.20 or 14.20, see above), which means you usually avoid queueing at the entrance, but it allows only 1.5 hours for the visit.

You can usually leave the museums from the Sistine Chapel (see below). A number of galleries containing exceptional masterpieces can remain comparitively deserted (at least before 11.00) simply because they are not 'on the way' to the Sistine Chapel. These include the Pinacoteca, the Etruscan Museum, and the Chiaramonti Museum, however when custodians are lacking these are the first galleries to be temporarily closed. The Gregorian Museum of Pagan Antiquities and the New Wing are also usually fairly peaceful, but these are both at present closed.

Getting there

The only access from St Peter's to the **entrance** on Viale Vaticano is by a long and rather unpleasant walk along Via di Porta Angelica to the north of Bernini's colonnade in Piazza San Pietro. At the beginning of the street is the battlemented covered way to Castel Sant'Angelo. The modern Piazza del Risorgimento marks the site of Porta Angelica. On the left is the Cancello di Sant'Anna, one of the entrances to the Vatican City. The road skirts the city wall and turns left out of Piazza del Risorgimento.

The **exit** (see p 396) is near the entrance, although it is also usually possible (except on Wednesdays) to leave the museums by the Scala Regia which leads directly down from the Sistine chapel to the portico of St Peter's (check if it is open with one of the guards at the Quattro Cancelli). This is a good way to avoid the crowds on the way back through the museums to the main exit, and the long walk back to St Peter's along Viale Vaticano.

Disabled visitors

Facilities for the disabled are provided. For information, and to book wheelchairs, ☎ 06 6988 3860.

Refreshments

There is a self-service restaurant and café below the courtyard outside the Quattro Cancelli, and in summer a small café is open near the Sistine Chapel. It is possible to eat a snack at some benches on the terraces and courtyard outside the Quattro Cancelli.

Numbering of sculptures

In the description below of some of the rooms the works have been identiffied by the numbers on the prominent labels (usually in red) attached below them. Some of these, however, are missing or difficult to decipher. The Vatican inventory numbers are inconspicuously marked in black on the right side or back of the works themselves, and so have been ignored here, although in some rooms the keyed plans to the most important works also carry these numbers.

The **main entrance** is on Viale Vaticano (**Map 1**; **3**, **4**; and see plan on pp 370–371) designed by Lucio Passarelli in 2000 in a bastion in the walls. On the ground floor is an information office and cloakroom, and an inappropriate sculpture by Giuliano Vangi (1999), and some Roman mosaics. A staircase (or lifts) leads up to the **ticket office** for individual visitors (separate office for students) and another cloakroom. Beyond the barrier there is a rather unattractive circular oblong stairway flanked by a long escalator. These emerge in the former Cortile delle Corazze, covered over in 2000 with glass and metal. A short flight of steps continues up to a corridor with a splendid view of the dome of St Peter's beyond an open court where the *base of the Column of Antoninus Pius* is exhibited. A monolithic block of Greek marble, it has high-reliefs on three sides showing the *Apotheosis of Antoninus and his wife Faustina*, who are being conducted to

Visiting the Vatican Museums

The number of guided tours in the Vatican can seriously impede other visitors' enjoyment of the museums, and at times the crowds can be such that it is virtually impossible to appreciate the visit. There are often queues and there are usually far too many people to make a visit rewarding. Well over three million people a year visit the Vatican, and the Sistine Chapel is the exclusive goal of almost all the tour groups that enter the palace. Although the number of visitors has doubled in the last 20 years, and the Vatican authorities themselves have admitted that they needed to work out a system to 'regulate the traffic'—which they themselves have compared to that in a small city—there seems to be little serious attempt on their part to meliorate this situation (the problem has been largely solved in many of the famous museums in Italy with the introduction of longer opening hours and booking services). There is also concern that some of the recently restored masterpieces such as the Stanze of Raphael and the Sistine Chapel itself are bound to suffer from the humidity caused by the incessant crowds of visitors. The museum guards are not very helpful, the labelling of the works of art poor, and the museums not as well kept as they might be. It is impossible to predict when the most crowded times will be (exceptionally crowded days can also be experienced in mid-winter). However, some suggestions as to how to attempt to avoid the crowds have been given above.

heaven by a winged genius personifying Rome, and delightful scenes of cavalcades (AD 138 61). It was found in 1703 in Via della Missone, near Montecitorio. Below the court are a self-service restaurant and café. On the right is the entrance to the Pinacoteca (see p 397) and on the left is a vestibule known as the **Quattro Cancelli** (where you can ask for information from the guards), from which all the various museums and galleries are signposted.

Four **one-way itineraries** have been imposed by the Vatican authorities—primarily to regulate the flow of people to the Sistine Chapel and you are expected to chose one of them depending on the time at your disposal. Tour groups have to take the signposted routes but if you are not in a tour they can be disregarded to some extent. If you want to see one particular collection only, however, the one-way systems are usually a hindrance, and in some cases access from one part of the museums to another is no longer possible.

The four separate tours suggested below can at present be made, taking into account the one-way systems.

Route I Quattro Cancelli, Simonetti Staircase, Egyptian Museum, Chiaramonti Museum, New Wing, Pio-Clementino Museum, upstairs to the Room of the Biga, Etruscan Museum, and return to the Quattro Cancelli.

Route II A very long and tiring route which should, if time permits, be taken in two stages. Quattro Cancelli, upstairs to the Gallery of the Candelabra, Gallery of Tapestries and Gallery of Maps, Hall of the Immaculate Conception, Raphael Rooms, Room of the Chiaroscuri, Chapel of Nicholas V, Chapel of Urban VIII, Borgia Rooms and Gallery of Modern Religious Art, Sistine Chapel, Museum of Christian Art, Sistine Hall and Library, returning to Quattro Cancelli.

Route III Quattro Cancelli, Vatican picture gallery, and back to Quattro Cancelli.

Route IV (these museums were closed for restoration in 2002). Vestibule,

Gregorian Museum of Pagan Antiquities, Pio Christian Museum, Ethnological Missionary Museum, and back to the Vestibule.

Route I

Egyptian Museum

The Egyptian Museum occupies rooms in the lower floor of the Belvedere Pavilion adjoining the Pio-Clementino Museum. The entrance is at the top of the first flight of the Simonetti Staircase (*Scala Simonetti*) outside the Hall of the Greek Cross (described below).

History of the Egyptian Museum

The museum was founded by Gregory XVI in 1839 and was arranged by Father Luigi Maria Ungarelli, one of the first Italian Egyptologists to continue the scientific research of Jean-François Champollion (1790–1832), the French archaeologist and founder of modern Egyptology. The rooms were decorated in the Egyptian style in the 19C by Giuseppe de Fabris. The collection was beautifully rearranged in 1989 and is well labelled.

Room I. Funerary stelae and tomb reliefs arranged in chronological order from c 2600 BC–AD 600. **Room II**. Wooden painted mummy cases (1000 BC); two marble sarcophagi (6C BC); jewellery, ornaments and figurines found in tombs (1500–525 BC); canopic jars (1500–500 BC); a model of a boat (2000 BC); and funerary masks and a painted fabric from the Roman period. **Room III**. *Sculptures from the Serapeum of the Canopus of the Egyptian Delta, built by Hadrian in his villa at Tivoli after his journey to Egypt in 130–31, including Serapis, a colossal bust of *Isis*, and statues of *Antinous*. **Room IV**. Colossal grey marble statue personifying the Nile (1C AD); two statues of Hapy, the god representing the Nile in flood; and works from the Serapeum in the Campus Martius.

Room V, the **Hemicycle**, follows the shape of the Niche of the Bronze Fir Cone (described below). Here are displayed a head in sandstone of *Mentuhotep II* (who reigned from 2010–1998 BC), the oldest portrait in the museum; statues in black granite of the lion-headed goddess *Sekhmet* (1390–1352 BC); a colossal statue of *Queen Tuaa*, mother of Rameses II, brought to Rome by Caligula; a colossal granite statue of *Ptolemy Philadelphos* (284–246 BC) and his wife *Arsinoë*; and a black bust of Serapis (2C AD). **Room VI** contains the Grassi collection of small bronzes of sacred animals and gods, and ritual objects. **Room VII** has terracotta statuettes from Alexandria, and limestone funerary reliefs from Palmyra in Syria (2C–3C AD). **Room VIII**. Finds from Syria and Palastine from the Neolithic to the Roman period and cylinder seals from Mesopotamia. **Room IX**. Exquisite *bas-reliefs from Mesopotamia (884–626 BC).

From the landing outside **room IX** of the Egyptian Museum, stairs lead down to the Chiaramonti Museum, and a door into the large **Cortile della Pigna** (Courtyard of the Fir Cone), one of the three sections into which Bramante's Courtyard of the Belvedere was eventually divided (see p 364). At the north end is a niche where Paul V (1605–21) placed the colossal bronze fir cone (*pigna*), over 4m high, found near the Baths of Agrippa. There are tiny perforations in the cone's scales and it originally formed the centrepiece of a fountain beside the

Temple of Isis, near the Pantheon, and gave its name to that district of the city, the Quartiere della Pigna. It was made by a certain Cincius Salvius in the 1C AD. In the Middle Ages it was in the portico of Old St Peter's, together with the two gilt-bronze peacocks (here replaced by copies; the originals are in the New Wing) on either side of it. The fir cone was seen in the portico by Dante and is mentioned in his *La Divina Commedia* (*Inferno*, xxxi, 53).

Also here are seated black granite statues of the goddess *Sekhmet*, and, in the courtyard below, two lions once part of a monument to Nectanebo I (XXXth Dynasty), removed by Gregory XVI from the Fontana dell'Acqua Felice. An incongruous sculpture, donated by Arnaldo Pomodoro, was installed in the centre of the courtyard in 1990. In 1981 a building was constructed 12m beneath this courtyard to house the Secret Archives of the Vatican Library.

Chiaramonti Museum

The Chiaramonti Museum is reached by stairs leading down from the landing outside the Egyptian Museum and near the Round Vestibule (see below). This gallery is named after its founder Pius VII of the Chiaramonti family and was arranged by Antonio Canova, who designed the lunette frescoes with scenes from the *Life of Pius VII* as patron of the arts by Francesco Hayez, Philippe Veit and others. The New Wing and the Gallery of Inscriptions are extensions of this museum. The Chiaramonti gallery, in Bramante's east corridor, is 300m long. The exhibits are divided into 59 sections, numbered on the wall above with roman numerals—odd numbers left, even numbers right. Here are displayed numerous Roman works, many of them copies of Greek originals made in the 5C or 4C BC (indicated as 'copy of a 5C original').

Section I. (3.) Sarcophagus of Caius Junius Euhodus and his wife Metilia Acte a priestess of the Magna Mater at Ostia, with a relief of the story of Alcestis: the faces of Alcestis and her husband Admetus are portraits of the Roman couple (2C AD). In the centre of **section II** is the herm of *Hephaistos* (Vulcan), copy of a 5C original, with a head which may be derived from a statue by Alkamenes. **Section IV.** (3.) Statue of *Hygieia*, part of a group of *Hygieia and Asklepios*, copy of a 4C original attributed to the sons of Praxiteles in the Asklepieion on the island of Kos.

Section X. (26.) Sepulchral monument of Nonnius Zethus and his family (1C AD), a square marble block with eight conical cavities for the remains of the various members of the family. The reliefs of a mill being turned by a donkey and of baking implements probably indicated the man's trade. In the centre of **section XI** is a portrait bust of *Cicero*. **Section XII.** (4.) Relief from a 3C sarcophagus, with a mule in blinkers turning a winepress. **Section XIII.** (1.) *Hermes*, from a 5C original; (4.) *Ganymede and the Eagle*, copy of a 3C Hellenistic original. In the centre of **section XV** is a portrait bust of *Pompey*.

Section XVI. (4.) Head of **Athena*, copy of a 5C original; the eyes are restorations but they indicate the skill with which Greek artists caught human expression. The whites of the eyes were probably of ivory, the pupils of semi-precious stone, and the lashes and brows of bronze. **Section XVII.** (3.) *Silenus with a Panther*, copy of a 3C Hellenistic original. **Section XXI.** (1.) *Eros*, bending his bow, probably a copy of a bronze original by Lysippos; statue of a **Boy*. **Section XXIII.** (3.) Fragment of a relief of **Penelope* in a characteristic pose, sitting on a chair and resting her head on her right hand, from a 5C original. **Section XXVI.**

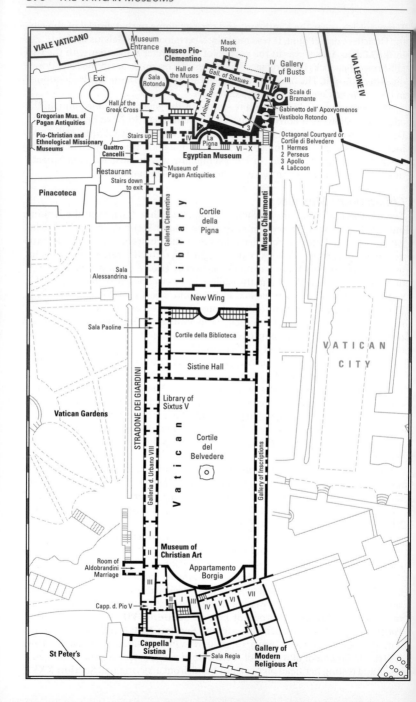

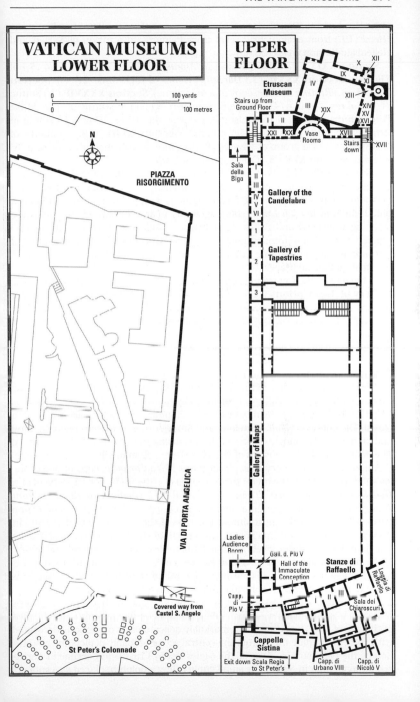

VATICAN MUSEUMS
LOWER FLOOR

0 — 100 yards
0 — 100 metres

N

PIAZZA RISORGIMENTO

VIA DI PORTA ANGELICA

Covered way from Castel S. Angelo

St Peter's Colonnade

UPPER FLOOR

Etruscan Museum

Stairs up from Ground Floor

X
XII
IX
XI
IV
XIII
III
XIX
XIV
XV
XVI
II
XVIII
XXI
XX
Vase Rooms
Stairs down
XVII

Sala della Biga

II
III
IV
VI
1

Gallery of the Candelabra

2

Gallery of Tapestries

3

Gallery of Maps

Ladies Audience Room

Gall. d. Pio V

Hall of the Immaculate Conception

Stanze di Raffaello

Loggia di Raffaello

Capp. di Pio V

I
II
III
IV
Sala dei Chiaroscuri

Cappella Sistina

Exit down Scala Regia to St Peter's

Capp. di Urbano VIII

Capp. di Nicolò V

(**15.**) Head of the *Discobolos* of Myron, copy of the 5C original; a limestone **Head* (**19.**) from a sepulchral relief from Palmyra, in a fusion of Syrian and Hellenistic-Roman styles (2C AD).

Section XXIX. (**2.**) Colossal head of *Augustus*; statue (**4.**) and head (**5.**) of *Tiberius*. **Section XXXII**. (**3.**) *Dacian Prisoner* of high rank (2C AD). **Section XXXVI**. (**3.**) *Resting Athlete*, copy of a 4C original. **Section XXXVII**. (**3.**) Statue of *Herakles*, from a 4C original. **Section XL**. (**1.**) Statue of the *Muse Polyhymnia*, copy of a Hellenistic original of the 3C or 2C BC; (**3.**) statue of *Artemis* (Diana), copy of a 4C original. **Section XLIII**. (**18.**) Statuette of **Ulysses*, part of a group of Ulysses offering wine to Polyphemus, copy of a 3C original. **Section XLV**. (**3.**) Colossal head of *Trajan*.

Section XLVII. (**14.**) Portrait bust of a *Lady of the Julio-Claudian Gens*, the hair is typical of the fashion of the age of Augustus (1C AD). **Section LVIII**. (**8.**) Personification of *Winter*—the female figure is wrapped in a cloak and holds a pine branch in her left hand; she is reclining near a stream where cupids are catching waterfowl and fishes—a Hellenistic-Roman work of the 2C AD; (**9.**) sepulchral relief of a Roman family (1C BC). **Section LIX**. (**7.**) Personification of *Autumn*, a companion piece to *Winter* (above); the female figure is surrounded by cupids gathering grapes.

At the end of the Chiaramonti Museum is a closed gate, beyond which is the **Gallery of Inscriptions** (*Galleria Lapidaria*), open only to scholars. It occupies the remaining part of Bramante's east corridor. The gallery was founded by Clement XIV and reorganised and classified by the epigraphist Monsignor Gaetano Marini (1742–1817). It contains over 5000 pagan and Christian inscriptions from cemeteries and catacombs.

Braccio Nuovo

On the right a door leads into the New Wing, or *Braccio Nuovo*, an extension of the Chiaramonti sculpture gallery constructed by Raffaele Stern (1817–22) for Pius VII. It contains some of the most valuable sculptures in the Vatican, but is often closed. The impressive hall, 70m long and 8m wide, has a vaulted coffered ceiling and an apse in the middle of the south side, facing the Courtyard of the Library. The floor is inlaid with mosaics of the 2C AD from a Roman villa at Tor Marancia.

Among the most important sculptures are: (**5.**) a *Caryatid*, copy of one of the caryatids of the Erechtheion on the Acropolis of Athens (5C BC); (**9.**) a head of a *Dacian*, from the Forum of Trajan (2C AD); and (**11.**) *Silenus Carrying the Infant Dionysos*, a copy of an original ascribed to Lysippos. The **Augustus of Prima Porta* (**14.**) is one of the most famous portraits of the Emperor, found in 1863 in his wife Livia's villa at Prima Porta, 12km north of the centre of Rome above the Via Flaminia. The statue celebrates the Emperor as a famous general and orator. Augustus, who appears to be about 40 years old, is wearing a cuirass over his toga; he held a sceptre in his left hand; his raised right hand shows that he is about to make a speech. The head is full of character and the majestic pose suggests the influence of Greek athletic statues of the 5C BC, such as the Doryphoros of Polykleitos. Augustus was always depicted as a young man, although he died at the age of 76. The cuirass, a remarkably delicate piece of work, is decorated with scenes that date the statue: the central scene probably depicts the restoration by the Parthians in 20 BC of the eagles lost by Crassus at Carrhae in northern Mesopotamia in 53 BC. The small cupid riding a dolphin, placed as a support for the right leg, may be a portrait of Gaius Caesar, grandson of Augustus. The statue is probably a replica of a bronze original, and numerous copies of it exist. Nearby is displayed *Modesty* (26.), probably *Mnemosyne*, a copy of an original of the 3C, and a statue of *Titus* (26.).

In the recess are exhibited: (32.) *Priestess of Isis*; (30.) bust of *Julius Caesar, one of the best examples to have survived of a posthumous portrait, dating from the time of Augustus; and (30a.) alabaster cinerary urn said to be that of Livilla, daughter of Germanicus. The two restored gilt-bronze *Peacocks* (30c, d) probably once stood at one of the entrance gates to Hadrian's Mausoleum. The six tombstones (30a, b, e–h) were found near the Mausoleum of Augustus; five of them belong to the Julian family and the sixth to that of Vespasian. (37.) *Wounded Amazon* (see below); (47.) bust of *Trajan*; (43.) *Selene* (the Moon) approaching the sleeping Endymion, copy of a Hellenistic original of the 4C–3C; (46.) statue of a *Tragic Poet* (the head of Euripides does not belong), copy of a 4C original, perhaps of Aeschylus; (53.) portrait bust of a *Roman (1C AD).

On the opposite wall is a statue of *Demosthenes (64.). This is a replica of the original statue by Polyeuctos of Athens, set up in Athens in 280 BC to the memory of Demosthenes, the orator and statesman. The hands were originally joined, with the fingers crossed. The mouth plainly suggests the stutter from which the great Athenian suffered. (65.) Portrait bust of *Ptolemy of Numidia* (1C AD); (67.) *Wounded Amazon, a replica of one of the statues from the Temple of Diana at Ephesus, by Polykleitos. According to Pliny the Elder, this statue won the prize in a competition in which Polykleitos, Pheidias, Kresilas and Phradmon all entered. The arms and feet were restored by Bertel Thorvaldsen in the early 19C. (74.) Bust of *Hadrian* wearing armour; (76.) statue of *Hera*, copy of a 5C original attributed to Alkamenes; (79.) *Fortune*, copy of a 4C statue—the head, though Roman, is from another figure; the oar and globe are Roman additions; (80.) portrait bust of an *Unknown Roman* of the 2C AD; (82.) statue of an *Unknown Man*, a Greek portrait of the 4C BC; (85.) statue of *Artemis, from a 4C original.

In the apse: bust of a *Man of the late Republican era, possibly Mark Antony; bust of *Marcus Aurelius* as a young man; statuettes of *Athletes*; statue of *Diana*; in the floor, mosaic of *Diana of the Ephesians*. (106.) The *Nile is a fine Hellenistic work, found in 1513 near the Temple of Isis with a statue of the *Tiber* (now in the Louvre). The river-god, who reclines near a sphinx and holds a horn of plenty, has the calm, benevolent expression of a benefactor who enjoys his munificence. The 16 children who frolic over him are supposed to symbolise the 16 cubits which the Nile rises when in flood. The plinth is decorated with characteristic scenes of life on the banks of the Nile.

(108.) Statue of *Julia*, daughter of Titus. (111.) The **Giustiniani Athena*, after a Greek original of the 4C BC, is the best existing copy of an original in bronze attributed to Kephisodotus or to Euphranor; it portrays the goddess's twofold function as the divinity of the intellect and of arms. (112.) Portrait bust of an *Unknown Roman* of the 1C AD, possibly Gnaeus Domitius Ahenobarbus; (114.) statue of a *Man Wearing a Toga*, with the head of Claudius; (117.) *Resting Satyr, copy of the famous statue by Praxiteles (there is a replica in the Gallery of Statues; others are in the Gregorian Museum of Pagan Antiquities and in the Musei Capitolini); (118.) bust of *Commodus* (180–92); (120.) statue of an *Athlete*, with the head of Lucius Verus—the body is a copy of a 5C original; (121.) bust of the Emperor Philip the Arabian (244–49); *Doryphoros of Polykleitos, one of numerous copies of the famous bronze statue of a young spear-bearer by Polykleitos, the greatest sculptor of the school of Argos and Sikyon, who made a careful study of the proportions of the human body; (**124**.) head of a *Dacian*, from Trajan's Forum; (**126**.) statue of **Domitian*, wearing a cuirass.

It is now necessary to return through the Chiaramonti Museum to the landing outside the exit from the Egyptian Museum.

Pio-Clementino Museum

The Pio-Clementino Museum has a superb collection of Greek and Roman sculptures, which together with the other sculpture museums in the Vatican Palace make up the largest collection of ancient sculpture in the world. The present entrance is from the landing outside the exit from the Egyptian Museum.

History of the Pio-Clementino Museum

The museum was founded in the 18C by Pius VI and is named after him and his predecessor, Clement XIV. It occupies the Belvedere Pavilion, which was adapted as a museum by Michelangelo Simonetti. The catalogue of the Museo Pio-Clementino was published in Rome 1784–1808. These collections owe their origin to the Renaissance popes, and in particular to Julius II. Many of the pieces originally collected were later dispersed, however, in particular by Pius V who made numerous gifts to the city of Rome and to private individuals. The popes of the late 18C and early 19C tried to reassemble the old collections and formed new ones. Paul IV decided that the nudity of each male sculpture should be covered with a fig leaf.

The contents of the sculpture galleries are mainly Greek and Roman originals, or Roman copies of Greek originals executed in the 1C and 2C AD. In some cases the Roman sculptor, when copying a Greek model, placed a contemporary portrait head on his copy; later restorers often made additions in marble, stone or plaster and also, in some cases, put heads on statues to which they do not belong.

In the first vestibule is the **sarcophagus*, in peperino, of Lucius Cornelius Scipio Barbatus, from the Tomb of the Scipios (see p 314); the sarcophagus is in the form of a Doric altar but the general character is Etruscan. The archaic inscription, in Saturnine verse, is said to be by Quintus Ennius, the great Roman poet. Above are two inscriptions, also from the Tomb of the Scipios, to the son of Scipio Barbatus, who conquered Corsica in 259 BC.

Ahead is the **Round Vestibule** (*Vestibolo Rotondo*). Here are a large bowl made of pavonazzetto and sculptural fragments. Beyond is the **Gabinetto dell'Apoxyomenos**, with the **Apoxyomenos*, a finely built athlete scraping the oil from his body with a strigil, from a bronze original by Lysippos; this was the masterpiece of the sculptor's maturity (c 330 BC) and illustrated his canon of proportions, and the increase in realism in Greek art of this period. The statue was found in Vicolo dell'Atleta in Trastevere in 1844. On the walls are inscriptions: those on the left in Archaic Latin are from the Tomb of the Scipios, and those on the right include one of Lucius Mummius Achaicus, the conqueror of Greece (146 BC). In the atrium beyond are three circus scenes (3C AD) and an intricately carved funerary niche from near Todi (late 1C AD). Through a glass door here can be seen the spiral **Staircase of Bramante**, which ascends to the floor above (only open in summer). The design is masterly; at each turn the order changes, starting with Tuscan at the bottom and ending with Corinthian at the top.

From the Round Vestibule is the entrance to the **Octagonal Courtyard of the Belvedere** (there is another, larger, courtyard of the Belvedere, to the south), formerly called the *Cortile delle Statue*, where Julius II placed the first Classical sculptures which formed the nucleus of the great Vatican collections, including the **Belvedere Torso** (see below). When Pius VI had the museum enlarged in 1775, Simonetti made the courtyard into an octagon by forming the recesses (*gabinetti*) in the four corners.

To the left is the **Gabinetto dell'Apollo**. Here is the famous *Apollo Belvedere*, a 2C Roman copy of a bronze original probably by Leochares (4C BC). The slender, elegant figure of the young god is stepping forward to see the effect of the arrow that he has just shot. The statue has been greatly admired as one of the master-pieces of Classical sculpture since it was brought to the Vatican in 1503, and was the centre of attention during the Grand Tour. Under the adjoining colonnade is a relief of a *Procession*, from the Ara Pacis (nearly all the heads are restorations).

The **Gabinetto del Laocoönte** contains the famous group of *Laocoön* and his two sons in the coils of the serpents, a vivid and striking illustration of the story related by Virgil in the *Aeneid*. Laocoön, priest of Apollo, warned his fellow Trojans against the trickery of the Greeks and entreated them not to admit the wooden horse into the city. In punishment Apollo or Athene sent serpents to crush him and his young sons to death. The violent realism of the conception as well as the extreme skill and accurate detail with which the agonised contortions of the bodies are rendered are typical of late Hellenistic sculpture.

This group, of Greek marble, is ascribed to the Rhodian sculptors Agesander, Polydoros and Athenodoros (c 50 BC). It was found on the Esquiline Hill in 1506, and was at once recognised as that described by Pliny though it is not carved from a single block, as he states, but from at least three pieces. It was purchased by Julius II and brought to the Vatican where it was greatly admired by the artists of the time; it has recently been suggested that one of the nudes in Michelangelo's *Tondo Doni*, now in the Uffizi gallery in Florence, may be a copy from the *Laocoön*. One of the best known Classical sculptures, it influenced other Renaissance and Baroque artists, and was particularly admired in the 19C. Byron, in *Childe Harold*, describes 'Laocoön's torture dignifying pain'.

The group was restored in 1957: its more familiar appearance—as restored by Giovanni Montorsoli on the advice of Michelangelo—is preserved in a plaster cast which can be seen from a window of the Gregorian Museum of Pagan Antiquities (see below).

Flanking the doorway beyond are two *Molossian Dogs* of the school of Pergamon. The **Gabinetto dell'Hermes** displays *Hermes* (formerly thought to be Antinous), perhaps Hermes Psychopompos, the conductor of souls to the underworld, a copy of an original by Praxiteles at Olympia. In the portico beyond (in a niche), is *Venus Felix* and *Cupid*: the body is copied from the *Venus of Knidos* in the Mask Room; the inscription on the plinth states that the group was dedicated to Venus Felix by Sallustia and Helpis. It has stood in the courtyard since Julius II began the collection here. Also here is a small marble funerary urn in the shape of a house or shrine, and beyond, a sarcophagus with a *Battle of the Amazons*, with Achilles and Penthesileia, grouped in the centre (3C AD).

The **Gabinetto del Canova** contains three Neo-classical statues of *Perseus*—inspired by the *Apollo Belvedere*—and of the boxers *Creugas* and *Damoxenes*, by Antonio Canova, placed here when most of the Classical masterpieces were taken to Paris by Napoleon in 1800, after the Treaty of Tolentino.

Beneath the following portico is the sarcophagus of Sextus Varius Marcellus, father of Elagabalus; and a sarcophagus with curved ends and a relief of a Bacchic procession. Beneath the porticoes are six granite basins, the four smaller ones from the Baths of Caracalla.

The door flanked by the two hounds leads out of the courtyard and into the **Animal Room** (*Sala degli Animali*). Most of the animal statues are by Francesco Antonio Franzoni (1734–1818), who made them for this room for Pius VI. Some are entirely Franzoni's work; others were made up by him from ancient fragments. The Roman pieces include, in the room on the left, a sow with a litter of 12, perhaps of the Augustan period, and, under the far window, the colossal head of a camel (a fountain-head), which is a copy of a Hellenistic original of the 2C BC.

In the niche at the end *Meleager with his Dog* and the head of a *Boar*, is a copy of a 4C original by Skopas. Other pieces of particular interest are: the *Triton* and *Nereid*, with cupids, perhaps a Hellenistic original of the 2C BC, and the head of a *Minotaur*, a copy of a 5C original. In the room on the right: *Mithras Slaying the Bull* (2C AD), and, on the wall behind, *mosaics with animals, from Hadrian's Villa at Tivoli (2C AD). In the pavement of each room are mosaics with animals and plants (2C AD).

The **Gallery of Statues** (right) is sometimes closed, together with the Gallery of Busts, and Mask Room: if this is the case, you should now proceed to the Hall of the Muses from the Animal Room, see p 377. The Gallery of Statues is part of the original Belvedere Pavilion built by Innocent VIII. Remains of paintings by Bernardino Pinturicchio may still be seen on the walls. To the right is the *Eros of Centocelle*, also called the **Genius of the Vatican**, found at Centocelle by Gavin Hamilton—a replica of an original of the early 4C, it is probably a statue of Thanatos, god of death, from an original attributed to Kephisodotos. The *Discobolos* of Polycletus is a replica of the second half of the 5C, and the seated statue of *Paris*, possibly a copy of an original by Euphranor (4C). The *Apollo Kitharoidos* was restored as *Minerva* in the late 5C, and the seated statue of *Penelope* has a head from another antique statue. The *Apollo Sauroctonos*, representing the god watching a lizard that he is about to kill, is a copy of the famous bronze original by Praxiteles, and the so-called *Mattei Amazon*, from an original attributed to Kresilas has a head which does not belong. The *Muse*, restored as *Urania*, belonged to the series of sculptures found at Tivoli (see above). On either side of the door are a pair of seated statues of *Poseidippos* and *Menander* (?), the comic poets, copies of Hellenistic originals. The statue of a *Roman* is traditionally identified as the Emperor Macrinus (AD 217–18), and the two *Children of Niobe* come from the Villa Medici group (now in the Uffizi gallery). Next to the *Danaid*, or nymph, holding a cup is a *Resting Satyr*, one of several known replicas of the famous statue of Praxiteles. At the end of the room: the *Barberini Candelabra*, with representations of divinities, from Hadrian's Villa at Tivoli, Roman works in neo-Attic style (2C AD); *Sleeping Ariadne*, copy of a Hellenistic original of the 3C or 2C; sarcophagus with a gigantomachia, 2C AD, after a Hellenistic original of the 2C BC; relief of *Bacchus and Ariadne*, from Hadrian's Villa; *Hermes*, copy of a 5C Greek original (school of Myron); and statue of *Augustus* of the 1C AD with the head of Lucius Verus (AD 161–69). On the bases of several of the statues are inscriptions relating to the gens Julia-Claudia found near the Mausoleum of Augustus.

At the end is the **Gallery of Busts** (also often closed), divided by arches into four little rooms. **Room I**. To the right, above: (**711**.) *Caracalla*; (**704**.) *Marcus Aurelius*; (**703**.) *Antoninus Pius*. Below: (**723**.) *Trajan*; (**718**.) *Nero*, idealised as *Apollo*; (**716**.) *Old Man wearing a crown of vine-leaves*, possibly a priest of Dionysos, Hellenistic, 2C BC; (**715**.) head of *Augustus as one of the Fratres Arvales* and (**714**.) as a boy; *Julius Caesar*; column with three dancing Hours, found near the Ara Pacis; (**598**.) porphyry bust of a *Youth*, perhaps Philip the Arabian, emperor in 244–49; (**592**.) portrait group of **Cato and Porcia*, probably from a Roman tomb, 1C BC. **Room II**. (**702**.) *Apollo*; (**698**.) *Saturn*, after an original of the 5C or 4C BC; above, (**689**.) colossal bust of *Serapis*; (**697**.) *Isis*; (**694**.) head of *Menelaus*, from a group of *Menelaus with the body of Patroclus* (see p 197). In the middle of the room, a base in the form of a rectangular chest standing on legs of winged lions, the lid decorated with flowers and foliage.

Room IV, the recess to the left. *Mask of Jupiter Ammon*, copy of a 4C original; *Woman in the Attitude of Prayer*, Augustan after a 5C original; bust of **Antinous*, an exquisite portrait; and head of *Juno*, after an original of the 5C. **Room III**. Seated statue of **Zeus (Jupiter Verospi)*, copy of a Hellenistic original, the lower part a restoration; celestial globe; head of one of the *Diadochoi* wearing a regal headband; *Augur*; *Mithras*, in the Phrygian cap; and *Pan*.

The so-called **Open Loggia** (*Loggia Scoperta*), also usually closed to the public, skirts the north side of the Belvedere Pavilion as far as the Mask Room. Here are exhibited a fragment of relief depicting a *Youth taking part in a Bacchic Procession* (3C AD); a frieze, in two sections, with scenes of farm activities and of the sale of bread in a baker's shop, 3C AD; and, over the door to the Mask Room, sepulchral relief of *Galatea*, a priestess of Isis, with her husband, 2C AD.

The **Mask Room** (*Gabinetto delle Maschere*) is usually locked, but is sometimes visible through a glass door. There is another entrance from the Gallery of Statues. It derives its name from four *mosaics of theatrical masks in the pavement. They came from Hadrian's Villa and date from the 2C AD. The border is of the time of Pius VI and bears his coat of arms. Opposite the entrance is the **Venus of Knidos*, a fine copy of the famous statue of Praxiteles. The goddess is about to bathe; she has a towel and, near by, a pitcher (*hydria*). The head belongs to another copy of the statue; the limbs are mainly restorations. On the left, the *Graces*, from an original perhaps of the 2C BC. In the niche opposite, *Satyr*, in rosso antico, from a Hellenistic bronze original (2C BC). On the wall between the doors, *Venus at her Bath*, a copy of a larger original by Doidalsas, a Bithynian sculptor of the 3C BC.

From the Animal Room (see above) is the entrance to the **Hall of the Muses** (*Sala delle Muse*), an octagon with a vestibule at either end, built in 1782 by Simonetti; the paintings are by Tommaso Conca. In the vestibule are herms, including one of *Sophocles*, and reliefs (note the Pyrrhic Dance, a 4C Attic work, and *Birth of Bacchus*). The octagon is a magnificent hall with 16 columns of Carrara marble: seven of the statues of the *Nine Muses* in this room were found, together with that of *Apollo*, in a villa near Tivoli, and are thought to be copies of originals, apparently of bronze, by Praxiteles or his school, but it is possible that they do not all belong to the same group. The statues alternate with herms which include portraits of *Homer*, *Socrates*, *Plato*, *Euripides*, *Epicurus*, and *Demosthenes*.

In the centre is the *Belvedere Torso*, bearing the signature of Apollonios, an Athenian sculptor of the 1C BC. The figure is sitting on a hide laid over the ground. In the past scholars have advanced various hypotheses about the identification of the statue including Hercules, Polyphemus, Prometheus, Sciron, Marsyas or Philoctetes, but recent studies have suggested that it may represent Ajax meditating suicide (in his right hand he probably held a sword with which he was about to kill himself).

Found in the Campo dei Fiori at the time of Julius II, the torso was formerly exhibited in the centre of the Cortile delle Statue (the Octagonal Courtyard of the Belvedere, see above) where it was greatly admired by Michelangelo and Raphael. It was frequently drawn by Renaissance artists, and in the 16C and 17C it was copied in small bronzes.

The domed **Circular Hall** (*Sala Rotonda*) was also designed by Simonetti (c 1782), and modelled on the Pantheon. In the pavement is a very well preserved polychrome mosaic from Otricoli, representing a *Battle between Greeks and Centaurs*, with tritons and nereids in the outer circle. The huge monolithic porphyry vase was found in the Domus Aurea. Around the walls are displayed important colossal busts and statues (described from right of the entrance): *Jupiter of Otricoli*, a colossal head of majestic beauty, attributed to Bryaxis (4C BC); *Antinous as Bacchus*, from a Greek prototype of the 4C, the drapery, originally of bronze, restored in the early 19C by Thorvaldsen; bust of *Faustina the Elder* (d. 141), wife of Antoninus Pius; *Female Divinity*, perhaps Demeter, wearing the peplos, after a Greek original of the late 5C BC; head of *Hadrian*, from his mausoleum; *Hercules*, a colossal statue in gilded bronze, an early Imperial copy of a work of the school of Skopas; bust of *Antinous*; *Juno* (the *Barberini Hera*), a Roman copy of a cult-image in the manner of the late 5C; head of a *Marine Divinity* (from Pozzuoli), believed to personify the Gulf of Baiae, an interesting example of the fusion of marine elements and human features; *Nerva* (or *Galba*), after a seated statue representing Jupiter; bust of *Serapis*, after a work by Bryaxis; *Claudius* as Jupiter; head of *Claudius*; *Juno Sospita* from Lanuvium, dating from the Antonine period; head of *Plotina* (d. 129), wife of Trajan; head of *Julia Domna* (d. 217), wife of Septimius Severus; *Genius of Augustus*; head of *Pertinax*.

The **Hall of the Greek Cross** (*Sala a Croce Greca*) is another Neo-classical room by Simonetti, dominated by two magnificent porphyry sarcophagi: that on the left belonged to St Helena, mother of Constantine, decorated with Roman horsemen, barbarian prisoners and fallen soldiers, and that on the right to Constantia, daughter of Constantine, decorated with vine-branches and children bearing Christian symbols of grapes, peacocks and a ram. It was moved here in 1791 from Santa Costanza (see p 441). In the centre is a mosaic pavement with a shield decorated with the head of *Minerva* and surrounded by the phases of the moon. Between two granite Sphinxes is another mosaic with a *basket of flowers.

Ahead is the landing of the **Simonetti Staircase**. It ascends to a second landing outside the Gallery of the Candelabra and the Room of the Biga on the right.

The **Room of the Biga** (with glass doors, usually locked) is a circular domed hall by Giuseppe Camporese. The *Biga*, or two-horsed chariot, is a reconstruction in 1788 by Francesco Antonio Franzoni from ancient fragments; only the body of the chariot and part of the offside horse are original. The chair was used as an episcopal throne in the church of San Marco during the Middle Ages. The bas-reliefs suggest that the *biga* was a votive chariot dedicated to Ceres and that it dates from the 1C AD. Also here are two statues of the *Discobolos*, one a copy of Myron's work with the head wrongly restored, and the other from a bronze original by Naucides, nephew and pupil of Polykleitos, a fine example of Peloponnesian sculpture of the 5C BC. The other works are difficult to see, but include a **Bearded Dionysos**, called **Sardanapalus**, a work of the early 4C BC attributed to Kephisodotos, and four sarcophagi of children (3C AD).

Etruscan Museum

The Etruscan Museum is reached by the Simonetti Staircase from the landing outside the Room of the Biga. At the top of the stairs, outside the entrance, is a beautiful krater in grey stone.

History of the Etruscan Museum

The museum was founded in 1837 by Gregory XVI, and its official name is the Museo Gregoriano Etrusco. One of the most important collections of its kind in existence, many of the objects come from Southern Etruria, but there are also outstanding examples of Greek and Roman art, and a notable collection of Greek vases. In 1989 the Giacinto Guglielmi collection of finds from Vulci—including Attic vases and Etruscan material—was acquired. The collection was beautifully rearranged and well labelled (also in English) at the end of the 20C. Apart from the first two rooms, the exhibits are subdivided according to material, i.e. bronze, stone, terracotta, precious objects and ceramics.

Room I. Early Iron Age material (9C–8C BC), in the case on the left are finds from Etruria with Villanovan cinerary urns, and in the case on the right objects from Latium Vetus (south of the Tiber), including a reconstructed chariot and weapons of the late 8C BC.

Room II. Interesting frescoes by Federico Barocci and Taddeo Zuccari, with good stuccoes. The room contains objects found in 1836 in an Etruscan necropolis south of Cerveteri, where a small group of tumulus chamber-tombs were unearthed; the most important is the *Regolini-Galassi Tomb*, named after its discoverers. Three important people were buried here in 650 BC, including a princess called Larthia, a warrior of high rank, and a priest-king who was cremated. Their funeral equipment includes gold jewellery (a gold *clasp*, with decorations in relief, necklaces and bracelets); ivories; cups; plates; silver ornaments of Graeco-Oriental provenance; a bronze libation bowl, with six handles in the shape of animals; and a reconstructed throne. Also here were found a *cremation urn*; a series of pottery statuettes; a bronze incense-burner in the shape of a wagon; a bronze stand with figures in relief; two five-handled jars; silverware including a drinking cup and jug; and small dishes of Eastern origin. The *biga* has been reconstructed, as well as a funeral carriage with a bronze bed and funeral couch. The two cases on the window wall contain finds from tombs in the immediate vicinity of the Regolini-Galassi Tomb, including Bucchero vases in relief, and ceramics from another tomb in the necropolis.

Room III. Frescoes (being restored) painted for Pius IV by Niccolò Pomarancio and Santi di Tito. Here is displayed a rich collection of bronze objects in common use, including an incense-burner, tripod, buckles, jars, small throne and candelabra, and two statuettes of children. In the centre is the *Mars of Todi*, wearing armour, a bronze statue dating from the beginning of the 4C BC, but inspired by Greek art of the 5C BC. The collection of mirrors includes a particularly fine one engraved with Herakles and Atlas, and another with Chalchas, the soothsayer, both designs derived from Greek models of 5C–4C BC. The *cistae*—caskets used by women for their jewellery or as toilet-cases—come mostly from Palestrina, and include a fine oval *cista found at Vulci, decorated with a **Battle between Greeks and Amazons**, with a handle formed by a satyr and a nymph riding on swans. Among the *paterae*, round flat dishes used for libations, is one with the figure of Eos (Aurora) carrying away Kephalos.

Two steps lead up to **room IV**, which exhibits works in stone. The two *Lions* (late 6C BC) used to guard a tomb at Vulci. The sarcophagus of Circeo has a polychrome relief of a procession from a tomb at Cerveteri (late 5C or early 4C BC) with the deceased lying on the roof. Beyond some small inscribed funerary cippi of the Volsinii type (4C–3C BC) is a cippus from Todi with a bilingual inscription in Latin and Celtic on both sides. A sarcophagus from Tuscania has a relief of the **Battle of the Centaurs**. Beyond is a seated female statue in sandstone, from Chiusi (3C–2C BC), and cippi in the form of pine cones from Palestrina. The sculpted heads include some from Vulci. A sarcophagus from Tarquinia (2C BC) shows the Thebans. The works from Vulci (4C BC) include two horses' heads and a funerary cippus in the form of a capital.

Steps lead up to room IX (described below), and on the left a modern flight of stairs continues up to rooms V–VIII (not always open). Rooms V–VI display works in terracotta. In **room V** are three antefixes. **Room VI**, on two levels, displays a group of votive statues and a high relief from the pediment of a temple in Tivoli. The polychrome ornament in the form of a winged horse comes from the corner or top of a pediment. In cases are numerous portrait *heads of both sexes and all ages, and models of legs and feet, all of them ex-votos. The bust of an *Elderly Woman*, dating from the 3C BC, is particularly remarkable. **Rooms VII** and **VIII** have a magnificent display of *gold jewellery, displayed chronologically from the 7C BC. Most of it is from Vulci and includes a necklace with pomegranate drops, coronets and diadems used as funerary wreaths, and beautiful earrings.

At the bottom of the stairs is **room IX** which displays the Guglielmi Collection from Vulci (half of it was donated to the Vatican in 1937, and the other half was purchased from the Guglielmi in 1988). It is especially important for its Attic black- and red-figure vases, a number of them attributed pieces displayed in the central cases. It also has Villanovan objects, bronzes—including fine stamnoi, bucchero vases and Corinthian ware. From the windows the view over the northern districts of the city extends to Monte Mario.

Room X. Alabaster cinerary urns from the Hellenistic period from Volterra and Chiusi. **Room XI**. Funerary monument with the figure of the *Dying Adonis* from Tuscania (second half of the 3C BC); cinerary urns in travertine from Perugia, and two urns from Bomarzo. The little **room XII**—with a view of the Borghese Gardens, Villa Medici and, to the right, Castel Sant'Angelo and the

Vittorio Emanuele II monument—displays the Falcioni collection acquired in 1898, typical of a 19C private collection, with a variety of objects including small bronzes, terracottas and jewellery, some from the neighbourhood of Viterbo, and others of unknown provenance. **Room XIII**. Three terracotta sarcophagi from Tuscania. The spiral staircase of Bramante which descends to the Pio-Clementino Museum is at present closed.

The **Antiquarium Romanum** is displayed in rooms XIV–XVI. **Room XIV**. Fragments of large bronze statues, including the portrait head of the *Emperor Treboniano Gallo* (251–53 AD); part of a bronze folding table; silver vases with a dedication to Apollo, from Vicarello on the Lago di Bracciano, dating from the 1C AD; Roman scales; a bronze weight in the shape of a crouching pig, marked C for 100 Roman pounds; armour in bronze and iron; rings, pins and keys. The view from the window takes in Castel Sant'Angelo, the dome of the Pantheon, the Vittorio Emanuele monument and the tower of Palazzo Senatorio on the Campidoglio, all of them backed by the Alban Hills.

Room XV. Architectural terracottas, lamps, glass and three fine terracotta panels with reliefs of the *Labours of Hercules*, from the Augustan age. Finds from the Ager Vaticanus, the area on the right bank of the Tiber near the Vatican, are displayed in **room XVI**.

A short flight of stairs leads down to **rooms XVII–XXI** which have a valuable *collection of Greek, Italic and Etruscan vases. Most of them come from the tombs of Southern Etruria, discovered during excavations in the first half of the 19C. At the time of their discovery the vases were all indiscriminately called Etruscan. In fact many of them are Greek in origin and illustrate the importance of the commercial relations between Greece and Etruria; from the end of the 7C to the late 5C BC many Greek vases were imported. By the middle of the 4C BC the Greek imports were largely replaced by the products of Magna Graecia, Lucania and Campania.

Room XIX, the **Hemicycle**, has charming 18C frescoes with views of Rome and the Vatican, and scenes of the Papal States and of the building which houses the sacristy of St Peter's, built at about this time. The hemicycle has a splendid display of Attic vases. At the right end, a case of black figure *oinochoi*; the black figure amphorae (500–490 BC) include one with a battle scene and chariot by the 'Edinburgh Painter'. Displayed in a case on its own is a *hydria* of the Leagros group (c 500 BC). Another case has four black-figure amphorae showing athletes in the presence of Athena, by the 'Berlin Painter' (500–480 BC). Beyond the door are kylixes of the 6C BC, including one with red-figure and black-figure decorations. In another case is a black-figure *amphora signed by Exekias, who worked in 530–520 BC. One side shows Achilles and Ajax playing with dice; on the other side Castor and Pollux are being welcomed on their return home by their parents, Tyndareus and Leda. The red-figure amphorae is attributed to the 'Kleophrades Painter' (510–500 BC). The wall case has red-figure vases including three signed hydria. In a case on its own is a red-figure amphora attributed to the 'Hector Painter', showing Hector carrying out libations before a battle, and taking leave of his parents Priam and Hecuba. In the last case are red-figure amphorae, and a *kylix by the famous 5C vase painter Duris, with Oedipus trying to solve the riddle of the Sphinx.

Room XX, frescoed by Pomarancio, contains the private collection left to the museum in 1967 by Mario Astarita of Naples. Exhibited on its own is a large krater of the late Corinthian period showing Ulysses and Menelaus asking for the return of Helen. **Room XXI**. Red-figure vases from Vulci and Cerveteri (6C BC), attributed to the 'Madrid Painter' and the 'Vatican Painter', and works in the Corinthian style (650–615 BC). The upper hemicycle (**room XXII**) has been closed for a number of years, but it will probably exhibit vases from Magna Graecia.

The Simonetti Staircase leads back down to the Quattro Cancelli.

Route II

From the Quattro Cancelli, at the foot of the Simonetti Staircase, you can visit a small room which houses the **Museum of Pagan Antiquities of the Library** (see p 396), a collection begun by Clement XIII in 1767, with additions from excavations in 1809–15. It was completed in the time of Pius VI, when this room was decorated by Luigi Valadier, with ceiling paintings symbolising *Time*. In the niches on either side of the entrance wall are a head of **Augustus* and a bronze head of *Nero*. In the cupboards (usually kept closed) in the left wall are carved Roman ivory, busts in semi-precious stones, a miniature torso, a mosaic from Hadrian's Villa at Tivoli, Roman bronze statuettes (1C–3C AD), and plaques with inscriptions. In the cupboards on the right wall are the head and arm of a gold-and-ivory statue of Minerva, claimed to be a 5C BC Greek original; Etruscan bronzes and carved Roman ivory. The other rooms of the Vatican Library, beyond, are described on p 395.

We now take the Simonetti staircase up two flights of stairs to the landing outside the Room of the Biga. Here is the beginning of Bramante's long west gallery, housing the Gallery of the Candelabra, the Gallery of Tapestries and the Gallery of Maps.

Gallery of the Candelabra

The Gallery of the Candelabra (80m long) is named after the pairs of marble candelabra, of the Roman Imperial period, placed on either side of the arches which divide it into six sections. The ceiling has frescoes by Domenico Torti and Ludovico Seitz illustrating events during the 16C pontificate of Leo XIII. In the pavement are marbles from the warehouses of ancient Rome.

Section I. (20.) Sarcophagus of a child, Roman, 3C AD; pair of candelabra from Otricoli, with reliefs of Bacchic rites and of Apollo and Marsyas, Roman, 2C BC. **Section II**. (10.) *Pan Extracting a Thorn from a Satyr's Foot*, copy of a 2C Hellenistic original; (22.) *Diana of the Ephesians*, 3C AD; candelabra of the 2C ad from a Roman villa; (83.) *Ganymede carried off by the Eagle*, after a bronze original by Leochares.

Section III. On the walls, fragments of frescoes from a Roman villa at Tor Marancia, near the Catacombs of Domitilla, with flying figures, 2C AD; (12.) mosaic of fish and fruit; (13.) *Apollo*, from an archaic Greek type; (40.) *Satyr*, with young Dionysos on his shoulders (1C AD).

Section IV. (30.) **Sarcophagus* with Dionysos and Ariadne and Dionysiac scenes, 2C AD; (38.) **Fisherman*, a realistic work of the school of Pergamon (3C BC); (66.) **Boy with a Goose*, from a bronze by Boethus of Chalcedon, 3C BC; (85.) **sarcophagus* with the *Slaughter of the Niobids*, a fine work of the 2C AD; (93.) *Boy of the Julio-Claudian Family*, 1C AD.

Section V. **Girl Running in a Race*, during a Peloponnesian religious festival,

Roman copy of a Greek bronze original of the 5C BC; (25.) *Young Satyr*, playing the flute. **Section VI**. Artemis, from a Praxitelean original, the head (which does not belong) a copy of a 5C bronze; (5.) statuette of a *Woman Wearing a Cloak*, copy of a Hellenistic original of the 4C or 3C BC; (8.) sarcophagus with Diana and Endymion; (20.) *Youth Wearing the Phrygian Cap*, in the manner of Praxiteles; (24.) *Niobid*, copy of a Hellenistic original of the 4C or 3C BC; (32.) *Fighting Persian*, statuette after an original bronze belonging to the series of statues given by Attalos I of Pergamon to the Athenians, which were placed on the Acropolis in Athens; (35.) sarcophagus with the rape of the daughters of Leukippos.

Gallery of Tapestries

The Gallery of Tapestries (*Galleria degli Arazzi*) is divided into three rooms, and contains the so-called New School series of tapestries executed after Raphael's death from cartoons by his pupils, some of which were copied from drawings he had left. Also displayed here are Roman and Flemish tapestries. **Room 1**. Raphael New School tapestries, woven in Brussels in the 16C: *Adoration of the Shepherds* and *Adoration of the Magi*. Opposite are tapestries illustrating the *Life of Urban VIII*, the most important product of the Barberini workshop, active in Rome 1627–83. **Room 2**. Raphael New School tapestries: *Massacre of the Innocents* (from a cartoon attributed to Tomaso Vincidor), in three parts; *Christ Appearing to Mary Magdalene*; *Resurrection of Christ*; *Supper at Emmaus*. Opposite are more 17C Roman tapestries illustrating the *Life of Urban VIII*. **Room 3**. *Death of Julius Caesar*, Flemish (1594). The late 15C tapestries include *Scenes of the Passion*; *The Creed*.

Gallery of Maps

The Gallery of Maps (*Galleria delle Carte Geografiche*) was decorated at the time of Gregory XIII with numerous *maps and plans painted in 1580–82 by Egnazio Danti, the celebrated Dominican cosmographer, mathematician, architect and painter. Danti had been appointed by the pope to sit on his commission set up in 1577 to reform the calendar— until that time the calendar in use had been that introduced by Julius Caesar. This was seen to contain a small error which Gregory XIII's new calendar, adopted in Italy in 1582, corrected by eliminating ten days. This new system of calculating the passage of time was not accepted in England until 1752.

The maps are extremely important to our knowledge of 16C Italy and represent the Italian peninsula, the Italian regions and the neighbouring islands, as well as some of its most important ports, and the papal territory of Avignon. It is the largest decorative scheme of its kind: it was intended to be seen from the far door, since the regions of northern Italy are at the southern entrance.

Taking the central axis of the gallery as the Apennine range, the west wall (overlooking the Vatican Gardens) represents the Adriatic and Alpine regions, and the opposite wall the Ligurian and Tyrrhenian side of Italy. Each map is labelled in Latin at the top. By the far door is *Venice, and two general maps showing the country under the Roman Empire (*Italia antiqua*) and in the 16C (*Italia nova*). The paintings were restored several times up until the 17C. The ceiling was decorated at the same time with stuccoes and frescoes illustrating the importance of history and geography to the Church, by a group of painters including Cesare Nebbia, under the direction of Girolamo Muziano.

Beyond the Gallery of Maps is the **Gallery of Pius V**. In the first room are four 17C tapestries made in Bruges and medieval and Renaissance ceramics, some of them found in excavations beneath the Lateran Palace and Palazzo della Cancelleria. In the second room are exhibited miniature mosaics made in the Vatican workshops from the late 16C onwards, and particularly in vogue in the late 18C and early 19C. This technique—which used tiny tesserae of glass enamel instead of stone—was used to reproduce large paintings in St Peter's and then to decorate boxes or precious objects often donated by the popes to illustrious visitors to the Vatican. Many of the mosaics displayed here have interesting views of Rome.

To the right is the Ladies' Audience Room (closed indefinitely), added by Paul V (1605–21) and frescoed by Guido Reni.

At the end of the gallery is the **Chapel of St Pius V**; to the left is the **Sobieski Room**. The floor is inlaid with mosaics from Ostia, and there is a painting by Jan Alois Mateiko (1883) depicting the *Liberation of Vienna* by John Sobieski on 12 September 1683.

Beyond is the **Hall of the Immaculate Conception**, a room decorated with frescoes by Francesco Podesti (1858) which illustrate the definition and proclamation of the dogma of the Immaculate Conception pronounced by Pius IX on 8 December 1854. The floor has 2C mosaics from Ostia. Beyond are the Stanze di Raffaello.

Stanze di Raffaello

The Stanze di Raffaello (Raphael Rooms) are a series of rooms built by Nicholas V as papal audience chambers, a library and a hall for the papal tribunal.

History of the Raphael Rooms

The walls were originally painted by Andrea del Castagno, Piero della Francesca and Benedetto Bonfigli. Julius II employed a group of great artists to continue the decoration, including Luca Signorelli, Perugino, Sodoma, Bramantino, Baldassare Peruzzi, Lorenzo Lotto and the Flemish painter Jan Ruysch. Bramante recommended a fellow citizen of Urbino, Raffaello Sanzio, known in English as Raphael, whom the Pope sent for and set to work immediately on his arrival in Rome in 1508. The result proved so satisfactory that Julius dismissed all the other painters, ordered their works to be destroyed, and commissioned Raphael to decorate the whole of this part of the Vatican.

The Stanze are the painter's masterpiece; they show the extraordinary development which took place in his art during the years between his coming to Rome in 1508 and his death at the age of 37 in 1520. Rome was of first importance during the High Renaissance, and when Raphael arrived he found the court of Julius II an intellectual centre of the first rank. The College of Cardinals and the Curia included among their members many celebrated savants, humanists and men of letters, and a crowd of artists, led by Bramante and Michelangelo, were at work in the city. In this highly cultured environment Raphael, who had great powers of assimilation, acquired an entirely new manner of painting.

Other works by Raphael in Rome can be seen in the Vatican picture gallery, the Cappella Chigi in Santa Maria del Popolo, and in Santa Maria della Pace and Sant'Agostino. He also designed the loggia of the Villa Farnesina and carried out a fresco there of Galatea. He painted a famous portrait of Julius II two years before the pope's death in 1513, now in the National Gallery in London, with a replica in the Uffizi gallery in Florence. The new Medici pope, Leo X, appointed Raphael head of the building works in St Peter's in 1514, and commissioned him to decorate the Vatican Loggia. In 1518 Raphael also painted Leo X, with two cardinals: this portrait is in the Uffizi gallery. Leo appointed him commissioner of antiquities to ensure that everything possible was done to preserve the ancient buildings of Rome. Raphael left the huge altarpiece of the *Transfiguration*, now in the Vatican picture gallery (see below) incomplete and it was displayed above his coffin at his funeral in 1520. He is buried in the Pantheon (see p 178).

Raphael began work in the Stanza della Segnatura (II), with the frescoes of *Astronomy, Apollo, Adam and Eve*, and the *Judgement of Solomon*, which were probably his trial works; he then carried out the other frescoes in this room. After this he decorated, successively, the Stanza d'Eliodoro (III), the Stanza dell'Incendio (I), and the Stanza di Costantino (IV). A careful programme of restoration of the frescoes was nearing completion in 2002.

Sala di Costantino

The entrance to the Stanze has been altered, so that the rooms now have to be visited in reverse chronological order, as described below. From the Hall of the Immaculate Conception a covered balcony overlooking the Cortile del Belvedere leads direct to the furthest room, **room IV**, the *Sala di Costantino*. This room was painted almost entirely in the time of Clement VII (1523–34), after Raphael's death, by Giulio Romano with the assistance of Francesco Penni and Raffaellino del Colle. On the wall facing the window is the *Victory of Constantine over Maxentius near the Pons Milvius*, for which Raphael had made some sketches. The reddish tint which suffuses the picture is characteristic of Giulio Romano. To the right are the figures of *St Urban, Justice and Charity*; to the left, *St Sylvester, Faith and Religion*.

On the entrance wall, *Constantine Addressing his Soldiers* and the *Vision of the Cross* are by Giulio Romano, perhaps from Raphael's design; to the right of this are the figures of *St Clement, Temperance and Meekness*; to the left, *St Peter, the Church and Eternity*. On the wall opposite the entrance, the *Baptism of Constantine by St Sylvester* (a portrait of Clement VII) is by Francesco Penni; at the sides to the right are *St Leo, Innocence and Truth*, and to the left *St Damasus, Prudence and Peace*. On the window wall, *Constantine's Donation of Rome to Sylvester* is by Raffaellino del Colle. At the sides on the right are *Gregory VII* (?) and *Fortitude*; and to the left *St Sylvester* and *Courage*. Below are other scenes from the *Life of Constantine*. On the ceiling is the *Triumph of Christianity*, interesting for its unusual iconography, by Tomaso Laureti. In the floor is a 2C Roman mosaic of the Seasons.

Room of the Chiaroscuri and Chapel of Nicholas V

It is now necessary to interrupt the visit to the Stanze in order to see the Room of the Chiaroscuri and the Chapel of Nicholas V. From the Sala di Costantino a door leads into the **Room of the Chiaroscuri**, or the Room of the Grooms (*Sala dei Palafrenieri*), with a magnificent carved and gilded *ceiling, with the Medici arms. The monochrome frescoes were restored in 1560 by Taddeo and Federico Zuccari and additions were made to them in 1582 by Giovanni Alberti.

The little adjoining **Chapel of Nicholas V** is entirely decorated with *frescoes by Fra Angelico, painted between 1448 and 1450, and restored in 2002. These represent scenes from the lives of the deacon saints *Stephen* (upper section) and *Lawrence* (lower section); especially fine is the painting of *St Stephen Preaching*. On the ceiling are shown the four Evangelists and on the pilasters the Doctors of the Church.

Loggia of Raphael

The Loggia of Raphael has been closed to the public for many years, but you can see a small part of it from the window of the room of the Chiaroscuri. The long gallery of 13 bays was begun by Bramante about 1513 and completed after Bramante's death by Raphael and his pupils. The vault of each bay has four little paintings of Old Testament scenes. The grotteschi of the borders are thought to have been inspired by those in the Domus Aurea of Nero (see p 279), which were discovered in the 15C and known to Raphael. The designs were carried out by Giulio Romano, Giovanni da Udine, Franceso Penni, Perino del Vaga, Polidoro da Caravaggio and others. Controversial restoration work was carried out on the paintings in 1978.

Stanza d'Eliodoro

A door leads back into the Stanze from the Room of the Chiaroscuri. **Room III**, the *Stanza d'Eliodoro*, was painted by Raphael in 1512–14; the subjects were nearly all chosen by Julius II (and restoration work is still in progress here). On the principal wall (to the right) is the *Expulsion of Heliodorus from the Temple at Jerusalem*, alluding to Julius II's success in freeing the States of the Church from foreign powers. The picture illustrates a story in the Apocrypha (Maccabees II, 3): King Seleucus sends his treasurer Heliodorus to Jerusalem to steal the Temple treasure, but the crime is avenged by a horseman assisted by two angels with whips. In the middle of the crowd on the left is Julius II, carried on the *sedia gestatoria* (the front bearer is a portrait of the engraver Marcantonio Raimondi). In the centre of the composition, under the vault of the Temple, the high priest Onias renders thanks to God before the Ark of the Covenant.

On the left is the *Mass of Bolsena*, representing the famous miracle which took place at Bolsena in 1263. A Bohemian priest who had doubts about the doctrine of Transubstantiation was convinced when he saw blood drop from the Host on to the altar cloth (the stained corporal is preserved in the cathedral at Orvieto). Julius II, on his first expedition against Bologna in 1506, had stopped at Orvieto to pay homage to the relic. He is shown kneeling opposite the priest in place of Urban IV, the contemporary pope. The warm colours, and especially, the harmony of reds in the composition, show how much Raphael was influenced by Venetian painters (Sebastiano del Piombo and Lorenzo Lotto arrived in Rome at this time).

On the long wall is *Leo I Repulsing Attila*, a subject originally selected by Julius II and taken up again at the suggestion of Leo X, when considerable changes were made in the design. It was executed partly by Raphael's assistants. The scene representing the banks of the Mincio, where the historic event took place, was replaced by the environs of Rome, and the figure of the pope, on a white mule, was brought from the back of the picture into the foreground in order to accentuate the allusion to the battle of Ravenna on 11 April 1512, at which Leo X, then a cardinal, had been present, and which resulted in the expulsion of the

French from Italy. Attila, mounted on a white horse, and the Huns behind him are struck with terror by a vision of St Peter and St Paul.

On the fourth wall is the *Liberation of St Peter*, alluding to the captivity of Leo X after the battle of Ravenna. Three night scenes, with remarkable light effects, illustrate three different episodes: in the middle, the interior of the prison is seen through a high barred window, with St Peter waking up as the angel frees him from his chains; on the left are the guards outside the prison; and on the right St Peter escaping with the angel.

The decoration of the lower part of the walls, with caryatids and four herms, is attributed to Perino del Vaga. The ceiling paintings of *God Appearing to Noah*, *Jacob's Dream*, the *Burning Bush*, and *Abraham's Sacrifice* are generally attributed to Peruzzi.

Stanza della Segnatura

Room II, the *Stanza della Segnatura*, where the pope signed bulls and briefs, has the most beautiful and harmonious frescoes in the series. It was painted entirely by Raphael in 1508–11. On the long wall opposite the entrance is the famous *Disputa* (or Disputation on the Holy Sacrament), representing a discussion on the Eucharist but essentially intended as a glorification of Catholicism. Given an extremely difficult subject, Raphael succeeded in making the relatively limited space occupied by the composition, which is divided into two zones, appear far larger than it is. In the celestial zone Christ appears between the Virgin and St John the Baptist; above is God the Father surrounded by angels; beneath, the Holy Dove between four angels holding the book of the Gospels; on the left are St Peter, Adam, St John the Evangelist, David, St Lawrence, and Jeremiah(?); on the right, St Paul, Abraham, St James, Moses, St Stephen and Judas Maccabaeus. In the middle of the terrestrial zone is a monstrance with the Host on an altar. On the right are St Augustine and St Ambrose, and on the left St Gregory and St Jerome; they are surrounded by an assembly of Doctors of the Church, popes, cardinals, dignitaries, and the faithful. Certain figures are thought to be portraits of the British medieval theologian Duns Scotus, St Dominic, St Francis, St Thomas Aquinas and St Nicholas of Bari. On the right is the profile of Dante crowned with laurel, and, beyond him (just visible at the back of the figures in a black hat), is Savonarola. Savonarola, the learned theologian and famous preacher had been excommunicated by Pope Alexander VI and executed for heresy and treason in Florence in 1498. On the extreme left are Fra Angelico, in the black Dominican habit, and, in the foreground, Bramante.

Beneath the picture are three monochrome paintings by Perino del Vaga: a *Pagan Sacrifice*, *St Augustine and the Child on the seashore*, and the *Cumaean Sibyl* showing the Virgin to Augustus.

On the wall nearest the Courtyard of the Belvedere is the *Parnassus*. Apollo is playing the violin in the shade of laurels, surrounded by the nine Muses and the great poets. Calliope is seated on the left, and behind her are Melpomene, Terpsichore and Polyhymnia; on the right, also seated, is Erato, and behind her are Clio, Thalia, Euterpe and Urania. In the group of poets on the left is the figure of the blind Homer, between Dante and Virgil; lower are Alcaeus, Corinna, Petrarch and Anacreon, with the voluptuous form of Sappho seated beside them. In the group on the right are Ariosto (?), Ovid, Tibullus and Propertius, and, lower, Sannazaro, Horace and the seated Pindar.

Below the picture are two monochrome scenes: that on the left is thought to show Alexander placing Homer's poems in the tomb of Achilles (or, possibly, the discovery of a sarcophagus containing Greek and Latin manuscripts on the Janiculum in 181 BC). The subject of the scene on the right is either Augustus preventing Virgil's friends from burning the Aeneid, or Roman consuls ordering the burning of Greek works considered harmful to the Roman religion. Below these again is some very fine painted intarsia-work by Fra Giovanni da Verona.

On the wall facing the *Disputa* is the splendid *School of Athens*, symbolising the triumph of Philosophy, and forming a pendant to the triumph of Theology opposite. The setting is a portico, representing the palace of Science, a magnificent example of Renaissance architecture, inspired by Bramante. The remarkable vaulting, well depicted in light and shade, recalls the Baths of Caracalla. At the sides are statues of *Apollo* and *Minerva*. On the steps the greatest philosophers and scholars of all ages are gathered round the two supreme masters, *Plato* and *Aristotle*. The figure of *Plato*—probably intended as a portrait of Leonardo da Vinci—points towards heaven, symbolising his system of speculative philosophy, while Aristotle's calm gesture indicates the vast field of nature as the realm of scientific research.

At the top of the steps, on Plato's side, is the bald head and characteristic profile of *Socrates*; near him, in conversation, are *Aeschines*, *Alcibiades* (represented as a young warrior), *Xenophon* and others. The beckoning figure next to *Xenophon* is presumably *Chrysippus*. At the foot of the steps on the left is *Zeno*, an old man with a beard, seen in profile; near him *Epicurus*, crowned with vine-leaves, is reading a book; in the foreground *Pythagoras* is writing out his harmonic tables, with *Averroës*, in a turban, and *Empedocles* looking over his shoulder. The young man sitting down holding a slate is *Federico Gonzaga*, who was included by order of Julius II; the handsome youth standing up is *Francesco Maria della Rovere*; beside him, his foot resting on a block of marble, is a figure who may represent *Anaxagoras*, *Xenocrates*, or possibly *Aristoxenus*. The seated figure of *Heracleitus*, isolated in the centre foreground, was not part of the original composition; obviously inspired by Michelangelo's work in the Sistine Chapel (where the first section of the vault was uncovered in 1510), it may, according to a recent suggestion, have been intended as a portrait of him.

On the right, around *Aristotle*, are the students of the exact sciences; standing at the foot of the steps—holding a globe and, because of a confusion with the Egyptian kings of the same name, wearing a crown—is *Ptolemy*, with his back to the spectator. Opposite him is *Zoroaster*, holding a sphere. On the extreme right of the composition, Raphael has introduced portraits of himself and *Sodoma*. To the left *Archimedes* or *Euclid* (with the features of Bramante), surrounded by his disciples, bends over a blackboard on which he is tracing figures with a compass. The solitary figure sprawling on the steps in the centre, with a blue tunic, is *Diogenes*.

The monochromes beneath the picture are by Perino del Vaga, and represent *Philosophy*, *Astrologers in Conference*, and the *Siege of Syracuse* with the death of Archimedes.

On the fourth wall, above the window, are the three Cardinal Virtues—*Fortitude*, *Temperance* and *Prudence*. On the left of the window, *Justinian Publishing the Pandects* represents Civil Law, and beneath, *Solon Haranguing the Athenians* is by Perino del Vaga. On the right, *Gregory IX* (in the likeness of Julius II) is shown handing the Decretals to a jurist (1227), to represent Canon Law. The prelates around the pope are portraits of Raphael's contemporaries; on the left, in front, is *Giovanni de'Medici*, afterwards Leo X, then *Cardinal Antonio del Monte*, *Alessandro Farnese* (Paul III), and others. Beneath, *Moses Bringing the Israelites the Tablets of Stone* is by Perino del Vaga. The ceiling was also painted by Raphael: above the *Disputa* is the figure of *Theology*; above the *Parnassus*, *Poetry*; above the *School of Athens*, *Philosophy*; and above the window wall, *Justice*. In the pendentives are frescoes of *Adam and Eve*, *Apollo* and *Marsyas*, *Astronomy* and the *Judgement of Solomon*. The small central octagon is attributed to Bramantino. The floor, in opus alexandrinum, shows the arms of Nicholas V and Leo X, and the name of Julius II.

Stanza dell'Incendio

Room I is the *Stanza dell'Incendio*. On the ceiling is the *Glorification of the Holy Trinity* by Perugino, Raphael's master, the only work not destroyed when Raphael took over the decoration of the Stanze. The walls were painted in 1517 from Raphael's own designs by his pupils Giulio Romano, Francesco Penni, and perhaps Perino del Vaga. The subjects chosen were events of the times of Leo III (795–816) and Leo IV (847–55), most of which, however, allude to episodes in the history of Leo X.

Facing the window is the *Incendio di Borgo*, illustrating the fire that broke out in Rome in 847 and which was miraculously extinguished when Leo IV made the sign of the Cross from the loggia of St Peter's. This was probably intended as an allusion to the achievement of Leo X in restoring peace to Italy. In the background, flames threaten the façade of the old church of St Peter's; on the right, the pope leaves the Vatican. On the left is a scene of the burning of Troy, with naked figures scaling the walls and Aeneas carrying his father Anchises on his back, followed by his wife Creusa and their son Ascanius.

Opposite the entrance wall is the *Coronation of Charlemagne by Leo III* in 800, an obvious reference to the meeting of Leo X and Francis I at Bologna in 1516, since Leo and Charlemagne have the features of the later pope and king. On the opposite wall the subject is the *Victory of Leo IV over the Saracens at Ostia* (849), an allusion to the crusade against the Turks proclaimed by Leo X, who is again represented in the figure of Leo IV. The two cardinals behind him are portraits of Cardinal Bibbiena and Giulio de'Medici. The window wall depicts the oath of Leo III, made in St Peter's on 23 December 800. On this occasion the Pope cleared himself of false charges, including perjury and adultery, that had been brought against him. This alludes to the Lateran Council held by Leo X

The monochrome figures below the paintings represent *Godfrey de Bouillon*, *Ethelwulf of England* (Astolfo), *Charlemagne*, *Lothair I* and *Ferdinand of Castile*.

From the Stanza dell'Incendio a door leads into the **Chapel of Urban VIII**, its ceiling richly decorated with frescoes and stuccoes by Pietro da Cortona.

Outside the chapel, a stairway (right) leads down to the Borgia Rooms and the Museum of Modern Religious Art. It is possible at this point to proceed left direct to the Sistine Chapel instead of approaching it through the Borgia Rooms and the Museum of Modern Religious Art. However, the first six Borgia Rooms have important frescoes by Pinturicchio which you should not miss; unfortunately it is now usually impossible to visit these alone since the guards direct you beyond them to follow the one-way system through the 50 subsequent galleries of modern religious art, the least interesting part of the Vatican museums.

Borgia Rooms

The six Borgia Rooms (*Appartamento Borgia*) are named after Alexander VI, who adapted this suite in the palace of Nicholas V for his personal use, and had it decorated with frescoes by Pinturicchio and his school (1492–95). The grotesques are inspired by the stucco and painted decorations discovered in the Domus Aurea (see p 279) at this time, and include Christian, Jewish and pagan elements as well as Egyptian subjects. After the death of Alexander VI and the disgrace of the Borgia family, the Borgia apartment was abandoned, and it was not until 1889 that Leo XIII had the rooms restored by Lodovico Seitz and opened them to the public. Incongruous modern paintings were hung here in 1973.

Room I (Room of the Sibyls) is square and has 12 lunettes each with a sibyl accompanied by a prophet. The juxtaposition of sibyls and prophets illustrates an ancient belief that the sibyls foretold the coming of the Messiah. Cesare Borgia was imprisoned here by Julius II in 1503, in the very room where he had had his cousin Alfonso of Aragon murdered in 1500. **Room II** on the left is now used to exhibit copes designed by Matisse.

Room III (Room of the Creed) is named after the scrolls held by the 12 Apostles depicted in the lunettes, on which the sentences of the Creed are written. Each Apostle is accompanied by a prophet holding an appropriate inscription. These frescoes are attributed to Pier Matteo d'Amelia, a successor of Pinturicchio.

Room IV (Room of the Liberal Arts) symbolises the Trivium—grammar, dialectic, rhetoric—and the *Quadrivium*—geometry, arithmetic, astronomy, music—which were the basis of medieval learning. The paintings are attributed to Antonio da Viterbo, a pupil of Pinturicchio. The Arch of Justice, in the middle, was painted in the 16C. The ceiling is decorated with squares and grotesques alternating with the Borgia bull. The fine chimneypiece is by or after Jacopo Sansovino.

Room V (Room of the Saints) has walls and vault covered with more splendid *frescoes by Pinturicchio, his masterpiece. The room is divided by an arch into two cross-vaulted areas forming six lunettes. On the ceiling is the *Legend of Isis* and *Osiris and the Bull Apis* (a reference to the Borgia arms), with reliefs in gilded stucco. Above the door is a medallion with the *Madonna and Child with Saints*. Entrance wall, the *Visitation*; *St Paul the Hermit* and *St Anthony Abbot in the Desert*, on the right. The end wall shows the *Disputation between St Catherine of Alexandria and the Emperor Maximian*; the figure of the saint was once thought to be a portrait of Lucrezia Borgia or Giulia Farnese. The figure behind the throne is a self-portrait by Pinturicchio, and in the background is the Arch of Constantine. The window wall shows the *Martyrdom of St Sebastian*, with a view of the Colosseum; and the exit wall, *Susanna and the Elders* and the *Legend of St Barbara*.

Room VI (Room of the Mysteries of the Faith) has frescoes partly by Pinturicchio, representing the *Annunciation*, *Nativity*, *Adoration of the Magi*, *Resurrection* (the kneeling pontiff is Alexander VI), *Ascension*, *Pentecost* and *Assumption of the Virgin*. The last fresco includes a portrait of the donor, perhaps Francesco Borgia. In the ceiling are stuccoes and paintings of prophets.

Room VII (Room of the Popes) was formerly decorated with portraits of popes. The frescoes and stucco decoration of the splendid vaulted ceiling were commissioned by Leo X from Perino del Vaga and Giovanni da Udine.

Gallery of Modern Religious Art

The Gallery of Modern Religious Art was arranged in 1973 in the Borgia Apartments, and in 50 or so lavishly renovated rooms. The 540 works by some 250 artists from all over the world were presented to Pope Paul VI by invited artists, collectors, and donors. The collection, arranged in no particular order but fully labelled, is disappointing despite the fact that it includes some of the most important artists of the 20C, such as Pietro Annigoni, Francis Bacon, Giacomo Balla, Bernard Buffet, Carlo Carrà, Marc Chagall, Salvador Dalí, Giorgio de Chirico, Filippo de Pisis, Max Ernst, Paul Gauguin, Renato Guttuso, Wassily Kandinsky, Paul Klee, Oskar Kokoschka, Fernand Léger, Carlo Levi, Giacomo Manzù, Marino Marini, Arturo Martini, Henri Matisse, Henry Moore, Giorgio Morandi, Edvard Munch, Ben Nicholson, José Clemente Orozco, Pablo Picasso, Auguste Rodin, Georges Rouault, David Alfaro Siqueiros, Mario Sironi, Ardengo Soffici, Armando Spadini, Graham Sutherland, Maurice Utrillo, and Maurice de Vlaminck.

Stairs lead up from the last gallery to the Sistine Chapel.

Sistine Chapel

The present entrance to the Sistine Chapel is in the west wall, to the right of the altar.

History of the Sistine Chapel

The chapel takes its name from Sixtus IV, who had it rebuilt by Giovanni de' Dolci in 1473–81 as the official private chapel of the popes, and for the conclaves for the election of the popes, which are still held here. Its fortified exterior is clearly visible from the piazza in front of St Peter's. The hall is a rectangle 40m long, 13m wide, and nearly 21m high, lit on either side by six windows, placed rather high up. Sixtus IV commissioned the greatest artists of his time to carry out the frescoes on the long walls, and the choir screen and beautiful pavement. The vault represented a blue sky covered with golden stars.

Julius II commissioned the famous frescoes by Michelangelo, perhaps the greatest pictorial decoration in Western art, which cover the barrel-vaulted ceiling. It is known that the artist was reluctant to take up this commission, but having accepted, he completed the vault between 1508 and 1512. The complex design, which has received various theological interpretations, combines Old and New Testament figures, as well as themes from pagan prophecy and Church history. The powerful sculpturesque figures are set in an architectural design with an effect of high relief and rich colour on a huge scale. Work on the ceiling was begun at the main entrance, in the area furthest from the altar: the development in the artist's skill and his facility in the technique of fresco painting can be seen in the later figures at the altar end. The scaffolding was taken down and the first half of the ceiling revealed in 1510 to the wonder of all who came to see it.

The frescoes were restored in 1980–94. They had been discoloured by dirt and candle smoke, and damaged by poor restorations in the past. Important details about the way in which Michelangelo worked on this great commission were discovered. Holes found beneath the windows would seem to confirm that the scaffolding bridge from which the whole ceiling was painted was without support on the ground. The lunettes were painted in three days directly onto the fresh plaster, without the help of a preliminary cartoon or the transfer of a preparatory sketch. There is now considerable concern about the conservation of the frescoes, since up to 20,000 people a day enter the chapel.

The ceiling

Looking towards the high altar, on the **lower curved part of the vault** are the Hebrew prophets and pagan sibyls sitting on architectonic thrones with mouldings in warm grisaille. Above the *Last Judgement* is the splendid figure of *Jonah*, issuing from the whale. On the left side, from nearest the altar, are the *Libyan Sibyl*; *Daniel writing*; the *Cumaean Sibyl*; *Isaiah*, in deep meditation; and the *Delphic Sibyl*. At the far end above the entrance is *Zachariah*. On the right side, from the altar end, are *Jeremiah*; the *Persian Sibyl*; *Ezekiel*, with a scroll; the *Erythrean Sibyl*; and *Joel*.

Along the centre of the vault are nine scenes from Genesis, from the Creation to events in the life of Noah. Again beginning from the altar, these are: *Separation of Light from Darkness*; *Creation of the Sun, Moon, and Planets*; *Separation of Land and Sea* and the *Creation of the Fishes and Birds*; *Creation of Adam*, perhaps the most beautiful work on the ceiling; *Creation of Eve*; *Temptation and Expulsion from Paradise*; *Sacrifice of Noah*; the *Flood*; and the *Drunkenness of Noah*. These are framed by decorative pairs of nudes, Michelangelo's famous *ignudi*, the most idiosyncratic elements in the ceiling and a remarkable celebration of the nude figure. In the lunettes over the windows are figures representing the forerunners of Christ. In the spandrels on either side of the prophet-sibyl sequence are scenes of salvation from the Old Testament; over the altar, *Moses and the Brazen Serpent* (right) and the *Death of Haman* (left); at the other end, *Judith and Holofernes* (right) and *David and Goliath* (left).

Last Judgement

More than 20 years later, in 1535–41, Michelangelo was commissioned byPaul III to paint his huge fresco (20m by 10m) of the *Last Judgement* on the **altar wall**. This involved the walling-up of two windows and the destruction of two frescoes (both by Perugino). Michelangelo introduced a new iconography for this scene, following none of his predecessors' interpretations, inspired by the spirit of the Counter Reformation.

The crowded composition, with innumerable nude figures, contains a remarkable sense of movement and high relief. The strong colour of the background was produced by Michelangelo's liberal use of lapis lazuli. In the upper centre is the enigmatic figure of *Christ*, beardless, and probably derived from Classical models. Near him are the *Madonna* and (probably) *Adam*, and on the right *St Peter* with the keys. At Christ's feet are seated *St Lawrence* and *St Bartholomew* with his flayed skin: the caricature of a face seen in the folds of the skin is a self-portrait of Michelangelo. In the lunettes high up above the figure of Christ are two groups of angels with the instruments of the Passion.

Beneath, in the central zone, on the left, the elect ascend to heaven with the help of angels; in the centre there is a group of angels with trumpets; on the right the damned are hauled down into hell. In this group is the famous figure of a soul in despair, known as the *Disperato*, looking down into the abyss. In the lowest zone, on the left, there is a scene representing the resurrection of the body; in the centre is a cave full of devils; on the right is the entrance to hell, with Charon's boat (as in Dante's description) and Minos, the guide to the infernal regions, with ass's ears. According to Vasari, the figure of Minos has the features of Biagio Martinelli, master of ceremonies to Paul III, who had objected to the nudity of Michelangelo's figures. Pius IV also protested about this and at one time intended to destroy the fresco, but in the end he commissioned Daniele da Volterra to paint clothes on some of the figures. In 1990–94 an extremely complex restoration operation was carried out on the fresco, which had deteriorated and been blackened by candle smoke and incense, as well as by the glues used as varnishes in restorations from the late 16C up to the 18C.

Sixtus IV commissioned from Mino da Fiesole, Giovanni Dalmata and Andrea Bregno the graceful marble screen that divides the chapel into two unequal parts, a larger choir and a small nave. The same artists were responsible for the cantoria. The mosaic pavement, a fine example of opus alexandrinum, also dates from this time.

The walls

The frescoes on the long walls were painted in 1481–83 for Sixtus IV by some of the greatest artists of the time; they were restored in 1999. They depict parallel events in the lives of Moses, on the left or south wall, and of Christ, on the right or north. There were originally fourteen scenes; the two on the altar wall were eliminated to make room for Michelangelo's *Last Judgement*.

Beginning from the altar, on the **left wall**: *Moses and Zipporah* (his wife in Egypt) and the Circumcision of their son by Pinturicchio; *Burning Bush*, with Moses slaying the Egyptian and driving the Midianites from the well by Sandro Botticelli; the *Passage of the Red Sea* by Biagio di Antonio; *Moses on Mount Sinai* and the *Worship of the Golden Calf* by Cosimo Rosselli; the *Punishment of Korah, Dathan and Abiram* (with the Arch of Constantine and the Septizodium in the background) by Botticelli; and *Moses Giving his Rod to Joshua*, with the *Mourning for the Death of Moses* by Luca Signorelli and Bartolomeo della Gatta.

Beginning from the altar, on the **right wall**: *Baptism of Christ* by Perugino and Pinturicchio; *Cleansing of the Leper*, and the *Temptation in the Wilderness* (with

Conclave, and the election of a pope

On the death of a pope, cardinals under the age of 80 are confined in a chosen locality, usually the Sistine Chapel, to elect a new pope. This practice is called conclave (from the Latin for a room that can be locked). The place chosen is locked both inside and outside and it includes rooms for the cardinals and their attendants. The internal guardian is the Camerlengo, the external guardian the commander of the Swiss Guard. The cardinals meet twice daily before the voting procedure takes place.

The result of the vote is indicated by the colour of the smoke which issues from a vent above the Sistine Chapel. If the smoke is black the election is still in doubt; if white, the new pope has been elected. The old practice of burning the voting papers (mixed with damp straw for the black smoke) to produce this signal was discontinued after the conclave of 1958. The new pope is proclaimed by the senior cardinal-deacon from the central balcony on the façade of St Peter's, from where the new pope gives his blessing. Since the proceedings take some time, there is always an interregnum between the death of a pope and the election of his successor; John Paul I died on 29 September and John Paul II was elected on 16 October 1978.

the hospital of Santo Spirito in the background) by Botticelli; the *Calling of Peter and Andrew* by Domenico Ghirlandaio (with a splendid landscape); *Sermon on the Mount*, with the *Healing of the Leper* by Cosimo Rosselli and Piero di Cosimo; *Christ Giving the Keys to St Peter* by Perugino with the help of Luca Signorelli; and the *Last Supper* by Cosimo Rosselli and Biagio di Antonio. On the east wall are two frescoes, the *Resurrection* by Domenico Ghirlandaio, and *St Michael Defending the Body of Moses* by Salviati, overpainted at the end of the 16C by Arrigo Fiammingo and Matteo da Lecce. In the niches between the windows are 28 portraits of the first popes by Fra Diamante, Domenico Ghirlandaio, Botticelli and Cosimo Rosselli. The celebrated tapestries designed by Raphael, now in the Vatican Pinacoteca, were first exhibited in the Sistine Chapel in 1519.

Through the main door of the Sistine Chapel the sumptuous **Sala Regia** can

sometimes be seen (no admission). It was begun by Antonio da Sangallo the Younger in 1540 for Paul III for the reception of ambassadors, and was used as a dormitory during conclaves. It contains stucco decoration by Perino del Vaga and Daniele da Volterra, and frescoes by Giorgio Vasari, Salviati and the Zuccari. The first official meeting between the pope and the archbishop of Canterbury since the Reformation took place here in 1966. The **Cappella Paolina** (also closed to the public), by Antonio da Sangallo the Younger, has two remarkable frescoes by Michelangelo, the *Conversion of St Paul* and *Crucifixion of St Peter*, painted in 1542–45 and 1546–50.

If you do not wish to continue the tour of the museums, you are often able to leave the chapel by the **Scala Regia** (usually open every day except Wednesday), an imposing staircase built by Bernini which descends past a statue of *Constantine* to the portico of

~Scala Regia

St Peter's. The other exit from the chapel is by a small door in the north wall of the nave, which leads to the Museum of Christian Art.

Museum of Christian Art

The Museum of Christian Art (*Museo Sacro*) was founded by Benedict XIV in 1756, and enlarged in the 19C, partly by the acquisitions of Pius IX but mainly by finds made during excavations in the catacombs by Giovanni Battista de Rossi and his successors.

Beyond a room with vestments is the **Chapel of St Pius V**, decorated by Giacomo Zucchi to designs by Vasari. In the wall-case is part of the treasury of the Sancta Sanctorum, the pope's private chapel. The relics were preserved in precious reliquaries inside a case made of cypress wood for Leo III (795–816). The 9C–12C works include: an enamelled *cross presented by St Paschal I (817–24), containing five pieces of the True Cross; a 9C case in the form of a cross; and the reliquary of St Prassede.

The **Room of the Addresses** (III; *degli Indirizzi*), was so called because in the time of Pius XI, the address or congratulatory documents sent to Leo XIII and Pius X were kept here. Here is displayed a splendid collection of liturgical objects in ivory, enamel, majolica, silver and other metals. In the cases opposite the window are *ivories, including diptychs and triptychs (9C–15C). The *Ramboyna diptych* (c 900) has Christian scenes with the representation of the Roman wolf in the bottom of the left-hand panel. A five-panelled *tablet with Christ blessing was part of the cover of a New Testament (the other half is in the Victoria and Albert Museum, London). Another *book cover from the Convent of St Gall, Switzerland, is illustrated with the Nativity. The collection of enamels includes Limoges enamels (12C–16C). Other cases display 14C–16C silver crosses and 18C–19C missals. On the window wall: church silver; crosses and amulets; 16C German, French and Roman silver; hammers used to open the Porta Santa in Holy Years; Roman silver made by Santi Lotti (1629–59); glass; seals and cameos.

The **Room of the Aldobrandini Marriage** on the left has been closed for many years. It is named after an ancient Roman *fresco of a marriage scene, a masterpiece of Augustan art, which combines realism and symbolism and was inspired by a Greek model of the 4C or 3C BC. It was found on the Esquiline in 1605, and acquired by Cardinal Pietro Aldobrandini. There are also detached *frescoes of the 1C BC, with scenes from the *Odyssey*, and a freize of famous women of antiquity and of children (1C AD). The ceiling frescoes are by Guido Reni. The **Room of the Papyri** (II) dates from 1774 when 6C–9C papyri from Ravenna were displayed here (now replaced by facsimiles). The frescoes are by Raphael Mengs and his assistant Christopher Unterberger. In the cases are *bozzetti* by Gian Lorenzo Bernini

The last room (I) displays early Christian antiquities from the Catacombs of St Calixtus, St Domitilla and St Sebastian, and other cemeteries. These include a collection of glass, some of the finer specimens gilded, engraved 4C glass from Ostia, and 2C–3C multicoloured glass. Christian and pagan lamps (1C–4C), some with symbols of the Good Shepherd, the fish, the peacock, and the monogram of Christ; terracottas; bronze lamps (3C–5C); fabrics including 11C–13C Church embroideries; and objects in gold.

Vatican Library

Beyond is the first of the exhibition rooms of the Vatican Library (*Biblioteca Apostolica Vaticana*). The exhibition rooms of the Library are the Gallery of Urban VIII, the Sistine Rooms, the Sistine Hall, the Pauline Rooms, the Alexandrine Room, the Clementine Gallery and the Museum of Pagan Antiquities. All the rooms, except the Sistine Hall, are in Bramante's west corridor.

History of the Vatican Library

The library was founded by Nicholas V with a nucleus of some 350 volumes, which he increased to 1200. Sixtus IV brought the total to 3650. The library was pillaged in the Sack of 1527, but before the end of the 16C Sixtus V commissioned Domenico Fontana to build the great Sistine Hall to accommodate it. Later popes adapted numerous rooms in Bramante's west corridor to house the steadily increasing collection of gifts, bequests and purchases. Among the most important acquisitions were the Biblioteca Palatina of Heidelberg (1623), the Biblioteca Urbinas founded by Federico, Duke of Urbino (1657),

Queen Christina of Sweden's library (1690), the Biblioteca Ottoboniana, formerly the property of Alexander VIII Ottoboni, bought in 1748, the Jesuit Library (1922), the Biblioteca Chigiana (1923), and the Biblioteca Ferraioli (1929). There are now about 60,000 manuscripts, 7000 incunabula, and 1,000,000 other printed books. Leo XIII added a reference library; Pius X reorganised the manuscripts and provided a study-room; and Pius XI carried out further reorganisation. The library and archives are open in the mornings to scholars with a letter of introduction.

The first room is the **Gallery of Urban VIII**. By the entrance wall are two statues: on the left *Aelius Aristides* (AD 129–89), dating from the 3C, and on the right the Greek orator *Lysias*, dating from the 2C. Astronomical instruments, sailing directions dating from the early 16C, and the Farnese Planisphere (1725) given to Leo XIII by the Count of Caserta are also shown here.

Beyond are the two **Sistine Rooms**, part of the Library of Sixtus V (see below). In the first are paintings of St Peter's as planned by Michelangelo and of the erection of the obelisk in Piazza San Pietro. Here, too, is a press designed by Bramante for sealing papal bulls. Over the doors of the second room are depictions of Sixtus V proclaiming St Bonaventura a Doctor of the Church in the church of the Santi Apostoli (Melozzo's frescoes are seen in their original place on the wall of the apse), and of the Canonisation of San Diego in old St Peter's.

The **Sistine Hall**, named after its founder Sixtus V, was built in 1587–89 by Domenico Fontana across the great Courtyard of the Belvedere, cutting it in two. It was later paralleled by the New Wing, the construction of which created a small central courtyard, known as the Courtyard of the Library. Beneath this an underground depository was constructed in 1983 to house the precious collection of Vatican manuscripts and incunabula. The hall is divided into two vaulted aisles by seven columns, and is decorated with themes glorifying literature and the pontificate of Sixtus V, with interesting views of Rome. Exhibitions are sometimes held here of the precious possessions of the library. In the vestibule, above the doors, are paintings of the Lateran Palace, before and after its reconstruction, by Domenico Fontana.

The two **Pauline Rooms** were added by Paul V, and decorated in the Mannerist style of 1610–11. The **Alexandrine Room** was adapted in 1690 by Alexander VIII, and decorated with scenes in the life of Pius VII by Domenico de Angelis.

The **Clementine Gallery**, in five sections, was added to the Library by Clement XII in 1732; in 1818, under Pius VII, it was decorated by De Angelis with paintings of scenes in the life of that pope. The last room has a bronze head of a *Muse*—a Roman copy of a Hellenistic original, and two bronze griffins of the Imperial period. On either side of the entrance are two Mithraic divinities. The main hall of the **Museum of Pagan Antiquities of the Library** (*Museo Profano della Biblioteca*), beyond, but no longer accessible from here, is described on p 382.

A new staircase has been constructed in the last room of the Clementine Gallery which leads down to the **exit from the museums** (used up until 2000 as the entrance to the museums), with a monumental double staircase built in 1932 by Giuseppe Momo with a bronze balustrade by Antonio Maraini. From the hall you can also take one of the two delightful old-fashioned lifts down to the street level. But to visit the museums described below, follow the signs.

Route III

Vatican Picture Gallery

The Vatican Picture Gallery (Pinacoteca Vaticana) is reached by the passageway from the open court beyond the Quattro Cancelli. The Vatican Picture Gallery owes its origin to Pius VI but under the Treaty of Tolentino (1797) he was forced to surrender the best works to Napoleon. Of these, 77 were recovered in 1815. The present building in the Lombardic Renaissance style, by Luca Beltrami, was opened in 1932.

Room I. Early Italian painters are displayed here. *St James and Mary Magdalene* by Antonio Veneziano; *Death of St Francis* by Jacopo da Bologna; *Madonna and Child* by Vitale da Bologna; *Christ in Judgement* by the 12C Roman school; *St Francis*, and panels illustrating his life by Giunta Pisano; **Last Judgement*, signed by a certain Giovanni and Niccolò who were at work in Rome in the late 11C (this is the oldest picture in the gallery). The portrait of *St Francis of Assisi* is by Margaritone d'Arezzo. On the window wall: *Madonna and Child with Saints* by Giovanni del Biondo; *Death of the Virgin* by Taddeo di Bartolo; *Madonna and Saints*, signed and dated 1371 by Giovanni Bonsi; and **Legend of St Stephen* by Bernardo Daddi. There are also works by Niccolò di Pietro Gerini and the Florentine school.

Room II. In the centre is the **Stefaneschi Triptych* by Giotto and assistants for the confessio of Old St Peter's. On the front: *Christ enthroned*, the *Martyrdom of St Peter and St Paul*, and the donor, Cardinal Stefaneschi at the foot of the throne; and on the back: *St Peter* accepting the triptych from the pope, and (at the sides), four *Apostles*; the other Apostles are depicted in the predella. Around the walls are some exquisite small paintings by mostly by Sienese and Florentine painters of the 14C and 15C: *Christ before Pilate, St John the Baptist, St Peter*, and the *Virgin*, all by Pietro Lorenzetti; the *Redeemer* by Simone Martini; **Madonna of the Magnificat* by Bernardo Daddi; *Nativity, St Nicholas Freeing Three Knights*, and *Annunciation*, all by Mariotto di Nardo; works by Sano di Pietro; *Nativity* by Giovanni di Paolo; *Vision of St Thomas Aquinas* and *Madonna and Child* by Sassetta; *Stories from the Life of St Benedict* by Lorenzo Monaco; *Stories from the Life of St Nicholas of Bari* by Gentile da Fabriano. On the window wall: *Madonna and Child* by Francesco di Gentile.

Room III. *Scenes from the *Life of St Nicholas of Bari*, and *Madonna and Child with Saints* by Fra Angelico. *Crucifixion*, and *Transition of the Virgin* by Masolino da Panicale; a triptych of the *Coronation of the Virgin* by Filippo Lippi; and *St Thomas Receiving the Virgin's Girdle* by Benozzo Gozzoli.

Room IV. Here are displayed some delightful fragments of a fresco of the **Ascension*, with eight angel musicians by Melozzo da Forlì, detached from the church of the Santi Apostoli (another part is in the Quirinal). Melozzo also painted **Sixtus IV and Platina*, a scene showing the pope conferring on the humanist the librarianship of the Vatican in the presence of Giuliano della Rovere (afterwards Julius II), his brother Giovanni, and Girolamo and Raffaele Riario (this was a fresco but it has been transferred to canvas). The *Madonna and Saints* on the right wall is by Marco Palmezzano.

Room V. Predella with *Miracles of St Vincent Ferrer* by Francesco del Cossa; *Pietà* by Lucas Cranach; and *Madonna and Child* by Giovanni Battista Utili.

Room VI displays some fine polyptychs by the Venetian school: *Madonna* dated 1482 and a *Pietà* by Carlo Crivelli; *Madonna with Saints*, dated 1481 by Vittorio Crivelli; *St Anthony Abbot* (in relief) and other *Saints*, signed and dated 1469 by Antonio Viviani. Also here are a *Crucifixion* and the *Polyptych of Montelparo* by Niccolò l'Alunno.

Room VII contains works of the Umbrian school: *Adoration of the Magi* (the Madonna della Spineta) by Lo Spagna; **Madonna Enthroned with Saints*, *Resurrection* (part of predella) with St Benedict, St Flavia and St Placidus, all by Perugino. The *St Jerome* is by Raphael's father, Giovanni Santi.

Room VIII. This, the largest room in the gallery, is devoted to **Raphael**. It contains three of his most famous paintings, as well as two exquisite predellas, and ten tapestries made from his original cartoons. The **Coronation of the Virgin* was his first large composition, painted in Perugia in 1503 when he was just 20 years old. Its predella is exhibited in front in a showcase, with scenes of the *Annunciation*, *Adoration of the Magi*, and *Presentation in the Temple*. The **Madonna of Foligno* is a mature work painted about 1511. It was a votive offering by Sigismondo Conti in gratitude for his escape when a cannon ball fell on his house during the siege of Foligno. He is shown with St Jerome, and in the background is Foligno during the battle. The painting was kept in the Convent of Sant'Anna in Foligno from 1565 until it was stolen by Napoleon in 1797. The **Transfiguration* is Raphael's last work, commissioned in 1517 by Cardinal Giuliano de'Medici for the cathedral of Narbonne. From 1523 to 1809 it was in the church of San Pietro in Montorio. The superb scene of the transfiguration of Christ is shown above the dramatic episode of the healing of the young man possessed of a devil. It is not known how much of the painting had been finished by the time of Raphael's death in 1520, and, although the composition is Raphael's, it seems likely that the lower part was completed by his pupils Giulio Romano and Francesco Penni.

The ten celebrated **tapestries** represent scenes from the Acts of the Apostles. Intended for the Sistine Chapel, where they were first exhibited in 1519, they were commissioned by Leo X and woven in Brussels by Pieter van Aelst from cartoons drawn by Raphael in 1515–16. Seven of the cartoons (the other three have been lost) are in the Victoria and Albert Museum, London, though some scholars believe that these seven, which were bought in 1630 by Charles I of England, are 17C copies and that all the originals have been lost. Other tapestries from the same cartoons, but of inferior quality, are in Hampton Court Palace near London, in the Palazzo Ducale at Mantua, and in the Palazzo Apostolico at Loreto.

The tapestries have borders of grotesques and broad bases decorated with bronze-coloured designs; most of this work is by Giovanni da Udine. The subjects are: (**A.**) *Blinding of Elymas* (the tapestry was cut in half during the Sack of Rome in 1527); (**B.**) *Conversion of St Paul*; (**C.**) *Stoning of St Stephen*; (**D.**) *St Peter Healing the Paralytic*; (**E.**) *Death of Ananias*; (**F.**) *St Peter Receiving the Keys*; (**G.**) *Miraculous Draught of Fishes*; (**H.**) *St Paul Preaching in Athens*; (**I.**) *Inhabitants of Lystra Sacrificing to St Paul and St Barnabas*; (**L.**) *St Paul in Prison at Philippi*. These tapestries belong to the so-called Old School series. Ten of the New School series are in the Gallery of Tapestries (see above). Also displayed here is a 16C Flemish tapestry of the *Last Supper*, after Leonardo's fresco in Milan.

Room IX. **St Jerome* by Leonardo da Vinci; *Madonna* by Lorenzo di Credi; *Christ at the Column*, and a supposed portrait of Bramante by the 16C Lombard school; **Pietà* by Giovanni Bellini.

Room X. *Madonna and Saints* by Girolamo Genga; *St Helena* by Paolo Veronese; *Madonna and Child enthroned with Saints* by Moretto; *Madonna of San Niccolò de'Frari*, and *Doge Niccolò Marcello* by Titian; *St George and the Dragon* by Paris Bordone; *Apparition of the Virgin to Augustus and the Sibyl* by Garofalo; *Madonna of Monteluce* by Giulio Romano and Francesco Penni; and *Madonna della Cintura* by the 16C Lombard school.

Room XI. *Stoning of St Stephen* by Vasari; *Annunciation* by Cavaliere d'Arpino; *Raising of Lazarus* by Muziano; *Assumption of the Virgin* by Cola dell'Amatrice; *Annunciation*, *Rest on the Flight into Egypt*, the *Blessed Michaelina*, *St Francis Receiving the Stigmata*, all by Barocci. In the centre there is a marble bas-relief of *Cosimo I* by Pierino del Vaga.

Room XII. Caravaggio, Guido Reni, Domenichino and Guercino. There is a fine view of the cupola of St Peter's from the window. The *Incredulity of St Thomas*, *St Margaret of Cortona*, and *Mary Magdalene* all by Guercino are displayed here. The *Communion of St Jerome* is signed and dated 1614 by Domenichino (this was his first important work, and there is a copy of it in mosaic in St Peter's). The works by Caravaggio include the *Descent from the Cross* (1602), and a copy of his *Denial of St Peter*. The *Crucifixion of St Peter*, *St Matthew* and *Virgin in Glory with Saints* are by Guido Reni. Also here: *Martyrdom of St Processus and St Martinian* by Valentin; *Vision of St Romauld* by Sacchi; *Holy Family* by Giuseppe Maria Crespi; and *Martyrdom of St Erasmus* signed by Nicolas Poussin.

Room XIII. *Madonna and Child* by Sassoferrato; *Judith* by Orazio Gentileschi; *St Francis Xavier* by Anthony Van Dyck; *Vision of St Bruno* by Pier Francesco Mola; *Appearance of the Virgin to St Francis and David and a Lion* by Pietro da Cortona; *Martyrdom of St Lawrence* by José Ribera (or his pupil Henry Somer); *Appearance of the Virgin to St John Nepomuk* by Pompeo Batoni.

Room XIV. 17C–18C Flemish, Dutch, German, French painters. Small paintings of religious subjects with flower borders by Daniel Seghers; *Hunter* by Rosa da Tivoli; *Orpheus, Pluto and Proserpina* by Matthias Stomer; *Triumph of Mars* by Peter Paul Rubens (but mainly executed by his pupils); *Astronomical Observations* by Donato Creti; *Gideon* by Nicolas Poussin; *Horses* by Van Bloeman.

Room XV. Portraits. *Francesco Sforza* by Bernardino Conti; *Philosopher* by Pieter Meert; *George IV of England* by Sir Thomas Lawrence; *Old Man* by David Teniers the Younger; *Gregory XII*, an idealised portrait of the pope who abdicated in 1415 by Muziano; *Pius VI* by Pompeo Batoni; *Cardinal Guglielmo Sirleto* by Scipione Pulzone; *Benedict XIV* by Giuseppe Maria Crespi (painted while still a cardinal—the papal robes were added afterwards); *Clement IX* by Carlo Maratta.

Room XVI. Works by Wenceslao Peter (1742–1829), including *Paradise* and a *Self-portrait*.

Room XVII. Clay models by Gian Lorenzo Bernini, including a *bozzetto* for the tabernacle of the Holy Sacrament in St Peter's and heads of Fathers of the Church and angels. The small inscription of 1638 commemorates the construction of one of the campaniles of St Peter's which was later demolished.

Room XVIII. Very fine collection of 16C and 17C Russian and Greek icons.

Route IV

The striking building housing the Gregorian Museum of Pagan Antiquities, Pio Christian Museum and Ethnological Missionary Museum was designed by a group of Italian architects headed by Fausto and Lucio Passarelli, and opened in 1970, when the collections formerly housed in the Lateran Palace were moved here. However, the building was closed for restoration in 2002 and the collections closed to the public. The arrangement described below may, therefore, be changed when they reopen.

Gregorian Museum of Pagan Antiquities

The Gregorian Museum of Pagan Antiquities (*Museo Gregoriano Profano*) is reached from the vestibule by the entrance to the museums. The Museo Profano was founded by Gregory XVI (1831–46) to house the overflow of the Vatican Museums and the yields of excavations at Rome, Ostia, Veio and Cerveteri during his pontificate. It was enriched by further excavations up to 1870, and at the end of the 19C by a collection of pagan inscriptions.

Near the entrance on the left are Roman copies of original Greek sculpture, including torsos, statuettes and heads, and ahead, *Marsyas*, a marble copy of a bronze by Myron which formed part of a group placed at the entrance to the Acropolis in Athens in the mid-5C BC. Marsyas is attracted by the sound of the double flute, which Athena had invented and just thrown away. He is foiled in his attempt to pick up the instrument by Athena's commanding gesture (the statue of Athena is a cast).

To the right are displayed some Greek originals, including a superb sepulchral stele, showing a *Young Man* whose slave is handing him a strigil and a flask of oil (5C BC); two heads (fragments from one of the metopes and from the north frieze of the Parthenon), and the fragment of a horse's head from the west pediment of the Parthenon, probably one of Athena's horses. The head of Athena is also a 5C BC original; it was made to wear a helmet, probably of bronze. The eyes are of polished grey stone in which were set glass pupils; the eyebrows and eyelashes were made of thin strips of bronze, and the ears had gold earrings. Two relief fragments of horsemen, perhaps part of a frieze, resemble in style the Parthenon frieze. The relief of *Dancing Nymphs* is an Attic work of the 4C BC. Stairs lead up to an area which contains the Lateran collection of pagan inscriptions, open only to scholars with special permission.

There follow a series of herms, and, on the floor, the *Heraclitus Mosaic* of an unswept floor from the triclinium of a house on the Aventine, showing the remains of a banquet. It is signed Heraclitus, and may be a copy of a celebrated work by Sosus of Pergamon. Other works in this section include a round altar, with a faun playing for two dancing women; a triangular tripod base, with reliefs of dancing figures taking part in Dionysiac rites, a neo-Attic work in Pentelic marble of the 1C BC, after a 4C BC original; a copy of the *Resting Satyr* of Praxiteles (others are in the Museo Pio-Clementino and the Capitoline Museum); a colossal statue of *Poseidon*, after a bronze original by Lysippos, with several restorations; and a colossal statue of *Zeus*.

In the next section, by the windows, is a relief of *Medea and the Daughters of Pelias* whom she is inducing to kill their father, a neo-Attic copy of a late 5C BC original. It is one of a series of four relating to the dramatic competitions in Athens.

Beyond a marble statue of **Sophocles** from Terracina, with fine drapery (a copy of a 4C BC work) are the remains of the large circular **Vicovaro Monument**, dating from the early 1C AD. In the next recess is the **Chiaramonti Niobid**, a fine Roman copy of an original by Leochares of the 4C BC. The head of a **Muse**, crowned with ivy, in the manner of Praxiteles, is a good copy of a 4C BC original. The torso of a statue of **Diana** is a Roman copy of a Greek original of the 4C BC; the motion expressed in the drapery is particularly fine. Also here are two Roman **Orators in togas** (1C AD), and fine Roman portrait heads, the last two perhaps portraits of Virgil.

The following sections contain Roman sculpture in chronological order, beginning with the late Republican era. Opposite two statues of the **Sleeping Silenus**, copies of Hellenistic works found in the Roman theatre at Caere (see below), are a series of funerary reliefs: the first with portraits of parents and a young son, and the second with five busts of members of the Furia family. The circular altar dedicated to Piety comes from Veio; it is decorated with garlands, lyres, and the attributes of Vulcan (1C AD).

Around to the left are a group of statues from the Roman theatre at Caere, mainly of the Julio-Claudian family: **Agrippina**, mother of Nero and wife of Claudius, as a goddess; a colossal seated statue of **Claudius** as Jupiter; a relief with figures symbolising the three Etruscan cities of Vetulonia, Vulci and Tarquinia, found with the statue and believed to have been part of the throne; a colossal head, probably of **Augustus**; a colossal seated statue of **Tiberius** idealised as Jupiter; a series of inscriptions found with the statues, explaining their identity; **Drusus and an Elder**, with a cuirass decorated with bas-reliefs of two griffins and above, a gorgon; an altar dedicated to Manlius, a censor of Caere, by his clients (1C AD); and a statue of an **Emperor** in a cuirass, decorated with reliefs.

Next comes the so-called Altar of Vicomagistri found near the Cancelleria (1C AD). The relief is of a sacrificial procession, followed by four figures carrying statuettes of household deities and by priestly officials known as *vicomagistri*. Two statues of **Young Boys** wearing togas, belonging to the Julio-Claudian family (one with a 3C head); more Roman portrait busts and heads.

To the left is an area with cinerary urns, among them one with finely carved reliefs: the head of Medusa in the centre, below a cock-fight, and festoons with eagles and genii at the sides. A covered urn has good reliefs and an inscription. The next section has architectural fragments, and some exquisite decorative reliefs with small Bacchic scenes and vine-leaves (1C AD). The area is dominated by two large Cancelleria reliefs, dating from the Flavian period (AD 70–96). The damaged frieze on the left represents the **Return to Rome of Vespasian**, who appears on the extreme right of the third panel. Surrounding the Emperor are Vestals, the Roman Senate and people, and the seated personification of Rome. The frieze on the right represents the **Departure from Rome of Domitian** who appears (restored as Nerva) in the second panel from the left, surrounded by Minerva, Mars and Victory to the left, and Rome with soldiers to the right.

Beyond more portrait busts is sculpture from the Tomb of the Haterii, probably dating from the late Flavian period, found near Centocelle in 1848. Two similar niches have well-modelled portrait busts of the freedman Quintus Haterius and his wife. The three reliefs are particularly interesting and rare as they show a woman's funeral: the body lying in state (the only Roman relief known of such a scene), surrounded by relatives and mourners in the atrium of a house; the funeral procession, passing buildings on the Via Sacra; and the sepulchral monument of the Haterii, with a view of the inside and the apparatus used in its construction. Above is a high-relief with three busts of gods of the underworld; a triangular pillar, beautifully carved, with candelabrum, rose branches and birds. In the relief of a procession of Roman magistrates in front of a temple (1C AD), one of the heads was restored erroneously in the early 19C by Thorvaldsen to represent Trajan.

Towards the windows, there is a large funerary relief of a *Woman Lying on a Bed* with a small dog (the head is a portrait). A sepulchral relief of a chariot race —with a side view of the circus seen from above—shows the organisers of the games, in whose memory the relief was made, on the left (early 2C AD). Two columns are carved with a papyrus motif and lotus leaves around the base.

To the right is a colossal statue of a *Dacian*, dating from the time of Trajan, found in 1841 in Via dei Coronari, on the site of a sculptor's studio of the Imperial era. A series of capitals and antefixes follow, with two fragments of an architectural frieze from the Forum of Trajan, with cupids and griffins and a neo-Attic amphora.

The next sections contain *pagan sarcophagi with mythological scenes. Among them, several depict the story of Adonis, of Hippolytus and Phaedra (with scenes of the wild boar hunt), of Orestes, and of the slaughter of the family of Niobe. Further on is a fine sarcophagus dating from the 3C AD, with a scene of the triumph of Dionysos: he is represented on his return from India in a triumphal carriage drawn by two elephants, being crowned by Nike (Victory). Beyond is a colossal statue of *Antinous* as the God Vertumnus, with finely modelled drapery (the head is modern); and a fragment of a relief with *Two Boxers*, presumably part of a large monument (2C AD).

The fragment of the large oval Plotinus Sarcophagus has figures in relief in philosophical discussion(?), and part of a lion hunt; on the wall behind is a sepulchral relief with the deceased man reading from a large scroll, surrounded by his family and pupils (3C AD); on the right, a funerary monument in high-relief shows a warrior saluting his seated wife; a horse stands ready, and a snake is depicted in the tree above. Nearby are fragments of draped Imperial porphyry statues. Towards the windows, a relief shows a nymph feeding an infant satyr from a large horn-shaped vessel, while in a grotto nearby a young Pan plays the syrinx. Known as the *Amaltheia Relief*, this was originally part of a fountain. To the right is a statue of *Dogmatius*. Another area contains Roman religious sculpture, including statues of *Mithras and the Bull* (3C AD), *Diana of the Ephesians* and *Asklepios*.

To the right of the stairs are fragments of a group with a boy riding a horse, and a river nymph on a sea centaur. Upstairs a walkway passes above a mosaic of athletes from the Baths of Caracalla and a black marble statue of a stag, a Roman copy of a 4C BC Greek original. The corridor has Hebrew inscriptions. Beyond, a balcony overlooks a second fine mosaic from the Baths of Caracalla and there is a view of the dome of St Peter's from here.

The rest of the upper floor is occupied by the **Pio Christian Museum** (also closed in 2002), founded by Pius IX in 1854 with objects found mainly in the catacombs, and displayed by subject matter. The display begins at the other end of the mezzanine floor, at the entrance to the building. The first section is devoted to the valuable collection of Christian sarcophagi of the 2C–5C, of the highest importance for the study of early Christian iconography; some famous sarcophagi owned by the Vatican but not on view here are represented by casts numbered with Roman numerals. At the beginning, on the left wall, are fragments of sarcophagi representing the **Nativity** and **Epiphany** of the 4C AD. Further on, to the right, is a sarcophagus showing the **Crossing of the Red Sea**.

Three steps lead up to the next section. In the middle is a cast of the sarcophagus of Junius Bassus (the original is in the Treasury of St Peter's). Round the corner to the left is a sarcophagus with five niches showing **Christ triumphant over death**, **Cain and Abel**, **Peter taken prisoner**, the **Martyrdom of Paul**, and **Job**. Another short flight of steps ascends past, on the right, the sarcophagus of the husband and wife Crescentianus and Agapene, found in the Vatican necropolis. At the top of the stairs, on the left, is a large sarcophagus with episodes from the Bible. To the right are panels with scenes from the Old and New Testaments; and a cast of a sarcophagus from Sant'Ambrogio in Milan. The next part of the gallery contains more sarcophagi (including one from the catacomb of St Calixtus) and some mosaic fragments. Three steps lead up to the last section of the museum. On the left is a well-preserved sarcophagus with traces of the original polychrome decoration. At the end is a sarcophagus illustrating the **Good Shepherd**.

On the right wall begins the collection of epigraphs from the **Museum of Christian Inscriptions**, the largest and most important collection of Christian inscriptions in existence (but closed in 2002). The whole collection was arranged and classified by Giovanni Battista de Rossi (1822–94) in four series. First series: inscriptions from public monuments connected with Christian worship; fragment of the sepulchral inscription of Publius Sulpicius Quirinus (Cyrenius), Governor of Syria, who took the census at the time of the birth of Christ; inscriptions of Pope St Damasus (366–84). Second series: dated copulohral inscriptions, dogmatic inscriptions, including the (fish) acrostic; inscriptions relating to the ecclesiastical hierarchy, virgins, catechumens, senators, soldiers, officials and workers. Third series: symbols and representations of Christian dogma. Fourth series: inscriptions (2C–6C) arranged topographically from cemeteries in Rome and Ostia.

The statue of the **Good Shepherd** is a fine work dating from the late 3C. A passage continues past a sarcophagus from San Lorenzo fuori le Mura, and the cast of a seated statue of the martyred doctor **St Hippolytus**. On the left of his chair is a list in Greek of the saint's works, and on the right a paschal calendar for the years 222–334. The original is now at the entrance of the Vatican Library, in the Courtyard of the Belvedere. On the balcony overlooking a mosaic from the Baths of Caracalla mentioned above is a fragment of the tombstone of Abercius, bishop of Hierapolis (Phrygia), who lived in the reign of Marcus Aurelius (161–80), discovered by Sir William Ramsay and presented to Leo XIII. The Greek text is in three parts: in the first part Abercius says that he is a disciple of Christ the Good Shepherd, in the second he mentions his journey to Rome and the East, in the third he asks the faithful to pray for him and threatens defilers of his grave.

Ethnological Missionary Museum

The Ethnological Missionary Museum (closed in 2002) occupies the whole of the area below ground-level. It was established by Pius XI in 1927 as a development of the Vatican Missionary Exhibition of 1924–26. The primitive and more recent cultures of each country have been arranged according to subject matter;

labelling is kept to a minimum. The exhibits illustrate the ways of life and religious customs in China, with fine Buddhist sculpture and religious figures of the Ming and T'ang dynasties; Japan, with ceremonial masks and paintings of martyrs; Korea; Tibet, Mongolia; Indochina, where examples of local art and manufacture show the adaptation of European sacred art to the local genius; the *Indian sub-continent, illustrating Shivaism and Vishnuism; Indonesia, Philippines; Polynesia; *Melanesia, with protective spirits, ceremonial masks and costumes, and the reconstruction of a hut of the spirits from New Guinea; Australia; North Africa; Ethiopia; Madagascar; West Africa, with statuettes of tribal gods; Central Africa; East Africa; Southern Africa; Christian Africa; South America, including ancient wood sculpture from Colombia; Central America; North America; Persia; Middle East; and Christian art from countries penetrated by the missions. A mezzanine floor contains study collections.

The Padiglione delle Carrozze, built by Paul VI in 1973, houses carriages and the first automobiles used by the popes, but is not at present open to the public.

34 • Vatican City and gardens

The Vatican City or Città del Vaticano (Map 1; 3, 4, 5, 6) is surrounded by a high wall skirted by Viale Vaticano for the whole of its length (see the plan on p nnn). With an area of 43 hectares (less than half a square kilometre) and a population of about 550, it is, in size, the smallest independent state in existence. The Vatican City has its own postal service and its own currency. Its newspaper, the Osservatore Romano, has a world-wide circulation, and it owns a radio transmitting station that was prominent in the Second World War. Policing is carried out by the Swiss Guard, a corps founded in 1506, which retains the picturesque uniform said to have been designed by Michelangelo. (The Noble Guards and Palatine Guards established in the 19C were disbanded by Pope Paul VI in 1970, and the Pontifical Gendarmes transformed into a private corps.)

This chapter describes the Vatican City and gardens, which are of relatively limited interest to visitors in comparison with St Peter's and the Vatican Museums (described in Walks 32 and 33).

Opening times

Individual visitors are not admitted, but tours of part of the Vatican City and gardens, on foot (c2 hrs), usually depart at 10.00 every day except Wed and Sun.

The tours are organised at the entrance to the Vatican Museums, ☎ 06 6988 4466. € 9. Tickets should be booked at least one day in advance.

History of the Vatican City

The temporal power of the popes officially ended with the breach of Porta Pia and the entrance of Italian troops into Rome on 20 September 1870, signifying the unification of Italy. Up until that time much of central Italy had been owned by the papacy: the States of the Church had extended for 44,547 square kilometres. On the same day an agreement was made with the Papacy that the Leonine City (see p 335) was excluded from the jurisdiction of Italian troops, and this led the way to the creation of the Vatican State in the Lateran Treaty (or Concordat), signed on 11 February 1929, which defined the limits of the Vatican City.

The Treaty also granted the privilege of extraterritoriality to the basilicas of San Giovanni in Laterano (with the Lateran Palace), Santa Maria Maggiore and San Paolo fuori le Mura, and to certain other buildings, including the Palazzo della Cancelleria and the pope's villa at Castel Gandolfo. Special clauses in the treaty provided for access to St Peter's and the Vatican Museums. Under the treaty, Italy accepted canon law on marriage and divorce and made religious teaching compulsory in secondary as well as primary schools. Italy also agreed to make a payment in final settlement of the claims by the Holy See for the loss of papal property taken over by the Italian Government. After the signing of the Treaty the pope came out of the Vatican for the first time since 1870. (A new Concordat—which made religious instruction in schools optional, and contained modifications regarding marriage—was signed between the Italian Government and the Vatican in 1984 in Villa Madama.)

There are three entrances to the Vatican City that are not open to the general public and are protected by members of the Swiss Guard. The **Portone di Bronzo** (1), in the colonnade to the right of St Peter's, is the official entrance to the Holy See. The **Arco delle Campane** (19), to the left of St Peter's, is the entrance for cars and the bus which runs from Piazza San Pietro to the Vatican Museums; it is also used for access to the Audience Hall, and for the organised tours of the gardens and City and of the necropolis below St Peter's. The **Cancello di Sant'Anna**, in Via di Porta Angelica, is used for the various offices of the Vatican State, including the Polyglot Printing Press, and the Vatican newspaper Osservatore Romano. The entrance to the Vatican Museums and the Sistine Chapel (see Walk 33) is in Viale Vaticano.

The pope and the hierarchy of the Vatican State

The pope is Sovereign Pontiff, the Bishop of Rome, successor to St Peter, and, as such, the head of the Roman Catholic Church and the Vicar of Christ. He enjoys the *primatus jurisdictionis*, that is, supreme jurisdictional power over the whole Church. By the Vatican City Law of Pius XI (1921), the pope is head of the legislature, executive and judiciary, and he nominates the General Council and the Governor of the Vatican. He is assisted by the Sacred College of Cardinals and by the Roman Curia.

The Sacred College of Cardinals was limited by Sixtus V to 70 members, but after the consistory of March 1962 the number was increased to 87. John XXIII created 46 new cardinals, and gave them all episcopal dignity. At present there is no limit to the number of cardinals who can be appointed. The College consists of six cardinal bishops (whose dioceses are the suburbicarian sees of Ostia, Velletri, Porto and Santa Rufina, Albano, Frascati and Palestrina), nearly 70 cardinal priests, and 14 cardinal deacons.

The Roman Curia comprises the 12 Sacred Congregations, which deal with the central administration of the Church, the three Tribunals, and the six Offices, which include that of the Cardinal Secretary of State, who represents the Vatican in international relations.

Vatican Gardens

The gardens, laid out in the 16C, cover the north and west slopes of the Vatican Hill. They are entered through the Arco delle Campane (**19**) which is protected by a sentry of the Swiss Guard, armed with a rifle instead of the halberd carried by the guard at the Portone di Bronzo (see p 405). The square beyond is Piazza dei Protomartiri Romani, the site of the martyrdom of the early Christians near the Circus of Nero. On the left is the **Camposanto Teutonico**, dating from the 8C, and probably the oldest medieval cemetery; it is still reserved for the Germans and Dutch. Adjacent is the Collegio Teutonico. Beyond, against the wall of the city, is the **Audience Hall** (**20**) by Pier Luigi Nervi (1971). Designed in the shape of a shell, it has seating for 8000 people.

In the pavement in front of the first arch of the passage beneath the sacristy of St Peter's (**18**), a slab marks the former site of the obelisk in Piazza San Pietro. A road leads beneath the sacristy to Piazza Santa Marta. Here, on the right, is a fine view of the south transept of St Peter's; on the left is the Palazzo dell'Arciprete di San Pietro. At the west end of the square is the Palazzo del Tribunale (**17**).

Opposite the majestic west end of St Peter's is the little church of **Santo Stefano degli Abissini**, built by Leo III as Santo Stefano Maggiore. In 1479 Sixtus IV conceded it to Coptic monks; it was rebuilt by Clement XI.

A road ascends past the Studio del Mosaico, with an exhibition room, and on the right the Palazzo del Governatorato (**16**; Governor's Palace), built in 1931 as the seat of the civic administration of the Vatican City. To the south is the little-used Vatican railway station (**15**). On the first floor a **Philatelic and Numismatic Museum** was opened in 1990. It preserves all the postage stamps and coins issued by the Vatican since 1929. It is open for group visits by request, ☎ 06 6988 4081.

Viale dell'Osservatorio continues up through the gardens past the Seminario Etiopico (**14**). At the western extremity of the city is a stretch of the wall built by Nicholas V on the site of the ancient walls put up by Leo IV. Here the **Tower of St John** (**13**), once an observatory, is now used as a guest house. On the westernmost bastion of the city walls is the heliport (**22**). The road passes a reproduction of the Grotto of Lourdes (**12**), presented by the French Catholics to Leo XIII.

A road leads down through exotic vegetation past the old **Vatican radio station** (**11**), designed by Guglielmo Marconi and inaugurated in 1931. Since 1957 Vatican Radio has transmitted from a station at Santa Maria di Galeria, 25km outside Rome. The **Fontana dell'Aquilone** (**10**), by Giovanni Vesanzio, has a triton by Stefano Maderno. Nearer the huge museum buildings is the **Casina of Pius IV** (**9**), two small garden buildings by Pirro Ligorio (1558–62), which are a masterpiece of Mannerist architecture. They were decorated by various artists including Santi di Tito, Federico Zuccari, Federico Barocci and Durante Alberti. In the villa, now the seat of the Pontifical Academy of Sciences, Pius IV held the Notti Vaticane, meetings during which learned discussions took place on poetry, philosophy and sacred subjects. Pius VIII and Gregory XVI used to give their audiences here.

Towards St Peter's a group of buildings include the Floreria, formerly the mint (*zecca*) founded by Eugenius IV, and the Fontana del Sacramento. The Stradone dei Giardini is an avenue which skirts Bramante's west corridor of the Vatican Museums. The exit is usually through Piazza del Forno (overlooked by the Sistine Chapel), around St Peter's, and through the Arco delle Campane.

Vatican City

The rest of Vatican City is normally closed to visitors. It consists of a series of small courtyards, including the **Cortile dei Pappagalli** (so called from its frieze of parrots, now almost obliterated). The larger Cortile di San Damaso is over-looked by the Loggia of Raphael (see p 386). The various offices of the Vatican State, near the Cancello di Sant'Anna, include the Polyglot Printing Press, the post office, the Casa Parrochiale, and the *Osservatore Romano* newspaper. Also here are the barracks of the Swiss Guard, a restoration centre for tapestries, and the restored church of San Pellegrino. In 1956 a pagan necropolis consisting of tombs of the 1C–4C was discovered beneath the car park. The cemetery was alongside Via Triumphalis, the line of which is now followed by Via del Pellegrino. Beside the Cancello di Sant'Anna is **Sant' Anna dei Palafrenieri** (**6**), the parish church of the Vatican City, built in 1573 by the Papal Grooms (Palafrenieri della Corte Papale) to the designs of Vignola.

To the south of St Peter's Colonnade is **Palazzo del Sant'Uffizio**. The Holy Office or tribunal, commonly known as the Inquisition, was established here in 1542 by Paul III to investigate charges of heresy, unbelief and other offences against the Catholic religion. The preparation of the Index of Prohibited Books was orig-inally entrusted to the Congregation of the Holy Office. In 1571 Pius V estab-lished a special Congregation of the Index, which survived until its suppression by Benedict XV in 1917, when these duties were resumed by the Holy Office. The tribunal was formally abolished by the Roman Assembly in February 1849, but it was re-established by Pius IX a few months later. The secret archives of the Inquisition were opened to students for the first time in 1998, covering the period from its inception to the first years of the 20C.

Outer Rome

35 • South of Porta San Paolo

Piazzale Ostiense, where the Porta San Paolo stands, is a very busy road junction at the site of the unexpected Pyramid, a well-preserved Roman monument, and the historic Protestant Cemetery. Nearby, on the otherwise uninteresing and unattractive Via Ostiense, the Centrale Montemartini, a disused electrical plant, was opened to the public in 1997 as a superb exhibition space to display a very fine collection of Roman sculptures from the Capitoline museums and is well worth visiting. Further along the Via Ostiense is the Basilica di San Paolo fuori le Mura, which is important as one of the four patriarchal basilicas of Rome, but it is a rather disappointing place to visit.

Getting there

Underground line B from Termini and Colosseum stations runs to Piramide station for Porta San Paolo and the Centrale Montemartini and to San Paolo station for the basilica of San Paolo fuori le Mura.

Bus No. 23 from Piazza Pia (Castel Sant'Angelo) follows the right bank of the Tiber past Trastevere to Ponte Aventino, where it crosses the river and follows Via Marmorata to Porta San Paolo. From there it runs along Via Ostiense past the Centrale Montemartini (the third request stop from Porta San Paolo) to the basilica di San Paolo fuori le Mura. On the return journey it follows the left bank of the Tiber.

Around Porta San Paolo

The well-preserved **Porta San Paolo** (Map 9; 7) was the Porta Ostiensis of ancient Rome; its inner side is original, with two arches from the time of Aurelian. The outer face, rebuilt by Honorius in 402, has been restored. The gate houses the **Museo della Via Ostiense**, which illustrates the history of the road to Ostia. Open Tues–Sun 09.00–13.30; Tues, Thur also open 14.30–16.30; closed Mon. ☎ 06 574 3193. It includes milestones and reliefs (some only casts), together with models of Ostia and its port in Imperial times (see p 448). Among the tomb-paintings are three frescoed lunettes from a tomb of the Servian period.

The square on the south side of the gate is called **Piazzale Ostiense**. An important traffic hub, it has an underground station and the railway station for the branch line to Ostia and Lido di Ostia, which is also on the branch line from Tiburtina station to Fiumicino.

On the west side of the square, across the line of the city wall, is the **Pyramid of Gaius Cestius** (Map 9; 7), praetor, tribune of the plebs, and member of the college of Roman priests called the Septemviri Epulones, who organised public banquets at important festivals. He died in 12 BC and the tomb is in the form of a tall pyramid of brick faced with marble, 27m high with a base 22m square. An inscription records that it was built in less than 330 days. It was included in the Aurelian Walls in the 3C, and remains one of the best-preserved monuments of ancient Rome (there were a number of similar pyramids in the ancient city). It is not open to the public. On the wall next to the pyramid is a plaque commemorates the liberation of Rome on 4 June 1944 by the US and Canadian 1st Special Service forces.

Beyond the pyramid, to the left, extends the so-called **Protestant Cemetery** or *Cimitero acattolico per gli Stranieri al Testaccio* (Map 9; 7). Open Tues–Sun 09.00–17.00 or 18.00; closed Mon. ☎ 06 574 1900. It is entered at no. 6 Via Caio Cestio; through a narrow slit in the wall along this road the tombs of Keats and Severn can be seen. In a romantic setting with tall cypresses and pine trees, it is beautifully kept, and inhabited by numerous friendly cats that are very well looked after (they are fed 14.00–17.00 every day near the Pyramid). Formerly reserved for Protestant or Orthodox foreigners—mostly English and German— since 1953 it has been open to all non-Catholics. Since the earliest recorded grave dating from 1738, some 4000 people have been buried here. The Catholic Church once stipulated that burials here had to take place after dark, and up until 1870 Papal censorship was exercised on the tomb decorations and epitaphs.

To the left, beyond a wall, is the **Old Cemetery**, from which there is a splendid view of the Pyramid. When Shelley saw the cemetery he wrote: 'It might make one in love with death to think that one should be buried in so sweet a place.' There are only a few graves here: in the far corner is that of 'A Young English Poet', **John Keats** (1796–1821), who wrote his own epitaph: 'Here lies one whose name was writ in water.' Keats spent the last three months of his life in Rome (see p 159) where he died from turberculosis, tended by his friend Joseph Severn (1793–1879), who is buried next to him. Severn returned to Rome as British Consul in 1860–72 and died here at the age of 85. Between the two graves is the little tombstone of Severn's son Arthur, who died at the age of one (Wordsworth was present at his baptism in Rome). Behind, a Celtic Cross marks the tomb of John Bell (1763–1820), the Scottish anatomist and surgeon. On the wall there is a plaque in memory of the writer Axel Munthe (1857–1949).

The **New Cemetery**, in use from 1822 onwards, is crowded with gravestones. On the highest ground, at the base of a tower in the walls, lies the heart of **Percy Bysshe Shelley** (1792–1822), the *cor cordium* ('the heart of all hearts'), brought here by his friend, the writer Edward Trelawny after his cremation on the beach at the mouth of the Arno. Shelley lived in Italy after 1818: in 1822 he and his wife Mary moved to the Casa Magni at Lerici in Liguria, and he was drowned at the age of 30 when his little boat sank off Viareggio. The great poet's monument is by Onslow Ford (1891). Trelawny was buried nearby, under a plain tomb slab, when he died in 1881 at the age of 88. In front, the grave of the American sculptor and poet William Wetmore Story (1819–95) and his wife is decorated with a sculpture by him entitled the *Angel of Grief*. Nearby lies J. Addington Symonds (1840–93), the historian of the Renaissance. Near the next tower in the walls, but on lower ground between two tall pine trees, is the tomb of Julius, the only son of Goethe, who died in Rome in 1830: his profile in relief is by Bertel Thorvaldsen. Others buried here include the sculptor John Gibson (1790–1886); the writers William Howitt (1792–1879) and his wife Mary (1799–1888); Robert Michael Ballantyne (1825–94), author of children's books; Hans von Marées (1837–87), the German painter; and Johann Christian Reinhardt (1761–1847), the German painter and engraver. At the far end of the cemetery is the grave of Antonio Gramsci (1891–1937), one of the founders of Italian Communism in 1921, who was imprisoned by the Fascist regime from 1926 until his death: his confinement is described in his famous *Lettere dal carcere* published in 1947.

Just beyond the Protestant Cemetery, at the end of Via Caio Cestio, and across Via Nicola Zabaglia, is the **Rome British Military Cemetery**, where 426 members of the three armed services are buried. The cemetery is beautifully sited along the line of the city wall. If the gates are locked, telephone the Area Office (the address and telephone number are given on a notice).

To the north of the British Military Cemetery and west of Via Nicola Zabaglia rises **Monte Testaccio** (Map 9; 7), an isolated mound 54m high and some 1000m round, entirely composed of potsherds (*testae*) dumped here from the Augustan period up to the middle of the 3C AD, from the neighbouring storehouses of the Republican port which lined the Tiber between Ponte Testaccio and Ponte Sublicio (now Ponte Aventino; see p 228). Among the finds here was a hoard of amphorae used to import oil from Spain, with official marks scratched on them, which are of fundamental importance to our knowledge of the economic history of the late Republic and early Empire. From the top of Monte Testaccio, which is entered from the corner facing Via Galvani and Via Zabaglia, there is a fine view. Jousts and tournaments were held in this part of the city during the Middle Ages. The district of Testaccio, near the 'ex-Mattatoio', a huge building of 1888–89 which used to be a slaughterhouse, has recently become a centre of cultural activities with several small theatres and a cinema complex. It is now also renowned for its restaurants of all categories (see p 38).

Centrale Montemartini

From Piazzale Ostiense the broad, uninteresting Via Ostiense leads almost due south through a depressing part of the town. It is not recommended to make this journey on foot; bus no. 23 follows the road to the basilica of San Paolo 2km away (get off at the third request stop from Piazzale Ostiense for the Centrale Montemartini). About half-way along, more or less opposite the Mercati Generali—the wholesale food markets of Rome—and set back from the road on the right (not well signposted), is the Centrale Montemartini with a superb display of Roman Classical statues from the Capitoline museums. Open 09.30–19.00; closed Mon. ☎ 06 574 8030. Combined ticket available with the Musei Capitolini, see p 78. There is a small café above the boiler room.

History of the Centrale Montemartini

Built in 1912, this was the first public electrical plant to be opened in Rome and was named after its designer Giovanni Montemartini. Operated by diesel and steam, it provided enough power to illuminate half the streets and piazze of the city. It continued to function throughout the Second World War and only fell into disuse in 1963. It was restored by the Rome water and electricity board (*ACEA*) in 1990 as a superb exhibition space and is also of the greatest interest as a monument of industrial archaeology.

Since 1997 some 400 Classical sculptures formerly exhibited in the Musei Capitolini (Palazzo dei Conservatori, the Museo Nuovo and Braccio Nuovo) have been exhibited here. They are beautifully displayed and labelled (also in English). Most of them were found in excavations in Rome at the end of the 19C or in the early 20C, when many villas and gardens were destroyed to make room for new buildings, including the famous Villa Ludovisi-Boncompagni (see p 237) between the Pincio and Quirinal hills.

The fine façade is preceded by palm trees and two elegant lamp posts designed by Duilio Cambellotti. On the **ground floor**, the **Sala delle Colonne** has exhibits from the earliest Archaic period. Here are displayed finds from the excavations around Sant'Omobono, near the foot of the Campidoglio; a fresco dating from the 3C BC with military scenes, found on the Esquiline Hill in 1873; finds from the tomb of the Cornelii discovered in Via Marco Polo in 1956; statues from the area sacra in Via Tiburtina; and the head of a *Girl in a Helmet* made out of peperino dating from the 2C BC, found near the Villa Aldobrandini on the Quirinal Hill.

At the end of the room is a fragment of a bed with very delicate inlaid decorations in bone, from Greece (late 1C BC), and exquisite small mosaics from Via San Lorenzo in Panisperna (early 1C BC). There is a case of finds from a domus unearthed in Via del Babuino, and the *Lettiga Capitolina*, a bronze litter found on the Esquiline.

The long hall displays statues and Republican heads including the well known *Togato Barberini*, the statue of a man in a toga carrying two busts, one of his father and one of his grandfather. In the hemicycle is an early portrait of *Augustus* (27–20 BC) found in Via del Mare. The headless statue of *Aphrodite* is a replica of a statue by Kallimachos (late 5C BC). The turbines and tools used when the electrical plant was still functioning can also be seen here.

A flight of iron stairs leads up to the **Sala Macchine**, or engine room, on the **first floor**, with a superb display of Roman sculpture inspired by Greek master-pieces. At the end are five very fine statues of *Athena*: the colossal statue found in Via del Corso is inspired by a Greek original by Kresilas of 430 BC (the head is a cast from a statue now in the Louvre). In the centre of the hall by the stairs are exhibited sculpted heads and, on the right, a *Young Athlete*, a head of *Hercules*, a beautiful head of an *Amazon*, a head of *Dionysus*, and a statue of a *Discus Thrower*. The statues in the centre of the room include a draped figure of *Apollo*—now damaged, but once portrayed as playing the *cetra*, two female fig-ures wearing the *peploe*, and *Aphrodite* from a Greek original by Praxiteles. The two grey statues nearby are particularly interesting: that of a praying female fig-ure has recently been identified as *Agrippina Minore*, wife of Claudius. It is made out of basanite, a precious stone from the Egyptian desert, and was unearthed on the Celian Hill: the original head was recently found in Copenhagen. The restored figure of the *Victory of Samathrace* is a Hellenistic work in bigio antico. Close by are statues and a metope of *Warriors*. In front of the temple pediment (see below) are sculptures from other such pediments including a colossal figure of *Jove* and a female figure, both found near the Teatro di Marcello and thought to date from the Augustan era.

Well displayed above steps is the reconstructed pediment from the **Temple of Apollo Sosianus**, dedicated to Apollo Medico in 433 BC and restored by the con-sul Sosius in 33 BC, three columns of which survive near the Teatro di Marcellus. The nine remarkably fine sculptural fragments represent a battle between Greeks and Amazons and are thought to date from 450–425 BC. At the end of the room, behind the pediment, are more fragments from the temple including a frieze with a triumphal procession, and the reconstructed aedicula of the cella of the tem-ple. Sculpture found near the Capitoline Hill, including three colossal heads of *Hercules* and two female statues, dating from the 1C BC, are also exhibited here. There follow finds from the temples in Largo Argentina and the Theatre of Pompey, including a statue of a *Seated Muse*, and fragments of a colossal statue of *Fortuna*—the head, arm and two feet show that it must have been some 8m high—attributed to a Greek artist working in Rome in 101 BC. The last two sec-tions in the corridor behind the huge generator display reliefs from the time of Claudius, a pastoral scene with two cows, and Imperial portraits. Along the win-dow wall are portrait heads and a statue of Icarus.

The **Sala delle Caldaie**, or boiler room, exhibits sculptures which used to dec-orate private residences, many of them the so-called *horti*, or grand villas with large gardens built on the hills of Rome and owned by the wealthiest citizens and members of the Imperial families. Finds from the Gardens of Maecenas on the Esquiline (see p 274) include the so-called *Auriga* or charioteer, a copy of a 5C original. It was formerly attached to a statue of a horse, also displayed here, and is now thought to represent a hero, possibly Theseus, driving his chariot. The sculptures were found in 1874. The beautiful *Dancing Maenad*, in relief, is from an original by Kallimachos, and the rhyton is a neo-Attic work signed by Pontios, and formerly used as a fountain. The statue of *Hercules in Combat* is from an original by Lysippos. Also from these gardens are the statues of *Muses*, a colossal statue of *Demeter*, and a very beautiful head of an *Amazon*, a copy of a famous bronze work by Polykleitos.

Finds from the Gardens of Sallust (see p 265) include a delicately carved fragment of a frieze, a kneeling statue of an *Amazon* from a temple pediment, and a herm of *Hercules* with a beard. The sculptures from the Gardens of Lamiani on the Esquiline include a funerary stele with the relief of a *Young Girl holding a Dove*, a Greek original of 500–490 BC, and the head of a *Centaur*. Also here is the *Esquiline Venus*, the figure of a beautiful young girl probably connected with the cult of Isis, an eclectic work dating from the 1C BC. Although the arms are missing, we know that the girl was depicted tying up her hair before taking a swim. Nearby are two fine female statues, similar in style and date to the Venus. To the right is a large marble vase, beautifully decorated with garlands of acanthus, and on the left two handsome large kraters, one with Dionisiac scenes and the other with a relief of the marriage of Paris and Helena. Near the side wall is a fragment of an exquisite polychrome mosaic found near Santa Bibiana, with hunting scenes. The charming statue of a *Muse*—probably Polimnia—leaning on a pillar of rock, was found near the Variani gardens. Close to the wall are statues found in the Gardens of Licinius (see p 298), including a charming *Seated Figure of a Girl*, a Hadrianic copy of a Hellenistic work, and a statue of *Dionysus with a Panther*. The three portraits of *Hadrian*, his wife *Sabina*, and *Matidia* were found in the Tauriani gardens. On the window wall are the head of a *Strategist*, two statues of *Pothos*, and a headless statue of a *Roman General* found in a domus beneath Via Cavour. A series of small sculptures are displayed together since they were found near Porta San Lorenzo and once probably decorated a nymphaeum. They include a *Wounded Satyr*, a fragment of a group of a giant fighting two satyrs, derived from the gigantomachia of Pergamon. Towards the end wall are a series of funerary monuments and two very fine sarcophagi.

Stairs lead up to a **balcony** with a good view of the mosaic with hunting scenes, where two cases display gilded bronze decoration and beautiful gems found in the Lamiani gardens.

On Via Ostiense a plaque marks the site of an oratory demolished in the 20C which, according to tradition, marked the spot where St Peter and St Paul greeted each other on their way to martyrdom.

In the middle of the road just before San Paolo fuori le Mura is a small necropolis known as the **Sepolcreto Ostiense**, which contained pagan and perhaps Christian tombs. The site, seen through railings, extended over a wide area; another part is visible left of the road.

San Paolo fuori le Mura

San Paolo fuori le Mura, 2km from Porta San Paolo (beyond **Map 9**; **7**) is the largest church in Rome after St Peter's. It is one of the four great patriarchal basilicas of Rome, and one of the three which have the privilege of extraterritoriality. The church commemorates the martyrdom of St Paul and is believed to contain the Apostle's tomb. The church is open daily 07.00–18.30. The cloisters are open daily 09.00–13.00 and 15.00–18.00.

History of San Paolo fuori le Mura

According to Christian tradition, a Roman matron called Lucina buried the body of Paul in a vineyard on the site of the church of San Paolo fuori le Mura. A small shrine existed here when, in 384, a large basilica was begun by Valentinian II and Theodosius the Great at the request of Pope Damasus. It was enlarged by Theodosius's son, Honorius, and decorated with mosaics at the expense of Galla Placidia, sister of Honorius. After the additions made by Leo III (pope, 795–816), it became the largest and most beautiful church in Rome. In the 9C it was pillaged by the Saracens and John VIII (872–82) enclosed it in a fortified village known as Giovannipolis. It was restored c 1070 by Abbot Hildebrand, later Gregory VII. The façade, overlooking the Tiber, was preceded by a colonnaded quadriporticus. Before the Reformation, the king of England was ex officio a canon of San Paolo and the abbot, in return, was decorated with the Order of the Garter. This great basilica was almost entirely destroyed by fire on the night of 15–16 July 1823.

Leo XII ordered the reconstruction, which was directed by Pasquale Belli, Pietro Bosio and Pietro Camporese, and afterwards by Luigi Poletti. In the rebuilding it was decided to use new materials instead of repairing the damaged stucture, although in plan and dimensions, if not in spirit, the new basilica follows the old one almost exactly. The transept was consecrated by Gregory XVI in 1840 and the complete church by Pius IX in 1854. In 1891 an explosion in a neighbouring fort broke most of the stained glass, which was replaced by slabs of alabaster. In March 1966 a service was performed here by Pope Paul VI and the Archbishop of Canterbury, when they issued a joint declaration of amity.

The present frigid 19C reconstruction, 'which looks outside like a very ugly railway station' (Augustus Hare, *Walks in Rome*), has none of the atmosphere of the other ancient basilicas in Rome, and the sale of souvenirs is disturbing.

The Romanesque campanile was pulled down to make way for the unattractive bell-tower by Luigi Poletti on Via Ostiense. Poletti was also responsible for the **north portico** which incorporates 12 Hymettan marble columns from the old basilica. On one of the nearest columns, beneath the frieze, is a 4C inscription of Pope Siricius (384–99). The façade (right) is preceded by a great quadriporticus with 146 enormous monolithic granite columns, added by Guglielmo Calderini (1892–1928). The elaborate frescoes on the façade date from 1885. The central **bronze doors** (1) are by Antonio Maraini (1928–30). The **Porta Santa** (2) has the bronze *doors that belonged to the old basilica (seen from the inside, light on the right). They were made at Constantinople by Staurakios in 1070, and have 54 panels of scenes from the Old and New Testaments inlaid with silver. They were opened for Holy Year in January 2000 by the pope together with the Archbishop of Canterbury and the Patriarch of the Orthodox Church.

The nave and transept form in plan a tau, or Egyptian cross, 132m by 65m; the height is 30m. The highly polished marble, alabaster, malachite, lapis and porphyry give an impression of Neo-classical splendour. The **nave**, with double aisles separated from one another by 80 columns of Montórfano granite, is the new part of the basilica. In the centre of the ceiling, which is richly decorated with stuccoes in white and gold, are the arms of Pius IX. The paintings between the windows, executed in the mid-19C and depicting scenes in the *Life of St Paul*, are by Pietro Gagliardi, Francesco Podesti, Guglielmo de Sanctis, Francesco Coghetti and Cesare Mariani; under these (and in the aisles), forming a frieze, are the portraits in

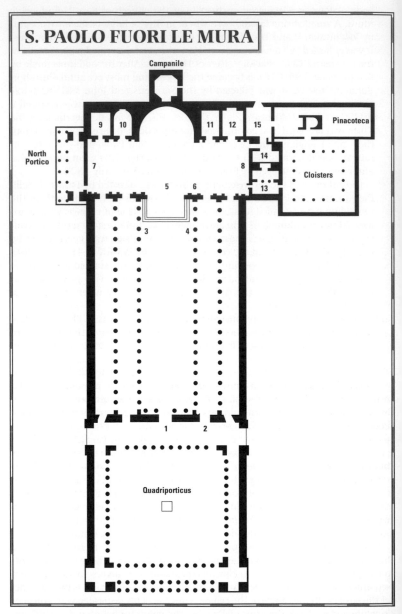

mosaic of all the popes from St Peter to John Paul II. In the outermost aisles are niches with statues of the Apostles. The six huge alabaster columns beside the doors were presented by Mohammed Ali of Egypt. The statue of *St Peter* (**3**) is by Alberto Giacometti and that of *St Paul* (**4**) by Salvatore Revelli.

The **triumphal arch**, a relic of the old basilica, is supported by two colossal granite columns. Its much-restored mosaics represent *Christ Blessing in the Greek Manner*, with angels, symbols of the Evangelists, the Elders of the Apocalypse, and St Peter and St Paul. On the other face of the arch are the remains of mosaics by Pietro Cavallini. Over the high altar, supported by four porphyry columns, is a splendid *tabernacle (5) by Arnolfo di Cambio and his companion Pietro (Oderisi?, 1285). The **tomb of St Paul** is traditionally supposed to be beneath the altar, where there is a 1C tomb surrounded by Christian and pagan burials. The inscription PAOLO APOSTOLO MART dates from the time of Constantine. The huge 12C paschal *candlestick (6) is by Nicolò di Angelo and Pietro Vassalletto.

The magnificent ceiling of the **transept** is decorated with the arms of Pius VII, Leo XII, Pius VIII and Gregory XVI, as well as with those of the basilica, an arm holding a sword. The walls are covered with rare marbles. The Corinthian pilasters are made up of fragments of the old columns. The great *mosaic of the apse was executed c 1220 by Venetian craftsmen sent by Doge Pietro Ziani at the request of Pope Honorius III. It was heavily restored in the 19C after damage in the fire of 1823. The subjects are: *Christ Blessing in the Greek Manner*, with St Peter, St Andrew, St Paul and St Luke; at the feet of Christ, Pope Honorius III; below this, a gem-studded cross on the altar, angels and apostles. On the outer face of the arch are the *Virgin and Child with St John blessing Pope John XXII*.

At either end of the transept is an altar of malachite and lapis lazuli, presented by Nicholas I of Russia: the *Conversion of St Paul* (7) is by Vincenzo Camuccini, and the mosaic (8) is a copy from the *Coronation of the Virgin* by Giulio Romano. The **Chapel of St Stephen** (9) has a statue of the saint by Rinaldo Rinaldi, and paintings of his *Expulsion from the Sanhedrin* by Francesco Coghetti, and of his stoning by Francesco Podesti. The **Chapel of the Crucifix** (10), by Carlo Maderno, was the only chapel saved in the fire. On the altar is a crucifix attributed to Tino da Camaino. Also here are statues of *St Bridget* by Stefano Maderno, and of a saint in wood. In this chapel, in 1541, St Ignatius de Loyola and the first Jesuits took the corporate oaths formally establishing their society as a religious order. The **Chapel of the Choir**, or of St Lawrence (11), with choir stalls, is by Guglielmo Calderini. It contains a 15C marble triptych. The **Chapel of St Benedict** (12) is a sumptuous work by Luigi Poletti, with a reproduction of the cella of an ancient temple; the 12 fluted columns are from Velo.

The **Sala del Martirologio** (13), with 13C frescoes, is inappropriately used for selling souvenirs. A door leads into the lovely **cloisters** (open 09.00–13.00 and 15.00–18.00; closed Sun) belonging to the old Benedictine convent. They have coupled colonnettes of different forms decorated with mosaics and with tiny couchant animals—most of which have now disappeared—between the columns. In the centre is a rose garden. The cloisters were begun under Abbot Pietro da Capua (1193–1208) and finished after 1228, and are the work, at least in part, of the Vassalletti family of sculptors. Along the walls are placed numerous inscriptions and sculptured fragments, both Christian and pagan. In the walk to the right is the statue of a *Prophet* (XX); an inscription recording the suicide of Nero (XIX), probably a 17C forgery; a large sarcophagus which retains its lid and very worn reliefs depicting the story of Apollo and Marsyas; and a seated statue (XIV) of *Boniface IX*. Off the cloister are the Chapel of Reliquaries, with a gilded silver cross, and the Pinacoteca, with works by Antoniazzo Romano

(*Madonna and Four Saints*) and Bramantino (*Flagellation*), as well as old prints showing the damage caused by the fire.

The **baptistery** (14), designed by Arnaldo Foschini on a Greek-cross plan in 1930, leads into the vestibule (15) preceding the south door of the church, which contains a colossal statue of *Gregory XVI* by Rinaldo Rinaldi, and 13C mosaics from the old basilica.

St Paul the Apostle in Rome

As a Pharisee, Paul's Hebrew name was Saul, and he apparently earned a living as a tent-maker. While on a journey to Damascus, on a mission to persecute the Christians, he had a dramatic conversion—vividly portrayed in Caravaggio's famous painting in the church of Santa Maria del Popolo. A Roman citizen by birth, he appealed to Caesar after he was arrested for his Christian beliefs around AD 60 in Jerusalem, and so was allowed to be tried in Rome. He travelled there as a prisoner by boat via Crete, Malta (where he was shipwrecked) and Sicily (as described in Acts). This was the fourth and last of the remarkably long journeys he made during his lifetime (the first three as a missionary).

Paul was met on the Via Appia outside Rome by Roman friends and lived for two years in the city under house arrest before his martyrdom, at about the same time as St Peter was crucified here. It is thought there must have been contact between St Peter and St Paul (an oratory, now demolished, on the Via Ostiense was supposed to mark the site where the two saints met). Paul is supposed to have been imprisoned in the Mamertine prison which can still be seen beside the Roman Forum, and to have been beheaded on the site of the abbey of the Tre Fontane, now near EUR.

Although he was little known outside the Christian world in his lifetime and numerous legends grew up around his name, St Paul is well known to us through his remarkable letters in the New Testament. It is now generally recognised that it was Paul who succeeded in transforming Christianity into a universal religion. As a result of Paul's preaching the new cult of Christianity took hold in Rome. St Paul is now honoured with St Peter as joint patron saint of Rome: their annual festival is held on 29 June.

36 • The Via Appia Antica and the catacombs

This walk describes the Via Appia Antica (see plan on pp 422–433) outside Porta San Sebastiano (Map 10; 8) in the Aurelian Walls. Since 1997 this ancient Roman road and the countryside close to it have been protected as a regional park which covers some 3500 hectares (larger than the historic centre of Rome itself). The Via Appia originally began at Porta Capena, a gate in the Servian Walls near the Circus Maximus (see p 310), but after Aurelian built his walls across it about 1.5km outside the Servian circle, this first stretch of the road was enclosed within the city limits and became known as the urban section (it is described in Walk 26).

The first stretch described in this walk, from Porta San Sebastiano to the church of Domine Quo Vadis, is now an unattractive, traffic-ridden road, extremely unpleasant to explore on foot except on Sundays, when it is officially (but not always) totally closed to traffic. Beyond the church the road, although very narrow (beware of fast cars), becomes prettier and passes the side entrance to the catacombs of San Callisto and then descends to the basilica and catacombs of San Sebastiano. These important catacombs along the Appia Antica, but not part of the Park, tend to be very crowded with tour groups, in contrast to the delightful peaceful atmosphere near the Roman monuments along the way. A short way beyond the basilica of San Sebastiano are the Circus of Maxentius and the Tomb of Cecilia Metella, two very interesting Roman monuments. Beyond is the most beautiful and characteristic section of the road.

Although this area was vandalised and neglected in the 1960s and 1970s, when luxury villas were also built near the road, it has, since 2000, been beautifully restored and is now looked after by the wardens of the park. There is a project to eliminate through traffic.

Information

Parco Regionale dell'Appia Antica, 42 Via Appia Antica; ☎ 06 52126314; ✉ www.parcoappiaantica.org.

Tours

Although the road is easy to explore on your own, there are also guided Sunday visits which can be booked at the Park office where bicycles can also be hired.

Getting there

Bus routes and timetables are subject to change, so telephone the park information office for up to date details. At present a special bus, called *Archeobus*, leaves every day every hour from Piazza Venezia, and although the ticket costs €14.70, it is valid for the whole day so that you can get on and off the bus at will to visit the monuments along the way. A guide on board indicates the most interesting sites, also in English.

It takes the following route and makes these stops: Piazza Venezia—Piazza Bocca della Verità—Circo Massimo—Terme di Caracalla—Porta San Sebastiano—Park office—Domine Quo Vadis (for the Caffarella Park)—Catacombs of San Callisto –Catacombs of San Sebastiano—Circo di Massenzio and Tomba di Cecilia Metella—Sant'Urbano (on Via Appia Pignatelli, near another entrance to the Caffarella park)—(Via Erode Attico back to the Appia Antica)—Villa dei Quintili—Casale Rotondo—(Via Casal Rotondo to the Via Appia Nuova)—Villa dei Quintili—Parco degli Acquedotti—(Via Appia Pignatelli back to Sant'Urbano)—Via Appia Antica (Catacombs of San Callisto) and back to the centre of Rome following the same route as the outward journey, except for Via Porta Latina instead of Via di Porta San Sebastiano.

ATAC bus 118 runs every 20-40 minutes from Piazzale Ostiense via the baths of Caracalla and Via di Porta San Sebastiano, along the Via Appia Antica as far as the Via Appia Pignatelli.

On weekdays bus no. 218 from San Giovanni in Laterano runs via the outside of the Aurelian Walls to Porta San Sebastiano and then follows Via Appia Antica as far as Via Ardeatina, near the catacombs of San Callisto and Santa Domitilla.

The catacombs of San Sebastiano can also be reached by **underground** Line A from Piazza di Spagna and Termini stations to Colli Albani, from where (on weekdays) bus no. 660 takes Via Appia Pignatelli to the Appia Antica at the catacombs of San Sebastiano.

Bicycles can be hired at the Park offices (see p 418)

Eating out

There are a few **restaurants** and **cafés** on the Via Appia Antica, but only in the stretch near San Sebastiano; otherwise it is a lovely place to picnic (especially the Parco della Caffarella and Parco degli Acquedotti).

History of the Via Appia

Called by Statius *regina viarum* (the queen of roads), the Via Appia was the most important of the consular Roman roads. It was built by the censor Appius Claudius in 312 BC as far as Capua, and later extended to Beneventum (Benevento) and Brundusium (Brindisi). In 37 BC Horace, Virgil and Maecenas travelled the 375km to Brindisi in 15 days.

For the first few kilometres the road served as a patrician cemetery, and was lined on either side by a series of family graves. Some of the tombs, usually in the form of a tower or tumulus, can still be seen, although often only their concrete cores survive. The solid bases were sometimes used in the Middle Ages as the foundations of watch-towers and small forts. The Via Appia was also used by the early Christians for their underground cemeteries, or catacombs, the most important of which are open to the public. When the road was reopened in 1852 many monuments were re-erected by Luigi Canina along its course.

Although the road survives as far as the twelfth Roman milestone (over 16km) and its junction with the modern Via Appia Nuova, little or no attempt was made to preserve it in the 20C, despite the fact that it was declared a public park in 1965. The ancient paving was almost totally covered with asphalt in the 20C up to the third milestone, the monuments were vandalised, and part of the historic area bordering the road was occupied by luxurious private villas in the 1940s and 1950s apparently without planning permission. The motorway circling Rome was even allowed to cut it in half at the seventh milestone.

However, largely thanks to the conservationist Antonio Cederna, who died in 1996, it finally became an official regional park in 1997, and in 1998 the administrative office (***Ente Parco***) was instituted. In 1999–2000 the circular motorway was diverted into a tunnel (1.5km) beneath the ancient road (an extremely rare instance where money has been spent purely to improve the scenery rather than facilitate the circulation of traffic). Then with special funds received during the Jublilee year important restoration was carried out on the ancient paving and sidewalks as far as the seventh milestone, and work is to continue beyond as far as the junction of the ancient road with the new Via Appia Nuova (the twelfth milestone, 16.5km in all).

The initial section of the Via Appia, the ancient *Clivus Martis*, is now a busy, unattractive road, not recommended for walkers, except on Sundays. It gently descends from Porta San Sebastiano, and about 120m from the gate is the site of the **first milestone**, marked by a column and an inscription (see the plan on pp 422–423). The Via Appia passes under an ugly flyover bearing a new fast road, where excavations have revealed ancient Roman remains, and then under the main Rome–Civitavecchia railway. It crosses the Almone (or Marrana della Caffarella), a brook where the priests of Cybele, the Magna Mater, used to perform the annual ceremony of washing the image of the goddess. Here, at no. 42, the seat of the *Parco Regionale dell'Appia Antica* and its information office is housed in a former papermill. This interesting monument of industrial archaeology, operational up until the 1950s, has a visitors' centre and is still being restored to house a museum and library devoted to the Via Appia. Beyond, tombs appear here and there. On the left, nearly 1km from the gate, is a conical Roman mound with a house on the top, and the little church of **Domine Quo Vadis**. This stands on the spot where—according to tradition—St Peter, fleeing the city, met an apparition of Jesus which shamed him into returning to Rome and martyrdom: the story was the subject of a novel by the Polish writer and Nobel prize winner Henryk Sienkiewicz, published in 1896. Inside a monument was erected to him by Polish residents in Italy in 1977.

By the church, Via Ardeatina branches off to the right to the Fosse Ardeatine 1km away (see below). At this fork is the entrance for cars to the catacombs of San Callisto.

Parco della Caffarella

About 100m from the church of Domine Quo Vadis is a turning to the left, onto Via della Caffarella which ends at a gate (open to walkers) into the remarkable protected area of the Caffarella. It is well worthwhile making a detour here through the countryside, as described below, and rejoin the Appia Antica just before the catacombs of San Sebastiano (see the Plan on pp 422–433).

This area, some 400 hectares of countryside and farmland, has been protected since 2000 when the Comune of Rome bought about half the land (the other half belongs to the Vatican). This is probably the area closest to the centre of the city where you can still see a landscape reminiscent of the famous Campagna Romana, the undulating plain around Rome between the sea and the low hills beneath the Sabine and Prenestine hills. It was characterised by its wide, open landscape of pastureland, green for most of the year, with a few wooded areas and others covered with typical low vegetation known as the *macchia mediterranea*. This landscape was praised and described by visitors, writers and artists up until the end of the 19C, when the countryside around Rome was gradually engulfed by new suburbs. In Roman times the wealthy Athenian Herodes Atticus, patron of arts and man of letters in the 2C AD, and famous above all for his numerous buildings in Greece, had his villa here, known as the Triopio.

After the first few hundred metres where the ugly suburbs of Rome are very conspicuous, we enter a well-preserved green valley from which there is a view back across fields to the Porta San Sebastiano and the dome of St Peter's in the far distance. In the other direction, on a clear day, the Alban hills and the Terminello mountains can be seen. This district has been used as farming land since the days of the ancient Romans, and some 5000–6000 sheep still graze here. Less than a kilometre along the lane is a path to the left, leading to the so-called **Temple of the Deus Rediculus**, by a mill near the Almone brook. The 'temple' is really a sumptuous tomb of the 2C, once identified as that of Annia Regilla, wife of Herodes Atticus (see below). Next to it is a medieval building. Both of these are to be restored and opened to the public. Beyond the lane passes a tumble-down medieval farm known as the Vaccereccia, still operating as such (on lease from the Vatican), where ricotta sheeps' cheese is made. On a clear day the Alban hills are clearly visible from here. After crossing a number of water channels (and a view left of a rock face with grottoes, used as huts by shepherds up until the early 20C), we come to the **Nymphaeum of Egeria**, a monumental fountain, recently restored and still a very picturesque and romantic spot even though it has been cleared of its centuries' old vegetation. The huge vault survives above a niche with a statue and Roman masonry in opus reticulatum. It is still fed by a branch of the Almone, although the water channel dates from the 19C. Here, according to myth, Numa Pompilius used to consult the nymph Egeria.

We now follow a lane up to a little hillock where three ancient ilexes mark the site of a **Bosco Sacro**. This 'sacred wood' has recently been replanted by the Park authorities. From here there is a splendid view of the Mausoleum of Cecilia Metella (see below) and below to the left the medieval Torre Valca can be seen. Beyond the ruins of an old cistern there is a good view of the Alban hills. The lane ends at a villa (privately owned, but due to be expropriated) beside the church of **Sant'Urbano**. This was originally a temple converted into a church in the 9C or 10C and was restored in 1634, when four fluted columns from the pronaos were incorporated into the wall of the church. Inside (not at present open) are remains of stucco ornamentation and extremely interesting frescoes by a certain Bonizzo (1011): over the door is the *Crucifixion*; on the end wall, *Christ Blessing*, with saints and angels; on the other walls, *Life of Jesus*, and the *Lives of St Cecilia and her Companions*, and of *St Vicolo*.

Sant'Urbano leads to Via Appia Pignatelli, a road opened by Innocent XII in the late 17C to link the Via Appia Antica with the Via Appia Nuova. We follow it to the right past the entrance to the **Catacombs of Praetextatus** (not open regularly to the public; see p 49), with pagan burials above ground and Christian sarcophagi below—including those of the martyred companions of St Cecilia—and 2C paintings. Via Appia Pignatelli rejoins the Appia Antica between the catacombs of St Calixtus and San Sebastiano (see below).

Beyond the church of Domine Quo Vadis (see above) the Appia Antica goes uphill past a trattoria at no. 87 on the left which incorporates remains of the so-called Columbarium of the Freedmen of Augustus, where some 3000 inscriptions were found. At no. 101 is the little Hypogeum of Vibia (no admission), with pagan paintings of the 3C AD. Beyond, at no. 103, is the site of the **second milestone**. At no. 110, on the right, is the entrance to the Catacombs of San Callisto.

The catacombs

The catacombs are a system of galleries of different sizes, often arranged on as many as five levels, and sometimes extending for several kilometres. Simple rectangular niches (*loculi*), where the bodies were placed wrapped in a sheet, were cut in tiers in the walls. The openings were closed with slabs of marble or terracotta on which the names were inscribed (at first in Greek, later in Latin), sometimes with the date or the words '*in pace*' added: almost all of these have now disappeared. Terracotta lamps were hung above the tombs to provide illumination in the galleries. A more elaborate type of tomb was the *arcosolium*, which was a niche surmounted by an arch and often decorated. Small rooms or *cubicula* served as family vaults. The shallowest of the galleries are 7–8m beneath the surface, while the deepest are some 22m below ground-level. Openings in the vaults, some of which survive, were used for the removal of earth during the excavations. Most of the tombs were rifled at some time over the centuries in the search for treasure and relics, but the inscriptions and paintings which survive are of the greatest interest.

History of the catacombs

The catacombs were used by the early Christians as underground cemeteries outside the walls of Rome, since burial within the walls was forbidden (pagan Romans were cremated). They were often situated on property donated by a wealthy Roman, after whom the cemetery was named (i.e. Domitilla, Agnese, Priscilla and Commodilla). Easily quarried in the soft tufa, the catacombs provided space for the tombs of thousands of Christians. They were in use from the 1C up until the early 5C. Many martyrs were buried here and the early Christians chose to be buried close to them. Later they became places of pilgrimage until the martyrs' relics were transferred to various churches in Rome. They were pillaged by the Goths (537) and the Lombards (755), and by the 9C they were abandoned. They received their name *ad catacumbas* (literally, 'by the caves') from the stone quarries on the site of the cemetery of San Sebastiano (see below).

In the 16C the archaeologist Antonio Bosio explored the catacombs and his remarkable study of them was published posthumously in 1632. They were not systematically explored again until 1850 when the archaeologist Giovanni Battista de Rossi carried out excavations—at first at San Callisto—and the Pontificia Commissione di Archeologia Sacra was set up. They were opened to the public and became one of the most famous sights of Rome, when visits by candlelight fired the romantic imagination of 19C travellers. The once popular belief that they were used as hiding places by the early Christians has been totally disproved.

The **Catacombs of San Callisto**, the first official cemetery of the early Christian community, are usually considered the most important of the Roman catacombs. Open 08.30–12.00 and 14.30–17.00 or 17.30; closed Wed and in Feb. ☎ 06 5130 1580. Visitors are conducted by an English-speaking priest. The catacombs were named after St Calixtus (San Callisto) who was appointed to look after the cemetery by Pope St Zephyrinus (199–217), and who enlarged them when he himself became pope in 217. They were the official burial place of the bishops of Rome. First investigated in 1850 by Giovanni Battista de Rossi (see above), they have not yet been fully explored.

The **Oratory of St Sixtus and St Cecilia** is a small basilica with three apses, where the dead were brought before burial in the catacombs. Here are inscriptions and sculptural fragments from the tombs, and a bust of De Rossi. Pope St Zephyrinus is generally supposed to have been buried in the central apse.

The catacombs, excavated on five levels, are reached by an ancient staircase. The tour usually remains on the second level, from which several staircases can be seen descending to other levels. The remarkable **papal crypt** preserves the tombs with original Greek inscriptions of the martyred popes St Pontianus (230–35), St Anterus (236), St Fabian (236–50), St Lucius I (253–54), martyred under Valerian's persecution, St Stephen I (254–57), St Dionysius (259–68) and St Felix I (269–74). In honour of the martyred popes, Pope St Damasus I (366–84) set up the metrical inscription seen at the end of the crypt.

In the adjoining crypt is the **Cubiculum of St Cecilia**, where the body of the saint is supposed to have been buried after her martyrdom at her house in Trastevere in 230. It is thought that in 820 it was moved by Paschal I to the church built on the site of her house. A copy of Stefano Maderno's statue of the saint in the church has been placed here. On the walls are very worn 7C–8C frescoes of the head of Christ, St Urban and other saints. Beyond the crypt, a 3C passage leads down a short flight of stairs, with Christian symbols carved on stone slabs, to the **Cubicula of the Sacraments**, with symbolic frescoes. In the first cubicle are frescoes of the *Raising of Lazarus* and, opposite, the *Miracle of the*

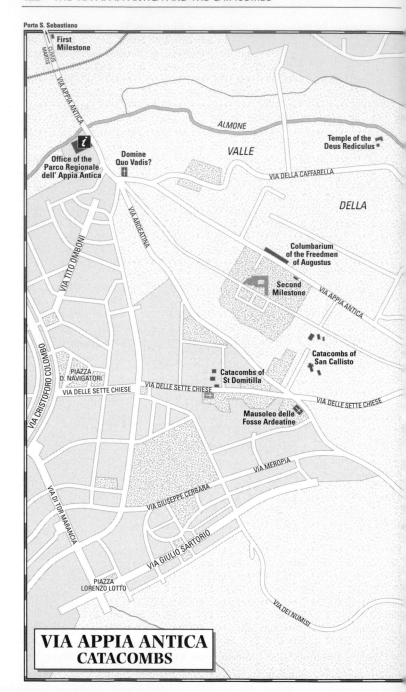

Porta S. Sebastiano

First Milestone

CLIVUS MARTIS

VIA APPIA ANTICA

ALMONE

VALLE

Temple of the Deus Rediculus

Office of the Parco Regionale dell' Appia Antica

Domine Quo Vadis?

VIA DELLA CAFFARELLA

DELLA

VIA ARDEATINA

VIA TITO OMBONI

Columbarium of the Freedmen of Augustus

Second Milestone

VIA APPIA ANTICA

Catacombs of San Callisto

VIA CRISTOFORO COLOMBO

PIAZZA D. NAVIGATORI

VIA DELLE SETTE CHIESE

VIA DELLE SETTE CHIESE

Catacombs of St Domitilla

VIA DELLE SETTE CHIESE

Mausoleo delle Fosse Ardeatine

VIA MEROPIA

VIA DI TOR MARANCIA

VIA GIUSEPPE CERBARA

VIA GIULIO SARTORIO

PIAZZA LORENZO LOTTO

VIA DEI NUMISI

VIA APPIA ANTICA
CATACOMBS

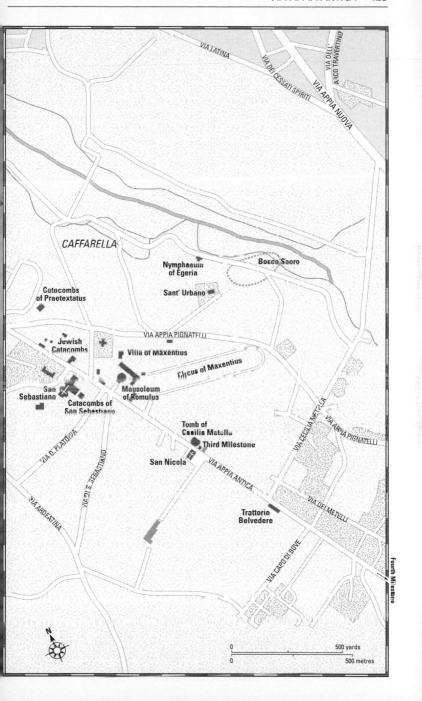

Loaves and Fishes. On the end wall is a fine double sarcophagus, with a lid in the form of a roof. The other cubicles have similar frescoes, several depicting the story of Jonah. Further on is the **Crypt of St Eusebius**, martyred in 310. In the adjoining cubicles are the sepulchral inscriptions of Pope St Caius (283–96) and two sarcophagi with mummified bodies. Next is the **Tomb of Pope St Cornelius** (251–53), with a contemporary Latin inscription containing the word 'martyr', and fine 6C Byzantine paintings. Adjoining is the **Crypt of Lucina**, the oldest part of the cemetery.

In 1991 remains of a 4C basilica used as a cemetery were discovered near the Via Ardeatina.

Back on the Via Appia, the **Jewish catacombs** (not regularly open; see p 49) at no. 119A, excavated in 1857, have tombs in the form of *loculi* or niches dating from the 3C to the 6C. The symbols include the cornucopia (Plenty), the palm-leaf (Victory), and the seven-branched candlestick, and the epitaphs are mostly in Greek.

The road descends to a small piazza in which, on the left, is a column set up by Pius IX in 1852 to commemorate his restoration of the ancient road. On the right are the **Basilica and Catacombs of San Sebastiano**, entered to the left of the church. Usually open 08.30–12.00 and 14.30–17.00 or 17.30; closed Sun and from mid Nov–mid Dec. ☎ 06 785 0350. Visitors are conducted by an English-speaking guide; the order of the tour is sometimes changed.

History of the Basilica and Catacombs of San Sebastiano

The basilica, one of the seven pilgrimage churches of Rome, was originally dedicated to St Peter and St Paul and called the *Basilica Apostolorum*. It was built in the first half of the 4C over the cemetery into which the bodies of the Apostles had been temporarily moved from their tombs in St Peter's and San Paolo fuori le Mura; this is said to have occurred in 258 during the persecution of Valerian. At a later date St Sebastian, who was martyred under Diocletian in 288, was buried here. After the 9C the association with the Apostles was forgotten and the church was named after St Sebastian. From the 3C to the 9C this was the most venerated area of subterranean Rome.

These catacombs have two special claims to fame: they are the only ones that have always been known, visited, and therefore damaged, and they were originally the only underground burial place to receive the name of catacombs, *ad catacumbas*, since they were built in an abandoned stone quarry here.

In the ticket office are fragments of sarcophagi and inscriptions. A stairway, with fragments of terracotta lids of sarcophagi bearing Imperial seals, leads down to the restored **Crypt of St Sebastian**, which contains a copy of a bust of *St Sebastian* attributed to Bernini. Beyond are the catacombs, excavated on four levels. The **Chapel of Symbols** has carved Christian symbols. An area below the basilica—the walls of which can be seen—known as the *Piazzuola* has three pagan tombs of the early 2C, extremely interesting for their architecture and elaborate decoration. They each have a façade with a terracotta tympanum. The first, on the right, has a fresco above the tympanum of a pastoral scene and a banquet. The marble inscription names this as the sepulchre of Marcus Clodius Hermes. Inside is a vault fresco with a Gorgon's head, and decorative frescoes on the walls include a beautiful composition with a vase of fruit and flowers flanked by two birds. The floor preserves a mosaic. The centre tomb has a magnificent stucco vault, dating from the early 2C, terminating in a shell design decorated with lotus and acanthus leaves and a peacock. It is believed both pagan and Christian burials took place in this composite tomb on several levels. The tomb to the left has a well-preserved stucco vault which descends to a lunette finely decorated with a grape and vine design. The cubicles here are also decorated with stucco.

A steep staircase ascends to the **Triclia**, a room reserved for the funerary banquets held in honour of the Apostles, Peter and Paul. There is a bench around the wall, and remains of red-painted decorations and fragments of pictures. The walls are inscribed with graffiti invoking the Apostles, including one dating from 260.

The **church** is usually shown at the end of the tour of the catacombs. It originally had a nave and two aisles; the aisles were walled up in the 13C. In 1612 it was rebuilt for Cardinal Scipio Borghese by Flaminio Ponzio; the façade has a portico with six Ionic columns, taken from the preceding 15C portico. The beautiful 17C wooden ceiling is by Giovanni Vasanzio. Off the south side is the apsidal Chapel of the Relics, containing a stone which was once believed to bear the imprint of Christ's feet, and other relics, and the Cappella Albani, built as a sepulchral chapel for Clement XI by Carlo Fontana. On the high altar are four columns of verde antico. On the third north altar, *St Francis of Assisi* is attributed to Girolamo Muziano. In a chapel off this side is a restored, late 14C wooden crucifix. An **archaeological museum** (usually closed) is arranged in the ambulatory, where remains of the 4C basilica can be seen. Another chapel on the north side has a very fine recumbent statue of *St Sebastian*, by Antonio Giorgetti, from a design by Bernini. Near the entrance is a stone from the catacombs with an inscription in honour of the martyr Eutychius, by Pope St Damasus.

Other parts of the catacombs not usually shown include the Platonia, the tomb of St Quirinus, and the Chapel of Honorius III, with 13C paintings, and an apsidal cubiculum bearing graffiti which indicate that this was the temporary grave of St Peter.

Just short of San Sebastiano, Via delle Sette Chiese, on the right, leads 600m to Via Ardeatina and 250m further on the Catacombs of St Domitilla (see below). In Via Ardeatina, a little to the left of its junction, is the **Mausoleo delle Fosse Ardeatine**, scene of one of the most horrifying events of the Second World War, during the German occupation of Rome. On 24 March 1944, as a reprisal for the killing on the previous day of 32 German soldiers by the resistance movement in Via Rasella, the Germans shot 335 Italians. The victims, who had no connection with the killing of the German soldiers, included priests, officials, professional men, about a hundred Jews, a dozen foreigners, and a boy of 14. The Germans then buried the bodies here under an avalanche of sand artificially caused by exploding mines. Local inhabitants provided a medico-legal commission with the means of exhuming and identifying the bodies after the German retreat. The scene of the massacre, below a huge tufa cliff, now has cave chapels. The victims, reinterred after identification, are commemorated by a huge single concrete slab placed in 1949 over their mass grave, with a group of standing figures, in stone, by Francesco Coccia (1950).

The **Catacombs of St Domitilla**, or Catacombs of St Nereus and St Achilleus, further along Via delle Sette Chiese, are among the most extensive in

Rome and may be the most ancient Christian cemetery in existence. They contain more than 900 inscriptions. Usually open 08.30–12.00 and 14.30–17.00 or 17.30; closed Tues, and in Jan. ☎ 06 511 0342. A friar conducts groups from the basilica to the catacombs. St Flavia Domitilla (niece of Flavia Domitilla, sister of Domitian) and her two Christian servants, Nereus and Achilleus, were buried here, as well as St Petronilla, another Christian patrician, perhaps the adopted daughter of St Peter.

At the foot of the entrance stairway is the aisled **Basilica of St Nereus and St Achilleus**, built in 390–95 over the tombs of the martyred saints. There are traces of a schola cantorum, and ancient columns probably from a pagan temple. The area below floor-level has sarcophagi and tombs. By the altar is a rare small column, with scenes of the martyrdom of St Achilleus carved in relief. The adjoining Chapel of St Petronilla (shown during the tour of the catacombs), with a fresco of the saint, contained her sarcophagus until the 8C, when it was removed to St Peter's.

The catacombs are excavated on two levels. The **Cemetery of the Flavians** (the family of Domitilla) had a separate entrance on the old Via Ardeatina. At this entrance is a vaulted vestibule probably designed as a meeting-place for the service of Intercession for the Dead, with a bench along the wall, and a well for water. A long gallery slopes down from here, with niches on either side decorated with 2C frescoes of flowers and genii. From the original entrance a gallery leads to another hypogeum, with four large niches decorated with 2C paintings (including *Daniel in the Lions' Den*). At the foot of a staircase is another ancient area; here is a cubicle with paintings of winged genii and the earliest known representation of the *Good Shepherd* (2C). On the upper level is the **Cubiculum of Ampliatus**, with paintings in Classical style. Other areas contain more painted scenes including the *Madonna and Child with Four Magi*, *Christ and the Apostles*, and a Cornmarket.

The **Catacombs of Commodilla** on the same street are not open regularly; see p 49.

The Via Appia beyond the catacombs

The Via Appia now leaves behind the area of the catacombs, and becomes more attractive and interesting for its Roman remains. On the left, in a hollow at no. 153, are the extensive ruins of the **Villa of Maxentius**. Built in 309 by the Emperor Maxentius, it includes a palace, a circus and a mausoleum built in honour of his son Romulus (d. 307). Open 09.00–17.00 or 19.00; closed Mon. ☎ 06 780 1324. Open-air concerts are held in the Circus in summer.

The **Circus of Maxentius** is the best-preserved of the Roman circuses, and one of the most romantic sites of ancient Rome. It has a good view of the Tomb of Cecilia Metella (see below). The circus was excavated by Antonio Nibby in 1825 for the Torlonia family, and restored in the 1960s and 1970s.

The stadium (c 513m by 91m) was probably capable of holding some 10,000 spectators. The main entrance was on the west side with the 12 *carceres* or stalls for the chariots and quadrigae, and, on either side, two square towers with curved façades. Two arches, one of which has been restored, connected the towers to the long sides of the circus and provided side entrances. In the construction of the tiers of seats, amphorae were used to lighten the vaults and these can still clearly be seen. In the centre of the left side is the conspicuous emperor's box, which was connected by a portico to his palace on the hill behind (see below). At the far end was a triumphal arch where a fragment of a dedicatory inscription to Romulus, son of Maxentius, was found identifying the circus with Maxentius (it had previously been attributed to Caracalla). In the centre is the round *meta* and the *spina*, the low wall which divided the area longitudinally and where the obelisk of Domitian, now in Piazza Navona, originally stood. The course was seven laps around the *spina*. The *spina* and the *carceres* were both placed slightly obliquely to equalise, as far as possible, the chances of all competitors, although it is likely that the circus was never actually used since Maxentius fell from power in 312.

Fenced off on the hillside to the left, towards Via Appia Pignatelli, are the overgrown remains of the **palace** which include fragments of baths, a basilica and a cryptoporticus. The conspicuous high wall near the west end of the circus belongs to the quadriporticus around the **Mausoleum of Romulus**, which faces the Via Appia. Some of the pilasters of the quadriporticus survive, as well as much of the outer wall. In the centre is the circular tomb preceded by a rectangular pronaos lying beneath a derelict house. The entrance is in front of a palm tree: beyond the pronaos is the mausoleum with niches in the outside wall for sarcophagi, and a huge pilaster in the centre also decorated with niches. The upper floor, probably covered with a cupola, has been destroyed. Nearby, beside the Via Appia, is the so-called **Tomba dei Sempronii**, probably dating from the Augustan era. It is closed to the public while excavations are still in progress.

The road rises to the **Tomb of Cecilia Metella**. Open 09.00–1 hour before sun set; closed Mon. ☎ 06 780 2465. A massive circular tower built in the Augustan period, 100 Roman feet (29.5m) in diameter, on a square base, and extremely well preserved, this is the most famous landmark on the Appia, and numerous drawings of it were made over the centuries. Much of the marble facing is still intact, as is also part of the elegant frieze surrounding the upper part, with garlands of fruit and bucrania (hence the name Capo di Bove, meaning heads of oxen, given to the adjacent ground), on either side of a very worn relief representing a soldier with Gallic shields and a prisoner from Gaul kneeling at his feet. Just below it is a large inscription to Cecilia, daughter of Quintus Metellus Creticus and wife of Marcus Licinius Crassus, elder son of the triumvir and one of Caesar's generals in Gaul.

A low corridor leads into the **sepulchral chamber** in the interior, now open to the sky and inhabited by pigeons. Its constructional technique is particularly interesting, using small flat bricks. It was built on a lava flow from the Alban hills: the volcanic rock can be seen at the bottom of a flight of steps outside (opened during excavations in 1999). In 1303 the Caetani transformed the tomb into a crenellated tower to serve as the keep of their large castle, which extended as far as the present Via Cecilia Metella, on both sides of the Appia. Several of its rooms can be seen here: in the largest one, still roofless, Antonio Muñoz arranged a little **museum** of sculptures from the Via Appia when he carried out more excavations here and restored the monument in the early 20C. His arrangement was kept when the building was restored in 2000, and the fragments include statues, capitals, friezes, urns and reliefs. Ceramic shards found on the site are exhibited in a little adjoining room, and more sculptures are arranged beside the ticket office. The original entrance to the castle from the road was closed up in the 19C and ancient inscriptions and sculptural fragments exhibited on the brick wall. Above can be seen the Caetani coat of arms. Beneath the two-light windows can be seen the (very worn) **third milestone**.

Part of the perimeter walls of the castle are now incorporated in the gardens of the private villas set back from the road here. The enciente also included the Gothic church of **San Nicola** opposite the mausoleum, now roofless and surrounded by a lawn and a group of pines, near a stretch of the perimiter walls of the castle. In 1306 the castle passed to the Savelli family and it was then owned in succession by the Colonna and Orsini.

The **Via Appia Antica** becomes more and more interesting as the view of the Campagna opens out (and to the left can be seen the imposing aqueduct of the Acqua Marcia and the Acqua Claudia). Excavated in 1850–59 between the third and eleventh milestones, this is the best-preserved part of the whole road, and it has recently been carefully restored. It was 4.2 metres wide (to allow two carts to pass each other) and the surface is now either covered with the massive polygonal blocks of grey basaltic lava from the Alban Hills, known as *basolato*, or by *sanpietrini* (small square blocks of stone). On either side were *crepidines* or sidewalks for pedestrians, and beyond these there are now low drystone walls.

For ten Roman miles or more it was bordered with tombs on both sides, and the picturesque remains of some of these were recovered and others reconstructed in the 19C by Antonio Canova and Luigi Canina. Some of the original sculptures have been removed to the Museo Nazionale Romano and replaced here by casts (easily identified by their yellow tint).

On a brick pilaster, on the left, opposite the site of the **fourth milestone**, are fragments of a tomb of a member of the Servilian gens. An inscription records that this was a gift made in 1808 by Canova, who, contrary to the general practice of his time, felt that objects found during excavations should be left in situ. Beyond on the left is the so-called Tomb of Seneca (replaced by casts), immediately followed by the Sepolcro Rotondo, a round cella with four loculi on a square base, and the Tomb of the Children of Sextus Pompeius Justus (partly replaced by casts). Beyond this, set back from the road, is a so-called Temple of Jupiter, square with apsidal niches. On the right, in the Proprietà Lugari near a clump of huge umbrella pines, is a superb monument in the form of a shrine—supposed to be that of St Urban—surrounded by the ruins of what was probably a villa.

In the next 550m are the scant remains of the Tombs of the Licinii, of Hilarius Fuscus (the five busts replaced by casts), of the Freedmen of the Claudian Gens, and of Quintus Apuleius Pamphilius. Beyond a sepulchre in the form of a temple is the Tomb of the Rabirii, where the three busts have been replaced by casts. Beyond more tombs, one in peperino and decorated with festoons and another with four busts (casts), the road crosses Via Erode Attico (where the *Archeobus* rejoins the Appia Antica) and Via Tor Carbone.

The Roman road is particularly well preserved here. It passes on the right the concrete core of a high tower and a round mausoleum, and on the left two sepulchres in the form of temples. At a point marked by a group of gigantic pines, near the **fifth milestone**, the road bends, probably to avoid some earlier tumuli, one of which on the right—now surmounted by a tower—is called the **Tumulus of the Curiatii**. There was a popular legend recorded by Livy that in this vicinity the Curiatii, three brothers from the Alban hills, engaged the Horatii, three brothers from Rome, in mortal combat, and this was traditionally believed to be the burial place of the three Curiatii. Opposite is a huge mausoleum in the form of a pyramid, which may have belonged to a member of the Quintili family.

Further on, on the right, surrounded by pines, is the so-called **Tumulus of the Horatii**, twin mounds, perhaps the burial place of two of the Horatii, or part of a monument erected here in the Augustan era to commemorate the Curiatii and Horatii. In the field to the right of the first are the remains of an *ustrinum* or cremation place which may have been connected with this famous battle. Opposite the second of the graves of the Horatii, an inscription of the 1C BC marks the tomb of Marcus Caecilius, in whose family grave was buried Pomponius Atticus, the friend of Cicero, thought to be the first owner of the Villa of the Quintili.

Just beyond, the magnificent and picturesque ruins of the **Villa of the Quintili** can be seen. Although remains of its nymphaeum are right on the Appia Antica, the entrance to the ruins, now owned by the State, is at present only from Via Appia Nuova (described on p 430). The nymphaeum was incorporated into a castle in the Middle Ages and restored by Antonio Munoz in 1905–13.

The Via Appia Antica now becomes more deserted, and the monuments more widely scattered. Some way beyond the nymphaeum of the Villa of the Quintili rises the **Casal Rotondo**, a large round tomb on a square base, with an incongruous modern house and an olive garden and pine tree on the summit. This was the largest tomb on the Via Appia, and dates from the Republican period; it was enlarged in early Imperial times. It was once thought to have been erected to the memory of the poet Messala Corvinus by his son Valerius Maximus Cotta. The stylobate is 120 Roman feet (c 36m) in diameter. Attached to a wall here, erected by Canina, are numerous Roman architectural fragments. Facing this monument is a smaller one attributed to the Aurelian gens.

Via di Casal Rotondo here leaves the Appia Antica and descends to the Via Appia Nuova. This is the route followed by the *Archeobus* to the entrance to the Villa dei Quintili and the Park of the Aqueducts (described below), but from here you can also explore the Appia on foot for another mile or so. On the left, just beyond the crossroads, where the Rome–Naples railway passes diagonally below the Appia Antica in a short tunnel, was the site of the **sixth milestone**. On the right is a tomb with reliefs of griffins and a columbarium. Opposite another columbarium, on the right of the road, is a tomb with four busts (casts). Some way further on, about 1km from the Casal Rotondo, is the **Torre Selce**, a pyramidal tumulus surmounted by a medieval tower, 107m above sea-level. Beyond inscriptions of Marcus Julius Pietas Epelides and Caius Atilius Eudos, a jeweller, the road swerves a little and begins to descend, and the arches of an aqueduct which formerly brought water from a sulphur spring near Ciampino to the villa of the Quintili are prominent. A column marks the **seventh milestone**. Near this point, the 68km ring road (Grande Raccordo Anulare) around the city, the first section of which was opened in 1951, is carried through a tunnel under the Via Appia. The tunnel was only built in 2000 and the area is still being replanted.

The remaining four kilometres of the Via Appia Antica (as far as its junction with the Via Appia Nuova) are to be restored. Beyond the site of the Torre Rossa or Torre Appia, a 12C–13C structure which collapsed in 1985, on a Roman base, at about the end of the eighth Roman mile, the Via Appia passes a sepulchral chamber (or possibly a sanctuary) and stumps of columns in peperino from a Roman portico. Once known as the Pillars of Hercules, these may have belonged to a temple dedicated to Silvanus. Further along the road, beyond the **Torraccio del Palombaro**, a monument preserved through having been turned into a church in the 10C, is a path that leads on the right to La Giostra, a little hill upon which the ruins, once identified with the ancient Latin city of Tellene, are now thought to be those of a 4C Roman fortified outpost. Then come other tombs, more or less ruined, including one called the Ruzzica d'Orlando; and at the ninth milestone is what is left of the Villa of Gallienus, with a fine circular ruin that is regarded as the mausoleum of that emperor. The road crosses the Rome–Terracina railway and, a little beyond the site of the **twelfth milestone**, joins the busy Via Appia Nuova.

Villa dei Quintili and the Parco degli Acquedotti

At present, since the gate into Villa dei Quintili from the Via Appia Antica is closed, these two districts should be reached by the *Archeobus* (see p 417), since there is no pleasant approach on foot.

Part of the site of a huge Roman residence called the **Villa dei Quintili**, now between the Via Appia Antica and the Via Appia Nuova, is enclosed in a park of some 24 hectares, owned by the State since 1985 and, for the first time, open to the public. Admission 09.00–15.30; summer 09.00–17.30; closed Mon.

The villa, the earliest parts of which date from the time of Hadrian, belonged to the wealthy and cultivated brothers Quintili, Maximus and Condianus, consuls under Antoninus Pius (AD 151) who wrote a treatise on agriculture. They were put to death by Commodus for the sake of their possessions, including this villa. The emperor enlarged the property and it was kept in repair by his successors up until the 4C.

As late as the 15C the area was known as *Statuario*, referring to the numerous ancient Roman statues and sculptures which were found here. In the 17C and 18C it was, instead, called *Roma Vecchia* as the ruins were so extensive as to suggest a small town rather than a villa. In 1797 the property was purchased by the Torlonia family and in 1828–29 Antonio Nibby carried out important excavations. Many of the finds made in the 19C are kept in properties still belonging to the Torlonia in Rome (see pp 221, 442), but these have not been open to the public (or scholars) for many years. The Vatican also carried out excavations here and some of the sculptures are now in the Vatican museums, but others found their way to the Louvre and the Hermitage. In the early 20C the archaeologist Thomas Ashby, director of the British School at Rome from 1906–25 carried out a systematic study of the villa. Excavations were renewed here from 1998 and are still in progress.

The **Antiquarium** is arranged in the stable block of a former farm house near the road. It contains finds from excavations carried out in 1929 on private property in the area between the Via Appia Pignatelli and Via Appia Nuova, as well as those in 1997–99 in the area of the villa itself. In the centre of the room is a large seated statue of *Zeus* dating from the 2C AD. In the middle of the right wall is a herm, thought to represent *Dionysus* (2C AD), and, on the opposite wall, another herm found in a room near the frigidarium of the Villa in 1998. A group of statues, mostly related to Oriental cults, were found in 1929 dumped together ready for use in a medieval kiln which produced lime. There are also two statuettes of *Hercules*, a relief with a Greek inscription to Astarte, and an alabaster slab reused in the Christian period. Brick stamps found in the Villa, some of which are exhibited here, date from 123 AD up until the early 3C. The capital decorated with fantastic animals (3C AD) is very unusual. The rare seated statue of *Zeus Bronton* representing the God of rain and thunder, is derived from similar cult statues in

Asia Minor. Also preserved here are architectural elements, a fragment of a fresco with flowers, and opus sectile work in marble.

Across a stream the impressive Roman buildings of the Villa can be seen along a ridge formed by an ancient lava flow from the Alban hills. Near the path are the **baths**, the most conspicuous of which is the rectangular calidarium, its walls still standing with four huge arched windows on two levels overlooking the valley. Low steps surround the rectangular pool which used to be filled with hot water. Beside it are the ruins of the tepidarium. The best preserved of the thermal buildings is the frigidarium, a little to the east, which also retains its walls and its splendid pavement of polychrome marble in opus sectile (2C AD). The two cipollino columns were recently returned here (they were removed many years ago and later found their way to the Baths of Diocletian).

In front of the baths was an oval edifice built in the 2C–3C AD (its shape can be seen clearly in the ground). This is usually called the **Teatro Marittimo** because of its similarity to a building at Hadrian's Villa in Tivoli (see p 473), but its precise function is unknown; it may have been a small amphitheatre or simply a garden to take the air. The residential area was further east, on the edge of the hill. Near the reception rooms was a large open courtyard paved with white marble. The service areas and private quarters are marked by a high arch. There is another small thermal complex to the south, on the line of an acqueduct which descended past several cisterns from the nymphaeum at the top of the hill on the the Via Appia Antica (see p 429), at the original entrance to the villa. The nymphaeum was enclosed in a castle in the 15C. Also in this area there was a garden, a hippodrome and a stadium.

Across the Via Appia Nuova a narrow road leads under two railway bridges to reach the **Parco degli Acquedotti** (for the *Archeobus* see p 417), a protected area of some 15 hectares, traversed by seven aqueducts and also forming part of the Park of the Appia Antica. Here can be seen long stretches of several aqueducts above ground (notably the Acqua Claudia) in open countryside where sheep are grazed. Beside an old farmhouse and group of pine trees (the Casale di Roma Vecchia) is a little public park with a pond fed by the Felice aqueduct, here channeled beneath a low vault. On a clear day there is a distant view of the dome of St Peter's. For a history of the aqueducts, see p 432.

From here the *Archeobus* returns to the centre of Rome (see p 417).

Off the Via Appia Nuova, on Via Arco di Travertino near the underground Line A *Arco di Travertino* stop, is the entrance to the **Parco delle Tombe Latine**, which is to be reopened; ☎ 06 7047 4619. It includes a group of tombs dating from the 1C and 2C. Most of them are square and brick-built, with recesses on the outside and interior chambers with interesting stucco ornamentation. On the right is the so-called **Tomb of the Valeri** (AD 160), a subterranean chamber decorated with fine reliefs of nymphs, sea-monsters and nereids in stucco on a white ground. On the left is the 2C **Tomb of the Pancrazi**, with landscape paintings, coloured stuccoes and four bas-reliefs of the *Judgement of Paris*, *Admetus and Alcestis*, *Priam and Achilles*, and *Hercules playing a lyre with Bacchus and Minerva*. Behind the tomb are the ruins of the 5C BC.

North of the park, on Via Tuscolana, is **Cinecittà**, the centre of the Italian film industry, opened in 1937. This is probably the only film studio in the world which provides facilities for complete motion picture production. It covers an area of 600,000 square metres, with 14 theatres. After the Second World War it was used by Visconti, De Sica and Rossellini and soon attracted international film directors and stars from Hollywood. In the 1950s and early sixties 'colossals' such as *Quo Vadis?* and *Cleopatra*, using some of the largest sets ever constructed, were made at Cinecittà. Antonioni and Pasolini worked here, but it is above all associated with the name of Federico Fellini (d. 1993), who created the grandiose sets for many of his films here. It is now also often used by television companies.

The aqueducts of Rome

Although a high proportion of the spring water brought to ancient Rome was channelled underground, stretches of aqueduct were also built above ground, and their magnificent arches crossing the Campagna used to be one of the most Romantic sights for travellers approaching the city. The abundant water supply they carried was needed for the huge public baths constructed in the ancient city, which were open to all the inhabitants. The water was also put to use in the baths attached to the private villas of the emperors, and in numerous decorative fountains. In later centuries the popes restored these aqueducts or built new ones.

Like roads and bridges all over the Empire, some aqueducts have survived to this day to demonstrate the skill of Roman engineers. The first aqueduct of all, the **Acqua Appia**, was built c 312 BC by Appius Claudius, the censor who also gave his name to the Via Appia: it was some 16km in length and entered Rome at the present Porta Maggiore, at a time when Rome was estimated to have around 200,000 inhabitants. Ten more aqueducts were constructed during the Republic and Empire. The **Anio Vetus**, the oldest aqueduct in the Park of the Seven Aqueducts, was built, mostly underground, between 272 and 269 BC, and supplies water from the valley of the Aniene, some 64 kilometres east of Rome. The **Acqua Marcia**, begun in 44 BC, also bought water from near Tivoli and reached all the way to the Campidoglio for a length of some 91 kilometres. It ran underground until it emerged in the present area of the Park (where it merges with the **Acqua Tepula** (125 BC) and **Acqua Julia** (33 BC), both from the Alban hills. Some of its low arches can still be seen in the Park; the rest of it was destroyed when the Acqua Felice was constructed in the 16C. The **Acqua Claudia** and the **Anio Novus**, or Acqua Aniene Nuova, were two of the finest of these, both of which also traverse the park. They were begun by Caligula in AD 38; the Acqua Claudia was completed by Claudius in AD 42, and the Anio Novus in 52. They were restored by Vespasian in 71 and by Titus in 81. The water of the Acqua Claudia came from two copious springs near Sublaqueum (Subiaco); its length was 74km. The Anio Novus was the longest of all the aqueducts (95km) and the highest; some of its arches were 28m high. The last aqueduct to be built in ancient Roman times was that by Alexander Severus c AD 226.

A fascinating account of the waters of Rome written in AD 97 by the man in charge of the city's water supply during the reigns of Nerva and Trajan, Sextus Julius Frontinus, was discovered in the 15C and it is through this document that we know so much about the ancient aqueducts. Frontinus helped to reorganise the supply, bringing water for the first time to the poorer districts of Rome. It seems that many of the aqueducts leaked and frequently needed repair but by AD 52, when nine aqueducts were in use, they were sufficient to supply nearly 1000 litres a day for each of Rome's estimated one million inhabitants. No other city at any time has been supplied with so much water (the present supply is around 500 litres per family).

The aqueducts were cut by the Goths in 537, and it was not until the 16C that attention was paid again to Rome's water supply, from then onwards under the care of the popes. The Acqua Vergine was restored by Pius V in 1570, Sixtus V built the new **Acqua Felice** in 1585 from Via Prenestina, and Paul V restored the **Acqua Traiana**, which comes from Lake Bracciano, to the northwest of Rome, in 1611, calling it the **Acqua Paola**. A new aqueduct called the **Pia Marcia**, built in part of cast-iron by a private Anglo-Italian company for the Papal States, used the same springs near Tivoli tapped by the ancient Acqua Marcia. This was inaugurated by Pius X in 1870, just ten days before Italian troops breached the walls beside Porta Pia and so brought to an end papal rule of the city.

These papal aqueducts are still functioning in modern Rome, but the water supply had to be greatly increased after 1870 to meet the needs of the growing population, which doubled in the 20 years between 1936 and 1956. The **Acqua Vergine Nuova** was inaugurated in 1937, and the **Peschiera-Capore aqueduct** was constructed between 1938 and 1980. It uses abundant springs near Rieti never before brought to Rome, and supplies much more water to the city now than all the other aqueducts put together. It is claimed to be the biggest aqueduct in the world using only spring water.

The aqueducts in the park are supplied from springs in the upper valley of the Aniene beyond Tivoli east of Rome, and in the Alban hills. The oldest aqueduct in the area of the park is that of the **Anio Vetus** (3C BC), but it is not visible here as it is almost totally underground. The most conspicuous aqueduct here is the **Acqua Claudia**, long stretches of which survive above ground, carried on high arches. The lower arches belong to the Acqua Felice.

37 • The EUR district

The monumental white marble buildings of the Esposizione Universale di Roma, now always abbreviated to EUR (prounced 'ay-oor'), are spaciously set out between wide avenues and empty roads, in a setting which recalls the metaphysical paintings of Giorgio de Chirico. An extremely interesting example of Fascist town planning, many of the edifices are now in need of restoration. Some of the huge buildings house museums, arranged for educational purposes and mostly visited by school parties. Nearby, to the east, is the Abbazia delle Tre Fontane, traditionally the site of the martyrdom of St Paul.

Getting there

EUR is about 6km from the Porta Ardeatina (**Map 10**; **8**) along the Via Cristoforo Colombo, which passes straight through the middle of the site as a ten-lane highway. It is easily reached in 12 minutes from Termini and Colosseum stations by underground Line B, on which it is the penultimate station. It is also reached by numerous buses, including no. 714 from Termini and no. 761 from San Paolo fuori le Mura.

History of EUR

EUR was begun in 1938 to the designs of Marcello Piacentini. An ambitious project to symbolise the achievements of Fascism, it was to have been opened for the 1942 World Expo, which was cancelled because of the Second World War. Its buildings were only partly completed, however, and the site suffered some war damage. After 1952 the original structures were restored, new ones were added, and government offices and public institutions were moved to the site, which was also developed as an exclusive residential district.

Piazza delle Nazioni (**Map 15; 1**) lies between twin palaces whose façades form two hemicycles. Viale della Civiltà del Lavoro leads right to the Palazzo EUR and, at the end, the **Palazzo della Civiltà Italiana** (**Map 14; 2**), built in 1938–43 by Giovanni Guerrini, Ernesto Bruno La Padula and Mario Romano and now called **Palazzo della Civiltà del Lavoro**. Known as the 'square Colosseum', it has statues symbolising the arts beneath the lowest arches. At the opposite end of Viale della Civiltà is **Palazzo dei Congressi** by Adalberto Libera (1938–54), with paintings by Gino Severini in the atrium.

In the centre of the vast **Piazza Marconi** (**Map 15; 3**) is a stele of Carrara marble (45m) by Arturo Dazzi (1938–59), dedicated to the inventor Guglielmo Marconi. On the right are two edifices with symmetrical fronts, the Palazzi dell'Esposizioni, while between them, further back, is a skyscraper known as the *Grattacielo Italia* (1959–60).

On the left, joined by a huge colonnade, are two palaces of similar design. The one to the left facing the colonnade contains the **Museo Nazionale delle Arti e delle Tradizioni Popolari** (**Map 15; 3**). The museum contains material collected by Lamberto Loria (1855–1913) for the Museo di Etnografia Italiana, founded in Florence in 1906, and illustrates with models and reconstructions various aspects of Italian life. Open 09.00–20.00; closed Mon. ☎ 06 592 6148. On the ground floor are exhibits relating to transport. The sections on the upper floor include furniture from rural houses, toys, crib figures, carnival and theatrical costumes, musical instruments used during local festivals, and puppets. There is a large collection of 19C and early 20C jewellery. A section on religious festivals includes ex-votos. On the stair landing is a gondola of 1882. The great hall, with frescoes of 1941, exhibits arts and crafts, with reconstructions of artisans' workshops. The next section illustrates agricultural life. The sections on seafaring and pastoral life are closed for rearrangement.

To the right of the colonnade is the Palazzo delle Scienze which contains the **Museo Nazionale Preistorico ed Etnografico Luigi Pigorini** (**Map 15; 3**). Open 09.00–20.00; closed Mon. ☎ 06 549 521. The museum, one of the most important of its kind in the world, is derived from the collection formed in the late 17C by Father Anastasius Kircher in the Collegio dei Gesuiti. From 1871 onwards it was greatly enlarged by Luigi Pigorini, and in 1876 it became the Museo Preistorico del Nuovo Regno d'Italia. After 1913 the protohistoric objects went to Villa Giulia, Classical and Christian antiquities to the Museo Nazionale Romano, and medieval exhibits to Palazzo di Venezia.

The Museo Preistorico is arranged geographically to indicate the way civilisation developed regionally through the Stone, Bronze and Iron Ages. Most of the exhibits are Italian, of the prehistoric period. They include material from all parts of the peninsula, so that a complete idea may be obtained of the growth of its civilisation and of the commercial and artistic influences of the East and of the countries bordering on the Aegean. The descriptive labels, maps and diagrams are very informative. The most interesting exhibits include: material from cemeteries in the Lazio area; finds of the Italian School in Crete; curious Sardinian statuettes of priests and warriors in bronze; a tomb from Golasecca, representative of the western civilisation of Northern Italy. The objects found in the cemeteries of western and southern Etruria (Vetulonia, Tarquinia, Vulci, Veio, etc.) are particularly interesting; among them are well-tombs (10C–8C BC), with ossuaries resembling those of Villanova, closed with a flat lid or shaped like a house, and trench-tombs (8C–7C BC) showing the influence of Greek commerce, especially on pottery.

The Ethnographical Collection includes material from the Americas, Africa, and Oceania collected by Lamberto Loria, Vittorio Bottego, Guido Boggiani and Enrico Hillyer Giglioli. There is a pre-Columbian archaeological collection from Mexico and the Andes, and artefacts made by the Inuits of the Arctic Circle. The collections from Oceania and Africa are at present closed: the African collection includes material from Angola and Zaire. Much of the material which belonged to Loria was collected by him in New Guinea.

Further along the colonnade, on the right, at Viale Lincoln, is the entrance to the **Museo dell'Alto Medioevo**, which is on the first floor of the Palazzo delle Scienze. A disappointing and small collection made in 1967, it contains Italian material from the fall of the Roman Empire to the 10C AD. Open 09.00–20.00; closed Mon. ☎ 06 5422 8199.

Room I. Heads of a Byzantine emperor and empress, and gold fibula, all of the late 5C found on the Palatine. **Room II**. Pottery, glass and gold work including beautiful jewellery—found in a 7C tomb at Nocera Umbra. **Room III**. Contents of a 7C tomb at Castel Trosino, including more very fine jewellery (B, 115, 16), a blue glass rhyton (119), a gold dagger case (E), glass containers (37–45), and fragments of a shield (T).

Rooms IV–V. Collection of 7C–10C church reliefs and friezes. **Room VI**. Finds from the site of Santa Cornelia, near Formello, excavated by the British School in 1963–65. Remains from three distinct phases were found: early Roman agricultural trenches, a farm and church built by Pope Hadrian I c 780, and a monastic complex (c 1035–41). Also in this room, 8C–9C pottery from the Roman Forum. **Room VII**. Finds from San Rufina, on the Via Cornelia, including mosaics. **Room VIII**. Coptic materials and fabrics of the 5C–8C.

Beyond the colonnade, Viale della Civiltà Romana leads to a piazza flanked by two symmetrical buildings, again joined by a colonnade, the building of which was financed by the *Fiat* organisation. Here the **Museo della Civiltà Romana** (Map 15; 4) was inaugurated in 1955. The entrance is in the right wing. Open 09.00–18.45; fest 09.00–13.30; closed Mon. ☎ 06 592 6041.

The museum, created to house the material from exhibitions held in Rome in 1911 and 1937, consists entirely of plaster casts of famous statues and monuments, and reconstructions of buildings which illustrate the history of ancient Rome and the influence of Roman civilisation throughout the world. They are displayed in 59 rooms of monumental proportions, which have been undergoing lengthy structural repairs for many years.

Each room illustrates a period of the history of Rome, in chronological sequence. **Room VI**. Origins of the city. **Room VII**. The conquest of the

Mediterranean. **Room VIII**. Julius Caesar. **Room IX**. Augustus, including a reproduction of the pronaos of the Temple of Augustus at Ancyra. **Rooms X–XIV**. The Roman emperors. **Room XV**. Christianity. **Rooms XVI–XIX**. The Roman army. **Room XXXVII** in the opposite wing of the museum—reached by returning to the entrance and crossing the piazza—contains a celebrated *model of Rome as it was in the 4C, on a scale of 1:250.

The other rooms include displays devoted to the navy; ports; central administration; the Imperial court; the 'triumphs' celebrated in Rome for victorious generals; the provinces of the Roman Empire; the 11 'regions' of Italy; methods of construction (quarries and mines); baths and aqueducts; theatres, amphitheatres and circuses; fora, temples and basilicas; military architecture; Roman roads; education; funerary monuments; domestic architecture; the family; religion; portraits; law; libraries; music; science and letters; medicine; artisans; agriculture; hunting and fishing; commerce; and art. In **room LI** is a complete collection of *casts from Trajan's Column made in 1860, and in **room LIX** the reconstruction of part of the Column of Marcus Aurelius.

Viale dell'Arte leads south; the second turning to the right is Viale Europa. Here are the ministries of Foreign Trade and Finance, built after the Second World War. On the corner of Via Cristoforo Colombo is the Ministry of Postal Services and Communications, with the well-arranged **Museo Storico delle Poste e delle Telecommunicazioni** (Map 14; 4). Open 09.00–13.00; closed Sat & Sun.

The postal display begins with a casket of 1300 used by the Pontifical Post Office of Urbino and 17C letter boxes, including a '*bocca di leone*', and there is a fine copy on tile of the Peutinger Table, an ancient map of the military roads of the western Roman Empire. Later postal history—pioneer air-mail flights, Ethiopian military cancellers, etc.—is well chosen. The electronic calculator invented by Enrico Fermi, made in 1956, is also displayed here. The history of telegraph and telephone is copiously illustrated by original appliances, including apparatus used by Marconi in his 1901 experiments between Cornwall and Newfoundland.

Viale Europa ends in steps which lead up to the massive church of **Santi Pietro e Paolo** (Map 14; 3), with a cupola almost as large as that of St Peter's. Dating from 1938–55, it was designed by Arnaldo Foschini. Returning to the centre of the EUR district, the first turning right at the foot of the steps leads to the Piscina delle Rose in Viale America and a large open-air theatre. Parallel to this road is a lake about 1km long, divided into three basins, the sides of which are planted with a thousand cherry trees from Japan. This area is perhaps the most successfully planned within the EUR complex. Bridges lead to the **Palazzo dello Sport** (Map 14; 8), designed by Pier Luigi Nervi and Marcello Piacentini for the Olympic Games of 1960, and an outstanding work of modern architecture. Constructed of prefabricated concrete, it is covered by a fine rib-vaulted dome 100m in diameter, and seats 15,000 spectators. The well-designed Velodromo Olimpico (**Map 14**; 5), for cycling events, is about 500m east.

Abbazia delle Tre Fontane

About 1km east of the point where Via Cristoforo Colombo crosses Via delle Tre Fontane, and reached by the latter and Via Laurentina, is the Abbazia delle Tre Fontane (**Map 15**; 4). This was built on the traditional site of the martyrdom of St Paul, whose severed head, rebounding three times, is supposed to have caused three fountains to spring up. A monastic community from Asia Minor was established here by 641. St Bernard is believed to have stayed here on his visit to Rome in 1138–40. Three churches were built, but the locality was afterwards abandoned as malarial. In 1868 it was acquired by the Trappists, who drained the ground and planted large groves of eucalyptus. A eucalyptus liqueur is distilled in the community. This and chocolate made by the monks are on sale.

An ilex avenue leads to a medieval fortified gate, with a frescoed vault. A small garden contains Classical fragments, and is filled with the sound of doves and a fountain. Ahead is the porch of **Santi Vincenzo ed Anastasio**. It was founded by Honorius I (625), rebuilt by Honorius III (1221), and restored by the Trappists. The spacious plain interior preserves its marble windows. In the nave are poorly restored frescoes of the Apostles (16C).

On the right, on high ground, is **Santa Maria Scala Coeli**, an old church with an octagonal interior, rebuilt by Giacomo della Porta (1582). The design can best be appreciated from the outside. It owes its name to the legend that St Bernard, while celebrating mass, saw in a vision the soul for which he was praying ascend by a ladder from purgatory to heaven. The Cosmatesque altar that was the scene of this miracle is still preserved in the crypt. The mosaics in the left hand apse, of Saints with Clement VIII and his nephew Cardinal Pietro Aldobrandini, are by Francesco Zucchi from designs by Giovanni de'Vecchi.

From the left of this church an avenue leads to **San Paolo alle Tre Fontane**, a 5C church, rebuilt by Della Porta in 1599, with a good façade. Inside to the right is the pillar to which St Paul is supposed to have been bound; on the floor are two Roman mosaic pavements from Ostia.

38 • The northern districts

This chapter describes the Via Nomentana, the Via Salaria and the Via Flaminia, once important Roman roads (see below) and still main traffic arteries, and the west bank of the Tiber north of the Vatican, with Monte Mario and the Foro Italico. All these districts are too far from the centre of the city to be approached on foot, and means of public transport have therefore been indicated.

On the Via Nomentana is the public park of Villa Torlonia where the charming little Casina delle Civette, a garden folly particularly interesting for its early 20C stained glass, has been restored and opened to the public. The other Neo-classical garden buildings in the park are being restored. Farther out along the Via Nomentana, beneath the 7C basilica of Sant'Agnese (which preserves its original apse mosaic) are some of the best-preserved catacombs in Rome, which are much less crowded than the more famous catacombs on the Via Appia Antica. In the peaceful garden beside Sant'Agnese is the centrally planned church of Santa Costanza, built by Constantine's daughter before 354 with remarkable early Christian mosaics dating from that time.

The catacombs of Priscilla some way out of the centre of Rome on the Via Salaria are also extremely interesting and rarely crowded with tour groups. On the hill of Monte Mario, which offers distant views of the city, the Villa Madama is an important building by Raphael which is unfortunately rarely open to the public. At the foot of the hill is the sports centre of Foro Italico, an interesting example of Fascist architecture.

Getting there

For Villa Torlonia and Sant'Agnese, take **express bus** no. 60 from Piazza Venezia and Via Nazionale which follows Via Nomentana. For the Catacombs of Priscilla, take bus no. 92 from Termini Station or no. 63 from Piazza Venezia (nearest stop, Via di Priscilla).

Tram 19 from Piazza del Risorgimento near the Vatican follows Via Flaminia. Piazza Maresciallo Giardino, at the foot of Monte Mario, and the Foro Italico are reached by bus no. 32 from the Mausoleum of Augustus.

Ancient Roman roads

The ancient Roman roads leading out of Rome in all directions are still partly in use, and still carry their Roman names. The **Via Aurelia Antica**, which leaves Rome at the Porta San Pancrazio, follows the line of an even older road which linked Rome with the Etruscan towns on the Tyrrhenian coast. It reached the shore at Alsium (Palo Laziale), a port of the Etruscan city of Caere (Cerveteri) and then followed the coastline to Pisa and Genoa. It ended in Gaul at Forum Julii (Fréjus) on the French Riviera. One of the most important ancient Roman roads, named after the Aurelia gens, it was built before 109 BC.

The **Via Cassia**, which leaves the city north of Ponte Milvio, was originally a rough road which ran from Rome north to Etruria. It was paved by Cassius Longinus, consul in 107 BC, and named after him. It runs through Viterbo to Siena and Florence. The **Via Flaminia**, which also leaves Rome north of Ponte Milvio, was begun in 220 BC and was named after Gaius Flaminius, censor and afterwards consul, who was killed at the Battle of Lago Trasimeno in 217 BC. It leads across Umbria to Fano and Rimini on the Adriatic. It leaves the Tiber at Prima Porta (12km from the centre of Rome) near the site of the battle of Sax Rubra where Constantine defeated Maxentius in 312, after being converted to Christianity by a vision of the flaming Cross with the words 'conquer by this'.

Via Salaria (see p 442) takes its name from its association with the salt trade between the Romans and the Sabines. This was probably formerly called the Via Caecilia, after the consul who built the road in 284 BC. Now the modern N4, it runs via Rieti and Antrodoco to Ascoli Piceno and the Adriatic near San Benedetto del Tronto.

Via Latina, probably in use as early as the 7C or 6C BC, ran south from Rome down the valley of the River Sacco in Latin territory and continued to the Campania around Naples. It was used by the armies of Pyrrhus and Hannibal, and in Roman times joined the Via Appia at Casilinum near Capua. The Via Appia Antica is described in Chapter 36.

The ancient **Via Tuscolana** ran to Tusculum, to the east of present-day Frascati. It was a short branch of the Via Latina, which left Rome by the Porta Capena, passed through Ferentinum (Ferentino), Frusino (Frosinone), Aquinum (Aquino), Casinum (Cassino) and Venafrum (Venafro) to Beneventum (Benevento) where it joined the Via Appia.

Via Ostiense was one of the earliest consular roads, and dates from the victorious campaign of the Romans against the inhabitants of Veio to secure their salt supply (5C BC). It ran to Ostia, and from there, under the name of Via Severiana, it followed the coast to Laurentum (near Castel Fusano), Antium (Anzio) and Terracina, where it joined the Via Appia.

Via Nomentana

Porta Pia (Map 4; 2) was Michelangelo's last architectural work, commissioned by Pius IV in 1561; the exterior face is by Virginio Vespignani (1868). It stands at the beginning of the wide **Via Nomentana** (Map 4; 2) which runs north-east, traversing a residential district of the city with palaces and villas, many with beautiful gardens. It follows the line of the ancient Roman consular road to Nomentum, now Mentana, c 20km from Rome.

The ancient Porta Nomentana, walled up by Pius IV, is in Piazza della Croce Rossa to the right of Porta Pia. The north tower has been preserved. The Castra Pretoria here and the area to the south are described in Walk 24. It was near the Porta Pia that the Italian troops under General Raffaele Cadorna entered Rome on 20 September 1870 and so brought to an end the temporal power of the popes. The breach was a few steps to the left of the gate, in Corso d'Italia, where there are commemorative inscriptions. In the small courtyard of the gateway is the **Museo Storico dei Bersaglieri** which documents the wars of independence, the African campaign, and the First World War, but which has been closed for several years (☎ 06 486 723). Outside the gate is a monument of 1932.

Inside the gate, on the left, is **Villa Paolina**, seat of the French Embassy to the Vatican. It was the home of Pauline Bonaparte from 1816 to 1824, and was once famous for its garden. On the other side of Via Venti Settembre is the British Embassy, a conspicuous building surrounded by water, designed by Sir Basil Spence and opened in 1971 on the site of a Torlonia villa, damaged by a terrorist's bomb in 1946.

Beyond Viale Regina Margherita, Via Nomentana passes on the left the public gardens of Villa Paganini, opposite which is the **Villa Torlonia**, which became the private residence of Mussolini after 1929. (There is another Villa Torlonia on the Via Salaria, see below.) It was expropriated by the Comune di Roma in 1977 and is now a municipal park of some 16 hectares. Open 07.30–dusk.

Giovanni and Alessandro Torlonia had most of the garden buildings erected in 1806–42 by Giuseppe Valadier, Quintiliano Raimondi, Giuseppe Jappelli and Giovanni Battista Caretti. All of them, except the Casina delle Civette, are in very poor condition although restoration work has at last begun on the Villino dei Principi (1920) on the right of the entrance gate. Preceded by a flight of steps lined with vases and near a granite obelisk and a grove of palm trees is the main Neo-classical villa built by Valadier in 1806. It has an Ionic portico with a tympanum and Doric colonnades on either side. The park, now well kept, includes cedars of Lebanon, magnolias and numerous palms.

A path leads left to the delightful little Art Nouveau **Casina delle Civette** ('garden house of the owls'), which was entirely restored and opened to the public in 1997. Open Tues–Sun 09.00–17.00 or 19.00; closed Mon. ☎ 06 4425 0072. Part of it was built in the form of a Swiss chalet by Giuseppe Jappelli in 1840, and it was rebuilt by Vincenzo Fasolo in 1916–21 as a charming folly with numerous interesting naturalistic details. It has weird gabled maiolica roofs, antique fragments, unusual windows and, inside, attractive panelling, stuccoes and tiled floors. It is especially interesting for its stained glass, made in 1908–30 by Duilio Cambellotti and Paolo Paschetto, some of it renewed during its recent restoration. There are long-term plans to restore the other interesting garden buildings in the park which include a theatre and an amphitheatre. The park is on the site of Jewish catacombs, which were in use in the 3C and 4C and were discovered in 1918. They originally extended for over 9km, but are now mostly caved in (no admission).

Sant'Agnese fuori le Mura
About 2km from Porta Pia, opposite a 19C fountain of the Acqua Marcia, stands the church of Sant'Agnese fuori le Mura, in an important group of early Christian buildings.

Opening times
The churches of Sant'Agnese and Santa Costanza are open Tues–Sat 09.00–12.00 and 16.00–18.00; Sun 16.00–18.00; Mon 09.00–12.00.

Catacombs open Tues–Sat 09.00–12.00 and 16.00–18.00; closed Mon afternoon and fest. mornings. ☎ 06 861 0840. Note. Santa Costanza is often in use for weddings.

History of Sant'Agnese fuori le Mura

According to a Christian tradition, St Agnes, having refused the advances of a praetor's son, was exposed in the Stadium of Domitian, where her nakedness was covered by the miraculous growth of her hair. She was then condemned to be burned at the stake, but the flames did not touch her, so that she was finally beheaded by Diocletian. The pallium or vestment worn by the pope is made of the wool of lambs blessed annually on the day of her festival, 21 January.

The buildings consist of the ruins of a large cemetery basilica built, probably after Constantine's death, by his elder daughter Constantia in 337–50 on her estate, next to the tomb where the martyred St Agnes had been buried in 304. Above the crypt sanctuary and catacombs, Honorius I (625–38) built a second church, when the Constantinian basilica was already in ruins. Next to the basilica, and with an entrance from its south aisle, Constantia built the mausoleum in which she and her sister Helena were buried.

The most direct entrance is through the garden on Via Sant'Agnese, but you can also enter through the gate of the convent of the Canonici Lateranensi on Via Nomentana, from which the campanile of the basilica of Honorius and the small colonnaded front can be seen. On the right of the court is a hall (originally a cellar) into which Pius IX and his entourage fell unharmed after the collapse of the floor of the room above in 1855.

Beyond a tower is the entrance to the 7C **basilica of Sant'Agnese fuori le Mura**, restored in 1479 by Giuliano della Rovere (later Julius II), by Cardinal Varallo after the sack of 1527, and by Pius IX in 1856. It is reached by a staircase of 45 white marble steps (1590), the walls of which are covered with inscriptions from the catacombs, including St Damasus's record of the martyrdom of St Agnes.

In the **interior** of the church (best light in the afternoon), the nave and aisles are separated by 14 ancient Roman columns of breccia and pavonazzetto, mottled and veined. There is a narthex for the *catechumens*, and a *matroneum* was built over the aisles and the west end in 620. The carved and gilded wood ceiling dates from 1606 but was restored in 1855. In the second chapel on the right, over a Cosmati altar, is a fine relief of *St Stephen and St Lawrence* by Andrea Bregno (1490), and a bust of *Christ*, probably the work of Nicolas Cordier after a lost work by Michelangelo. In the second chapel on the left there is a 15C fresco of the *Madonna and Child*. On the high altar, in which are preserved the relics of

St Agnes and St Emerentiana, her foster-sister, is an antique torso of Oriental alabaster restored in 1600 as a statue of *St Agnes*, beneath a baldacchino (1614) supported on four porphyry columns. On the left of the altar is a fine candlestick, thought to be a neo-Attic work of the 2C. In the apse is the original plain marble decoration and an ancient episcopal throne. Above is a *mosaic (625–38) representing *St Agnes between Pope Symmachus and Pope Honorius I*, two restorers of the basilica, a model of which is held by Honorius. The simplicity of the composition against a dull gold background is striking. The dedicatory inscription below records how much Honorius spent on the church.

In the left aisle is the entrance to the **Catacombs of Sant'Agnese**. The best-preserved and among the most interesting Roman catacombs, they were discovered in 1865–66. The atmosphere in these catacombs, not normally visited by large groups, offers a striking contrast to that in the more famous catacombs on the Via Appia (see Chapter 36), which are usually crowded with tours. They are shown by a well-informed guide on a tour which normally takes about 40mins. They contain no paintings but there are numerous inscriptions and many of the *loculi* are intact and closed with marble or terracotta slabs. They may date from before 258 but not later than 305; the oldest zone extends to the left of the basilica. A chapel was built where the body of St Agnes was found, and a silver coffer provided in 1615 by Pope Paul V.

On the other side of the entrance court and garden a path leads to the round mausoleum of Constantia, known as the church of **Santa Costanza** since the 9C. This was built by Constantia as a mausoleum for herself and her sister Helena, daughters of the Emperor Constantine, probably before 354. It is remarkably well preserved and in a lovely peaceful spot. The charming **interior** is annular in plan: 24 granite columns in pairs with beautiful Corinthian capitals and pulvinated imposts support the dome, which is 22.5m in diameter. There are 12 large windows with restored transennae beneath the dome. The pavement is in terracotta except between the columns where it is marble, and there are bare brick walls. On the barrel vaulting of the encircling ambulatory are remarkable early Christian *mosaics (4C), pagan in character and designed in pairs on a white ground. They were restored by Vincenzo Camuccini in 1834–40. Those flanking the entrance have a geometric design, and the next a circular motif with animals and figures. Vintage scenes and vine tendrils with grapes follow, and the fourth pair have roundels with a leaf design, busts and figures. On either side of the sarcophagus are leaves, branches, amphorae and exotic birds. Over the sarcophagus only a fragment remains of a mosaic with a star design. The two side niches also have fine mosaics (5C or 7C). The mosaics in the dome were destroyed when they were replaced by the frescoes in 1620. Constantia's magnificent porphyry sarcophagus was replaced here by a cast when it was removed to the Vatican in 1791 (see p 378); Helena's sarcophagus was removed in 1606.

Two small gates on the right of the mausoleum lead into an overgrown garden and orchard with the remains of the huge **Constantinian basilica** (see above), identified in 1954 and still being excavated. They include the outer walls with a round window in the apse, sustained on the outside by huge buttresses. In plan it was typical of the early cemetery basilicas of Rome, such as San Lorenzo fuori le Mura and San Sebastiano.

Just beyond the church of Sant'Agnese, on the opposite side of Via Nomentana, are the gardens of the **Villa Blanc**, which were designated a public park in 1974 but are still not open to the public and are in a state of abandon. The villa, built in an eclectic style with Art Nouveau elements, is in urgent need of repair. Incorporated in the garden wall is a 2C circular tomb looking like a small copy of the Mausoleum of Cecilia Metella (see p 427). Nearly 2km further north the Nomentana crosses the river Aniene, the ancient Anio which rises near Tivoli. On the right of the new bridge the Roman **Ponte Nomentano**, rebuilt by Narses in 552 and guarded by a medieval watchtower, survives.

The Catacombs of Nicomedes, at 32 Via dei Villini, and of the Cimitero Maggiore on Via Asmara, which has interesting frescoes, are both off Via Nomentana. They are not regularly open to the public; for admission, see p 49.

Via Salaria and the Catacombs of Priscilla

Piazza Fiume (**Map 4**; 1) is on the site of the Roman Porta Salaria. The gate no longer exists but the bases of two tombs in the square define its width. The **Via Salaria** (**Map 4**; 1; 13; 7, 5, 4, 1) begins here, running one-way south, one of the oldest Roman roads. Off Via Nizza, at no 24 Via Reggio Emilia, is the entrance to the former Stabilimento Birra Peroni (there is another entrance at no. 29 Via Cagliari). This was a brewery up until 1971 and has been restored and rebuilt to house part of the **Galleria Comunale d'Arte Moderna e Contemporanea**. At present the permenent collection is displayed in Via Francesco Crispi (see Walk 8) and these premises are used for exhibitions. Open 09.00–19.00; summer 10.00–21.00; closed Mon. ☎ 06 6710 7900.

Some 300m further along Via Salaria on the right is the large park, with umbrella pines, of **Villa Torlonia** (**Map 13**; 7, 8), formerly Albani. The villa and collection are still privately owned by the Torlonia, and permission to see them is rarely granted, although you are asked to apply in writing to the *Amministrazione Torlonia*, 30 Via della Conciliazione.

History of the Villa Torlonia

The villa was built in 1760 by Carlo Marchionni for Cardinal Alessandro Albani, whose valuable collection of Classical sculpture was arranged here in 1765 by Johann Winckelmann, the German archaeologist who had become superintendent of Roman antiquities in 1763. By order of Napoleon 294 pieces of the villa's original collection of Classical sculptures were taken to Paris; after Waterloo nearly all of them were sold at Munich instead of being returned. The rest of the collection continued to increase, and in 1852 it passed into the possession of the Chigi. In 1866 it was bought, with the villa, by Princess Alessandra Torlonia.

The Casino, surrounded by a formal garden, has a hemicycle with 40 Doric columns. In the portico are niches with busts of Roman emperors. Beyond an atrium with caryatids, the first gallery has a collection of herms. The staircase, with Roman reliefs, leads up to the Oval Hall with a statue of an *Athlete*, signed by Stephanos (1C BC). In the Great Hall the ceiling painting of **Parnassus* is by Raphael Mengs. Here is displayed the *Albani Pallas*, a statue of the Attic school. In the right wing are paintings by Alunno, Perugino, Giovanni Paolo Pannini, Gerard van Honthorst, Pompeo Batoni, Anthony Van Dyck, Taddeo Zuccari, Jacopo Tintoretto, José Ribera and Guercino.

The left wing has a relief of **Antinous*, from Hadrian's Villa, the only piece brought back from Paris in 1815; the so-called *Leucothea*, a relief dating from the beginning of the 5C BC; a 5C relief of a **Battle Scene*, showing the influence of Pheidias; the **Apollo Auroktonos*, an ancient copy after Praxiteles; a bust of **Quintus Hortensius**; and the **Apotheosis of Hercules*, in the style of the Tabula Iliaca in the Capitoline Museum. The so called *Aesop* is a naturalistic nude statue of a hunchback, possibly a portrait of a court dwarf of the time of Hadrian. The paintings include sketches by Giulio Romano for the story of Psyche in Palazzo del Te at Mantua, and works by Borgognone, Luca Giordano and Gaspare Vanvitelli. On the ground floor is the Stanza della Colonna, a room with 12 fine columns—one fluted, in alabaster—in which is displayed a **sarcophagus with a scene of the marriage of Peleus and Thetis, considered by Winckelmann to be one of the finest in existence. The Kaffehaus contains Roman mosaics.

West of Villa Torlonia is the circular **Mausoleum of Lucillus Peto** (Map 13; 7), dating from the time of Augustus and recently restored.

Also near the Via Salaria are a number of catacombs not regularly open to the public; for admission, see p 49. These are the Catacombs of Sant'Ermete, with a large underground basilica containing an 8C fresco which includes the earliest known representation of *St Benedict*; the catacombs of Panfilo and of Santa Felicità (or Massimo), with a small underground basilica (**Map 13**; **5**); the catacombs of the Giordani, the deepest catacombs in Rome with five tiers of galleries, which contain a fine 4C mural of a woman in prayer; and the catacombs of Via Anapo, with interesting frescoes of Old and New Testament scenes, dating from the 3C and 4C.

At no. 430 Via Salaria is the entrance to a monastery of some 25 Benedictine nuns and the **Catacombs of Priscilla** (Map 13; 2), among the most important and interesting in Rome, and much more pleasant to visit than the overcrowded catacombs on the Via Appia Antica. Open Tues–Sun 08.30–12.30 and 14.30 (or 15.00) till dusk; closed Mon. and in Jan. ☎ 06 8620 6272. Visitors are taken in groups by an English-speaking nun or guide; the tour lasts about half an hour, and is easy under foot and well lit.

These catacombs, where many popes were buried between 309 and 555, were discovered in 1578. They extend for some 13km and it is estimated that there must have been about 40,000 burials here. They are on three levels, but only the uppermost level, dating from the 2C AD, is accessible. The first area shown is that of the '*arenario*', probably a pozzolana stone quarry, where the **Cubiculum of the Velata** has well-preserved late-3C paintings, including a woman in prayer, representing the deceased woman who was buried here, between scenes of her marriage and her motherhood. In the pretty vault, the *Good Shepherd* can be seen, surrounded by sheep, trees, peacocks and other birds. In the side lunettes are scenes from the Old Testament (three Hebrew youths being saved from fire by an angel, and the *Sacrifice of Abraham*). Above the entrance is a depiction of *Jonah and the Whale*. In the long corridors can be seen the burial places of both adults and children and fragments of the marble slabs carved with Christian symbols that once closed the tombs. Some tombs are preserved intact behind a wall dating from the 4C. In another area of the catacombs, presumed to be near a martyr's tomb, there is a remarkable fragment of stucco decoration combined with painting, in a vault dating from 220 AD. The *Good Shepherd* is depicted here again, flanked by two sheep amongst graceful trees. The figures of the *Madonna* *and Child* are the oldest known representations of this subject: next to the Virgin stands a prophet pointing up to a star.

The **criptoporticus**, with cross-vaulting, was part of a villa of Priscilla's family, the Acilii, which probably existed above the cemetery and later became a chapel. Here there are photographs which help you to identify the frescoes in the so-called Greek Chapel which is shown next. This funerary chapel, named after the Greek inscriptions found here, is interesting for its 3C decorations in stucco and fresco. A banquet scene against a bright red ground, on the apse arch, includes the figure of a veiled woman (the third figure from the right), and there are biblical scenes (the *Three Wise Men*, *Susanna and the Elders*, *Moses Striking the Rock*) as well as a pagan bust representing Summer.

On the opposite side of Via Salaria is the garden wall of the huge **Villa Ada**, formerly Savoia (**Map 13**; **1**, **2**). This was once the private residence of Vittorio Emanuele III, and is now the Egyptian Embassy. Part of the grounds are open as a public park: the entrance is on Via Panama.

Adjoining the park to the north is **Monte Antenne**, the site of the ancient Sabine town of Antemnae, said to have been founded by the Siculi. It had probably already disappeared by the time of the Roman kings. At the foot of the hill, with an approach road from the Parioli district (see below), is Rome's first **mosque**, built in 1984–93 and designed by Paolo Portoghesi, Vittorio Gigliotti and Sami Monsawi. The mosque, which can hold up to 3000 people and is the largest in Europe, was financed by some 24 Arab countries. There is also a cultural centre and library here.

Via Salaria crosses the Aniene about 1km north of the Catacombs of Priscilla, near its confluence with the Tiber, by the Roman **Ponte Salario**, rebuilt in 565 by Narses and reconstructed after it was blown up by papal troops in 1867. Only two side arches are original.

Via Flaminia and Ponte Milvio

The **Via Flaminia** begins outside Porta del Popolo (**Map 2**; **2**). Continuing the line of the Corso it runs north to cross the Tiber by the Ponte Milvio. It passes the wooded grounds of the Villa Strohl-Fern and on the left Via Pasquale Stanislao Mancini, where the **Museo Hendrik Christian Andersen** was opened in 1999. Open 09.00–18.30; closed Mon. ☎ 06 321 9089 or 06 322 4152. This was the home and studio of the sculptor and painter Hendrik Andersen, who was born in Norway in 1872 and whose family emigrated to America. Anderson came to Rome in 1894 and remained here until his death in 1940. In 1899 he met Henry James, who admired his work, and an interesting collection of letters from the writer to him survives. The Bostonian writer Olivia Cushing, his sister-in-law, inspired his work which was to have decorated a 'world city' under the auspices of the World Conscience Society, founded by Andersen in 1913. The house, owned by the State since 1978, and now a satellite museum of the Galleria Nazionale d'Arte Moderna, remains as he built it in 1925, together with his monumental sculptures displayed in a gallery and studio on the ground floor (visitors are given a hand list). The upper floor is used for exhibitions, and there is a museum café.

The vast Marine Ministry (*Ministero della Marina*) was built in 1928 by Giulio Magni. At the corner of Viale delle Belle Arti is the elegant **Palazzina of Pius IV**, attributed to Pirro Ligorio, and a fountain erected by Julius III beneath an imposing façade, originally of only one storey, by Bartolomeo Ammannati (1553); the second part was added by Pirro Ligorio in 1562. Viale delle Belle Arti leads right to the Museo Nazionale di Villa Giulia and the Galleria Nazionale d'Arte Moderna (see Walk 18) and on the left is Ponte del Risorgimento (1909–11), the first bridge to be built in the city in reinforced concrete, with a single span of 100m.

Via Flaminia continues to the graceful little circular church of **Sant'Andrea in Via Flaminia** by Vignola (1550–55), erected by Julius III to commemorate his deliverance from Charles V's soldiers while he was a cardinal. It is now between Via Flaminia and Viale Tiziano.

On the right of the Via Flaminia is the exclusive **Parioli** residential district (**Map 12; 3**), the centre of which is at Piazza Euclide, with the huge church of the Sacro Cuore Immacolato di Maria by Armando Brasini (1923).

Further north is the district of **Flaminio** with, to the right, the **Stadio Flaminio**, designed in reinforced concrete by Pier Luigi and Antonio Nervi in 1959. In addition to the football ground, which can accommodate 45,000 spectators, there are gymnasiums, a fencing school and a swimming-pool. On the left of Piazza Apollodoro, in Via Guido Reni, is the church of Santa Croce, built by Pius X in 1913. In a former barracks nearby, a museum designed by Zaha M. Hadid is to be built to house the modern and contemporary art collections (works dating from the 1970s and later) of the Galleria Nazionale d'Arte Moderna. Nearby the first part of the **Città della Musica**, consisting of three concert halls (the largest with 2700 seats) and designed by Renzo Piano, was inaugurated in 2002. On the other side of the Via Flaminia is the **Palazzetto dello Sport**, an adventurous and striking construction by Pier Luigi Nervi and Annibale Vitellozzi, designed for the Olympic Games in 1960. Beyond is the Villaggio Olimpico, built to accommodate athletes in 1960, and now a residential district.

Further east is the **Parco di Villa Glori** (**Map 12; 1**), converted in 1923–24 by Raffaello de Vico into the Parco della Rimembranza to commemorate the heroism of the brothers Enrico and Giovanni Cairoli, who were killed in 1867 during Garibaldi's attempt to liberate Rome from papal rule. The park is planted with cypresses, oaks, elms, maples and horse chestnuts. A clump of oak trees commemorates heroes of the First World War. There is a fine ·view of the Tiber valley. Beyond is the mineral spring called Acqua Acetosa; the well-head (1661) is probably by Andrea Sacchi.

On the south side of Ponte Milvio is Piazza Cardinal Consalvi, with a shrine containing a statue by Paolo Taccone, erected by Pius II in 1462 on the spot where he had met Cardinal Bessarion returning from the Morea (Peloponnese) with the head of St Andrew.

Ponte Milvio or Ponte Molle (*Pons Milvius*), which once carried the Via Flaminia over the Tiber but is now used only by pedestrians, was built by the censor Marcus Aemilius Scaurus in 109 BC. It was here that Cicero captured the emissaries of the Allobroges in 63 BC during the Catiline conspiracy; and it was from this bridge that the Emperor Maxentius was thrown into the Tiber and drowned after his defeat by his co-emperor Constantine on 28 October 312. Remodelled in the 15C by Nicholas V, who added the watchtowers, it was restored in 1805 by Pius VII, who commissioned Giuseppe Valadier to erect the triumphal arch at the entrance. Blown up in 1849 by Garibaldi to arrest the advance of the French, it was again restored in 1850 by Pius IX.

Monte Mario and the Foro Italico

Monte Mario (**Map 16**; **5**), the ancient *Clivus Cinnoe* and medieval Monte Malo, takes its present name from the Villa Mario Mellini built on the summit (139m). Via di Villa Madama climbs the east slope of the hill to **Villa Madama** (**Map 16**; **3**), a lovely suburban villa, now used by the Italian Government as accommodation for prominent visitors, and so rarely open to the public. The villa was designed by Raphael and begun for Cardinal Giulio de' Medici (later Clement VII) by Giulio Romano. It was altered by Antonio da Sangallo the Younger. Later it came into the possession of Madama Margaret of Parma and was afterwards owned by the kings of Naples. The beautiful loggia, decorated with stucco reliefs by Giovanni da Udine and paintings by Giulio Romano (1520–25) after Raphael's designs, rivals and even excels the famous loggia of the Vatican. In one of the rooms is a frieze of cupids by Giulio Romano. There is a lovely view of Rome from the balcony of the main façade. The attractive hanging garden served as a model for many Italian gardens.

On the south slope of the hill is the round church of **Santa Maria del Rosario** (**Map 16**; **5**), built in 1650 by Camillo Arcucci, from which there is a good view. Beyond the ditches of the fort of Monte Mario, a road leads right to the summit at the **Villa Mario Mellini**, now incorporated in the **Astronomical and Meteorological Observatory**, with the **Copernican Museum**, founded in 1873. It contains mementoes of Copernicus, astrolabes, sextants, quadrants and telescopes, and a large collection of globes. For admission, ☎ 06 3534 7056 or 06 3534 7802.

At the foot of Monte Mario, extending along the riverfront, is the **Foro Italico** (**Map 16**; **3**, **2**), an ambitious sports centre built in 1928–31 by the former Accademia Fascista della Farnesina, one of the most impressive building projects carried out by Mussolini in imitation of ancient Roman Imperial architecture. Designed by Enrico del Debbio, and finished by Luigi Moretti in 1936, it was altered during work on preparations for the World Cup in Italy in 1990. Facing the entrance is Ponte Duca d'Aosta (1939).

A marble monolith, 17m high, inscribed *Mussolini Dux*, rises at the entrance in front of an imposing avenue paved with marble inlaid with mosaics designed by Gino Severini, Angelo Canevari and others. It ends in a piazza decorated with a fountain and with a huge marble sphere. On either side of the avenue are marble blocks, with inscriptions recording events in the history of Italy. At the end, beyond the piazza, is the **Stadio Olimpico**, finished for the Olympic Games in 1960, with accommodation for 100,000. It was reconstructed for the World Cup in 1990, with little respect for the setting. To the right is the **Stadio dei Marmi**, capable of seating 20,000 spectators, with 60 colossal statues of athletes. There are open-air and enclosed swimming-pools, the latter with mosaics by Giulio Rossi and Angelo Canevari. Another building has mosaics by Gino Severini. There are also lawn-tennis and basketball courts, running tracks, gymnasiums and fencing halls.

Lungotevere Maresciallo Diaz continues along the Tiber passing the Casa Internazionale dello Studente and, behind it, the Italian Foreign Office (1956), known as the **Farnesina** from the name of the road here. The sculpture is by Arnaldo Pomodoro (1968). The French Military Cemetery, with the graves of 1500 French who died in the Second World War, is also in this district. The Lungotevere ends at Piazzale Milvio, at the north end of Ponte Milvio (see above).

The church of the **Gran Madre di Dio** was designed by Cesare Bazzani in 1933. Ahead, Viale di Tor di Quinto continues along the river to Ponte Flaminio, opened in 1951, a seven-arched entrance to the city from the north.

Days out of Rome

Ostia Antica and Fiumicino

The extensive excavations of the Roman city of Ostia Antica are one of the most interesting and beautiful sights near Rome. They are extremely easy to reach from Rome by public transport in half an hour: the frequent Ostia train service (every 15 minutes) has a stop a few minutes walk from the entrance to the site. The ancient ports of Claudius and Trajan are near Fiumicino, Rome's main airport, served by an express train service from Termini station.

The excavations of Ostia Antica

The ruins, in a beautiful park of umbrella pines and cypresses, give a remarkable idea of the domestic and commercial architecture prevalent in the Empire in the late 1C and 2C AD, hardly any of which has survived in Rome itself, and are as important for the study of Roman urban life as those of the older cities of Pompeii and Herculaneum.

At least half a day is needed for the visit, and it is a splendid place to have a (discreet) picnic (food can be bought in the village, close to the entrance to the excavations). There is also a café with refreshments, near the museum. Some of the *mosaics discovered in the ruins are occasionally covered with wind-blown sand. In the description below only the most important monuments are mentioned as the ruins are well labelled (in English as well as Italian).

Getting there from Rome

The fastest way of reaching Ostia is by **train** from Stazione Ostiense beside Porta San Paolo (**Map 9**; **7**): services run every 15 minutes for Ostia Antica (30mins; for the price of a bus ticket) going on to Ostia Lido. For information, free phone ☎ 800 431 784. Stazione Ostiense is very close to the Piramide stop on underground Line B from Stazione Termini, and is served by numerous buses, including no. 95 from Piazza Venezia. From the station of Ostia Antica, cross Via Ostiense and Via del Mare by a footbridge which leads to the entrance to the excavations.

For the Museo delle Navi Romane and the ports of Claudius and Trajan there is a direct rail link from Stazione Termini to Fiumicino airport (30mins).

By car, take the Via del Mare (N8) from Viale Marconi beyond San Paolo fuori le Mura, a fast *superstrada* that was opened in 1928 when the Lido di Ostia became Rome's seaside resort. You should take care not to miss the turning right (23km from Rome) signposted for Scavi di Ostia Antica: there are no more exits off the fast main road until it reaches the coast (28km) at the west end of the Lido di Ostia—now usually called just Ostia—an ugly modern suburb of Rome, with a complicated system of one-way roads. There is also a motorway link to the airport (26km). There is a car park beside the entrance to Ostia Antica.

The old Via Ostiense (see below) runs parallel to the Via del Mare for the whole of its length.

Opening times

Tues–Sun 09.00–17.00; 09.00–18.00 or 19.00 in summer; closed Mon. ☎ 06 5635 8099. The museum has the same opening hours.

History of Ostia Antica

According to legend, Ostia, now called Ostia Antica, was founded by Ancus Marcius, fourth king of Rome, to guard the mouth (*ostium*) of the river Tiber. (The river formerly flowed past the city in a channel to the north, the Fiume Morto, dry since a great flood in 1557.) The surviving remains are not, however, older than the 4C BC, and the city, which was probably the first colony of Rome, may have been founded about 335 BC. It was originally a fortified city (*castrum*), the walls of which survive in part; later it became a much larger commercial city (*urbs*), also enclosed within walls. Its first industry was the extraction of salt from the surrounding marshes, but it soon developed into the commercial port of Rome and, shortly before the outbreak of the First Punic War (264 BC), it also became a naval base. The link between the port and the capital was the Via Ostiense, which, carrying as it did all Rome's overseas imports and exports until the construction of the Via Portuensis, must have been one of the busiest roads in the ancient world.

The commerce passing through Ostia was vital to the prosperity and even the existence of Rome. One of its most important functions was the organisation of the *annona*, the supply of produce, mainly grain, to the capital. At the head of the *annona* was the *quaestor ostiensis*, who had to live at Ostia. He was appointed by lot and his office, according to Cicero, was burdensome and unpopular. By 44 BC the *quaestor* was replaced by the *procuratores annonoe*, answerable to the *praefectus annonae* in Rome. The organisation involved the creation of a large number of commercial associations or guilds covering every aspect of trade and industry. Numerous inscriptions referring to these associations are preserved on the site in the Piazzale delle Corporazioni. Ostia suffered a temporary setback in 87 BC, when it was sacked by Marius, but Sulla rebuilt it soon afterwards and gave it new walls.

As the city continued to thrive, it outgrew its harbour and by the 1C AD, the construction of another port had become an imperative necessity. Planned by Augustus, this Porto was built by Claudius to the north-west of Ostia, and later enlarged by Trajan (see below). For a time Ostia remained the centre of the vast organisation for the supply of food to the capital. It added to its temples, public buildings, shops and houses, and it received special marks of favour from the emperors.

The decline of Ostia began in the time of Constantine, who favoured Porto. The titles conferred by the emperor on the newer seaport must have been particularly galling to the inhabitants of Ostia. But even in the 4C, though it had become a residential town instead of a commercial port, it was still used by notable people travelling abroad. In 387 St Augustine was about to embark for Africa with his mother, St Monica, when she was taken ill and died in a hostel in the city. In the following centuries, Ostia's decline was accelerated by loss of trade and by the increase of malaria. Its monuments were looted: columns, sarcophagi and statues stolen from the ruins have been found as far afield as Pisa, Amalfi, Orvieto and Salerno. An attempt to revive the city was made by Gregory IV, when he founded the borgo of Ostia Antica. In 1756 the city, which at the height of its prosperity had had a population of some 80,000, had 156 inhabitants; half a century later only a few convicts of the papal government lived here; Augustus Hare, writing in 1878, speaks of one human habitation breaking the utter solitude.

Excavations of the site began on a small scale at the beginning of the 19C, under Pius VII. Further work was instituted in 1854 under Pius IX, but systematic excavations did not begin until 1907. They have been continued, with few interruptions, until the present day. The work carried out in 1938–42 by Guido Calza and others brought to light many monuments of great interest. The excavated area is now c 34 hectares, or two-thirds of the area of the city at its greatest extent.

The city of Ostia seems to have been divided into at least five districts or *regiones*. The various monuments have been classified according to the area to which they are believed to have belonged: the streets and buildings are marked with signs indicating (a) the number of the region, (b) the number of the block, (c) the type of construction, such as temple, warehouse, insula or domus, (d) the traditional name of the street or building.

Beyond the entrance to the excavations is a stretch of the Via Ostiense, outside the walls. Parallel on the south is **Via delle Tombe**, also outside the walls, since Roman law forbade burials within the city limits: here can be seen a few terracotta sarcophagi and sealed graves, as well as columbaria for the urns holding the ashes from cremations.

The entrance to the city is by the **Porta Romana**, with remains of the gate in walls of the Republican period; some fragments of a marble facing of the Imperial era have been found and placed on the inner walls of the gate. The Piazzale della Vittoria is dominated by a colossal statue of Minerva Victoria, dating from the reign of Domitian and inspired by a Hellenistic original that may once have decorated the gate. On the right of the square are the remains of *horrea* (warehouses), later converted into baths. In the Baths of the Cisiarii on the far side of the warehouses are several mosaics, one with scenes of life in Ostia.

The **Decumanus Maximus**, the main street of Ostia, begins here. It runs right through the city and is c 1200m long. On the right is Via dei Vigili (Street of the Firemen), the construction of which involved the demolition of some earlier buildings, to which belonged the mosaic at the end of the street representing the Four Winds and Four Provinces (Sicily, Egypt, Africa, Spain). On the Decumanus a flight of steps leads to a platform, on the second story of the Baths of Neptune. From here can be seen the tepidarium and calidarium, remains of columns, and the floor of the large entrance hall with a mosaic of *Neptune* driving four sea-horses and surrounded by tritons, nereids and dolphins. In an adjoining room is a mosaic of *Amphitrite Escorted by Hymen*. The platform also provides a fine view of the excavations. Nearby is the palaestra (gymnasium), a large colonnaded courtyard surrounded by rooms.

Beyond the baths on the Decumanus is the **Tavern of Fortunatus**, in which there is a mosaic pavement with the broken inscription *Dicit Fortunatus: vinum cratera quod sitis bibe* ('Fortunatus says: drink wine from the bowl to quench your thirst'). Here is Via della Fontana, one of the best-preserved streets in Ostia, with typical apartment houses, with shops and living-rooms over them. It ends at the Caserma dei Vigili (firemen's barracks), built in the 2C AD, with a large arcaded courtyard, a shrine dedicated to Fortuna Santa, and an *Augusteum*, or shrine for the cult of the emperors. Nearby Via della Fullonica is named from its well-equipped fuller's workshop for cleansing cloth, complete with a courtyard for drying.

The domestic architecture of ancient Rome

One result of the research at Ostia Antica has been the great increase in knowledge of the various types of house occupied by Romans of the middle and lower classes. Since it is not likely that the domestic architecture of Ostia differed radically from that of the capital, the examples that have been unearthed of the lower-grade house here may be taken as typical of such buildings in Rome itself, though not of dwellings throughout the empire. The middle- and lower-class house at Ostia (*insula*) was in sharp contrast to the typical Pompeian residence (*domus*), with its atrium and peristyle, its few windows and its low elevation: houses of this type are rare at Ostia.

The ordinary Ostia insula usually had four storeys and reached a height of 15m, the maximum permitted by Roman law. It was built of brick, probably not covered with stucco, and had little ornamentation, although sometimes bricks of contrasting colours were used. The entrance doors had pilasters or engaged columns supporting a simple pediment. There were numerous rooms, each with its own window. The arches over the windows were often painted in vermilion. Mica or selenite was used instead of glass in the windows. The façades were of three types: living-rooms with windows on all floors; an arcaded ground floor with shops and living-rooms above; and a ground floor with shops opening on the street, and living-rooms above. Many of the houses had balconies of various designs. The apartment houses contained numerous flats or sets of rooms designated by numbers on the stairs leading to them. They, too, were of different types; some were of simple design and others were built round a courtyard.

The rare domus, built for the richer inhabitants, was usually on one floor only and dates mostly from the 3C and 4C. Such houses were decorated with apses, nymphaea and mosaic floors, and the rooms often had columns and loggias.

The next street to the west is Via delle Corporazioni; in it is a well-preserved apartment house, with paintings on the walls and ceilings. On the other side of the street is the **Theatre**, built by Agrippa and enlarged by Septimius Severus in the 2C. It has two tiers of seats (originally there were three), divided by stairways into five sections or *cunei*. It could accommodate 2700 people. A tufa wall with some marble fragments and three marble masks survive from the stage, behind which some cipollino columns that once decorated the third tier of the auditorium have been set up. In the main façade, towards the Decumanus Maximus, is a series of covered arcades, formerly shops. Between the arcades and the street are areas paved with travertine and, at either end, a fountain. A Christian oratory in honour of St Cyriacus and his fellow-martyrs of Ostia was later built over the fountain on the east side.

Behind the theatre extends the spacious **Piazzale delle Corporazioni** (Square of the Guilds). In this square were 70 offices of commercial associations ranging from workers' guilds to corporations of foreign representatives from all over the ancient world. Their trademarks are preserved in the mosaic floors of the brick-built arcade running round the square. The trademarks of the foreigners tell where they came from (e.g. Carthage, Alexandria, Narbonne) and what their trade was, and those of the citizens indicate their trade, such as ship repair and construction, maintenance of the docks, warehouses and embankments, dockers, salvage crews, and customs and excise officials. In the middle of the square are the stylobate and two columns of a small temple in antis known as the Temple of Ceres, and the bases of statues erected to the leading citizens of Ostia.

Beyond the square is the handsome **House of Apuleius**, of the Pompeian type rare at Ostia, with an atrium and rooms decorated with mosaics. Beside it is a **Mithraeum**, one of the best-preserved of the many temples dedicated to Mithras in the city. It has two benches for the initiated, on which are mosaics illustrating the cult of the god. There are also casts of the marble relief of Mithras which was found here, with several inscriptions. In front are four small tetrastyle temples, erected in the 2C BC on a single foundation of tufa. They are supposed to have been dedicated to Venus, Fortuna, Ceres and Hope. In the square in front of the temples are the remains of a nymphaeum and of a sanctuary of Jupiter. In Ostia, as elsewhere in the Roman world, different religious cults flourished without disharmony. As well as temples dedicated to the traditional deities such as Vulcan, Venus, Ceres and Fortuna, there was a popular cult of the emperors and a surprisingly large number of eastern cults, such as the Magna Mater, Egyptian and Syrian deities, and especially Mithras. Singularly few Christian places of worship have been found.

Horrea, large warehouses for the storage of corn, can be seen on the right from the Decumanus Maximus. They have over 60 small rooms, some of them arranged round a central colonnaded courtyard. At the corner of the next street on the right, Via dei Molini, with a building containing millstones, are the remains of a Republican temple. Here is the **Porta Orientale**, the east gate of the original fortified city or *castrum*; to the left are the original tufa walls. At this point the Decumanus Maximus has been excavated down to the level of the ancient city and is liable to flooding in bad weather.

A street on the west side of Via dei Molini, Via di Diana, takes its name from a house called the **Casa di Diana**. It has a characteristic façade with shops on the ground floor, rooms with windows on the first floor, and a projecting balcony on the second floor. The house is entered through a vaulted corridor. On the ground floor a room on the left has a ceiling and walls that have been restored with fragments of frescoes. The small interior courtyard has a fountain and a relief of Diana. At the back of the premises are two rooms converted into a Mithraeum. Opposite the entrance to the Casa di Diana, Via dei Lari opens into Piazzetta de Lari, with a round marble altar dedicated to the lares (household gods) of the district.

In Via di Diana, beyond the Casa di Diana, on the left is the remarkable **Thermopolium**, which bears a striking resemblance to a modern Italian bar. Just outside the entrance, under the balcony, are two small seats. On the threshold is a marble counter, on which is a small stone basin. Inside the shop is

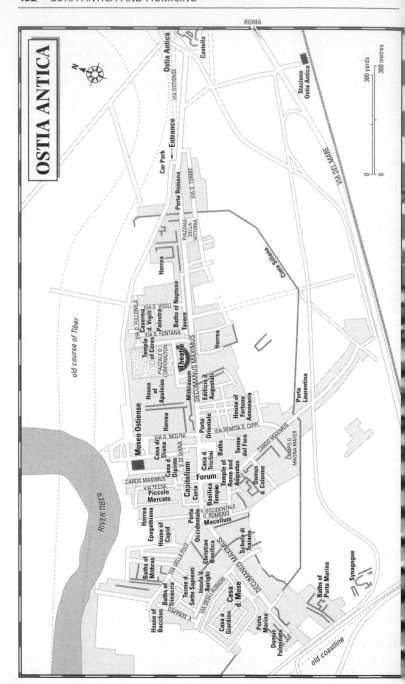

OSTIA ANTICA

ROMA

Ostia Antica
Castello
VIA OSTIENSE
Stazione Ostia Antica
VIA DEL MARE

Entrance
Car Park
Porta Romana
VIA D. TOMBE
PIAZZALE DELLA VITTORIA
Horrea
Cippa Silline
Porta Laurentina

VIA D. FULLONICA
VIA D. VIGILI
Caserma d. Vigili
VIA D. FONTANA
Temple of Ceres
Baths of Neptune
Palestra
Tavern
Horrea

old course of Tiber

House of Apuleius
Mithraeum
Theatre
PIAZZALE CORPORAZIONI
DECUMANUS MAXIMUS
Edificio d. Augustali
House of Fortuna Annonaria
Porta Orientale
VIA SEMITA D. CIPPI
CAMPO D. MAGNA MATER
CARDO MAXIMUS

Museo Ostiense
VIA D. MOLINI
Casa d. Diana
Casa d. Dipinte
V. DI DIANA
Casa d. Triclini
Baths
Terme del Faro
Domus d. Colonne

Horrea
Forum
Capitolium
Curia
Temple of Rome and Augustus
Basilica Tempio

RIVER TIBER

CARDO MAXIMUS
VIA TECTA
Piccolo Mercato
Porta Occidentale
V. OCCIDENTALE D. ROMERIO
Macellum
Schola di Traiano
DECUMANUS MAXIMUS

Horrea
Epagathiana
House of Cupid
VIA DELLA FOCE
Christian Basilica
V. SERAPEO

Baths of Mithras
Baths of Trinacria
Terme d. Sette Sapienti
Insula d. Aurighi
VIA DEGLI AURIGHI
Casa d. Muse
Baths of Porta Marina
Synagogue

House of Bacchus
Casa a Giardino
Porta Marina
Domus Fulminata

old coastline

300 yards
300 metres

another counter for the display of food dishes; above are wall-paintings of fruit and vegetables. On the rear wall is a marble slab with hooks for hats and coats. Beyond is a delightful court and fountain.

At the end of Via di Diana on the right is an apartment house, originally of four storeys, called the **Casa dei Dipinti**. A staircase leads up to the top floor from which there is a fine view of the excavations. The ground floor (entered around the corner from Via dei Dipinti) has a mosaic floor and 'architectural' wall-paintings in a corner room; beyond is a fine *hall painted with mythological scenes, human figures and landscapes. In the garden of the house are numerous *dolii*, large terracotta jars for the storage of corn and oil. At the end of the street is the museum, which contains the principal finds from the excavations.

Museo Ostiense

The Museo Ostiense is housed in a building dating from 1500 and originally used by the authorities concerned with the extraction of salt; it was given its Neo-classical façade in 1864. The rooms are un-numbered in situ. In the atrium are three charming marble table legs, and a statue of *Apollo Kitharoidos* of 2C AD. **Room 1** on the left has *Mithras Slaying the Bull*, from the Baths of Mithras, signed by Kritios of Athens (1C BC); next to it is displayed a copy made a few years later known as the *Torso Giustiniani* which was for years kept in the garden of the Odescalchi in Bassano Romano from which it was stolen. In 1980 it was exhibited at the J. Paul Getty Museum in California, and retrieved by the Italian police in 1999. In the niche to the right is a group of 18 cult statues found in the Sanctuary of Attis (AD 140–70). The circular *altar with reliefs of the Twelve Gods is a neo-Attic work of the 1C BC.

Steps lead down into **room 2** which displays sculpture inspired by Greek art of the 4C and 3C BC; two copies of *Eros Drawing his Bow*, one a replica of an original by Lysippos; a cult statue of *Asklepios* (?); two herms of *Hermes* of the Alcamene type; a *Dionysos* with elements inspired by Praxiteles. In the centre is a fragment of a group of *Wrestlers* dating from the Trajan era on a Hellenistic model. On the left is **room 3** with sculpture inspired by Greek art of the 5C BC: inscribed bases testifying to the presence of Greek artists; a head of *Hermes*; a votive relief (an original Greek-Italiot work of the first half of 5C BC); three heads of *Athena*, from originals of the Phidias type, the Kressilas type, and the Kephisodotos type (first half of 4C BC); the upper part of a herm of *Themistocles*, a copy of an original of the 5C; *Omphalos Apollo*, from the 5C original; head of an *Unknown Man*. On the right of room 2 is **room 4** with sculpture inspired by Hellenistic works. Heads of a *Satyr* and of a *Barbarian* of the Pergamene type (2C BC); two heads of *Korai*; head of *Victory* from the Giulio-Claudian era; *Perseus with the Head of Medusa*; *Cupid and Psyche* from the House of Cupid and Psyche; replica of the crouching *Venus* of Doidalsas (3C BC); statue of the *Three Graces*.

Room 5 is the next large room which displays Roman sculpture from the 1C BC to the mid-2C AD. The headless *male statue, nude except for the drapery over the left arm, is signed with the name of the donor Curtilius Poplicola, whose sarcophagus is near Porta Marina. It is regarded as the best extant copy of the type known as the *Hero in Repose*. Also here are portraits of *Augustus*, *Trajan* (including a statue of him wearing a cuirass), *Hadrian*, *Sabina, wife of Hadrian*, and a group of portraits of members of the family of Marcus Aurelius. The herm of *Hippocrates* is from an original of the 3C BC. Beyond a funerary statue of Giulia Procula, a relief—a fragment of an architectural frieze—shows the sacred geese in front of the Temple of Juno Moneta on the Capitoline. The last large room, **room 6**, has Roman sculpture (end of 2C to 4C AD): *Maxentius*(?) as Pontifex Maximus, found in the Edificio degli Augustali; statue of *Fausta*, sister of Maxentius (AD 310–12); *Giulia Domna*, in the semblance of Ceres; bust of *Septimius Severus*, her husband; statue in grey marble of *Isis Pelagia*, with two fragments of a serpent, also in grey marble, at her feet. In **room 7**, to the left, are Roman sarcophagi of the 2C–3C AD. The *sarcophagus of a boy, from the Isola Sacra Necropolis, is a magnificent example of the Attic type, dating from the 2C AD; on the lid is the figure of a boy lying on a couch decorated with bas-reliefs; and the three sides have reliefs of Dionysiac rites with a charming frieze of putti, illustrating the direct influence sarcophagi of this type had on artists of the Renaissance. On the back is the scene of a wrestling match which was left in a rough, unfinished state. The *sarcophagus from Pianabella (c 160 AD) has scenes from the *Iliad*, and another sarcophagus has a scene of Lapiths and Centaurs. Off this room a small room displays fragments of wall paintings dating from the Imperial period.

Not at present on show are some magnificent opus sectile *panels found in an edifice near Porta Marina (5C–4C AD): they are decorated with various portraits, a head (with a halo) thought to be that of Christ, and two scenes of a lion attacking a horse. The collection also includes *bas-reliefs showing scenes of everyday life including various arts and crafts, the scene of a birth, and a surgical operation; and two bas-reliefs with the plan of a temple and the topographical plan of a city.

Parallel with Via dei Dipinti, on the west, is the wide **Cardo Maximus** with arcaded shops, which runs from the Tiber to the Forum and from there to the Porta Laurentina. To the west of this street and also parallel is the narrow Via Tecta, on the brick walls of which are displayed many of the best-preserved inscriptions found in the ruins. Via Tecta runs beside a grain warehouse called the **Piccolo Mercato**. Several layers of the tufa blocks of the primitive city walls have been incorporated in the south wall. The Cardo Maximus runs south to the **Forum**, which is traversed from east to west by the Decumanus Maximus. At the north end of the Forum is the **Capitolium**, the city's most important temple, dedicated to Jupiter, Juno and Minerva. This prostyle hexastyle building, dating from the first half of the 2C, had six fluted white marble columns. The pronaos is reached by a wide flight of steps, in front of which is a reconstituted altar. In the cella are niches and a plinth for statues of the deities. During the Barbarian invasions the temple was stripped of nearly all its marble facing, but a magnificent slab of African marble is still in place on the threshold and a few surviving marble fragments have been placed to the east of the building under a colonnade, which defined the sacred area.

Opposite the Capitolium, on the south side of the Forum, are the remains of the 1C **Temple of Rome and Augustus**. Like the Capitolium it had six fluted marble columns across the front, but with two side staircases. Fragments of the pediment have been placed on a modern wall to the east; the cult statue of Rome as Victory, dressed as an Amazon, has been placed inside the temple on a plinth, and a headless statue of Victory near the rearranged pediment fragments.

On the east side of the Forum are the **Baths of the Forum**, built in the 2C and restored in the 4C. When restored the baths were decorated with mosaics and cipollino columns; some of the columns have been re-erected. The frigidarium survives, together with a series of rooms warmed by hot air. Off the north side is the town **forica** (public lavatory), its 20 seats almost perfectly preserved. Also on the east side, at the corner where the Decumanus Maximus enters the Forum, is the **Casa dei Triclini**, so called from the couches in each of the three rooms on the right wing of the central courtyard. Behind the courtyard is a room with a high podium decorated with coloured marbles.

Opposite, on the west side of the Forum, is the **Basilica**, or law courts and place of assembly. The façade towards the Forum had a portico of marble arches with a decorated frieze. Fragments of this decoration and of the columns have been preserved. To the south of the Basilica is the **Tempio Rotondo**, dating from the 3C and probably an Augusteum, or temple erected to the worship of the emperors. The peristyle was paved with mosaics and surrounded by marble-faced niches. It was reached by a flight of steps, which have been preserved: these led to the pronaos which comprised a portico with brick piers faced with marble and with cipollino columns. In the cella are seven niches, three rectangular and four circular. Between the niches are column bases; to the right are the remains of a spiral staircase that led to the dome.

Also on the west side, north of the Decumanus Maximus, is the **Curia**, or senate house. The inscriptions on the walls are lists of *Augustales*, citizens of Ostia belonging to the cult of the emperors. Beside the Curia is the **Casa del Larario**, or House of the Shrine of the Lares, a combination of a house and shopping centre.

Leaving the Forum the Decumanus Maximus continues to the **Porta Occidentale**, the west gate of the original *castrum*; the ancient walls are seen clearly in Via degli Horrea Enagathiana a turning on the right. In this street are the **Horrea Epagathiana et Epaphroditiana**, warehouses in a remarkable state of preservation, and used as a shard store (no admission). They were built by two Eastern freedmen, Epagathus and Epaphroditus, whose names are preserved on a marble plaque above the entrance; this is a brick portal with two engaged columns supporting a

One of the horrea in Ostia Antica

pediment. The inner courtyard was surrounded by an arcade of brick piers, repeated on the upper floor. On the walls of the vestibule and courtyard are four intact aediculae. In a large vaulted room at the rear of the horrea are further remains of the primitive town wall.

The region to the west of the Decumanus Maximus was excavated in 1938–42. The Decumanus Maximus now forks. The right fork is Via della Foce (Street of the River Mouth); it has been excavated for c 270m. The left fork is the continuation of the Decumanus Maximus and runs south-west to the Porta Marina (see below).

In Via della Foce, on the left, a long passageway leads to the **Mitreo delle Pareti Dipinti** (Mithraeum with Painted Walls), built in the 2C into a house of the Republican period. The Mithraeum is divided into two sections by partly projecting walls with ritual niches. The two stucco-faced galleries of the inner section also have niches. In the rear wall is the brick-built altar, with a marble cippus on which is a bust of Mithras. On the north wall are paintings of initiation rites.

A short street to the right leads to the sacred area of three Republican temples. The central and largest is the prostyle hexastyle **Temple of Hercules Invictus**. The pronaos, paved with mosaics, is reached by a flight of nine steps as wide as the façade. Inside the cella was a small marble column carved to represent the club of Hercules with the lion skin thrown over it. The temple, which may date from the time of Sulla, was given an altar in the 4C AD by Hostilius Antipater, *praefectus annonae*. On the north side of the sacred area is a tetrastyle temple of the same date as the first, its dedication unknown. Between the Temple of Hercules and Via della Foce is the **Temple of the Amorini**, named after a round marble altar with winged cupids found there. It was built in the early Republican period and rebuilt under the Empire. Its final form was in antis with just two columns in the portico.

Behind the temple is a street leading to the **House of Cupid and Psyche**, a domus dating from the end of the 3C. It is named after a marble group found in it and now in the museum. On the west side of the central atrium are four rooms, one with a pavement of coloured marbles and a copy of the statue; on the east is an attractive nymphaeum in a courtyard with columns and brick arches. At the north end of the atrium is a large room paved with opus sectile, and preserving some marble mural facing. Further along Via della Foce is Via delle Terme di Mitra to the right. The **Baths of Mithras** date from the time of Trajan and were rebuilt in the 2C. They had elaborate systems for heating and for pumping water. In the basement is a Mithraeum, in which was found the group of Mithras slaying the bull, now in the museum.

On the left side of the main street are three blocks of small apartment houses; then follows a complex of two apartment blocks with baths between them. The **Insula di Serapide** is named after a figure of Serapis in an aedicula in the courtyard. The **Terme dei Sette Sapienti** were so called from a satirical painting of the *Seven Sages* found in one of the rooms. The Sages are distinguished by name in Greek; to each of them is attached a crude inscription on the subject of health. The baths have a round central hall that was once domed and is paved with a beautiful *mosaic with five concentric rows of hunting scenes, including what appears to be a tiger. In a room next to a marble plunge pool is a painting of *Venus Anadyomene*. A passage leads to the extensive Insula degli Aurighi (of the charioteers), an apartment block with a large central courtyard. Two small paintings of charioteers belonging to opposing factions in the east wall of the arcade give the house its name. Off the north walk is a flat of six rooms with interesting paintings. Beyond the east side of the courtyard is a shrine, presumably of Mithras.

Further along Via della Foce, on the left, is a group of buildings of Hadrian's time. The **Baths of Trinacria** preserve good mosaics and interesting installations for heating and conducting the water. On the other side of Via Serapeo is the **House of Bacchus and Ariadne**, with rich floral mosaics. The **Serapeum**, behind, was dedicated in AD 127, and included a temple, with a courtyard flanked by porticoes and cult rooms. To the west, originally connected with the Serapeum, is a fine domus, with more mosaics.

Beyond the Insula degli Aurighi is Via degli Aurighi, which runs east to join the extension of the Decumanus Maximus. In this street on the left is the **Insula delle Celle**, a type of warehouse with small rooms, and, opposite, a modest hotel with a stable called **Albergo con Stalla**. This inn faces a street named after the Insula delle Volte Dipinte (no admission), with painted ceilings. Across the street is the **Casa delle Muse**, dating from the time of Hadrian. This house has a central courtyard with a covered arcade. The restored wooden roof of the arcade rests on the ancient brick cornice. Several rooms contain paintings, and on a wall of the arcade are some graffiti, one of them representing the lighthouse of Ostia.

To the right is the **Casa a Pareti Gialle** (House with the Yellow Walls). This looks on to a vast square of four large apartment houses built round a garden and known as the **Case a Giardino**. The scale of construction, the provision of a private garden and the absence of shops all indicate that the flats in these buildings were intended for the wealthier inhabitants of Ostia.

The Decumanus Maximus, and its extension from the fork outside the Porta Occidentale, continues south-west and runs for 350m to the Porta Marina and, beyond it, to the sea-coast. The **Porta Marina** (Sea Gate) was an opening in the walls built by Sulla, remains of which may be seen. Just inside the gate is a wine-shop, the Caupona di Alexander, and, outside, a large square. The extension of the Decumanus Maximus beyond the gate, built in the time of Augustus, ran through an earlier cemetery (see below). On this section is the **Santuario della Bona Dea**, a small prostyle tetrastyle temple dedicated to a goddess worshipped exclusively by women, where four column bases survive. Further towards the sea is the **Domus Fulminata**, with a small monument recording the fact that the house had been struck by lightning. Opposite, Via di Cartilio Poplicola leads to the **Baths of Porta Marina** past the tomb of L. Cartilius Poplicola, a prominent citizen. The surviving fragment of its decorative frieze shows a trireme with the helmeted head of a goddess. This and another tomb close by attest to the existence of a cemetery in the Republican era.

On the outskirts of the town towards the shore, and between the sea and the ancient Via Severiana (on the south-west side of this street), is the most ancient Jewish **synagogue** known from monumental remains. It was in continuous use from the 1C to the 5C AD. Ritual carvings and poorly preserved mosaics have been found; several Ionic columns have been re-erected. It was discovered in 1961–63 when the new road to Fiumicino airport was constructed.

The Decumanus Maximus returns past the charming **Fontana a Lucerna**. In a street to the south, beyond the junction with Via degli Aurighi, is a block of shops with windows beside their doors. Close by is the **Schola di Traiano**, seat of an Ostian corporation named after a statue of Trajan found in it. In the courtyard, which has stuccoed brick columns, is a long basin provided with niches. The central room has a headless statue of *Fortuna* and a mosaic pavement. The school overlays earlier constructions, among them a 1C domus; its nymphaeum has been partly restored.

On the opposite side of the main street is the **School of the Naval Smiths**, with a temple. The arcade of the courtyard in front of the temple was evidently a marble store: unused and partly finished columns, bases and capitals have been found in it. The store appears to have belonged to Volusianus, a senator of the 4C, as his name is carved on some of the column shafts. Adjoining is the **Christian Basilica**, an unpretentious structure with two aisles divided by columns and ending in apses. Vico del Dionisio leads south to the Cortile di Dionisio, surrounded by several houses, and to the **Mitreo delle Sette Porte**, which displays in seven arches the seven grades of the Mithraic cult.

The **Macellum**, or market, on the right, occupies the area between the Decumanus and a street running south, Via Occidentale del Pomerio. The market has numerous shops; two fish shops open on to the Decumanus. Behind them is the market-place. Via Occidentale del Pomerio and Via del Tempio Rotondo, behind the Tempio Rotondo at the south end of the Forum, lead to the south continuation of the Cardo Maximus. On the right here is the **Domus di Giove Fulminatore**, a house of the Republican period remodelled in the 4C, with a striking phallic 'doormat' mosaic. Beside it is the **Domus della Nicchia a Mosaico**, another Republican house, twice rebuilt. It is named after a semicircular niche faced with polychrome mosaic in the room (*tablinum*) beyond the atrium. Adjoining is the **Ninfeo degli Eroti**, with well-preserved marble floor and walls and niches in which were found two copies of the *Eros of Lysippos*. The next building is the **Domus delle Colonne**, a large corner house with façades on the Cardo Maximus and on Via della Caupona del Pavone to the right. In the centre of the courtyard is a stone basin with a double apse and short white marble columns; beyond is the large tablinum with its entrance between two columns.

In the side street is a wine-shop, the 3C **Caupone del Pavone**. One of its rooms is decorated with paintings of flying *Bacchanals and Muses*; beyond is the bar, with a counter and small basins. On the opposite side of the street is the **Domus dei Pesci**, evidently a Christian house. A vestibule has a mosaic showing a chalice and fish. A large room on the south side, with two marble columns, has a fine *mosaic floor.

The Cardo Maximus passes on the right the **Portico dell'Ercole**; opposite is a fulling mill. Adjoining are the **Terme del Faro**. In a floor of the frigidarium of the baths is a mosaic depicting fish, sea monsters and a lighthouse (*pharos*), after which the baths were named. One of the rooms has a white marble pool and frescoed walls in the 3C style. A ramp leads from the Cardo to the triangular **Campo della Magna Mater**, one of the best-preserved sacred areas of the Roman world. At the west corner is the prostyle hexastyle Temple of Cybele. At the east corner the Sanctuary of Attis has an apse flanked by telamones in the shape of fauns. On the same side is the **Temple of Bellona**, the goddess of war, dating from the time of Marcus Aurelius, and, opposite, the **Schola degli Hastiferes**, seat of an association connected with the cult of Bellona. The sanctuary is close to the **Porta Laurentina**, which retains the tufa blocks of Sulla's circumvallation (c 80 BC).

Some way south of Porta Laurentina, along the line of the ancient Via Laurentina, is the **Cemetery of the Porta Laurentina**, first excavated in 1865 and systematically explored in 1934–35. Many of the inscriptions relate to freedmen. Beyond the motorway, in the locality called Pianabella, excavations begun in 1976 revealed a necropolis and Christian basilica.

A short distance back along the Cardo Maximus, the Semita dei Cippi leads to the right (north). This street is flanked by two cippi and contains a 3C domus, the **Casa del Protiro**, its reconstituted portal prettily flanked by cypresses. To the north a right turn leads into a street named after the **House of Fortuna Annonaria**, which has a garden in its peristyle. On the west side of the peristyle is a large room with three arches, columns and a nymphaeum. At the end of the street, on the right, is another **Temple of Bona Dea**, with a Mithraeum next door, notable for its mosaic pavement. Also in the street is the **Domus Republicana**, with four Doric columns; it is adjoined by the **Edificio degli Augustali**, the headquarters of the *Augustales*, those in charge of the imperial cult. This building has another entrance in Via degli Augustali, which leads to the Decumanus Maximus, and the main entrance.

Ostia Antica

Across the road from the entrance to the excavations are a few houses outside the borgo of Ostia Antica, a **fortified village** whose walls are still standing, founded by Gregory IV in 830 and given the name of Gregoriopolis. The walls enclose a tiny picturesque hamlet of russet-coloured houses beside the castle, bishop's palace and church. The **castle** (open 09.00–13.00; closed Mon; on Tues and Thur 14.30–16.30; excellent guided tours) is a splendid building erected in 1483–86 by Baccio Pontelli for Julius II while he was still a cardinal.

From the courtyard there is access to a remarkable spiral stone staircase used by the guards, an old oven, a bath-house, and a room from which cannon were fired. A spiral ramp (designed for use by horses) leads up to the residential area with traces of frescoes by the school of Baldassarre Peruzzi. From the battlements and terrace there are views towards Fiumicino and the present site of the Tiber (which formerly flowed beneath the castle walls). An old fortified tower which predates the castle can be seen from here, and the site of a drawbridge which connected it to the main building.

The church of **Santa Aurea**, by Baccio Pontelli or Meo del Caprina, contains the body of the martyred St Aurea (d. 268) and, in a side chapel, a fragment of the gravestone of St Augustine's mother, St Monica, who died at Ostia in 387. The **Episcopal Palace**, with fine monochrome frescoes on the first floor inspired by Trajan's Column in Rome, attributed to Baldassare Peruzzi (1500–13), is the residence of the Bishop of Ostia.

Via del Mare continues to **Lido di Ostia** (61,600 inhabitants), now usually just called Ostia, on the coast. The lido became Rome's seaside resort after the First World War, and under the Fascist regime was planned as a district of the capital and connected to EUR by a fast road, Via Cristoforo Colombo, in 1936. Ostia is now an ugly suburb of Rome with numerous high-rise blocks of flats, but is still used as a resort by thousands of Romans in summer. It has some monumental edifices erected in 1916–40, but has been ruined by indiscriminate new building. On the seafront, in Piazza Anco Marzio, a monument by Pietro Consagra was set up in 1993 to the writer and film director Pier Paolo Pasolini, found murdered on 2 November 1975 at the Idroscalo, a former seaplane station near the mouth of the Tiber west of the esplanade (where another neglected monument stands). Nearby survives the **Tor San Michele**, built in 1568 by Nanni di Baccio Bigio to a design by Michelangelo.

To the east is the **Lido di Castel Fusano** in a beautiful pine forest. The first pines were planted here c 1710, and in 1755 the property was acquired by the Chigi family and was afterwards let as a royal hunting reserve. It has belonged to the Comune di Roma since 1932 and part of it is open as a public park. There are long-term plans to connect it, as one huge nature reserve of some 6000 hectares, to the forests of Castel Porziano and Capocotta to the south. This is the largest coastal forest left in the country.

From Ostia Antica a branch road signposted to Fiumicino (see below) skirts the fence protecting the excavations, curving right on a spur from Via del Mare. It passes close to the remains of the synagogue (described above). Beyond the Tiber and a set of traffic lights, the road passes a huge old industrial building, and at a pedestrian crossing with traffic lights a narrow road—with an inconspicuous sign for Necropoli di Porto—leads right. The first byroad left ends at the entrance to the **Necropoli di Porto** or Isola Sacra, in a pretty group of trees. Open Tues–Sun 09.00 till sunset. ☎ 06 658 3888.

History of the Necropoli di Porto

This was the necropolis of the port of Claudius and the later port of Trajan that came to be known as Porto (see below), particularly important for its 2C–3C tombs. It is situated on the Isola Sacra, a tract of land made into an island by the cutting of the Fossa Traiana from Porto to the sea. Once a flourishing horticultural centre, the island was abandoned after the fall of the Western Empire, and became an uninhabited malarial marsh. It was reclaimed in 1920 when the swamps were drained, roads ballasted and canals dug. Only part of the site has been excavated as much of it is under cultivation, and some of the tombs have recently been restored.

Since the necropolis was the burial place of the middle- and lower-class inhabitants of Porto, such as merchants, artisans, craftsmen and sailors, there are no elaborate mausolea. The tombs, which have been preserved by the sand that covered them for centuries, are arranged in groups. They have or had barrel vaults of brick and masonry faced with stucco; some of them had gable roofs. Internally they are decorated with stuccoes, paintings and mosaics. Sarcophagi and urns in columbaria have been found, often in the same tomb, evidence of the simultaneous practice of burial and cremation. Many of the sarcophagi are adorned with mythological reliefs; terracotta reliefs have representations of arts and crafts, indicating the trade of the deceased. Nearly every tomb has a name inscribed over the door. The tombs of the wealthier citizens have sepulchral chambers, with fanlights. Outside, by the door, are couches for funeral feasts.

Some of the tombs are like old-fashioned round-topped travelling trunks, and recall similar examples in North Africa. The poorest citizens, who could not afford the cost of a monument, buried their dead in the ground and marked the place with amphorae through which they poured libations; or they set up large tiles to form a peaked roof over the remains.

The road through the cemetery, the Via Flavia, is a section of the ancient road from Ostia to Porto. The tombs are numbered with small marble plaques. Of particular interest are a chamber tomb (**11**), with a marble sarcophagus with a scene of a funeral feast, and two other sarcophagi; the Tomb of the Children (**16**), with an entrance mosaic of the *Nile*; the Tomb of the Smith (**29**), with a façade divided by three pilasters and terracotta reliefs indicating the man's trade; the Tomb of Telesphorus and Julia Eunia (**39**), with the Christian symbols of the lamb, dove and anchor, apparently unique in this cemetery; a two-storeyed tomb (**41**); a tomb with a mosaic of a ship and the lighthouse of Porto (**43**). In the row behind are two tombs (**55, 56**), the first pedimental, the second with a square-corniced façade, both preserving their inscriptions. Close by is a series of four chamber tombs (**77–80**), with pedimental façades bearing reliefs.

Near the necropolis is the church of **Sant'Ippolito** where excavations, still in progress, have revealed interesting early Christian remains and a large medieval basilica (not yet open to the public).

Fiumicino and the ports of Claudius and Trajan

The main **airport** of Rome is usually called Fiumicino after the ugly seaside town nearby, which was heavily bombed in the Second World War, although its official name is Leonardo da Vinci. The airport, with graceful cantilevered buildings, was opened in 1961.

At the entrance, at 35 Via Alessandro Guidoni near a war memorial, is the **Museo delle Navi Romane**, a fine purpose-built museum, opened in 1979, that stands in the area once occupied by the Port of Claudius (Porto). Open Tues–Sun 09.00–13.30; Tues, Thur also 14.30–16.30. ☎ 06 652 9192 or 06 6501 0089.

History of the ports of Claudius and Trajan

When the harbour of Ostia (see p 448), already inadequate for its trade, began to silt up with the action of the Tiber, Augustus planned a larger seaport. In AD 42 Claudius began operations. The work was completed in 54 by Nero, who issued commemorative coins stamped Portus Augusti. With an area of some 80 hectares, and a wharf frontage of 800m, it was the most important commercial port in the Mediterranean, and was connected to the Tiber by a canal. Part of the site is now covered by the airport buildings, and by the grassy fields near the museum, in which fragments of the quays and buildings can be seen. Still extant is part of the quay incorporating the form of Caligula's ship (104m by 20m), which brought from Egypt the obelisk now in Piazza San Pietro. The ship was sunk and used as the base of a huge four-storeyed lighthouse.

Even this harbour soon silted up, however, and in 103 Trajan constructed a hexagonal artificial basin, the Port of Trajan, further inland to the south and better protected. It was connected to the Port of Claudius by a series of docks. This is reached from the airport by Via Portuense, an ancient road which followed the right bank of the Tiber from Rome to the port. More than one hundred ships could be moored here at any one time, and it was surrounded by warehouses. The area is to be opened to the public.

The museum houses the remains of five Roman boats found here at the entrance to the port of Claudius. They include four flat-bottomed cargo ships or barges used to carry goods upstream to Rome (AD 300–400) and a fishing boat (1C AD). Various objects found in the excavations, including lead seals and anchors, are also displayed here, and explanatory diagrams illustrate the history of the ports. There is a good view of the boats from the balcony.

The remains of the **Port of Trajan** include the hexagonal basin (650m across), perfectly preserved, constructed with travertine blocks. It shows up excellently from the air when landing at Fiumicino, but it is fenced off and can only be visited with special permission or on guided tours organised by the *Soprintendenza Archeologica di Ostia* (information at the Museo delle Navi; or ☎ 06 5635 8099).

The area is still the private property of the Sforza Cesarini family, and is occupied by a safari park. Attempts have been made to expropriate it and save it from further destruction, and there are long-term plans to create a coastal archaeological park and nature reserve here. Excavations have unearthed the remains of granaries, a wall, a high arch in red brick and an underground passageway. To the west are more ruins, including a monumental portico, at present still overgrown and abandoned. Like Claudius, Trajan also dug canals in connection with the seaport. The **Fossa Traiana** (now the Canale di Fiumicino) survives as a navigable canal between the Tiber and the sea. Numerous marble columns and coloured marbles, imported from all over the Empire and destined for ancient Rome, have been found in the area.

The village of **Porto**, 2km from the airport on the Via Portuensis, takes its name from the ancient city of Portus, which grew up around the ports of Claudius and Trajan. It was favoured as a seaport by Constantine at the expense of Ostia; in 314 it had its own bishop and became known as Civitas Constantina. In the village are the rebuilt church of Santa Rufina (10C), an old episcopal palace, and the Villa Torlonia. The suburbicarian see of Porto and Santa Rufina is one of the six held by the cardinal bishops.

Tivoli and Hadrian's Villa

Tivoli is one of the most famous places to visit outside Rome, and numerous sight-seers come here on day-trips by coach. In the centre of the little town is the Villa d'Este. well-known because of the numerous abundant fountains in its gardens, and below the town is Hadrian's villa, one of the most important archeological sites in Italy. However, if you are using public transport it is a very strenuous one-day trip from Rome, combining the underground railway and a bus along the extremely ugly and traffic-ridden Via Tiburtina for the town of Tivoli (from which there is an infrequent bus service to near Hadrian's Villa). At the same time it is not the best place to spend a night as there are no hotels (except 4-star category) in pleasant peaceful locations in the old town.

Getting there from Rome

Tivoli is not a pleasant place to visit by public transport. It can be reached by the **underground** Line B from the Colosseum or Termini railway station to Ponte Mammolo (the stop before the terminus at Rebibbia) which is connected by a *COTRAL* **bus service** (about every 20 minutes) to Tivoli (20km along the ugly traffic-ridden Via Tiburtina, in about 45 minutes). If you take this bus and wish to visit Hadrian's Villa before Tivoli, you can get off at a requst stop at Via di Villa Adriano (but this is over one kilometre from the entrance to Hadrian's Villa). There is also a **bus** (c every hour) from Ponte Mammolo along

the Via Prenestina, which has a stop closer to the entrance of Hadrian's Villa.

There is a local bus service (no. 4) about every 20 minutes from Tivoli (with a stop outside the tourist office) to near the entrance of Hadrian's Villa.

By **rail**, there is a somewhat roundabout route (infrequent service) from Rome (Tiburtina) to Tivoli via Guidonia,

By **car**, Tivoli, 31km east of Rome, is reached by the ugly Via Tiburtina, now extremely busy with traffic, on the line of the old Roman road to Tibur (Tivoli). It passes Bagni di Tivoli and a branch road (right), at Bivio Villa Adriano, for Hadrian's Villa.

Information

IAT office of the *APT della Provincia di Roma*, Largo Garibaldi, ☎ 0774 311 249.

Where to stay

The only hotel in the old town is the ☆☆☆☆ *Sirene*, 4 Piazza Massimo, ☎ 0774 330 605; 📠 0774 330 608, in a lovely position above cascades near the Ponte Gregoriano. Near the Villa Adriano, below the town: ☆☆☆☆ *Il Maniero*, 33 Via Villa Adriano,

☎ 0774 530 208, and ☆☆☆ *Adriano*, 194 Via di Villa Adriana. There are also a number of places which offer bed-and-breakfast (information from the IAT tourist office).

Eating out

Numerous restaurants all over the town. Hadrian's Villa is a superb place to picnic.

Market day on Wednesday in the streets around Ponte Gregoriano.

Tivoli

Tivoli, the Classical *Tibur*, is now a busy noisy town (population 52,000), surrounded by ugly high-rise buildings. In the centre of the town are the famous gardens of the **Villa d'Este**, and below the hill, protected by a beautiful park, are the magnificent ruins of **Hadrian's Villa**. Tivoli was built in a delightful position on the lower slopes (230m) of the Sabine Hills at the end of the valley of the Aniene, the Classical *Anio* which here narrows into a gorge and forms spectacular cascades. The river makes a wide loop round the town and borders it on three sides. It joins the Tiber north of Rome, near the Ponte Salario, and in Roman times its waters were carried to Rome by two aqueducts, the *Anio Vetus* (70km), begun in 273 BC, and the *Anio Novus* (95km) begun in AD 36.

History of Tivoli

Tibur is supposed to have been founded four centuries before the birth of Rome, by the Siculi, who were later expelled by Tiburtus and his brothers, grandsons of Amphiaraus. It was captured by Camillus in 380 BC. By the end of the 1C BC numerous wealthy Romans came to live or pass the summer here: the area was noted for its abundance of water and its cool climate. Temples were erected to Vesta, Hercules and other deities. Marius, Cassius, Sallust, Maecenas and Quintilius Varus all had sumptuous villas in the town or nearby. Augustus and the poets Catullus, Propertius and Horace frequently visited the town. Trajan also favoured Tibur, but it reached its greatest fame when Hadrian chose it as his residence and built his remarkable villa on the outskirts of the town. Tibur was sacred to the cult of the Sybil Albunea. Later it was used for the confinement of state prisoners.

In the 6C Totila, the Ostrogoth, sacked the town, but then rebuilt it as his capital. By the 10C it had recovered its prosperity, and withstood a siege by Otho III. It became independent as an Imperial free city, and was occupied by the Caraffa in the 16C. It did not lose its autonomous character until 1816. Among its natives were Munatius Plancus (consul 42 BC), the founder of Lyons, Pope Simplicius (468–83) and Pope John IX (898–900).

The road from Rome, Via Tiburtina, enters the town from the southwest and ends at Largo Garibaldi, a busy traffic hub. On the left is the **Giardino Garibaldi**, with a splendid view of the open country below: almost due west is Rome, and to the southwest the Roman Campagna extends to the sea.

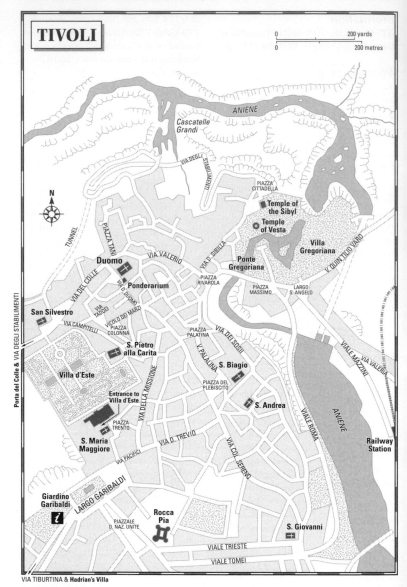

VIA TIBURTINA & **Hadrian's Villa**

Villa d'Este

At the end of the gardens on the left, numerous booths selling souvenirs precede the entrance a short distance away (in Piazza Trento) to the Villa d'Este, celebrated for its remarkable gardens decorated with spectacular fountains. These were created by Pirro Ligorio for Cardinal Ippolito II d'Este (1509–72), a rich Renaissance prince and collector and patron of the arts, who was a friend of

Ariosto, Tasso, Benvenuto Cellini, and the musician Pierluigi da Palestrina. The gardens and villa were restored in 2000 and the waters of the Aniene which feed the fountains were cleaned.

Opening times

Daily except Mon 08.30 to dusk; in March it closes at 17.00, and in April at 18.30; from May to Aug at 19.00, in Sept at 18.30 and in Oct at 17.30; winter at 16.00 or 16.30. ☎ 0774 312 070.

History of the villa

Originally a Benedictine convent, the property was confiscated as a residence for the governor of Tivoli. When Cardinal Ippolito II d'Este became governor in 1550 he commissioned Pirro Ligorio to transform the convent into a sumptuous villa. The district of the town below the convent was destroyed and the hillside was levelled to provide space for the gardens. An underground conduit was constructed from the Aniene, to increase the water supply. The use of water as the main theme of the gardens may have been inspired by Hadrian's Villa and the plan, based on a series of terraces, is similar to that of the Temple of Fortune at Palestrina. The work had not been completed by the time of the cardinal's death in 1572, and it was continued by his successor Cardinal Luigi d'Este who employed Flaminio Ponzio after 1585.

In the 17C numerous additions and restorations were carried out for Cardinal Alessandro d'Este, and (by Gian Lorenzo Bernini) for Cardinal Rinaldo d'Este. In the 19C the villa and gardens were neglected, and all the Roman statues were sold. It passed by bequest to Austria, but after 1918 the Italian Government resumed possession and undertook a general restoration. The top floor was the Italian home of Franz Liszt (1811–86) from 1865 to the year of his death; from this base he travelled to many parts of Europe and while here, he composed the third book of his *Années de Pèlerinage*, in which one of the most popular pieces is *Les Jeux d'Eau à la Villa d'Este*. A fine Roman mosaic pavement was found beneath the villa in 1983.

The **entrance** (formerly the back entrance) leads into a courtyard designed in 1567 on the site of the cloister of the convent. The Fountain of Venus here incorporates a Roman statue.

A staircase leads down through a room of the villa on the piano nobile (other rooms in the villa are visited after the gardens) and a door leads out to the terrace in front of the main façade of the villa overlooking the gardens, filled with the sound of water. In the centre there is an elegant **loggia** (1567) on two storeys, connected to the gardens by a double flight of steps. The gardens are laid out on terraces which descend from the villa and are connected by steps and paths. The original vegetation (which included many plane trees and elms) was altered when evergreen trees (ilexes, pines and cypresses) were introduced in the 17C, and sequoia and cedars were planted in the 19C. The terrace along the front of the palace is called the **Passeggiata del Cardinale** with a balcony on which is a pretty fountain basin. Beneath it is a grotto overgrown with ferns, and a series of fountains on lower levels.

A path leads straight from the terrace to the far left end of the gardens with the **Grotto of Diana** (at present closed), with Mannerist decorations (in stucco, mosaic, coloured glass, and shells) by Lola and Paolo Calandrino. From here the

Fontana di Roma, described below, can be seen. A ramp leads back down to the centre of the gardens and the **Fontana del Bicchierone**, added in 1661 by Gian Lorenzo Bernini beneath the terrace. From here we return on our steps to follow another path down to the elaborate **Fontana di Roma**, or Rometta, designed by Pirro Ligorio and executed by Curzio Maccarone. This has numerous fountains and sculptures including a model of the Tiber with an islet (representing the Isola Tiberina) in the form of a boat, on which is an obelisk, a seated statue of Rome, the wolf suckling Romulus and Remus, and miniature reproductions of the principal buildings of ancient Rome.

From here the **Viale delle Cento Fontane** leads right across the garden, parallel to the villa. It is skirted by a long narrow basin lined with hundreds of jets of water, surmounted by a frieze of obelisks, models of boats, Estense eagles, and lilies of France, overgrown with maidenhair fern and moss, and below, water-spouts in the form of animal heads. At the far end, against the perimeter wall of the gardens, in a courtyard shaded by four splendid old trees, is the grandiose **Fontana di Tivoli** or dell'Ovato, by Pirro Ligorio, with the end of the conduit from the Aniene, one of the water supplies for the fountains, which descends in an abundant cascade in the middle of a hemicycle which used to be decorated with statues of nymphs, by Giovanni Battista della Porta.

Beyond an archway a path between two marble columns leads to the monumental **Fontana dell'Organo**, built around a water-operated organ (1568) in the centre of the niche (later protected by a little temple). This was one of the most original and famous features of the garden. The mechanism of the organ was destroyed in the 18C; only the outer structure survives. The apse of the church of San Pietro alla Carità, just outside the gardens, is conspicuous here. The fountain overlooks the **Fontana di Nettuno**, with high jets of water, created in 1927 and the three *peschiere* or fish ponds which cross the gardens on the same axis.

From here we descend to another walk, the Viale del Drago, which runs parallel to the villa façade, in the middle of which is the **Fontana del Drago** by Pirro Ligorio. This was probably intended as a homage to Gregory XIII (it reproduces the dragons in his coat of arms), who was a guest at the villa in 1572. It has two monumental flights of steps which ascend above the fountain basin and a grotto to the Viale delle Cento Fontane, but we continue straight along the Viale, crossing the Scala dei Bollori an ingenious water staircase designed in 1567 (but at present dry) to the other side of the gardens where the bizarre **Fontana della Civetta**, once used water power to produce birdsong interrupted by the screech of an owl. It was begun in 1565 by Giovanni del Duca, and finished by Raffaello Sangallo in 1569. Next to it is the **Fontana di Proserpina** (1570) which was used as an outside dining room.

From here we descend to the three fishponds on the lowest level of the gardens. There is a splendid view of unspoilt countryside from this side of the gardens. The gardens here have box and laurel hedges enclosing more fountains, and in the centre of the perimetre wall, decorated with climbing roses, is the **Fontana della Madre Natura**, with a statue of *Diana of the Ephesians*. From here there is a vista back up across the gardens to the villa on the hillside.

Nearby is the **Rotonda dei Cipressi**, surrounded by some of the mightiest cypresses in Italy (three of them survive, albeit propped up, from the 17C). New trees have replaced some that were struck by disease and had to be felled. From here the central path leads straight through the gardens and back up steps to the villa.

The exit is through the **Appartamento Nobile** on the ground floor, a series of rooms off a long corridor, overlooking the gardens. The largest room is the **Salone with the Fontana di Tivoli**, a wall fountain in mosaic, begun by Curzio Maccarone and completed in 1568 by Paolo Calandrino. The frescoes are by the school of Girolamo Muziano and Federico Zuccari. On the walls are views of the garden painted by Matteo Neroni in 1568. The two rooms behind the fountain were decorated by Cesare Nebbia and assistants, and the rooms on the other side of the Salone have frescoes by Federico Zuccari and assistants. The **Sala della Caccia** has 17C frescoes. Stairs lead up to a series of rooms, part of the **Appartamento Vecchio**, with ceiling frescoes by Livio Agresti, and a balcony overlooking the gardens. The chapel was frescoed in 1572 by the workshop of Federico Zuccheri.

In the Piazza outside is the Romanesque church of **Santa Maria Maggiore**, with a fine rose-window attributed to Angelo da Tivoli above a later Gothic narthex (which contains a 13C fresco of the *Madonna and Child*, in a fine tabernacle). The **interior** contains remains of the original floor at the east end. In the presbytery are two triptychs, the one on the right dates from the 16C, and the one on the left is signed by Bartolomeo Bulgarini of Siena (14C). Above the latter is a *Madonna and Child* by Iacopo Torriti. Over the high altar is a Byzantine *Madonna* (12C?); in the right aisle there is a crucifix attributed to Baccio da Montelupo.

The old town

From Largo Garibaldi (see above) Via Pacifici and Via del Trevio lead towards Piazza del Plebiscito (see the plan), the town centre with a daily market. Here is the church of **San Biagio**, founded in the 14C. Rebuilt in 1887, the **interior** is a remarkable example of the neo Gothic style, with three impressive stained-glass windows (replaced in 1950 after their destruction in the last War). On the second south altar is a good 15C painting of San Vincenzo. Behind the altar is a 15C detached fresco of the *Crucifixion*. Off the north side are interesting fresco fragments of the *Madonna enthroned* and the *Glory of St Thomas*.

To the south, in Via Sant'Andrea, is the church of **Sant'Andrea**, with a Romanesque campanile.

From Piazza del Plebiscito, Via Palatina leads down to **Piazza Palatina** with the fine Palazzo Bonfiglietti, incorporating numerous Roman fragments, including six columns, low down on its façade. In the adjoining **Piazza dell'Erbe** is an old fountain and an ancient house which has part of a Roman statue supporting the masonry on the corner. Via Ponte Gregoriana, with a view of the hilly countryside outside the town, leads to Piazza Rivarola beside **Ponte Gregoriana** over the Aniene, with picturesque waterfalls and a fine view of the Temple of Vesta (see below). The area beyond the bridge, with the Villa Gregoriana (at present closed) is described on p 469.

This side of the bridge, the picturesque Via della Sibilla with interesting houses leads to a little secluded piazza beside a restaurant, already famous in the 19C, with an entrance (at present closed) to the so-called **Temple of Vesta** (covered for restoration), a circular Roman temple famous for its picturesque position above the Aniene valley, frequently drawn and painted by travellers in the 18C and 19C. It is not known to whom the temple was actually dedicated; it is circular peripteral and dates from the last years of the Republic. It was converted in the Middle Ages into the church of Santa Maria della Rotonda. Ten of its 18 fluted Corinthian columns survive, and there is a frieze of bucrania, garlands, rosettes and paterae. The doors and windows of the well-preserved cella are trapezoidal.

Close by is an earlier temple, known as the **Temple of the Sibyl**, also of uncertain attribution. It is rectangular with a tetrastyle Ionic façade. Until 1884 it was the church of San Giorgio. The road ends in Piazza della Cittadella, the site of the Roman acropolis, and to the left a lane leads out to the edge of the cliff which dominates the valley. Here begins **Via degli Stabilimenti**, a road which was restored with *sanpietrini* paving in 2002 and which encircles the town past old paper mills and re-enters it close to San Silvestro (see below).

From Piazza Rivarola (see above) Via San Valerio leads downhill to Piazza Tani, with a huge sarcophagus serving as a wall fountain, and a side entrance to the **Duomo** (San Lorenzo), rebuilt in 1650 but retaining a Romanesque campanile of the 12C. In the **interior**, the fourth chapel in the south aisle (light on right), contains a 13C group of five carved wooden figures representing the *Descent from the Cross* (temporarily removed because of problems of humidity). The third chapel in the north aisle has a superb silver and gilt *Macchina del Salvatore*, made in the mid 15C by silversmiths from Lucca to enclose a precious 11C or 12C triptych, painted in tempera. The triptych is exhibited only on high religious festivals on the adjoining altar. Also in this aisle are two episcopal tombs (late 15C and early 16C).

From the little Piazza Duomo, the medieval **Via del Duomo** (partly stepped) leads past (no. 78) the entrance to the **Ponderarium** (being restored), the office which controlled weights and measures, containing two tables with measures of capacity, used by the Roman inspectors. At the top, take Vicoli dei Marzi downhill right to Piazza Colonna, where steps (Via Cordonato) lead down to Via della Missione, across which more steps (Via Taddei) continue under an arch with a column fragment above it, to **Via Campitelli**, also stepped, which traverses one of the most pictureque parts of the town with some very old houses close to the garden wall of Villa d'Este.

We emerge on Via del Colle beside a house with Roman columns. Outside the Romanesque church of **San Silvestro** there is a picturesque fountain, overgrown with ferns. Inside are interesting 12C or 13C frescoes in the apse. Via del Colle continues down hill past a locked garden gate of Villa d'Este to the abandoned church of San Nicola opposite an ancient group of houses (and the Porta del Colle over the road can be seen a short way further on downhill). Here Via degli Stabilimenti re-enters the town (see above). A short way along it on the left is the entrance to the site of the **Sanctuary of Hercules Victor**, in a large area until recently occupied by a paper mill. It is being excavated and studied and there are long-term plans to open it to the public (for information, ☎ 0774 330 329). This huge Hellenistic sanctuary was mentioned by numerous Classical authors as being the most important in the city. There was an oracle here similar to the one in Palestrina. The buildings are thought to date from the end of the 2C BC. The most conspicuous remains are the Cyclopean substructures to the northwest where the hill descends to the Aniene valley. Above the mighty foundations are arches and vaults which supported a huge piazzale, with a portico on three sides, a temple, and a theatre. A market was connected to the sanctuary.

The quicket way back to the Largo Garibaldi is by the stepped Via Campitelli (see above) and Via della Missione, which passes the church of **San Pietro alla Carità**, which contains ten cipollino columns, probably from a Roman villa, and an interesting crypt.

Villa Gregoriana

On the far side of Ponte Gregoriana (see above) beyond the large Piazza Massimo with the bus station, is the entrance (at present closed) to the Villa Gregoriana, a park on a very steep hillside with the cascades of the river Aniene and which extends all the way down to the floor of the valley. There are long-term plans to restore the villa which may be purchased by the *FAI*.

The park commemorates Gregory XVI, who took decisive steps to put an end to the periodic local floods, which in 1826 had seriously damaged the town. On his accession to the papacy in 1831, he instructed the engineer Folchi to build a double tunnel under Monte Catillo, to ease the flow of the river. From this tunnel (300m and 270m), known as the Traforo Gregoriano, which bears inscriptions recording the visits of popes and kings, the water plunges down in another waterfall, known as the Great Cascade. In other parts of the park there are also remains of a Roman villa, the fantastic **Grotto of the Siren**, a limestone cavern in which the water tumbles down a narrow ravine and the **Grotto of Neptune**, through which the Aniene originally flowed.

From Piazza Massimo Viale Mazzini leads south to the station. Here, in a park, the ancient Roman tomb of a Vestal Virgin called Cossinia has been set up.

Beside Villa Gregoriana, Via Quintilio Varo leads to **Via della Cascatelle** (3km long) which winds above olive plantations, and passes several times beneath the viaducts of the Rome–Tivoli railway. From the belvedere there is a fine view of the Great Cascade, and, after crossing beneath the railway for the last time, there is an excellent view of the Great Cascade, the Cascatelle, the town of Tivoli, and the Campagna. The road passes the church of Sant'Antonio (left) and the ruined arches of the **Acqua Marcia**. This aqueduct, 58km long and dating from 144 BC, ran from Via Valeria to Rome. Five hundred metres further on, a byroad (left; unsignposted) diverges from the main road and leads down past a group of houses to the conspicuous **Santuario di Santa Maria di Quintiliolo**, near the ruins of a Roman villa, said to have been that of Quintilius Varus who married Augustus' grand-niece. He was legate of the Rhine army in 9 BC and committed suicide after a crushing defeat.

The road soon deteriorates and becomes less interesting. Further on it crosses the Ponte dell'Acquoria over the Aniene, and, going straight on, begins to climb the Clivus Tiburtinus, partly levelled by Constantine. On the right, is the so-called **Tempio del Mondo**, with a large interior chamber and further on, also on the right, is a Roman building known as the Tempio della Tosse. Probably dating from the 4C, this is an octagonal building with a circular exterior. Traces of Byzantine decoration suggest it may have been adapted for Christian worship. The road passes round the ruins of the Temple of Hercules Victor (see above), and re-enters Tivoli by Porta del Colle.

From Largo Garibaldi there is a good view of the imposing **Rocca Pia** which has been closed to the public for many years, a castle built by Pius II (1458–64) to dominate the inhabitants of Tivoli. It is rectangular in shape and has four crenellated cylindrical towers, two large and two smaller. The castle was built over the ruins of a Roman amphitheatre, best seen from Vicolo Barchetto to the north.

Hadrian's Villa

About 5km below the town of Tivoli, beyond a beautiful olive grove on the hill-side, and reached off the Via Tiburtina, the main road to Rome, is Hadrian's Villa, the largest and richest Imperial villa in the Roman Empire. Hadrian became emperor on the death of Trajan in 117, and began the villa the following year, completing it ten years later. It is known that Hadrian prided himself on his abilities as an architect, and it is therefore presumed that the remarkably original buildings, many of them inspired by famous buildings in Greece and Egypt, were directly designed by him. They were spaciously laid out between numerous gardens. It seems to have been used as a residence for the emperor and his court, particularly in the summer months. Of all the splendid buildings left which were erected by Hadrian throughout the empire this is probably the most interesting. It is now one of the most evocative classical sites to survive in Italy, protected by a beautiful park.

Getting there

The villa is not very easy to reach by **public transport** and it is mostly visited by coach tours.The road for the Villa leaves the Via Tiburtina (the main road from Rome to Tivoli) at the Bivio Villa Adriana, 28km from Rome, and 4km from Tivoli. From the turn an ugly byroad (1.5km) continues to the entrance. For transport from Rome and from Tivoli, see p 462.

Opening times

Daily except 25 Dec, 1 Jan, and 1 March from 09.00 to dusk; in winter it closes at 16.00; in Feb at 17.00; in March at 17.30; in April at 18.00; from May–Aug at 18.30; in Sept at 17.30, and in Oct at 17.00.

The villa is a splendid place to picnic, and at present there is no café open here.

History of Hadrian's Villa

It is difficult to understand why Hadrian, with all the resources of the Empire at his disposal, should have chosen such an unprepossessing site for his magnificent estate. Though little over 5km from the scenic Roman health resort of Tivoli, the low-lying surroundings of the villa have no particular attraction. In the emperor's day the flat plain was not even healthy. One reason for the choice of this site is probably the fact that its owner was the Empress Sabina; another reason may have been the emperor's desire to keep himself apart from his courtiers, many of whom owned villas on the hills around Tivoli. Parts of a smaller country house of the 1C BC, overlooking the Vale of Tempe, were incorporated into the emperor's villa.

Many of the buildings of the villa are derived from famous Classical monuments, some of which Hadrian saw during his prolonged travels in the empire. These were the Lyceum, the Academy, the Prytaneum and the Stoa Poikile in Athens; the Canopus of the Egyptian Delta; and the Vale of Tempe in Thessaly. He also included a representation of Hades, as conceived by the Greek poets. An extensive system of underground passages (only some of which are now open), some mere corridors and others wide enough for a horse and carriage, exist beneath the villa; these were presumably service areas. Hadrian's successors enlarged the villa, but Constantine is supposed to have stolen some elements to decorate Byzantium. Barbarian invaders plundered the site, and it later became a quarry for builders and lime-burners. Until the Renaissance the ruins continued to be neglected or abused.

The first excavations were ordered by Alexander VI and Cardinal Alessandro Farnese. Soon after he took up residence at the Villa d'Este in 1550, Cardinal Ippolito II d'Este employed Pirro Ligorio to continue excavations, but he took many of the finds to decorate his villa. Further excavations were carried out in the 17C–19C. Giovanni Battista Piranesi drew a plan of the site, and made engravings of the buildings and sculptures (now in the Calcografia Nazionale in Rome). In 1730 Count Fede planted cypresses and pines among the ruins. In 1870 the Italian Government acquired most of the site, and systematic excavations were begun (still far from complete). The works of art discovered in the villa (more than 260) are scattered in museums all over Europe, as well as in Rome (the Museo Nazionale Romano, the Capitoline Museum, and the Vatican Museums).

The general plan of the villa, which covers some 120 hectares, is capricious, although the buildings are grouped round four principal structures: the Poikile, the Canopus, the Academy, and the Imperial Palace. Excavations and restorations are in progress on the hillside overlooking the Canopus. Recent studies and excavations suggest that the traditional interpretation of many of the buildings is probably wrong (see the description below), and some of them were used for different purposes than those formerly ascribed to them. Numerous areas between the buildings were reserved for gardens and open courtyards. All the ruins are labelled with explanatory diagrams (also in English). It is not easy to understand the connection between all the buildings since the order of the visit does not begin at the main entrance to the villa (only recently identified). A whole day is needed for a detailed visit to the vast site.

From the **ticket entrance** (with the car park), a short drive leads on to a building which houses a model of the villa. On the far right (not well signposted, and at present closed) an 18C villa is used as a museum with an excellent didactic display on three floors, providing a useful introduction to the ruins. On the ground floor are models of various parts of the villa. The first floor illustrates its architecture, with fragments of friezes, capitals, and a Roman marble model of a stadium. The building techniques are illustrated, and the various brick stamps shown. The finds from the villa now in museums are recorded by photographs. On the second floor are engravings of the site (including copies of Piranesi's works) and examples of the various marbles used in the buildings. Fragments of floors, mosaics and painted plaster are displayed.

The **entrance to the ruins** is through the massive north wall of the **Pecile**, or portico which seems to have been inspired by the Stoa Poikile (painted porch) in Athens, famous for its paintings by Polygnotos and Panainos, and for its association with the Stoic philosophers. Hadrian's version is a rectangular peristyle (232m x 97m) with the ends slightly curved, similar to a Greek gymnasium. The huge north wall (9m high), running almost due east and west, still exists. On the south side the wall is no longer standing, but there are remains of a pavilion with three exedrae and a fountain. This was probably a monumental atrium. On both sides of the Pecile ran roofed colonnades; here the sun or shade could be enjoyed at any hour of the day, and either warmth or coolness, depending on the season. In the middle of the rectangle the fish pond has been restored. The free area round it was probably used for exercise. On the southwest the Pecile had as a substructure a huge sustaining wall with three rows of small chambers, now called the **Cento Camerelle**,

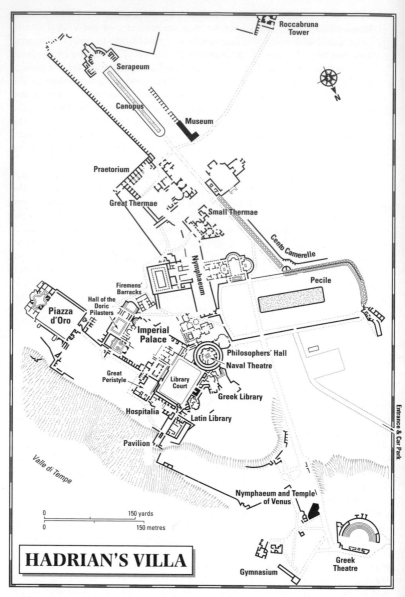

HADRIAN'S VILLA

or the 'hundred small rooms' which are thought to have been used as accommodation for the Praetorians. Excavations are at present in progress here.

At the northeast angle of the Pecile, a few steps lead up to the so-called **Philosophers' Hall** (17m x 9m), with an apse, seven niches and four side-doors. This is now thought to have been a large throne room, or auditorium, where the emperor held audiences, and met in council with court dignitaries. It was probably part of the complex which includes the Pecile and the so-called *Terme con Eliocamino*. Beyond is a charming circular building, with an Ionic marble peristyle, known as the **Naval Theatre**, almost certainly a private retreat for the emperor, where he could be totally isolated. Unfortunately it is now only possible to see it from outside. A circular moat (3.5m broad), lined with Luni (Carrara) marble, encloses an island on which stand an atrium with fluted Ionic columns in an intricate design, and a series of living-rooms, and baths. It could be reached only by two small wooden (removable) bridges.

On the east side, stairs lead up to the first nucleus of buildings belonging to the **Imperial Palace**, which is disposed parallel to the Vale of Tempe (see below); its elements are grouped round four peristyles. The so-called *Cortile delle Biblioteche* is now a secluded olive plantation. The '**Greek and Latin Libraries**' on the northwest side have been identified by some scholars as the monumental entrance to the villa, with towers, on three floors. The third floor had a heating system and may have been used by the emperor before the villa had been completed. Behind, excavations have revealed part of a delightful walled garden with a long fountain basin.

To the north of the *Cortile delle Biblioteche* is the **Hospitalia**, a residential wing used by the high-ranking staff of the villa who were particularly close to the emperor. Here are ten well-preserved small rooms leading off either side of a wide corridor. Rectangular alcoves indicate space for the beds (three in each room). Lighting was provided by the high openings. The rooms are decorated with well-preserved mosaics. Steps lead down to a triclinium, a dining room with (left) some capitals with a lotus motif, and a mosaic floor. To the right is a long corridor with oblique openings in the vault, to allow the light of midday to enter. This leads to a pavilion which overlooks a valley with a stream which is thought to have been landscaped by Hadrian to recreate the Vale of Tempe in Thessaly, famed for its beauty. The stream, now called the Pussiano, represented the ancient Peneios.

From here steps lead up to a path (south) which leads to the **Great Peristyle** of the palace, with a private library and other small rooms overlooking the **Library Court**. Here also is a well proportioned room with two rows of small columns. Nearby, stairs lead underground to a cryptoporticus, with well-lit corridors. At the other end of this nucleus of the palace is the **Hall of the Doric Pilasters**, with a fine entablature, which connected the east and west parts of the villa. The so called **Firemen's Barracks**, beyond the apse of the basilican hall (right), was more probably a storehouse near the kitchens. Beyond it is a quadriporticus, with a pool and a portico of fluted Composite columns. This is now considered to be at the centre of the most important part of the Imperial palace and the residence of Hadrian. The upper floors were supplied with heating systems. Beneath it is a well-preserved extensive cryptoporticus. Beyond it, on a lower level, is the large nymphaeum, described below.

On the left is another **nymphaeum**, which had two round fountain basins, and from here a path leads to the **Piazza d'Oro**, a rectangular area at the southeast end of the palace. It was so named because excavations here yielded such rich finds. It is entered through the fine octagonal vestibule. The peristyle was formed of alternate columns of cipollino and granite in two rows. On the far side (southeast) is an intricate series of exedrae and nymphaea; the central one seems to have been a summer triclinium. This was an open courtyard with a remarkable Greek-cross plan, with alternate convex and concave sides. The plan of the portico recalls Greek gymnasiums. It was formerly thought that this was used for banquets, but a recent interpretation is that it was in fact a stoa with libraries, similar to that which Hadrian had built in Athens in this period.

A path continues west past the back of the Caserma dei Vigili and of the main nucleus of the palace, and descends to a clump of mighty cypresses and the **Small Thermae** and the **Great Thermae**. The small baths are well preserved (they are visited from a wooden walkway) with a large rectangular hall, perhaps the frigidarium, and an octagonal hall with a domed vault. They were particularly elegant and refined and may have been reserved for the use of the emperor alone. The large baths, on a simpler design, were probably used by court dignitaries and visitors. They include a circular hall, with cupola and skylight. The huge hall with an apse and a superb cross-vault, now mostly collapsed. Opposite is another cross-vaulted room decorated with exquisite stucco reliefs. On the east is a swimming-pool, bounded on the northwest by a cryptoporticus with, on its ruined walls, numerous graffiti of the 16C and 17C. This gives access to the so-called **Praetorium**, a tall edifice which was divided into three storeys by wooden floors. It may have been used as a warehouse, or as a service wing.

Beyond a row of six huge ilexes is the celebrated **Canopus**, designed to imitate the famous sanctuary of Serapis which stood at the 15th milestone from Alexandria. Hadrian dug a hollow (185m by 75m), in which he constructed a basin, bordered on the east by a block of 20 rooms and a portico, and on the west by a heavy buttressed wall (238m long), against which were more rooms (some of them now used for the museum; see below). Around the curved north end of the canal, reproductions of statues found on the site have been set up between marble columns surmounted by an epistyle arched over alternate pillars. Along the west side are reproductions of colossal caryatids and telamones (the originals were found in the basin in the 1950s). At the south end is the so-called **Serapeum**, a monumental triclinium, in the form of a temple of Isis, with a half-dome formerly covered with mosaics, above a semicircular banqueting table (reconstructed) from which the diners had a scenic view of the canopus. Some scholars think this may have been intended as a symbolic representation of the Nile: a series of fountains represent its source (in the niche behind), the cataracts, and its delta (in the piscina in front). The basin would then have represented the Mediterranean, with Athens to the west (represented by the caryatids), and Ephesus to the east (represented by statues of Amazons). The canopus may have been built by Hadrian in honour of his lover Antinoos, who was represented as an Egyptian divinity in numerous statues found here. Most of the Egyptian sculptures now in the Capitoline and Vatican museums come from here (those in the Museo Gregoriano Egiziano have recently been rearranged, according to the above interpretation).

There is a fine view of most of the villa from the hill behind. On the northwest side of the hollow is the **museum** (at present closed) housing finds from excavations since 1950. The statues include: a bust of *Caracalla*; *Venus*, copy of a work by Praxiteles; *Wounded Amazons*, one a mutilated copy of a Polykleitan original, the other a fine replica of the famous original by Pheidias; portrait of *Verres*; *Athena* and *Mars*, both from mid-5C originals; two *Athletes*; a *Crocodile*; tondo with the bas-relief of a *Satyr*; four marble *Caryatids*, copies of the 5C originals on the Erechtheion at Athens; and two sileni.

A path leads from here west to the **Roccabruna Tower**, a belvedere which has square outer walls and is circular inside. This is possibly an imitation of the Tower of Timon of Athens, which stood near the Academy. It stands in an olive grove, famous for the size of its olive trees, one of them (the *Albero Bello*) claimed to be the largest in the Tivoli district.

To the southeast, in another olive grove, is the so-called **Accademia**, a complex of buildings which some scholars identify as a secondary palace. The group includes a round hall, known as the **Temple of Apollo**, a peristyle, and the remains of three rooms with delicate stucco ornamentation. About 300m southeast are the remains of an **Odeion**, or theatre (45m in diameter), with the imperial box in the centre of the cavea. To the east of the odeion a path descends to a hollow (150m long), hewn in the tufa and overshadowed by thick vegetation, which leads to a semicircular vestibule (once perhaps guarded by an image of Cerberus). This was the entrance to Hades or the Inferi, represented by a quadrangle of four subterranean corridors, 5.5m wide and 91m in total length, with 79 apertures for light. Smaller tunnels connected Hades with various parts of the villa.

A broad main path returns towards the entrance. To the right, just before the Poikile, is the large **Nymphaeum**, formerly called the *Stadio* from its elongated form. It was a decorative garden surrounded by porticoes, and a building with three exedrae. Between it and the **Maritime Theatre** are remains of the first baths constructed in the villa, formerly known as the **Heliocaminus Baths**, which had a large circular room with a heating system used for steam baths. On the other side of the nymphaeum, reached by steps which lead up past a well-preserved cryptoporticus, is the main part of the imperial palace (see above). A path leads back across the Pecile to the entrance.

From here a fine avenue of cypresses leads north to the Greek Theatre, passing the Casino Fede (now the excavation office), built on part of the ruins of the so-called nymphaeum, a semicircular portico. This frames a small **Temple of Venus**, a goddess particularly venerated by Hadrian. The temple was modelled on the Temple at Cnidos; a statue of *Aphrodite of Cnidos* discovered here, a copy of the famous statue by Praxiteles, has been replaced by a cast (original in the museum, see above). Beyond, to the right, a walk leads to the modernised **Fontana di Palazzo**, near which are a few traces of the Gymnasium. Beyond this extends the Vale of Tempe (see above). Descending (left) through olives and cypresses, the path passes the Greek Theatre, c 36m in diameter; its cavea, or auditorium, is carved out of the hillside.

A few kilometres west of Hadrian's Villa, on Via Tiburtina, is **Bagni di Tivoli**, a spa (hotels of all categories) which uses the water from two nearby lakes. These are fed by hot springs (24°C), the Roman *Aquae Albulae*, charged with sulphuretted hydrogen which gives a strong smell to the locality. There are remains of the Roman baths. Nearby are travertine quarries which provided stone for the Colosseum, St Peter's, and many other buildings in ancient and modern Rome. The stone is the lapis tiburtinus, which hardens after cutting. The five-arched **Ponte Lucano**, a Roman bridge over the Aniene, was named after Lucanus Plautius and rebuilt at various times from the 15C to the 19C. Next to the bridge is the tower like **Tomb of the Plautii**, dating from AD 10–14, and resembling the Tomb of Cecilia Metella on the Via Appia. Aulus Plautius commanded the army which invaded Britain in AD 43.

Popes

Various points in early papal history are still uncertain: the evidence for Dioscuros as legitimate pope is perhaps stronger than the evidence for Boniface II (No. 55); Leo VIII (No. 132) is an antipope if the deposition of John XII (No. 131) was illegal, and if Leo VIII was a legitimate pope, Benedict V (No. 133) is an antipope; and if the triple deposition of Benedict IX (No. 146) was illegal, Sylvester III, Gregory VI and Clement II (Nos. 147, 149, 150) must rank as antipopes. Among the popes named John there was never a John XX. The title 'pope' was first assumed by John VIII (d. 882); the triple tiara first appears on the sepulchral effigy of Benedict XII (d. 1342). Adrian IV (d. 1159) was the only English pope, Gregory XI (d. 1378) the last French pope and Adrian VI (d. 1523) the last non-Italian pope before John Paul II. Anacletus II (d. 1138) was a converted Jew. 'Pope Joan' is placed between John V (d. 686) and Conon.

The names of antipopes and of illegal occupants of the papal chair and particulars as to papal tombs imperfectly identified or no longer in existence are enclosed in square brackets [ ]. Conjectural dates are followed by a query (?). The title of each pope is given, together with the date of his consecration (for the early popes) or of his election (from Gelasius II onward; No. 162), the date of his death, the duration of his pontificate, and, as far as possible, his birthplace and family name. Martyred popes are indicated by the letter M. The letter B stands for 'Blessed' or beatified by the Church.

St Peter's remains are preserved beneath the confessio in St Peter's and the thirteen following popes are believed to have been interred close by.

1. **St Peter**; M.; 42–67
2. **St Linus**, of Tuscia (Volterra?); M.; 67–78
3. **St Anacletus I**, of Rome; M.; 78–90 (?)
4. **St Clement I**, of the Roman Flavian gens; M.; 90–99 (?)
5. **St Evaristus**, of Greece (or of Bethlehem); M.; 99–105 (?)
6. **St Alexander I**, of Rome; M.; 105–115 (?)
7. **St Sixtus I**, of Rome; M.; 115–125 (?)
8. **St Telesphorus**, of Greece; M.; 125–136 (?)
9. **St Iginus**, of Greece; M.; 136–140 (?)
10. **St Pius I**, of Italy; M.; 140–155 (?)
11. **St Anicetus**, of Syria; M.; 155–166 (?)
12. **St Soter**, of Campania (Fundi?); M.; 166–175 (?)
13. **St Eleutherus**, of Epirus (Nicopolis?); M.; 175–189
14. **St Victor I**, of Africa; M.; 189–199
15. **St Zephyrinus**, of Rome; M.; 199–217
16. **St Calixtus**, of Rome; M.; 217–222 [**Hippolytus**, 217–235]
17. **St Urban I**, of Rome; M.; 222–230

18. **St Pontianus**, of Rome; M.; 21 July 230–28 Sept 235
19. **St Anterus**, of Greece; M.; 21 Nov 235–3 Jan 236
20. **St Fabian**, of Rome; M.; 10 Jan 236–20 Jan 250
21. **St Cornelius**, of Rome; M.; March 251–June 253 [Novatian, 251–258]
22. **St Lucius I**, of Rome; M.; 25 June 253–5 March 254
23. **St Stephen I**, of Rome; M.; 12 May 254–2 Aug 257
24. **St Sixtus II**, of Greece (?); M.; 30 Aug 257–6 Aug 258
25. **St Dionysius**, of Magna Graecia (?); M.; 22 July 259–26 Dec 268
26. **St Felix I**, of Rome; M.; 5 Jan 269–30 Dec 274
27. **St Eutychianus**, of Luni; M.; 4 Jan 275–7 Dec 283
28. **St Gaius**, of Dalmatia (Salona?); M.; 17 Dec 283–22 April 296
29. **St Marcellinus**, of Rome; M.; 30 June 296–25 Oct 304
30. **St Marcellus I**, of Rome; M.; 27 May 308–16 Jan 309

31. **St Eusebius**, of Greece; M.; 18 April 309–17 Aug 309 or 310
32. **St Melchiades or Miltiades**, of Africa; M.; 2 July 311–11 Jan 314
33. **St Sylvester I**, of Rome; 31 Jan 314–31 Dec 335
34. **St Mark**, of Rome; 18 Jan 336–7 Oct 336
35. **St Julius I**, of Rome; 6 Feb 337–12 April 352
36. **Liberius**, of Rome; 17 May 352–22 Sept 366
   [**St Felix II**, 355–22 Nov 365]
37. **St Damasus I**, of Spain; 1 Oct 366–11 Dec 384
   [**Ursinus**, 366–367]
38. **St Siricius**, of Rome; 15 Dec 384–26 Nov 399
39. **St Anastasius I**, of Rome; 27 Nov 399–19 Dec 401
40. **St Innocent I**, of Albano, 22 Dec 401–12 March 417
41. **St Zosimus**, of Greece; 18 March 417–26 Dec 418
42. **St Boniface I**, of Rome; 29 Dec 418–4 Sept 422
   [**Eulalius**, 27 Dec 418–3 April 419]
43. **St Caelestinus I**, of Campania; 10 Sept 422–27 July 432
44. **St Sixtus III**, of Rome; 3 July (?) 432–19 Aug 440
45. **St Leo I the Great**, of Tusculum; 29 Sept 440–10 Nov 461
46. **St Hilarius**, of Sardinia; 19 Nov 461–29 Feb 468
47. **St Simplicius**, of Tivoli; 3 March 468–10 March 483
48. **St Felix III** (II), of Rome, of the gens Anicia; 13 March 483–1 March 492
49. **St Gelasius I**, of Africa; 1 March 492–21 Nov 496
50. **St Anastasius II**, of Rome; 24 Nov 496–19 Nov 498
51. **St Symmachus**, of Sardinia; 22 Nov 498–19 July 514
   [**Laurentius**, Nov 498–505]
52. **St Hormisdas**, of Frosinone; 20 July 514–6 Aug 523
53. **St John I**, of Tusculum; M.; 13 Aug 523–18 May 526. Died at Ravenna
54. **St Felix IV (III)**, of Samnium (Benevento?); 12 July 526–22 Sept 530
55. **Boniface II**, of Rome; 22 Sept 530–7 Oct 532

   [**Dioscurus**, 22 Sept 530–14 Oct 530]
56. **John II**, of Rome; 2 Jan 533–8 May 535
57. **St Agapitus I**, of Rome; 13 May 535–22 April 536. Died at Constantinople
58. **St Silverius**, of Frosinone; M.; 8 June 536–deposed 11 March 537. Died in exile on the island of Ponza 538 (?)
59. **Vigilius**, of Rome; June 538 (?)–7 June 555 (but elected 29 March 537). Died at Syracuse
60. **Pelagius I**, of Rome; 16 April 556–4 March 561
61. **John III**, of Rome; 17 July 561–13 July 574
62. **Benedict I**, of Rome; 2 June 575–30 July 579
63. **Pelagius II**, of Rome; 26 Nov 579–7 Feb 590
64. **St Gregory I the Great**, of Rome, of the gens Anicia; 3 Sept 590–13 March 604
65. **Sabinianus**, of Tusculum; 13 Sept 604–22 Feb 606
66. **Boniface III**, of Rome; 19 Feb 607–12 Nov 607
67. **St Boniface IV**, of Valeria de' Marsi; 25 Aug 608–8 May 615
68. **St Deusdedit I**, of Rome; 19 Oct 615–8 Nov 618
69. **Boniface V**, of Naples; 23 Dec 619–25 Oct 625
70. **Honorius I**, of Campania; 27 Oct 625–12 Oct 638
71. **Severinus**, of Rome; 28 May 640–2 Aug 640
72. **John IV**, of Dalmatia; 24 Dec 640–12 Oct 642
73. **Theodore I**, of Jerusalem (? or Greece); 24 Nov 642–14 May 649
74. **St Martin I**, of Todi; M.; 21 July 649–exiled 18 June 653–16 Sept 655. Died at Sebastopol
75. **St Eugenius I**, of Rome; 16 Sept 655–2 June 657
76. **St Vitalian**, of Segni; 30 July 657–27 Jan 672
77. **Deusdedit II**, of Rome; 11 April 672–17 June 676
78. **Donus**, of Rome; 2 Nov 676–11 April 678
79. **St Agatho**, of Sicily; 27 June

678–10 Jan 681

80. **St Leo II**, of Sicily; 17 Aug 682–3 July 683

81. **St Benedict II**, of Rome; 26 June 684–8 May 685

82. **John V**, of Antioch; 23 July 685–2 Aug 686

83. **Conon**, of Thrace; 21 Oct 686–21 Sept 687
[**Theodore**, 22 Sept 687–Oct 687]
[**Paschal**, 687]

84. **St Sergius I**, of Palermo; 15 Dec 687–8 Sept 701

85. **John VI**, of Greece; 30 Oct 701–11 Jan 705

86. **John VII**, of Greece; 1 March 705–18 Oct 707

87. **Sisinnius**, of Syria; 15 Jan 708–4 Feb 708

88. **Constantine**, of Syria; 25 March 708–9 April 715

89. **St Gregory II**, of Rome; 19 May 715–11 Feb 731

90. **St Gregory III**, of Syria; 18 March 731–10 Dec 741

91. **St Zacharias**, of Greece; 10 Dec 741–22 March 752

92. **Stephen II**, of Rome; 23 March 752–25 March 752

93. **St Stephen III**, of Rome; 26 March 752–26 April 757

94. **St Paul I**, of Rome; 29 May 757–28 June 767
[**Constantine II**, 5 July 767–murdered 769]
[**Philip**, elected 31 July 768–abdicated 768]

95. **Stephen IV**, of Sicily; 7 Aug 768–3 Feb 772

96. **Hadrian I**, of Rome; 9 Feb 772–26 Dec 795

97. **St Leo III**, of Rome; 27 Dec 795–12 June 816

98. **St Stephen V**, of Rome; 22 June 816–14 Jan 817

99. **St Paschal I**, of Rome; 25 Jan 817–11 Feb 824

100. **Eugenius II**, of Rome; 21 Feb 824–27 Aug 827

101. **Valentine**, of Rome; Aug (?) 827–Sept (?) 827

102. **Gregory IV**, of Rome; Oct 827–25 Jan 844

103. **Sergius II**, of Rome; Jan 844–27 Jan 847

[**John**, 844]

104. **St Leo IV**, of Rome; 10 April 847–17 July 855

105. **St Benedict III**, of Rome; 6 Oct 855–17 April 858
[**Anastasius**, 29 Sept 855–20 Oct 855]

106. **St Nicholas I the Great**, of Rome; 24 April 858–13 Nov 867

107. **Hadrian II**, of Rome; 14 Dec 867–14 Dec 872

108. **John VIII**, of Rome, 14 Dec 872–16 Dec 882

109. **Marinus I** (Martin II) of Gallesium; 16 Dec 882–15 May 884

110. **St Hadrian III**, of Rome; 17 May 884–17 Sept 885

111. **Stephen VI**, of Rome; Sept 885–Sept 891

112. **Formosus**, bishop of Porto; 6 Oct 891–4 April 896

113. **Boniface VI**, of Gallesium; April 896

114. **Stephen VII**, of Rome; May 896–Aug 897. Strangled in prison

115. **Romanus**, of Gallesium; Aug 897–end of Nov 897

116. **Theodore II**, of Rome; Dec 897

117. **John IX**, of Tivoli; Jan 898–Jan 900

118. **Benedict IV**, of Rome; Jan 900–end July 903

119. **Leo V**, of Ardea; end of July 903–Sept 903. Deposed and imprisoned
[**Christopher**, of Rome; 903, deposed in Jan 904]

120. **Sergius III**, of Rome; 29 Jan 904–14 April 911

121. **Anastasius III**, of Rome; April 911–June 913

122. **Lando**, of Sabina; end of July 913–Feb 914

123. **John X**, of Ravenna; March 914–May 928. Strangled in prison

124. **Leo VI**, of Rome; May 928–Dec 928

125. **Stephen VIII**, of Rome; Jan 929–Feb 931

126. **John XI**, of Rome; son of Pope Sergius III and Marozia; March 931–Dec 935. Died in prison

127. **Leo VII**; 3 (?) Jan 936–13 (?) July 939

128. **Stephen IX**, of Germany (?); 14 (?) July 939–end of Oct 942

129. **Marinus II** (Martin III), of Rome; 30 (?) Oct 942–May 946

130. **Agapitus II**, of Rome; 10 May

946–Dec 955

131. **John XII**, Ottaviano, of the family of the Counts of Tusculum, aged 19; 16 (?) Dec 955–deposed 14th May 964

132. **Leo VIII**, of Rome, 4 Nov 963–1 March 965

133. **Benedict V**, Grammatico, of Rome; 22 (?) May 964–expelled from the pontifical see 23 June 964; died at Bremen 4 July 966

134. **John XIII**, of Rome; 1 Oct 965–5 Sept 972

135. **Benedict VI**, of Rome; 19 Jan 973–June 974. Strangled in prison [**Boniface VII**, Francone, of Rome; June–July 974 for the first time]

136. **Benedict VII**, of the family of the Counts of Tusculum, of Rome; Oct 974–10 July 983

137. **John XIV**, of Pavia; Dec 983–20 Aug 984; killed by Francone (Boniface VII) [**Boniface VII**, Francone; for the second time, Aug 984–murdered July 985]

138. **John XV**, of Rome; Aug 985 March 996

139. **Gregory V**, Bruno, of the family of the Counts of Carinthia; 3 May 996–18 Feb 999 [**John XVI**, John Philagathus, of Greece; March 997–Feb 998]

140. **Sylvester II**, Gerbert of Aurillc, Auvergne; 2 April 999–12 May 1003

141. **John XVII**, Sicco, of Rome; June (?) 1003–6 Nov 1003

142. **John XVIII**, of Rapagnano; Jan (?) 1004–July (?) 1009

143. **Sergius IV**, of Rome; 31 July 1009–12 May 1012

144. **Benedict VIII**, John, of the family of the Counts of Tusculum, of Rome; 18 May 1012–9 April 1024 [**Gregory**, 1012]

145. **John XIX**, of Rome, brother of Benedict VIII; April 1024–1032

146. **Benedict IX**, Theophylact, of the family of the Counts of Tusculum; elected (aged 15) for the first time in 1032–deposed in Dec 1044; elected for the second time 10 March 1045–deposed 1 May 1045; elected for the third time 8 Nov 1047–deposed 17 July 1048

147. **Sylvester III**, John, bishop of Sabina; 20 Jan 1045–deposed 10 March 1045

148. **Gregory VI**, Gratian, of Rome; 5 May 1045–banished 20 Dec 1046; died 1047

149. **Clement II**, Suidger, bishop of Bamberg; 25 Dec 1046–died at Pesaro 9 Oct 1047

150. **Damasus II**, Poppo, bishop of Bressanone, of Bavaria; 17 July 1048–9 Aug 1048. Died at Palestrina

151. **St Leo IX**, Bruno, of Germany, bishop of Toul; 12 Feb 1049–19 April 1054

152. **Victor II**, Gebhard, of Germany, bishop of Eichstätt; 16 April 1055–28 July 1057. Died at Arezzo

153. **Stephen X**, Frédéric, of the family of the Dukes of Lorraine; 3 Aug 1057–29 March 1058 [**Benedict X**, of Rome; 5 April 1058–deposed 24 Jan 1059]

154. **Nicholas II**, Gérard de Bourgogne; 24 Jan 1059–27 (?) July 1061

155. **Alexander II**, Anselmo of Milan; 30 Sept 1061–21 April 1073 [**Honorius II**, appointed by Imperial Diet of Basle 1061–1072]

156. **St Gregory VII**, Hildebrand di Bonizio Aldobrandeschi, of Sovana; 22 April 1073–25 May 1085 [**Clement III**, Ghiberto; 25 Jan 1080–Sept 1100]

157. **B. Victor III**, Desiderio Epifani, of Benevento; elected 24 May 1086, consecrated 9 May 1087–16 Sept 1087

158. **B. Urban II**, of Reims; 12 March 1088–29 July 1099

159. **Paschal II**, Rainiero, of Breda; 14 Aug 1099–21 Jan 1118 [**Theodoric**, Sept–Dec 1100] [**Albert**, Feb–March 1102] [**Sylvester IV**, 18 Nov 1105–12 April 1111]

160. **Gelasius II**, Giov. Caetani, of Gaeta; 24 Jan 1118–28 Jan 1119 [**Gregory VIII**, Maurice Bourdain, of Limoges, 8 March 1118–deposed April 1121]

161. **Calixtus II**, Gui de Bourgogne, of Quingey; 2 Feb 1119–13 Dec 1124

162. **Honorius II**, Lamberto Scannabecchi, of Fanano

(Modena); 15 Dec 1124–13 Feb 1130

163. **Innocent II**, Gregorio Papareschi, of Trastevere; 14 Feb 1130–24 Sept 1143
[**Anacletus II**, Pierleone, a converted Jew; 14 Feb 1130–25 Jan 1138]
[**Victor IV**, Gregorio da Monticelli, elected 15 March 1138, abdicated 29 May 1138]

164. **Celestine II**, Guido, of Città di Castello; 26 Sept 1143–8 March 1144

165. **Lucius II**, Gerardo Caccianemici dell'Orso, of Bologna; 12 March 1144–15 Feb 1145

166. **B. Eugenius III**, Bernardo Paganelli, of Montemagno (Pisa); 15 Feb 1145–8 July 1153

167. **Anastasius IV**, Corrado, of the Suburra, Rome; 12 July 1153–3 Dec 1154

168. **Hadrian IV**, Nicholas Breakspeare, of Bedmond (Hertfordshire, England); 4 Dec 1154–1 Sept 1159. Died at Anagni

169. **Alexander III**, Rolando Bandinelli, of Siena; 7 Sept 1159–30 Aug 1181. Died at Civita Castellana
[**Victor IV** (V), Ottaviano; 7 Oct 1159–20 April 1164]
[**Paschal III**, Guido da Crema; 22 April 1164–20 Sept 1168]
[**Calixtus III**, John of Strumio, a Hungarian, Sept 1168, abdicated 29 Aug 1178]
[**Innocent III**, Lando Frangipane of Sezze, elected 29 Sept 1179, deposed in Jan 1180]

170. **Lucius III**, Ubaldo Allucingoli, of Lucca; 1 Sept 1181–25 Nov 1185. Died in exile at Verona

171. **Urban III**, Uberto Crivelli, of Milan; 25 Nov 1185–20 Oct 1187. Died at Ferrara

172. **Gregory VIII**, Alberto di Morra, of Benevento; 21 Oct 1187–17 Dec 1187

173. **Clement III**, Paolino Scolare, of Rome; 19 Dec 1187–Mar 1191

174. **Celestine III**, Giacinto Bobone Orsini, of Rome; 30 March 1191–8 Jan 1198

175. **Innocent III**, Lotario dei Conti di Segni, of Anagni; 8 Jan 1198–16 July 1216. Died at Perugia

176. **Honorius III**, Cencio Savelli, of Rome; elected in Perugia, 18 July 1216– died at Rome, 18 March 1227

177. **Gregory IX**, Ugolino dei Conti di Segni, of Anagni; elected at the age of 86; 19 March 1227–22 Aug 1241

178. **Celestine IV**, Castiglione, of Milan; 25 Oct 1241–10 Nov 1241

179. **Innocent IV**, Sinibaldo Fieschi of Genoa; 25 June 1243–7 Dec 1254. Died at Naples

180. **Alexander IV**, Orlando dei Conti di Segni, of Anagni; 12 Dec 1254–25 May 1261. Died at Viterbo

181. **Urban IV**, Hyacinthe Pantaléon, of Troyes; elected at Viterbo 29 Aug 1261; died at Perugia 2 Oct 1264

182. **Clement IV**, Gui Foulques Le Gros, of St-Gilles; elected at Viterbo 5 Feb 1265–died at Viterbo 29 Nov 1268

183. **Gregory X**, Teobaldo Visconti of Piacenza; elected at Viterbo 1 Sept 1271–died at Arezzo 10 Jan 1276

184. **Innocent V**, Pierre de Champagny, of the Tarentaise; 21 Jan 1276–22 June 1276

185. **Hadrian V**, Ottobono de' Fieschi, of Genoa; elected at Rome 11 July 1276–18 Aug 1276

186. **John XXI**, Pedro Juliao, of Lisbon; elected at Viterbo 8 Sept 1276–20 May 1277

187. **Nicholas III**, Giov. Gaetano Orsini, of Rome; elected at Viterbo 25 Nov 1277–died at Soriano nel Cimino 22 Aug 1280

188. **Martin IV**, Simon de Brion, of Montpincé in Brie; elected at Viterbo 22 Feb 1281–died at Perugia 28 March 1285

189. **Honorius IV**, Iacopo Savelli, of Rome; elected at Perugia 2 April 1285–3 April 1287

190. **Nicholas IV**, Girolamo Masci, of Lisciano di Ascoli; 15 Feb 1288–4 April 1292

191. **St Celestine V**, Pietro Angeleri da Morrone, of Isérnia; 5 July 1294–abdicated 13 Dec 1294. Died in the Castello di Fumone near Alatri 19 May 1296

192. **Boniface VIII**, Benedetto Gaetani, of Anagni; 24 Dec 1294–11 or 12 Oct 1303

193. **B. Benedict XI**, Niccolò Boccasini, of Treviso, 22 Oct 1303–died at Perugia 7 July 1304

194. **Clement V**, Bertrand de Got, of Villandraut, near Bordeaux; elected at Perugia 5 June 1305–died at Roquemaure 14 April 1314

195. **John XXII**, Jacques d'Euse, of Cahors; elected at Avignon 7 Aug 1316–died at Avignon 4 Dec 1334
[Nicholas V, Pietro da Corvara, 12 May 1328–30 Aug 1330]

196. **Benedict XII**, Jacques Fournier, of Saverdun, near Toulouse; 20 Dec 1334–25 April 1342

197. **Clement VI**, Pierre Roger de Beaufort, of Château Maumont, near Limoges; 7 May 1342–6 Dec 1352

198. **Innocent VI**, Etienne d'Aubert, of Mont, near Limoges, 18 Dec 1352–12 Sept 1362

199. **Urban V**, Guillaume de Grimoard, of Grisac, near Mende in Languedoc; 16 Oct 1362–19 Dec 1370

200. **Gregory XI**, Pierre Roger de Beaufort, nephew of Clement VI, of Château Maumont, near Limoges, elected at Avignon 30 Dec 1370–died at Rome 27 March 1378

201. **Urban VI**, Bart. Prigano, of Naples; 9 April 1378–15 Oct 1389

202. **Boniface IX**, Pietro Tomacelli, of Naples; 2 Nov 1389–1 Oct 1404

203. **Innocent VII**, Cosimo de'Migliorati, of Sulmona; 17 Oct 1404–6 Nov 1406.

204. **Gregory XII**, Angelo Correr, of Venice; 30 Nov 1406–abdicated 4 June 1415–died at Recanati 17 Oct 1417

Popes at Avignon
[Clement VII, Robert of Savoy, of Geneva; elected at Fondi 20 Sept 1378–16 Sept 1394]
[Benedict XIII, Pedro de Luna, of Aragon; 28 Sept 1394–23 May 1423]

Antipopes at Avignon
[Clement VIII, Gil Sanchez Muñoz, of Barcelona; 10 June 1423–16 July 1429]
[Benedict XIV, Bernard Garnier; 12 Nov 1425–1430 (?)]

Popes at Pisa
[Alexander V, Pietro Filargis, of Candia; 26 June 1409–3 May 1410]
[John XXIII, Baldassarre Cossa, of Naples; 17 May 1410, deposed 29 May 1415–died at Florence 23 Dec 1419]

205. **Martin V**, Oddone Colonna, of Genazzano; elected (aged 50) at Constance, 11 Nov 1417–20 Feb 1431

206. **Eugenius IV**, Gabriele Condulmero of Venice; elected (aged 48) 3 March 1431–23 Feb 1447
[Felix V, Amadeus, duke of Savoy; 5 Nov 1439–7 April 1449; died 1451 at the Château de Ripaille on the Lake of Geneva]

207. **Nicholas V**, Tommaso Parentucelli, of Sarzana; electe (aged 49) 6 March 1447–24 March 1455

208. **Calixtus III**, Alfonso Borgia, of Xativa, in Spain; elected (aged 78) 8 April 1455–6 Aug 1458

209. **Pius II**, Aeneas Silvius Piccolomini, of Corsignano (Pienza); elected (aged 53) 19 Aug 1458–15 Aug 1464

210. **Paul II**, Pietro Barbo, of Venice, elected (aged 48) 30 Aug 1464–26 July 1471

211. **Sixtus IV**, Fr. della Rovere, of Savona; elected (aged 57) 9 Aug 1471–12 Aug 1484

212. **Innocent VIII**, G. B. Cibo, of Genoa; elected (aged 52) 29 Aug 1484–25 July 1492

213. **Alexander VI**, Roderigo Lenzuoli-Borgia, of Valencia, Spain; elected (aged 62) 11 Aug 1492–18 Aug 1503

214. **Pius III**, Fr. Todeschini Piccolomini, of Siena; elected (aged 64) 22 Sept 1503–18 Oct 1503

215. **Julius II**, Giuliano della Rovere, of Savona; elected (aged 60) 31 Oct 1503–21 Feb 1513

216. **Leo X**, Giov. de' Medici, of Florence; elected (aged 38) 9 March 1513–1 Dec 1521

217. **Adrian VI**, Adrian Florisz. Dedel, of Utrecht; elected (aged 63) 9 Jan 1522–14 Sept 1523

218. **Clement VII**, Giulio de' Medici, of Florence; elected (aged 45) 19 Nov 1523–25 Sept 1534

219. **Paul III**, Aless. Farnese, of Camino (Rome) or of Viterbo (?), elected (aged 66) 13 Oct 1534–10 Nov 1549

220. **Julius III**, Giov. Maria Ciocchi del Monte, of Monte San Savino, near Arezzo; elected (aged 63) 7 Feb 1550–23 March 1555

221. **Marcellus II**, Marcello Cervini, of Montefano (Macerata); elected (aged 54) 9 April 1555–30 April 1555

222. **Paul IV**, Giov. Pietro Caraffa, of Capriglio, Avellino; elected (aged 79) 23 May 1555–18 Aug 1559

223. **Pius IV**, Giov. Angelo de'Medici, of Milan; elected (aged 60) 26 Dec 1559–9 Dec 1565

224. **St Pius V**, Ant. Ghislieri, of Bosco Marengo, near Tortona; elected (aged 62) 7 Jan 1566–1 May 1572

225. **Gregory XIII**, Ugo Boncompagni, of Bologna; elected (aged 70) 13 May 1572–10 April 1585

226. **Sixtus V**, Felice Peretti, of Grottammare; elected (aged 64) 24 April 1585–27 Aug 1590

227. **Urban VII**, G. B. Castagna, of Rome; elected (aged 69) 15 Sept 1590–27 Sept 1590

228. **Gregory XIV**, Niccolò Sfondrati, of Cremona; elected (aged 55) 5 Dec 1590–15 Oct 1591

229. **Innocent IX**, Giov. Ant. Facchinetti, of Bologna; elected (aged 72) 29 Oct 1591–30 Dec 1591

230. **Clement VIII**, Ippolito Aldobrandini, of Fano; elected (aged 56) 30 Jan 1592–3 March 1605

231. **Leo XI**, Aless. de' Medici, of Florence; elected (aged 70) 1 April 1605–27 April 1605

232. **Paul V**, Camillo Borghese, of Rome; elected (aged 53) 16 May 1605–28 Jan 1621

233. **Gregory XV**, Aless. Ludovisi, of Bologna; elected (aged 67) 9 Feb 1621–8 July 1623

234. **Urban VIII**, Maffeo Barberini, of Florence; elected (aged 55) 6 Aug 1623–29 July 1644

235. **Innocent X**, G. B. Pamphilj, of Rome; elected (aged 72) 15 Sept 1644–7 Jan 1655

236. **Alexander VII**, Fabio Chigi, of Siena; elected (aged 56) 7 April 1655–22 May 1667

237. **Clement IX**, Giulio Rospigliosi, of Pistoia; elected (aged 67) 20 June 1667–9 Dec 1669

238. **Clement X**, Emilio Altieri, of Rome; elected (aged 80) 29 April 1670–22 July 1676

239. **Innocent XI**, Bened. Odescalchi, of Como; elected (aged 65) 21 Sept 1676–11 Aug 1689

240. **Alexander VIII**, Pietro Ottoboni, of Venice; elected (aged 79) 6 Oct 1689–1 Feb 1691

241. **Innocent XII**, Ant. Pignatelli, of Spinazzola (Bari); elected (aged 76) 12 July 1691–27 Sept 1700

242. **Clement XI**, Giov. Fr. Albani, of Urbino; elected (aged 51) 23 Nov 1700–19 March 1721

243. **Innocent XIII**, Michelangelo Conti, of Rome; elected (aged 66) 8 May 1721–7 March 1724

244. **Benedict XIII**, Vinc. Maria Orsini, of Gravina (Bari); elected (aged 75) 29 May 1724–21 Feb 1730

245. **Clement XII**, Lor. Corsini, of Florence; elected (aged 79) 12 July 1730–6 Feb 1740

246. **Benedict XIV**, Prospero Lambertini, of Bologna; elected (aged 65) 17 Aug 1740–3 May 1758

247. **Clement XIII**, Carlo Rezzonico, of Venice; elected (aged 65) 6 July 1758–2 Feb 1769

248. **Clement XIV**, Giov. Vincenzo Ganganelli, of Sant'Arcangelo di Romagna (Forlì); elected (aged 64) 19 May 1769–22 Sept 1774

249. **Pius VI**, Angelo Braschi, of Cesena; elected (aged 58) 15 Feb 1775–29 Aug 1799. Died at Valence, France

250. **Pius VII**, Giorgio Barnaba Chiaramonti, of Cesena; elected (aged 58) at Venice; 14 March 1800–died at Rome, 20 Aug 1823

251. **Leo XII**, Annibale della Genga, born at La Genga, near Foligno; elected (aged 63) 28 Sept 1823–10 Feb 1829

252. **Pius VIII**, Francesco Saverio Castiglioni, of Cingoli; elected (aged 69) 31 March 1829–30 Nov 1830

253. **Gregory XVI**, Bart. Cappellari, of Belluno, elected (aged 66) 2 Feb 1831–1 June 1846

254. **Pius IX**, Giov. Maria Mastai Ferretti, of Senigallia; elected (aged 54) 16

June 1846–7 Feb 1878

255. **Leo XIII**, Gioacchino Pecci, of Carpineto Romano, elected (aged 68) 20 Feb 1878–20 July 1903

256. **St Pius X**, Giuseppe Sarto, of Riese (Treviso); elected (aged 68) 4 Aug 1903–20 Aug 1914

257. **Benedict XV**, Giacomo della Chiesa, of Genoa; elected (aged 60) 3 Sept 1914–22 Jan 1922

258. **Pius XI**, Achille Ratti, of Desio (Milan); elected (aged 65) 6 Feb 1922–10 Feb 1939

259. **Pius XII**, Eugenio Pacelli, of Rome, elected (aged 63) 2 March 1939–9 Oct 1958

260. **John XXIII**, Angelo Roncalli, of Sotto il Monte, Bergamo; elected (aged 77) 28 Oct 1958–3 June 1963 (beatified 2000)

261. **Paul VI**, Giov. Battista Montini, of Brescia; elected (aged 65) 21 June 1963–6 August 1978

262. **John Paul I**, Albino Luciani, of Forno di Canale, Belluno; elected (aged 65) 26 August 1978–29 September 1978

263. **John Paul II**, Karol Wojtyla, of Wadowice (Krakow), Poland; elected (aged 58) 16 October 1978–

Glossary

Acrolith statue with the body made from a different material than the head

Aedicule small opening framed by two columns and a pediment, originally used in classical architecture

Ambo (pl. **ambones**) pulpit in a Christian basilica; two pulpits on opposite sides of a church from which the gospel and epistle were read

Amphora antique vase, usually of large dimensions, for oil and other liquids

Antefix ornament placed at the lower corners of the tiled roof of a temple to conceal the space between the tiles and the cornice

Antiphonal choir-book containing a collection of antiphonae—verses sung in response by two choirs

Antis in antis describes the portico of a temple where the side-walls are prolonged to end in a pilaster flush with the columns of the portico

Apodyterium dressing-room in a Roman bath

Apse vaulted semicircular end wall of the chancel of a church or of a chapel

Arca wooden chest with a lid, for sacred or secular use. Also, monumental sarcophagus in stone, used by Christians and pagans

Archaic period in Greek civilisation preceeding the classical era: from about 750 BC–480 BC

Architrave the lowest part of an entablature, the horizontal frame above a door

Archivolt moulded architrave carried round an arch

Aryballus (pl. **aryballoi**) small Greek pottery vase for oil or perfume with a globular body, narrow neck and single handle

Atlantes (or **telamones**) male figures used as supporting columns

Atrium forecourt, usually of a Byzantine church or a classical Roman house

Attic topmost storey of a classical building, hiding the spring of the roof

Baldacchino canopy supported by columns, usually over an altar

Basilica originally a Roman hall used for public administration; in Christian architecture, an aisled church with a clerestory and apse, and no transepts

Biga chariot

Borgo a suburb; a street leading away from the centre of a town

Bottega the studio of an artist; the pupils who worked under his direction

Bozzetto sketch, often used to describe a small model for a piece of sculpture

Bucchero Etruscan black terracotta ware

Bucrania a form of classical decoration—heads of oxen with flower garlands

Caldarium or **calidarium** room for hot or vapour baths in a Roman bath

Campanile bell-tower, often detached from the building to which it belongs

Camposanto cemetery

Canephora figure bearing a basket, often used as a caryatid

Canopic vase Egyptian or Etruscan vase enclosing the entrails of the dead

Carceres openings in the barriers through which the competing chariots entered the circus

Cardo the main street of a Roman town, at right angles to the Decumanus

Cartoon from *cartone*, meaning large sheet of paper. A full-size preparatory drawing for a painting or fresco

Caryatid female figure used as a supporting column

Cavea the part of a theatre or amphitheatre occupied by the row of seats

Cella sanctuary of a temple, usually in the centre of the building

Chiaroscuro distribution of light and shade in a painting

Chiton linen tunic worn by the ancient Greeks

Ciborium casket or tabernacle containing the Host

Cipollino a greyish marble with streaks of white or green

Cippus sepulchral monument in the form of an altar

Cista casket, usually of bronze and cylindrical in shape, to hold jewels, toilet articles, etc., and decorated with mythological subjects

Clerestory upper part of the nave of a church above the side aisles, with windows, usually a feature of Gothic architecture

Cloisonné type of enamel decoration divided by narrow strips of metal, typical of Byzantine craftsmanship

Columbarium a building (usually subterranean) with niches to hold urns containing the ashes of the dead

Confessio crypt beneath the high altar and raised choir of a church, usually containing the relics of a saint

Corbel a projecting block, usually of stone

Cornice topmost part of a temple *entablature*; any projecting ornamental moulding at the top of a building beneath the roof

Cosmatesque or **Cosmati** inlaid marble work using mosaic and coloured glass and stone to decorate pavements, pulpits, choir screens, columns, cloisters, etc. Its name comes from the Roman stonemason surnamed Cosmati or Cosma active in Rome and Lazio from the 12C to 14C.

Cryptoporticus vaulted subterranean corridor

Cuneus wedge-shaped block of seats in an antique theatre

Cyclopean the term applied to walls of unmortared masonry, older than the Etruscan civilisation, and attributed by the ancients to the giant Cyclopes

Decumanus main street of a Roman town, running parallel to its longer axis

Diaconia early Christian welfare centre

Dipteral temple surrounded by a double peristyle

Diptych painting or ivory tablet in two sections

Entablature upper part of a temple above the columns, made up of an *architrave*, *frieze*, and *cornice*

Ephebus Greek youth under training (military or university)

Exedra semicircular recess

Ex-voto tablet or small painting expressing gratitude to a saint

Forum open space in a town serving as a market or meeting-place

Fresco (in Italian, *affresco*), painting executed on wet plaster. On the wall beneath is sketched the sinopia, and the cartoon is transferred onto the fresh plaster (intonaco) before the fresco is begun, either by pricking the outline with small holes over which a powder is dusted, or by means of a stylus which leaves an incised line on the wet plaster. In recent years many frescoes have been detached from the walls on which they were executed

Frieze strip of decoration usually along the upper part of a wall; in a temple this refers to the horizontal feature above the columns between the *cornice* and *architrave*

Frigidarium room for cold baths in a Roman bath

Gens Roman clan or group of families linked by a common name

Giallo antico red-veined yellow marble from Numidia

Gigantomachia contest between giants

Gonfalone banner of a medieval guild or commune

Graffiti design on a wall made with an iron tool on a prepared surface, the design showing in white. Also used loosely to describe scratched designs or words on walls

Greek cross cross with the arms of equal length

Grisaille painting in various tones of grey

Grotesque (or *grotteschi*) painting or stucco decoration based on the style of the ancient Romans found during the Renaissance in the Domus Aurea in Rome (then underground, hence the name, from 'grotto'). The delicate ornamental decoration usually includes patterns of flowers, sphinxes, birds and human figures, against a light ground

Herm (pl. **hermae**) quadrangular pillar decreasing in girth towards the ground, surmounted by a bust

Hexastyle temple with a portico of six columns at the end

Hypogeum subterranean excavation for the interment of the dead (usually Etruscan)

Impasto early Etruscan ware made of inferior clay

Imperial Period Period of ancient Roman history under the Roman emperors (48 BC–475 AD) see pp 68–69.

Insula (pl. **insulae**) tenement house

Intarsia (or **tarsia**) inlay of wood, marble or metal

Intonaco plaster

Krater antique mixing-bowl, conical in shape with a rounded base

Kylix wide shallow vase with two handles and short stem

Laconicum room for vapour baths in a Roman bath

Latin cross cross with a long vertical arm

Loggia covered gallery or balcony, usually preceding a larger building

Lunette semicircular space in a vault or ceiling often decorated with a painting or relief

Matroneum gallery reserved for women in early Christian churches

Meta conical turning-post for chariot races in a circus or stadium

Metope panel between two triglyphs on the frieze of a Doric temple

Mithraeum temple of the god Mithras

Monolith single stone (usually a column)

Narthex vestibule of a Christian basilica

Naumachia mock naval combat for which the arena of an amphitheatre was flooded

Niello black substance used in an engraved design

Nimbus luminous ring surrounding the heads of saints in paintings; a square nimbus denoted that the person was living at that time

Nymphaeum a cave inhabited by nymphs; an artificial grotto decorated with a fountain in a Roman villa

Octastyle a portico with eight columns

Oinochoë wine-jug, usually of elongated shape, for dipping wine out of a krater

Opus Alexandrinum mosaic design of black and red geometric figures on a white ground

Opus incertum masonry of small irregular stones set in mortar (a type of concrete)

Opus quadratum masonry of large rectangular blocks without mortar; in

Opus Etruscum the blocks are placed alternately lengthwise and endwise

Opus reticulatum masonry arranged in squares or diamonds so that the mortar joints make a network pattern

Opus sectile mosaic or paving of thin slabs of coloured marble cut in geometrical shapes

Opus spicatum masonry or paving of small bricks arranged in a herring-bone pattern

Opus tessellatum mosaic formed entirely of square tesserae

Opus vermiculatum mosaic with tesserae arranged in lines following the design contours

Palazzo any dignified and important building

Palombino fine-grained white marble

Patera small circular ornamental disk, usually carved; Greek or Roman dish for libations to the gods

Pavonazzetto yellow marble blotched with blue

Pax sacred object used by a priest for the blessing of peace, and offered for the kiss of the faithful; usually circular, engraved, enamelled or painted in a rich gold or silver frame

Pendentive concave spandrel beneath a dome

Peperino earthy granulated tufa, much used in Rome

Peplos draped women's woollen mantle made from a single piece of cloth usually open at the side

Peripteral temple surrounded by a colonnade

Peristyle court or garden surrounded by a columned portico

Piano nobile main floor of a palace

Pietà group of the Virgin mourning the dead Christ

Piscina Roman tank; a basin for an officiating priest to wash his hands before mass

Pluteus (pl. **plutei**) marble panel, usually decorated; a series of them used to form a parapet to precede the altar of a church

Podium a continuous base or plinth supporting columns, and the lowest row of seats in the cavea of a theatre or amphitheatre

Polyptych painting or tablet in more than three sections

Pozzolana reddish volcanic earth (mostly from Pozzuoli, near Naples) largely used for cement

Predella small painting or panel, usually in sections, attached below a large altarpiece

Presepio literally, crib or manger. A group of statuary of which the central subject is the Infant Jesus in the manger

Pronaos porch in front of the cella of a temple

Propylaea columned vestibule approaching a temple

Prostyle temple with columns on the front only

Pulvin cushion stone between the capital and the impost block

Pulvinar Imperial couch and balcony on the podium of a theatre

Putto (pl. **putti**) figure sculpted or painted usually nude, of a child

Quadriga four-horsed chariot

Republican period Period of ancient Roman history dating from c 509 BC to 31 BC (preceeding the Imperial period)

Rhyton drinking-horn usually ending in an animal's head

Rosso antico red marble from the Peloponnese

Rostra orator's platform; and ships prows captured in battle, which were often used to decorate these platforms

Sanpietrini (or sampetrini) small rectangular flint paving stones used in Piazza San Pietro (hence the name) but also used in numerous old streets and squares of Rome. Also the name used in past centuries for the workmen employed on the maintenence of St Peter's

Schola cantorum enclosure for the choristers in the nave of an early Christian church, adjoining the sanctuary

Sinopia large sketch for a fresco made on the rough wall in a red earth pigment called sinopia (because it originally came from Sinope, a town on the Black Sea). When a fresco is detached for restoration, it is possible to see the sinopia beneath, which can also be separated from the wall

Situla water-bucket

Skyphos drinking cup with two handles

Solomonic column barley-sugar or twisted column, so called from its supposed use in the Temple of Solomon

Spandrel surface between two arches in an arcade or the triangular space on either side of an arch

Spina low stone wall connecting the turning-posts (metoe) at either end of a circus

SPQR *Senatus Populusque Romanus* ('the Senate and the Roman People') These letters have represented the Romans since the days of the Republic and are now used to denote the municipality

Stamnos big-bellied vase with two small handles at the sides, closed by a lid

Stele upright stone bearing a monumental inscription

Stemma coat of arms or heraldic device

Stereobate basement of a temple or other building

Stoa a porch or portico not attached to a larger building

Strigil bronze scraper used by the Romans to remove the oil with which they had anointed themselves

Stylobate basement of a columned temple or other building

Telamones see **Atlantes**

Temenos a sacred enclosure

Tepidarium room for warm baths in a Roman bath

Tessera a small cube of marble, glass,

etc., used in mosaic work

Tetrastyle having four columns at the end

Thermae originally simply baths, later elaborate buildings fitted with libraries, assembly rooms, gymnasia, circuses, etc.

Tholos (Greek) a circular building

Tondo round painting or bas-relief

Transenna open grille or screen, usually of marble, in an early Christian church

Travertine tufa quarried near Tivoli; the commonest of Roman building materials

Triclinium dining-room and reception-room of a Roman house

Triglyph small panel of a Doric frieze raised slightly and carved with three vertical channels

Triptych painting or tablet in three sections

Trompe l'oeil literally a deception of the eye. Used to describe illusionist decoration, painted architectural perspectives, etc.

Tropaeium (or **Trophy**) victory monument

Tumulus a burial mound

Velarium canvas sheet supported by masts to protect the spectators in an open theatre from the sun

Verde antico green marble from Tessaglia

Zoöphorus frieze of a Doric temple, so-called because the metopes were often decorated with figures of animals

Index to artists

This index lists Italian painters, sculptors and architects mentioned in the guide. Only a few foreign artists who worked in the city are included.

F

G

Index

W

Z

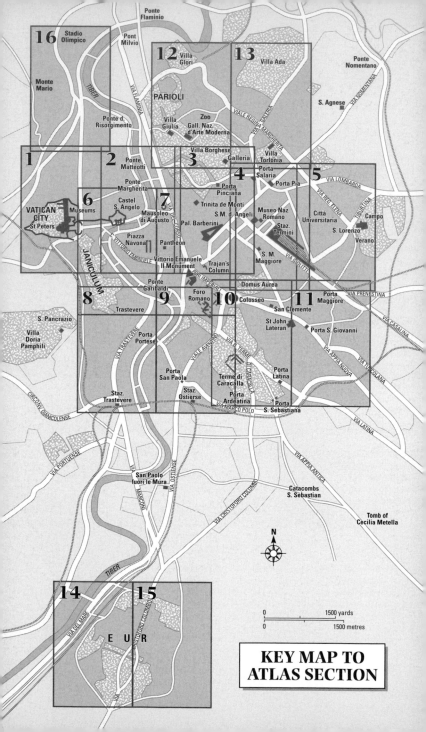

16 Stadio Olimpico

Monte Mario

Ponte Flaminio

Pont Milvio

Ponte d. Risorgimento

VIA FLAMINIA

TIBER

12 Villa Glori

PARIOLI

Villa Giulia

Zoo

Gall. Naz. d'Arte Moderna

13 Villa Ada

S. Agnese

VIALE REGINA MARGHERITA

Ponte Nomentano

VIA NOMENTANA

1 VATICAN CITY St Peters

Museums

6 Castel S. Angelo

Ponte Matteotti

Ponte Margherita

2

JANICULUM

VITTORIO EMANUELE

Mausoleo di Augusto

Piazza Navona

7

VIA DEL CORSO

3 Villa Borghese

Galleria

Porta Salaria

4 Porta Pinciana

Trinita de Monti

S.M. d. Angeli

Pal. Barberini

Pantheon

Vittorio Emanuele II Monument

Trajan's Column

Villa Torlonia

Porta Pia

Museo Naz. Romano

Staz. Termini

S. M. Maggiore

5

VIA LOMBARDA

VIA REG. ELENA

TIBURTINA

Città Universitaria

Campo

S. Lorenzo

Verano

FORI IMPERIALI

VIA GIOLITTI

Domus Aurea

8

S. Pancrazio

Villa Doria Pamphili

Trastevere

Ponte Garibaldi

Foro Romano

9

Porta Portese

VIA TRASTEVERE

Porta San Paola

Colosseo

10

VIALE AVENTINO

San Clemente

St John Lateran

11

Porta Maggiore

VIA PRENESTINA

VIA CASALINA

Porta S. Giovanni

VIA DELLE TERME DI CARACALLA

Terme di Caracalla

Porta Latina

VIA APPIA NUOVA

VIA TUSCOLANA

Staz. Trastevere

Staz. Ostierse

Porta Ardeatina

VIA MARCO POLO

Porta S. Sebastiana

Porta

VIA LATINA

VIA CIRCON V. GIANICOLENSE

VIA PORTUENSE

San Paolo fuori le Mura

VIA OSTIENSE

MARCONI

VIA CRISTOFORO COLOMBO

VIA APPIA ANTICA

Catacombs S. Sebastian

Tomb of Cecilia Metella

N

TIBER

14

VIA DEL MARE

15

E U R

VIA CRISTOFORO COLOMBO

| 0 | | 1500 yards |
| 0 | | 1500 metres |

KEY MAP TO ATLAS SECTION

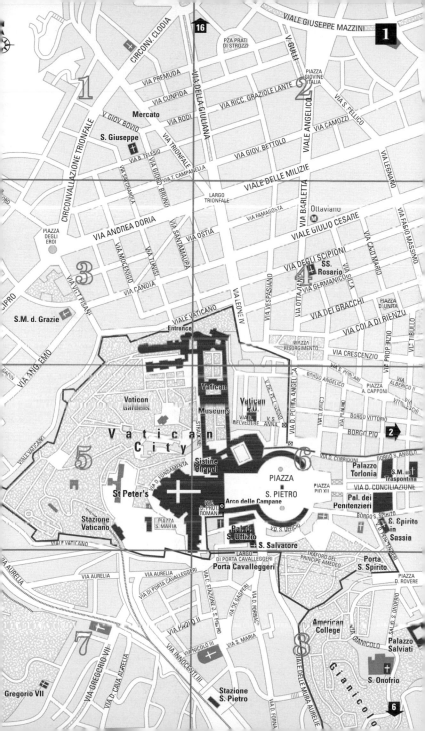

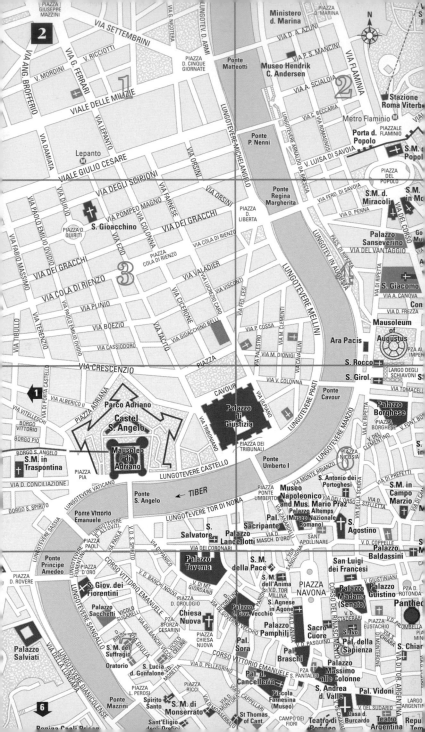

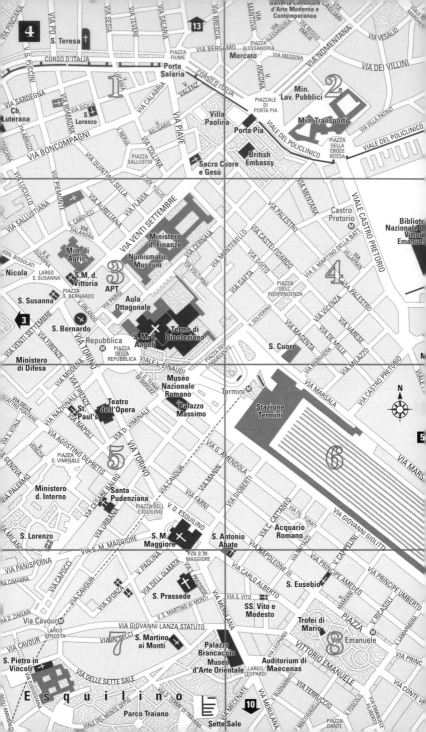

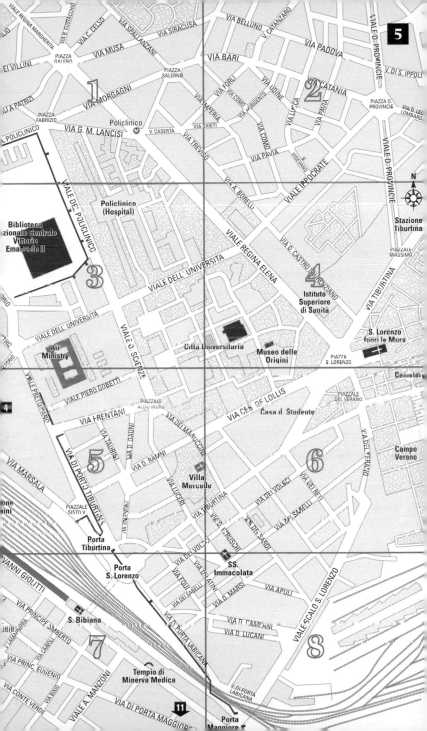

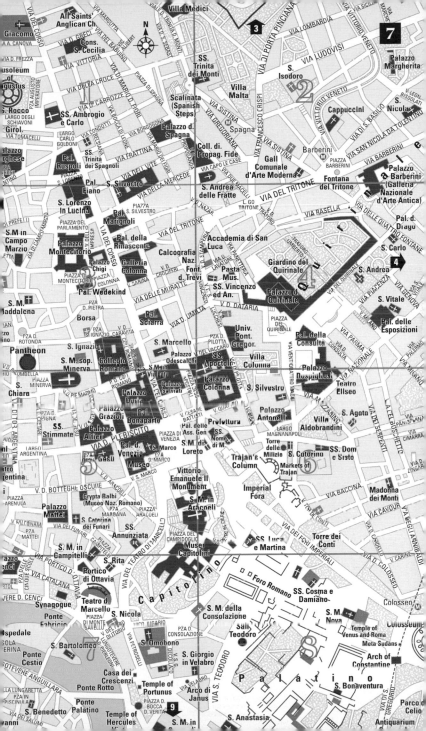

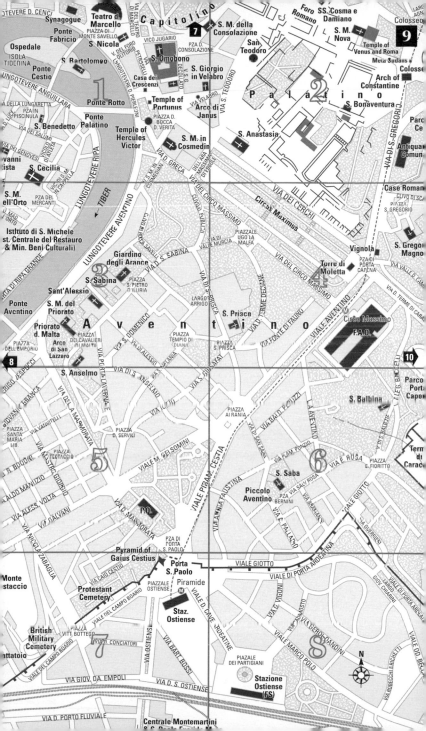

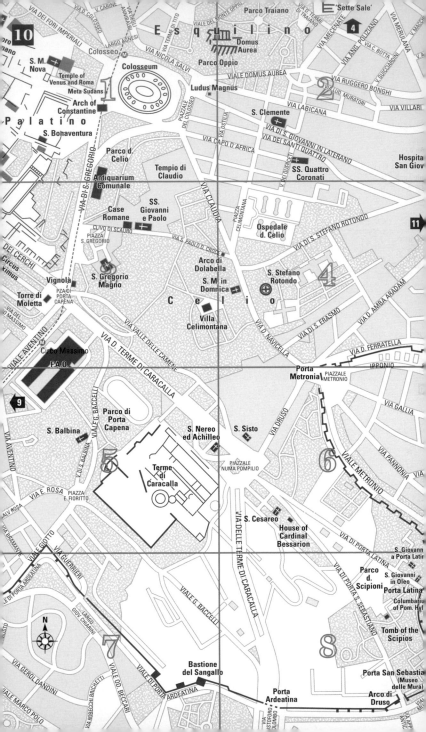

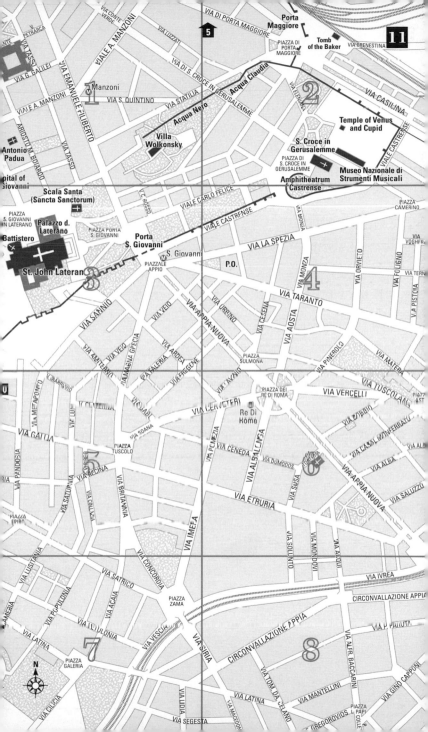

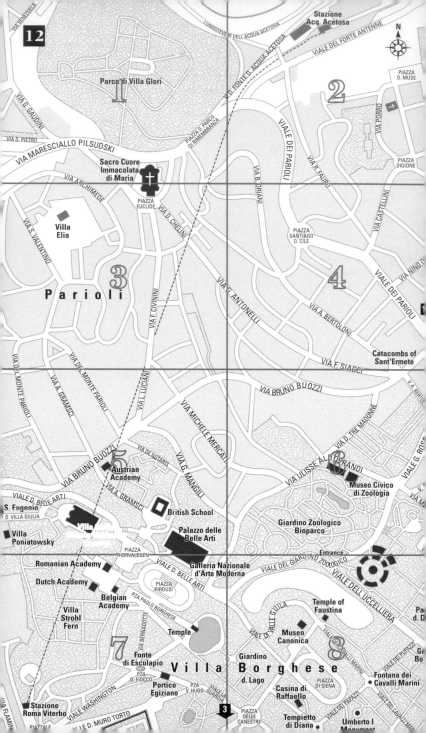

12

Parco di Villa Glori

1

Stazione
Acq. Acetosa

VIALE DEL FORTE ANTENNE

PIAZZA
D. MUSE

2

VIA G. GAUDINI

VIA D. PIETRO

VIA MARESCIALLO PILSUDSKI

VIA ARCHIMEDE

Sacro Cuore
Immacolata
di Maria

PIAZZA
EUCLIDE

PIAZZA D. PARCO
DI RIMEMBRANZA

VIA D. FONTE D. ACQUA ACETOSA

LUNGOTEVERE DELL'ACQUA ACETOSA

VIALE DEI PARIOLI

VIA B. ORIANI

VIA R. FAURO

PIAZZA
DIGIONE

VIA S. VALENTINO

Villa
Elia

3

P a r i o l i

VIA F. CIVININI

VIA D. CHELINI

VIA G. ANTONELLI

PIAZZA
SANTIAGO
D. CILE

4

VIALE DEI PARIOLI

VIA NINO B

VIA A. BERTOLONI

VIA F. SIACCI

Catacombs of
Sant'Ermete

VIA CASTELLINI

VIA DEL MONTE PARIOLI

VIA A. GRAMSCI

VIA DEL MONTE PARIOLI

VIA L. LUCIANI

VIA MICHELE MERCATI

VIA BRUNO BUOZZI

VIA D. TRE MADONNE

VIALE G. ROSS

VIA BRUNO BUOZZI

VIA DE NOTARIS

VIA G. MANGILI

VIA ULISSE ALDROVANDI

6

Austrian
Academy

5

VIA A. GRAMSCI

British School

Museo Civico
di Zoologia

VIALE D. BELLE ARTI

S. Eugenio

S. VILLA GIULIA

Palazzo delle
Belle Arti

Giardino Zoologico
Bioparco

Villa
Poniatowsky

Villa

PIAZZA
THORVALDSEN

Entrance

Romanian Academy

Galleria Nazionale
d'Arte Moderna

VIALE DEL GIARDINO ZOOLOGICO

VIALE DELL'UCCELLIERA

Dutch Academy

PIAZZA
FIRDUSI

VIALE D. BELLE ARTI

Belgian
Academy

P.ZA PAOLO BORGHESE

Temple of
Faustina

Villa
Strohl
Fern

VIA BERNADOTTE

Temple

PZA
D. FIOCCO

7

Fonte
di Esculapio

Museo
Canonica

VIALE DI VIALE GIULIA

VIALE DI VIALE GIULIA

Portico
Egiziano

PZA
V. HUGO

Villa Borghese
d. Lago

Giardino
d. Lago

PIAZZA
DI SIENA

8

Stazione
Roma Viterbo

VIALE WASHINGTON

VIA D. MURO TORTO

PIAZZA
DELLE
CANESTRE

Casina di
Raffaello

Tempietto
di Diana

Fontana dei
Cavalli Marini

Umberto I
Monument

3

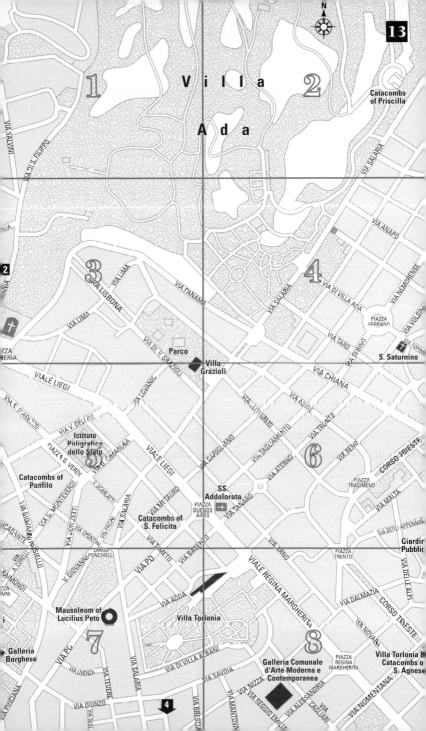

Villa

1

2

Ada

Catacombs
of Priscilla

VIA SALVINI

VIA DI S. FILIPPO

VIA ANAPO

VIA NEMORENSE

VIA SALARIA

3

VIA LIMA

VIA LISBONA

VIA PANAMA

VIA LIMA

VIA SALARIA

4

VIA DI VILLA ADA

VIA VOLSINI

PIAZZA
VERBANO

VIA TARO

VIA SEBINO

VIA DI V. GRAZIOLI

Parco

S. Saturnino

Villa
Grazioli

VIA CHIANA

VIALE LIEGI

VIA LOVANIO

VIA ADIGE

VIA S. PAOLO

VIA V. BELLINI

VIA TIRSO

VIA CIRVIGLIANO

VIA TAGLIAMENTO

VIA TRIESTE

Istituto
Poligrafico
dello Stato

VIALE LIEGI

VIA CADAMOSA

VIA TAGLIAMENTO

6

VIA RENO

CORSO TRIESTE

PIAZZA
G. VERDI

PIAZZA
TRASIMENO

Catacombs of
Panfilo

V. SCARLATTI

VIA METAURO

SS.
Addolorata

VIA ATERNO

VIA MALTA

VIA G. MONTEVERDI

V. SPONTINI

VIA PACINI

PIAZZA
BUENOS
AIRES

VIA TAMARO

VIA DEGLI APPENNINI

VIA GIOVANNI PAISIELLO

Catacombs of
S. Felicita

VIA SALARIA

VIA SIMETO

VIA BASENTO

VIA ARNO

Giardir
Pubblic

ARCADI SANTE

VIA DON ZETTI

PIAZZA
TRENTO

VIA PO

V. CIMELLI

LARGO
PONCHIELLI

VIA DELLE ALPI

RAIMONDI

V. GIOVANNI

VIA PO

VIA SIMETO

VIA ADDA

VIALE REGINA MARGHERITA

VIA DALMAZIA

CORSO TRIESTE

PIAZZA
MAZZINI

Mausoleum of
Lucilius Peto

VIA NOVARA

7

Villa Torlonia

8

Villa Torlonia &
Catacombs o
S. Agnese

Galleria
Borghese

VIA PO

VIA TEVERE

VIA SALARIA

VIA DI VILLA ALBANI

VIA SAVOIA

VIA NIZZA

PIAZZA
REGINA
MARGHERITA

Galleria Comunale
d'Arte Moderna e
Contemporanea

VIA NOMENTANA

VIA PINCIANA

VIA LIVENZA

VIA ISONZO

VIA SESI

VIA BRESCIA

VIA SEGGIO EMILI

VIA MANTOVA

VIA ALESSANDRIA

VIA CAGLIARI

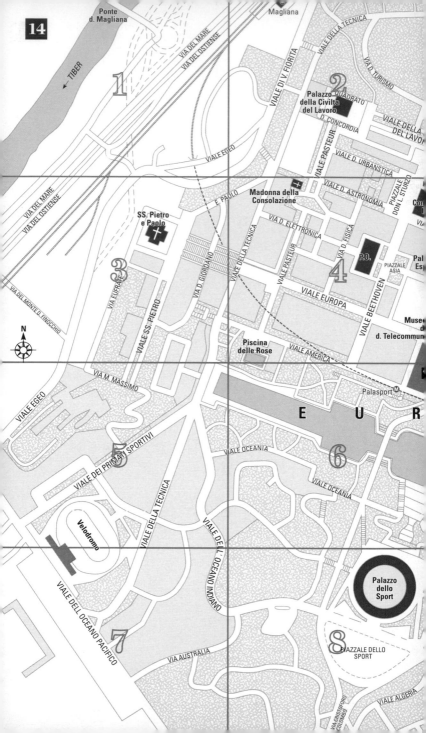

14

Ponte
d. Magliana

Magliana

← TIBER

1

VIA DEL MARE
VIA DEL OSTIENSE

VIALE DELLA TECNICA

VIALE DI V. FIORITA

VIA D. TURISMO

2
QUADRATO

Palazzo
della Civiltà
del Lavoro

VIALE DELLA
DEL LAVOR

D. CONCORDIA

VIALE PASTEUR

VIALE D. URBANSTICA

VIA DEL MARE
VIA DEL OSTIENSE

VIALE EGEO

E. PAOLO

Madonna della
Consolazione

VIALE D. ASTRONOMIA

PIAZZALE
DON L. STURZO

Co
V

VIA D. ELETTRONICA

SS. Pietro
e Paolo

VIA D. FISICA

P.O.

Pal
Esp

VIALE DELLA TECNICA

VIA D. GIORDANO

VIALE PASTEUR

3

4

PIAZZALE
ASIA

VIA EUFRATE

VIA DEL MONTE D. FINOCCHIO

VIALE SS. PIETRO

VIALE EUROPA

VIALE BEETHOVEN

N

Muse
d
d. Telecommun

Piscina
delle Rose

VIALE AMERICA

VIA M. MASSIMO

VIALE EGEO

Palasport M

E   U   R

VIALE DEI PRIMATI SPORTIVI

5

VIALE OCEANIA

6

VIALE DELLA TECNICA

VIALE OCEANIA

Velodromo

VIALE DELL' OCEANO INDIANO

Palazzo
dello
Sport

VIALE DELL' OCEANO PACIFICO

7

8

PIAZZALE DELLO
SPORT

VIA AUSTRALIA

VIA CRISTOFORO COLOMBO

VIALE ALGERIA

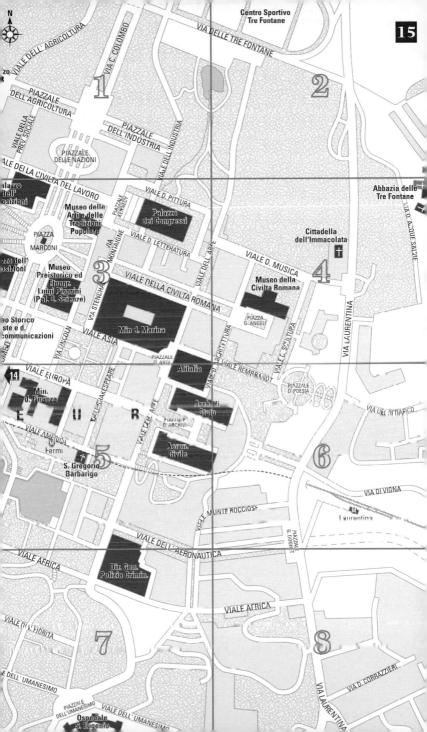

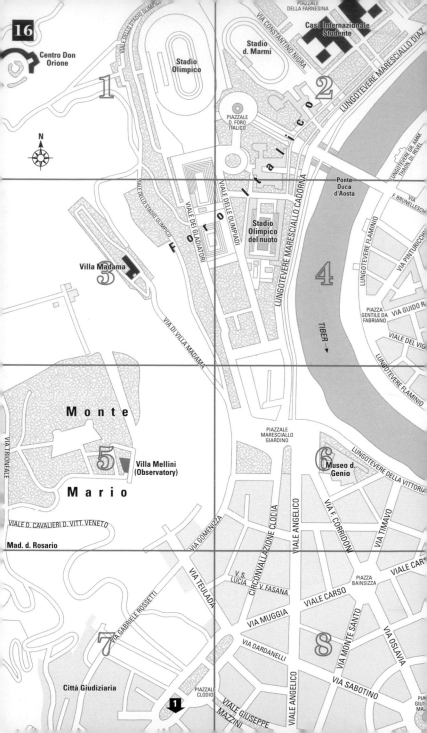